A Perfect Frenzy

Also by Andrew Lawler

Under Jerusalem:
The Buried History of the World's Most Contested City

The Secret Token: Myth, Obsession,
and the Search for the Lost Colony of Roanoke

Why Did the Chicken Cross the World?
The Epic Saga of the Bird
That Powers Civilization

A Perfect Frenzy

A Royal Governor, His Black Allies, *and* the Crisis That Spurred the American Revolution

ANDREW LAWLER

Atlantic Monthly Press
New York

FIRST EDITION

Published simultaneously in Canada
Printed in the United States of America

This book is set in 11.75-pt. Dante by Alpha Design & Composition of Pittsfield, NH

First Grove Atlantic hardcover edition: January 2025

Library of Congress Cataloging-in-Publication data is available for this title.

ISBN 978-0-8021-6413-1
eISBN 978-0-8021-6414-8

Atlantic Monthly Press
an imprint of Grove Atlantic
154 West 14th Street
New York, NY 10011

Distributed by Publishers Group West

groveatlantic.com

25 26 27 28 10 9 8 7 6 5 4 3 2 1

To Ann Fitzpatrick Lawler

Lord Dunmore has commenced hostilities in Virginia . . . It has raised our countrymen into a perfect frenzy.

—Thomas Jefferson

No longer shall thou dread the iron chain
Which wanton tyranny with lawless hand
Had made, and with it meant t'enslave the land.

—Phillis Wheatley

I am willing to allow the colony great merit for having produced a Washington; but they have been shamefully duped by a Dunmore.

—Abigail Adams

Contents

Author's Note

The way people describe themselves and others is always in flux. Eighteenth-century literate Americans, who were overwhelmingly of English or Scottish descent, commonly used the terms white, black, Indian, savage, Negro, master, and slave. I have preserved their words in quotations but typically employ more modern terminology elsewhere. Those in bondage are enslaved or unfree, while those who held them in bondage are owners. Occasionally, the word slave may be used outside quotations to avoid repetition or to emphasize an eighteenth-century perspective. African or European describes those born on these continents and, occasionally, those of African or European descent. Black is capitalized to emphasize a shared ethnic identity, while the more amorphous white is not. People descended from those who lived in North America when the Europeans arrived are, when possible, referred to by their own contemporary names for themselves or by familiar Anglicized ones, and more generically as indigenous, Indian, or Native American. Patriot is synonymous with rebel, and loyalist with Tory. Given that the era was a time of creative spelling, punctuation, and capitalization, some letters and words in quotations have been standardized to make them less jarring to modern eyes. Thus, Thomas Jefferson's "perfect phrenzy" becomes "perfect frenzy." For those seeking the precise texts and sources, references to all quotations are contained in the endnotes. Finally, in exploring this era, we confront the challenge of having voluminous writings from (and portraits of) Europeans and those of European descent, primarily men, while records made by, or even of, those of African and indigenous American heritage are, by contrast, few. I've attempted to glean what is available from this skewed historical record to give all players in the drama of Virginia's early revolutionary struggle their due.

Prelude

When I was a child, my grandparents often took me to the scene of the single biggest war crime of the American Revolution. Climbing out of their Chevrolet Impala, we strolled into the shaded churchyard of St. Paul's in the heart of our hometown, Virginia's port city of Norfolk. The colonial-era sanctuary, surrounded by tilted tombstones and gnarled water oaks, stood marooned in a bleak urban desert of parking lots, two-story public housing units, and austere high-rise office buildings. We never entered the church. Instead, we walked to one corner of the exterior wall and gazed up. Protruding from the red brick just beneath the eave was a black hemisphere the size of a cantaloupe. A plaque affixed below read, FIRED BY LORD DUNMORE, JAN. 1, 1776.

Lord Dunmore ruled as King George III's last royal governor of Virginia, the largest, wealthiest, and most populous of the thirteen American colonies. By the first day of the fateful year 1776, my grandparents explained, liberty-loving patriots had driven the wicked Scottish earl aboard one of the British warships anchored in the harbor of what was the largest city in Virginia and the busiest port between Philadelphia and Charleston. The frustrated nobleman, they said, unleashed a deadly barrage on the defenseless town; one cannonball smashed through a home, shattering the leg of a nursing mother. I was told that the subsequent raging fires reduced the church to four charred walls and the entire port to ashes. A single dovecote was the only structure left standing. Thousands were rendered homeless and destitute at the start of a bitter winter. No other city in North America, before or since, has suffered such a complete calamity.

Today, inured to twentieth-century horrors like Coventry, Dresden, and Hiroshima, we tend to forget that even in the most vicious eighteenth-century European conflicts, settlements were sacked but never purposely leveled.

The ball in the wall spoke more powerfully than any history book of the terrible price of freedom. Dunmore was, to my young mind, an entitled and thuggish terrorist who vainly tried to stem the flooding tide of independence. I was in good company. George Washington called him "that arch traitor to the rights of humanity." Richard Henry Lee, the Virginia delegate to the Continental Congress who introduced the resolution to separate from the mother country, said that if the king's ministers "had searched through the world for a person best fitted to ruin their cause, and procure union and success for these colonies, they could not have found a more complete agent than Lord Dunmore." On the floor of Congress, Lee derided the governor as a drunk, while other Americans labeled him a pirate, a monster, and a rapist. He was said to deflower young white virgins and entertain Black women at orgies. One prominent planter suggested that he "be placed securely chained in some madhouse." Virginia patriot Judith Bell declared, "There was never a viler wretch than the Earl of Dunmore," adding, "It appears that he takes pleasure in killing his fellow man." The royal governor was, noted one historian, "the first full-fledged villain to step from the wings as the Revolutionary War unfolded."

His infamy contrasted sharply with the saintly glow around my childhood hero, invariably referred to as "Mr. Jefferson," as if he might at any moment knock on our front door and ask me to recite the Declaration of Independence. The two men were the fixed poles in my American identity as a youth: the humble humanitarian who bravely asserted that all were created equal and the arrogant aristocrat intent on maintaining brute authority. Jefferson's aura faded over the years, as I became aware that his defiant ownership of people and his sexual relationship with the enslaved Sally Hemings were at painful odds with his soaring rhetoric. Dunmore, however, never lost his dirty taint. There was, after all, that ball in the wall.

Decades later, a magazine editor asked me to come up with an idea to mark Black History Month. At the time, I had returned to

Virginia to visit my mother, and we made the familiar hour-long drive to Colonial Williamsburg. The old capital was restored with money from the Rockefeller family to resemble the town in Dunmore's day, and charming brick and clapboard homes line the tidy streets, as they did on the eve of revolution. There is even a careful reproduction of the elegant mansion where the governor lived for four years. During the tour of what was dubbed the Palace, our lace-capped guide pointed out the earl's stately grandfather clock, which, unlike his reputation, had survived the ravages of time.

Leafing later through books at a nearby gift shop, I stumbled on a startling mention of "Lord Dunmore's Ethiopian Regiment," a corps of armed Black men who fought for the British against their patriot owners. In that era, four out of ten Virginians were enslaved workers; the governor himself owned more individuals than all but a handful of white planters. As the Revolution gathered steam in the summer of 1775, he fled the Palace for Royal Navy ships anchored off Norfolk. He needed troops to make a stand against the rebels, while those in lifetime servitude yearned for liberty. Defying threats of torture, imprisonment, and death, enslaved people flocked to his side. More than thirty years before Abraham Lincoln was born, Lord Dunmore formally emancipated any enslaved people owned by patriots who would fight for the king, gave them weapons, and sent them into battle against those who had held them in bondage.

After writing a brief article on this bit of history neglected by my grandparents and school texts, I sensed there was more to the story. My journalistic instincts whetted, I set out to uncover what else had been omitted or obfuscated. I traced Dunmore's steps, drinking tea in his Scottish garden pavilion topped with a massive stone pineapple, crossing the ocean on a ship that followed his route to the New World, and visiting ballrooms and battlefields where the rebellion had unfolded. I interviewed eighth-generation descendants of enslaved Virginians who had found freedom on the rocky coast of eastern Canada, spoke with archaeologists, and sought out reenactors of the Revolutionary era who could explain the finer points of a skirmish. I pestered professional historians for clues and clarifications amid a blizzard of letters, reports, newspaper articles, and scholarly papers, all the while struggling to read eighteenth-century scrawl.

Again and again, I returned to Norfolk, puzzling over a long-lost colonial city that had been the scene of a series of dramatic events but contained almost no physical trace of those events beyond the churchyard perimeter.

Much of what I uncovered contradicted what I had been taught. The most stunning revelation was that Dunmore did not destroy Norfolk. That brutal act was, I learned, encouraged by Thomas Jefferson, perpetrated by the colony's patriot authorities, and then blamed on the royal governor. The church had survived the cannonade, only to be torched, along with any other buildings still intact, by patriot troops on the orders of the rebellion's leadership. Not even outhouses were spared. A patriot investigation later documented this intentional act in detail, but the report was kept secret for sixty years, and Dunmore remains the prime culprit in the public imagination. Even the irrefutable evidence of the ball in the wall proved ambiguous. The chunk of iron had fallen to the ground in the aftermath of destruction. Nearly a century passed before an enslaved worker dug it out of the ground and cemented it back in place at his owner's direction.

The tumultuous events in and around Norfolk had an immediate and profound impact on the unfolding American Revolution. The unlikely alliance between the man at the apex of Virginia society and those at the bottom turned into the largest insurrection of enslaved people in North America prior to the Civil War, terrifying millions of white Americans and threatening to upend the patriot cause. In the fall of 1775, an alarmed Continental Congress considered kidnapping the earl, and dispatched the first fleet of what would become the United States Navy to crush the British and African forces. Dunmore's erstwhile friend George Washington, commander of the Continental Army, warned in December that the royal governor was well on his way to becoming America's "most formidable enemy."

As 1776 opened, the idea of independence from Britain was still not embraced by most Americans. Dunmore's move to free and arm Black men coupled with his alleged New Year's Day burning of a major American city shocked even those wary of separation. Together with the simultaneous publication of Thomas Paine's persuasive tract *Common Sense* and news that the king had declared the colonies in rebellion, the emancipation of the enslaved and the port's obliteration turned the tide in favor of those eager to abandon the British Empire. In the stormy spring and summer that followed, the governor oversaw an enormous fleet crammed with thousands of Black and white civilians and soldiers. Dubbed "Lord Dunmore's floating town," this was the largest settlement in all of Virginia at that time, and its multiracial multitude threatened to snatch the strategic prize of Virginia from patriot hands. Without that colony's full backing, the Revolution might easily have fizzled into regional revolts more easily crushed by Britain.

In the end, a devastating epidemic, lack of British military support, and a surprise patriot attack forced Dunmore and this remarkable community to withdraw from Virginia one month after the Declaration of Independence was adopted. Yet the impact of that struggle rippled through the war that followed, and long after. Within weeks of the royal governor's emancipation proclamation, Washington was forced to accept an integrated Continental Army, while British generals went on to support and expand Dunmore's edict with the tacit approval of Parliament and King George III.

Tens of thousands of enslaved people abandoned their American owners over the course of the Revolution—precise figures remain a matter of hot dispute among historians—and thousands of those would seed free communities outside the young United States in a vast diaspora that extended from Sierra Leone to New South Wales. Black veterans, meanwhile, gave vital momentum to the growing abolitionist movement on both sides of the Atlantic. Lincoln's more famous decree, and the liberation of four million enslaved Americans in the wake of the Civil War, began with a middle-aged Scottish aristocrat and the brave but largely forgotten men, women, and children who risked their lives to reach British lines and achieve freedom.

"The American war is over, but this is far from being the case with the American Revolution," wrote Pennsylvania patriot Benjamin Rush in 1787, as the Constitutional Convention prepared to meet. That remains true today as we feud over gun control, immigration, race relations, the proper role of government, and even the virtues of country versus city living. We are, in effect, still fighting our revolution, albeit with sound bites rather than bullets.

The roots of these controversies can be found in the conflict that unfolded five hundred miles south of Lexington Green. The popular leader Patrick Henry stoked white Virginian fears of a race war when he warned that the British intended to seize colonists' guns and ammunition, spawning what would become the constitutional "right of the people to keep and bear arms." Norfolk's ruination owed much to rural contempt for a cosmopolitan port dominated by foreigners who, in turn, feared and disdained those native-born. Such enmity lives on in today's rivalry between urban and rural areas and in arguments over immigration. And it was in the Virginia of 1776 that patriots came up with the notion of states' rights to ensure that Congress could not dictate like Parliament. The subsequent conflict over the federal government's capacity to limit slavery culminated in the Civil War. Americans continue to argue over how much power the nation's central authority should wield.

What I discovered in the wake of my Williamsburg visit eclipsed my childhood ideas of reliably sinister redcoats and virtuous patriots. My American Revolution is not that of my grandparents, but it is, I hope, a more accurate depiction, as well as a richer and rawer realm of physical suffering, cynical subterfuge, and remarkable courage and tenacity. Those who fought to remain or break with Britain were intimate players in a fast-paced drama filled with impossible choices, ruthless deeds, and unintended consequences.

We can feel revulsion for the acts of patriots and respect for their enemy without betraying the founders' call for a more just and equitable society. The Black men who shouldered muskets, wielded swords, and wore uniforms emblazoned with LIBERTY FOR SLAVES are surely as deserving of our homage as rifle-toting white minutemen with LIBERTY OR DEATH adorning their hunting shirts. They fought on opposing sides, but for the same cause, that of liberation from tyranny.

EASTERN NORTH AMERICA, 1775
N
Gulf of St. Lawrence
QUEBEC
Quebec City
Halifax
NOVA SCOTIA
Montreal
L. Superior
NEW HAMPSHIRE
Falmouth
Portsmouth
MASSACHUSETTS
L. Huron
L. Michigan
L. Ontario
NEW YORK
Boston
Providence
CONN.
RHODE ISLAND
New Haven
Detroit
L. Erie
PENNSYLVANIA
New York
Pittsburgh
Philadelphia
Trenton
Wilmington
NEW JERSEY
Disputed area
Baltimore
DELAWARE
Annapolis
MARYLAND
PROCLAMATION LINE OF 1763
Chesapeake Bay
Williamsburg
Ohio River
Norfolk
VIRGINIA
Mississippi River
LOUISIANA (SPAIN)
New Bern
NORTH CAROLINA
Wilmington
SOUTH CAROLINA
Atlantic Ocean
Charleston
GEORGIA
Savannah
Claimed by the thirteen British colonies
WEST FLORIDA
Pensacola
St. Augustine
EAST FLORIDA
0 Miles 500
0 Kilometers 500
New Orleans
BAHAMAS
Gulf of Mexico
CUBA (SPAIN)
© 2024 Jeffrey L. Ward

CHESAPEAKE BAY
Baltimore
Patuxent River
Potomac River
Annapolis
Georgetown
Alexandria
Mt. Vernon
(Washington home)
Gunston Hall
(Mason home)
M A R Y L A N D
NEW
JERSEY
Delaware River
Delaware
Bay
Cape Henlopen
DELAWARE
Fredericksburg
St. George Island
Chantilly
(Lee home)
Potomac River
Edmundsbury
(Pendleton home)
Chesapeake Bay
Rappahannock River
Scotchtown (Henry home)
Pamunkey River
Mattaponi River
Hanover
V I R G I N I A
N
Ruffin's Ferry
Chickahominy River
Gwynn's Island
Richmond
York River
Doncastle Ordinary
Rosewell (Page home)
Williamsburg
Petersburg
Yorktown
Jamestown
Cape Charles
James River
Hampton
Cape Henry
Norfolk
Kemp's Landing
Atlantic Ocean
Blackwater River
Suffolk
Great
Dismal Swamp
Great Bridge
Lake Drummond
N O R T H C A R O L I N A
0 Miles 10 20 30
0 Kilometers 30
Chowan River
© 2024 Jeffrey L. Ward

Part One

February 1774 to July 1775

Chapter One

A Kind of Friction

"Clear, with very little wind, and exceeding pleasant—being warm," noted George Washington at his Mount Vernon plantation. On that unusually mild February day in 1774, a cannon crew one hundred miles to the south strained their eyes to be the first to spot a sail in the east. The "bold, gravely cliff" on which they stood commanded "a full view of the river down towards the Bay of Chesapeake," a contemporary visitor wrote, "and a pretty land view, which contains some of the best lowlands in the province." To their backs loomed the hundred or so homes, shops, and taverns of the little tobacco port of Yorktown. Below, people lined the wharves along the sandy shore of the York River.

The mood was festive that Saturday afternoon as the crowd eagerly anticipated a glimpse of the highest-ranking woman to visit Virginia since its founding more than a century and a half before. Lady Charlotte Stewart Murray, Countess of Dunmore, was the niece of an admiral, daughter of one Scottish earl, and wife of another. She and six of her seven living children had braved a hazardous winter ocean crossing from England to New York before journeying south to Virginia to join Lord Dunmore, her husband and governor of the southern province. Another ship sailing the stormy Atlantic for British North America that season wrecked, drowning three crew and eighty of the one hundred enslaved Africans chained beneath the deck.

After an unusually swift five-week crossing, the vessel carrying the Scottish aristocrats anchored off Manhattan on New Year's Day. "I take the liberty of congratulating your Lordship upon the safe arrival of Lady Dunmore and the rest of your right honorable family at New York," Washington wrote the governor in January, assuring him that he was "your Lordship's most obedient servant." He even offered his "carriage, horses, and best services in case her ladyship should travel by land." In the end, the family traveled by water from Maryland, sailing south through the bay and then up the York River, bypassing Mount Vernon on the Potomac.

A stir arose when an elegant town coach driven by an enslaved African in baby-blue-and-white livery rolled down the steep path from town to the docks. A coat of arms featuring a wild man and a beast, with the Latin motto FURTH FORTUNE—"go forth and seek your fortune"—ornamented both doors. John Murray, Fourth Earl of Dunmore, stepped out to the cheers of onlookers. One colonist described him as "short, strong built, well-shaped with a most frank and open countenance," while another recalled him as "muscular and healthy," though "of low statue."

His friend Sir Joshua Reynolds had painted him a decade before as a stocky man with large calves, a tartan kilt, prominent ruddy cheeks, shining brown eyes, and a full head of red hair. At the time, he was a middling Scottish aristocrat with a rapidly growing family, rising debts—he never paid for the portrait—and few career prospects. His wife and her sister used their connections to secure him a lucrative job as royal governor of New York, and in September 1770 he left his children and pregnant wife behind to take up the post. Transferred to Virginia in 1771, he served as King George III's representative in the colony's capital of Williamsburg, which lay eleven miles to the west of Yorktown. Lord Dunmore was now a graying forty-two-year-old with a paunch, though he still had an athletic air reflecting his love of hunting and hiking.

A cry went up from the bluff as the vessel carrying Lady Dunmore appeared on the horizon and swiftly approached the wharves below, carried by the incoming tide. The cannon crew, made up of Yorktown tavern owner Thomas Archer, his friend Benjamin Minnis, and two unnamed Black men, snapped into action to fire a celebratory shot welcoming the countess. One man swabbed the iron barrel with a wooden pole wrapped in rags, while another prepared to ram a gunpowder charge wrapped in cloth down its mouth. The explosive was a carefully ground and sifted combination of charcoal and sulfur, with saltpeter—potassium nitrate—to oxidize the volatile mixture. But the crew proved either too inexperienced or too excited. "By ramming the rod too violently against the iron within, it occasioned a kind of friction, which communicated to the powder," reported eyewitness Clementina Rind, who edited one of the colony's two newspapers.

The powder exploded prematurely as the men hovered over the barrel. The blast hurtled a searing wave of superheated particles and burning cloth into their bodies. Archer's "arms, face, and eyes" were "bruised in a most terrible manner," while Minnis suffered a severe burn on his thigh. The worst injuries of the explosion were inflicted on the two Africans. Each was "dreadfully mangled, one of them having lost three fingers off his right hand; the other much burnt in the face, and his eyes are so much hurt, that it is thought he will never recover their use." Their screams of agony drowned out the cheers below.

The thirty-four-year-old countess disembarked soon after the accident. The tragedy, Rind reported, "gave great pain to all present, and particularly, it is said, to Lady Dunmore." She had auburn hair, rosy cheeks, a delicate nose, kind eyes, and a lilting Scottish accent. One smitten Philadelphia attorney called her "a very elegant woman" who "looks, and speaks, and moves, and is, a lady." After four years of separation, the governor hugged his wife of fifteen years to his chest, and then embraced their three sons and three daughters, including two "sprightly, sweet" teenage girls one colonist called "the two greatest beauties in America." Missing were a toddler deemed too young to make the journey and a son who had died the previous May at age ten.

They climbed into the waiting carriages, helped by enslaved coachmen, as physicians tended to the wounded on the bluff. The accident proved a sinister portent. Seven years later, at this same site, four hundred cannon would roar as more than twenty-five thousand troops from four nations battled amid mud and gore, leaving much of the town in ruins. The outcome would humble an empire, birth a nation, and doom millions to lifetime servitude.

Following the slanting winter sun, the procession rolled out of Yorktown for the hour-long journey to the capital. Tidewater Virginia was an alien place to Scottish eyes used to stone villages, green pastures, and craggy mountains shrouded in gray mist. The port's bluff was an exception in this otherwise relentlessly horizontal terrain of scraggly forest edged with marsh. One visitor at the time found it "so very low and flat and so divided by creeks and great rivers that it appears, in fact, redeemed from the sea and entirely a very recent creation." Chesapeake Bay dominated the eastern portion of the colony, a vast estuary that stretched two hundred miles from north to south and was as wide as forty miles. Like fingers extending from a palm, four great rivers—the Potomac, Rappahannock, York, and James—flowed from the distant Appalachian Mountains to the bay, which in turn emptied into the Atlantic Ocean through a single twelve-mile-wide passage.

Indigenous peoples who spoke an Algonquian language had thrived for millennia on the region's abundant game, seafood, and vegetation. When the English arrived in 1607 to build their first permanent colony in the New World, they found a confederation of tribes called Powhatans, who grew corn, squash, beans, and tobacco, a wild herb domesticated some three thousand years earlier in the high Andes. Prized in the Americas for its spiritual and medicinal values, tobacco quickly became popular among Europeans, who believed it dissolved gallstones, cured asthma, relieved headaches, and disinfected open wounds. Blown in the ear, they thought, it could restore hearing, and, properly administered, it was said to bring the drowned to life.

Virginia's early English settlers crossed the Powhatans' tobacco variety with a milder Caribbean strain to produce a sweet and aromatic leaf that proved a sensation on the international market. In the rush to profit, white immigrants pushed the native peoples, already weakened by European disease, from the most productive lands. Within twenty years of the colony's founding, King Charles I was complaining that Virginia was "wholly built upon smoke, tobacco being the only means it hath produced." Fantastic fortunes could be made by those who obtained fertile land. "We have no merchants, tradesmen, or artificers of any sort here but what become planters in a short time," reported one immigrant in 1757. By the time Lady

Dunmore arrived, tobacco still accounted for three-quarters of the colony's exports, but annual production had soared from half a million pounds in the 1620s to one hundred million pounds.

This enormous increase was made possible by enslaved Africans, who by the early 1700s had largely replaced indentured servants, the urban poor, and prisoners brought from England to labor in the fields. The new hands were mostly Efik, Ibibio, and Igbo from what is now Nigeria, Cameroon, Gabon, and Equatorial Guinea who had been crammed into the holds of British merchant ships. "The shrieks of the women, and the groans of the dying, rendered the whole a scene of horror almost inconceivable," recalled Gustavus Vassa, an African who wrote an account of a 1750s crossing in an autobiography composed after he achieved freedom and reached Britain. Those who survived the fearsome Middle Passage were sold on Virginia wharves. By 1774, more than 200,000 enslaved people—two out of five inhabitants—powered the colony's tobacco boom, the vast majority employed in the fields. Nineteen out of twenty had been born within the province, spoke fluent English, and worshipped as Christians, though Islamic and traditional African beliefs inflected their religion.

On that unusually warm late Saturday afternoon, Lady Dunmore undoubtedly would have glimpsed enslaved Black workers covering precious young tobacco seedlings with pine boughs or pale linen cloth to protect them from late frosts. They would return at dusk to an outbuilding or a shack for a meal of hoecake and salted fish. At Mount Vernon, Washington allocated daily rations of one quart of cornmeal and five to eight ounces of shad or herring to his adult unfree workers. One English visitor noted that those in bondage rarely received meat, unless their master "be a man of humanity" who provided "a little fat, skimmed milk, and rusty bacon."

Not surprisingly, pilfering food was the most common crime among those enslaved. "I wish you could find out the thief who robbed the meat house at Mount Vernon, and bring him to punishment," Washington later wrote an overseer. Penalties were severe. A week before Lady Dunmore arrived, an unnamed Norfolk man in bondage was convicted of stealing a hog and received the legally mandated "thirty-nine lashes, on his . . . bare back, well laid on, at the public whipping post." This was nearly double the flogging decreed for free people for a similar crime, though owners had the right to exceed that number. David George, an enslaved Virginian born the same year as Thomas Jefferson, recalled his sister was scourged until her back was "all corruption," while his brother endured five hundred lashes for an attempted escape. George himself was beaten until blood ran down "over my waistband," but added that his greatest trial "was to see them whip my mother, and to hear her, on her knees, begging for mercy." There were other forms of punishment, including branding, shackling, and disfigurement. While laboring on a Virginia plantation, Vassa encountered a Black cook with a metal device secured on her head "which locked her mouth so fast that she could scarcely speak; and could not eat nor drink. I was much astonished and shocked at this contrivance, which I afterward learned was called the iron muzzle."

These enslaved Africans were at the bottom of Virginia's social pyramid. "They live in huts and hovels near the houses of their owners," one British visitor observed, "and are treated as a better kind of cattle." Above them were some sixty thousand indentured servants—often convicts—from England, Ireland, and Scotland who toiled for as long as seven years to pay off their passage, food, and shelter. Then came tenants and day laborers. Roughly half of the colony's 260,000 whites were small tobacco planters and corn and wheat farmers, who typically lived in plain one-and-a-half-story dwellings and might have owned a couple hundred acres and one or two people in bondage. Their diet was heavy with bread, beer, and stew.

Near the pyramid's top, making up some 10 percent of white Virginians, were the elite tobacco growers who dominated the colony's legislative assembly, the House of Burgesses, and mimicked the fashion, manners, and architecture of well-to-do Britons. They dined on beef, pork, lamb, seafood, sweetmeats, puddings, and pastries served by liveried Africans on imported china within stately homes resembling those of the English landed gentry. "Freedom is to them not only an enjoyment, but a kind of rank and privilege," wrote British politician Edmund Burke.

At the apex of the hierarchy were a hundred or so of the richest planters, such as John Page, a close friend of Thomas Jefferson. On her way to Williamsburg, Lady Dunmore would have spotted, across the York River to the north, the twin massive chimneys that marked Page's home of Rosewell. The twelve-thousand-square-foot, three-story brick pile was the continent's largest private home, with an imported mahogany-and-marble interior, walls three and a half feet thick, and a lead roof. Page's feudal domain, extending over twenty-seven thousand acres, included more than one hundred enslaved Africans. While most labored in the fields, others were skilled workers, including Emmanuel, a shoemaker, Oliver, a blacksmith, and Mary, a dairy maid, along with coopers, spinners, weavers, carpenters, and laundresses.

While those trapped in lifetime servitude had little chance of altering their status, any reasonably lucky and hardworking white man might aspire to join the ranks of the gentry. Unlike sugar cultivation in the Caribbean and rice farming in South Carolina, tobacco husbandry did not require massive start-up capital and a concentrated labor force, and it lent itself to smaller parcels. Even major plantations were usually broken up into fields called quarters, where a dozen or so enslaved people were "quartered" and managed by an overseer. With a bit more land, a few more skilled enslaved workers, and several good harvests, a small planter might find himself asked to join the local church vestry or even seek election as a burgess. At the same time, a swift downward trajectory was also possible. An epidemic, a hailstorm, or the feared tobacco budworm could plunge even the richest family into sudden financial ruin.

One in four of the three million Americans in the thirteen colonies was a Virginian, twice the number of Massachusetts residents, and no other North American province could match its total wealth. The key to this prosperity was relentless expansion. Tobacco sucked sulfur, magnesium, phosphorus, and potassium from the soil, and planters were quick to abandon exhausted fields, which then reverted to weeds and pines, giving the countryside a desolate and deserted air. Virginia's four great rivers served as highways into the interior, allowing settlers to displace indigenous peoples from the rich and rolling hills of the Piedmont, the region that lay between the coastal plain and the Appalachian Mountains. "There are an incredible number of creeks, most of which are also navigable," Dunmore explained to his superior in London in 1773. "Upon the whole I may venture to say no country for two hundred miles back from the sea can be more commodiously situated for water carriage than this is."

These waterways also made towns largely superfluous, as almost every gentleman planter loads "whatever he has for sale at his own door, and at the same place receives his goods from Great Britain." Courthouses and churches sprang up to serve these tobacco growers as new counties proliferated. This rapid yet orderly growth set Virginia apart from the other southern colonies of Maryland, the Carolinas, and Georgia. There, the wealthy elite remained largely clustered along the coastal plain, and their capitals were ports with easy access to the sea. Small farmers and recent immigrants dominated those colonies' poorer inland territories, which were less accessible to British markets.

By the middle of the 1750s, Virginians were already pressing up against the forested mountain ridges that divided the Atlantic watershed from that of the Mississippi. Beyond the Appalachians lay the rich bottomlands of the Ohio Valley, which the colony's planters considered to be part of a province that they maintained extended to today's Michigan, Wisconsin, and even to the distant Pacific Ocean. The valley was home to Shawnees, Mingos, Delawares, and other tribes. In 1754, a party of Virginians and their indigenous allies, led by the young militia colonel and land speculator George Washington, ambushed a French delegation in what is now western Pennsylvania, sparking the French and Indian War, which spread to Europe as the Seven Years' War. By early 1763, Britain had triumphed over France, gaining nominal control over the French province of Quebec and those lands between the Appalachians and the Mississippi River.

White Virginians like Washington were ecstatic, since this removed their European enemy and opened the door to further westward expansion. Britain, however, was deeply in debt and feared another expensive war between its colonists and the indigenous peoples that were now technically under the protective mantle of the empire. In the summer of 1763, a bloody uprising against the British occupiers by a confederation of tribes led by the warrior Pontiac prompted King George III to forbid colonists from settling west of the highest Appalachian ridges. This Proclamation Line irritated members of the gentry, who needed legal grants from the king to enlarge their tobacco kingdoms. Less-well-heeled white settlers ignored the boundary, filtering over the mountains in small armed bands, often with their enslaved workers, to rent, buy, or take land from the indigenous inhabitants. To the Native peoples of the Ohio, the cutlass-carrying Virginians were "Assarigoe," an Iroquois term translated as "Long Knives."

For the first century and a half, the British government imposed no tax on North American colonists. That changed when Parliament passed a series of duties on imports after 1763 aimed at paying off the war debt. This new policy particularly angered New Englanders, who profited heavily from the sea trade, but it drew fierce resistance from all the colonies. They employed lobbyists, wrote petitions, established boycotts, and convinced Parliament to rescind these measures. British legislators, however, stubbornly maintained their right to raise revenue from the colonies and refused to repeal a small tax on tea to make that point. Tensions came to a head in March 1770. Redcoats killed five Bostonians in a brawl on an icy street—including a Black sailor named Crispus Attucks—but the British quickly withdrew troops from the city to calm tensions. By the time Dunmore arrived in New York that fall to serve as governor, the crisis between Crown and colonists seemed to have passed.

Then came the devastating recession of 1773 that threatened to sink the troubled East India Company. London judged the tottering private business too big to fail and allowed the company to sell heavily discounted Chinese tea directly to the colonies with the small levy. Parliament did not expect any pushback; even with the duty, tea would be cheaper than in the past, and consumers as well as company shareholders would benefit. The legislation, however, highlighted the detested tax and angered American merchants, particularly those in the north who profited from smuggling goods, including tea, from abroad.

The first shipment of the East India Company leaf arrived in Boston in late November, as Lady Dunmore and her family were speeding across the Atlantic. Two weeks later, men disguised as Mohawks clambered aboard a vessel docked in the Massachusetts capital, chopping up 342 chests of tea and dumping 46 tons of it into the harbor's chilly waters. The countess arrived in New York on the first day of 1774, soon after two hundred leading citizens had signed a petition branding anyone who purchased legally imported tea "an enemy to the liberties of America." They argued that executing Parliament's plan "involves our slavery, and would sap the foundation of our freedom, whereby we should become slaves to our brethren." Three thousand people had gathered outside city hall to protest the duty. Talk of the crisis permeated the drawing rooms where the countess and her children spent their next month, making social rounds in the bustling port of twenty-five thousand people.

When the Dunmore family reached Philadelphia—then the largest urban area in North America after Mexico City—the town was likewise abuzz. The *Polly* had arrived in Delaware Bay on Christmas Day with 697 chests of tea, and 7,000 residents packed the square in front of the Pennsylvania State House to protest the shipment. It was the biggest gathering up to that point in American history. "What think you, captain, of a halter around your neck—ten gallons of liquid tar decanted on your pate—with the feathers of a dozen wild geese laid over that to enliven your appearance?" read one handbill. The captain chose to return with the cargo to England rather than endure the torture of tarring and feathering. At a reception held in her honor at the city's Lodge Alley in February, the countess danced as the city's affluent businessmen fretted over the deepening crisis.

The upheaval largely bypassed Virginia. No immediate tea shipments were planned, so there were no petitions and no mass demonstrations. The province's white inhabitants preferred British beer or Jamaican rum to the Chinese beverage, and Scottish and English merchants owned most of the seagoing ships plying its waters. Of far greater concern was the slump in tobacco prices and the growing debt planters owed to those merchants. There were also ominous clashes between indigenous peoples and white settlers pressing west, and a worrisome uptick in escapes by enslaved Africans.

Some white Virginians were happy at the prospect of cheaper tea, while others feared it was a first step toward what one called the "unlimited extension of taxes in America by the British Parliament."

Virginia's gentry, however, agreed that the urban mob had gone too far by disregarding the sanctity of private property. "The Bostonians did wrong in destroying the tea," concluded Edmund Pendleton, an influential slave-owning lawyer and burgess. "Americans will never be taxed without their own consent," insisted George Washington, quickly adding, "not that we approve their conduct in destroying the tea." One planter worried that the rash act by "our northern brethren" might "end in the annihilation of our American legislatures and introduce a military government." Such fears, however, seemed overblown. The colonists in the past had mostly succeeded in getting their way, and they had little reason to think this time would be different.

Dozens of riders were waiting for the governor and his family on the road outside Williamsburg, their hands clutching the reins of their finest horses. "A great number of the most respectable citizens, and many from the country, who had been informed of her arrival, attended the carriages, in order to see her ladyship safe at the Palace," Rind's paper noted. Leading the retinue was Peyton Randolph, the portly Williamsburg lawyer who had long served as speaker of the House of Burgesses. His younger brother John, the attorney general, would also have been present, along with George Wythe, the gaunt lawyer and mentor to Jefferson. Members of the town council and the governor's council—nearly all wealthy planters chosen by the king—filled out the company. After greeting the countess and her children, the men formed an honor guard to see them to the governor's mansion.

The trip that winter evening was short. Though Williamsburg was the second-largest settlement in Virginia, it was home to fewer than two thousand people and would barely have qualified as a neighborhood in Philadelphia, which had a population twenty times that of the Virginia capital. The only city of note in the colony was Norfolk, the port that lay forty miles to the southeast, near the entrance to Chesapeake Bay.

Williamsburg straddled the spine of land separating the watersheds of the York and James Rivers. Originally called Middle Plantation, it lay halfway along a palisade built in the 1620s across the width of the peninsula to divide the territory between settlers and Powhatans. Six miles to the south, on a small, marshy James River island plagued with malaria-bearing mosquitoes and brackish water, stood Virginia's original capital of Jamestown, established in 1607.

In 1693, King William III and Mary II granted a charter that made Middle Plantation home to Virginia's first institution of higher learning, the College of William and Mary. At that time, the colony's governor lived in Britain, delegating the unpleasant job of living at the unhealthy site of Jamestown to Lieutenant Governor Francis Nicholson. In 1699, Nicholson conspired with the first college president, Scottish cleric James Blair, to have the capital transferred from Jamestown to Middle Plantation. They wrote speeches for students to present at a college ceremony arguing that the new location would be "free from the plague of mosquitoes and the noisome stinks and thick fogs of fenny, marshy, and swampy grounds." Along with plentiful springs, the interior location made it impervious "to great guns and bombs of any enemies' men of war" as well as the "rudenesses of great gangs of sailors."

The combination of education and political institutions would create a welcome synergy. "The college will help to make the town, and the town to make the college," one student asserted. Laying out the capital as a proper city also would "retrieve the reputation of our country, which has suffered by nothing so much as by neglecting a seat of trade, wealth, and learning." They dreamed that it would someday "equal if not outdo Boston, New York, Philadelphia, Charles Town, and Annapolis."*

The House of Burgesses readily agreed. The new city was dubbed Williamsburg for the Dutch-born reigning British king. Nicholson personally designed it so as to avoid both the repetitive grid of Philadelphia and the twisting alleys of Boston. He centered the town on a grand mile-long, ninety-nine-foot-wide boulevard that led east from the college building to the new seat of the provincial government. He called it Duke of Gloucester Street, after the eldest son of Queen

* The South Carolina capital, named for King Charles II, was renamed Charleston in 1783. Hereafter, the modern name is used.

Anne. Not one inclined to modesty, he named the parallel streets Francis and Nicholson after himself.

The lieutenant governor then ordered construction of a massive brick capitol, paid for with revenues from a twenty-shilling tax imposed on each imported African and built with the help of enslaved labor. The innovative H-shaped structure consisted of an east wing, with a legislative chamber modeled on Westminster's House of Commons on the first floor and committee rooms above, and a west wing, which housed a general court at ground level and the governor's council chamber on the second floor. An enclosed gallery connected the two wings on the first level, with a spacious room above. A thin glassed-in cupola perched on the cypress-shingled roof, topped with a flapping Union Jack. The west wing faced the distant college. A governor's residence took longer to complete, but it eventually rose at the end of a grassy mall halfway down the main street. At the time, it was the largest single residence in British North America. The three-story brick building had a steeply sloping roof, slender cupola and four large chimneys. "A magnificent structure built at the public expense, finished and beautified with gates, fine gardens, offices, walks, a fine canal, orchards, etc.," enthused one college professor in the 1720s.

The new capital attracted tavern keepers and small merchants, yet Nicholson's dream of a thriving urban center never materialized. Williamsburg served primarily as a stage set for Virginia's wealthy planters, who overwhelmingly lived in distant rural seats. On court days and when the House of Burgesses was in session, they promenaded, drank, danced, gambled, and raced horses. Their coaches, landaus, phaetons, and chaises, steered by Black men in livery, bumped along the unpaved streets. "On those occasions, there are balls and other amusements," wrote an Anglican minister from Britain. Virginians were said to "dance or die," and one governor bragged, "There was not an ill dancer in my government."

Half the town's residents were enslaved Africans who served the drinks, prepared the food, assisted in the shops, and took care of the horses, gardens, and farm animals, while white residents typically worked as artisans, clerks, and shop owners. Williamsburg "resembles a good country town in England," noted Lord Adam Gordon when he visited in 1765, if one subtracted the enslaved population. Wary of public expenditures, legislators balked at the cost of planting shade trees, building sidewalks, or digging drainage ditches along the boulevard, which was alternatively deep in dust or thick with mud. Walking the street was "very disagreeable," one visitor complained, "especially in summer, when the rays of the sun are intensely hot" and "there is no shade or shelter to walk under." The capital retained a raw look, like a late-nineteenth-century frontier town. Even Washington, who had never seen a city larger than Philadelphia, sarcastically referred to it in 1752 as "the great polis."

The Anglican minister noted that as soon as legislators finished their work, "they return to their plantations and the town is in a manner deserted." The appearance of a countess near the end of a drab winter understandably caused a welcome stir. "Our city has long expected the arrival of Lady Dunmore," a Williamsburg pastor informed Washington, while one excited college student wrote his father that "great preparations are being made."

The sky was dark by the time the carriages rolled past the Capitol and down Duke of Gloucester Street, but the windows of apothecaries, milliners, tailors, wigmakers, barbers and hairdressers, and private homes were bright with hundreds of tallow candles, in what was called "an illumination." The procession crossed the broad and grassy Market Square, dominated by the octagonal armory and new courthouse. Turning right at Bruton Parish Church, they rode down Bowling Green, lined by catalpa trees and elegant brick homes, before coming to a halt before the governor's imposing home, the Palace, its dozens of multipaned sash windows glowing with light.

A low brick wall at the entrance was broken by two pillars, one topped with England's lion and the other with Scotland's unicorn, which represented the 1707 union of the two countries. The family climbed the imported-stone stairs and stepped into a foyer with a brightly gleaming polished floor of black-and-white marble quarried in England and Belgium. Hundreds of pistols, muskets, bayonets, small swords, and broad swords were "arranged upon the walls in an ornamental manner, as in the Tower of London." The countess would have felt immediately at home; such martial displays were still common in Scottish castles, where they served a useful function in case of enemy attack.

Less familiar was the staff of enslaved Africans who stood at attention before their new mistress in crisp blue-and-white uniforms. Their fine clothes were designed to reflect the wealth and power of their owner, the governor. Those Black residents who waited tables for less distinguished white families or for tavern customers wore simpler garments, while enslaved children often wore few or no clothes. A few years later, a traveler from Philadelphia was taken aback by "boys of ten and twelve years of age going through the streets quite naked." He added that "this is so common a sight that even the ladies do not appear to be shocked at it."

The Palace was far grander than any residence Lord and Lady Dunmore had previously inhabited. Like other men of his station, the governor delighted in luxury even if he could ill afford it. He had furnished the twelve-thousand-square-foot home containing twenty-five rooms with "beds, bedding, looking glasses, bureaus, bookcases, valuable tapestry, damask curtains, carpets, etc.," as well as "a number of valuable pictures by Sir Peter Lely, and a number of costly prints." The governor had amassed a fine collection of china, glass, and household utensils, along with a "valuable library consisting of upwards of 1300 volumes," one of the largest in the colonies. The music room and ballroom featured "three organs, a harpsichord, a pianoforte, and other musical instruments." There was even a small organ housed in a walnut box used to encourage birds to mimic popular tunes. The cellar was packed with 5,000 gallons of wine—mostly fine Madeira—and 480 gallons of aged rum. The children delighted in Glasgow, the governor's prize bulldog, as well as the spiral staircase on the top floor that led to grand views of the James and York Rivers, ideal for sky gazing with Dunmore's state-of-the-art telescope.

The mansion operated much as any large plantation, with some twenty outbuildings clustered around the main house and a large staff of enslaved people, as well as white employees on a salary. Reception and dining areas took up much of the downstairs, and a wing with an elaborate ballroom and supper room extended into the formal garden. The second floor, accessed by a grand staircase, included bedrooms and the library, while the third floor with its many dormers provided ample space for Dunmore's large brood.

Two buildings flanking the Palace entrance served as office space and accommodations for white staff and guests. In the rear was a blacksmith's forge, a cabinetry shop, stables. Enslaved men lived and worked in a building housing a variety of coaches, carriages, and phaetons, as well as assorted wagons and carts. In the kitchen, scullery, laundry, smokehouse, and other structures, women and children in bondage spun wool and flax, washed and ironed clothes, baked bread, brewed beer, prepared meals, and cleaned the pots and pans and plates. The spacious garden on the north and west ends of the compound was lined with boxwoods and edged with a canal. A stout brick wall enclosed the compound, which lay at the northern limit of town.

In the days that followed Lady Dunmore's arrival, Williamsburg's elite hosted lavish dinners and firework displays, eager to impress the countess with their hospitality. A local lawyer wrote Jefferson that the colony's first lady was "well pleased with everything hitherto; every mark of respect having been shown her." The town's two newspapers competed to see which could publish the lengthiest panegyrics to the governor's wife. Both were called the *Virginia Gazette*, the name required if they were to qualify for lucrative government contracts to publish official notices. In a year, editor Clementina Rind would be dead of cancer and a third *Gazette* would be born, each of the three typically published on a different day of the week. Their jumble of letters, news reports, gossip, and advertisements for real estate and runaway slaves were the colony's primary sources of information.

"While cannon roar to hail thee, bonfires blaze, and joy 'round every heart exulting plays," went one verse dedicated to the countess. "Fair Murray"—her husband's family name—"deigns to tread the savage plain, each muse, and soft-eyed grace, are in her train." Another poem praised the governor while gingerly hinting at trouble to come. "May his example liberty inspire" and "unite in freedom's glorious cause . . . the Crown's prerogative, the people's right, equally poised, and ever in their sight."

A fast ship had delivered news of Boston's mid-December "tea party" to London by late January 1774, as Lady Dunmore was making her way south from New York. The king's Cabinet, furious about the destructive act, determined to take "effectual steps . . . to secure the dependence of [the] colonies on the Mother Country." As Virginians celebrated Lady Dunmore with pomp and circumstance, ministers in London drafted a bill to close Boston harbor to all shipping. Another month would pass before Parliament approved the drastic measure, and another six weeks before word of this reached Williamsburg. The balance between people and Crown had begun to wobble.

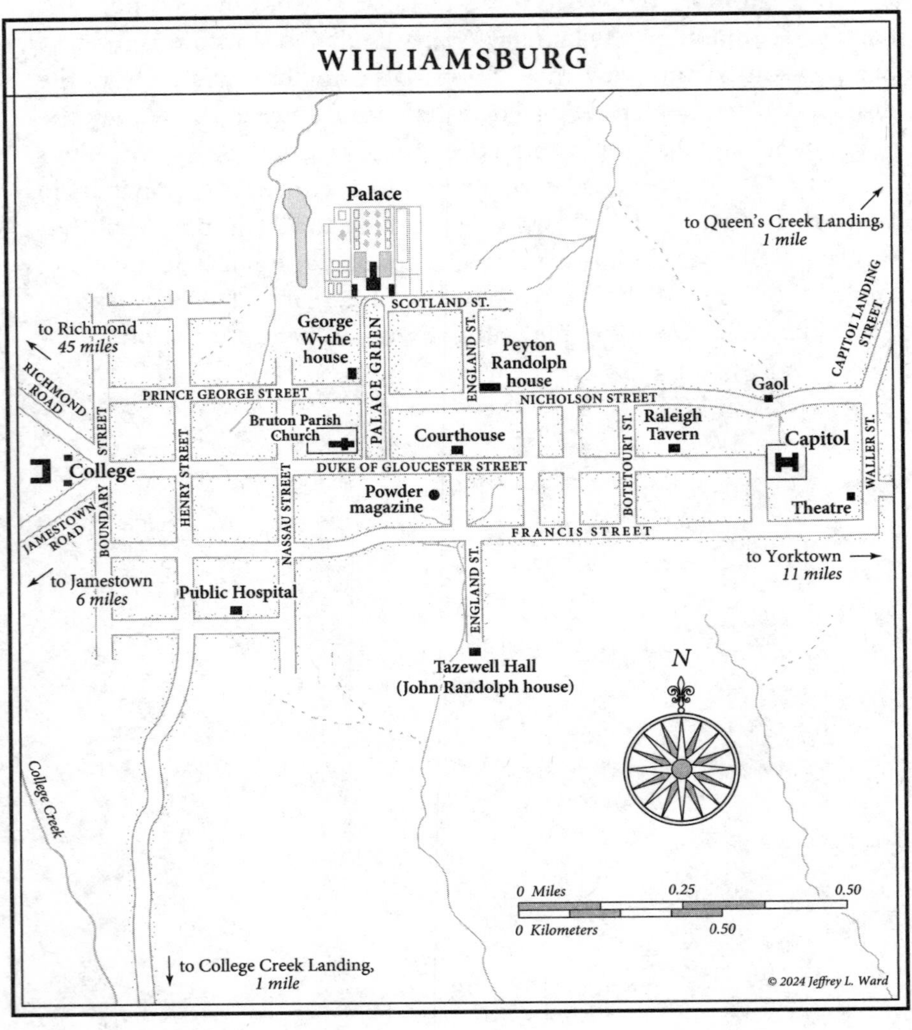
WILLIAMSBURG
Palace
to Queen's Creek Landing,
1 mile
CAPITOL LANDING STREET
SCOTLAND ST.
to Richmond
45 miles
George
Wythe
house
PALACE GREEN
ENGLAND ST.
Peyton
Randolph
house
RICHMOND ROAD
PRINCE GEORGE STREET
NICHOLSON STREET
Gaol
BOUNDARY STREET
Bruton Parish
Church
Courthouse
BOTETOURT ST.
Raleigh
Tavern
Capitol
WALLER ST.
College
HENRY STREET
DUKE OF GLOUCESTER STREET
NASSAU STREET
Powder
magazine
Theatre
JAMESTOWN ROAD
FRANCIS STREET
to Yorktown
11 miles
to Jamestown
6 miles
Public Hospital
ENGLAND ST.
Tazewell Hall
(John Randolph house)
N
College Creek
0 Miles
0.25
0.50
0 Kilometers
0.50
to College Creek Landing,
1 mile
© 2024 Jeffrey L. Ward

Chapter Two

A Gentleman of Benevolence

Dunmore had not wanted the job. "Damn Virginia!" he is said to have roared when he received orders from the king in early 1771 to leave New York for Williamsburg. "Did I ever seek it? Why is it forced upon me?" He preferred the bustle of Manhattan to life in a torpid and sickly rural backwater, and immediately tried to reverse London's decision. "Virginia, where the climate is such that I never could think of carrying my lady or any of the children," he wrote his superior, the colonial secretary in London, "as there are eight months in the year, that they are hardly ever free from fever and ague." Raised in the Scottish Highlands, Dunmore hated heat and humidity. As if this were not bad enough, the gregarious earl would have to endure the "tiresome" prospect of "little or no society."

The governor was unaware that his wife and sister had deftly pulled strings in the British capital when the previous governor died the same month he had arrived in New York. Overseeing the continent's largest and wealthiest British colony was, after all, a plum assignment with a larger salary and greater prestige; a friend congratulated Dunmore on "a more distinguishing mark of his Majesty's favor" which put him at the apex of "the first American government." Transatlantic communication was, in any case, a slow and uncertain business. A typical square-rigger of the day traveled at an average of less than two miles an hour, and a three-thousand-mile crossing could last four weeks or three months, depending on wind and weather. Added time was needed by sailors, riders, or coachmen to convey the message to and from the ship. For Dunmore to receive news from Britain and get a reply might easily take a third of a year.

Dunmore's confided to a friend that he preferred "health and good society to a greater salary," but his frantic attempts to decline the job led a piqued King George III to order the obstinate aristocrat "to fit yourself with all convenient speed, and to repair to our said colony of Virginia." The royal governor sent his baggage and hunting dogs south but lingered awkwardly in New York City after his replacement arrived, fruitlessly trying to convince him to swap jobs. When that failed, he headed north to inspect some fifty thousand acres in the Green Mountains of what is now Vermont that he was angling to buy. He spent a pleasant summer with two guides named John and Abraham, who were either indigenous men or of African descent, describing them as "perfectly sober, faithful, and indefatigable." They provided him with his first intimate introduction to non-Europeans.

By the time Dunmore finally sailed into Yorktown in September 1771, the worst of the Tidewater summer was over. By then, it was common knowledge among the gentry that the earl had not wanted the job. This made many ready to believe rumors that he was "a gamester, a whoremaster, and a drunkard." A second- or thirdhand report claimed that he had even sliced off the tails of the horses owned by New York's chief justice in a late-night prank fueled by too much liquor. The earl's arrival in New York had been marred by a petty quarrel over his salary—paid for, fatefully, with revenues from the tea tax—and his penchant for keeping others waiting irritated legislators. He proved, however, an able administrator in a colony dominated by bitterly feuding families. In his brief tenure he convinced the colony's fractious gentry to tackle a ballooning public debt and pay for British troops stationed there. This last accomplishment earned him the gratitude of General Thomas Gage, the British officer based in New York who commanded the North American forces.

Dunmore exuded a vitality atypical of royal governors. One contemporary New Yorker called him "a very active man, fond of walking and riding, and a sportsman." Another said he was "easy and affable in his manners, very temperate, and a great lover of field sports, indefatigable and constant in pursuit of them." He also enjoyed fine wine, good food, and lively conversation; a newspaper editor praised his "convivial disposition." This love of entertaining as well as the outdoors soon dispelled the Virginia elite's initial trepidation. He was not the debauched rake of the rumor mill, and he quickly embraced the gentry's way of life. Among the first friends he made was an ambitious planter three years his junior who lived a two-day's ride to the north. Within two weeks of the new governor's arrival, George Washington was dining at the Palace and treating the new governor to performances at the theater next to the Capitol.

At first glance, the tall and reticent Virginian from the lush southern countryside would seem to have little in common with the short and voluble aristocrat who grew up in the stony Scottish Highlands. "He may be described as being as straight as an Indian, measuring six feet two inches in his stockings," wrote one burgess of Washington. His frame was "padded with well-developed muscles, indicating great strength," and he had "colorless pale skin, which burns with the sun." The planter kept his mouth closed to hide "defective teeth" and was as abstemious with his words as Dunmore was garrulous.

Yet their lives had taken eerily parallel paths. Both grew up on the fringe of empire, lost their fathers at an early age to death or disgrace, and were shaped by strong-willed and well-educated mothers. Washington and Dunmore were born into families less affluent than many of their peers', and as youths chose soldiering as a path to success. Each fought in the Seven Years' War, only to quit the military in disgust when they failed to achieve the rank they felt they deserved.

Both men found wealth and recognition through marriage to formidable women. In the first week of January 1759, Washington wed Martha Custis, one of Virginia's richest widows, with vast estates and some three hundred enslaved Africans. Six weeks later, Dunmore married Charlotte Stewart, his first cousin once removed. Though she lacked significant financial assets, Stewart came from a well-connected family with substantial social capital. Both couples settled on feudal-style estates with dramatic water views, Mount Vernon on the Potomac and Dunmore Park on Scotland's broad Firth of Forth.

They also launched their political careers almost simultaneously. Washington used his wife's resources to buy voters beer, rum punch, wine, and cider to win a seat in the House of Burgesses—a time-honored Virginia tradition—while the new King George III appointed the earl to the House of Lords. Neither man, however, showed much interest in the intricacies of legislating. They spoke little in sessions, initiated no major bills, and were frequently absent. They preferred riding, hunting, and betting on horse races to the tedious business of governing.

Throughout the 1760s, both indulged their love of fashionable clothes, good wine, and the latest styles in transport and architecture. Washington turned his modest six-room farmhouse into a grand mansion while purchasing more land and enslaved Africans. Dunmore constructed an elaborate neoclassical garden pavilion on his country estate, while keeping a house in nearby Edinburgh as well as one in London. The Virginian ordered an ornate carriage from England, while the earl was seen "cutting a flash" through Edinburgh's cobbled streets in a "splendid coach" while wearing a waistcoat sewn with gold lace. When he arrived in New York, Dunmore had packed a wardrobe that included forty-five new shirts, forty-two pairs of white silk stockings, and thirty velvet and cloth coats. Their wives also enjoyed profligate spending. Martha Washington collected fine china and embroidered silk-and-leather pumps, while Lady Dunmore made frequent trips to Italy to escape the dreary British winters.

By the second half of the decade, both couples were living far beyond their means. Mount Vernon's clay soil proved unsuitable for tobacco, and Washington found it expensive to replace "such hazardous and perishable articles as Negroes, stock, and chattels, which are to be swept off by innumerable distempers and subject to many accidents and misfortunes." Illness killed many of his enslaved workers. "God knows I have losses enough in Negroes," he wrote. With bills piling up, Washington took the radical step in 1766 of shifting his plantation's crop from tobacco to wheat. He renovated an old mill and soon was earning a handsome profit by selling bushels of fine flour. "G Washington" became a sought-after regional brand. This move also insulated him from the unpredictable swings in tobacco prices that battered his neighbors.

Dunmore's income derived primarily from tenant farmers working Scotland's rocky soil. Flour shortages in 1766 sparked riots "among the poorer folk," who found it difficult to survive while also paying rent to their spendthrift landlord. The earl was reduced to asking for a loan from the Duke of Atholl, who led the primary branch of the vast Murray clan. The duke reluctantly agreed. "Though none but the good deserve our friendship yet the imprudent have often a title to our assistance," he wrote a friend, noting that his cousin possessed "good qualities," while adding that weeds "have grown up with the wheat."

The earl's prospects brightened with the discovery of a coal seam running through his garden, which, together with the loan, stabilized his finances. Still, he needed a high-paying job. The 1768 marriage of his wife's sister to the Earl of Gower, a leading British politician, opened the door to the lucrative upper levels of civil service. His sister-in-law "teased every minister for every little office that fell in his department," complained a disapproving Horace Walpole, who, like most of the era's elite, played the same game. When New York's governor died in the fall of 1769, the two women quickly exploited the sudden opening. By November, Dunmore had "kissed his Majesty's hand . . . on being appointed governor of New York." He wrote a grateful letter to Lord Gower on New Year's Day 1770, hoping the job "may turn out to be both pleasant to myself, and advantageous to my family." His anxious patron could not have agreed more. "The welfare of a good wife and eight children depends upon his succeeding," Gower confided later to a friend.

Wheat and a three-thousand-pound-a-year job, respectively, rescued Washington and Dunmore from looming financial disaster, but they did not much alter their spending habits. As a member of the House of Lords, the earl was expected to entertain lavishly in London, which was then, as now, one of the world's costliest cities. And the Virginian feared that reducing expenses would "create suspicions of a decay in my fortune and such a thought the world must not harbor." Selling a prize horse or dressing enslaved house servants in old clothes was a public sign of personal distress.

The antidote was land. As early as 1766, Dunmore had his eye on the vast acreage of the New World. That winter, during an outing to an abbey outside London, he regaled his friend Lord Shelburne with plans for "a settlement in North America where he has a scheme of going some time or other" and even drew a sketch for his "habitation on the banks of the Ohio." For his part, Washington had coveted the fertile soil along the broad western river since he was a teenage surveyor. Like many members of the gentry, the planter viewed this region beyond the Appalachians as the key to his personal fortune as well as the colony's future prosperity. The 1763 Proclamation Line—drawn, ironically, by Lord Shelburne at the king's request—prevented this. "I can never look upon that proclamation in any other light (but this I say between ourselves) than as a temporary expedient to quiet the minds of the Indians," Washington wrote to a friend.

In subsequent years, bowing to settler and speculator pressure, British agents negotiated treaties with indigenous elders to push the line further west, but restrictions on white settlement beyond the boundary remained in place. While speculators like Washington needed official title to buy or sell acreage, poorer white colonists ignored the king's decree. "Not even a second Chinese wall, unless guarded by a million soldiers, could prevent the settlement of the lands on the Ohio," one writer in a *Virginia Gazette* noted in 1773. Washington feared these squatters would obtain all the best bottom land.

Dunmore's arrival in Williamsburg revived the planter's hopes that he could win permission to survey the Ohio, using the chains and compasses that indigenous people called "land stealers." During long afternoon dinners at the Palace, rides through the countryside, and evenings at the capital's theater, Washington had little trouble firing the earl's imagination. The governor of New York had been reluctant to come to Virginia in part, no doubt, because he stood to lose his claim to fifty thousand acres in the Green Mountains of what is now Vermont. He soon realized that the more temperate Ohio Valley promised even greater returns. The royal governor was under strict instructions from London to uphold the king's policy and respect the lands of indigenous peoples. The temptation to find loopholes, however, was great, and Washington proved tenacious. He proposed they visit the Ohio Valley together in the summer of 1773; months in the saddle would give Mount Vernon's owner a golden opportunity to press his case. He promised that any request the governor had in planning the expedition would be "punctually obeyed." If the earl wanted "to have an Indian engaged," for example, he would "have one provided."

Abandoning the sultry capital for cool mountain air appealed to Dunmore. During the earl's first summer in Virginia, in 1772, he contracted a fever and lay sweltering for weeks in his four-poster Palace bed. He dreaded another torrid Tidewater summer, when a thick haze typically enveloped the capital. During the day, complained one visitor to the South, "the atmosphere seemed in a glow, as if fires were kindled round us, the air being so thick and smoky, that the sun appeared as a ball of redhot metal." Night offered little relief. "With all the doors and windows open, we were constantly bathed in sweat."

The sudden death of Martha's sole daughter in June 1773 derailed Washington's well-laid plan. The seventeen-year-old expired after an epileptic fit, plunging her mother into deep grief just weeks after her only son had left for college in New York. Washington reluctantly begged off the trip, though he promised to find Dunmore the necessary guides, and urged him to stop at Mount Vernon on his way west. "I do sincerely condole with you, and poor Mrs. Washington, for your loss," the governor responded, though he tactfully took a route that bypassed the grieving family. Dunmore crossed the length of Virginia, past the hardscrabble farms of Scotch-Irish settlers, who one traveler that year noted were "much addicted to drinking parties, gambling, horse racing, and fighting." The journey, three hundred miles as the crow flies, was at least double that on horseback, through dense forests, up steep slopes, and across dozens of rocky creeks and rushing rivers.

When he reached Pittsburgh, the strategic site where the Allegheny and Monongahela Rivers meet to form the Ohio, Dunmore was welcomed as a savior by the white Virginians who lived there uneasily with Pennsylvanians; both colonies claimed the area, which served as the gateway to the Ohio Valley. The recent British withdrawal of troops from crumbling Fort Pitt, undertaken as a cost-cutting measure, had left a power vacuum. "Upon my arrival the people flocked about me and beseeched me [regarding] grievous inconveniences under which they labored," he later wrote London. They feared an Indian uprising and suspected that Pennsylvania traders were in league with indigenous peoples to drive out the Long Knives.

The unofficial leader of the resident Virginians was John Connolly, a savvy physician and experienced military officer fluent in several indigenous languages. Washington judged him "a very sensible and intelligent man who had traveled over a good deal of this western country," and encouraged the governor to meet him. Dunmore hired the doctor on the spot to serve as his real estate agent and secretly agreed to grant him several thousand acres of prime land on the river, a dubious promise given London's restrictions on such grants. Connolly, in turn, assured Washington that the earl was "a gentleman of benevolence and universal charity, and not unacquainted with either man or the world." He was, in other words, someone willing to do business. On his return in September 1773, Dunmore formally declared Virginia's jurisdiction over the Pittsburgh area, drawing an angry protest from Pennsylvania's governor. The dispute threatened to embroil the two colonies in war, though the earl tried to keep London in the dark about his expedition west and the brewing conflict.

At home with his grieving wife, Washington regretted missing the trip. He wrote the governor that he was "exceedingly sorry and disappointed in not having the honor of your Lordship's company, as it was my intention to have waited on you." He even suggested that if the governor had chosen to stop at Mount Vernon on his way west, Washington might "have been tempted to accompany you." He then lamented his inability to be present to further "any schemes your Lordship might have of procuring lands to the westward of us, for yourself."

While eager to obtain western acreage for himself and his friends, Dunmore could ill afford to openly antagonize his patrons in London or provoke an indigenous backlash. That fall, he and his council ordered the return of one surveying party for fear that it was "likely to give discontent to the Indians and bring on a war with them." Dunmore told Washington, "I do not mean to grant any patents on the western waters, as I do not think myself empowered to do so." Though a blow to the planter, this declaration did not cool his courtship. He brought Martha and his stepson to Williamsburg in November to dine at the Palace. Later that month, on a clear, still, warm autumn day, the two men inspected the governor's newly acquired farm called Portobello, a six-hundred-acre spread seven miles north of the capital on a creek that emptied into the York. "Its situation beautiful, the land good, fine meadows, plenty of fish, no end to oysters, close at the door, and the orchard accounted one of the finest on the continent," read the real estate advertisement. By then, Dunmore had relented and allowed surveying in the Ohio Valley to resume.

On December 14, 1773, two days before the Boston Tea Party, Washington shipped milled wheat to a merchant in Norfolk, where he did frequent business. "With the flour, you will receive a barrel of white thorn berries for His Excellency the governor," he informed the buyer. The planter asked him to send the fruit, a popular holiday decoration in Scotland, to the Palace "by the first opportunity—charge the freight to me." On Christmas Eve, a fellow speculator reported to Washington that moves were afoot to assert Virginian control over the Ohio region and as far as the Great Lakes. "Should this prove true," he wrote, "I should think it much in our favor, as it would extend the powers of Lord Dunmore to the western waters."

By the time Lady Dunmore arrived two months later, the earl had put down roots. Along with Portobello, he owned livestock, a saw and grist mill, and two large plantations near the mountains. Such purchases, he explained to London, "may be advantageous to my family" while proving a "means of ingratiating myself very much with the people of the colony." He also had acquired a dozen indentured white servants and at least fifty-seven enslaved Africans. In 1773 he bought one hundred pairs of shoes and "strong coarse stockings" for field workers, as well as equipment for six coachmen and new livery for his unfree Palace servants. He may have owned well over a hundred people in bondage, making him one of the colony's largest slaveholders. The burgess and country lawyer Patrick Henry confided to a friend that "his Lordship was determined to settle his family in America," and later reiterated that he had a "determined resolution to settle his family on this continent."

Chapter Three

A Notion Now Too Prevalent

With thoroughbred horses in his stable, fine wine in his cellar, and an army of enslaved people to serve at his table and work his plantations and farms, Dunmore in 1774 was a prosperous member of the landed elite. Yet his ethnicity still made him something of an outsider. "He is as popular as a Scotsman can be among weak and prejudiced people" wrote James Parker, a Scottish merchant in Norfolk.

Barely half of white Americans were of English origin in that day, with German, Scots, Irish, and Swedish settlers forming a majority in some regions. Virginia's western counties included many Germans and Scots, but most of the colony's white population were of English descent. The merchant class, however, was dominated by Scots from the booming city of Glasgow. The two ancient rivals lived uneasily together. Those of English heritage often criticized "North Britons" as brutish drunks prone to Catholicism, sympathetic to despotism, and driven by greed. Scots, in turn, quietly scorned the English as lazy, untrustworthy, and poorly educated.

When the English settlers landed in Virginia in 1607, Queen Elizabeth was dead and her successor, James I, had assumed the throne. He was the first in a series of members of the Scottish Stuart family who ruled England for a tumultuous century during which Parliament and the monarchy battled for control. The family's opponents were mostly strict Protestants who saw the Stuarts as bent on imposing an autocratic regime friendly to Catholic Spain and France; they would become known as Whigs. The Stuarts' supporters, eventually called Jacobites, from the Latin name for "James," denounced the Whigs as intolerant religious fanatics. James I's son, Charles I, lost his head at the end of a bloody civil war, but his son, Charles II, was later installed as monarch. In 1688, Charles's younger brother, James II, was deposed and exiled. From then on, reliably Protestant and pliant Dutch and German princes, with powers carefully limited by Parliament, held the throne.

When a Scottish scheme to colonize Panama in the late 1690s failed, virtually bankrupting the entire nation, England offered to cover the losses in exchange for merging the two kingdoms. The 1707 union was resisted by some English and by many Scots who yearned to put a Stuart back on the throne. Support for the Stuarts was particularly strong in the rugged Scottish Highlands, where the inhabitants periodically rose up against the foreign-born rulers in London. Dunmore's own father, William Murray, had thrown in with the rebels in 1745, while the future earl was still a young teenager.

This last rebellion against the British monarchy was led by Charles Edward Stuart, known fondly to his supporters as Bonnie Prince Charlie. Grandson of James II, the handsome and charismatic twenty-five-year-old intended to seize the throne from the German-born King George II for his father, who lived in Rome. The French fleet that was to assist in the coup had turned back, so the prince improvised when he landed in northern Scotland in the summer of 1745. He issued decrees calling on people to free the land "from the usurpation of foreigners" and set off across the moors to raise a local force to march on distant London. During a halt at Blair Castle, home to the large Murray clan's leader, the Duke of Atholl, Charles met the future earl and his father, William, relatively poor members of the extended family. They joined the prince, apparently more out of clan loyalty and desire for economic gain than out of political conviction. William Murray became vice chamberlain of the prince's household, while young John Murray served as a page and perhaps an occasional messenger, receiving a master class in an armed uprising against a king.

The prince assembled a ragtag army of mercenaries, tough Highlanders, and English sympathizers to unseat the head of one of the world's largest empires. They came within a hundred miles of London, only to retreat and then be badly defeated in April 1746 outside the Scottish village of Culloden. Hundreds were rounded up and executed in the aftermath, the victors systematically dismantled many Scottish clans and traditions—wearing a kilt or carrying a weapon became a punishable offense—and thousands fled to the American colonies. Dunmore's father turned himself in and was convicted of treason. Barely escaping the chopping block, he was sentenced to a lifetime of house arrest. His son was deemed too young to be punished, though the family shame weighed heavily on the young man. He was reduced to begging King George II for a minor appointment as an army officer.

The wrenching upheaval paradoxically ushered in an era of unprecedented prosperity and intellectual ferment in what was still primarily an impoverished land of tenant farmers. By the 1750s, the old capital of Edinburgh, still a maze of medieval alleys, drew an astonishing array of philosophers, scientists, and radical thinkers. In 1764, the French philosopher Voltaire admired "the progress of the human spirit" made in a country far removed from Parisian salons. "From Scotland come rules of taste in all the arts, from epic poetry to gardening," he added. Benjamin Franklin later noted that the only sensible people who fall into disputes are "lawyers, university men, and men of all sorts that have been bred at Edinburgh."

Dunmore, who assumed the title of Fourth Earl of Dunmore on his father's death in 1756, found himself in the thick of one of the Western world's most remarkable moments, the Scottish Enlightenment. His mother had encouraged a love of books, and he became a fixture in the town's proliferating salons and societies, spurred in part by the fact that Scotland's dominant Presbyterian Church ensured the world's highest literacy rate. Dunmore took walks with economics pioneer Adam Smith, dined with the celebrated philosopher David Hume, and listened to the lectures of Adam Ferguson, who defined modern sociology. James Boswell, the famed biographer of Samuel Johnson, thought the earl "talked very well," high praise from a man who didn't suffer fools; the earl also could talk and write in Gaelic, French, and German as well as English. Dunmore was one of the few aristocrats admitted to exclusive groups like the Select Society and the Poker Club, where intelligence, wit, and a capacity for broad thinking, rather than titles, status, or money, were the prime entry requirements.

Mid-eighteenth-century Edinburgh was a place where freethinkers confronted urgent intellectual and social issues of the day. At the time, Britain led the world in human trafficking, and the morality of the lucrative business was hotly debated in the town's clubs and taverns. "No one is born a slave; because everyone is born with all his original rights," wrote Ferguson, adding that the "supposed property of the master in the slave is therefore a matter of usurpation not of right." Smith, for his part, insisted, "There is not a Negro from the coast of Africa who does not . . . possess a degree of magnanimity which the soul of his sordid master is too often scarce capable of receiving." Africans and American Indians were "nations of heroes" for enduring "the refuse of the jails of Europe." Smith may have been thinking of Virginia when he warned that in a rich state, slaveowners would live "in continual fear of their slaves, so they will treat them with the greatest severity." The freer the nation, he added, "the more intolerable is the slavery of the slaves." Smith viewed the institution as antiquated, but, like Ferguson, seemed unsure why it persisted or whether it could be eradicated. "Love of dominion and authority over others will probably make it perpetual," he concluded pessimistically.

Not all Scottish thinkers sweated over slavery's morality. "I am apt to suspect the Negroes . . . to be naturally inferior to the whites," Hume infamously wrote in 1753. "There never was a civilized nation of any other complexion than white." He argued that an educated Black man was merely "a parrot."

The students who flocked to Edinburgh's famous university often returned home with notions that mortified their elders. Arthur Lee, the youngest son of one of Virginia's oldest and richest families, came back to the grand family mansion of Stratford Hall on the Rappahannock River in 1767 with a burning desire to wean his home colony from the iniquities of human bondage. A *Virginia Gazette* printed the first installment of his radical essay, boldly addressed to the House of Burgesses. "As freedom is unquestionably the birthright of all mankind," he wrote, Africans as well as Europeans, to keep the former in a state of slavery is a constant violation of that right, and therefore of justice." This bald statement stunned the colony's slaveowners, and the editor dropped plans for a second installment. Lee eventually abandoned his youthful crusade.

There is no evidence that Dunmore embraced antislavery views at a time when emancipation societies had yet to form, and the tiny number of abolitionists were pious Christians widely dismissed as misguided altruists. He certainly did not hesitate to purchase people once he reached Virginia. Yet in the Edinburgh clubs cloudy with the smoke of slave-produced tobacco, he was exposed to and almost certainly participated in debates about the pros and cons of the practice, as well as arguments about the equality of the races, to an extent unusual among white Britons and Americans of the day.

Debates about slavery that were confined to Edinburgh's salons or to gatherings of Quakers and Methodists suddenly burst into the public consciousness in 1772 during a contentious trial in London. The saga had begun in 1749, when an eight-year-old African boy who had endured the Middle Passage was purchased by a Scottish merchant named Charles Steuart in Virginia's port of Norfolk. Steuart gave him the name James Somerset. Two decades later the merchant relocated to the British capital with his enslaved servant. One autumn evening in 1771, just as Dunmore arrived in Virginia, Somerset failed to return from a London errand. Steuart hired slavecatchers, who captured their quarry two months later. The furious owner had Somerset shackled and taken aboard a Jamaica-bound ship in the Thames, with orders that the captain should sell him and return the proceeds. Three of the Black man's Christian abolitionist friends learned of his plight and sought out England's chief justice, William Murray, First Earl of Mansfield. The justice was Dunmore's older cousin; they grew up in the same county in the Highlands and were undoubtedly acquainted.

Lord Mansfield was a conservative jurist who felt little sympathy for abolitionists, yet he and his childless wife were raising their nephew's daughter, Dido Elizabeth Lindsay, whose mother was an enslaved African. Somerset's friends asked the judge to intervene in what they claimed was an illegal imprisonment. Even royal officials were required to prove the necessity of detaining an individual, a principle at the heart of English jurisprudence. Mansfield agreed, ordering Somerset's release from his shackles on the ship. The judge subsequently encouraged both sides to reach an out-of-court settlement so that he could avoid ruling on the controversial matter of whether slavery was legal in England. Somerset, however, insisted on his freedom, while Steuart would not give up his human property. The trial pitting the enslaved man against his owner quickly riveted London.

On June 22, 1772, Mansfield and two other jurists declared that Steuart had no right to detain and deport Somerset, given the absence of domestic English laws pertaining to slavery, and immediately set the African-born man free. "Near 200 Blacks, with their ladies, had an entertainment at a public house in Westminster," London's *Public Advertiser* reported that same evening, "to celebrate the triumph which their brother Somerset had obtained over Mr. Steuart, his master." They paid five shillings each to toast the judge's health and attend the feast and the ball that followed.

Though the ruling technically applied only to Somerset, newspapers across England declared that it extended to all those in bondage. This was a policy only Parliament could set, yet the public perception persisted that June 22 was a day of emancipation of enslaved people in England. Somerset himself encouraged this view. On July 10, one of Steuart's business associates complained that a man he held in bondage "was determined to leave me, which he did without even speaking to me" after receiving a letter from "Uncle Somerset, acquainting him that Lord Mansfield had given them their freedoms."

The ruling came as a shock to Virginia's white inhabitants. The Scottish judge was already unpopular for his stance supporting American taxation, and his decision seemed yet one more attempt by London to limit their freedoms—in this case, the freedom to own human property. "Slaves are devils, and to make them otherwise than slaves will be to set devils free," worried Virginia planter Landon Carter. One Caribbean sugar planter warned in a letter reprinted in a *Virginia Gazette* that "slave holding might perhaps be well discontinued in every province of the North American continent." Another owner of unfree West Indian laborers feared that British abolitionists would "put into the heads of our colony-negroes to rebel and occasion much bloodshed."

Yet instead of sparking revolts, news of the Somerset case prompted many enslaved people to quietly slip away to seek passage to England. One slaveowner in Surry County, south of Jamestown, complained that a husband and wife were attempting to make their way to England, "where they imagine they will be free." He added, in an obvious reference to Somerset, that this was "a notion now too prevalent among the Negroes, greatly to the vexation and prejudice of their masters." Advertisements for runaways in the pages of *Virginia Gazettes* doubled after the court ruling became known. By spring of 1773, the figure had tripled, and remained high for the rest of that year. These numbers suggest a notable increase in escapes by those in bondage. The owner of Bacchus, a literate enslaved man, assumed that his human property fled in the spring of 1774 "to get on board some vessel bound for Great Britain, from the knowledge he has of the late determination of Somerset's case."

There were other factors behind this apparent surge, including the economic crash that began the same day that Mansfield and his fellow judges ruled on the Somerset case. This recession, which would prompt Parliament to grant the East India Company a monopoly on American tea sales, led some slaveowners to reduce clothing and food rations; such material deprivation, historians believe, was often the trigger for escapes and uprisings. A religious revival of a more egalitarian and charismatic Christianity often critical of slavery was also spreading through the colonies at that time. One enslaved Baptist shoemaker with "a large scar on his breast from whipping" fled his owner, while another white man blamed "the mischief" of a Baptist preacher for the flight of a twenty-year-old unfree worker named Primus. Whatever their individual reasons, enslaved Africans during Dunmore's tenure began to flee their owners in greater numbers than in the past.

As the Somerset drama unfolded in London in the spring of 1772, Virginia's House of Burgesses approved a resolution far more radical than Mansfield's emancipation of a single man. The legislators called for a total halt to the slave trade plied in the colony since 1619. Addressing their petition to the king, they argued that the business was one "of great inhumanity," which "we have too much reason to fear will endanger the very existence of your Majesty's dominions."

At first glance, this stance seems surprising coming from the very people who depended on unfree workers for much of their wealth and status. The gentry's concern, however, centered on their own physical and economic security rather than morality. They feared that a continued influx of enslaved people would flood the market and lower the value of their human property, which often accounted for half or more of a wealthy white planter's net worth. They also preferred to produce their own enslaved workers rather than buy them from abroad. Richard Corbin, a leading tobacco magnate, instructed his overseers "to be kind and indulgent" to his "breeding wenches" who were pregnant with future enslaved laborers. English merchants, by contrast, opposed any limits on the lucrative slave trade, arguing in a petition to London that planters stood to benefit at their expense "as the number of Negroes" carried from Africa "is diminished."

Those newly arrived from that continent at the time accounted for only 5 percent of Black Virginians, and they were deemed more liable to escape or rebel than those born in the colonies. George Mason, Washington's neighbor and a major slaveowner, had asserted years before that "the introduction of a great numbers of slaves" was the prime cause of the fall of the Roman Empire. Dunmore tried to find middle ground, begging London to approve a modest increase in the duty, citing "the evil consequences of having too many slaves imported into the colony." His plea was rejected. The carping of distant colonial planters could not compete with Britain's powerful slave-trading lobby.

The governor had more success convincing the gentry to embrace new ways of thinking about agriculture, infrastructure, and science. The burgesses were traditionally averse to collecting taxes, even those necessary to fund a militia, and were hostile to public improvements. While beacons had long guided ships safely into ports like Boston, New York, and Charleston, for example, Virginia lacked a single lighthouse. Dunmore urged legislators "to infuse that spirit of industry, which alone can make a country flourish," and encouraged a raft of bills to build bridges, add ferries, improve roads, construct canals, and place a light tower at the entrance to Chesapeake Bay.

A provocative letter in a 1772 issue of a *Gazette* by "Academicus" attacked tobacco cultivation for "restraining the progress of population and national wealth." The writer urged adoption of "grasses and grains best adapted to our soils and seasons," such as the wheat Washington grew. Academicus also lambasted Virginia's lack of cities, arguing that this deficiency made it difficult to find the "intercourse and association which is necessary to the perfection of every power of man." The identity of the writer is unknown, but the pseudonym strongly suggests that the caustic criticism came from Dunmore or an academic ally. The governor's two teenage sons were enrolled in the College of William and Mary, the colony's sole institution of higher learning, and he served as its titular head.

The *Gazette* letter sparked the creation of the Virginia Society for the Promotion of Useful Knowledge, the colony's first scientific organization. One inspiration would have been the Edinburgh Society for Encouraging Arts, Sciences, Manufactures, and Agriculture in Scotland, created in 1755 by the city's Select Society, which included Dunmore in its ranks. Philadelphia's American Philosophical Society almost certainly was another. Founded in 1743 by Benjamin Franklin, it had absorbed the American Society for Promoting Useful Knowledge to form the colonies' most important intellectual club.

Dunmore visited the city in 1771 while on his way to take up his new post in Virginia, and would have encountered members of the distinguished group. Franklin and Philadelphia's pioneering physician Benjamin Rush quickly became corresponding members of the new Virginia society, with Dunmore as its royal patron. At a 1774 meeting at the Capitol, attended by Washington, an inventor demonstrated an ingenious device capable of threshing wheat and won a gold medal and cash, believed to be the first prize for a practical invention in the colonies. Detailed records are missing, but Thomas Jefferson, a member of the Philadelphia society, would certainly have been associated with this elite Virginia group.

If Dunmore and Washington shared a passion for the theater, horses, and hunting, Jefferson and the governor collaborated in agricultural and architectural innovations. The red-haired twenty-nine-year-old planter admired the ancient Roman authors Horace and Virgil, who praised rural life, and he gave his unique home in western Virginia the romantic Italian name of Monticello. He joined the governor and several senior burgesses in funding an ambitious private venture by Italian entrepreneur Philip Mazzei to grow grapes from soil not far from the hilltop plantation, and to produce silk, oils, and other exotic products as lucrative alternatives to tobacco.

While Jefferson lauded the simplicity of country living, he also championed impressive and innovative public buildings that might rival those of Europe. The earl emerged as the first patron of his architectural ambitions. In the fall of 1772, "at the request of Lord Dunmore," Jefferson produced a "plan for an addition to the College of William and Mary," according to a sketch in his own hand. The ambitious blueprint doubled the building's size, creating a European-style courtyard in the center.*

The two men also seem to have discussed renovating the Palace, which at more than six decades old was showing its age. Jefferson wrote that the unfashionable building was "capable of being made an elegant seat," and drew an ambitious neoclassical makeover, adding immense porticoes to the front and rear. The drawings were long thought to date from Jefferson's tenure as governor in the late 1770s, but recent analysis suggests that they are contemporary with the college drawing. Given Dunmore's fascination with neoclassical design, it is not difficult to imagine the two men sifting through thick volumes in the upstairs Palace library, dreaming of transforming the dusty little capital into a New World showplace.

If there was correspondence between these two men who shared so many interests, the letters were lost or destroyed. Unlike Washington, Jefferson left no detailed diary, so it is difficult to gauge how frequently he and Dunmore met, and he is largely silent in later writings about his relationship with the governor. If they drew close, by the spring of 1773 they would have drifted apart. Jefferson joined a small cabal of burgesses that included the country lawyer Patrick Henry and Richard Henry Lee and Francis Lightfoot Lee, brothers of Arthur, who was then living in London. They were anything but outsiders. All were sons of prosperous slave-owning planters, and one

* Archaeological digs in the 1950s confirmed a foundation based on his scheme was dug, though work was abandoned at the onset of the Revolution.

historian likened Virginia's Lee dynasty to the Medici, Hapsburg, or Rothschilds families of Europe. But they shared a desire to show more "forwardness and zeal" than their more conservative colleagues in opposing British policies. This was before Parliament passed the Tea Act, but they already were disturbed by "various rumors and reports of proceedings tending to deprive" Virginians "of their ancient, legal, and constitutional rights."

These affronts would have included the king's refusal to limit slave imports and grant western lands, as well as his threats to extradite Americans accused of burning a Royal Navy ship in Rhode Island. The ominous Somerset decision by Mansfield also would have weighed on the minds of men who depended on people in bondage for most of their income. What was needed, Jefferson recalled later, was "unity of action." To accomplish this, they needed to win the approval of cautious legislators and avoid alarming the governor.

One chilly March night in 1773, the half-dozen men met in a private room in Raleigh Tavern to craft a proposal to form a committee, led by Speaker Peyton Randolph, to share news and information with other colonial legislatures. It seemed an innocuous enough idea, and the burgesses approved the plan the next day with little debate. Dunmore wrote London that while the resolve demonstrated "a little ill humor," he found it "so insignificant that I took no matter of notice." He placed his seal of office on the document, unwittingly planting the seed that would grow into the Continental Congress.

When the resolution reached Boston, a delighted Samuel Adams predicted it would have important consequences, and had three hundred copies printed and distributed. One historian later noted that while Massachusetts had organized a province, Virginia promoted a confederacy.

These committees of correspondence were quickly adopted by all the colonies, save Pennsylvania, and served as the connective tissue that would transform scattered protests into mass rebellion.

Chapter Four

The Mysterious War Dance

As New Englanders in early 1774 looked nervously east to Britain for its reaction to the Boston Tea Party, white Virginians looked west as violence threatened to set the frontier on fire. John Connolly, Washington's acquaintance in Pittsburgh, lit the fuse. On January 1, 1774, a few months after Dunmore's visit and just as Lady Dunmore was arriving in New York, Connolly gathered a group of armed Virginians and seized the town's abandoned and decrepit Fort Pitt. He renamed it Fort Dunmore and set about strengthening the wood-and-earth redoubt, declaring that the region would become a new Virginia county.

"Possession is eleven points in the law, and they say there are but twelve," went an old Scottish saying doubtless known to the governor, who had encouraged Connolly's aggressive move. His proclamation and preparations for war alarmed not just the Pennsylvanians but the Shawnee, Mingo, and Delaware peoples who lived in the vicinity. Through the late winter and spring, tensions mounted between the Virginians and Pennsylvanians, and between Virginians and indigenous peoples. Britain's Indian agents warned of an impending conflict, but those Virginians dreaming of owning Ohio land were pleased, hoping that events might force the Indians to retreat while putting pressure on London to ease its ban on land grants in indigenous territory.

When Connolly learned on April 21 that Shawnee warriors had intimidated surveyors measuring and mapping their tribe's hunting grounds, he urged armed Virginians to act. On the last day of the month, settlers lured several Mingos—including a woman named

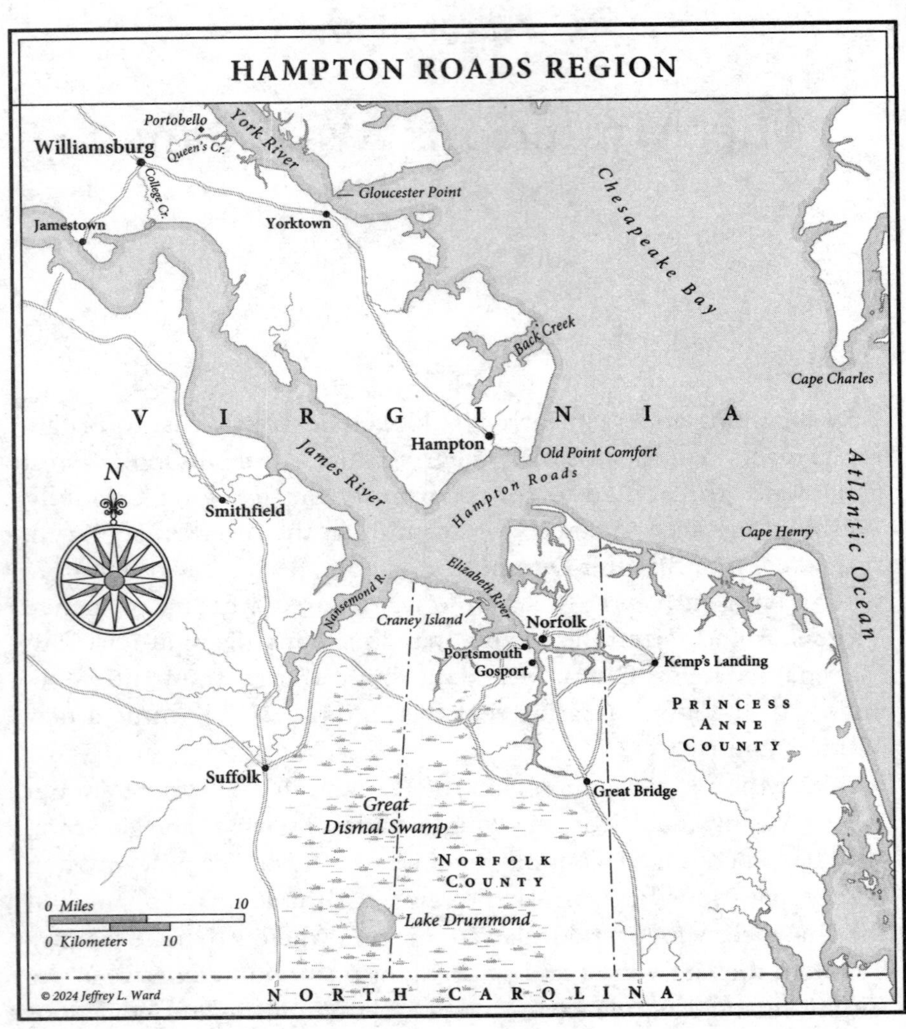
HAMPTON ROADS REGION
Portobello
York River
Williamsburg
Queen's Cr.
College Cr.
Gloucester Point
Jamestown
Yorktown
Chesapeake Bay
Back Creek
Cape Charles
V I R G I N I A
Hampton
Old Point Comfort
N
James River
Hampton Roads
Atlantic Ocean
Smithfield
Cape Henry
Nansemond R.
Elizabeth River
Craney Island
Norfolk
Portsmouth
Gosport
Kemp's Landing
PRINCESS ANNE COUNTY
Suffolk
Great Bridge
Great Dismal Swamp
NORFOLK COUNTY
0 Miles 10
0 Kilometers 10
Lake Drummond
© 2024 Jeffrey L. Ward
NORTH CAROLINA

Koonay, who was with her infant—to drink in a smoky tavern that stood about fifty miles downstream from Pittsburgh, where Yellow Creek emptied into the Ohio. The white men waited until the alcohol took effect, then murdered the Mingos. Koonay managed to rush outside, only to be shot in the head by one of the assailants; her infant was taken captive. A rumor later spread that she had been pregnant, and the fetus had been torn from her womb. Though likely false, the story was widely circulated and believed. The men subsequently killed several more Mingos who had crossed the river in canoes to investigate the shots and screams. They then scalped the dead. What made this grisly event—one violent act among many on the frontier—so notorious was the identity of the victims. They made up the entire family of Tachnechdorus (or Soyechtowa), known to white settlers as James Logan, an elder respected on both sides who had long urged his people to avoid antagonizing the invaders. The dead Koonay was his sister.

In the wake of the bloodbath, a devastated Logan took up his musket and hatchet. He insisted that he was bent solely on avenging the deaths of his relatives rather than fighting a full-scale war, but white residents of the region panicked. They feared a grand alliance of indigenous peoples along the western frontier, from the Cherokees in the south to the Iroquois in the north, finally united in their determination to push the colonists back over the Appalachians. Thousands who had seized Indian land or paid trifling sums for their acreage now fled their isolated farmsteads. A friend of Washington wrote the retired colonel of "many hundreds having gone over the mountain, and the whole country evacuated as far as the Monongahela," one of the two rivers that converge to form the Ohio. He estimated that a thousand people a day were in flight, many crowding into Pittsburgh as others made for the Appalachian slopes and the safety of the East. Another settler warned of "an entire depopulation" of the region "unless something was done."

On the day of the Yellow Creek massacre, but before word of the gruesome slaughter reached the capital, Lord and Lady Dunmore and their children left Williamsburg to attend a ball at the Mason's Hall in Norfolk. The land route involved ramshackle ferries, rough roads, and a harrowing trek across the northern edge of the Great Dismal Swamp. This million-acre wetland was thick with mosquitoes, snakes, and bears, and served as "a general asylum for everything that flies from mankind and society," according to one colonist, particularly refugees from slavery. The journey by horse or carriage to the port could take two or three days. With a brisk wind and the right tide, a sailing ship could make the trip in two or three hours. The family therefore traveled the eleven miles to Yorktown, with enslaved servants and trunks packed with their finest clothes, and then boarded a boat to Norfolk.

The vessel glided five miles downstream to the mouth of the York River, then tacked south through Chesapeake Bay and into the broad channel known as Hampton Roads. The five-mile-wide mouth of the James River, named for King James I, and the two-mile-wide entrance of the Elizabeth River, named for his daughter, formed this spacious but sheltered anchorage. The ship passed the little harbor of Hampton at the end of the peninsula formed by the York and James Rivers, facing the twin capes Henry and Charles, named for two sons of James I. For Lord and Lady Dunmore, these monikers were not simply those of long-dead royals; they were the names of family—both husband and wife were related to the Stuart line.

The breeze and current carried the ship past Craney Island, standing sentinel at the entrance of the Elizabeth River. Unlike the James and the colony's three other mighty streams, this was a short estuary with no source of its own and a flow regulated solely by the ocean tides. For the first half dozen miles, the deep channel formed what sailors called a reach, a relatively straight passage with favorable prevailing winds. Pines, marsh, and narrow beaches edged the shore, with the occasional farmhouse and a scattering of outbuildings looming in a field beyond.

Ahead, at the end of the reach, lay Norfolk. Hundreds of chimneys would have bristled from low-peaked roofs beneath a hazy brown pall of wood smoke. Lady Dunmore had marveled at New York's dramatic harbor, dotted with wooded isles and framed by high bluffs. In Philadelphia she had admired the white church towers and State

House cupola that rose gracefully over tall brick warehouses lining sturdy stone wharves. Virginia's premier port, by contrast, lacked a single steeple or bucolic hill. The tallest objects in this otherwise flat landscape were two enormous windmills and an iron crane rising from the shore opposite the town. As the ship approached a line of floating wooden docks that stretched far into the river, the smell of sunbaked seaweed, fresh excrement, and rotting garbage wafted through the spring air. Even the cawing seagulls circling the ship were specked with grease and grime.

What the town lacked in scenic charm it made up for in practical geography. In an era before diesel-powered dredges, accurate weather forecasts, and precise nautical charts, the speed and safety of every sea voyage hinged on unpredictable winds, currents, tides, and depths. Boston was exposed to storms and rimmed with a rocky coast, while Baltimore and Philadelphia lay inconveniently far inland. The shifting sandbars at the entrance to New York and Charleston harbors made for a tricky passage to and from the ocean. Vessels approaching the East Florida port of St. Augustine ran aground so frequently "that disasters of the sort have ceased to arouse sympathy," one local reported. Norfolk, by contrast, was easily reached from the Chesapeake capes yet protected from fierce gales and high surf. The bar across the river's mouth was a safe thirty feet down, sufficient for the keel of any ship of that era. Dunmore enthused to London that the town's harbor was "as fine a one as any I ever saw, it would contain the whole fleet of England." One patriot officer later called it "perhaps the most noble place for arms . . . the world ever produced," while another would assure Washington it was "the finest and most advantageous port in America."

Norfolk owed its existence to this favorable topography and King Charles II. By 1680, the Stuart monarch had grown impatient with a colony that seven decades after its founding remained resolutely rural. One member of the Royal Society reported six years later to London: "The country is thinly inhabited; their living is solitary and unsociable; trading confused and dispersed." The king insisted that towns were essential for growth, and the House of Burgesses duly resolved to create twenty settlements, including one on a stubby peninsula jutting into the north side of the Elizabeth River. An English lord whose family had once held the title of Duke of Norfolk originally owned the parcel, giving the county and, later, the city its name. Few of the other proposed towns thrived, but by the turn of the century the little port on the Elizabeth boasted a church, a wharf, and a scatter of homes and shops.

The area's dense and sandy soil proved ill-suited for tobacco but ideal for indigenous corn, European pigs and cattle, and African peanuts, while extensive pine and cypress forests supplied the material for barrel staves, shingles, lumber, pitch, and tar. The port also served northeastern North Carolina, which lacked a reliable deep-water port on its upper coast. "Norfolk has more the air of a town of any in Virginia," wrote the wealthy planter William Byrd II when he passed through in 1728. "There were then near twenty brigantines and sloops riding at the wharves, and oftentimes they have more. It has all the advantages of situation requisite for trade and navigation." The good harbor was "so near the sea, that its vessels may sail in and out in a few hours." He noted pine logs lashed together to serve as floating piers. From these, stevedores loaded heavy barrels of beef, pork, rum, flour, and building materials onto ships bound for other Chesapeake harbors and Caribbean sugar plantations.

While Byrd was sure Norfolk would "remain in a happy and flourishing condition," he noted that "it lies under the two great disadvantages that most of the towns in Holland do, by having neither good air nor good water." Even by colonial standards, it was an unhealthy place. "The sewage ditches are open, and one crosses them on little narrow bridges made of short lengths of planks nailed on cross pieces," a later visitor noted. These fetid waterways served as "receptacles of the filth of all the privies, and the nurseries of mosquitoes." Another observer complained that "putrid bilious fevers are common" and "verminous diseases are frequent."

Byrd was amused at the way seaport residents gaped at the rare sight of rich tobacco tycoons, though he lived a mere sixty miles upstream on the James River. When he and his companions attended Sunday service at the Anglican church, he wrote, "people could not attend their devotion for staring at us, just as if we had come from China or Japan." Norfolk was indeed a foreign land to the rest of Virginia. The town was separated from the bulk of the colony by more than geography, and that gulf only grew as it prospered. A visitor in 1736 was impressed by a harbor crowded with vessels from distant ports, and the "spirit of trade" pervading the town. "The inhabitants are, from their great intercourse with strangers, abundantly more refined," he added. Yet the planters who dominated the colony were careful not to let this economic gain translate into more political power. That year, the House of Burgesses granted the town's request to be incorporated as a borough but imposed a strict charter that concentrated power in the hands of a small circle of aldermen who served for life. Wary legislators preferred to see the increasingly cosmopolitan port run like a plantation, with residents—half of whom were enslaved—kept on a short leash.

Scottish merchants such as Charles Steuart, who purchased James Somerset on a Norfolk wharf, and Steuart's close friend James Parker arrived in the wake of the failed 1745 rebellion by Bonnie Prince Charlie. The subsequent peace spawned an economic boom in Glasgow, which lay a few days' sail closer to the Chesapeake than its English competitors. Businessmen there quickly captured the bulk of the lucrative tobacco trade, assisted by a Scottish legal code permitting partnerships that protected individuals from lawsuits. Experimenting with new corporate structures, long-term loans, and derivatives, these early capitalists helped spark the industrial revolution. Rather than building country houses like their English counterparts, they plowed their immense tobacco profits into iron, coal, textiles, and other products they could sell to the Americans. Gigantic warehouses soon lined Glasgow's River Clyde, which led to the Atlantic, and Scottish companies established trading posts far up Virginia's rivers.

"All the merchants and the shopkeepers . . . through the province are young Scotchmen," noted one Virginian in 1774. These entrepreneurs bought tobacco from planters, sold them imported goods and people, and made loans in a land where mints were forbidden and hard currency was rare. The town on the Elizabeth River became their headquarters and soon emerged as a flourishing node in the fast-expanding British Empire, more like Bridgetown in Barbados and Kingston in Jamaica than like sleepy Williamsburg. "Norfolk is the port of most traffic in Virginia," wrote Lord Adam Gordon a decade before the Revolution. "It contains above 400 houses, has depth of water for a forty-gun ship or more, and conveniences of every kind for heaving down and fitting out large vessels." When Lord and Lady Dunmore arrived in May 1774, the town had burgeoned into a sprawling settlement made up of 1,300 buildings and some 6,500 residents, three times more than the capital had. This made it the eighth-largest city within the thirteen colonies and the most populous center between Philadelphia and Charleston.

Scottish profits and slave labor fueled the borough's industrial expansion. One company employed its fifty unfree workers to churn out "Negro shoes," as well as footwear for "ladies and gentlemen" who desired red, green, and blue Moroccan leather as good "as any from London." The neighboring tannery, also staffed with men in bondage, produced saddles, books, coach seats, and the whips used by plantation overseers. Ropewalks manufactured the lines critical for ships, while sailmakers profited from Royal Navy contracts. Across the Elizabeth River, Scottish investors built one of the largest distilleries in the colonies, capable of producing seven thousand gallons of rum annually with molasses imported from the West Indies. The most impressive facility lay a mile upstream. The Gosport shipyard was a sprawling complex of warehouses, wharves, repair slips, blacksmith's shops, and a crane, imported from England, all controlled by a slave-owning Scottish-born industrialist.

The financial success of Norfolk's Glasgow merchants and their employees along Virginia's rivers drew the suspicion and envy of the colony's gentry. Much like European Jews of the era, Scottish businessmen were criticized for their supposed monetary savvy, tight-knit clans, and international networks. This animosity occasionally flared into violence. In 1768, the borough's Scottish inhabitants inoculated themselves against the smallpox virus, a procedure the English feared would spread the deadly illness. Angry mobs rioted, smashing windows and burning the home of a Scottish doctor. James Parker "put out the muzzle of a gun" to protect his barricaded compound from an armed crowd that included a carpenter who owed him money. He suspected the man's fury had as much to do with his debt as with the disease.

The economic boom gave many enslaved people an opportunity to hire themselves out for pay on their own time, and even negotiate a share of the profits from their owner. Such arrangements were rare in the colony's few other towns and unthinkable in the strictly policed tobacco fields, a reason the harbor became a magnet for unfree laborers. Here, a refugee from bondage might pass as free and join a ship's crew. "Perhaps he may go to Norfolk, and endeavor to get on board a vessel," one distraught slaveowner wrote in June 1772 of a man called Ned. This was a common refrain in Virginia advertisements for runaways.

The port's Black residents had long had a reputation among white colonists for unruly and rebellious behavior. As early as 1718, "a great concourse of Negroes" were "caballing together" at "unseasonable hours in the night." A dozen years later, a rumor circulated that the king had declared that baptized slaves would be granted freedom, launching one of the largest slave uprisings recorded in colonial America. Two hundred people in bondage chose leaders to demand the governor honor the alleged proclamation. "When they saw nothing come of it, they grew angry and saucy, and met in the nighttime in great numbers, and talked of rising," reported one alarmed colony official. The revolt was quelled "by imprisonment and severe whipping of the most suspected." Others fled south into the nearby Great Dismal Swamp, which the governor at the time called "a common sanctuary to all our running servants." A few weeks later, swamp residents chose "officers to command them in their intended insurrection," but patrols captured the ringleaders and hanged two dozen.

White men were subsequently required to carry a firearm to church or face a five-shilling fine, and the pastor was said to keep a loaded pistol on his lectern. Town leaders periodically passed new laws to prevent "insult and abuses from the Negroes" and to halt "unlawful and tumultuous meeting[s] of Negroes on Sundays, holidays, etc.," a sign that this behavior was frequent and difficult to control. Slaveowners were fined if their human property did not obey a 10:00 p.m. curfew, and the enslaved person was whipped.

A British officer who visited Baltimore in 1774 described a prospering port with "a good market and a great number of whores." Norfolk was undoubtedly similar, and especially rich in taverns. Between 1755 and 1770, the town magistrate granted an impressive

155 tavern licenses, half of which were renewals. This rough-and-tumble tavern culture brought together people of all colors, genders, and backgrounds. A multiracial couple, the white man Walter Bruce and a free Black woman named Susannah, were accused of "keeping a disorderly house and entertaining gentlemen's slaves." There were repeated court cases "of lewd life and conversation and common disturbers of the peace," and one of the colony's first jails was built in Norfolk in 1753. The court docket listed fights at bordellos and a resident's assault on a militia sergeant. A 1741 regulation forbade the sale of liquor to indentured or enslaved servants, but this seems to have been only sporadically enforced.

Women also thumbed their noses at white male authority. For swearing in court, a resident named Jennit Long was fined five shillings and given ten lashes. White females even competed in a footrace to win a fine piece of underclothing, a contest that would have scandalized Williamsburg's far more staid society. Pirates, prostitutes, and prisoners on the lam haunted the dimly lit rum bars, and multiracial gangs bet, argued, and cheered together at bull-baiting contests. A night watch continually struggled to enforce the order to "dispose or apprehend any Negroes that shall assemble or be tumultuous." A powder magazine was built at the north end of town in 1774, in part to secure ammunition in case of an uprising of the enslaved. Those in bondage still felt the bite of the lash and the humiliation of bondage, but the southeast corner of Virginia was far removed from the more rigid regimes of forced labor camps like Mount Vernon and Monticello.

Downtown Norfolk crowded along a fifty-acre oblong peninsula, moored like a ship to the mainland by a narrow isthmus and pierced by swampy creeks. The governor and his family would have landed at the public wharf fronting the main plaza. Taverns and shops lined the east and west sides of the square, with a large market house in the center and an imposing brick courthouse and squat jail on the north end. Two Scottish aristocrats and their fashionably attired sons and daughters, surrounded by town dignitaries in their finest wigs and waistcoats, would have captured the attention of shoppers, storekeepers, and stevedores. Stepping into waiting carriages, the party trundled past fine shops, elegant homes, and narrow alleys shadowed by tall tenements.

The ball was to be held just north of the isthmus in the grand two-story brick Mason's Hall, just past the borough church, at the intersection of Freemason and Cumberland Streets. Cumberland Street, named for the duke who defeated Bonnie Prince Charlie at Culloden in 1746, was home to many of the town's well-to-do artisans, merchants, and doctors.

Among them were the Thompsons, who lived in a neat two-story frame house with a small orchard, garden, pigpen, and milking barn in the rear. Jane Thompson was an industrious woman in her mid-fifties, while her husband, Talbot, was a respected sailmaker with Royal Navy contracts. Like most of their prosperous neighbors, they owned enslaved Black servants. Unlike their neighbors, however, the Thompsons were not white. They had, against tremendous odds, prospered in the burgeoning borough as free Black residents, and the people they held in bondage were relatives and friends.

Both husband and wife were born into slavery. Talbot's Scottish slaveholder had owned Raleigh Tavern in Williamsburg but moved to Britain in 1758. The thirty-three-year-old Talbot Thompson was given the rare choice of a new owner of his "own liking," due to his "long, faithful, and extraordinary services." The person of Thompson's "own liking" was himself. He subsequently negotiated his own purchase with the estate's executor for sixty British pounds within five years. At a time when the average white colonist earned less than fourteen pounds annually, this was a huge sum, and nearly twice the going price for the average enslaved African. He accomplished this impressive feat with two years to spare, thanks to his savvy in sail making. A single merchant ship required acres of canvas, a word derived from the Latin term for "hemp," "cannabis." The fabric had to be strong enough to withstand fierce winds but light enough to be handled in foul weather by sailors far above the deck of a swaying ship. An experienced and disciplined free sailmaker could make a good living in a busy port like Norfolk.

Buying himself, however, was simply a first step toward liberation. Under Virginia law, Thompson could only achieve legal manumission by convincing the royal governor and his council that he had performed "meritorious service" warranting such an unusual move. That 1723 statute was designed, the governor at the time admitted, to curb the "pride of a manumitted slave" lest he believe himself "to be as good a man as the best of his neighbors." It had long proven a barrier that only a handful surmounted. Encouraged by a wealthy white acquaintance, Thompson carefully prepared his petition, including proof of payment and the testimony of an influential Williamsburg lawyer. The governor ordered him emancipated "according to his prayer." This protected him from re-enslavement and provided some legal rights; he once sued a white man for failing to pay a debt—and won.

Jane Thompson had been living as Talbot's wife since about 1750, after bearing at least two children with a previous partner. She and Talbot subsequently had two sons. She remained the property of Norfolk merchant Robert Tucker, a former mayor and burgess. As a youth, he had inherited a palatial home with an entry hall filled with thirty-nine paintings, cabinets bulging with fifty-seven silver serving dishes, a library of religious, history, and navigation tomes, and nineteen Africans in bondage. His business expanded hugely in the 1750s and 1760s, and he invested heavily in ships, industry, and humans. Like many local merchants, he employed enslaved men to crew and pilot his fleet of ships.

Others worked as bakers and millers at his wind-powered flour plant and bakery—one of the largest in the South—that he constructed just downstream from Norfolk at Tucker's Mill Point, and which his son later expanded. Two wind-powered mills crushed unprocessed wheat between four pairs of turning French-imported quartzite stones, and the resulting flour was sent to an enormous bakehouse. Workers kneaded the dough on long stone tables before placing the sticky masses into one of four massive ovens built out of some 200,000 bricks. The plant produced three thousand loaves a day, enough to provide nearly every inhabitant of Norfolk with half a loaf, and the complex included brick dwellings for the overseer as well as the enslaved workers.

At least some of Tucker's enslaved laborers—including Jane Thompson—lived in town with their spouses, and some were able to hire themselves out to earn an income during their time off. Tucker seems to have grasped that stable families made for more productive skilled workers, and he likely was the unnamed white acquaintance who encouraged Talbot Thompson to seek official freedom. Emboldened by his success, Thompson set out to purchase his wife, children, and stepchildren. That plan went awry when Tucker died deeply in debt in 1767, forcing his widow to sell his property, including those enslaved, to satisfy creditors.

On September 16, 1768, Thompson attended the auction where his own family was put up for sale. In what must have been a harrowing experience, he bid the modest sum of five pounds for Jane. No one made a higher offer, and he also gained ownership of an older man named Joseph Tucker, possibly Jane's father. But two sons, local ship pilots, were sold to white owners. Another, Sam, remained the property of the white Tuckers, though the Thompsons seem to have bought him at a later date. A small consolation was that all their children remained in the area. With the help of Robert Tucker's son, Talbot then succeeded in winning official freedom for Jane in 1769. No other Black couple in colonial Virginia would achieve this remarkable feat.

Thompson was widely known as a hard worker; a merchant later characterized him as "an honest, industrious man." He negotiated lucrative Royal Navy contracts and continued to save money. He and Jane celebrated Christmas 1770 in their new home on Cumberland Street. The frame house had a footprint of 450 square feet—spacious for a city house of the day—and included a cellar below and Talbot's sail loft upstairs. The property featured a dairy and a second outbuilding, and room for two cows, three pigs, and an orchard. The couple invested in other property as well, buying three homes and at least one enslaved person, likely a friend or family member. Their net worth was far above that of the average white colonist.

Jane Thompson lived "in a way that no black woman in Virginia could realistically aspire to," notes historian Cassandra Pybus, who traced the family's story. "More than a few white women might envy such a life." Envy, however, may have made their lives more difficult.

Free Black residents, adds Pybus, confronted deeper suspicion and hostility from white inhabitants than did many of those enslaved. And despite manumission, Talbot Thompson was not equal under the law. He could not vote, serve on juries, or join the militia. He paid higher taxes than his white neighbors and needed written permission from white authorities to own a weapon. And for all their diligence and success, the couple certainly did not receive an invitation to the ball that took place just down their street.

At one o'clock on the afternoon of May 2, 1774, a cannon blast echoed across Norfolk's harbor, sending startled seagulls into the air. The twenty-one-gun salute marked the start of the port's annual celebration of St. Tammany. The name was a corruption of Tamanend, a seventeenth-century leader of the Lenni-Lenape who signed a peace treaty with Pennsylvania's founders, which stated that the two peoples would "live in peace as long as the waters run in the rivers and creeks and as long as the stars and moon endure." Later, he came to be viewed by colonists as America's patron saint, spawning secret societies in which white men performed mock Native rituals in faux Native gear. Norfolk's chapter of the "Sons of the Saint" sponsored that evening's ball, held in America's first purpose-built hall for another secret society, the Freemasons. Lady Dunmore's father had been Grand Master of Scotland, while her husband's cousin had served as England's Grand Master. Both Dunmore and Washington were members of the fraternal order.

Four hundred people crowded the ballroom, dressed in yards of fine English wool, Chinese silk, and French taffeta. Eight Royal Navy officers stood out in their splendid dark-blue uniforms and polished black boots, in stark contrast to "their heads powdered as white as they could be," recalled one partygoer. Among them was twenty-three-year-old George Montagu. He had assumed command of the *Fowey*, a small warship with twenty-four guns, just two weeks before. The room was awash with the merchant-captains of Norfolk, Scottish manufacturers, and local rural gentry. Enslaved Black servants in livery proffered chilled wine and rum punch.

The cannon battery boomed a second salute precisely at six o'clock, and a member of the House of Burgesses opened the event "in the character of King Tamm[a]ny, properly accoutered in the ancient habit of this country," a newspaper recounted. At a signal, the orchestra struck up. White Virginians of all classes favored English country dancing and the Scottish step called the Virginia reel, but French minuets, gavottes, and allemandes typically began a formal ball, accompanied by lively pieces composed by Haydn, Mozart, or Boccherini, often played by Black musicians. One participant remembered vivid details some forty years later. "By and by, the fiddles struck up; and there went my Lady Dunmore in the minuet, sailing about the room in her great, fine, hoop-petticoat, (her new-fashioned air balloon as I called it)." A local dandy in "his famous wig and shining buckles" was tasked with offering the countess the first dance. "Bless her heart, how cleverly she managed her hoop—now this way, now that—everybody was delighted. Indeed, we all agreed that she was a lady sure enough, and that we had never seen dancing before."

A nervous Mayor George Abyvon, a Barbados-born merchant more at home on a ship's deck than on a ballroom floor, took her hand for another minuet. "But the poor captain was laboring hard in a heavy sea all the time," the observer remembered, "and, I dare say, was glad enough when he got safe moored in his seat." After candles were lit as darkness fell, the intricate and stiffer European dances gave way to more familiar steps. "Then came the reels; and here our Norfolk lads and lasses turned in with all their hearts and heels."

Still later, the dancers would have cut loose with jigs derived from African dances, with couples likely gyrating "to some Negro tune," as one English visitor to Virginia noted in 1775. He was shocked by its "lack of method or regularity" and objected to what "looks more like a bacchanalian dance than one in polite assembly." The Norfolk ball lasted until four in the morning, when the candles had sputtered out, and exhausted musicians could play no more. As dawn approached, the remaining Sons of the Saint "encircled their king and practiced the ancient mysterious war dance." Across the distant Appalachians, real combat between white settlers and tribal peoples had just begun.

Chapter Five

Twenty-Two Days for Nothing

On May 6, two days after an unusual late-spring snowstorm blanketed the colony and destroyed fruits and crops, Virginia's burgesses converged on the capital, picking their way through the thawing mud of Duke of Gloucester Street to begin their first session of 1774.

Like Britain's king, Virginia's governor was no dictator. His role was strictly limited by the provincial legislature, which alone, like Parliament in London, could approve resolutions, pass bills, and appropriate funds. Unlike the monarch, the governor was not chosen for life but served at the king's pleasure. Although members of the House of Burgesses—two for each county—stood for regular election, in practice delegates often retained their seats for decades, amassing significant power. A governor could veto a measure and, on rare occasions, even dissolve the legislature and force new elections. Such moves, however, were sure to antagonize the gentry, and even prompt demands for the governor's recall.

Dunmore had quickly discovered the limits of his authority. In 1773, colony officials exposed a ring of counterfeiters that threatened to wreak economic havoc in the province, which was perpetually short of hard currency (most daily transactions were made with tobacco promissory notes that fluctuated wildly in value). He promptly consulted with his council, the group of well-to-do Virginians who had been chosen by the king to be his closest advisors and who served as an additional check on his power. They agreed he should bring the accused to Williamsburg for trial rather than leave the pressing matter to the distant local court. He did so immediately, and then called an emergency meeting of the House of Burgesses to address the crisis.

When the burgesses assembled, the spare and acerbic thirty-seven-year-old Patrick Henry attacked the governor rather than the counterfeiters. A failed farmer, indifferent tavern keeper, and good fiddler, Henry had found his calling as a lawyer and quickly developed a reputation as a fine orator in county courtrooms across the colony. "You would swear he had never uttered or laughed at a joke," one friend later said. "His manner was so earnest and impressive, united with a contraction or knitting of his brows which appeared habitual." Henry argued that transferring the case to Williamsburg was an alarming breach in due process and complained that the earl had deprived Virginians "of their ancient, legal, and constitutional rights." The burgesses agreed, and a chastened Dunmore was forced to apologize. The incident marked his first clash with the brash Henry. The case against the alleged counterfeiters was later tried in the capital but fell apart when one prisoner escaped and a key witness fled. The proliferation of fake notes, meanwhile, shook the confidence of other colonies in Virginia's economy.

A year later, as the burgesses gathered on that chilly May morning, there was still no news from London regarding the tea destruction in Boston. Aware that a harsh response was sure to anger the delegates, the governor gave a short opening speech to the burgesses counseling "prudence and moderation." Washington arrived ten days later with Martha, who typically remained at Mount Vernon during legislative sessions but was no doubt eager to meet the countess. The couple dined with Lord and Lady Dunmore at the Palace, waited on by the governor's many enslaved servants.

On May 19, word finally reached Williamsburg of Parliament's decision to close Boston harbor, British North America's second-largest port, until its citizens paid for the destroyed tea and gave up their rebellious ways. The blockade was set to begin June 1. The shocking news at first drew little response from the burgesses, who were focused on the brewing conflict between frontiersmen and indigenous peoples across the Appalachians. The chamber, after all, was dominated by speculators in western land rather than ocean-going merchants concerned with tariffs and taxes. Many gentry also felt little sympathy for those urban Northerners who had wantonly destroyed private property.

This indifferent response dismayed Jefferson, Henry, and the Lee brothers, who had drafted the previous year's plan for committees of correspondence among the colonies. Letters from these official groups set up by legislatures were now traveling up and down the Eastern Seaboard, sharing news and grievances and establishing important ties among colonial leaders. Yet Virginia's gentry remained largely detached from the turmoil enveloping New England. Four days after the Boston news arrived, when the legislators had adjourned for the day, Jefferson and his allies met secretly in the governor's council chamber on the second floor of the Capitol's west wing. The room, dominated by the oval council table, also housed a legal library. "We were under conviction of the necessity of arousing our people from the lethargy into which they had fallen," Jefferson later wrote.

Direct criticism of Parliament was sure to draw opposition from many burgesses as well as from Dunmore, so the men sought an inoffensive alternative. Piling books on the long table, they found a suitable precedent in a thick volume called *Historical Collections*. During the Parliamentary revolt against the Stuart monarch Charles I in the 1640s, the legislature's leader Oliver Cromwell ordered a day of "fasting, humiliation, and prayer." Using this example, Jefferson and his friends "cooked up" a resolution imploring the divine to avert the "destruction of our civil rights, and the evils of civil war."

The date was set for June 1 to coincide with the port's closure. Given their reputations as troublesome radicals, the men then convinced the colony's pious treasurer, Robert Carter Nicholas, to sponsor the measure. Though a political conservative, he was pleased by the religious nature of the resolution, which was agreed to the following day with little dissent. A more pressing matter was consideration of a complaint by land speculators that British refusal to grant western lands would "much retard the settlement and cultivation of that part of the country."

The next afternoon, Washington "dined and spent the evening at the governor's." Severe thunderstorms pummeled the capital that evening, and he may have stayed the night in a Palace bedroom. The next day, May 26, dawned warm and sunny, and the two men rode the seven miles to the earl's Portobello estate to share breakfast. They ambled down the muddy path winding through fields and woods, reveling in the fresh air of the clear dawn. Dunmore was constantly buying and selling prize mounts, while Jefferson—no mean rider himself—called Washington "the best horsemen of his age, and the most graceful figure that could be seen on horseback."

Later that morning, as gray clouds again began to gather in the west, they trotted back to Williamsburg, with Washington proceeding to the Capitol for the morning House session and Dunmore returning to the Palace. By early that afternoon, as a light drizzle began to fall, the governor had obtained a copy of the resolution. Whether Washington or another person was the source of the leak isn't clear, but the governor's response was unambiguous. He called for his state carriage, which was soon splashing through the puddles on the way to the Capitol.

Jefferson and his clever coterie had miscalculated. Dunmore was well versed in history and the law, and knew that only the king, as head of the Anglican Church, could decree a legitimate day of fasting and prayer. The allusion to Cromwell only made the resolution more offensive, given that he had later ordered the execution of Dunmore's Stuart ancestor, King Charles I. When the governor reached his council chamber—the same one where the resolution had been hammered out—he took his seat at the end of the table with his dozen councilors and summoned the burgesses. A crimson, fur-lined robe covering his bulky frame, Speaker Randolph led the procession from the House chamber. Sixty-odd legislators crowded around, spilling into the hallway beyond. With his unusual height, Washington would have towered above most of the members.

"Mr. Speaker and gentlemen of the House of Burgesses," Dunmore began. "I have in my hand a paper published by order of your House, conceived in such terms as to reflect highly"—that is, poorly—"upon his Majesty and the Parliament of Great Britain; which makes it necessary for me to dissolve you; and you are dissolved accordingly." His councilors unanimously backed the governor's decision. At that moment, Virginia's legislature ceased to exist, and could not meet again until after new elections. "This dissolution was as sudden as unexpected," Washington later wrote to a friend, "for there were other resolves of a much more spirited nature ready to be offered to the House which would have been unanimously adopted." The assembly, he added, "sat in 22 days for nothing." If he had alerted his friend to the resolution during the previous evening and that very morning, but had failed to convince the governor to accept the measure, he never admitted to it.

Dunmore explained later to the colonial secretary in London that he was indeed aware the House might introduce what Washington called "resolves of a much more spirited nature." He worried that these would "inflame the whole country and instigate the people to acts that might arouse the indignation of the mother country against them." Dissolving the assembly, he admitted, "will not be effectual," but he calculated it was the best way to calm a tense situation that threatened to spin out of his control.

This was not the first time the king's representative had dissolved their legislature, and the burgesses did what they had done in the past. "The governor dissolved us as usual," Jefferson wrote matter-of-factly. "We retired to the Apollo as before." This was the grand reception room in Raleigh Tavern, a five-minute stroll down the street, with a Latin phrase carved above its mantle that translated as "Jollity, the offspring of wisdom and good living." The next morning, meeting as "former members" of the House, they chose Peyton Randolph as their "moderator." Freed from fears of offending the governor and in the absence of those conservative gentry who declined to attend, they voted to create an association to protest a system "formed and pressed for reducing the inhabitants of British America to slavery" through unjust taxes and the arrival of a hostile army and navy on their shores. They also urged Virginians to "avoid all commercial intercourse with Britain." This was, in essence, a reprise of their actions during the Stamp Act crisis a decade previously.

In addition, the men proposed that colonial representatives "meet in a general congress, at such place annually as shall be thought most convenient." The purpose would be to "deliberate on those general measures which the united interests of America may from time to time require." Others had called for such a gathering, but these Virginia planters were the ones who lobbied successfully for a formal continental assembly. Philadelphia, as the largest and the most central city, was the obvious site.

This abrupt rift between the earl and the gentry did not spoil that evening's long-planned entertainment. Though the House of Burgesses was no more, it sponsored a ball in honor of Lady Dunmore. The event took place, fittingly, in the large upstairs room reserved for negotiations between the legislature and governor. The spring air was crisp and clear, and the breeze from the open windows cooled the partygoers as uniformed enslaved Africans served drinks and food. George and Martha Washington were there, as were Peyton Randolph and his wife, Betty. Thomas Jefferson and Patrick Henry attended, though their wives, both ill, did not make the journey to the capital. The music continued until dawn as the colony's elite chatted with the earl, admired his teenage sons and daughters, and took turns on the floor with the energetic countess. If New Englanders were grimly readying for war, Virginia's gentry continued to dance with the British.

June 1, 1774, dawned hot and still in Williamsburg, a prelude to what would prove a dry and scorching summer. Though it was Wednesday, those House members still in Virginia's capital dressed in their Sunday best. This was the day the blockade of Boston began, and they intended to express solidarity with the New England port and ignore Dunmore's attempts to forbid their day of prayer.

From the windows of the Palace, the governor could observe fasting legislators and locals parade past on their way to Bruton Parish Church. Peyton Randolph led the procession, which included the Washingtons, who had so recently shared the earl's table. The honor of giving the sermon had been offered to Thomas Gwatkin, an Anglican chaplain who tutored Dunmore's children, but he declined, cheekily citing "a disorder in his breast." His replacement delivered a fiery address drawing on the biblical story of Sodom and Gomorrah that underscored the calamity that Boston faced that day, as British warships sealed off its harbor from the outside world.

Other churches across Virginia held similar services. Though a notorious skeptic of established religion, Jefferson recalled that "the effect of the day through the whole colony was like a shock of electricity." Peyton Randolph's nephew Edmund wrote that the prayer resolution served as a "cement among the colonies" and even as "the seed of a revolution." His loyalist father, John Randolph, the colony's attorney general and Peyton's younger brother, dismissed the entire exercise as a cynical misuse of faith. He scoffed at the idea that "the postponing of a dinner will induce the supreme being to prevent a hostile invasion or the horrors of a civil war."

Prayers certainly did not prevent the horrors then erupting in the west. On June 1, Logan killed and scalped a family of four as part of his campaign of revenge against any white Virginians he encountered. Settlers conducted their own reprisals, prompting the Shawnee leader Colesqua—known to white colonists as Cornstalk—to join with Mingos to combat the Long Knives. Virginian farmer William Spier was found with an axe in his chest, his wife and children "murdered and scalped." Washington wrote a friend on June 10 that "since the first settlement of the colony, the minds of people in it were never more disturbed, or our situation so critical as at present." He was referring to the west, not Boston. John Connolly wrote an urgent letter to Washington, urging him to support construction of forts in Shawnee territory to "send terror into their country for the present and keep them from annoying our settlements." This would also "forever deter" indigenous attacks on Ohio surveyors critical for land grants.

The same day, Dunmore sent a memo to militia commanders ordering them to raise men, build forts, and protect civilians and their animal stocks. One commander wrote that he hoped "this useless people may now at last be obliged to abandon their country, their towns may be plundered and burned, their cornfields destroyed, and they distressed in such a manner as will prevent them from giving us any future trouble." A desperate British agent insisted that the "crisis could be managed without a war," while Pennsylvania's governor warned that Connolly's actions "may have a dangerous tendency to involve the colonies in general in an Indian War." Backed by Dunmore, Connolly rebuffed negotiation with the Native peoples. "I am determined no longer to be a dupe to their amicable professions, but, on the contrary, shall pursue every measure to offend them."

Washington remained in Williamsburg to attend a June 15 meeting of the Virginia Society for the Promotion of Useful Knowledge at the Capitol, where Dunmore would have presided. The following afternoon, the two men enjoyed a leisurely dinner at the Palace, though the impending western war and the growing tensions with London would have made for sober conversation. Given Washington's extensive combat and travel experience in the Ohio, the earl would have been eager to draw on the retired militia colonel's knowledge of the region and its indigenous peoples. It would be their last meal together. On the same day, the governor's council warned Dunmore of "the growing discontents of all orders of men, even as those that were well affected to government." At their urging, and no doubt with Washington's prompting, the governor called for July elections so that a new House of Burgesses could convene in August.

Within days, Logan took thirteen additional scalps and left a message that his vengeance was sated. "The Indians is not angry, only myself," he explained. It was too late. As Logan penned his note, Dunmore ordered Connolly to attack Shawnee settlements. The Virginians were to take "as many prisoners as they can of women and children," who would serve as hostages "to reduce those savages to sue for peace" and ensure "their future good behavior."

Many of the colony's gentry, including Washington and Jefferson, realized this could clear the Ohio of illegal settlers as well as indigenous people. Even Henry, an avid real estate investor despite his populist credentials, was enthusiastic about war. "Lord Dunmore is your greatest friend," he candidly told a fellow speculator. "What he is doing will forever hereafter secure the peace of your colony by driving the Indians to an amazing distance from you." Revenge for white killings was merely an excuse. The earl, he explained, "was really pursuing this war in order to obtain by purchase or treaty from the natives a tract of territory" along the Ohio. Jefferson later agreed that the governor was "conscious of the injustice of the war," but saw it as an opportunity to "compel the Indians to accept a peace on reasonable terms"—terms, that is, favorable to Virginia. Yet while the war had broad support from a gentry eager to obtain Ohio Valley territory, the tightfisted House of Burgesses refused to advance funds. Dunmore would have to raise and equip an army on credit.

Meanwhile, the committees of correspondence had sent invitations for representatives of Britain's American colonies to meet in September in Philadelphia for a "general congress" to consider ways to counter British policies. The former burgesses planned to gather in the Capitol on August 1 for what they called the Virginia Convention to select their colony's delegates. The assembly was not meant to replace the House of Burgesses, and the Philadelphia session was designed only to consider the "united interests of America." In the eyes of the British, however, these bodies lacked legitimacy since they were not authorized by the king or Parliament.

Only a dozen colonies on mainland North America agreed to participate in the Continental Congress. East and West Florida, Quebec, Nova Scotia, Newfoundland, and St. John's—now Prince Edward Island—declined to attend. Given the large French, Spanish, and Native American populations in these provinces, a patriot movement dominated by rabid anti-Catholics largely hostile to indigenous peoples held little appeal. Georgia, meanwhile, wanted British troops to quell Indian unrest on its borders, while the outnumbered white inhabitants of Caribbean islands such as Jamaica depended on army regiments to discourage and, if need be, put down slave rebellions.

In late June, Washington departed the capital for Mount Vernon to campaign for reelection to the new House of Burgesses. A few days later, Dunmore invited a visiting young Swiss-born British lieutenant named Augustine Prevost to dinner. The son of a British colonel with the same name, Prevost had just arrived from the Maryland capital of Annapolis, where he heard customers in a coffee shop "very warm in a debate about the situation of the Bostonians." Virginians, by contrast, seemed oblivious to the crisis. "Scarcely during our whole stay in the province did we hear of any politics nor any undecent reflections upon king or government," he noted with surprise.

Dunmore's daughters entertained the young officer, who was impressed by "the masterly manner" with which fourteen-year-old Catherine Murray played harpsichord and guitar, while thirteen-year-old Augusta "sings to admiration." Prevost was also taken with the countess. "His lady is a most agreeable pretty woman," he noted. While he found the earl hospitable, he believed talk that he was "a consummate rake" and felt he did not pay his wife sufficient consideration. The governor paid the countess at least some attention: she was three months pregnant with their ninth child. The lieutenant also relayed Williamsburg gossip that the earl's wife was "extremely jealous . . . of a young lady whom it is reported was very dear to him."

In the social hothouse of the little capital, rumors had long swirled that Dunmore had carried on extramarital affairs before his family had arrived. Such acts by a powerful man in that era might have spurred gossip, but they were not particularly shocking; Virginians had even raised a statue to the governor's predecessor, who had fathered an illegitimate son without damaging his reputation. White men also could use their positions of authority to have sex with the enslaved without fear of consequences. By law, any resulting progeny grew up in bondage, and mixed-race children were a common sight in colonial Virginia's forced labor camps, including Monticello.

Two years into Dunmore's tenure, a town widow demanded a share of the estate of her wealthy physician husband, who died soon after their wedding without consummating their marriage. Thomas Jefferson defended the dead man's side, arguing that the wife was guilty of "hatred, ill-temper, disobedience," as well as adultery and "refusal of conjugal rights." The widow hired Patrick Henry to press her case and accused her late husband of "impotence and hidden causes of disgust." As the colony's chief judge, the governor decided in the widow's favor. The loss irked Jefferson, who noted that "the suspicions of adultery were with Lord Dunmore, who, presiding at the court at the hearing of the cause, might be the reason why those suspicions were not urged." The governor had, in fact, paid the college tuition fees of her younger brother, though this may have been a simple act of charity. The earl also was whispered to have had an affair with John Randolph's daughter, which Norfolk merchant James Parker asserted was not simply known of but was approved by the attorney general himself. Given social mores of that day and class, however, this seems highly improbable.

Two weeks after Prevost's departure, the earl said goodbye to Lady Dunmore, his children, and Williamsburg's dreaded season of "fever and agues." Instead of a sightseeing adventure, his second journey to the Ohio Valley was a military campaign to defeat the Shawnees and their allies, and, in so doing, open western lands to white settlement. He left behind a gentry increasingly incensed by Parliament's actions, and with a growing sympathy for embattled Bostonians.

Two months after the June 1 day of fasting and prayer, more than a hundred aging white men in wigs and waistcoats crowded into the stuffy brick Capitol in Williamsburg during a crippling drought that brought searing temperatures. Despite the torrid weather, the numbers were impressive. "We never before had so full a meeting of delegates at any one time as upon the present occasion," marveled Washington. All the participants in the Virginia Convention were former members of the House of Burgesses, the colony's upper crust. Like most white Americans, they were sympathetic to Britain's Whig faction that emphasized personal liberties and staunchly supported an empire opposed to the hated Catholic regimes of France and Spain. The men immediately professed their "inviolable and unshaken fidelity and attachment to our most gracious sovereign," blaming the crisis on "several unconstitutional acts of the British Parliament." Their goal was not to overturn the established order but to ensure the "restoration and continuance" of the era preceding the French and Indian War, when Britain did not tax white Virginians, unduly interfere with their human property, or restrict their westward expansion. They wanted to resurrect a previous era, not to forge a new one.

Some argued that petitions might not suffice to overturn legislation from London that patriots had begun to call the "Intolerable

Acts," including the one that closed the continent's second-largest port. A South Carolina visitor reported that the normally reserved Washington stood to propose a bold act of violent rebellion. "I will raise a thousand men, subsist them at my own expense, and march myself at their head for the relief of Boston," he quoted him as saying. Word of his promise, even if apocryphal, spread as far as New England, establishing his reputation as a determined patriot willing to defend the American cause by force of arms paid for out of his own pocket.

The Convention was already buzzing with a document Washington and his neighbor George Mason had drawn up for their home county of Fairfax to articulate American grievances. These Fairfax Resolves accused Parliament of attempting to "reduce us from a state of freedom and happiness to slavery and misery" and called for a sweeping boycott against British goods. Central to the resolves was the demand for an immediate halt to the "wicked, cruel, and unnatural trade" in humans.

Other county committees dispensed with the humanitarian fig leaf. "The African trade is injurious to this colony, obstructs our freemen, manufacturers, and others who would emigrate from Europe and settle here," stated the patriots in Caroline County. The practice, they added, put slaveowners dangerously in debt. By 1773, Jefferson estimated Virginia planters owed at least two million pounds to British merchants, much of it from buying people on credit. No county committee, however, suggested abolishing the domestic sale of enslaved Africans or softening the harsh penalties imposed by the gentry on enslaved people. Extending new liberties to nearly half of the adult male population was not on the Virginia patriot agenda.

The Convention also agreed to halt all British imports as of November 1, 1774, excepting medicines. The men pledged to "neither ourselves import, nor purchase any slave, or slaves, imported by any person" after that date. As for tea, "we view it with horror." Merchants would be carefully monitored for price gouging or smuggling; if they broke the boycott, their wares would be impounded and they would be labeled "inimical to this country." This embargo would fall particularly hard on the Scottish traders who dominated the import business. Virginia planters, however, were not prepared to stop tobacco exports, which provided their major source of income. That cutoff date was pushed back to 1775.

Before adjourning, the men chose seven delegates to travel to Philadelphia for the Continental Congress in September. They carefully balanced vociferous British critics like Patrick Henry and Richard Henry Lee against those more eager for accommodation, including the wealthy libertine Benjamin Harrison and the silver-tongued attorney Edmund Pendleton. Washington, who still counted as a centrist, was elected, and the respected long-time House speaker, Peyton Randolph, headed the team. Only New York sent a larger delegation.

Jefferson, still an obscure junior legislator, was passed over. Illness had forced him to turn back before reaching Williamsburg, but he sent his enslaved servant Jupiter Evans to deliver copies of "A Summary View of the Rights of British North America" to Henry and to Peyton Randolph, Jefferson's cousin. Henry apparently ignored the tract, with Jefferson archly calling the lawyer "the laziest man in reading I ever knew." Randolph, however, was intrigued. At an informal August 1774 gathering at the speaker's mansion in the heart of Williamsburg, just opposite the arsenal called the Powder Magazine and two blocks from the Palace, numerous burgesses gathered to hear the document read aloud. "Open your breast, sire, to liberal and expanded thought," the young burgess wrote, boldly addressing the king directly. Independence, he assured the monarch, "is neither our wish, nor our interest." Simply by raising the idea of separation, Jefferson introduced a concept unfathomable to men who prided themselves on being loyal members of what they viewed as the world's most enlightened and powerful empire.

Even in his absence, Jefferson shocked the assembly of slaveowners by calling for an end to British America's culture of bondage. "The abolition of domestic slavery is the great object of desire in those colonies," he bluntly asserted, "where it was unhappily introduced in their infant state." Before that radical step could be taken, however, it would be "necessary to exclude all further importations from Africa." The king had failed to impose "duties which might amount to a prohibition," he noted, echoing a host of county resolutions. Jefferson's stance placed the burden of overthrowing the institution of slavery, the engine of Virginia's economy, on distant slavers rather than on those who held human beings in lifetime bondage. He also challenged King George III's right to grant territory, ridiculing "the fictitious principle that all lands belong originally to the king." Only Americans should allot American lands through their legislatures, and if these bodies eschewed restriction, he maintained, then an individual "may appropriate to himself such lands as he finds vacant, and occupancy will give him title." The rights of the roughly quarter million indigenous peoples living west of the Appalachians were not addressed, though it was their land that white settlers presumably would declare vacant.

When the reading ended, some enthusiastically applauded while others heaped scorn on the document; one attendee complained of its "most indecent and unmitigated language." Printed as a pamphlet, Jefferson's words quickly spread throughout the colonies and to Britain, establishing his reputation as an audacious writer.

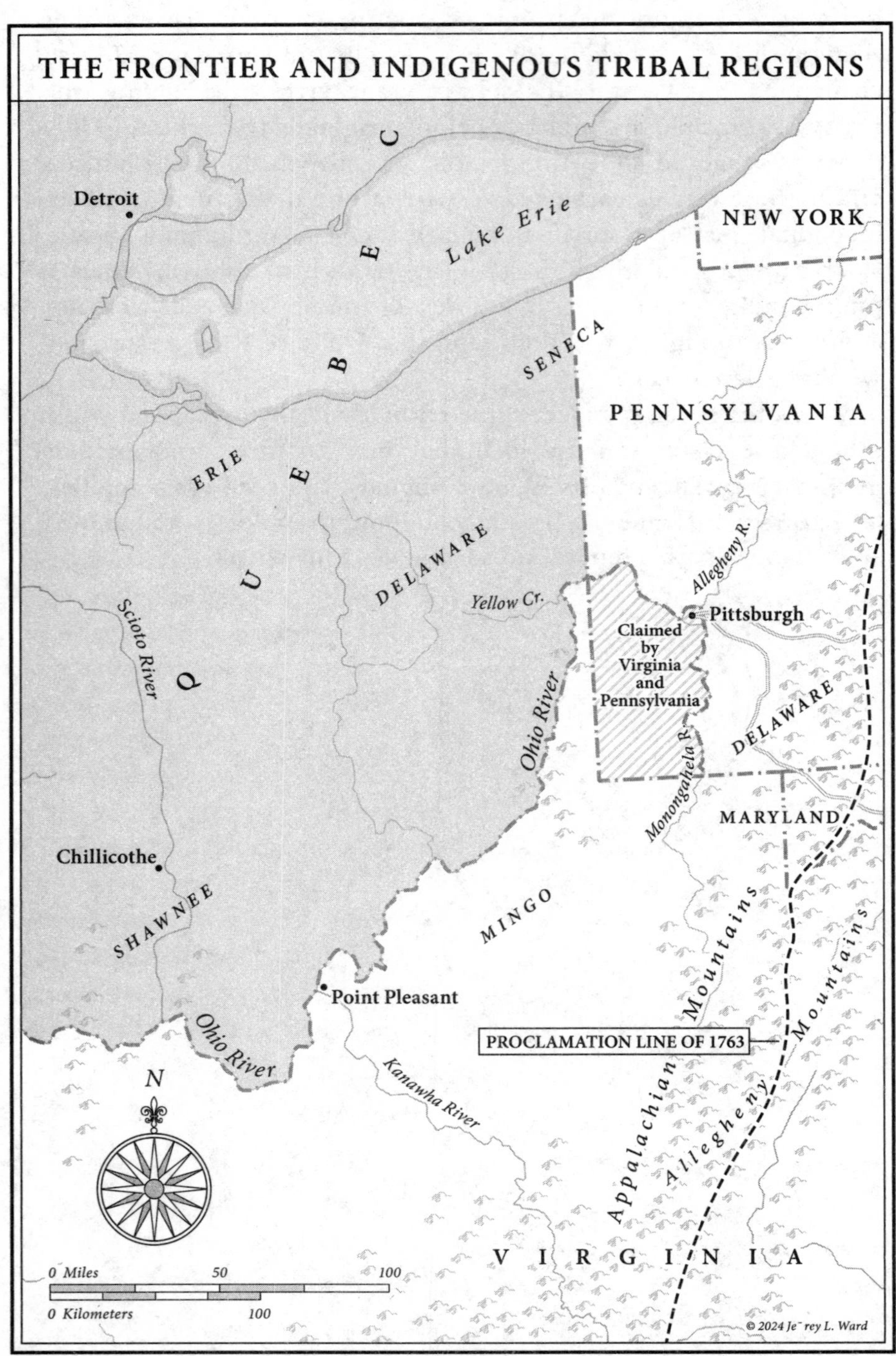
THE FRONTIER AND INDIGENOUS TRIBAL REGIONS
Detroit
Lake Erie
QUEBEC
NEW YORK
SENECA
PENNSYLVANIA
ERIE
DELAWARE
Yellow Cr.
Allegheny R.
Pittsburgh
Scioto River
Claimed by Virginia and Pennsylvania
Ohio River
DELAWARE
Monongahela R.
MARYLAND
Chillicothe
SHAWNEE
MINGO
Point Pleasant
Ohio River
Kanawha River
PROCLAMATION LINE OF 1763
Appalachian Mountains
Allegheny Mountains
N
VIRGINIA
0 Miles 50 100
0 Kilometers 100
© 2024 Je rey L. Ward

Chapter Six

Lord Feathers and the Big Knife

The First Continental Congress convened September 5, 1774, in Carpenters' Hall in Philadelphia, three blocks from the Pennsylvania State House. As a man of compromise and the speaker of the largest colony, Peyton Randolph was elected president and settled his large frame into an oversized high-backed chair to supervise discussion among the fifty-six delegates. Five days later and two hundred fifty miles to the west, Dunmore arrived in Pittsburgh in a canoe with no fanfare. A surprised sentry at the fort, which Connolly had renamed for the earl, quickly doffed his hat and welcomed him with enthusiasm, "which made my Lordship laugh heartily," one eyewitness reported.

Dunmore had spent two months traveling west and building an army out of scratch. Virginia had no standing force and militia were called up only in rare emergencies, though armed slave patrols always kept a close watch on the movements of Africans in bondage. Since legislators had refused to provide funding, Dunmore could only promise recruits that they might be paid in money or land at some future date. On his journey across the Piedmont and over the Appalachians, he gathered an impressive force of twelve hundred men. Most were small farmers who sowed corn and tobacco on steep slopes, while others hunted deer and cured hides that became either gentlemen's breeches in London or machinery belts in Glasgow after disease decimated European cattle herds.

Many wore hunting shirts over their clothes, a "kind of loose frock, reaching halfway down the thighs, with large sleeves, open before, and so wide as to lap over a foot or more when belted." Made of the same cheap but sturdy linen used in clothing for the enslaved, the garment was unique to the region. Some were dyed and fringed, the latter style adopted from local indigenous tribes. A thick leather belt secured a tomahawk, gan item also borrowed from Native Americans.

These mountain men preferred rifles to the cumbersome five-foot-long Brown Bess muskets that were far more common in Britain and the colonies. German immigrants brought the typically shorter and more accurate firearm to the Appalachians in the 1740s. They were still so unknown up and down the East Coast that John Adams had to explain to his wife Abigail that these "peculiar" weapons fired a shot "with great exactness to great distances," and their owners were "the most accurate marksmen in the world." Spiral grooves inside the iron barrel made it possible to shoot game at more than triple the distance of a musket, and with greater accuracy. That feature, however, made loading a more delicate and time-consuming task. While this was not a great disadvantage for a hunter in the woods, it could be fatal when facing men with muskets, which could be quickly reloaded. Nor could rifles be fitted with bayonets. Properly protected by other troops, however, riflemen could serve as highly effective snipers against a well-entrenched enemy or exposed crews on distant ships.

Prevost, the lieutenant who had dined the previous month at the Palace, was visiting Pittsburgh to sort out family real estate matters. One day he ran into Dunmore hunting alone with his hound and joined him in the "amusing" search for squirrels. "His Lordship . . . is by no means a bad man," he wrote in his diary. "On the contrary, he is a jolly, hearty companion, hospitable and polite at his own table." Yet the officer added that the governor was "the most unfit, the most trifling, and the most uncalculated person living" to command a military expedition. He suffered from a "weak will," was surrounded by "evil counselors" like Connolly and embraced disastrous strategies "very much like those of a novice." The militia "had no store either of provisions, ammunition, or what is worse, money." By his account, Dunmore was headed for a disaster unmatched "in the annals of

Virginia." A Delaware elder was likewise unimpressed. "What old little man is that yonder playing like a boy?" he is said to have asked when he spotted the diminutive governor. The earl was known to the Ohio tribes, with apparent irony, as Big Knife.

While in Pittsburgh, Dunmore irritated other indigenous leaders who had come to negotiate a settlement by keeping them waiting. Prevost, however, insisted the earl was sincere in his attempts to avoid bloodshed, though the talks went nowhere.

Meanwhile, a second Virginia army of about fifteen hundred men commanded by the imposing and stoic French and Indian War veteran Andrew Lewis was on its way west along a more arduous southern route. It was still making its way to the rendezvous point south of Pittsburgh, on the Ohio. With winter approaching and no word from Lewis, an impatient Dunmore crossed the river on September 23 with his farmers and frontiersmen on a bold eighty-mile march into the heart of enemy territory. He was determined, he claimed later, "to put an end to this most horrid war in which there is neither honor, pleasure, nor profit."

Prevost watched the ragtag army cross the river with "little or no provision, only a few canoes, very bad men, and those all inclined to quit him." Yet the governor proved far more popular and enterprising than the young lieutenant suspected. He had secured funds from local traders to pay his soldiers and buy supplies, while his long experience with rough Scottish Highlanders prepared him to lead independent-minded mountain men. He delighted the men by walking and carrying his own knapsack, a radical departure from British military tradition; officers typically remained aloof—literally on a high horse. One militia member penned a poem during the march that read, in part:

> Great Dunmore, our general valiant and bold
> Excels the great heroes – the heroes of old
> When he does command, we will always obey
> When he bids us fight, we will not run away

Lewis and his men arrived two weeks later south of Pittsburgh, at the confluence of the Kanawha and Ohio Rivers, unaware that the

Shawnee leader Cornstalk had monitored their progress. Seven hundred Indian warriors—Shawnee, Mingo, Delaware, Miami, Ottawa, and Wyandot—prepared to ambush the oblivious white militiamen. The night before the battle, Cornstalk attempted to dissuade his men from launching an assault he knew was doomed, but he was rebuffed. At dawn, the warriors crept toward the makeshift fort, but lost the element of surprise when they were spotted by a party of white soldiers who were hunting. "Be strong! Be strong!" shouted Cornstalk to his men as they attacked Lewis's camp. One militia officer marveled at their opponents' bravery. "Never did the Indians stick closer to it, nor behave bolder," he said. Fifty Virginians were killed in the hand-to-hand fighting, including Lewis's brother, but the indigenous allies were outgunned and withdrew by nightfall.

Cornstalk retreated west across the Ohio to urge his people to sue for peace. "The Big Knife is coming on us, and we shall all be killed," he told a tribal gathering at the Shawnee capital of Chillicothe. Dunmore and his army were soon within a dozen miles of the town. A Pennsylvania trader rode up to his camp with a white flag and a proposal from Cornstalk to discuss terms. The governor refused. The next day, almost in sight of Chillicothe, the earl halted his men in a field surrounding an ancient oak. He scrawled "Camp Charlotte" on the tree in red chalk—in honor of his wife, that of King George III, or both. Negotiations began that evening. The proud Shawnee leader spoke directly to Dunmore, leaving one Virginian awed. "I have heard the first orators of Virginia, Patrick Henry and Richard Henry Lee," he recalled, "but never have I heard one whose powers of delivery surpassed those of Cornstalk on that occasion."

The Shawnee leader railed against dishonest white traders and called for a ban on rum sales to Indians, then let subordinate chiefs discuss surrender terms. Amid the negotiations, word came that Lewis's army was fast approaching. Dunmore sent a message ordering them to halt immediately so as not to spook the Shawnees. The men, however, kept marching. Eager to avenge their dead comrades and set on plunder and pillage, "they could not be stopped," one of Lewis's sons later explained. Only after the earl sent a second urgent dispatch did Lewis make camp.

On October 19, the defeated indigenous tribes agreed to give up their hunting rights south of the Ohio as far as the Mississippi River. In return, the governor pledged that no white colonists would settle to the north of the Ohio and promised to forbid "any violence upon, or doing any injury to, Indians of whatsoever tribe or nation, and from every encroachment upon their territory." Both sides would provide hostages to guarantee peace, and the Indians would return captured whites as well as enslaved Africans. Cornstalk and his lieutenants found the terms milder than expected. Logan, however, refused to negotiate, and some of his Mingo followers fled north. The governor dispatched a unit that killed several Mingo warriors, took prisoners, and torched two villages. Chastened, the remaining Mingos returned to lay down their arms. The two sides agreed to meet again in the spring of 1775 to work up a final peace agreement.

With a single battle, Dunmore's forces had secured more than forty thousand square miles, much of which would later become the state of Kentucky, for white settlers and speculators. The governor then rode to Lewis's camp to forbid the troops from pillaging or looting. The grumbling men returned east to their Ohio River redoubt, dubbed Fort Gower after the earl's brother-in-law and primary patron. Dunmore galloped on to Williamsburg. His officers, meanwhile, received news of the suffering in Boston and of the Continental Congress meeting in Philadelphia. On November 5, they signed a statement pledging allegiance to the king while resolving to "exert every power within us for the defense of American liberty." This would be done, they promised, "not in any precipitate, riotous, or tumultuous manner." Yet they also boasted, "Our men can march and shoot with any in the known world," in what was the first public call to arms against Britain.

Yet they professed to "entertain the greatest respect for His Excellency the Right Honorable Lord Dunmore, who commanded the expedition against the Shawnees," adding that he "underwent the great fatigue of the singular campaign from no other motive than the true interest of this country." When news of the Fort Gower Resolves reached London, politicians were aghast. One alarmed member of the House of Lords accused Dunmore of failing to suppress a "military league."

What came to be called Dunmore's War reverberated throughout the colonies and in Britain in unexpected ways. "We look upon the peace which Lord Dunmore made with the Indians to be conclusive and certain," Washington wrote, "and . . . I dare say it will be of lasting duration." The treaty ensured relative quiet on the frontier at a moment when patriots could ill afford a second front. It also brought together three thousand armed Virginia men, more than ever before in the colony's history, who linked their fight to expel indigenous peoples from the Ohio with the growing calls in the East for freedom and liberty. The residents of one mountain county passed a resolution insisting that their effort to punish "those cruel and savage people" was proof that they were "never to surrender" their liberty. The committee of a nearby county declared its citizens would defend with their lives their rights to range the woods. "The original purchase was blood, and mine shall seal the surrender." The Indians to the west and the British to the east were now seen as common threats to their way of life. "When the honest man of Boston, who has broke no law, has his property wrested from him, the hunter on the Allegheny must take the alarm," said one.

Men who gave little thought to taxes and tariffs and were far removed from the seats of political power suddenly felt solidarity with distant New England. Their hunting shirts and tomahawks quickly became symbols of the homegrown American fight against what they saw as the tyranny of an out-of-touch elite that sought to restrict their freedoms. The riflemen who had rallied to Dunmore's side soon would be among his most feared foes.

Williamsburg's citizens greeted the governor with cheers and acclamations when he reached the capital on December 4 after an absence of nearly half a year, his arrival sweetened by news that Lady Dunmore had given birth the previous morning to a baby girl. A *Virginia Gazette* reported that the Ohio River was the colony's new and undisputed western boundary, and the Indians promised to "never more take up the hatchet against the English." One admirer composed a ballad praising the victory, the generous treaty terms, and the earl's "cheerfully undergoing all the fatigues of the campaign."

Two weeks later, Dunmore rode to the capital's outskirts to greet four Shawnee hostages, who would be treated more like diplomats than prisoners. Among them was Cornstalk's son Wisscapoway, known to colonists as Captain Morgan. One observer described the new arrivals as "tall, manly, well-shaped men, of a copper color with black hair, quick piercing eyes, and good features." With their plucked eyebrows and eyelashes, vermillion-painted faces, and silver nose rings, earrings, and arm bracelets, they cut striking figures. "They are in white man's clothes," the observer added, "except breeches which they refuse to wear," preferring instead a loincloth. Williamsburg's residents gawked as they rode to the Palace, where they were given living quarters to ensure their safety. Dunmore also ordered Virginians "strictly to refrain from committing any violence upon, or doing any injury to, Indians of whatsoever tribe or nation, and from every encroachment upon their territory."

The one sour note amid the accolades came from London's colonial secretary, Lord Dartmouth. The earl had led an unauthorized war against people who were nominally under the protection of the empire. It was just the sort of conflict King George III had sought to avoid; the monarch himself was furious. London officials also were startled that the governor's aggressive actions had come close to provoking a war with Pennsylvania. In a long letter written on Christmas Eve 1774, Dunmore defended his actions, touting his victories while predicting that the British government could never "restrain the Americans" in their relentless surge westward. "They acquire no attachment to place," he explained. "Wandering about seems ingrafted in their nature." They constantly "imagine the lands further off are still better than those upon which they are already settled."

During Dunmore's long absence, anger at British policies had intensified and begun to spread beyond the gentry. "Everything here is in the utmost confusion," noted one British visitor to the colony in October. "The New Englanders by their canting, whining, insinuating tricks have persuaded the rest of the colonies that government is going to make absolute slaves of them." Those who failed to go along with the boycott now were derisively labeled "Tories." This term referred to the king's faction that opposed the Whigs in Parliament, though Americans who resisted patriot measures often were themselves Whigs; they preferred the term loyalists and derided their adversaries as rebels. The visitor added that loyalists "have been tarred and feathered, others had their property burnt and destroyed by the populace."

The humiliating torture of tarring and feathering, used by a medieval British king to punish thieves, was first employed by Americans in Norfolk. In 1766, during the Stamp Act crisis, William Smith was accused of reporting a fellow merchant's smuggling operation to British authorities. Furious patriots seized and stripped him on a downtown wharf, covered him with heated tar, rolled him in feathers, and pelted him with eggs and rocks. They then "carried me through every street in town," he recalled. Bound with a rope and tossed in the harbor to drown, he was rescued by a passing boat. Several patriot merchants—including the mayor—were indicted for "inhumane treatment" but never brought to justice. The practice soon caught on in New England and was revived in Virginia in the summer of 1774, though more often as a threat than an actual punishment.

That August, a group of patriots in a village south of Richmond put the British prime minister, Frederick North, on trial. Lord North was "universally condemned," and his effigy was tarred and feathered before being led through the streets by a "deformed African" as a warning of what white Virginians might expect if North had his way with the colonists. The effigy was then hanged and burned before a cheering crowd.

Virginia's thousands of Scottish residents were widely suspected by patriots to be enemies of the American cause. The colony's Scot-dominated merchant association gathered in the capital for a regular meeting in early November. The town was already crowded with burgesses preparing to attend the House session that had been slated to start on November 3 but repeatedly postponed until Dunmore returned from the Ohio. William Aitchison, a Norfolk trader, wrote James Parker on November 14 that patriots had placed a barrel of tar close to Raleigh Tavern, with a mop and feathers suspended above. The message was clear: publicly agree to the boycott on British goods imposed by the First Continental Congress or face public torture. "Lord Feathers was thought the slightest punishment they could get," noted Parker dryly. Two Scottish merchants accused by patriots of importing tea were swarmed by a Williamsburg mob, and their "lives were threatened," according to Aitchison. One account had Peyton Randolph, the Continental Congress president, personally intervening in the street to prevent violence.

During Dunmore's absence, news arrived from London of a new measure passed by Parliament and approved by the king that further angered many Americans, especially white Virginians. French Quebec had fallen under Crown control in 1763, and Britain struggled to govern an enormous province peopled mainly by French Catholics and indigenous tribes. After more than a decade of hesitation, Britain allowed French property laws to remain in effect and granted residents the right to practice the Catholic faith, which was illegal in Britain. To avoid the awkwardness of a French-dominated assembly, unelected British administrators were put in charge. The plan also tripled Quebec's size by including indigenous lands that reached to the north shore of the Ohio River within its borders. For Protestant white Virginians, this placed an enemy on their frontier and an obstacle to their future growth. It did not help that the legislation was championed by Lord Mansfield, the judge who had freed James Somerset. From the Americans' perspective, the Quebec Act confirmed fears that Britain was hostile to their interests. The bill was lumped together with others that restricted trade and fishing rights as one of the "Intolerable Acts."

Little wonder that the governor returned home to find the king's authority in the colony "entirely disregarded, if not overturned," as he told Dartmouth. The courts had closed, county government was largely in the hands of patriot committees, and the Virginia Convention passed resolutions as if it were a legal body. Unauthorized militias in each county were even "arming a company of men . . . to be employed against government, if occasion requires," he wrote. He was, however, confident that the boycott on British goods would backfire. "The people of Virginia are very far from being naturally industrious," and the instigators of the trouble would confront their own rebellion when "the lower class of people discover that they have been duped by the richer sort." The result would be "quarrels and dissensions" that would drive Virginians back into the British fold. In the meantime, he suggested the Royal Navy blockade Chesapeake Bay to ensure "their own schemes be turned against them."

Publicly, however, Dunmore was careful not to criticize the Fort Gower Resolves or the gentry leaders, who increasingly resembled the Jacobite rebels of his youth. With no British troops and only a small ship or two patrolling the colony's waters, the governor chose not to alienate Virginia's fierce riflemen and powerful planters.

Enslaved people, meanwhile, continued to slip away from their owners. Sam, though "very dim-sighted" and lacking shoes and stockings, made his break the same week the governor returned to Williamsburg. He carried with him "a remarkable scar on his breast, which seems as if occasioned by the lash of a whip, his sides and back are much scarified by whipping." His owner was nevertheless convinced that the mutilated man had no cause to run away. "I have great reason," he insisted, "to imagine he was stolen."

Gunpowder was the essential explosive of the eighteenth century. It made cannons boom, muskets fire, and rifles crack. Since the 1600s, rulers in India had held a global monopoly on its primary ingredient, saltpeter. Making this substance, potassium nitrate, was a complicated and smelly business requiring urine, sewage, or toxic salts. Along with its use in explosives, it was handy for tanning hides, bleaching cloth, and even preserving meat. The hunt for saltpeter was a major reason that European colonial powers competed to gain a foothold on the Indian subcontinent.

Yet even with high-quality saltpeter on hand, making gunpowder was a tricky business. The right amount had to be mixed with a fine-tuned combination of charcoal and sulfur, then meticulously sifted and granulated into neatly rounded particles. The highly volatile material was then dried in a special outbuilding. Extreme care was essential at every stage. A single spark could ignite a disastrous explosion; during the Revolution, a patriot mill built near Valley Forge went up in a thunderous cloud of smoke and flame. Before the war, Americans depended almost entirely on British stocks of gunpowder. The only domestic source was a small factory outside Philadelphia that opened in 1774, but its output was small, and the plant was incapable of making the higher-grade ammunition needed to fire artillery. Americans could hardly expect to fight a skirmish, much less a war, without the vital munition. The conflict with Britain ignited in both northern and southern colonies a scramble to secure the limited gunpowder stocks.

In the summer of 1774, Massachusetts militias quietly withdrew their towns' powder, kept in an arsenal across the Charles River from Boston. When British troops removed what remained to a well-defended fort in the harbor, thousands gathered in nearby Cambridge, ready to fight the redcoats, prompting the startled army commander, General Thomas Gage, to fortify Boston and request reinforcements from Britain. That fall, as the First Continental Congress met and Dunmore was negotiating the Shawnee surrender, King George III prohibited any exports "of gunpowder or any sort of arms or ammunition" to the colonies. He also ordered the governor of each colony to "take the most effectual measures for arresting, detaining, and securing any gunpowder, or any sort of arms or ammunition which may be attempted to be imported into the province under your government," excepting military stores.

New England patriots rushed to grab what they could. In early December, Rhode Island patriots seized forty-four cannon and a large cache of gunpowder from a British fort near Newport. On December 14, militias near Portsmouth, New Hampshire, used the cover of a snowstorm to steal some one hundred barrels of gunpowder from Fort William and Mary, but not before the small garrison there fired on the attackers, in the first organized violence of the war. At nearly the same moment, the October 1774 petition from the Continental Congress, drafted by Patrick Henry, Richard Henry Lee, and Pennsylvania's John Dickinson, arrived in London. The document urged the king to repeal the "Intolerable Acts," but with Parliament in recess for the holidays, the plea was set aside.

A month later, on the afternoon of January 19, rain and sleet pattered on the shingled roof of Bruton Parish Church as the earl and countess stood in the icy sanctuary for the christening of their ninth child with the chill water in the stone baptismal font. They named her Virginia in tribute to their new home. The baby's godfather was a member of the gentry; years later, an elderly Lady Dunmore recalled that it was George Washington, though he was not in the capital that day. The planter had been reviewing the newly formed Fairfax County militia in Alexandria, one hundred miles to the north, and returned to nearby Mount Vernon that afternoon for "dinner alone." The more likely candidate was John or Peyton Randolph, each of whom were the governor's colleague and neighbor.

After the ceremony, the family hurried home with their carefully swaddled newborn to prepare for a party celebrating the baptism, the official birthday of the German-born Queen Charlotte, and the fourth anniversary of Dunmore's appointment to his post. After dark, carriages drew up before the Palace, and the town's elite climbed the slick stone steps. The earl would have greeted partygoers in his most elaborate suit. Lady Dunmore doubtless wore a hooped skirt, perhaps covered in Chinese silk. The wealthier women were clothed in Indian printed cottons or British knockoffs, while less affluent callers—or those eager to display their patriotic fervor—wore plainer linen, cotton, or wool spun at home. The faces of the guests were not all white; protocol demanded attendance of the four Shawnee men who still served as hostage-diplomats. Dozens of enslaved African attendants—butlers, footmen, and sub-footmen—stood arrayed in their blue-and-white uniforms with elaborate collars, velvet breeches, and frock coats.

Visitors crossed the length of the house and passed through a door framed by an immense neoclassical pediment. Beyond was one of North America's grandest rooms. The Palace ballroom glowed with the flickering light from dozens of tall tapers in candlesticks, candelabras, and the crystal chandelier hanging from the high arched ceiling. Prussian-blue walls edged in gilt served as the backdrop for the governor's collection of portraits of King George III and Queen Charlotte, as well as the Stuart king, Charles II, and his queen, Catherine of Braganza. Some were painted by Dunmore's acquaintance Allan Ramsay, one of Britain's most famous artists. On the floor lay a brightly patterned wall-to-wall carpet, a breathtaking luxury in an era when even small carpets were both rare and expensive. Off to the side stood a large stove called a Dutch "warming machine," stoked with coal shipped from Dunmore's country home outside Edinburgh. Musicians in one corner played his harpsichord, as well as violas, cellos, violins, mandolins, and German flutes, as guests danced minuets, reels, and rigadoons. For those who tired of dancing, there were gaming tables and private seating areas.

Supper was served later in the next room, decorated with pagoda-like pediments and Chinese-inspired wallpaper of brilliant green. Meats, sugared nuts, pastries, and candied fruits covered the tables. A 1746 Palace banquet had included "near 100 dishes, after the most delicate taste" and toasts drunk to the king, his family, and the governor, with "a great variety of the choicest and best liquors." Such affirmations of loyalty, even in early 1775, were unlikely to cause discomfort among Virginia's gentry, who still prided themselves on their devotion to the British sovereign. As enslaved servants refilled glasses and replenished platters, an army of white and enslaved workers—butchers, dishwashers, skilled chefs, and their many assistants—labored in serving rooms on the west side of the Palace, and in the kitchen and scullery outbuildings. The gathering lasted until near dawn, marking the last social event shared by royal governor and gentry.

The next morning's *Virginia Gazette* printed Dunmore's order for the newly elected burgesses to convene at the Capitol in May 1775. London had forbidden provincial assemblies from meeting "until his Majesty's pleasure be known," but the earl wanted to show that the provincial government was still in operation. Next to the notice, however, was Peyton Randolph's own decree. The Second Virginia Convention would meet on March 20 in the scruffy village of Richmond, fifty miles northwest of the capital, to select delegates to the next Continental Congress.

In an adjacent column was a letter lambasting Virginia's "clannish" Scottish merchants suspected of disloyalty to the American cause. "If we should be so unhappy as to come to a rupture with Great Britain, will they not be ready to come at our backs, and cut our throats?" the writer asked. "Let us then, my friends, whilst the disorder is curable, purge this our sickly colony of such filth." The anonymous author recommended "sending them from where they came." This suggestion of a forced deportation to Scotland was a sinister call for ethnic cleansing. The item appeared above notice of a sale of a dozen enslaved "men, women, and boys" to be auctioned "to highest bidders."

As Dunmore read the paper and his enslaved staff cleared the plates and glasses from the previous night's party, Parliament reconvened in Westminster. News of the theft of critical military supplies in late 1774 had hardened the stance of many lawmakers, including some Whigs sympathetic to the American cause. The petition from the Continental Congress, a body London deemed to lack legal standing, was paid little heed. In succeeding days of debate, a few voices urged members to accede to American demands. "There is no time to be lost," insisted the old and ailing former prime minister William Pitt, now Lord Chatham, on January 20. "It will soon be too late," he warned, predicting "years of calamity" if the legislation was not repealed. His call for reconciliation was rejected by an overwhelming majority. With neither Parliament nor patriots willing to compromise, all that was needed was a spark to ignite full-fledged war.

Chapter Seven

My Right Well-Beloved Cousin

"The cherry buds were a good deal swelled" when Washington set off from Mount Vernon for the Second Virginia Convention on March 15, 1775. He rode for five blustery days over rutted late-winter roads to reach what one contemporary called a "collection of villages lying around a trading place." Richmond's roughly 600 residents lived in some 150 buildings strewn along hills on the north side of the James River, which tumbled wildly over seven miles of rock before turning into a broad tidal stream that flowed past Jamestown to join the Elizabeth and empty into Hampton Roads. The small frame church built by Thomas Jefferson's great uncle was the only structure large enough to accommodate the 102 delegates.

The session began on March 20, the first day of spring, which also marked the start of what was known as campaign season, when armies traditionally took to the field. On the meeting's third day, March 23, snow threatened outside but the delegates opened the windows to relieve the heat generated by the packed mass of men. The Convention delegates agreed it was their "most ardent wish . . . to see a speedy return to the halcyon days when we lived a free and happy people." These men did not imagine building a new nation on radical principles of liberty and equality. They yearned for a bygone era.

Curious townspeople gathered along the open sashes when an "animated debate" broke out over Patrick Henry's call to establish "a well-regulated militia of gentlemen and yeomen" in each county, a force excluding the poor and the enslaved. He championed putting the colony "immediately into a posture of defense." Richard Henry Lee seconded the motion, and Jefferson also supported it. More conservative men, such as Peyton Randolph and Edmund Pendleton, bridled at a step they saw as needlessly provocative. They urged members to wait for a reply to the October 1774 petition sent by the Continental Congress to London. Then Henry rose from his pew to give one of the most influential speeches in American history.

All those present knew of his deep personal grief. The orator's mentally ill wife, Sarah, had been confined to the cellar in their home of Scotchtown, a plantation two dozen miles to the north. Mother of six, she may have been suffering from bipolar disorder or schizophrenia. A straitjacket had prevented her from harming herself or others, and she had been attended by an enslaved Black woman. The thirty-seven-year-old had died a few weeks prior, possibly by her own hand in an effort to free herself from suffering. Henry, not quite forty, told his family physician that her passing had turned him into "a distraught old man."

Henry's mother was drawn to the Baptist and Methodist preachers roaming the Virginia countryside. They were held in contempt by most members of the gentry, who disdained their more egalitarian and emotional approach to Christianity. They often suffered arrest and imprisonment, but their oratorical talents had impressed young Patrick Henry. While he remained a staid Anglican, he used evangelical methods to forge a unique and powerful speaking style. "Every word he says, not only engages, but commands the attention, and your passions are no longer your own when he addresses them," recalled George Mason.

The haggard attorney began mildly, according to later accounts. "It is natural to man to indulge in the illusions of hope," he said, adding that to delay creating a militia might result in white Virginians finding themselves "totally disarmed" with "a British guard stationed at every house." He then predicted that violence would soon erupt in Massachusetts. "There is no retreat," he added, with growing passion, "but in submission and slavery." Henry warned delegates that the king's ministers intended to place colonists in a servitude similar to that endured by Virginia's unfree workers. "Is life so dear, or peace so sweet, as to be purchased at the price of chains and slavery?" he asked the riveted audience, his rising voice filled with righteous indignation. "Forbid it, Almighty God!" The delegate is then said to have raised his hand as if holding "an imaginary dagger," concluding, "I know not what course others may take; but as for me, give me liberty, or give me death."

In that moment, "he plunged it into his heart and sank back into his seat," a witness recalled. Educated listeners would have caught his reference to the popular play *Cato*, in which a republican Roman commits suicide rather than fall into the hands of a tyrannical Caesar—but not before giving his faithful daughter to a virtuous African prince. It was Washington's favorite play. The impassioned rhetoric swept away even cautious members of the gentry, such as Thomas Nelson, the governor's senior counselor and a wealthy Yorktown merchant. He immediately pledged to "repel the invaders at the water edge." It was no idle boast. His mansion stood exposed on the bluff overlooking the York River.

Still, the controversial measure to create a militia passed by a thin margin of just five votes, and then only after it was watered down. Militia members would receive no pay, and these volunteers would have to provide their own firearm, cartouche box, and tomahawk, a pound of gunpowder, and four pounds of shot. This limited the fighting force to those few with deep pockets. Washington was among those selected to "prepare a plan for embodying, arming and disciplining" the new force.

The call to arms was not aimed at unseating Dunmore. The Convention went on to unanimously praise the governor "for his truly noble, wise, and spirited conduct on the late expedition against our Indian enemy" and his "attention to the true interests of this colony." His tireless executive work made the people "grateful to live under his administration." As if to reassure him, they explained that the militia was designed to protect the province from "invasion or insurrection," meaning an attack by an outside British force, indigenous peoples, or those enslaved. Yet they went on to criticize his recent decree, made by order of the king, to put all vacant lands in the colony up for sale. The highest bidder would pay a small fee per acre to the

Crown. Speculators were outraged, and the delegates appointed a committee that included Henry and Jefferson—both investors in land companies—to consider a response. Jefferson, of course, had insisted that the monarch had "no right to grant lands of himself." Freed from British constraints, the gentry stood to reap the tremendous wealth of the Ohio Valley. Dunmore's War had paved the way for Virginia's next phase of expansion.

The young planter's star was on the rise. As tall as Washington, though with a lankier frame, Jefferson "has rather the air of stiffness in his manner, his clothes seem too small for him," and he has "a loose shackling air," said one acquaintance, who added that "his face has a sunny aspect." Before the Convention disbanded on March 27, members selected him to serve as an alternative member of the Philadelphia delegation should the chronically ill Randolph be unable to serve. With that, the men scattered to their plantations. Washington rode back to Mount Vernon with the task of preparing the colony for military conflict.

Since his return from the Ohio Valley, Dunmore had maintained a resolute public silence on the growing rebellion. Two weeks after the January Palace ball, white male property owners had gathered at the capital's courthouse to select Peyton Randolph as their Convention delegate. Though he lived just a few blocks away, the governor had declined to interfere. He also had been careful not to openly criticize the March Convention held less than a day's ride from Williamsburg.

As the Richmond gathering broke up, Dunmore received strict instructions from London that made it impossible to cling to this diplomatic policy of neutrality. All royal governors were told to halt appointments to the Second Continental Congress, planned to convene in May. To obey the king would be to alienate Virginia's gentry, lose his position at the apex of colonial society, and even forfeit his farms, plantations, enslaved people, and livestock. Yet if he rejected the king's demand and sided with the patriots, he would be in rebellion against the empire, risking his titles, his reputation, his life, and the lives of his wife and six of his seven surviving children and the baby Virginia. If there was ever a moment Dunmore pondered which side to back, it was March 28, 1775.

Other governors took an array of positions that spring. Maryland governor Robert Eden, long a friend of Washington, maintained cordial relations with that colony's patriots. Rhode Island's Joseph Wanton refused to take sides, while New Jersey's William Franklin, son of Benjamin, remained a devout loyalist. Connecticut governor Jonathan Trumbull, by contrast, openly backed the rebels. Trumbull rejected the request by General Thomas Gage that he send troops to Boston, insisting such an action would "disgrace even barbarians." He also castigated Tories as "depraved, malignant, avaricious and haughty." A grateful Washington dubbed him "the first of the patriots."

Unlike Dunmore, Wanton and Trumbull were local men in the handful of colonies where the governor was elected by voters, not appointed by the king. Yet the earl had sunk his substantial fortune into Virginia and settled his family there. He also had just led an army of crack provincial riflemen to victory, and he did not share the smug view of many British leaders at the time who dismissed the colonials as undisciplined and cowardly. The earl, after all, had witnessed the defeat of the vaunted British army more than once at the hands of a hastily assembled Jacobite force.

At the same time, no royal governor knew better the price of joining a failed rebellion. Highland culture had suffered as a result, and his own father had been convicted as a traitor and only narrowly escaped death. The governor had seen the severed heads of the less fortunate rebels hanging from London Bridge. Unlike the vast majority of patriots, he understood too well the terrible consequences of defeat.

Yet in the topsy-turvy world of eighteenth-century British politics, Dunmore was now the monarch's "right trusted and right well-beloved cousin," in charge of his most important North American domain. Without an army or navy, however, he seemed doomed to lose Virginia to the rebels and return home in disgrace, forced to rely again on relatives for a career and financial support. If he allied with Virginia's planters, on the other hand, he stood to gain an honored place in the new government. The gates to the Ohio might then open, and thousands of fertile acres could ensure a comfortable life for him and his many sons and daughters. Washington, Jefferson, and Peyton Randolph would have welcomed Dunmore into the fold; the defection of a member of the House of Lords to their cause would have been a major coup. And were he to cast his lot with the patriots, there was little doubt that the colony's riflemen would again flock to his side, this time to march against any redcoats who might threaten Virginia.

Lady Dunmore, however, would have strongly objected to any notion of joining the rebellion. Their daughters were rapidly coming of age, and the colony lacked suitable aristocrats for them to marry, an important consideration in those days. She also had grown up within a Jacobite family in the traumatic aftermath of Bonnie Prince Charlie's revolt. More immediately, their youngest son remained in Britain, as did her family, friends, and extensive political connections. She might enjoy dancing with Virginia's gentry, but staking her future on them would have been a different matter.

If the couple indeed debated what to do, they came to a decision on March 28, hours after the Richmond meeting recessed. Dunmore set the governor's heavy seal on an official document criticizing the Continental Congress for its "unwarrantable proceedings" and disparaging its attempts to redress "pretended grievances" in a manner "so highly displeasing to His Majesty." A copy was dispatched to the print shop of a *Virginia Gazette*. "Had the above proclamation made its appearance but a day sooner," the editor commented, the Convention delegates likely would have issued a strong condemnation of the governor. That edition also reported on Parliament's January debate and concluded that "all hopes of an accommodation are at an end."

At the onset of the Revolution, one in five Americans was held in lifetime bondage. All were either born in Africa or of African or mixed descent. In the north, they made up a small percentage of the overall population and were heavily concentrated in towns and cities, where they typically performed menial tasks. The vast majority of enslaved people labored as unpaid field hands in the rural regions of Maryland,

Virginia, the Carolinas, and Georgia. In many areas in coastal South Carolina and along Virginia's rivers, Black residents outnumbered those who were white. About 10 percent of Black Americans were free, though still denied many of the rights accorded residents with a European background.

White Americans in that era commonly viewed those with dark complexions not as an oppressed minority but as a permanent lower caste. Given that slave labor was so central to the American economy, European-Americans preferred to ignore the moral quandaries posed by the widespread practice. "Would anyone believe that I am master of slaves of my own purchase?" Patrick Henry wrote in a frank letter to an abolitionist in January 1773. Henry, who owned a dozen individuals, acknowledged the practice was as "repugnant to humanity as it is inconsistent with the Bible, and destructive of liberty." Yet he was, he said, "drawn along by the general inconvenience of living without them." Wealth, convenience, and habit trumped moral considerations.

The same month that Henry made this stark admission, a Black Bostonian named Felix Holbrook launched the first public campaign for manumission and equal rights for Black Americans. He submitted a heart-wrenching petition to Massachusetts authorities in April, surely inspired by the recent Somerset decision. "We have no property! We have no wives! No children! We have no city! No country!" he wrote. "We pray for such relief only, which . . . to us will be as life from the dead." A legislative committee which included merchant John Hancock and activist Samuel Adams tabled the appeal. Holbrook made another bold but fruitless plea the following year. "We have in common with all other men a natural right to our freedoms," he insisted. On August 17, 1774, the *Essex Journal* published a letter from a free Black man named Ceasar Sarter. "Would you desire the preservation of your own liberty?" he asked. "As the first step, let the oppressed Africans be liberated."

For many whites, however, the enslaved class was a useful and powerful reminder of liberty's value. One week after Sarter made his plea, Washington shivered at the prospect of a Parliament that "will make us as tame and abject as slaves, and the Blacks we rule over with such arbitrary sway." As one Southern planter later explained, "the constant example of slavery" did not contradict patriot ideals, but "has, in fact, a tendency to stimulate and perpetuate the spirit of liberty."

As the patriot cause gathered strength, many white patriots came to fear Black Americans, both free and unfree, as a fifth column. Though no friend of slavery, Abigail Adams warned her husband in September that a group of enslaved men told the military governor, Thomas Gage, "they would fight for him provided he would arm them and engage to liberate them if he conquered." By late 1774 and early 1775, rumors of slave uprisings traveled up and down the East Coast, mirroring increased white demands for liberty from oppressive British laws. A handful of enslaved New Yorkers "confessed that their design was to convey ammunition to the Indians" along the Hudson River. They had allegedly collected "a large quantity" of gunpowder and bullets as well as hundreds of indigenous allies. "We are to set fire to the houses and stand by the doors and windows to receive the people as they come out," one defendant said.

Alleged plots to murder white people agitated residents of New Jersey and Long Island, while a Massachusetts man of color was accused of enlisting others to commit "some disturbance" that would draw away the militia as a signal to "destroy the white people." It was, one shaken resident wrote, an "infernal scheme." Several Georgians in bondage killed four white men and wounded three others; two were found guilty and burned at the stake.

In November 1774, the twenty-three-year-old Virginia slaveowner and aspiring politician James Madison revealed to a Philadelphia friend that some "unhappy wretches" in an unnamed Virginia county "met together and chose a leader who was to conduct them when the English troops should arrive." He added that "they foolishly thought" this would take place "very soon, and that by revolting to them they should be rewarded with their freedom." The plot was discovered "and the proper precautions taken to prevent the infection." Insurrection was, in other words, a dangerous malady that must be contained. The young planter declined to provide details lest the news spread. "It is prudent," he explained, "such attempts should be concealed as well as suppressed."

Madison dreaded an alliance between those in bondage and the emperor's armed forces. "If America and Britain should come to a hostile rupture, I am afraid an insurrection among the slaves may and will be promoted," he wrote. His concern was shared by his Pennsylvania correspondent. "Your fear with regard to an insurrection being excited among the slaves seems too well founded," his friend responded, conveying a piece of gossip that must have struck Madison with terror. While visiting a Philadelphia coffeehouse the day before, the man had heard that in case of a split with the colonies, the British government planned to declare "all slaves and servants free that would take up arms against the Americans."

He was referring to a pamphlet then circulating in London by Englishman William Draper, who had just returned from the colonies. The text has since been lost, but Arthur Lee, the Edinburgh-educated Virginian and former abolitionist, reported from the British capital that it advocated "emancipating your Negroes by royal proclamation and arming them against you." The idea, he added, "meets with approbation from ministerial people." This assertion was patently false. In January 1775, Parliament briefly debated whether to abolish American slavery, thus "humbling the high aristocratic spirit of Virginia and the southern colonies," but the measure was soundly defeated. Such a move, it was feared, might spread rebellion across Britain's Caribbean possessions. Still, in patriot minds, emancipation was part of Parliament's plot to destroy American liberties and reduce the colonists to the same state as their human chattel.

Dunmore had long been aware that the sheer number of enslaved people made white Americans vulnerable. "The people with great reason trembled at the facility that an enemy would find in procuring such a body of men," he noted soon after arriving in Virginia. Those in bondage were "attached by no tie to their masters or to the country, on the contrary, it is natural to suppose their condition must inspire them with an aversion to both." That made them ripe "to revenge themselves by which means a conquest of this country would inevitably be effected in a short time." At the time, he was thinking of Spanish or French invaders, but he apparently realized by the time of his return from the western war that those enslaved might challenge the patriot cause. After all, nearly half of all those in bondage in the colonies, more than 200,000 people, were Virginians. And, lacking a census, Dunmore estimated their numbers at twice that.

"I am informed by unquestionable authority, that he, Lord Dunmore, has wrote to the ministry that the Negroes have a notion the king intends to make them all free," wrote London-based William Lee—yet another of the Lee brothers—to Robert Carter Nicholas in March 1775. If his source was correct, the governor was already considering an alliance with the enslaved to counter the growing rebellion at the end of 1774. "The folly of this plan is only to be equaled by its wickedness," Lee added. He went on to propose a solution that echoed his brother Arthur's youthful ideas. "The best method of defeating so dreadful a scheme," he advised Nicholas, "would be to emancipate all the Negroes yourself by an act of the assembly, and instead of their being slaves, make them your tenants."

Virginia's gentry, however, showed no sign of loosening their control over their unfree workers. If anything, they tightened their grip amid a surge of unsettling incidents in April 1775. On April 15, an African man named Toney living west of Richmond was whipped after he was found guilty of plotting murder and insurrection. Three days later in an adjacent county, a white man reported, "We patrol and go armed" against "a dreadful enemy"—not redcoats but vengeful Africans. In Norfolk, meanwhile, two enslaved men, both named Emanuel, were jailed on suspicion of conspiring against white residents. And in a county near Washington's home, two men in bondage were said to have lit "a parcel of straw fixed to the end of a pole" and dangled it over a patriot militia officer's house, setting it aflame.

Such violence was the stuff of white nightmares, but it was the exception rather than the rule. Instead of taking revenge, those in bondage were far more apt to simply disappear. In January 1775, Richard Hipkins reported that his house servant Peg, "about fifteen to sixteen years of age and of a middle size," had run away from his plantation on the Rappahannock River in a brown linen jacket and plaid stockings with a stash of other clothes. She was, he said, a sensitive person, "greatly surprised and apt to cry" when accused of wrongdoing, and she had never traveled more than five miles from her home. Peg nevertheless found the courage to hail a passing sloop and gave the skipper a false name, telling him that "she wanted to go to Norfolk." Her owner was baffled that a person in forced servitude would flee. She left, he wrote, "without the least provocation."

Chapter Eight

The Smoldering Spirit of Revolt

In the freezing predawn hours of April 19, 1775, seven hundred red-coated troops marched out of Boston to seize and destroy arms and ammunition secreted in the town of Concord "for the avowed purpose of raising and supporting a rebellion against his Majesty." The force reached the village of Lexington at five that morning to find armed patriots on the town green. It is not clear who fired first, but seven local men soon lay dead. Three hours later, the British were in Concord, drawing hundreds of patriot militiamen. Another shootout ensued, but this time the British suffered more casualties. The Revolutionary War had begun.

Five hundred miles to the south, Williamsburg's voters gathered that morning at the courthouse to select Peyton Randolph as their representative to the Second Continental Congress, where he was all but certain to be renamed its president. Despite the king's order that he halt elections for what London considered an illegal gathering, Dunmore ignored this blatant act of civil disobedience taking place a short stroll from his Palace. He had, however, secretly taken steps to secure the ammunition kept across the street in the whimsical octagonal brick building known as the Powder Magazine.

The colony's only major arsenal was old and deteriorating, its window frames and doors filled with rot and its interior resembling more an unkempt attic than a major colony's weapons cache. Camp kettles, canteens, canvas tents and poles, swords, scabbards, and powder horns littered the dusty space. There were 342 new muskets and "a large number of old muskets and other small guns, almost useless." A reinforced room on the south side held gunpowder stored in twenty-one wooden kegs called half barrels, each containing fifty pounds of the explosive. To fire a musket required a quarter ounce of powder, while launching a single twelve-pound cannonball consumed two and a half pounds. The Magazine stockpile was enough to fight a skirmish or two, but hardly a war.

The building's contents were legally under the governor's control, though a designated keeper held the keys. Dunmore quietly obtained these following the Virginia Convention's call in late March for an independent militia. He wrote Lord Dartmouth that this resolution "made me think it prudent to remove some gunpowder which was in a magazine in this place." The ammunition, he added, "lay exposed to any attempt that might be made to seize it, and I had reason to believe the people intended to take that step." Dunmore planned the seizure with Lieutenant Henry Collins, captain of a small naval schooner called the *Magdalen* that had recently arrived in Virginia. The vessel now lay anchored off Jamestown, six miles south of the capital.

Word quickly leaked that Dunmore had the Magazine keys, and by April 16—Easter Sunday—local patriots had posted guards to keep an eye on the arsenal. The earl postponed the operation to avoid bloodshed. Five days later, in the early morning hours of April 21, chilly gale-force winds whipped across Market Square, and the patriot sentries sought shelter. The governor's spies reported their absence. Roused from sleep with this welcome news, Dunmore ordered a messenger to ride to Jamestown to deliver the keys and a note to Collins ordering him to set their plan into motion.

By three o'clock in the morning, twenty marines and sailors were on the road to Williamsburg, the chill gusts masking the thud of their horses' hooves and the clank of the wagon wheels as they rode into the capital under a waning moon. Collins dismounted and unlocked the north-facing outer gate, and the men entered the courtyard surrounding the building. Hurrying to the south end, they squeezed through the small door leading into the powder room. Either working in the dark or using a special lantern that prevented a spark from setting off the high explosives, the sailors and marines passed the half barrels—each weighing about sixty-five pounds—out the door and stacked them in the wagon. They ignored four barrels that were empty or contained rotted powder. Then an early riser spotted the intruders and sounded the alarm. As patriot drums beat, the wagon rolled toward the James River, where the cache was piled into a waiting boat and then transferred into the *Magdalen*'s hold.

One of those awakened by the early Friday morning clamor was William Pasteur, a London-trained surgeon who was sympathetic to the patriot cause and served on the town council. He pulled on his breeches and waistcoat and rushed into the street to find "a great commotion." Most of the city's white male inhabitants were already there, he recalled, "many of them under arms." Dunmore later said an angry crowd gathered on the green in front of the Palace and made "continued threats . . . to my house." He claimed that they resolved "to seize upon or massacre me, and every person found giving me assistance, if I refused to deliver the powder immediately into their custody."

With the marines on board the *Magdalen*, Dunmore's only defenders were the young Shawnee hostage-diplomats, white servants, and enslaved Black men inside the Palace. They had plentiful weapons, given the large cache of swords, knives, and guns lining the foyer walls. The governor undoubtedly ordered his wife and children to a secure storeroom or outbuilding beyond the range of patriot muskets and rifles. He knew that in Boston, royal officials had had their homes ransacked and even leveled for much less than what he had done.

Williamsburg, however, was not a city of mobs. Half of the population were enslaved Black workers kept under careful scrutiny by its white inhabitants, while indentured servants were bound by contract to obey their masters. Most of the rest were innkeepers, shopkeepers, and upscale artisans. Town leaders quickly gathered at the courthouse and drew up a petition to calm citizens. They then sent a delegation, which would have included Peyton Randolph and Pasteur, to knock politely on the Palace door. The wary governor had them shown in. The men presented the petition, which "humbly" asked the governor's motive and requested the gunpowder be returned. "We have much reason to believe that some wicked and designing persons"—presumably Royal Navy officers—"have instilled the most diabolical notions into the minds of our slaves," the document stated. Rumors were rife that enslaved Africans were poised to rebel in or near the capital. From his plantation outside Williamsburg, Edmund Pendleton wrote to Washington the same day of "some disturbance" in Williamsburg by enslaved workers. He thought the matter serious enough that Randolph might postpone his impending departure to the Continental Congress.

Prepared for a violent showdown, the earl was relieved that the petition was made "milder in terms than I expected." Privately, he considered it a high insult or even a "treasonable proceeding," yet he did not dare say so. "I had removed the powder," he assured the delegation, "lest the Negroes might have seized upon it." The ammunition, he promised, was now in "a place of perfect security." If there should be trouble, he promised "to deliver it to the people" within a mere half hour. He then expressed surprise to find men under arms. Given the volatile situation, the earl said, he "should not think it prudent to put powder in their hands." This response satisfied the delegation, which withdrew as cordially as it had arrived.

The armed crowd waited on Bowling Green in front of the Palace to hear Dunmore's reply. The governor would have watched anxiously from a Palace window as Randolph and Robert Carter Nicholas "by persuasion" convinced the people to disperse and "retire peaceably to their habitations." Pasteur later said that he "saw no further commotion that day." During the afternoon, he spotted Dunmore's personal secretary, Edward Foy, "walking down the main street unmolested." Foy, an army captain who had arrived with the governor in 1771, was accompanied by Collins, as well as Captain George Montagu of the *Fowey*, the frigate stationed in Norfolk that was now anchored off Yorktown. The ship carried some 130 crew members, along with a dozen and a half marines.

That evening's calm was broken when word spread that the marines intended to attack the capital. Armed patriots gathered at the Powder Magazine. Foy, according to one source, went from house to house to dispel the rumor. In his letter to Washington, Pendleton reported that some citizens "had a strong inclination to go immediately and secure the arms and ammunition" still in the building, but a local reported that the men "soon dispersed except a few who acted as patrol that night." Dunmore would have endured a sleepless night. His position, and the safety of his family and his few allies, was suddenly tenuous.

For the two Emanuels incarcerated in Norfolk's dank jail, sleep that night would have been far more difficult. They had been tried that day on "suspicion of felony," although the specific crime was plotting an insurrection. One Emanuel pled not guilty and "was fully heard in his own defense." Found guilty, he was asked why he should be spared execution. "He has nothing to say but what he has said before," the clerk wrote. A judge then read the sentence. "Therefore, it is considered by the court that the said Emanuel be hanged by the neck until he be dead." The deed was to be done by the end of the week. He was valued at 125 pounds, which would be paid to his owner in compensation for his financial loss.

The next morning, April 22, a resident of the Palace woke with an inflammatory disorder. Pasteur was summoned. Just one week previously, he and a partner had opened the Pasteur & Galt Apothecary Shop on Duke of Gloucester Street to "practice physic and surgery to their fullest extent" and provide imported medicines "as soon as the situation of the times will admit." He prescribed the patient honey and barley water and charged the exorbitant sum of four pounds for the house call.

Before he reached the door, he bumped into the earl. They were well acquainted; Pasteur was married to the daughter of the president of the College of William and Mary, where Dunmore chaired the board and his two teenage sons were students. When the governor on April 3 offered to resign given the political upheaval, the faculty prevailed upon him to remain. According to Pasteur's later deposition, Dunmore that morning seemed "exceedingly exasperated at the people's being under arms" the previous day. The doctor sought to allay his concern, noting that "this was done in a hurry and confusion, and that most of them seemed convinced it was wrong." His temper rising, the governor "proceeded to make use of several rash expressions." He charged that Foy and Collins had been insulted while strolling the streets of the capital on the previous afternoon.

Then Dunmore voiced words that would echo up and down the colonies and across the ocean. He "swore by the living God and many such expressions that if a grain of powder was burnt at Captain Foy or Captain Collins, or that if any injury or insult was offered himself or either of them, he would declare freedom to the slaves and reduce the city of Williamsburg to ashes." The governor also warned that he would consider "setting up the royal standard." The standard was the flag representing the British sovereign, and to raise it was a call for all loyal subjects to rally to the Crown's defense. Pasteur reported that the earl "did not say he would actually do it," but if he was forced to, he was certain those "people and all the slaves on the side of government" would rush to his support. The governor then issued a blunt threat. "He has once fought for Virginians," the doctor recalled Dunmore saying, and "by God, he would let them see he could fight against them." The result, he warned, would "depopulate the whole country."

What appeared a chance meeting and spontaneous outburst may well have been scripted. The governor was composed enough to tell Pasteur to "communicate to the speaker"—Peyton Randolph—"and gentlemen of the town and to do it immediately, that there was not an hour to spare." This suggests he feared an imminent attack on the Palace, and the dramatic threat by this theater lover was an effective way to deter violence. The stunned physician did as he was told. Those gentlemen, Pasteur recalled, responded with "great uneasiness" to the governor's warning, and some sent their wives and children out of the capital. The town's committee immediately resolved "that His Excellency's menacing declaration" had "tended greatly to irritate the minds and excite commotions among the people." The king's representative was expected to prevent a slave insurrection, not encourage one. Pasteur's story was later confirmed by loyalist John Randolph. He said under oath that the earl intended to "fix up the royal standard to distinguish the friends of government from its foes." He also verified Dunmore's stance on enslaved Africans. "If any Negroes had offered their services upon that occasion," Randolph said, they would have been "well received."

Several days after the incident, Dunmore visited a local judge and patriot named Benjamin Waller, who had helped Norfolk's Talbot

Thompson gain his freedom. Much of the seized powder, the governor complained, turned out to be of poor quality and useless. Waller was forthright. The half barrels were beside the point. The governor, he said, "had lost the confidence of the people not so much for having taken the powder as for the declaration he made of raising and freeing the slaves." The latter was the real explosive. The governor was unapologetic, telling Waller that he "would do that or anything else to have defended himself in case he had been attacked."

As Waller predicted, white colonists quickly lashed out, as much for the emancipation threat as for the munitions' removal. "You will see what diabolical (horrible to relate) measures he fell upon by robbing the Magazine of powder" and "stirring up the Negroes to rebellion," wrote one Virginian. The Henrico County committee denounced the powder removal as "an insult to every freeman in this country," and as a "cruel" measure, given that the town was "threatened with insurrection." It also helped "destroy the pleasing idea . . . of His Excellency's regard for the happiness and true interests of this colony." Dunmore, wrote another committee, "has justly forfeited all title to the confidence of the good people of Virginia."

Outrage spread as couriers carried the news beyond the colony's borders in subsequent weeks and months. White South Carolinians, heavily outnumbered by their enslaved population, were particularly aghast. A June 6 issue of a Charleston paper fulminated over "the monstrous absurdity that the governor can deprive the people of the necessary means of defense at a time when the colony is actually threatened with an insurrection of their slaves." In doing so, he had "worked up the passions of the people there almost to a frenzy." A senior South Carolina patriot worried that the enslaved "entertained ideas that the present contest was for obliging us to give them their liberty." Whatever their views on British taxation or Boston's travails, many white Southerners were sure to oppose anyone threatening to raise a slave army.

News of Dunmore's declaration also circulated that spring among Virginia's enslaved people and to those in other colonies. "The Negroes have a wonderful art of communicating intelligence among themselves," John Adams observed that same year. "It will run several hundreds of miles in a week or fortnight." For those in bondage, the words spoken by the king's representative offered the welcome prospect of liberty.

On Monday, April 24, patriot militiamen were drilling on the green in Fredericksburg, the inland town on the Rappahannock River eighty miles northwest of the capital, when a messenger arrived with news of the gunpowder seizure three days earlier. Four of their leaders immediately drew up a declaration calling for the colony's citizens to "embrace this opportunity of showing zeal in the grand cause by marching to Williamsburg" to "take such steps as may best answer the purpose of recovering the powder and securing the arms now in the Magazine." They urged patriots to assemble on the Fredericksburg green by Saturday, April 29.

They also sent a letter to Washington, who lived a few hours' ride to the east. Since Dunmore's actions constituted a "public insult," they wrote, the militia planned, "with your approbation, to join any other bodies of armed men who are willing to appear in support of the honor of Virginia as well as to secure the military stores yet remaining in the Magazine." They pleaded for additional gunpowder and reinforcements. One of the officers, Hugh Mercer, was a close friend of the Mount Vernon owner. The Scottish physician counted Washington's mother as a patient in his Fredericksburg medical practice, and he had purchased the planter's boyhood home across the river from the little tobacco port. Mercer was one of the colony's few experienced officers, having fought for Bonnie Prince Charlie in 1745 before fleeing to the colonies after the defeat at Culloden. He quickly took up a musket to fight under Washington for the British in the French and Indian War. His former superior was at his Potomac plantation that week, yet there is no evidence that he answered the urgent letter.

As many as six hundred men did heed the call, and two thousand were expected to gather by Saturday. When the governor heard this, he sent Lady Dunmore and their children to the *Fowey*, anchored off Yorktown. On the morning of Thursday, April 27, two days before the march to the capital was to commence, Pasteur paid another a house call at the Palace and again encountered the earl. This time, the governor told him that "if a large body of people came below Ruffin's Ferry"—a crossing point about thirty miles west of Williamsburg—"he would immediately enlarge his plan and carry it into execution." If the patriot militia crossed this Rubicon, in other words, Dunmore would arm loyalists, indentured servants, and enslaved Africans to defend the capital. He made it clear that he had two hundred loaded muskets in the Palace to fight off an assault. Pasteur rushed through the gun-filled foyer and out of the door. He had only to turn left on Scotland Street and right on England Street to reach Peyton Randolph's home, where the speaker and his wife were preparing to leave on the ten-day journey to Philadelphia the next morning.

The governor's latest ultimatum came as a shock. Randolph, aging and ailing, confronted a terrifying scenario. In just a few days, hundreds or even thousands of armed white men under the command of experienced officers might swarm into the capital. They would confront armed Black men allied with white loyalists led by the royal governor and possibly backed up with British marines and artillery from the *Fowey*. Word of the battles at Lexington and Concord, fought a week before, had yet to reach Williamsburg. The colonies and Britain remained, as far as he knew, at peace. If Randolph encouraged the patriot army, the governor might well follow through on his threat. A bloody civil war might be unleashed at the doorstep of the president of the Continental Congress; he could see the Magazine from his office window. The crisis was not one that Randolph was well equipped to handle. Jefferson, his first cousin once removed, described the speaker as good-natured and logical, but more comfortable with conciliation than confrontation. And "being heavy and inert in body, he was rather too indolent and careless for business."

Within an hour or two, confirmation of the danger came from three mud-splattered and exhausted men on horseback who dismounted at Randolph's door. Sons of wealthy planters, these patriots had been sent by the militia gathering in Fredericksburg to determine if the governor had returned the powder and to alert Randolph "that upwards of two thousand men" planned to march if it remained in Dunmore's custody.

A distraught Randolph chose to calm passions even at the price of fudging the truth. He hurriedly dictated what he called "a candid relation of the disturbance" to the Fredericksburg officers. The speaker explained that the earl "thinks he acted for the best" and that "His Excellency has repeatedly assured several respectable gentlemen that his only motive in removing the powder was to secure it, as there had been an alarm from the County of Surry," just across the James River. Enslaved Africans there were said to be planning an insurrection, a rumor that "at first seemed too well founded," though it later proved groundless. Randolph claimed that the earl had given his word "that the powder shall be returned to the Magazine, though he has not condescended to fix the day." The speaker concluded, "The governor considers his honor at stake," and therefore "will not be compelled" to reverse course. It would be more effective to let him return the powder of his own volition rather than by force. Randolph begged the militia to stand down, warning that "violent measures may produce effects, which God only knows the consequences of."

One of the trio put the letter in his saddlebag, and they pounded west down Duke of Gloucester Street. Before they departed, Randolph assured them he would stop in Fredericksburg on his way to Philadelphia to make a personal appeal for peace. The riders heading up the peninsula would have passed a lone traveler galloping in the opposite direction. Hours later, the solo messenger reached Williamsburg and tied his exhausted horse to the post outside the office of a *Gazette*. He pulled a paper from his saddlebag and handed the printer a few lines from a brief report scribbled ten days earlier at ten o'clock in the morning. Six patriots lay dead and four wounded at the Massachusetts village of Lexington after being fired on "without provocation" by British troops. "I have spoken with several who saw the dead and wounded," stated the correspondent.

Later, word arrived of the afternoon clash in nearby Concord. The final bloody tally of deaths that day was forty-nine Americans and seventy-three British. "The sword is drawn," intoned the day's *Gazette*, "and God knows when it will be sheathed." The issue also reported on the trial of the two Emanuels, noting "a sentence of death passed upon two Negroes lately tried at Norfolk, for being concerned in a conspiracy to raise an insurrection in town."

The patriot call to arms doubled Fredericksburg's population. On the morning of Saturday, April 29, more than a thousand "well armed and disciplined men, friends of constitutional liberty and America," stirred in the makeshift camp on the green, which soon was smoky with cooking fires. As a mild spring sun warmed the volunteers, talk of the battles to the north swirled with the smoke. More than one hundred of their leaders, representing fourteen militia companies, gathered nearby in what one participant called "a council of war." There was still no word from Washington, who remained silent at Mount Vernon.

During the stormy debate, the messengers from Williamsburg arrived after a long night on the road. Ushered into the meeting hall, one of the tired and muddy travelers read Randolph's plea to the hushed assembly. Only after further contentious debate did the officers agree to disband their forces. They confirmed in a statement their preference for "peaceable measures" to avert "the horror of a civil war," but pledged to gather "at a moment's warning" to defend Virginia or its sister colonies. The document also condemned Dunmore's actions as "ill-timed and totally unnecessary." The result was "alarming to the good people of this colony, tending to destroy all confidence in government, and to widen the unhappy breach between Great Britain and her colonies." Many had marched with Dunmore less than six months before, and the officers felt obliged to remind them that he now represented a threat to "our injured and oppressed country."

The militia on the green reluctantly accepted the resolution by their leaders and packed up to return home. "I am glad to inform you, that, after a long debate, it was at last agreed we should not march on Williamsburg," one of Mercer's colleagues, Alexander Spotswood, wrote Washington the next day. Though married to Washington's niece, he, too, received no reply. Throughout April 1775, arguably the most consequential month in American history, Washington remained strikingly removed from the critical events unfolding around him.

This detachment did not extend to his campaign to obtain western lands. The speculator had sent a survey team to lay claim to twenty thousand choice Ohio acres that promised to make him one of North America's single largest landowners. When he learned that Dunmore had rejected the surveyor's credentials and ordered his return east, he wrote his longest known letter to the royal governor. The April 5 missive described news of the surveyor's rejection as "incredible," and went on to praise the earl's "inclination to hear, and disposition to redress, any just cause of complaint." He asked that the surveyor be allowed to finish his job, and then begged the earl to forgive "the length and freedom of this epistle," closing with, "I profess myself to be, with your utmost respect, your Lordship's most obedient and humble servant." He made no mention of the brewing conflict with Britain.

Ten days later, an impatient Washington had yet to receive a response, though a letter from Williamsburg might take a week or more to arrive at Mount Vernon. "I despair of it at this time," he wrote to a friend in Pennsylvania, "as his Lordship is, I know, under a prohibition, by a late instruction, to grant no more lands to the westward of us (but on certain conditions) till His Majesty's further pleasure be made known." He had not given up hope that his carefully cultivated ties with the earl would open the west, but he was pessimistic, "so strange and inconsistent is the policy of the times."

Washington must have feared that taking a public stance against the governor might dash his hopes of obtaining Ohio Valley acreage, a dream he had nurtured for nearly a quarter of a century. This would explain his resolute silence during what came to be known as the "the gunpowder incident." He was not alone in seeking to avoid open conflict. Washington, Peyton Randolph, Pendleton, and even Richard Henry Lee failed to back the militia initiative for fear that British reprisals might endanger their property, charged James Madison. In a May 9 letter to a friend in Philadelphia, he accused these leading patriots of "a pusillanimity little comporting with their professions or the name of Virginian." The young Madison's western plantation and his enslaved workers, however, lay safely removed from any Royal Navy attack.

Only after the militia in Fredericksburg disbanded did Washington receive a brief and curt response from the earl, dated one day before the battles of Lexington and Concord and two days before the gunpowder incident. Dunmore confirmed that he had ordered the surveyor's return because the man seemed to lack the necessary credentials. "If this is the case," he concluded, not entirely closing the door, the land patents would "of consequence be declared null and void." So would the intimate relationship between Washington and Dunmore. This is the last known direct communication between the two men.

Chapter Nine

Virginia's Rubicon

While Dunmore holed up in the Palace, other governors were in flight. Less than a week before, North Carolina's Josiah Martin had watched from the window of his own stately home in New Bern as patriots made off with six cannons that had been arrayed at his front door. He promptly sent his family to New York and boarded a naval ship off the coast. The earl might easily have joined his own family on the *Fowey*, putting himself out of reach of the rebels. Instead, he transformed his stately residence into a secure military compound. "He has fortified his house, with swivel guns at the windows, cut loopholes in the Palace, and has plenty of small arms," wrote Norfolk merchant James Parker. The mansion now resembled the sturdy Scottish castles Dunmore knew well.

On May 1, before word arrived that the patriot militia in Fredericksburg had disbanded, Dunmore begged three senior British officials for aid. "The inhabitants of most of the counties of this colony are in commotion, and a body of two thousand men are now actually preparing to march to the assault of my house," he told General Gage, commander of six thousand troops stationed in Boston. "I have daily received fresh insults from other bodies of armed men appearing in town from the country." He doubted that he could "make an effectual resistance" from the Palace. Dunmore asked the general to provide "two or three hundred men or even one hundred" to hold out "on an entrenched post on the bank of one of the rivers under the protection of the guns of a man of war."

He also pleaded with Admiral Samuel Graves, who oversaw a fleet of more than one hundred Royal Navy vessels in Boston's harbor, for "one of the large ships of war now under your command." It would "strike awe over the whole country" and allow Dunmore to retain a land base. The governor argued that the extensive network of broad and deep rivers made it possible for a small number of ships to control the colony. Virginia had not a single working fort, its patriots had no ships, and most of its towns and plantations lay exposed on navigable waters. Dunmore also warned Lord Dartmouth in London that saving Virginia could not "be effected without force to support it," and requested "arms, ammunition, and other requisites." With these supplies, he said, "I could raise such force from among Indians, Negroes, and other persons, as would reduce the refractory people of this colony to obedience."

Until then, the earl assured Dartmouth, "I shall remain here until I am forced out," then retreat to Yorktown, build trenches under the guns of the *Fowey*, and "wait for His Majesty's orders." He specifically planned "to arm all my own Negroes and receive all others that will come to me whom I shall declare free." If the rebels did not cease their resistance, the earl pledged that he would "consider the whole country in a state of rebellion" and would "not hesitate at reducing their houses to ashes and spreading devastation wherever I can reach."

The letters to Gage and Graves were sent by boat to Boston, a journey that might take a week or two, so he could not expect a response for up to a month. By land, letters from Virginia might take three weeks or more to reach Boston and were also subject to patriot interception. The same month Dunmore made his pleas, the Continental Congress established its own postal system, effectively disabling the Crown's land network, making the sea route the only viable option. His correspondence to Dartmouth would require much longer to reach London and elicit a reply. This communications lag meant that Dunmore often had to make critical decisions without direction from the British command in North America or the king's ministers across the sea. By the time his superiors responded to his urgent messages, events had already outpaced their capacity to intervene.

The next day he assembled his councilors in the armed Palace, a safer venue than the exposed Capitol. "Commotions and insurrections have suddenly been excited among the people which threaten the very existence of His Majesty's government in this colony," he began. The governor defended his right and responsibility to secure the gunpowder. "I acted in this manner," he said, "to anticipate the malevolent designs of the enemies of order and government, or to prevent the attempts of any enterprising Negroes." As for the colonists' grievances, he maintained that they could only be redressed "by constitutional applications" rather than by force. Councilor John Page, Jefferson's friend and Rosewell's owner, suggested the governor return the powder. "Mr. Page, I am astonished at you," Dunmore replied, banging his fist on the table. The men then adjourned, and the next morning hammered out a conciliatory decree pledging to combat any "foreign enemy or intestine insurgents," while urging colonists to suppress "the spirit of faction."

News that the patriots in Fredericksburg had abandoned their planned march had by then reached Williamsburg, but a new threat emerged. What for Peyton Randolph was a crisis to defuse and for George Washington one to avoid, for Patrick Henry was an opportunity not to be squandered. The famed orator saw in Dunmore's words and actions a way to engage the colony's vast majority of white inhabitants—mostly small farmers, planters, and laborers—who remained largely on the quarrel's sidelines. The militia that assembled in Fredericksburg was a fraction of the army recently raised by Dunmore, and most counties had yet to form independent armed units.

Henry was a successful trial lawyer who had traveled the colony's rough back roads. Unlike most of Virginia's gentry, he understood that his clients cared little about taxes and tariffs. "You may in vain talk to [the people] about the duties on tea, etc.," he wrote a friend in April. "These things will not affect them. They depend on principles too abstracted for their apprehension and feeling. But tell them of the robbery of the Magazine, and that the next step will be to disarm them," he wrote. "You bring the subject home to their bosoms, and they will be ready to fly to arms to defend themselves."

In colonial Virginia, a white man's musket and powder stash were essential possessions. They were vital tools for killing animals for meat and skins, but they were, first and foremost, the means of preserving his personal safety and independence. The foes were not British troops but enslaved and indigenous people. The belief that the Crown intended to take their guns and powder made "too abstracted" notions of tyranny suddenly concrete. A patriot later wrote that white Virginians "believed at the time, and more strongly suspected from what happened afterwards, that [Dunmore] designed, by disarming the people, to weaken the means of opposing an insurrection of the slaves." The capital's arsenal, though poorly maintained and stocked, symbolized the Crown's promise to protect white citizens from such a rebellion.

Henry lived a few dozen miles south of Fredericksburg in Hanover County, but he had not joined those on the green. When the militia disbanded, the Hanover committee met on May 1 at a tavern near his plantation of Scotchtown. They spent the day arguing over what to do next, "there being some disagreement among them," one officer later recalled. An impatient Henry saw his chance to launch the southern rebellion against Britain. Though he lacked military training, his soaring rhetoric had the power to sway. The next day, he gave a rousing speech to the militia, which, according to one biographer, "spread before their eyes in colors of vivid description, the fields of Lexington and Concord, still floating with the blood of their countrymen, gloriously shed in the general cause." The skilled orator then "showed them that the recent plunder of the Magazine in Williamsburg was nothing more than a part of the general system of subjugation." He closed by ensuring the men that if they struck the first blow in the colony in the "great cause of American liberty," they "would cover themselves with never-fading laurels."

Henry's enthusiastic audience immediately elected him commander of the county militia and presented him with the hunting shirt that had become their standard uniform. On the morning of May 3, they left in high spirits and crossed Dunmore's Rubicon. Along the way they sang patriotic songs in the warm sunshine, then halted that afternoon at Doncastle's Ordinary, an inn frequented by burgesses like Washington on their travels to and from the capital, which lay a dozen miles to the east. By then, the militia had swelled to some 150. It was not, however, a mob of the downtrodden. One observer called them "all men of property," who gave "a very martial appearance." To deny the earl intelligence of their movements, they detained anyone they came across who was heading to Williamsburg. Henry also sent a message to Yorktown patriots asking them to intercept the governor if he tried to escape to the *Fowey*.

A few travelers, however, slipped past the militia to warn of the rebels' approach. Some of Dunmore's councilors worried about "the many innocent persons who would suffer by [Henry's] precipitate entrance into Williamsburg." Without a force to oppose him, the king's representatives chose to pay him off. Carter Braxton, a wealthy and conservative young planter, was sent to offer the radical leader the cash value of the gunpowder.

The governor also sent a warning to Captain Montagu of the *Fowey*. After midnight, Montagu wrote to Thomas Nelson, the governor's senior counselor. Henry's Richmond speech had persuaded Nelson to back military force even though he still served the governor and his Yorktown mansion stood within range of the ship's cannon. Montagu told him that Henry's men planned to attack the Palace "at daybreak this morning," adding that he was sending troops to protect the governor. The captain, unaware that Nelson was in Williamsburg, urged him to "prevent the party from being molested and attacked." If his men encountered resistance on the way to the capital, Montagu warned, "I must be under a necessity to fire upon this town."

At three o'clock that morning, forty-three marines landed upriver at the earl's Portobello plantation to begin their seven-mile march to the Palace. Montagu stationed a small sloop named *Liberty* at the site to evacuate the governor if necessary. The earl later reported that he was "defending myself by arming the persons of my family." A nineteenth-century historian who interviewed participants wrote that the earl "armed his servants together with the Shawnee hostages" and "parties of Negroes mounted guard every night at the Palace."

Braxton had arrived at Doncastle's Ordinary on the previous evening as the sliver of the new moon set. Henry agreed to take a promissory note to cover the cost of the powder—but not from the young man, due to his "political attachments." The lawyer insisted the money come from someone he trusted, or he would march at first light. After another hurried exchange of midnight messengers,

Nelson was chosen to negotiate the deal. The middle-aged merchant rode fast through the night to reach the inn before dawn. When he arrived, Henry put the gunpowder's value at 330 pounds, about $33,000, triple its actual worth. This was no time to haggle, so Nelson wrote out a receipt, and Henry handed him a letter agreeing that the powder affair was "now settled." The money was designated to pay for patriot arms. The orator, despite his reputation, did not wholly lack a sense of humor. He slyly offered to send armed guards into the capital for Nelson's "protection," an offer the tired advisor politely declined.

The immediate crisis was over. Henry and his men retreated to Hanover County, and the attorney soon left for the Continental Congress in Philadelphia. John Page later concluded that Henry "did actually bully" the governor but added that "they appeared to be mutually afraid of each other." Nelson, meanwhile, shared Montagu's letter threatening to bomb Yorktown with the York County Committee, which accused the captain of "a spirit of cruelty unprecedented in the annals of civilized times." In New England, this would have been a call to board and burn the ship. The committee instead imposed a peculiarly Virginian punishment, advising citizens to avoid contact with the officer, offering only "what common decency and absolute necessity requires."

Tensions, however, remained high. After dark on May 4, patriots broke into the Magazine and took "a great number of guns, cartouche boxes, swords, canteens, etc., for which His Excellency, the governor, has ordered a diligent search be made," a *Gazette* reported. Dunmore inspected the site the next day, while Williamsburg's leaders dutifully expressed their "abhorrence of such unlawful proceedings" and told citizens to return the stolen materials and "prevent the like outrage in future."

In the aftermath of Henry's attempted coup, Dunmore had to address the armed intimidation in public. Declaring the popular politician an outlaw would only make matters worse, so he ordered colonists "not to aid, abet or give countenance to the said Patrick Henry." Even this mild rebuke only increased the lawyer's renown. Madison wrote on May 9 that Henry's planned attack "gained him great honor in the most spirited parts of the country." Men in hunting shirts with rifles and muskets began to drift into the capital. "Even in the place where I live," the governor wrote Dartmouth on May 15, "drums are beating and men in uniform . . . with arms are continually in the streets, which my authority is no longer able to prevent." The danger forced the governor "to shut myself in and make a garrison of my house expecting every moment to be attacked."

That same day in Boston, General Gage wrote Lord Dartmouth in London that the Virginia governor's situation "appears so very alarming that I fear the assistance in my power to give him will avail but little." Gage and Dunmore had been allies when they served in New York, but the military leader was preoccupied with the crisis in New England. "Gage's ignorance about the South was especially damaging," notes one historian. "He scarcely mentioned Virginia in his letters home." The general ordered a handful of soldiers dispatched from the old Spanish fort of St. Augustine, then an important British military base, in the hope that they "might be of some use" to the beleaguered governor.

News of Dunmore's late April threat to emancipate enslaved Africans had reached Gage by mid-May. "We hear by private letter that a declaration his lordship had made, of proclaiming all Negroes free who should join him, has startled the insurgents," he noted without comment. When he received the news later that spring, Dartmouth made no move to reprimand the governor. In fact, he seems to have been sympathetic to the idea of emancipation. The colonial secretary was a pious Methodist with abolitionist friends; the enslaved Black Massachusetts poet Phillis Wheatley dedicated a poem to the minister and met with him during her 1773 visit to London.

Those in bondage, meanwhile, acted on Dunmore's words. A *Gazette* reported on May 4 that several Black men had "offered to join him to take up arms" after Henry menaced the capital. According to the paper, however, Dunmore "threatened [them] with the severest resentment should they presume to renew their application." Loyalist John Randolph later confirmed this under oath, reporting that the earl had rejected their help, ordering them "to go about their business." Dunmore had no intention of further inflaming the patriots by openly recruiting indigenous and African soldiers as armed white men paraded through the capital's dusty streets. "The rebels are called 'shirtmen' from their uniforms," a Royal Navy sailor later noted, "a long shirt down to their heels with a leaden medal at their breasts in the shape of an old English shield, on which is inscribed 'Liberty or Death.'" Other reports suggest the men sewed the motto directly into their clothing.

The governor had made his threat and put weapons in the hands of his unfree servants as a temporary expedient to protect himself and his family. In the short term, this had proved a remarkably effective strategy. The patriot militia had twice abandoned their intention to attack the capital and, presumably, to arrest and imprison the governor. Yet long after the men stood down, the earl's words continued to send shock waves through the colonies and on to Britain. For nearly a century, Virginia law had forbidden enslaved persons from carrying "any club, staff, gun, sword, or any other weapon of defense or offense." As punishment, the offender would receive "twenty lashes on his bare back well laid on." Lifting a hand "in opposition against any Christian" incurred thirty lashes. Arming those enslaved was more than a crime; it was a betrayal. If anyone had crossed Virginia's Rubicon, it was not Henry, but Dunmore.

On a damp and gusty February afternoon in 1775, members of Parliament had gathered at the king's residence at St. James Palace in London to present their bill declaring Massachusetts to be in rebellion. The monarch then pledged to take "the most speedy and effectual measures" to stamp out the uprising. Lord North, a canny politician, was determined to give the Americans a carrot as well as a stick. Two weeks later, he proposed a "conciliatory resolution" to grant the colonies control over their domestic affairs, including taxation. In exchange, they would contribute to the empire's defense. Parliament and the king reluctantly approved the measure. The resolution was sent not to the Continental Congress, which the British government did not recognize, but to the elected assemblies of individual colonies. Dartmouth ordered royal governors to convene their legislatures to present the proposal, and Dunmore set June 1, 1775, as the new date for the House of Burgesses to meet.

North's proposal was widely seen by patriots as a cynical attempt by the British politician to divide the colonies. "I would make the meanest American I know piss upon him," wrote Virginia militia officer Adam

Stephen. The earl was not hopeful. "It is no longer to be doubted that independence is the object and view," he warned Dartmouth. To help put Williamsburg back in its usual somnolent state, Lady Dunmore and their children returned after two weeks aboard the *Fowey*. Her flight reflected poorly on the patriots, and a newspaper reported that her arrival brought the "great joy of the inhabitants." White colonists, the article noted, felt "an unweighted regard for her ladyship, and wish her long to live amongst them." Norfolk's James Parker, an inveterate collector of gossip, heard there was another reason for her to disembark; she was again pregnant. If the countess was expecting while still nursing her five-month-old daughter, shipboard life in the late spring heat would have been a trial.

On May 22, ten days after the family returned, the Palace came under surprise attack. In three minutes, more than three hundred panes of precious imported glass in the mansion windows shattered, sending shards skittering across the wide-plank floors. The culprit was a barrage of hail accompanying a storm that unleashed a tornado, which tore through a nearby county, killing four and laying waste to homes and crops. "Such a scene of horror and devastation was never seen before by winds in this country," said one eyewitness. Enslaved workers nailed wooden planks across some of the gaping holes, giving the Palace an embattled air.

At five in the afternoon on Tuesday, May 30, the bells of Bruton Parish Church began to clang, and town residents rushed to the main street. Onlookers cheered as an elaborate coach with the ailing Peyton Randolph and his wife rolled past Bowling Green accompanied by patriot militiamen. Randolph had departed Philadelphia to reassume his role as speaker of the House of Burgesses, leaving the presidency of the Continental Congress in the hands of Massachusetts merchant John Hancock. When rumors spread that Randolph might be arrested by a Royal Navy contingent, a militia unit escorted him from Ruffin's Ferry to his house off Market Square. The governor, who watched the retinue from his broken windows, called it "a pompous military exhibition." The men and "other respectable gentlemen" then decamped to Raleigh Tavern for several rounds of patriotic toasts. The next morning, a crowd gathered outside Randolph's large clapboard home to praise him as the "father of [his] country and the friend to freedom and humanity."

Two days later, on the first anniversary of the day of fasting and prayer marking the closure of Boston harbor, the colony's burgesses gathered at the Capitol. Amid the usual velvet waistcoats and powdered wigs were linen hunting shirts and steel tomahawks tucked into broad leather belts. Some even carried rifles as they filed into the governor's council chamber in the west wing. "I have called you together to give you an opportunity of taking the alarming state of the colony into your consideration," Dunmore calmly began. The earl urged them to consider North's reconciliation plan with an eye to preventing "the disputes, which have unhappily raged between the mother country and the colonists." He assured them that "well-founded grievances, properly represented," would receive a fair hearing. The members then politely took their leave to begin their work. Jefferson was appointed to the committee designated to respond to the governor's brief speech.

The habitual civility masked patriot rage. That day's *Gazette* referred caustically to "a nominal itinerant governor, who for some time past has been suspected of acting the part of an incendiary in this colony," a sly reference to the Magazine incident. This man "is to take the field as generalissimo at the head of the Africans." The writer concluded that "the Black ladies, it is supposed, will be jollily entertained" in the Palace. The anonymous author was likely Theodorick Bland, a cousin of Randolph and Jefferson. He subsequently accused the governor of hosting "convivial banquets" for Black men and women, as well as "nightly orgies within the walls of your Palace." Such allegations of social and sexual transgressions drew on common contemporary English tropes about barbaric and libidinous Scotsmen. They became a hallmark of attacks on a governor who, until just months before, had been widely respected and praised.

His Jacobite past, once politely ignored, now made him a target of criticism. Whigs had long castigated those who sought to bring the Stuart family back to the throne, viewing them as sympathetic to Britain's Catholic enemies. The May 25, 1775, *Gazette* heralded the governor as "his most catholic excellency." The winking phrase may have been used to link the earl with France, Spain, and the hated Church of Rome.

Dunmore, a lifelong member of the Scottish Episcopal Church, ignored the public taunts, and on June 2 he sent Lord North's proposal to the House chamber. Meanwhile, the burgesses focused on the backlog of petitions that formed much of their day-to-day work. A large number came from white slaveowners seeking compensation for lost or damaged human property. One asked to be paid the worth of an enslaved woman named Juda said to have murdered her son and burned her owner's dwelling before she died in the flames. Another enslaved worker had been jailed for stealing pigs and "was frostbitten during his confinement." Jailers often denied their charges the warmth of a fire for fear they would torch the prison. Indeed, one slaveowner sought repayment after his human property died in a conflagration while incarcerated.

The burgesses adjourned the next day to celebrate Whitsunday, also called Pentecost, a major religious festival accompanied by games and contests in England. In Virginia, it was a day when white inhabitants feared that raucous celebrations would encourage an "unlawful concourse of Negroes." The colony's militia typically was on high alert to prevent any disturbances. That night, residents woke with a start to gunfire and anguished cries echoing across the town's Market Square. White male citizens rushed outside expecting to confront armed Black men or British marines—or both. Instead, they found three local white teenagers writhing on the ground by the door of the Magazine. One had suffered only minor injuries, but a second had lost two fingers on his right hand while the third "was very much lacerated by small balls, which entered his arm and shoulder." The first blood spilled south of New England in the American Revolution was drawn by an anonymous boobytrap. The youthful intruders had intended to rob the arsenal of weapons and ammunition in the dead of night but had tripped a cord that ran through the triggers of two loaded guns placed just inside the building. The uninjured ringleader was the mayor's son.

Dunmore insisted he had no knowledge of the snare, but the incident hardened patriot opinion against him. "The cry among the people was for vengeance," he wrote Dartmouth. While the burgesses sat in session that Monday, another group of teenagers broke into the armory in broad daylight and made off with at least four hundred low-quality guns kept for distribution to indigenous trappers. Jefferson and Richard Henry Lee were assigned to a panel tasked with investigating the break-ins, and asked Dunmore to provide them with the magazine key. The governor demanded a signed request, which offended these men whom the earl had known for years. The earl then pledged to return the removed powder "as soon as I see the Magazine is in a proper state." The committee found the building in poor repair and poorly stocked, with 157 guns for the Indian trade, 180 new muskets lacking locks, and 527 older models, "the barrels very rusty, and the locks almost useless." Several half barrels of powder buried in the magazine's yard were now "totally destroyed by the late rains." Conspiracy theories nevertheless proliferated. One issue of a *Gazette* repeated a rumor that the governor had buried a fuse that led from the Palace to the Magazine and could "blow up the town in an instant."

On June 7, the House of Burgesses extended Dunmore its "thanks for his kind tender of services in the war against the Shawnees." The members requested a meeting with the governor in his Capitol council room the next day at one o'clock, to which he agreed. That afternoon, the earl felt comfortable enough to stroll from the Palace to Tazewell House, the grand white-columned mansion of his loyalist ally John Randolph. The quarter-mile walk took him through the heart of town and back. At some point that evening, perhaps on his return home, he apparently received a dire warning of a patriot plot to kidnap or assassinate him.

By two o'clock the next morning, candles in the Palace were lit, and servants rushed to and fro with piles of clothes and stacks of important papers. Lady Dunmore and the children assembled with the governor's secretary Captain Foy, the Anglican pastor Thomas Gwatkin, and a handful of free and enslaved servants. Dressed in traveling clothes, they entered the darkened ballroom and crossed the low pile of the carpet before passing through the deserted supper room. Filing through the wide double doors at the northern end of the wing, they stepped into a late spring night loud with cicadas. Their footfalls crunched on paths shining pale with broken oyster shells in the waxing moon. Exiting the back garden gate, the party climbed quietly into waiting carriages, coaches, and carts filled with a few hastily packed chests and bags of belongings.

As a gesture of goodwill, Dunmore had permitted Cornstalk's son to return home, but the three other Shawnees remained at the Palace. Also left behind were most of the earl's possessions, including dozens of enslaved men, women, and children. With muted cries, the coachmen urged the horses forward, and the vehicles sprang into the dark and rolled through the back streets of the silent town. None of those who left that night would see the Palace, or Williamsburg, again.

Chapter Ten

Black as an Ethiop

The next morning, June 8, the burgesses convened as usual at ten o'clock. Dunmore's councilors arrived later at the Capitol to prepare for their one o'clock meeting with the House. Instead of the governor, they found a letter signed by him. He explained that he was "now fully persuaded that my person, and those of my family, likewise, are in constant danger of falling sacrifices to the blind and unmeasurable fury" of the people. He was certain that they planned to take advantage of his defenseless state "and perpetrate acts that would plunge this country into the most horrid calamities and render the breach with the mother country irreparable."

Dunmore was gone. He and his family had fled in the night to Portobello, where a boat was waiting to transfer them before dawn to the *Fowey*, anchored just downstream off Yorktown. Rather than wishing him good riddance, the stunned lawmakers quickly sent a messenger pounding down the dirt road to assure "His Excellency" that they viewed "with horror every design that may be mediated against the persons of his lordship, his very amiable lady, or family." They promised their "cheerful concurrence in any proper measure for their future safety." His return, the legislators agreed, was "the most likely means of quieting the minds of the people." For all their criticisms, the gentry feared that the hasty departure of the king's representative would sow chaos. They warned Dunmore, however, that it would be "impracticable" to continue the session "whilst your lordship is so far removed from us and so inconveniently situated."

The governor did not elaborate on the "acts" planned against him. Not even his friends knew for sure. The earl had spent time the previous evening with John Randolph, but the attorney general later insisted under oath that Dunmore had not mentioned any threat to his life at the time. In Norfolk, James Parker had "no doubt some private injury was intended him." He claimed that one radical patriot made "some foolish speeches" on the floor calling for the governor to be hanged. Yet a man who had recently foiled two armed attacks was not easily frightened.

There was, in fact, a plot to kidnap the earl. A Virginia delegate to the Second Continental Congress later revealed in open debate that "it was from a reverence for this Congress that the Convention of Virginia neglected to arrest Lord Dunmore." The delegate was George Wythe, a respected attorney and mentor to Jefferson who lived on Bowling Green near the Palace and knew the governor well. He explained that the plot was never carried out for fear of the repercussions of jailing a member of the House of Lords. Dunmore may have gotten wind of this plan late on June 7, perhaps from an enslaved servant who had overheard details and whispered a warning as the governor strolled back from Tazewell House in the dark. Either the governor foiled the plot by abruptly abandoning Williamsburg or, as Wythe maintained, the burgesses had already chosen not to follow through.

The legislators nevertheless continued their work. The day's first order of business was to consider a petition from the sheriff of Accomack County on the colony's Eastern Shore, the rural tongue of land between the Chesapeake and the Atlantic. "Daniel, a Negro man slave," had been accused of "attempting to ravish a white woman" and condemned to castration by the local court. Daniel's owner, William Ward, had incurred "considerable expense" as a result, having had to pay "a surgeon for performing the operation, and healing the wound." The sheriff wanted him reimbursed, and the House later granted him seven pounds and ten shillings, about $800 today, in taxpayers' money. They adjourned that afternoon after considering a host of such pleas.

The following morning, they took up Lord North's proposal for a compromise between the patriots and Parliament to avert violence, only to be startled by distant thunder through the open windows. This was no spring storm but the sound of cannon firing. "At eleven a.m. His Excellency the Earl of Dunmore came on board," reported Captain Matthew Squire in his log of the sloop *Otter*, which had just dropped anchor next to the *Fowey*. "Saluted him with fifteen guns, the same on his leaving her." Hearing a report that the patriots were holding Dunmore captive—another hint that there might have been a patriot plot—Admiral Graves in Boston had rushed the ship south. Less than one hundred feet in length and armed with only small cannon, it was not the formidable man-of-war the earl had requested. The new arrival was smaller than the *Fowey*, but it was newer and nimbler and drew less water, making it well suited for the colony's broad and shallow waters. It was accompanied by an even smaller vessel, the schooner *Arundel*.

The little squadron—*Fowey*, *Magdalen*, *Otter*, and *Arundel*—was humble compared to the enormous fleet of a hundred or so Royal Navy ships crowding Boston harbor, but it gave the British clear naval superiority in this water-crossed land. Washington would later call such an advantage "the pivot upon which everything turned." Squire, young but experienced, welcomed the governor on deck to the cannon's boom and the shrilling of pipes. In his stern cabin he gave the earl the good news that sixty soldiers would soon be on their way from St. Augustine. "Small as it is," Dunmore later wrote Gage, the numbers of ships and men "will possibly serve to strike some degree of awe upon the inhabitants, who mostly lie exposed along the river sites here." He hoped that they would "contribute to restore the lawful authority of government."

The newly confident governor sent a message to Williamsburg urging the burgesses to accept Lord North's peace plan. If they did, he promised, "I will return with the greatest joy and shall consider it as the most fortunate event of my life." The earl would, he said, work for "the undisturbed enjoyment of your rights and liberty, and I shall be well pleased, by bringing my family back again." It was his deepest wish "to cultivate a close and lasting intimacy with the inhabitants." His conditions, however, were onerous. The patriots had to agree to reopen the courts, disarm the militia, and return the stolen arms to the Magazine. He also called on the Virginians to end "that spirit of persecution" that menaced "all persons who differed from the multitude in political opinion." If these demands were not met, he added, "my return to Williamsburg would be as fruitless to the people as possibly dangerous to myself." As a compromise, he suggested the legislators move to Yorktown to continue their work.

The burgesses were divided. Some conservatives feared that rejecting Dunmore's conditions would prompt him to dissolve the assembly again. Jefferson saw instead an opportunity to repudiate the mother country's policies. He was still working on a response to Dunmore's June 1 address. "The British Parliament has no right to intermeddle with the support of civil government in the colonies," his draft boldly asserted. "We alone are the judges of the condition, circumstances, and situation of our people." The statement also criticized Parliament's act "extending the boundaries and changing the government and religion of Quebec," a move that threatened to halt Virginia's westward expansion. By placing the border of this Catholic-dominated province against Virginia's newly won frontier along the Ohio River, British ministers seemed determined to restrict the planters' wealth and power.

Liberty, Jefferson added, overrode reconciliation. He also argued that Virginians could not accept North's proposal without making themselves "base deserters of that union." The Continental Congress had to be consulted first. Before the House of Burgesses approved a final version of the response, Jefferson was already on his way to Philadelphia to fill Randolph's vacant seat in the congress. He stashed a fresh copy of the draft resolution in a trunk for the journey north. He rode out of the capital on Sunday, June 11, in a sporty phaeton drawn by four horses steered by an enslaved African.

The next morning, the burgesses dispatched a messenger to the Yorktown docks with the legislators' response to Lord North's plan. "We examined it minutely; we viewed it in every point of light in which we were able to place it," the delegates told the governor, "And with pain and disappointment we must ultimately declare it only changes the form of oppression, without lightening its burden." The burgesses also declined to meet in Yorktown, while assuring Dunmore that there was not "the least danger in his returning to the Palace" and expressing "the sincerest disposition on our part to have the utmost harmony and most perfect tranquility restored." Dunmore responded that he saw not the least inclination on the part of the legislators for "a reconciliation with the mother country," yet he did not dissolve the House.

He wrote Admiral Graves that he intended to remain on the *Fowey* "for the preventing of the shedding of blood." Williamsburg was, according to James Parker, awash with men who resembled "a band of assassins," and Dunmore's spies reported that the gentry and town residents feared the rural men with guns who roamed the town spoiling for a fight. At least some legislators yearned for the governor's return to prevent disorder from enveloping the capital. But Williamsburg, Dunmore insisted, was now "an improper place for the residence of the governor."

For the next week, messages flew back and forth between the *Fowey* and the Capitol, alternatively threatening and cajoling, like those between a separated couple trying to determine if they should make up or divorce. It was as if neither side wanted to be the first to break the spell cast by Virginia's 157-year-old political system, the oldest in British North America. On June 19, the burgesses acknowledged to the earl "some irregularities" committed by "country" patriots. The protocol-minded planters even apologized to Dunmore for rejecting a dinner invitation he had proffered a few weeks previously.

Yet the delegates doubled down on their criticism of the powder removal amid "a well-grounded apprehension of an insurrection of the slaves," and echoed Henry's warning that London intended to seize not just powder but the colonists' guns. "A general plan they had heard was recommended in England" to "disarm the people" and thereby deprive white colonists of "the only means of defending their lives and property." The burgesses also lambasted "a scheme, the most diabolical . . . to offer freedom to our slaves and turn them against their masters." The June 19 missive by the burgesses declared that Britain plotted to "subjugate America" by seizing their firearms while unleashing a slave rebellion. Patriots viewed this prospect with dread, though neither policy was seriously considered in London.

"It is imagined our governor has been tampering with the slaves," Madison wrote to a Philadelphia friend that same day. "He has it in contemplation to make great use of them in case of a civil war in this province. To say the truth, that is the only part in which this colony is vulnerable; and if we should be subdued, we shall fall like Achilles by the hand of one that knows that knowns the secret."

As the letter from the House of Burgesses made its way from the Capitol to Dunmore on the *Fowey*, the Second Continental Congress meeting in Philadelphia's Pennsylvania State House chose George Washington to serve as "general and commander in chief of the army of the United Colonies." New Englanders preferred a Virginian to lead the new force to demonstrate unity, and Washington was the obvious candidate. As the only delegate who wore a military uniform, he had made his availability plain. "No harum scarum ranting swearing fellow," wrote one Connecticut delegate of the former militia colonel, "but sober, steady, and calm."

Soon after, word arrived of the bloody June 17 clash on Breed's Hill, across the Charles River from Boston, which came to be known as the Battle of Bunker Hill. More than a thousand British and nearly five hundred colonists lay dead or wounded. Washington left Philadelphia on June 23 to assume command of the nascent Continental Army bivouacked opposite British-occupied Boston in Cambridge. That day, the House of Burgesses made one final plea for Dunmore to return to the capital so they could close the session. The tobacco crop demanded their "immediate presence at home," they explained. He refused.

The next day, without waiting for the governor's permission, they adjourned with a final assurance to the earl: "We do and will bear faith and true allegiance to our most gracious sovereign, George the third, our only lawful and rightful king." By then, the Palace stood deserted, aside from a few free or unfree servants. The three Shawnee diplomat-hostages, fearing enslavement or prison, had slipped away, making a harrowing journey across the mountains while dodging patriot patrols. Not everyone, however, was aware of the governor's departure to Yorktown. An unfortunate fifteen-year-old enslaved girl sought refuge at the Palace door after she was discovered having sex with her owner's daughter, only to find the governor gone. Recaptured, she was subjected to eighty lashes; hot embers were then poured on her wounds.

On the night of the 23rd, an intruder opened a window on the first floor of the mansion and threw open the double doors at the entrance. "A considerable body of men" rushed into the foyer and "carried off all the arms they could find," the earl later reported. The trespass almost certainly had the approval of the House, which had complained to Dunmore that the mansion's weapons collection was "exposed to your servants," including enslaved Africans. They had warned that a "rude invader" might loot the king's arms to keep them out of enemy hands. In a letter the following day to Dartmouth, Dunmore admitted that his threat to emancipate those enslaved had "stirred up fears" among white colonists "which cannot easily subside, as they know how vulnerable they are in that particular." Yet the earl expressed no regret, on the "grounds of self-preservation." He had used the only obvious strategy available to forestall patriot assaults—and succeeded. "I had full right to make use of any means I could avail myself of, for my defense against a furious people."

For many white Virginians, however, the genial hero was now a monstrous tyrant. "We never imagined him an enemy," wrote "Virginius" in the June 29, 1775, *Gazette*. Once considered "an inoffensive, easy, good-natured man," he had become "suddenly as black as an Ethiop," a reference to the African kingdom of Ethiopia. The man heralded as the colony's champion was now derided as a liar, blunderer, and worse. "Can any confidence," the writer asked, "be reposed in a murderer?"

As the House members were leaving the sweltering Capitol, Richard Henry Lee scratched a few lines from Shakespeare on the pillars linking the building's two wings. When would they meet again? "When the hurly-burly's done / When the battle's lost and won." The quote was drawn from the first scene in *Macbeth*, the tragedy of an ambitious Scottish lord who murders his king and numerous others, and in turn is murdered by those he had wronged.

On the morning of June 28, the people of Yorktown were still sleeping when the crews of the *Fowey* and *Magdalen* lifted their anchors, unfurled their sails, and rode the outgoing tide downriver into Chesapeake Bay. Residents awoke to rumors that the governor had fled to Boston or Britain. His four-year-long tenure finally seemed over. The

Magdalen was indeed bound across the Atlantic. On board were Lady Dunmore, her seven children, Reverend Gwatkin, John Randolph, and other staunch loyalists. The earl stood on the deck of the *Fowey* to accompany the vessel as far as the Virginia capes. The governor had struggled to convince his pregnant and nursing wife to depart the colony. "He tried every stratagem to get his amiable lady away," one Virginia merchant wrote a friend. She was, despite the obvious dangers, just as adamant on staying. Dunmore "at last almost forced her and her family" to board the Britain-bound ship. The countess was saying a reluctant farewell to a husband in a hostile land. She was also leaving their real estate and most of her valuable possessions, including enslaved Africans, and suddenly faced a precarious financial future.

At noon, waving from their respective decks, the couple parted, and the *Magdalen* faded into the pale eastern haze. Lady Dunmore carried with her a letter from Dunmore to be delivered to Dartmouth. He laid out his plan to secure a land base in Virginia "difficult to be attacked and under the protection of the men of war." From there he would rally loyalists while awaiting reinforcements from Boston.

Dunmore's unilateral decision to send a naval vessel back to Britain would infuriate Graves, but it ensured his family's safety, and the countess would make his dire situation known in London.

By dusk, the *Fowey* was again moored off Yorktown. The news quickly reached Williamsburg, where patriots feared an attack was imminent. According to Dunmore's spies in the capital, Peyton Randolph called for a meeting of white patriots in the area to form a militia "to assist the citizens in their nightly watches to guard against any surprise from their enemies." This drew "great numbers of people, horse and foot, from various parts of the country." A Virginia delegate in Philadelphia estimated that some 150 armed men gathered to protect the city from "any attempts that [Dunmore] may make with his boil'd crabs," a reference to the governor's handful of red-coated marines.

By then, the shirtmen had set up camp near the Capitol and on the Palace grounds, "wantonly cutting and maiming my cattle which they found there," the earl complained. A second Palace incursion cleaned out any remaining arms, as well as, presumably, the governor's extensive wine cellar. The leader of the daytime break-in was the son of colony treasurer Robert Carter Nicholas. The governor could only sputter that the raid was "an atrocious outrage against the king's authority." Dunmore's remaining "domestics" fled to his Portobello farm.

On July 7, Captain Montagu and Dunmore boarded a barge to travel upstream to Portobello. The governor may have been eager to question his enslaved servants as well as to escape the heat belowdecks as summer gathered steam. Montagu needed a new mast for a small vessel and brought along two carpenters to find a suitable tree on the governor's farm. Lookouts in Yorktown immediately spotted the barge and relayed word to Williamsburg. The unsuspecting governor and captain enjoyed a leisurely meal in the modest brick farmhouse where the earl and Washington had breakfasted six weeks before. Suddenly, servants—almost certainly enslaved Black workers—burst in to warn that seventy shirtmen were fast approaching. At their head was Patrick Henry's brother-in-law.

"We had but just time to get into our boat and to escape," the governor wrote, though the carpenters at work in the woods were captured. A delegate in Congress told Washington that the British had been "within three or four minutes of being all taken." He insisted that "no injury was intended" the governor, and that their only goal was to "put him in the Palace and promise him protection." Dunmore, however, reported that his assailants took aim at the departing boats. "A servant, who got into a canoe to follow me a very little time afterwards, was fired at four or five different times." The governor owed his last-minute escape to his own enslaved Africans. Without their quick action, Dunmore's fight against the rebels would have ended before it began.

Two sultry weeks passed with no word from Boston. Then, on July 11, a small warship named the *Mercury* appeared on the murky horizon under the command of a brash young captain named John McCartney. He had orders to replace Montagu's *Fowey*, which was needed in Nova Scotia. McCartney brought welcome news of "a complete victory" over the patriots at Breed's Hill. From Norfolk, a jubilant James Parker predicted, "If the head of the serpent is effectively crushed in the North, we will soon be quiet here." The terrible human cost of that victory was not yet clear.

The *Mercury*'s arrival panicked the patriots. The twenty-four-gun ship, the pro-patriot *Norfolk Intelligencer* reported, was "full of men, but we know not for what purpose." The editor scoffed, "We have now four men of war and an armed schooner for our 'protection and defense!'" The patriots expected the new British force to march on Williamsburg, and hundreds of Virginia militia flooded into Yorktown to prevent a landing. "The men are continually parading in arms along the shore close to us," Dunmore wrote Dartmouth the next day, "and at night we hear them challenge every boat or person that approaches them." The governor declared that "the people of Virginia manifest open rebellion by every means in their power."

Montagu was more worried about his own diminishing provisions, as well as military orders to send food to hungry Boston. The British army there was besieged by Washington's nearly twenty thousand soldiers, most of them New England farmers. "The great scarcity of provisions in their army has led me to take every precaution to prevent a supply," Washington wrote on July 14 to John Hancock in Philadelphia. Congress had forbidden Americans from supplying warships, though Montagu was able to purchase enough flour in and around Yorktown to feed the hundreds of men now anchored offshore. The rest would have to come from raiding farms and plantations along the shoreline. "What he now procured must be by stealth," Graves later informed London.

The captain confiscated a ship loaded with pork bound for the West Indies and diverted it to Massachusetts. He also sent soldiers across the York River to the patriot bastion of Gloucester County to seize sheep and cows. Montagu soon earned patriot contempt for another reason. A midshipman from the *Otter* went ashore to negotiate the release of fellow seamen who had been captured by the rebels. He was escorted to their camp, which he described as "a few pales covered with leaves." A patriot told him that "if they caught any belonging to the *Fowey* man of war, they would never let them go." One Gloucester patriot argued in the July 13 *Gazette* that "Negro slaves, now on board the *Fowey*, were under the governor's protection" and were "in actual rebellion, and punishable as such." If taken, the legal punishment was death. The writer then suggested that the patriots counter "their bloody plan by arming our trusty slaves ourselves," an idea that failed to gain traction.

How many enslaved Africans found sanctuary on the British ships off Yorktown in July 1775 is unclear, but their presence enraged colonists, who considered them valuable property stolen by Montagu. His decision to grant refuge to those in bondage, a radical step that Dunmore surely would have had to approve, challenged not just Virginia's laws but the very foundation of its society.

Not all the fleet's commanders agreed with Montagu. As the *Fowey* readied to leave, its captain asked McCartney to take on the Black refugees. McCartney refused to "harbor the slaves of any individual in this province." The *Otter*'s Captain Squire stepped in to take the refugees aboard his already crowded ship.

By then, Dunmore and the naval officers realized that Yorktown was more a trap than a strategic base of operations. The rebels had already taken the high bluff, from which they could observe every British move and launch cannonballs at any ship. Retreat was the only option. The *Fowey* sailed on July 13 with the governor, followed by the *Otter*; the *Mercury* would bring up the rear. "We have not been able to learn where Lord Dunmore intends fixing his residence," a *Gazette* reported. "Some say Portsmouth, but we only mention it as a report."

Two days later, the ships lay moored near the small port of Hampton at the end of the peninsula, where in 1619 a Dutch ship sold enslaved Africans to English settlers. The *Fowey*'s crew paused to prepare for the eight-hundred-mile voyage to Nova Scotia.

At dawn on July 15, Dunmore bade farewell to Montagu and his long-time secretary, Captain Edward Foy, who would be traveling to Boston to assume a position under General Gage. A former commanding officer recalled that Foy was "not to be contradicted." He was certainly eager to escape from under the shadow of the governor to find glory in battle. "Lord Dunmore is not a character from which, in any difficult times, I should hope for any great advantage," he wrote a friend, adding that he preferred not to "share of all disgrace attending his proceedings." That "disgrace" may have been Dunmore's moves to free those in bondage. Like McCartney, Foy may have strongly objected to confiscating what was legally considered private property. "I am no longer interested in the fate of Lord Dunmore," he declared, without noting that the earl had intervened to win him a place on Gage's staff.

The royal governor climbed down the swaying gangway into a bobbing launch for the short trip to the *Otter*. He had left behind his family, friends, and allies, along with his fine residence, his books, and most of his musical and scientific instruments. He had been cast out of the inner circle of Virginia's gentry, demonized as a race traitor, and mocked as a lecher. And this time, there would be no escaping the sickly heat of the Tidewater summer he so loathed. His only companions were a handful of "domestics." These were likely enslaved as well as white servants from the Palace.

General Gage was unlikely to send an army, Graves would not part with his major warships, and white loyalists were hesitant to take up arms against their countrymen. Dunmore's only path to victory lay in building a force of enslaved Africans to combat the patriots. A small number had already wielded guns to protect his family from attack, risked death to find refuge, and rescued him from patriot clutches at Portobello. As word spread that the British offered sanctuary, larger numbers were sure to follow. Their support was crucial to combat the growing strength and determination of the patriots. Yet this path was sure to unleash even greater white fury.

Almost exactly thirty years earlier, Bonnie Prince Charlie had confronted a curiously similar situation. He had landed in Scotland in July 1745 in a single ship with only seven supporters and the almost ludicrous intention to overthrow the head of one of the world's most powerful empires. The prince had rallied people of all classes, ethnicities, and political opinions to his cause, assembling a multinational army that included at least one Black man. This force repeatedly defeated the British military. The Jacobites had come tantalizingly close to victory. Now it was the Scottish earl's turn to battle the odds. This time, however, he would be fighting to preserve the very regime he and his father had risked their lives to topple.

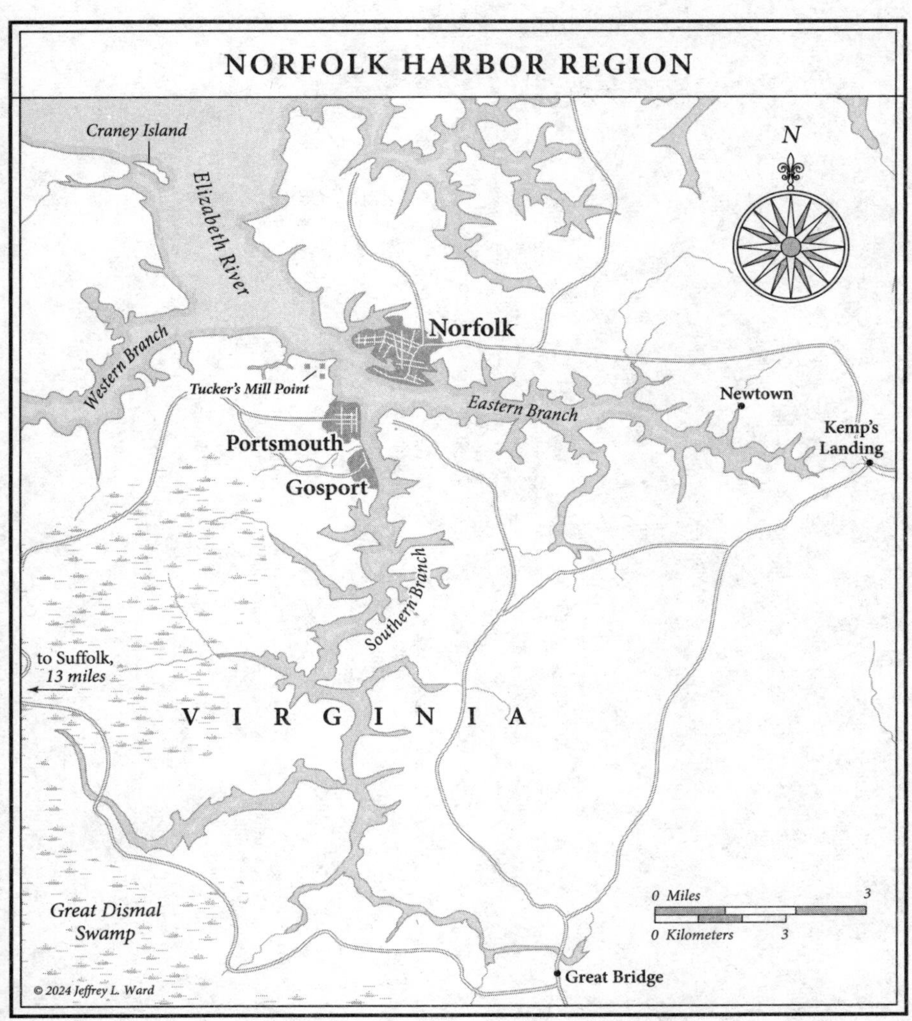
NORFOLK HARBOR REGION
Craney Island
Elizabeth River
Western Branch
Tucker's Mill Point
Norfolk
Portsmouth
Gosport
Eastern Branch
Newtown
Kemp's Landing
Southern Branch
to Suffolk, 13 miles
VIRGINIA
Great Dismal Swamp
Great Bridge
N
0 Miles 3
0 Kilometers 3
© 2024 Jeffrey L. Ward

Part Two

July 1775 to December 1775

Chapter Eleven

Lieutenant Governor of Gosport

At eight o'clock on the muggy morning of Saturday, July 15, 1775, the *Otter* glided into Norfolk harbor. There were no celebratory cannon salutes to mark the arrival of the royal governor in the colony's premier port, and the town's dockworkers, shoppers, and merchants would have watched the ship with a mixture of relief and anxiety. Though small by Royal Navy standards, the vessel boasted fourteen cannon that could hurl a six-pound iron ball a half mile, and a well-trained crew could rain down seven shots per minute.

Here, Dunmore would make his stand against the patriots. The excellent anchorage was home to shipyards, supply depots, and industrial facilities, while being safely removed from Virginia's patriot heartland. He could count on the support of the area's wealthy Scottish merchants, who were strongly attached to Great Britain. The enslaved Africans who labored in the warehouses, on the docks, and aboard ships as crew, pilots, and watermen, also had ample reason to support the king's cause. Many of the region's white farmers, who mostly raised corn and hogs, also might prove sympathetic to his campaign against the tobacco gentry.

As Captain Squire ordered sails furled amid the dozens of merchant ships riding at anchor, the earl was nevertheless unsure what sort of reception to expect. The previous August, Norfolk's town leaders had denounced the Boston blockade and forced a brigantine to return to Britain with nine chests of tea. Most of its traders, whether of

English or Scottish descent, had agreed to abide by Congress's import ban and the impending ban on exports. Some were ardent patriots, while others calculated that opposing the boycott was futile.

Dunmore's arrival heartened those who backed the Crown. Among them was James Parker, a prosperous Scottish merchant who had married a local woman, purchased more than a dozen enslaved workers, and built an impressive walled compound in the western suburbs with a large home, numerous outbuildings, and the city's finest garden. He and his wife, Margaret, dubbed it Little Eden. For him, the governor and Royal Navy offered not only protection from the rebellion but a chance to remake the colony's power structure. Parker argued in May 1775 that it was time to shift Virginia's political gravity from its little rural capital to an economic hub with easy access to the sea. "Williamsburg did well enough for the seat of government during the golden age," he noted. "It will not do now, it should be here, Norfolk, or someplace where a ship can go."

For now, the governor remained on board the cramped *Otter*, with its crew of more than one hundred and a number of refugees from slavery. Patriots in Norfolk whispered that he feared assassination were he to set foot onshore. Dunmore soon requisitioned a Jamaica-based merchant ship called the *William* for his new flagship, and the *Mercury* arrived from Yorktown. On Monday morning, the squadron lifted anchor and sailed with the rising tide into the mouth of the southern branch of the Elizabeth River, opposite Norfolk.

On the west side of the branch's entrance stood the tidy suburb of Portsmouth, with its Scottish mansions, busy wharves, and popular jockey club. The ships passed the town, and then the mouth of a marshy creek, halting just beyond at what was known as Gosport. The shipyard was among British North America's most advanced maritime facilities, covering an area the size of a dozen football fields. At its heart stood a five-story warehouse with a footprint of 3,600 square feet, one of the largest buildings on the continent. It would not have been out of place among the warehouses on Glasgow's bustling River Clyde; it was, in fact, modeled on those enormous depositories of goods. The bottom three stories were built of stone, quarried far to the west, and the upper two of wood. The entrance was by "broad stairs of hewn stone, mostly brought from Britain at great expense."

Adjacent were three smaller warehouses, a blacksmith's shop, and a counting house. Wide wharves lined the river's edge, with docks projecting into the river interspersed with ramps that allowed ships to be hauled onto land to be refitted, repaired, and cleaned of barnacles, worms, and algae. Above it all loomed a massive English-imported iron crane with brass pulley wheels.

The duke of this domain was sixty-five-year-old Andrew Sprowle, who reigned from an impressive mansion overlooking the complex. An eccentric and savvy entrepreneur, he was reputed to be the richest man in Virginia and therefore one of the wealthiest in the colonies. Sprowle grew up near Glasgow and as a child witnessed Virginia tobacco transform what had been a middling Scottish port into a rich and thriving metropolis. As a teenager, he crossed the ocean and settled in Norfolk to trade in lumber, wine, and people; at least two of his ships carried Africans from the West Indies to sell in his slave mart. When George Washington sailed as a youth from Virginia to Barbados, it was on a Sprowle-owned forty-ton sloop. For a time, the merchant also prospered as a privateer, capturing enemy French and Spanish merchant vessels during the Seven Years' War. More than once he failed to report his prizes to the authorities, retaining the valuable ships and their cargoes for himself. One previous governor judged Sprowle's actions "scandalous."

Such behavior did not prevent him from serving as the president of the Virginia association of merchants for more than thirty-five years. In the capital he was treated with a combination of amusement, disdain, and respect. The balding businessman "cuts as droll a figure as you ever saw," with his "silk coat and two or three holes in his stockings," wrote one planter after a 1768 meeting in Williamsburg. He went on to praise Sprowle for speaking with an "elegance and simplicity [that] far outdoes the studied performance of the professors and masters" of the College of William and Mary.

The entrepreneur plowed his profits into Norfolk and Portsmouth real estate, and in 1767 purchased the vacant land across the creek from the latter, dubbing it Gosport after the naval town adjacent to the English maritime center of Portsmouth. He obtained government contracts, and Royal Navy ships regularly tied up there "in the winter months for the convenience of watering and other necessities." He also did a thriving retail business; by 1771, he was selling Washington candles to light Mount Vernon.

Sprowle kept a close eye on his fiefdom. "No one does anything without his advice and direction," wrote Katherine Hunter, his nephew's widow, who lived in the Gosport mansion. Enslaved workers were an essential part of the operation. Sprowle occasionally leased those in bondage to bolster his workforce—a common practice in the Norfolk area—and didn't shy away from selling them to distant places.

The Scotsman profited greatly from slavery with no obvious moral qualms, yet he was also an evangelical Christian at a time when most upper-crust Virginians were devout members of the official Anglican Church. The radical movement of Methodism spawned by England's John Wesley took a more emotional approach to faith and welcomed Black men and women into the ranks of believers. Norfolk became a hotbed of the persecuted sect. In 1772, an itinerant Methodist preacher startled town leaders when he climbed the courthouse steps overlooking Market Square to sing hymns and preach, drawing a crowd of white as well as Black residents. The mayor was aghast. "If we permit such a fellow as this to come here," he warned, "we will have an insurrection of the Negroes."

Wesley decried slavery as immoral in 1774, though most Methodist ministers in Virginia were careful to steer clear of the charged subject and made sure that Black worshipers were subordinated to whites. At the time of Dunmore's arrival, Methodist preacher Francis Asbury ministered to a growing flock, and regularly preached to more than 150 people in "an old, shattered building, which has formerly been a playhouse." At one meeting, whites were seated first, with Black worshipers left to peer through the door and windows. When the floor began to sag under the weight of the massed bodies, the revival was moved outdoors for what became an enormous interracial service. Sprowle and Jane and Talbot Thompson, who had also embraced Methodism, could well have been among those at this enthusiastic gathering.

The governor knew his fellow Scot from his frequent business trips to Williamsburg; the merchant had been there as recently as June 12, just three days after the earl's departure. That same month, a man was accused of smuggling a detailed map of the Virginia coast to the governor at Sprowle's behest. He was acquitted, but the incident suggests that the earl and the industrialist had been secret allies for some time. For Dunmore, Gosport had a deep anchorage and facilities ideal for fighting a naval war. Surrounded by water and marsh, it was easy to defend. Norfolk lay less than two miles away, within view but safely out of cannon shot. For Sprowle, whose business had suffered with the boycott, hosting the governor ensured both profits and protection. Hunter reported that the earl was soon jokingly referring to himself as "lieutenant governor of Gosport."

As Sprowle greeted Dunmore at the shipyard, delegates to the Third Virginia Convention jammed the wooden pews of Richmond's church, eighty miles up the James River. The first act of the hundred-odd delegates that morning was not to address the military crisis but to consider surveyors' complaints that the governor restricted their work in "lands in the uninhabited parts of this colony," a reference to indigenous territory. This, they predicted, would lead to "much confusion and litigation." Three full days passed before the Convention resolved to raise a force to confront Dunmore. With Washington's Continental Army busy besieging the British in Boston, Virginia patriots had to rely on their own initiative to counter the governor.

The delegates did not mention tea or taxes when they laid out their reasons for opposing Britain, citing instead Dunmore's threat to "set fire to the city of Williamsburg, lay waste the country, and emancipate our slaves." They noted with alarm that several unfree workers had "already been received and detained on board" the *Fowey*. This "hath plainly demonstrated the most hostile and inimical designs against the good people of this colony, and thereby compelled us for the security and preservation of our lives, liberties, and estates, to take the most effectual measures to defeat such wicked intentions." This blunt explanation was later excised from the official record.

Just how to organize a "sufficient armed force" would confound the Convention for weeks to come. Until Dunmore's April threats, the county militias were primarily made up of well-to-do men who could afford to volunteer and provide their own equipment. George

Mason even boasted that the Fairfax County independent company "consisted entirely of gentlemen." Their numbers were embarrassingly small. In Jefferson's home county of Albemarle, fewer than 2 percent of adult white males had enlisted before the gunpowder incident. These few dozen owned an average of nearly a thousand acres and fifteen enslaved Africans each. With Dunmore's actions and threats, the militia immediately tripled in size, with the average member now owning three hundred acres and five slaves. "Gone," wrote the historian who made these painstaking calculations, "were the white-stockinged gentlemen volunteers."

The new recruits also brought a contempt for authority. They insisted on electing their own officers and on coming and going as they pleased. According to Washington's cousin, Lund Washington, some believed that soldiers and officers should be paid the same and march immediately into battle rather than "shilly shally . . . until all the poor people are ruined."

Such egalitarian and democratic attitudes were at odds with elite Virginians' expectations of dutiful subservience. The rich old planter William Byrd III protested the "many insults" directed his way when he refused to join the fight. Another wealthy Virginian warned against "the ravages of the populace, or the plunder of a licentious army" that might turn against its betters.

The new citizen soldiers were also impatient with the gentry's timid approach to Dunmore, and skeptical that Norfolk's residents were sufficiently patriotic. Four days after the earl arrived, fourteen militia officers in Williamsburg told the port's patriot committee that they were "truly alarmed" by word that Norfolk men were "deserting the Glorious Cause" and even assisting the enemy at Gosport. The committee called the charge "totally devoid of truth," adding that "the time may come when we many stand in need of your assistance, surrounded as we are by armed vessels." In that case, they would welcome the men "with willing hearts and open arms."

A grove east of the Capitol was soon crowded with some five hundred shirtmen. Lieutenant George Gilmer wrote to Jefferson in Philadelphia that the men's senior commander had "a fear to offend" his own troops, who were "rather disorderly." Discipline was lax; those deserting their posts were given three strikes before they were expelled. "We appear rather invited to feast rather than fight," Gilmer lamented. To keep the men occupied, he proposed "laying hands on all his Majesty's money immediately." This plan to seize customs duties and other Crown revenues gained favor among the bored officers, who wanted to get at the money before Dunmore. They sent a threatening letter to the colony's elderly receiver general, Richard Corbin, implying that he would suffer consequences if he did not account for every penny. "The independent companies are riding over all the country to seize what money is in the public offices," Parker wrote on August 4.

Only belatedly did the officers inform the Convention in Richmond of their intention, and then only after securing nearly 1,700 pounds, or almost $170,000. The delegates viewed Gilmer's move as banditry, yet they feared antagonizing men with rifles, tomahawks, and scalping knives. Peyton Randolph sent a message asking the men to abandon their scheme, while gingerly praising their "very laudable motives" and assuring them that "no censure was passed" on their actions. The chastened officers apologized for their "precipitate conduct" and promised to be guided in the future by civilian rule and "to execute any matters under your authority." The incident nevertheless highlighted the challenges faced by Virginia's patriot leaders. They had to curb what one called the militiamen's "wild irregular sallies" without dampening their enthusiasm. The colony's gentry had to lead a rebellion without fomenting one that would threaten their own grip on power.

Among the most prized enslaved Virginians in the colonial era were pilots. The economy was almost wholly dependent on moving cargoes safely and efficiently through the many rivers and bays. This required experts who could steer a vessel safely amid shifting weather, currents, and shoal waters; a single grounding or shipwreck could spell death for the crew and bankruptcy for the owner. By the 1770s, men in bondage dominated this critical trade. Many lived at Hampton, the small port at the end of the peninsula formed by the James and York Rivers, which emptied into the Chesapeake opposite the Virginia capes. "Hampton town, which lies upon a narrow creek, barred with sand at the entrance, and having only shoal water, can never be a place of any consequence," concluded a British customs official in 1770. But it was the perfect location from which pilots could set out in small boats to rendezvous with regional watercraft or oceangoing vessels to guide them to their destinations.

The port's pilots included one of the Thompsons' sons, James Jackson, who remained enslaved. Another was Joseph Harris, described as a diminutive man of mixed race. In mid-July, Harris passed "intelligence concerning a smuggling schooner" to the crew of the *Fowey* as their vessel prepared to depart for Nova Scotia. Patriots soon learned of Harris's act, and Captain Montagu reported that "the people of Hampton and some other places have threatened his destruction." With his pilot boat impounded, the resourceful Harris found another vessel and reached the safety of the British warship. He would have understood that his knowledge of local waters would be highly valuable to naval officers who lacked detailed nautical charts.

After boarding the ship, Harris was shown to Montagu's stern cabin for questioning. Though records show he was enslaved by a Hampton man, the new arrival posed as a freeman, to discourage the British from returning him to shore as Virginia law demanded. To test his abilities, the captain gave him a variety of tasks to perform and watched him closely. The officer determined that the pilot "always appeared very sober and prudent," and he was particularly impressed by his intimate familiarity with the colony's myriad waterways. On July 20, he wrote Squire of the *Otter* that Harris was "too useful to His Majesty's service to take away, he being well acquainted with many creeks on the Eastern Shore, at York, James River, and Nansemond, and many others." He was also "a very useful person, especially in tenders," the boats that "tended" larger vessels by shuttling goods and people. "I could wish strongly to recommend him to such indulgence as his endeavors may merit," Montagu concluded.

He handed the letter to the pilot and sent him up the Elizabeth River to Gosport to report to Squire. Harris became one of many enslaved Africans—exactly how many is not known—who quietly slipped into the shipyard that summer. His risky decision to spy for the British set off a chain of events that would cause the war in New England to spread to Virginia.

Harris landed at Gosport as Jefferson dismounted from his phaeton in Philadelphia. The new Virginia delegate immediately went for a shave and shopped for books, butter mints, and shoes. Perhaps appalled by the urban squalor, he also put a few coins in the poor box. "His happy talent for composition" was already well known when he reported to the Continental Congress. Jefferson was immediately assigned to help Pennsylvania's John Dickinson draft a document to explain the rebellion to the public on both sides of the Atlantic.

The "Declaration of the Causes and Necessity for Taking Up Arms," adopted July 6, served as a rough draft of the Declaration of Independence, though it denied "ambitious designs of separating from Great Britain." The document claimed that "schemes have been formed to excite domestic enemies against us," a clear reference to Dunmore's threat to arm those enslaved, and also cited "certain intelligence that General Carleton, the Governor of Canada, is instigating the people of that province and the Indians to fall upon us."

The same day, Indian leaders meeting at Pittsburgh with a Virginia delegation led by John Connolly agreed to a preliminary peace treaty. Connolly explained to the tribal elders that their "brother the Big Knife"—Dunmore—expected them to keep their people from settling or hunting south of the Ohio. A final treaty meeting was slated for fall 1775. Many members of his own delegation suspected Connolly of working for Dunmore at the expense of the patriots. The Virginia Convention had sent "a committee of their own body to inspect my conduct," he recalled, which concluded that he had acted "in the most open and candid manner." Connolly later claimed he had "secretly frustrated the machinations of the republicans" by winning private assurances "from the Indian chiefs to support his Majesty." They gave him "a large belt of wampum" to be presented to Dunmore and forwarded to King George III "as a symbol of their inviolable attachment to his royal person." Such belts, tantamount to solemn treaties, confirmed military alliances.

Connolly rode east at the talks' conclusion, only to be arrested by suspicious Pennsylvanians. They had previously jailed him for his role in claiming Pittsburgh for Virginia. Once again talking his way out of custody, he crossed the mountains. On August 1 he sent a letter to the Virginia Convention in Richmond. "I have finished a treaty with the Shawnees," he reported, denying accusations that he was "a ministerial tool" who was "ready to support every measure which Lord Dunmore might recommend." Such insinuations, he insisted, were "malicious and far foreign to truth." He asked permission to present the preliminary agreement to the assembly, and the grateful delegates agreed.

On his way, he stopped in Fredericksburg for the night. There he spent an uncomfortable evening with several patriots, including his old friend Hugh Mercer, who had called the militia to march on the capital in April. His hosts became suspicious when Connolly refused to drink what he called "inflammatory and unconstitutional toasts" against the king. They had him followed when he left the next morning, but he gave his tail the slip. Turning off the road to Richmond, he galloped hard through heavy rain past Williamsburg, arriving at Yorktown after midnight "thoroughly drenched and excessively fatigued." The following morning, August 8, he made it to Hampton, where "by a little finesse with the waterman," he secured a boat to Norfolk.

That afternoon he landed at Gosport and "immediately obtained the ardently wished-for pleasure of an interview" with the governor. "I had been twice a prisoner, twice rescued; had passed the Appalachian Mountains, and come upwards of four hundred and fifty miles, through a country where every eye seemed intuitively suspicious," he wrote with a dramatic flourish. "My heart swelled with the hopes of doing something eminently conspicuous." His goal was to "convince the infatuated people of their folly" and cure them of "the ridiculously called 'patriotic spirit' of the rebels."

In the privacy of Dunmore's stern cabin on the *William*, the governor and Connolly concocted one of the American Revolution's most fantastic schemes, one that would instill horror and dread in George Washington and the Continental Congress. The plan was as ambitious in scope as it was unwieldy in title. Called "Proposals for raising an army to the westward for effectually obstructing a communication between the southern and northern governments," it laid out their bold approach to crush the rebellion.

The two men agreed that Connolly would sail to Boston to win approval for the plan from General Gage. He would then journey by water to Quebec City, Montreal, and on to British-controlled Detroit. During the long winter there, he would assemble a force of redcoats and indigenous people, as well as artillery, stores, and boats, while recruiting "such serviceable French and English partisans as I can engage by pecuniary rewards or otherwise." With the spring thaw, this combined force would march two hundred miles to the southeast, gathering tribal allies along the way. They would then attack Pittsburgh with "such pieces of light ordinance as may be thought requisite for the demolishing of Fort Dunmore . . . if resistance should be made by the rebels."

The multiethnic army would then pour over Virginia's poorly defended frontier, supported by loyalists who joined the fight with the promise of gaining three hundred acres. By the time the cherry trees were again in bloom at Mount Vernon, the troops would be swarming down the Potomac River valley. In the meantime, Dunmore would recruit his own force and rendezvous with Connolly at Alexandria, the port just upstream from Washington's home.

The date for their meeting was set at April 20, 1776, the day between the first anniversary of the Battles of Lexington and Concord and the Williamsburg gunpowder incident. Virginia patriots would find themselves overwhelmed by French, indigenous, and white loyalist troops, bolstered by Dunmore's loyalists—presumably white as well as Black recruits. Isolated from northern allies, their resistance would crumble, and the governor would return to the Palace to mete out justice to the traitors. "This would not only be productive to the restitution of the royal authority of this colony," the two argued, "but have a general tendency to promote the success of his Majesty's arms, and the like happy effects universally." They suggested Gage launch a spring 1776 offensive in Massachusetts to tie down Washington's troops during the Virginia invasion. To succeed, they needed secrecy, timing, and luck.

As the plan's indispensable man, Connolly demanded extraordinary powers, including a military commission to lead "such troops as I may raise and embody on the frontier." The Detroit commissary was to "furnish such provisions as I may judge necessary." He also wanted the power to "make such reasonable presents to the Indian chiefs and others" to ensure that they would "act with vigor."

Dunmore agreed, and the two men then crafted a letter to Koquethagechton, known to the British as Captain White Eyes, who led the Delaware, or Lenni-Lenape. The governor pledged British help to counter white expansion. "Our foolish men shall never be permitted to have your lands, but on the contrary, our great king will protect you and preserve you in the possession of them," the earl promised. He criticized the "impudent" behavior of the settlers and called himself "your friend and brother." He asked the tribal leader to "acquaint the Cornstalk"—the respected Shawnee leader—"with these my sentiments also as well the chiefs of the Mingos and the other Six Nations," a reference to the powerful Iroquois confederation. Ensuring their support was crucial to building a formal alliance between the Crown and the peoples of the Ohio Valley. The letter was sent to one of Connolly's trusted contacts in Pittsburgh, with orders that it be translated into the Lenape language and read to the chief.

On August 22, Connolly set off from Gosport for Boston on the *Arundel* with his white servant William Cowley, an Englishman who had served the major at Fort Pitt and was then in Dunmore's employ. Patriot leaders in Williamsburg, meanwhile, fretted over the growing possibility of an indigenous attack. Four days after Connolly set out, a *Gazette* notice reported that "many of the more western and southwestern tribes seem determined to take up the hatchet against us." A subsequent article reported that British officials intended .to dispense 40,000 pounds—roughly $4 million today—among the Canadian Indians "to induce them to fall upon the colonies." A Maryland newspaper put it more bluntly. This huge sum was designed "to see the Indians cut our throats." The race was on to see which group of feuding whites could lure the most Native peoples to their side.

Chapter Twelve

The First Law of Nature

On the last day of July, the British troops deployed from St. Augustine arrived on a transport in Norfolk's harbor. A young Scottish captain named Samuel Leslie led the sixty redcoats, nine officers, and one drummer, part of the Fourteenth Regiment. "He was not handsome, but very genteel," recalled Helen Maxwell, a local woman whose Scottish father was the captain's cousin. Though she was sympathetic to the patriot cause, her family welcomed Leslie often to their home, where he enjoyed leafing through their sheet music and humming tunes.

Norfolk's town council assured the Virginia Convention in Richmond that despite the redcoats' arrival, they were "under no apprehensions of an attack." What most concerned the city's leaders was the "exceeding bad effects" the men's presence would have on "the Blacks from the neighborhood of the men of war." An increased troop presence would encourage defections among those in bondage. Council members had already asked the naval captains to pledge that they would refuse to accept runaways. The *Mercury*'s McCartney had assured Norfolk mayor Paul Loyall—who, despite his name, was a patriot—that he would "protect the property of all loyal subjects," including human property. He promised "not to harbor the slaves of any individual in this province."

The *Otter*'s captain, the thirty-year-old Squire, had already shown sympathy for people fleeing bondage by accepting those McCartney had refused at Yorktown. According to local patriots, he had since taken on board "a number of slaves belonging to private gentlemen" from the Norfolk area. When this became known in Williamsburg, on August 1, outraged militia officers urged the Virginia Convention to order Dunmore's arrest. It was, they asserted, high time "to establish the doctrine of reprisal and to take immediate possession (if possible, of his person), at all events of his property."

The *Norfolk Intelligencer* reported the next day that "this town and neighborhood have been much disturbed lately with the elopement of their Negroes, owing to a mistaken notion which has unhappily spread amongst them, of finding shelter on board the men of war." By protecting fugitives, the British proved themselves to be of a "most unfriendly disposition to the liberties of this continent." The publication called for residents to "have no connections or dealings with Dunmore, Squire, and the other officers of the *Otter* sloop of war." McCartney was pointedly excluded from this blacklist.

Angry slaveowners rowed to the *Otter* to demand return of their unfree workers, and some later claimed they were "ill-treated" by the captain and his crew. Amid this growing hostility, Squire eventually relented. "Last week several slaves, the property of gentlemen in this town and neighborhood, were discharged from on board the *Otter*," the Norfolk newspaper noted on August 16, "where it is now shamefully notorious, many of them for weeks past have been concealed." Those unlucky people would have endured stiff punishment or death for their defiance. The article's author hinted that Dunmore himself had ordered their return.

Since April, the earl had avoided public mention of emancipation to dampen patriot ire, but many white colonists remained convinced he was secretly encouraging insurrection. "The governor of Virginia, the captains of the men-of-war, and mariners have been tampering with our Negroes, and have held nightly meetings with them; and all for the glorious purpose of enticing them to cut their masters' throats while they are asleep," asserted an outraged Maryland pastor on August 2. "Gracious God! That men, noble by birth and fortune, should descend to such ignoble base servility."

That day, Dunmore wrote to Dartmouth that the Continental Congress was raising an army and establishing "a new government at Philadelphia." While grateful for the Florida reinforcements, he argued that their numbers were too small to regain control of the wayward province, "considering the situation of this distracted country." He was, however, careful to exude confidence. "I am still persuaded, was I speedily supplied with a few hundred more, with ammunition and other requisites of war, and with full powers to act, that I could in a few months reduce this colony to perfect submission." In the meantime, he ordered the new troops to drill on a makeshift Gosport parade ground; Sprowle provided warehouse space for their barracks.

The earl was reviewing the soldiers when an aide, John Schaw, pointed out a man in a hunting shirt observing the drill. The governor ordered the intruder taken into custody, and personally questioned him aboard the *Otter*. The patriot freely admitted he was a fifer in a militia unit and the governor had him released. The man promptly reported the incident to Norfolk's patriot committee, which then recommended that residents "furnish themselves with a hunting shirt and cockade" as well as "all the necessary accoutrements of war." The panel also summoned Schaw, a local debt collector whom the governor had put in charge of securing naval supplies. He was labeled an enemy to American liberty and signed a confession declaring his "sincere repentance" and promised to be "a zealous advocate for the rights and liberties of America."

Before this abject apology could be published, a gang of patriots spotted him on a Norfolk street. Schaw was already unpopular as a debt collector, and a mob quickly seized him. Dunmore later claimed his aide was stripped bare by the enraged people before being "beat and bruised . . . in a most cruel manner," all as a prelude to tarring and feathering. The August 16 Norfolk newspaper gave a more lighthearted account. "The populace were parading him into town to the tune of Yankee Doodle, as played by the fifer he had caused to be apprehended." With the help of sympathetic bystanders, the battered man was spirited into the house of a town alderman, where he hid in a chimney and avoided further abuse. The city leader dispersed the crowd by promising to turn Schaw over the next morning to the Norfolk County committee.

The panel chose not to punish Schaw further, but it did summon Sprowle for questioning. It was no secret the shipyard owner was hosting Lord Dunmore, but the rich merchant had signed and endorsed the embargoes approved by the Continental Congress. He had testified before the House of Burgesses following the April gunpowder incident and was even appointed to serve on the patriot committee, though "a severe fever" prevented him from accepting the position. After learning of Schaw's fate, he now feared for his life. If a man had been nearly beaten to death for pointing out a patriot in a crowd, the host of enemy troops and ships might expect far worse.

Sprowle responded to the summons by insisting that he was an unwitting victim of the British occupation. "Suppose yourselves in my situation," he said in a letter to the committee. "What would you have done under the guns of two men of war and sixty soldiers?" Given the circumstances, "moderation appears to me to be most advisable." He was, he assured the patriots, "as much attached to the American cause as anyone (but more moderate than many)." He declined to appear before the committee, pleading age. "Self-preservation is the first law of nature," he wrote, adding that he was too old to survive the sort of drubbing suffered by Schaw. He suggested that the patriots come to "my house in daylight," where he would "answer all reasonable questions asked of me." There he would be safe under the guns of British soldiers and warships.

Captain McCartney's good relations with the patriots made him the ideal go-between. "Such accusations should be alarming to Mr. Sprowle," he wrote the mayor, "particularly after the cruel and oppressive treatment Mr. Schaw lately received from a mob in Norfolk." He vowed not to be "an idle spectator, should any violence be offered." The mayor then assured the officer that Sprowle would be treated with respect. "I will take proper care, that he shall not be molested or injured by a riot or mob, if he shall think fit to attend to the committee."

McCartney or one of his subordinates accompanied Sprowle across the river on August 16 for the eleven o'clock appointment in Norfolk. The officer was conspicuous in his formal dress uniform and sword as the anxious Scotsman followed in his wake. When they arrived at the meeting room, Sprowle faced twenty-one Norfolk patriots, merchants, and planters he knew well. He explained that he had tried to dissuade Dunmore from using his warehouse, insisting in vain that it would "give great offense to the community." The earl had then assured him that the occupation would last only a week or two while the ships were refitted to accommodate the new troops.

The panel accepted this obvious lie, merely chastising him for being "remiss in not giving this committee the earliest information that his private property had been seized upon, soldiers quartered in his house, contrary to his inclination and solicitations." Sprowle, however, was taking no chances. A few days later, a member of the committee sent him "a letter of thanks" for "early information" he had provided relating to British forces. Whatever secret intelligence he revealed, it prompted the panel to convey their "warmest acknowledgements." Moderation was no longer a sufficient strategy. For "self-preservation," Sprowle had turned double agent.

By August, Gosport was an armed camp echoing with shouted commands and the stomp of soldiers' feet amid the metallic groans of the swiveling crane and the loud clanks from the blacksmith's shop. The earl ordered the *William* outfitted with thirteen cannon and welcomed seven army officers sent from Boston by General Gage. Other arrivals included escaped people in bondage from throughout the colonies, such as Cato Winslow, who had fled New York City that summer for the relative safety of the shipyard, as well as Rose from Boston—a Black "wench of forty years"—who disembarked with her son Toby. She and Winslow would later marry.

Dunmore was quick to negotiate loans from the area's wealthy Scots, promising that the British government would make good on repayment. These funds were essential for purchasing supplies, renting vessels, and paying a fighting force. Less than a month after his arrival in Gosport, the governor had fully secured a suitable beachhead for building up his forces while protected by armed vessels.

He also formed alliances with local loyalists, including a band led by Josiah Philips, a white laborer who lived in Princess Anne County, the isolated rural area between Norfolk and the Atlantic Ocean. According to a patriot memo, Philips "commands an ignorant disorderly mob," apparently a reference to a group of armed Black and white loyalists. An August issue of the *Gazette* claimed that Philips and his multiracial band fled into a swamp when threatened by local patriots. The renegade leader mistook "stumps and roots of trees for Indians, which his imagination, it is said, swelled to five hundred." He emerged three days later "disfigured and deformed" by swarms of mosquitoes so "that scarcely his own dog knew him." Philips was not so skittish. Jefferson would later describe this guerrilla fighter as a man "of daring and ferocious disposition."

An army of redcoats, white loyalists, and Black men with weapons backed by artillery and warships and led by an experienced militia leader like Dunmore was the stuff of Virginia patriot nightmares. "It is likely he will pay us a visit in this city," warned the August 4 issue of the *Gazette*. "He cannot expect the same cordial reception as on former occasions," the report added with bravado, "but will probably be received with such illuminations as may make him forget his way to the Palace." The governor was, announced one editor, "their mortal enemy" surrounded by "minions" who would come to "rue, before long, their ill-timed, base, and ungenerous conduct." Militia officers in Williamsburg sent an urgent message to the delegates in Richmond urging action. "It is our desire," they wrote, "to crush these matters in embryo."

The Virginia Convention was too busy arguing over what sort of army to create and who would lead it to address the imminent threat. After more than two weeks of haggling, members resolved on August 4 to raise five hundred men "for the defense and protection of the towns of Norfolk and Portsmouth and the neighborhood thereof." They agreed on little else. "We are of as many different opinions as we are men," despaired one delegate. The endless squabbling dismayed George Mason, who suffered from long bouts of poor health. "I never was in such a disagreeable situation," he wrote Washington, "and almost despaired of a cause which I saw so ill conducted." The infighting made him physically sick. "Vexation and disgust threw me into such an ill state of health" that "I was sometimes near fainting," he wrote, adding, "We had frequently no other way of preventing improper measures, but by procrastinations."

The bitterest quarrel revolved around who would lead an army that did not yet exist. Fredericksburg's Hugh Mercer, an experienced soldier who had served with Washington in the French and Indian

War, was the best qualified candidate, but his Scottish birth made him suspect. Patrick Henry was the other leading contender. The orator felt awkward and ineffective in the Continental Congress and yearned for battlefield glory. Many conservative planters, however, distrusted the fiery populist who, one argued, was "very unfit to be at the head of troops."

On August 5, Mercer won on the first ballot, but Henry triumphed on the second. "He was chosen by a party merely through opposition to a Scotchman," sneered one delegate. Washington, who did not share the common prejudice against Scots and was Mercer's former commander, was appalled. "My countrymen made a capital mistake when they took Henry out of the senate to place him in the field," he subsequently wrote. "And pity he does not see this." But Henry was wildly popular with rural whites, and his selection helped draw new recruits. When he made a triumphal entry into Williamsburg the following month, "he was met and escorted to town by the whole body of volunteers, who paid him every mark of respect and distinction in their power," one witness recalled.

He would now serve as both overall commander of the colony's army and head of its Virginia First Regiment. The Second Regiment was put under the authority of William Woodford, a forty-year-old gentry insider. His father and grandfather had served on the governor's council, his mother was related to Washington, and a first cousin had served as the capital's mayor. As a youth he served in the French and Indian War and later became the neighbor and protégé of the polished conservative lawyer Edmund Pendleton. Not surprisingly, the aristocratic Woodford and the iconoclastic Henry disliked each other.

Jefferson appeared at the Richmond church door on August 9, while on leave from Philadelphia to visit his ailing wife. By then, many delegates had returned home out of frustration or illness, but the smaller number eased decision-making. The following day, they approved the creation of a Committee of Safety to serve the same role as the governor's council. The eleven-member panel would run the colony when the Convention was not in session. It would also oversee the militia and county committees that served as the local patriot organizations, keeping in check challenges to gentry power.

This quiet bureaucratic move marked the real birth of Virginia's new revolutionary government, the first without ties to Great Britain. Jefferson himself tallied the results.

The Committee of Safety was, however, no one's idea of a revolutionary cabal. Each member was either a planter or a well-to-do lawyer, all owned enslaved Africans, and all but one hailed from the Tidewater and Piedmont regions. There was "an old man, almost deprived of sight," another "lost in melancholy," and a third who begged to resign. The committee president would serve, in effect, as Dunmore's successor in Williamsburg. Edmund Pendleton was chosen for the post.

An orphan apprenticed as a lowly church clerk, he had grown into a tall frame with "the first order of manly beauty." His marriage to a wealthy woman and his skill as an attorney vaulted him to prominence. Pendleton bought land and dozens of enslaved workers and built a mansion west of the capital that he dubbed Edmundsbury. Dunmore admired his eloquence, and Jefferson, who sparred often with him in the courtroom, characterized him as "cool, smooth and persuasive" and concluded he was "the ablest man in debate I have ever met with." When named Virginia's deputy attorney general, Pendleton had been quick to enforce the colony's draconian laws against those in bondage. In the 1760s, he ordered three enslaved Africans hanged in a single month.

Like many members of his class, Pendleton dismissed direct democracy as "the worst form" of government. The Virginia Convention chose him in 1774 as a reliable conservative in the colony's delegation in Philadelphia. He was a counterweight to Henry, a man he despised as an uncouth and dangerous demagogue. While there, Pendleton authored a resolution reassuring Britain that America's dispute with its mother country was "not an inclination on our part to set up for independency, which we utterly disavow." The measure failed, but Congress did approve a call by Pendleton and Pennsylvania's John Dickinson to petition the king for a peaceful resolution. Privately, Pendleton denounced "rash measures without consideration" and complained that Henry's aborted effort to attack Dunmore divided patriots and was therefore "very injurious to the common cause." His July 20 departure from Congress to attend the Virginia Convention was no doubt a relief to radicals like John Adams and Jefferson.

Residents in the capital, meanwhile, were living in perpetual fear of British attack. The August 11 *Gazette* reported that the earl "intends soon to put into motion" his plan to sail his fleet up the James or York River to land troops. On August 14, from the safety of Richmond, the Convention warned that "Lord Dunmore was meditating a hostile march, with an armed force to attack the city of Williamsburg," and urged the volunteer companies "to repel such troops by force." The threat did not deter delegates in Richmond from pondering ways for white speculators and settlers to obtain indigenous lands in the west. On August 15, they questioned "whether the king may of right advance the terms of granting lands in this colony," and ordered Virginians "not to pay any regard" to the governor's powers over surveying and granting territory. Not until August 25, after a month of squabbling and stalemate, did the delegates officially abolish the troublesome and ineffective volunteer companies and approve the two Virginia regiments to supplement the county militias while creating sixteen minuteman battalions. All were to be under Henry's command.

With this, Virginia's gentry put into place an organization with which they hoped to guide the rebellion, and to keep poorer white farmers firmly under their control. They adjourned the next day after criticizing Dunmore for "his repeated and horrible threats." The governor had connived "at the detention of some of our slaves" and "solicited troops to be sent amongst us," proof of his "fixed determination to do this unhappy country every injury in his power." As the summer's heat waned, each side marshaled its forces for what threatened to be a bloody autumn.

There was even concern among patriots that Dunmore intended to send a party of soldiers up the Potomac River to Mount Vernon to kidnap Martha Washington. Informed of the alleged plot, the commander in Cambridge was skeptical, but wary. "I can hardly think that Lord Dunmore can act so low, and unmanly a part, as to think of seizing Mrs. Washington by way of revenge upon me," he wrote to his cousin and estate manager Lund Washington on August 20. "If there is any sort of reason to suspect a thing of this kind, provide a kitchen for her in Alexandria, or some other place of safety elsewhere for her and my papers." Lund, who managed Mount Vernon in Washington's absence, reassured his cousin. "You may depend I will be watchful, and upon the least alarm persuade her to move." He also said he was prepared to defend the plantation from a British attack with a multiracial force. "I would endeavor to find the men, black or white, that would at least make them pay dear for the attempt." Just five months earlier, the Dunmores and the Washingtons had shared a convivial table.

"Englishmen, and more especially seamen, love their bellies above anything else," noted the seventeenth-century diarist Samuel Pepys, who expanded and modernized the Royal Navy, setting the stage for the British Empire. One of his innovations was to provide standard rations. If the Achilles' heel of the patriots was the colony's enslaved Africans, the prime British vulnerability was the need to provide adequate victuals for their troops and sailors. Virginia's early revolutionary struggle amounted to a contest by each side to exploit the other's principal weakness.

Aboard the *Mercury*, *Otter*, and *William*, sailors sat at tables of six to share salted and pickled pork and beef, dried peas and oats, several kinds of cheese, and hard biscuits and butter. They washed it down with a gallon of beer each day—"the very cement that keeps a mariner's body and soul together," one contemporary wrote—topped off with a daily ration of rum or brandy mixed with water. The full complement on the *Otter* and *Mercury* consumed more than two hundred gallons of beer per day. Sauerkraut and currants kept scurvy at bay. Coffee, sugar, and chocolate were usually available, while tea, so controversial onshore, was rare in shipboard messes. Fresh fish offered a substitute protein at sea, but fresh meat while in port was more highly prized. Senior officers ate better than common seamen, but they were expected to provide a good table for more junior officers.

Before the summer of 1775, any British ship arriving in Norfolk was swarmed by bumboats, small craft steered by vendors hawking eggs, fruit, baked goods, and vegetables. Crews were glad to part with their meager earnings for a ripe pear or fresh cucumber, and their hard currency was welcome in cash-poor colonial Virginia. The ship's purser would disembark to obtain supplies, from flour to fowl, from the stalls in Market Square. For longer stays in port, he would sign contracts with a ship chandler, a supplier of maritime needs, from fresh water and sides of pork and beef to brooms, boat hooks, and the pine pitch used to plug leaks.

In spring, the Continental Congress had banned colonists from supplying British warships, and by summer Virginia's patriot committees cracked down on offenders. When Anthony Warwick in the nearby port of Suffolk was found guilty in August of selling his region's sought-after peanut-fed pork to British-occupied Boston, he was given "a fashionable suit of tar and feathers." After he endured that excruciating torture, he was placed on a horse, and his tormentors "drove him out of town, through a shower of eggs." Such violent acts infuriated ship captains, who viewed this intimidation as an act of aggression directed at the Royal Navy.

On August 12, Captain McCartney sent Norfolk mayor Loyall an ultimatum. He warned that he would defend any merchants "unjustly censured for their loyal conduct" in selling supplies to the British. He was even willing, he wrote, to position his vessel "abreast of the town" and "use the most coercive measures in my power to suppress all unlawful combinations and persecutions within the province of Virginia." This thinly veiled threat to bombard Norfolk underscored the officer's desperation at the prospect of running low on food and water at harvest time in an abundant land. "I confess I feel myself somewhat astonished," the mayor responded, but he promised the captain he would "take every legal method" to suppress further persecutions, affirming "the earnest desire of the inhabitants of this borough to live in the most perfect harmony with the gentlemen of the Navy." He trusted that "no little incident may interrupt it."

When Loyall shared this correspondence with the town council on August 21, his colleagues were shocked by the threat and Loyall's tepid response. Council members castigated the *Mercury* captain for his attempt to "alarm and intimidate the inhabitants of this borough" and denounced "this haughty declaration" that threatened "utter destruction of their lives and estates." They went on to promise never to abandon "the righteous cause of their country, plunged as it is into dreadful and unexpected calamities." They insisted, perhaps with hyperbole, that they would rather see their "utterly defenseless city" ruined than submit to military rule.

Chapter Thirteen

Terror of Oyster Boats and Canoes

Strong gusts rattled the rigging of McCartney's *Mercury*, anchored off Gosport, as the light faded on the first day of September 1775. Bands of rain provided welcome relief from the long summer drought, but the barometer in the captain's stern cabin began an ominous plunge. The captain donned a black tarpaulin hat and brown oilcloth coat over his dark-blue uniform to assess the weather and climbed the stairs to the swaying quarterdeck above.

He surveyed a harbor crowded with dozens of large merchant vessels bucking in the mounting whitecaps. Black and white stevedores struggled to haul huge barrels and heavy pallets out of the cavernous buildings lining the wooden wharves. Moving down the floating docks that rose up with every swell, they wrestled the ungainly containers into the holds of docked ships or lowered them onto barges to row them to vessels anchored in the choppy channel.

The Continental Congress had set September 10, 1775, as the deadline for halting all exports to Britain, and Norfolk's merchants raced to get the materials to sea before the boycott went into effect. "Many vessels had taken on board part of their cargo, and the remainder were afloat, and would have been ready for sea before the tenth of this month," noted the borough's newspaper. Dozens had just departed, their packed hulls low in the water. Those heading for the West Indies slipped south along North Carolina's Outer Banks, an elbow of sand thrust into the ocean nicknamed the Graveyard of the Atlantic. There, the rains and wind grew in ferocity, forcing the crews to reef their sails and steer away from the treacherous shoals. For most, it was too late. They were trapped in the deadly spiral of a hurricane charging north up the Gulf Stream current, its summer-warmed water feeding the storm's power. Norfolk merchant James Parker was in North Carolina that night and reported "only one vessel out of thirty-eight escaped" and "most of the crews perished." There was no one onshore to rescue any survivors; whole villages on the narrow barrier islands were swept away.

The next morning the storm lumbered into the lower Chesapeake Bay. Norfolk's densely built downtown stood only a few feet above sea level and was almost completely surrounded by water. The burgeoning borough in recent years had filled in adjacent marshes without thought for adequate drainage or storm protection. The Scottish-owned factories and shantytowns clustered along the low-lying east side of town were particularly vulnerable to flooding. With little warning, the entire port was suddenly immersed in "one of the severest gales within the memory of man," the town newspaper reported, and it "continued unabated for eight hours."

Dunmore and Squire were absent that day, having set out in different vessels to scout sites along the James and York Rivers for landing spots to retake Williamsburg. A worried McCartney ordered his crew into the rigging to lower the topgallant masts and spars to the deck to keep them from splintering in the "strong gales" and "constant rain" buffeting the boat. "We had to turn our heads to take a breath, or the wind simply jammed the air down our throats," recalled one British seaman forced to climb into the rigging during a hurricane. "The rain stung our faces and our bare legs like hard pellets. It was almost impossible to open my eyes." Just after noon, amid "violent hard squalls," the vessel was pulled into shallower water.

The captain then told the men to make "all as snug as possible." All they could do was hunker down and wait for the storm to pass, but the winds continued to scream. At five in the afternoon, "very heavy squalls and rain" shoved the *Mercury* inexorably toward land until it was "drove onshore on Portsmouth Point." The crews of the *Otter* and *William* watched helplessly as the ship lurched against the muddy shore and tilted dangerously on its port side as waves pounded the hull. Shouting into the blast, McCartney and his officers exhorted the drenched and exhausted crew to shift the cannon on the gun deck to starboard "to heel the ship into the bank" and stabilize its precarious position.

Three hours later, the sun's setting rays above the dense clouds bathed the seething harbor in an otherworldly glow. The captain had an emergency anchor thrown over the port side to refloat the stranded vessel, "but the violence of the wind continuing and the sea breaking over the ship prevented her from getting off." As darkness fell, the crew hauled additional portside guns to starboard and hoisted up the ship's longboat to lessen the tilt. The rhythmic hammering of the water against the wooden planks threatened to rip the beached vessel apart. A brackish flood poured into the bilge, and the water inside the hull began to rise.

"She being in great danger," McCartney had only one last option to rescue the *Mercury*. Over the side went the massive cooking stove, 2,100 pounds of bread, 930 gallons of beer, 216 gallons of rum, 620 pounds of butter, a cask with beef and another with pork, and a dozen eight-ton, ten-ton, and twelve-ton water casks. Tossing the vital supplies overboard saved the vessel. By midnight the immediate danger had passed with no casualties, though the ship was stuck with "three feet of water inside."

Squire and the governor endured their own ordeals. "Lord Dunmore, it seems, fared but poorly in this hurricane," a *Gazette* reported. The earl's ship was caught in the middle of the James River when the storm hit. "By some accident or other, occasioned by the confusion in which the sailors were, his Lordship fell overboard" and was briefly submerged, according to the report. "But according to the old saying, those who are born to be hanged will never be drowned."

Squire, meanwhile, was traveling on the York River in a tender named *Liberty*, having left his second-in-command in charge of the *Otter*. His odyssey proved far more harrowing than Dunmore's; a *Gazette* reported that he "had very near perished." The *Liberty* was a small but sturdy craft with an iron stove for cooking meals and an awning for protection from rain and sun, armed with six swivel guns and five sets of muskets and cutlasses. On board was an Englishman, two Scottish sailors recently seized from a merchant ship, and Aaron and Jimmy, two enslaved Africans owned by Hampton patriot Wilson-Miles Cary. Aaron and Jimmy had escaped in June from Cary's plantation on the upper York River and found their way to Gosport. They were probably serving as Squire's local guides. Also on board Squire's vessel was Joseph Harris, the "small mulatto man" who had narrowly escaped patriot wrath by defecting in July to the *Fowey*. Given his knowledge of local waters, he would have taken the helm.

Unfortunately for the men aboard the *Liberty*, Hampton was the nearest safe harbor when the storm struck. If the three men who had escaped bondage were captured, they could face the death penalty, while the tender—and Squire himself—would be valuable rebel prizes. Amid mountainous waves and heavy spray, Harris made a run for Back Creek, a small estuary adjacent to the York's mouth and to Hampton's rear. He adroitly maneuvered the tender into the shallow waterway, tacking into a small creek branching to the south. All reached shore soaked but unscathed, proof of Harris's remarkable seamanship. But their trials were just beginning. The multiracial crew split up, making their way through the surrounding woods as branches flew from the wildly swaying trees. Squire followed Harris to a cabin owned by a Black acquaintance of the pilot. As the storm abated, they dried their wet clothes and ate whatever their surprised host could offer.

That night, the still-powerful hurricane roared north up the Chesapeake, rolling up the copper-sheeted roof of the new Maryland statehouse in Annapolis "like scrolls of parchment," according to one newspaper account. The Continental Congress had just adjourned, and Philadelphia suffered "much heavy rain, lightning, and thunder" as an enormous tide did "much damage to the stores on the wharves" and "many boats and small craft were sunk or beat to pieces."

In Hampton, the next morning dawned silent and fair as shaken residents ventured out to inspect the damage. Three ships had sunk in its little harbor, including one in which "every soul on board perished, except the master and the boy." Soon, local whites stumbled upon the beached *Liberty*. After "securing the rigging, guns, etc.," they set it alight to avenge Squire's "harboring gentlemen's Negroes, and suffering his sailors to steal poultry, hogs, etc."* They then captured three of the tender's white crew, who had overnighted with a white inhabitant nearby. They were marched under guard into the debris-littered town for questioning.

Harris and Squire eluded the patrols sent to capture them. In a daring escape, the enterprising pilot secured a canoe, and the two men paddled past the mouth of Hampton's harbor as the smoke from the burning *Liberty*, beached on Back Creek, rose behind them. They crossed the wide expanse of Hampton Roads before making their way up the Elizabeth River. The sight of the port would have been a shock. Ships were strewn along neighboring marshes and perched at odd angles on Norfolk's shattered wharves. "During the gale much damage was done," Squire's second-in-command wrote that day, "many vessels being onshore, others dismasted and some entirely lost." Some two dozen ships were "irrecoverably gone," a *Gazette* reported, while the winds and water "made great destruction in the warehouses and among the wharves." The article concluded that "the devastation at Norfolk was inexpressible."

Francis Asbury, Norfolk's Methodist minister, was appalled by the damage. "Houses were blown down; docks torn up; bridges carried away; abundance of trees broken and torn up by the roots; and several tracts of land overflowed with water," he wrote. An unknown number of residents and sailors perished, suffered injuries, or were left homeless. Those living in rickety tenements, particularly the enslaved, would have fared the worst, but all suffered. Even well-to-do citizens feared starvation and disease. Parker's wife, Margaret, their children, and her half dozen servants in bondage weathered the storm in their sturdy brick house, but there was little to eat in the aftermath. "Everything at home looks desolate and we have nothing left in our garden," she wrote her absent husband three days later. "There is not a plant of broccoli left, nor can I find any seed to sow." A neighbor delivered a baby the night of the storm, which, Margaret wrote woefully, was "at the point of death."

The devastation inevitably spawned a large refugee population and would have disrupted white control over those in bondage. Enslaved

* The patriots missed at least one swivel gun, which was found buried in Back Creek sand in the 1920s.

survivors suddenly had the opportunity to flee into the Great Dismal Swamp or seek Dunmore's protection.

Squire and Harris pushed their canoe through broken planks, bobbing kegs, and torn canvas, making for the cluster of British ships now anchored near the Portsmouth shore. One of them heeled at a precarious angle. Squire would have felt some relief at seeing the *Otter* intact. The *Mercury*, however, remained stuck, and the other two ships had drawn up at either end of the stranded vessel. The *Mercury* crew had had little rest. At four that morning, after the storm had blown itself out, they hauled supplies from the hold and sent empty casks to shore while rerigging the battered ship. The men began the backbreaking task of transferring all but two of the heavy guns and all of the cannonballs into a waiting sloop to lighten the *Mercury*'s burden. The rest of Dunmore's fleet was battered but largely unscathed: the *William* was undamaged, while the *Otter* lost only six hogsheads and two large casks swept off a Gosport wharf.

The two tired and hungry refugees clambered aboard the *Otter*, relieved to have escaped both the hurricane and the Hampton patriots. The two Africans on the tender had not been so fortunate. Dunmore called their owner, Willson-Miles Cary, "one of the most active and virulent of the enemies of government." The Hampton patriot had been searching for his lost human property for weeks and suspected they had fled to Gosport. Shortly before the storm, he had had his overseer obtain Sprowle's leave to search for them, but "as the captain had taken them upon a cruise, they were not then to be found." Soon after the hurricane passed, Cary reported that "two of my neighbors brought in to me Aaron, taken up near the wreck," while Johnny was captured and returned a few hours later. For Cary, the storm seemed like divine providence, for it dropped the runaways virtually on the doorstep of his plantation home on Hampton's outskirts.

In a September 4 letter published in a *Gazette*, he made the most of this happenstance. "You will be pleased, through your paper, to return Captain Squire, of his Majesty's ship *Otter*, my warmest thanks for his very kind hospitable treatment of my two slaves Aaron and Johnny . . . during their stay on board his ship." The taunt began a bitter feud of words that would build to bullets and cannonballs.

Mired in the mud, the *Mercury* was a source of patriot merriment. "And there may she stick fast, fast!" chortled a writer in a *Gazette*. The sailors spent days laboriously emptying everything out of the ship, including the iron ballast deep in its hold. On September 6, with the tide running high, the *Otter* tugged at the stranded ship. "At four began to heave," recorded Squire. "At five she came off, on which we gave her three cheers, which she answered." An hour later, McCartney floated his ship into deeper water.

The captain's relief and elation were short-lived. At four o'clock the next afternoon, the naval sloop *Kingfisher* "anchored abreast of the town of Norfolk in five fathoms," close to the *Mercury* and *Otter*. Eleven guns boomed out a salute, startling residents cleaning up the debris, as Lord Dunmore boarded the newly arrived vessel amid the pomp of pipes. He was welcomed by twenty-three-year-old Captain James Montagu, younger brother of the *Fowey* commander who had left in July for Nova Scotia. His was an aristocratic seafaring family; their father was an admiral. The younger Montagu's unpleasant job was to replace the *Mercury* while that ship took McCartney to Boston for a court martial. Angered at the young officer's fraternizing with the enemy at Yorktown, Dunmore had written Admiral Graves in Boston to complain, and the commander had, reluctantly, ordered McCartney's arrest. The disgraced captain was called aboard the *Kingfisher* and divested of his command. Dunmore had since come to tolerate and even respect the brash McCartney. He wrote Graves on September 12 urging leniency. His only fault, the earl explained, was naivete in the face of "a very artful, subtle set of people," and "a want of knowledge of mankind."

The letter gave the governor another opportunity to request more British forces, suggesting that Graves and Gage winter in Norfolk, "as nature will block up all the northern ports for three or four months at least." They could retake Williamsburg, destroy patriot resistance, and quash the rebellion. It was a creative but vain request. Gage had written Dunmore two days earlier, politely acknowledging the earl's "disagreeable" situation but denying his earlier plea for reinforcements. "I am not supplied in the manner your Lordship may imagine," he replied curtly, adding, "At present I can neither assist you with men, money, arms or ammunition, for I have them not to spare." Even if he could, the general's intelligence on "affairs in Virginia" suggested there was "no probability of landing the men, there being no fort or stronghold" and "neither cannon nor ammunition." He advised Dunmore to raise a force of local loyalists, adding, "I don't doubt government will gladly defray your expense."

The patriot press wished McCartney good riddance while ridiculing Squire. The September 6 edition of the *Norfolk Intelligencer* jeered at the latter, a man who thought "the service of their sovereign consists in plundering his subjects, and in committing such pitiful acts of rapine as would entitle other people to the character of robbers." Another commentator railed against "the crimes daily committed by this plunderer." These offenses, he added, deserved a death sentence. One issue of a *Gazette* mocked Squire as "a saucy coward" who was the "terror of oyster boats and canoes."

Norfolk residents also came in for their share of criticism. An anonymous September 21 letter to a *Gazette* complained that the town's patriots had missed a golden chance to burn the *Mercury*, "the terror of Norfolk and a refuge to our slaves," while it lay helpless in the hurricane's wake. This would have avenged "the captain's bloody threats to destroy their town." The port's rebels, however, seemed so "destitute of courage as to be afraid to make the attempt." The letter concluded with a warning. "We, sir, who live at a distance are at a loss to account for the strange remissness of the inhabitants of Norfolk in neglecting to seize the opportunity which heaven has kindly thrown their way." The writer made the startling suggestion that the destruction of the colony's largest city was worth the sinking of a single small British warship, warning that "thousands are resolved to burn the devoted vessel, even if the consequences of it should be the total ruin of Norfolk."

Once the *Mercury* was refloated, an irate Squire turned his attention to the Hampton rebels who had captured his men, burned his vessel, and confiscated its contents. He insisted that the town's committee return the king's property. If they refused, he said, "the people of Hampton, who committed the outrage, must be answerable for the consequence." The members tartly responded that they would do so after the captain compensated them for "the several slaves he has harbored (some of whom he employs in the king's service) as well as for the number of robberies he has suffered to be committed, in hogs and poultry, from sundry plantations." The caustic reply invited a British raid, and the nervous patriots dispatched an urgent message to Williamsburg pleading for "a sufficient force to protect the inhabitants of Hampton from any insult that might be offered to them by Captain Squire." One hundred armed men eagerly volunteered. After months of tedium camped at the capital, they set off on the thirty-mile march. But when Royal Navy vessels failed to appear in Hampton's harbor, the disappointed troops trudged back to Williamsburg.

Hampton's patriots continued to bait Squire. They sent the captain a long letter defending their actions. He had led "a pillaging or pleasuring party" on a tender they claimed was seized from a private owner. The patriots denied stripping the boat, insisting that the *Liberty*'s white crew had given its gear to a man named Finn, "near whose house you were drove onshore, as a reward for his entertaining you with respect and decency." The crew, however, made no mention of this in their depositions. The patriots also laid out their "just and equitable terms" for resolving the dispute. Squire was to return "Joseph Harris, the property of a gentleman of our town, and all our other slaves whom you may have on board." They also demanded all confiscated boats and crew belonging to Hampton citizens. Finally, they insisted that the captain agree not to "insult, molest, interrupt, or detain, the persons or property of anyone passing to and from this town, as you have frequently done for some time past." After Squire agreed to these conditions, the patriots would "endeavor to procure every article left on our shore."

The British officer was not likely to hand over the man who had saved his life and kept him from falling into patriot hands. The *Norfolk Intelligencer* delighted in reporting Squire's alleged response. The captain damned "the impudence of these people" and "swore he would make them no other reply than what his cannon could give them." On September 9, "a servant of Lord Dunmore" carried Squire's brief but angry letter ashore to the office of the *Norfolk Intelligencer* on Main Street.

The editor, John Hunter Holt, had taken the publication's helm that spring with financial backing from his patriot uncle, a Williamsburg merchant. Holt was the thirty-year-old adopted son of John Holt, a former Williamsburg mayor who now published the resolutely pro-patriot *New-York Journal*. John Hunter followed in his famous father's footsteps, turning the Norfolk press into a powerful platform to broadcast patriot sentiments, ridicule the British, and lambaste loyalists. The *Intelligencer*'s August 30 issue warned that Parliament intended to enslave the colonists so that, as Holt put it, "we shall cease to look with horrors upon the prostitution of our wives and daughters."

In his brief letter, Squire denounced Holt for spreading "many falsities" and warned, "If I am ever again mentioned therein, with reflections on my character, I will most assuredly seize your person, and take you on board the *Otter*." Though the captain's maritime actions suggest that he was a competent and compassionate naval officer, he was woefully out of his depth tangling with Holt, a savvy activist-journalist. The editor was only too delighted to print Squire's sputtering protest four days later, taking the opportunity to seize the moral high ground in the very public dispute. The press stood only a few hundred yards from the *Otter*, and Royal Navy artillery drills shook the building and rattled the glass panes. The practice salvos were so frequent that British authorities sent "an old woman or two out of town, that are afraid of having their brains addled with the noise of the cannon," one patriot reported. In the subsequent two weeks, Holt nevertheless continued his gleeful attacks.

There are no known surviving copies of the September 27 edition of the *Intelligencer*, which would prove to be its last. According to notes from those who read it, the editor took his verbal assault to new highs—or lows—by reporting that Squire had been "too free with people, sheep, and hogs." According to Parker, Holt also included "a few anecdotes of the rebellious principles of Lord Dunmore's father." The editor seems to have detailed William Murray's role in the 1745 uprising against King George II that left him convicted of treason and confined to house arrest for the rest of his life. Airing the earl's dirty family laundry in public was clearly designed to embarrass the governor and diminish his standing as the king's representative.

That Wednesday morning, Squire was chasing a Norfolk sloop bound for Yorktown with smuggled rum, sugar, and chocolate. After firing small arms at the fleeing vessel, his crew boarded it. By four o'clock in the afternoon, the *Otter* dropped anchor off Portsmouth with its prize, the latest in a series of seizures designed to tighten the economic noose around the rebels. Two uneventful days passed. On the morning of Saturday, September 30, Squire sent Holt another letter, reiterating that the editor should "desist in his personal attacks." Without waiting for a reply, and with Dunmore's blessing, the captain now took more decisive action.

At two o'clock that afternoon, Dunmore stood on the deck of the *William* as a crowded boat shoved off from the *Otter*. Eight sailors rowed it to the county wharf at the western end of Main Street. Squire, resplendent in his naval uniform with its silk sash, and with a sword at his side, disembarked and formed the men into ranks. First came seven musket-bearing Royal Grenadiers, in high black bearskin hats designed to make these tall men look even more imposing. Led by Captain Samuel Leslie, they wore scarlet coats and shiny black boots that reached above their knees. Originally tasked with throwing grenades at their enemies, the grenadiers had evolved into the British army's elite troops. Behind them were a half dozen marines in ribboned tricornered hats, carrying pistols and swords. This special force, which twenty years earlier had come under the control of the admiralty, sported bright-red uniforms with gleaming buttons. Unarmed sailors fell in line at the rear of the procession. According to Samuel Edwards, an *Otter* mate who took part in the raid, their mission was to seize the press to prevent "inflaming the minds of the lower sort of people to rebellion."

The streets were crowded with Saturday afternoon shoppers and noisy with the din of hammers and saws as workmen repaired the wharves and warehouses damaged in the hurricane. Pedestrians and cart traffic made way as the troops followed the captain east along Main Street, toward the town's heart. Passersby stared at the line of soldiers and marines, a sight that few Virginians had ever witnessed. The armed force arrived at Holt's establishment and surprised the pressmen. Edwards estimated that "five hundred spectators" gathered outside to watch. No one made a move to intervene.

Leslie ordered the building searched and arrested two employees and a bookbinder. A startled Holt hid and then escaped, possibly by climbing through a window in a side alley. The landing party methodically dismantled the heavy iron press and boxed up "all the types and every necessary for printing." The sailors carried the materials out the door and down Main Street as the crowd silently gave way. "After getting to the water side with their booty, [the British] gave three huzzas," according to one *Gazette* account. "A crowd of Negroes" who had gathered nearby joined in the celebratory cry—a sign that the town's Black community viewed Holt and his rebel allies with contempt. Scottish traders were also relieved. "It was prostitute to the worst of purposes," merchant George Rae wrote of the *Intelligencer*. "They paid no respect to any person whatsoever."

By then, patriots "were beating to arms," said Edwards, who acidly observed that "those valiant heroes who pretend to stand up so much in defense of liberty" offered no resistance during an operation that lasted an hour and a quarter. One Williamsburg paper said that the drumming drew a small number of "spirited gentlemen," but they "were joined by few or none." A loyalist estimated some thirty patriots eventually materialized, "but these were all officers; they could not get but eight privates and these were mustered after the soldiers were gone." This lackluster response and the acquiescence of hundreds of residents, suggests that Holt, a newcomer from New York, was unpopular outside the ranks of the port's gentry.

The town council met in an emergency session later that afternoon to protest the raid. Squire and his men had "landed in the most public part of this borough in the most daring manner, and in open violation of the peace and good order, seized on the printing-utensils belonging to an inhabitant of this town as also the persons of two of his family," the councilors informed the governor. They called the foray "both illegal and riotous." Instead of blaming Dunmore, however, they sought his intervention. The councilors "most earnestly entreat your Lordship" to "put a final stop to such violent infringements of our rights; and to order the persons seized on by Captain Squire to be immediately put onshore, and the property to be replaced from whence it was taken."

The message conveyed their desire for compromise. "We have ever preserved the peace of this town," they reminded the earl, "and have never prevented the ships of war and others from being supplied with provisions or any other necessaries and have carefully avoided offering any insult to any of His Majesty's servants"—a claim that Schaw, still recovering from his wounds, would have hotly disputed. Norfolk's leaders requested only to be allowed to go about their "lawful business." To prevent them from doing so was "a gross violation of all that men and freemen can hold dear." They spun the failure of the town to interfere in the raid as "another proof of their peaceable intentions."

Dunmore had kept clear of the dispute between Squire and Holt, no doubt acutely aware of the futility of feuding with the press. The editor's accusations of September 27, however, infuriated the governor. Rather than take up the olive branch offered by Norfolk's leaders, he vented about the newspaper "poisoning the minds of the people, and exciting in them a spirit of rebellion and sedition" that would only bring "inevitable ruin and destruction on themselves and [their] country." Holt had maligned royal officials "in the most false and scandalous manner" and instigated "treason and rebellion."

If Holt and his other associates turned themselves in, Dunmore said, they could resume publication so long as they confined their reports "to truth, and representing matters in a fair, candid, impartial manner on both sides." The goal, he added, was to provide the public "with a fair representation of facts." This, he added, "never would happen, if the press was to remain under the control of its present dictators." The town fathers must rein in such traitorous behavior, or they would "not be surprised if the military power interposes." In an October 5 letter to Dartmouth, he defended his action in seizing "the public press of the little dirty borough of Norfolk" because it was "wholly employed in exciting in the minds of all ranks of people the spirit of sedition and rebellion by the grossest misrepresentation of facts both public and private."

The earl had more in mind than shutting Holt down; he had the press reassembled on the *Eilbeck*, a "fine new ship lately launched, frigate built, and pierced for 22 guns" that Dunmore had recently leased from a Norfolk company. The machine would churn out copies of what would be called, inevitably and confusingly, the *Virginia Gazette*. The prospect of a government-controlled publication was "so diabolical a scheme only fit to be accomplished among Turks," wrote one editor in Williamsburg. Another mockingly welcomed the competition of "the *Gosport Chronicle*, published by authority" with the help of "Dicky Squire" and "little white-headed Montagu."

Dunmore faced stiff competition from Virginia's three Williamsburg papers, all run by staunch patriots and experienced journalists with loyal readerships and extensive circulations. Luckily for the governor, two of the captured printers were Scots with loyalist leanings; they would go on to serve as the British military's official printers in New York. According to Parker, the enterprising men secured "some ink and paper belonging to the press, which was delivered very quietly."

Within weeks, the first issue of Dunmore's *Virginia Gazette* rolled off the floating press. It was, as the governor promised, far more balanced than the competition, printing letters and news from patriots and loyalists alike. Yet it lacked the hot scoops, wicked wit, and sophisticated propaganda that made the others required reading, and it never reached a wide audience. Holt's purloined press would soon prove useful for a more important task.

Chapter Fourteen

Burn the Scoundrels

On September 11, after a ten-day voyage from Norfolk, John Connolly and his white servant William Cowley stepped onto a Boston wharf. The port was now more a grim military base than a town; most residents had fled as food and fuel grew scarce amid the siege by Washington's army. The men climbed the stairs of Province House, the formidable three-story brick mansion that served as headquarters for Thomas Gage, provincial governor and military commander of British forces. Connolly was quickly shown into Gage's office cluttered with maps, letters, and reports. After presenting letters from Dunmore, the major made his pitch for opening a second front in the west against the Virginia patriots.

A cautious man, Gage was notoriously skeptical of ambitious military plans, but Connolly's timing was propitious. The general had recently learned that Washington had welcomed a few Stockbridge Indians into his ranks. He had informed Lord Dartmouth, "We need not be tender of calling upon the savages, as the rebels have shown us the example." He had ordered commanders at British forts along the frontier to "cultivate the friendships of the Indians on all occasions, as they may be wanted for his Majesty's service."

There was a second reason to gamble on the scheme proposed by Dunmore and Connolly. American troops even then were marching north to conquer Quebec. If the British threatened Virginia's frontiers, Washington might be forced to divert troops south and abandon the invasion.

"When my proposition was laid before General Gage," Connolly recalled later, he "saw the advantages that were likely to result from their being put in execution." The general immediately posted a letter to Quebec City asking Canadian governor Guy Carleton to back the endeavor. The next day he sent a similar message to the British agent in charge of relations with tribes south of the Ohio. Gage asked him to encourage them to "take arms against his majesty's enemies and to distress them in all their power."

Word of the British effort to secure Indian alliances quickly reached Philadelphia, prompting the Continental Congress to seek its own indigenous confederates. The rush to secure western tribal allies had begun. Before Connolly departed, the general advised him to scrap his plans to sail into Canada, given the American incursion. He suggested instead that he return to Virginia and take a land route to Detroit. Connolly and Cowley promptly sailed for Virginia on the Royal Navy's *Viper*, passing the time discussing details of the plan.

On September 30, the same day Squire seized Holt's press, the vessel made a brief stop in Newport, Rhode Island. Another passenger disembarked to visit his parents in the port, and Cowley asked to accompany him. Once onshore, Connolly's servant betrayed him. He found a local patriot to deliver his written account of Dunmore's scheme to Washington's headquarters. The report, addressed directly to the general, provided full details of the "outrageous actions and rebellious works which are going to be put into execution," down to the nine twelve-pounders needed to smash the walls of Fort Dunmore. "As Your Excellency knows what state that country is in," Cowley added, referring to Virginia, "I thought it most fitting to disclose it." Once Washington verified the information, he alerted the Continental Congress and Virginia's Committee of Safety.

Cowley never returned to the ship, and Connolly continued on to Virginia. After reaching Gosport on October 12, he succumbed to "a short fit of sickness, occasioned by excessive fatigue and anxiety," which forced him to postpone his departure for Detroit. During the subsequent weeks, word of the plot spread through patriot networks. "Your good friend Lord Dunmore is endeavoring to raise all the powers on earth to demolish poor Virginia," Francis Lightfoot Lee in Philadelphia wrote to planter Landon Carter on October 21. With his Indian and French allies, Connolly would proclaim "freedom to all servants that will enlist," while the governor sailed with his fleet from Norfolk to launch an amphibious assault on Alexandria.

The British seizure of Holt's press was part of a struggle on both sides to control information. In May 1775, the Sons of Liberty burned the publishing house of James Rivington, editor of the loyalist *New-York Gazetteer* and competitor of John Holt and his pro-patriot *New-York Journal*. Rivington fled, though New York's provincial assembly later allowed him to resume publishing. He obtained a new press, but the revived *Gazetteer* proved short-lived. When news reached Connecticut of the Norfolk incident, some one hundred militia descended on New York on November 23 and marched to Rivington's shop with bayonets drawn. "A small detachment entered it, and in about three-quarters of an hour brought off the principal part of his types, for which they offered to give an order on Lord Dunmore," one account reported. "They then faced and wheeled to the left and marched out of town to the tune of Yankee Doodle." It was a sardonic reenactment of Squire's raid, except that the heavy lead type was cast into bullets to fire at the British.

Though patriots throughout the colonies harshly criticized Virginia's governor, they were no less outraged by those Norfolk residents who had stood passively by during the September raid. "You will no doubt have heard of the disgraceful conduct of Norfolk, in suffering Lord Dunmore, with a few men, to take away their printing press," Richard Henry Lee in Philadelphia wrote Washington. "It happened when the good men of that place were all away, and none but Tories and Negroes remained behind." Lee assured the earl's former friend that "Virginia is much incensed, and five hundred men are ordered immediately down to Norfolk. I expect by every post to hear of the demolition of that infamous nest of Tories."

At least one leading citizen of the Virginia city was ready to perpetrate that act of destruction. Joseph Hutchings was a Norfolk merchant, planter, and slaveowner from an old family of English descent. He served as a borough representative in the House of Burgesses, as a Virginia Convention delegate, and as colonel in the county militia. His failure to halt the raid reflected poorly on his leadership, and he took out his frustration in a public tantrum. A Scottish merchant complained to the town council that Hutchings had, "in the hearing of women, children [and] the Negroes," sworn that he would round up those who refused to fight the British and "drive the scoundrels out of town." The outburst prompted respected tavern owner Mary Ross to close her business and flee for the safety of the countryside. Hutchings's wife confirmed to friends that her husband and his followers were resolved "to set fire to the town and burn the scoundrels out of it, that would not take up arms."

A *Gazette* article from October 27 offered a more nuanced explanation of residents' refusal to intervene to protect Holt and his press. "The situation of Norfolk and Portsmouth was very different from that of any other place in Virginia," the writer explained. The residents faced "an open and powerful enemy in full array of war before their town," with "two men of war always prepared to fire on them." Those opposing the British also confronted "a host of internal enemies." These included "almost to a man, merchants and mechanics, and a majority of them Scotchmen and rank Tories" in a town "full of slaves, ready for an insurrection at the beck of their leader." Dedicated patriots therefore were surrounded by "base and perfidious fellow-citizens . . . and dangerous and deadly enemies in their very houses. What then could be expected from a people whose whole property was at stake in their houses, and whose lives were beset on all sides!"

In the aftermath of the raid, personal attacks on Dunmore by the patriot press proliferated. He was suddenly deemed a dangerous sexual predator who posed a threat to Virginia's young white women. The governor was long rumored to have had lovers before his family arrived in 1774, though there had been no suggestion that he was a rapist or pederast. In the October 19 issue of the *Gazette*, "Cato" claimed that the earl "dared to offer violence to the chastity of a poor innocent girl" taken from Norfolk's poorhouse to serve as "an unhappy victim to his lawless lust." Dunmore allegedly had her brought to his ship as his "instrument of pleasure" until he was supplied "with more charming objects." The hapless victim was then "thrown upon the world, robbed of all she held most dear." The writer offered no evidence for this sensational claim.

"Ye inhabitants of Norfolk!" the author exclaimed. "Why were ye passive here? Why suffer such an outrage to go unpunished?" It was, "Cato" maintained, high time to act. "To let the sword, therefore, remain a moment longer within the scabbard, will be criminal. What! Shall the sons of *Virginia* be idle spectators, while one of her daughters is ravished?" Norfolk's patriots were advised "to give vent, then, to every sentiment of revenge; let it, like the obstructed torrent, burst forth with gathered fury." Rebellion was not without risk, and it might "cost the lives of a few" and "either the partial or total destruction of one of our seaport towns." The outraged author assured readers that the city's brave residents were ready to do their part "when the general good requires it."

No senior patriot is reliably recorded urging the annihilation of Boston, though it had long been in British and loyalist hands. Norfolk, by contrast, was not even occupied by the enemy. For nearly a decade, its merchants had supported patriot boycotts and been the first to tar and feather those deemed enemies to America. Patriots still retained control of its government. Yet "Cato" was urging Norfolk's citizens to raze their own homes and businesses in atonement for an alleged and otherwise undocumented rape. Eliminating the city altogether was a moral necessity, required for no other reason than to placate "the guardian deities of American liberty and those of Virginian chastity."

Such logic revealed the rift between the more diverse and industrial port, with its rich merchants and skilled Black workforce, and the tobacco culture dominated by the gentry that defined the rest of the colony, a divide that William Byrd II had noted with amusement a half century before. Dunmore's presence in the harbor amplified suspicions among many Virginia patriots—including some who called it home—that the port was enemy territory. The underlying struggle was not with Britain, but between two competing Virginias, one led by rural planters and another by urban merchants. This tension would come to define the new nation.

By the autumn of 1775, what one delegate called the "very threatening condition" in Virginia set off alarms from Philadelphia to Cambridge. George Mason warned Washington that "the principal families are removing from Norfolk, Hampton, York, and Williamsburg, occasioned by the behavior of Lord Dunmore." On October 6, the representatives gathered in the assembly room in Pennsylvania's State House debated how to address the challenge posed by the governor. "Lord Dunmore has been many months committing hostilities versus Virginia, and has extended his piracies to Maryland," complained that colony's Samuel Chase, a prominent attorney. He accused his sister colony of inaction.

Richard Henry Lee blamed the impotence of the colony's patriots on geography. "Virginia is pierced in all parts with navigable waters," he explained. "His Lordship knows all these waters, and the plantations on them." The British had unquestioned naval superiority, as well as experienced pilots like Harris. Lee shared intelligence that the Royal Navy in Boston "is coming to assist him in destroying these plantations," since Dunmore's influence "is sufficient to obtain what he pleases." The result, he warned, could be "decisive destruction to Maryland and Virginia." The governor, in other words, posed a lethal threat to the patriot cause in not one, but two colonies. Lee proposed a joint naval assault against the governor's forces before the ships from Boston arrived. "I wish Congress would advise Virginia and Maryland to raise a force by sea to destroy Lord Dunmore's power," he said.

Congress's sudden burst of concern was apparently triggered not just by fears of a British invasion but by evidence that Dunmore would free those in bondage. "I look on the plan we heard of yesterday to be vile, abominable, and infernal, but I am afraid it is practicable," said one Georgia delegate who seems to have been referencing a report, since lost, of the governor's intention to arm Black Virginians. "Infernal" and "diabolical" were common terms patriots applied to the notion of emancipation. John Adams was already deeply concerned. On September 24, "two gentlemen from Georgia" had appeared at his Philadelphia lodgings to warn that if a thousand redcoats landed in their colony and proclaimed those enslaved to be free, then twenty thousand Black men would join the British.

The obvious solution was to kidnap the royal governor before he could emancipate those in bondage, a controversial notion that kicked off a contentious debate. "I wish he had been seized by the colony months ago," said an impatient Chase. His Maryland colleague Thomas Johnson disagreed. Though he saw reconciliation with Britain as unlikely, he did not want to "render it impossible" by imprisoning a member of the House of Lords. Another delegate chimed in that "seizing the king's representatives will make a great impression in England, and probably will be carried on afterwards with greater rage." Eliphalet Dyer from Connecticut retorted that "they can't be more irritated at home than they are; they are bent upon our destruction." He argued that kidnapping Dunmore could prove useful. "His connections in England are such that he may be exchanged to advantage" with an American prisoner of war.

Richard Henry Lee, injecting some levity into the tense discussion, suggested the earl's abduction might best be accomplished during one of his alleged alcoholic binges. "He is fond of his bottle, and may be taken by land, but ought to be taken at all events." George Wythe, Dunmore's former neighbor in Williamsburg, then revealed that "it was from a reverence for this Congress that the Convention of Virginia neglected to arrest Lord Dunmore" while he was still in the capital, evidence that the earl had fled the Palace upon learning of this plot. "If Maryland[ers] have a desire to have a share in the glory of seizing this nobleman, let them have it," Wythe said. "I don't say that it is practicable, but the attempt can do no harm." New York's Francis Lewis then proposed an amendment that Virginia's Convention delegates "take such measures to secure themselves from the practices of Lord Dunmore, either by seizing his person, or otherwise, as they think proper." Though the outcome is not recorded, it appears to have been adopted.

During the debate, Connecticut's Dyer noted in passing that the Scottish earl was the sole civilian representative of the king posing a serious threat to the patriot cause. New Hampshire's royal governor had fled to Boston, and the others were not to be feared. "Franklin is not dangerous, Penn is not, Eden is not," he added, citing the royal governors of New Jersey, Pennsylvania, and Maryland. Outside of the British high command in Boston, Dunmore was now the patriots' prime opponent—and target.

Norfolk in the second half of 1775 was the spy capital of the South. British forces remained at Gosport rather than risk the complications that would go with occupying the city, but the patriot hold on the town—as demonstrated by the seizure of Holt's press—was weak. People of all political persuasions mingled in the shops, taverns, and warehouses. As tensions between patriots and their opponents mounted, both sides desperately sought accurate data on troop levels, armaments, munitions stores, and provision supplies. Operatives ranged from enslaved Black watermen to genteel patriot women who collected drawing-room gossip in the town's imposing brick townhouses. They reported intelligence to the Committee of Safety, gave tips to Dunmore, and sometimes—as in the case of Sprowle—passed information to both.

"An informer is such a mean and despicable character that I shudder to think I should be branded by such a name," wrote an anonymous person to Captain Montagu on October 1, the day after Squire's raid. The incident had inspired the correspondent. "It's now high time to annoy by every possible means these damned rebels," the novice informant explained, and then revealed that a small sloop in port was preparing to rendezvous off the Virginia capes with a ship loaded with gunpowder destined for Williamsburg. After confirming the information, Montagu seized the ship and captain.

Enslaved men such as Harris served important roles in relaying intelligence to the British, and their ubiquity and subservient positions often made them less visible to whites. The prospect of earning freedom was a powerful incentive to cooperate with Dunmore's forces. At the other end of the social hierarchy, wealthy Scots like James Parker made up a tight-knit fraternity determined to combat a patriot menace that threatened to destroy their lucrative livelihoods.

At the center of this formidable network was Dunmore. "No man can give more attention to business than his Lordship," Parker wrote on October 9. "He is seldom out of his ship which lay on the mouth of the [Elizabeth's] south branch, sees and hears all that is going forward." From the deck of his flagship, Dunmore could scan the ships coming and going with his telescope. He stationed five tenders at strategic points around the region to serve as his remote eyes. From the security of his stern cabin, the earl opened confiscated patriot mail and sent orders using free or enslaved Africans as reliable messengers. A frustrated Pendleton in Williamsburg complained when details on an important shipment of arms and ammunition leaked. "A villain has given Lord Dunmore information of it, and he has six or seven tenders flying out for it."

The patriots had their own impressive spy ring, as attested by the speed and accuracy with which Williamsburg's three papers published the smallest details of British troop and ship deployments. In October, the earl received word of a two-ton rebel shipment of gunpowder from the West Indies approaching the coast and notified his naval captains. Alerted to the risk of sailing through the well-patrolled Virginia capes, the patriot captain picked his way through the dangerous shoals of a North Carolina inlet, transferring 150 barrels of the critical munition to ox carts, which took the grueling land route to Williamsburg. The shipment arrived on October 15 and was stored in the Powder Magazine, now protected by trenches and shirtmen.

Dunmore countered that rebel success when he received an intercepted letter the same day implicating a Portsmouth captain in the plot. The man was promptly arrested, brought aboard the *Otter*, and questioned by the earl. When the prisoner's father learned of his son's arrest, he came on board to express "sincere repentance." In exchange for his son's freedom, he offered to place his extensive merchant fleet at the governor's disposal. The earl was only too happy to oblige. He needed what he called "a spirited, active, industrious family" on his side more than he needed a culprit in irons. The merchant ships were promptly signed over to "government service."

On October 17, Dunmore learned of "a great quantity of artillery, small arms, and all sorts of ammunition" at a village called Kemp's Landing that was rumored to be the site of rebel military maneuvers. The settlement lay ten miles to the east, at the head of navigation of the Elizabeth River's eastern branch. The small but prosperous port served as an important trading mart for Princess Anne County, the rural area bounded on the north by the Chesapeake, on the east by the Atlantic, and on the south by the Great Dismal Swamp and other wetlands. This isolation provided a secure base for loyalist renegades like Josiah Philips as well as for roving bands of patriots who wanted to keep their distance from the governor's forces.

At three o'clock on the next afternoon, Captain Montagu of the *Kingfisher* ordered a small schooner loaded with guns, ammunition, twenty marines, and a dozen sailors. They were joined by the seventy privates and a dozen officers of the Fourteenth Regiment in a cluster of smaller boats. An hour later, curious Norfolk residents watched the little flotilla vanish up the channel. Patriot spies saddled their horses to take the parallel land route to warn the rebels at Kemp's Landing. "Many people rode out of town when the vessel passed and carried intelligence," Parker noted. Moving upstream with the rising tide, the ship and boats drifted past small farms cut out of pine forest dotted with oaks and maples tinged with fall colors. White and enslaved people would have paused to gape at the remarkable sight of a small convoy filled with bright redcoats toting muskets with flashing bayonets.

The troops disembarked two miles shy of their goal at the small village of Newtown. They formed a column led by Dunmore and the army officer Leslie. "Our men all went out in full expectation of a smart resistance," one marine wrote later. More than two hundred armed rebels, nearly double the British force, lay in wait at Kemp's Landing. "A fine ditch was pointed out to them where they might attack the enemy," Pendleton later informed the Continental Congress. The patriot force included a contingent under Captain Thomas Matthews and another led by Colonel Joseph Hutchings, the Norfolk burgess no doubt eager to regain his honor after the debacle of Holt's raid. As dusk fell, both sides prepared for what seemed certain to be the first battle between American and British forces south of New England.

To fortify their spirits, the patriot officers had been drinking on that cool fall afternoon. As dusk fell and the measured tramping of the approaching redcoats grew louder, the spooked officers frantically called a last-minute retreat. "The captain then gave orders for all to run away, which was performed with instantaneous exactness by all," Parker wrote with delight. Hutchings, he added, "had made rather too free with the bottle" and collapsed in a heap while fleeing on a back road. "A town butcher driving some cattle found and took him into the woods," the Norfolk merchant wrote, "and covered him with trash by which he escaped." The essence of this account was later corroborated by local resident Helen Maxwell, who knew the Hutchings family. The colonel was, she recalled, "full of Dutch courage." She also saw Captain Matthews "racing off at a fine rate through Kempsville." He was "whipping his horse and crying out as loud as he could bawl to take care of the powder, take care of the powder." British troops quickly intercepted him.

When the redcoats arrived at the landing's wharves, they were puzzled at the absence of an enemy. "Is it thus you stand up in defense of your rights and liberty?" wrote Beesly Joel, a marine from the *Otter*. "Two hundred Virginian troops ran away from scarce ninety regulars." He added that the British "demanded the keys of all the stores" from the nervous owners. "Most of them was delivered up, those which [were] not they broke open." The party uncovered a "good many small arms, musket locks, a little powder and ball, two drums, and a quantity of buckshot, all which we either brought off or destroyed," an officer later reported. One patriot complained that the soldiers "broke open a blacksmith's shop and destroyed about fifty muskets, which the smith had to repair, then pillaged a number of houses in the neighborhood." The patriots had wisely moved their gunpowder elsewhere the night before.

The rummaging redcoats enraged an inebriated William Robinson, a Princess Anne County delegate to the Virginia Convention who was hiding nearby. "Poor Robinson went up to them drunk when in one of the stores, declaring he would not allow such doings while he had the honor to be a delegate," Parker said. He was promptly arrested. By eleven o'clock that night, the British were marching back to Newtown to catch the ebbing tide. By two in the morning the schooner dropped anchor in Norfolk's harbor. *Otter* mate Samuel Edwards said senior patriots either fled north after the rout or "delivered themselves up to the governor and have sworn their recantation."

According to Parker, the captured Matthews quickly "turned king's evidence," providing details on arms and ammunition caches in exchange for mercy. Dunmore acted quickly on the information. At noon the next day, some forty regimental troops landed at a Norfolk wharf. Pedestrians again made way as the men marched in close formation down Main Street and turned north on Church Street, crossing the isthmus into the suburbs, and passing the church. Two miles beyond, they uncovered "twenty pieces of cannon (from six to three-pounders) concealed in a wood; thirteen of which they destroyed," Leslie reported to his new commanding officer, General William Howe, who had recently replaced General Gage in Boston as head of North American ground forces. These likely were the ordinance pieces the patriots had previously moved from Kemp's Landing. The remaining seven cannon were hauled back to Norfolk and loaded onto boats that afternoon.

At ten o'clock that night, another shore party yielded "some powder" and thirty-seven casks of Dutch gin. The raids continued until the end of the month "without the smallest opposition," according to Leslie. A total of seventy-seven field pieces were captured. This second landing of troops in Norfolk "was done in the face of day and without any opposition," wrote one scandalized Alexandria patriot. "Indeed, none could be expected, as the principal people of that town are Tories."

One mate on the *Otter* was disgusted by the patriots' continued timidity. "The people of this province and Maryland are equally as refractory as those to the northward," he noted, but they lack "both force and courage to act." He estimated the rebels had some ten times more men under arms, yet "they take care to keep themselves up the country," around Williamsburg. Like many British military men of the day, he belittled their method of attacking "when under cover of woods, houses, and where they are sure you can't come at them." The patriots, he assured a friend, "strictly adhere to the old maxim of Sir John Falstaff: him that fights and runs away, may live to fight another day."

The arms seizures and rebel disarray throughout October gave the British effective control over southeastern Virginia, an area nearly inaccessible by land from the rest of the colony and rich in cattle and corn farms capable of feeding Dunmore's crews and troops. On October 20, fifty-five additional soldiers from the Fourteenth Regiment in St. Augustine, accompanied by nine officers and two drummers, arrived at Gosport with a welcome supply of ammunition, bedding, and other necessities. Leslie, however, remained worried that they lacked a sufficient force to attack Williamsburg. "As our situation is so extremely critical," he wrote General Howe, "I flatter myself that you will be so good as to send us a reinforcement as soon as possible." He cited the successful raids as "a proof that it would not require a very large force to subdue this colony."

However, the new commander had no intention of diverting troops in Boston to Virginia, the Carolinas, or Georgia. At least some of his officers in Boston were confident that Dunmore could build a fighting force of indentured servants, convicts, and enslaved people in Maryland and Virginia without need of additional redcoats. The royal governor's name, according to a memo written in the fall of 1775 by an officer who had spent time in Gosport, was "half an army in the Chesapeake Bay." His proposal noted that those in bondage in the area were "full of intelligence, fidelity, and courage" and emphasized that Dunmore "may and indeed should add the bravest and most ingenious of the Black slaves whom he may find all over the bay." Howe never formally approved the plan, nor did he stand in Dunmore's way as the governor set it in motion.

Crisp days and patriot setbacks raised morale in the little community of Gosport. Joel, the *Otter* marine, assured his mother in England that he enjoyed "the most agreeable situation imaginable," and asked her to send "a neat collection of prints, a few old magazines, and a goodly collection of hair pencils"—paintbrushes for artwork. He and his comrades clearly intended to stay through winter. The shipyard was now a busy military base, with soldiers drilling on the makeshift parade grounds accompanied by a band, while the Royal Navy's cannon crews continued to practice their speed and accuracy. Three hundred soldiers bivouacked in one warehouse, while those assigned to the vessels frequently came ashore. "Indeed, Gosport is the only place [that] can be called" peaceful in the colony, wrote Katherine Hunter on October 29, in a letter to her daughter attending school in Scotland. "We all are one family."

The Glasgow-born Hunter had lost her husband, Sprowle's nephew, on Christmas Eve 1774, leaving her with seven children. The aging bachelor uncle housed her in his mansion and supported her children's education in Britain. Hunter quickly became the doyenne of the Gosport social scene, as well as gatekeeper for those seeking permission to leave the compound. "The old gentleman"—Sprowle—"says I am directress of both army and navy, as all passes and permits are asked by me," she told her daughter with delight. Hunter was a "formidable, outspoken, and educated woman," according to one historian, and she made powerful men, from Dunmore to Jefferson, uncomfortable. One correspondent would later warn Benjamin Franklin that she was "a very bad woman with, I am assured, no mean talents of insinuation and address."

The widow was soon "very great folks" with the distantly related "good old major called Leslie"—Captain Samuel Leslie. Gosport gossips whispered that she was secretly engaged to him, but she assured her daughter that "my gratitude to the worthy Sprowle will ever prevent me from leaving him on all your accounts." An eighteenth-century Scottish widow with seven children had to be practical, and the pay of a military officer could hardly compare with the income of one of North America's wealthiest men.

Hunter conveyed a picture of a tight-knit circle of civilian loyalists and British military men bound together by their faith in the king and their aversion to the rebels. "The officers of both army and navy spend the evening here and we have often balls in the storehouse, where they all lodge," Hunter wrote. The wide planks of the building echoed with the strains of fiddles and the stamping of feet, while Sprowle held lavish dinners at his home for the governor, officers, and loyalist gentry. Except for her concerns for her distant children, she told her daughter, "I should be envied!" Her sunny description of life on the isolated military base was no doubt burnished to put her daughter's mind at ease. Hunter suggested lightheartedly that her son could find a job in the armory that was "well paid," while "Peggy might have made a fortune by washing and dressing."

There is little doubt Gosport provided a haven for loyalists, yet it was also a fragile bubble. Outside of the shipyard, wrote Samuel Edwards of the *Otter*, "the only people we now associate with" were Scottish residents.

Within the boundaries of the carefully patrolled military zone was another community, one largely excluded from the white social whirl. Many Black refugees from patriot servitude, as well as those still enslaved by loyalists, lived and worked at Gosport, including pilots, house servants, sailors, carpenters, fieldhands, cooks, blacksmiths, coopers, and other laborers. Some served in the usual menial roles, with lesser rations, inferior housing, and little or no pay, while those with specialized skills, like Harris, would have fared somewhat better. The shipyard was nonetheless unique in the southern colonies, if not in all British North America. Those still enslaved mixed with free skilled and unskilled Black workers, and the social barrier between the races that was so impermeable elsewhere would have been far more porous here. There is no mention of whipping posts, gallows, or the harsh punishments regularly meted out by slaveowners to their human chattel in the rest of the region, though this fact may simply be an omission in the historical record.

Gosport was nonetheless no paradise for people of color. Those owned by loyalists on the base remained in bondage, while those who had fled loyalist owners outside its boundaries would have feared that at any moment they might be returned to servitude. And whatever their expertise, all those of color, including those who were free, were still expected to be subservient to whites. Nonetheless, by the fall of 1775, Sprowle's shipyard had become a sanctuary for those fleeing slavery, and word of its existence under the aegis of the royal governor spread to unfree Black people in all corners of the colony, and beyond.

Fleeting mentions of armed Black men in uniform by local patriots and Williamsburg's newspapers suggest that Dunmore was secretly training select enslaved people to handle weapons, march in formation, and serve alongside British soldiers. This was not the first time Black Americans had borne arms in conflict. A few took part in the aborted 1676 Virginia rebellion led by Nathaniel Bacon and, later, in the French and Indian War. More recently, several dozen had fought at Lexington, Concord, and Bunker Hill. Yet now, for the first time in British North America, a fully multiracial army had begun to take shape.

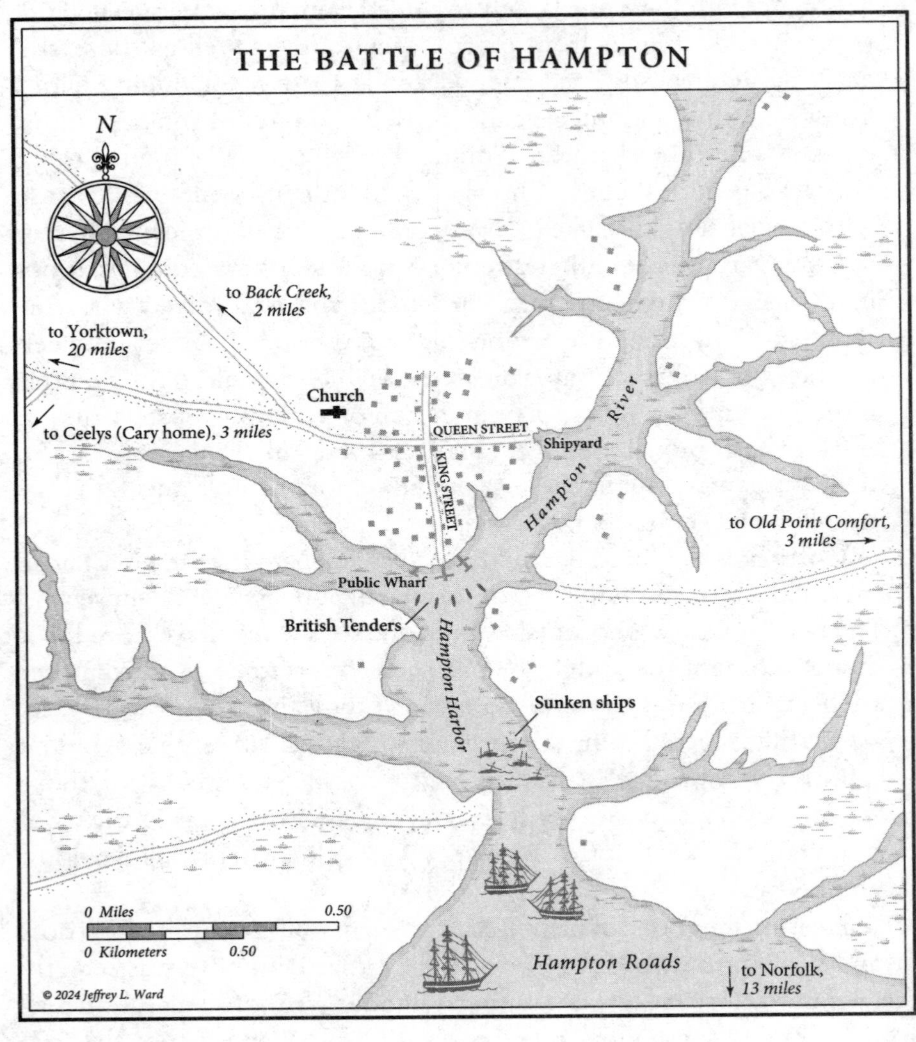
THE BATTLE OF HAMPTON
N
to Back Creek,
2 miles
to Yorktown,
20 miles
to Ceelys (Cary home), 3 miles
Church
QUEEN STREET
KING STREET
Shipyard
Hampton River
to Old Point Comfort,
3 miles
Public Wharf
British Tenders
Hampton Harbor
Sunken ships
0 Miles 0.50
0 Kilometers 0.50
Hampton Roads
to Norfolk,
13 miles
© 2024 Jeffrey L. Ward

Chapter Fifteen

A Most Disagreeable Step

By early August, Lady Dunmore and her children were back home, though she appears to have miscarried on the long voyage. Her husband's decision to stay and fight had made him a popular figure in Britain. "He has acquitted himself so well and gained so much applause from everybody," a Scottish woman wrote the governor's aunt on August 3. "Indeed, his courage nobody could ever doubt but his conduct has been admirable." The countess quickly delivered Dunmore's pleas for help to Lord Dartmouth, the colonial secretary.

Across the ocean, Virginia's patriots worried that the governor's political muscle would translate into additional land and sea forces. On October 10, Jefferson wrote to a friend in the colony that "a great number of frigates and small vessels of war" were on their way "at the express and earnest intercessions of Lord Dunmore . . . to lay waste all the plantations on our river sides."

The next day, the *Pennsylvania Journal* reported that a twenty-eight-gun frigate was being fitted for sea at a British port. The vessel was said to be complete with a captain's cabin "lined with crimson baize" and "everything commodious and proper for her intended destination, which is Virginia, where she is to accommodate the governor, Lord Dunmore." The London correspondent added that the luxurious interior was designed to impress Indian delegations, and "to induce them to take up the hatchet and boil the war-kettle." On October 15, a panicked Pendleton wrote Richard Henry Lee that Royal Navy ships were headed for their colony "to put a stop to all foreign trade . . . and so starve us into submission."

Worse news soon arrived. The "olive branch" petition approved by the Second Continental Congress reached Britain soon after Lady Dunmore. Since the Crown did not recognize the Philadelphia body, the government of King George III ignored the document and on August 23, the monarch declared the colonies in a state of "open and avowed rebellion." This put the southern provinces in British sights for the first time. As Pendleton wrote to Lee in mid-October, Lord North penned a proposal to the king to snuff out the rebellion there. "A very considerable number of the people in those provinces wish for a speedy accommodation," he noted, so that "a small force from home would quickly turn the scale."

The prime minister was also aware that Virginia and the Carolinas were in a "perilous situation" given the "great number of their Negro slaves, and the small proportion of white inhabitants," though he stopped short of proposing emancipation to those in bondage. He recommended sending five British regiments, or more than 3,300 men—hardly a "small force"—before the year was out. They would vanquish the southern rebels by the spring of 1776 and then head north to break the Boston siege by summer.

North favored an attack on Georgia or the Carolinas, in part because winter operations there were more viable than in the chillier Chesapeake. He also believed there were larger numbers of loyalists in these colonies' hinterlands waiting for British support. The king responded in less than three hours. "Every means of distressing America must meet with my concurrence," he wrote. The fleet was to anchor two hundred miles south of Norfolk, off the Cape Fear River that led inland to Wilmington, North Carolina's primary port. After joining loyalists there, they would sail south to Savannah or Charleston.

Virginia's patriots, however, believed the British wolf was nearly at their door. During the weekend of October 21, 1775, Pendleton huddled with those members of the Committee of Safety healthy enough to attend the meeting. They were under pressure from the Continental Congress to act before the expected enemy fleet arrived. The committee members were also convinced that an armed uprising by enslaved Africans was underway. In an October 24 public statement, they charged Dunmore with "withdrawing himself unnecessarily from the administration of government and exciting an insurrection of our slaves." The patriot leadership also accused him of commencing "hostilities against his Majesty's peaceable subjects in the town and neighborhood of Norfolk." He had captured "and seized the property of others, particularly slaves, who are detained from the owners."

Government seizure of private property was a serious violation in Britain's unwritten constitution. It was, in effect, an act of tyranny. Under Virginia law, an enslaved person was as much a possession as a cow. Any appropriated person in bondage under British jurisdiction in the colony was stolen goods and therefore an affront to American liberties.

The dual threats of invasion and insurrection finally convinced the patriots to send armed men to confront the governor's growing forces, in what amounted to a declaration of war against the British. Though Patrick Henry commanded the army, he was pointedly passed over for this assignment. Instead, Colonel William Woodford, commander of the Second Virginia Regiment, was "to march to the neighborhood of Norfolk or Portsmouth" with expert riflemen from distant Culpeper County. These western hunters intimidated Williamsburg residents; one wrote that the townspeople "seemed as much afraid of us as if we had been Indians." Their reputation rapidly spread. "I hope the riflemen who have shown themselves very savage and even bloodthirsty" are not typical of Virginians, Abigail Adams wrote her husband a few months later. "Are they not like the uncivilized natives Britain represents us to be?"

Woodford was ordered to protect patriots and kill or capture any enemies and sever all communications with the port. "More particularly, you shall stop and detain all slaves, who may so attempt to pass; if in arms, to proceed against them according to the rules of war." He was to return those belonging to patriot owners or "dispose of them as prudence may direct." Armed Black men were already presumed to be a danger, another sign that Dunmore had some in training at Gosport. The committee also advised Woodford to use his own "humanity and discretion" to avoid "wanton damage or destruction of any person's property whatsoever."

Richard Henry Lee begged Washington on November 13 for armed ships to counter the governor. "Two or three vessels of tolerable force . . . may affect a stroke or two of greatest consequence." The general, however, could not help. "There are none of any tolerable force belonging to this government," he replied. Without ships, Woodford and his troops would have to reach Norfolk by the long and circuitous land route. Like Dunmore, Virginia's patriots were essentially on their own. Pendleton could do little more than count on the slim hope that Britain would recall or rein in Dunmore. If that occurred, he wrote Lee, "our affairs may, perhaps, take another turn."

On October 25, 1775, the day after the patriots decided to attack the governor's stronghold, the *Otter* and *Kingfisher* each fired a fusillade that echoed across Norfolk harbor, followed by the thunder of guns mounted near Gosport's barracks. The booms unnerved local residents. "Make no doubt," *Otter* marine Beesly Joel wrote to a friend, "that the people in the country were very apprehensive for the fate of Norfolk." The volley celebrated the anniversary of King George III's ascension to the throne fifteen years before.

Following the barrage, Squire climbed down the *Otter* gangway and boarded a waiting sloop. This was a shallow-draft and single-masted vessel, perhaps sixty feet long, on which typically would be mounted four cannon in the bow and six in the stern, all capable of launching six-pound cannonballs. The crew may have numbered three to four dozen. Another sloop, a schooner, and two pilot boats filled with troops and Black crewmen stood ready.

Hampton's patriots still refused to hand over the guns and gear taken from the *Liberty* in the hurricane's aftermath, and the captain had blockaded the little port. Now, with Norfolk's hinterland secure—and after weeks of enduring patriot jeers—Squire was determined to teach a lesson in British naval superiority. The outgoing tide carried the ships past Norfolk's damaged wharves, down the Elizabeth, and into Hampton Roads. At dusk, part of the convoy sailed into a small creek east of Hampton. According to a patriot report, a party of redcoats landed and set fire to the home of a local and "took away a valuable Negro man slave and a sail from the owner."

At dawn the next morning, Hampton's patriots awoke to find the enemy vessels anchored about three hundred yards off the mouth of Hampton River. Old boats sunk by the patriots blocked the channel that led to the town, about a half mile inland. According to Dunmore, a dozen militiamen led by George Nicholas, son of the colony's treasurer, came to the shore to reconnoiter.

As with the early morning clash six months earlier on Lexington Green, there is no agreement on who first pulled the trigger first. "So soon as the rebels perceived them," wrote Dunmore, Nicholas "fired at one of the tenders, whose example was followed by the whole party." A patriot, however, blamed the British for "two volleys of musketry" aimed at the men onshore, who promptly fired back in self-defense. A tender's crew responded by launching a four-pound iron ball at the patriots. For an hour or so, bullets and balls intermittently soared between the ships and shore to no apparent effect.

The colonial militia eventually withdrew into nearby woods, either for cover or in hopes of drawing the landing party ashore. When the redcoats didn't follow, the thirsty patriots retreated that afternoon to a town tavern. A messenger was already pounding up the road to Williamsburg to request patriot reinforcements. It was dark by the time the rider galloped into the capital as a chill rain began to fall. He roused the sleepy Pendleton, who in turn ordered Woodford to march immediately to the port's defense. The Norfolk campaign would have to wait. If Hampton were lost, Williamsburg would be open to a British attack. The rain grew heavy as Woodford mustered his men and they made their way down a dark thoroughfare that quickly turned into a ribbon of thick mire. In the gray and drizzly dawn of October 27, the shirtmen struggled into Hampton's outskirts.

Most of the town's wood-and-brick buildings clustered along its primary avenue, King Street, which ran directly to the wharves on the creek. The remainder stood along Queen Street, which intersected King Street just above the port area. A sturdy brick Anglican church anchored one end of Queen while the other was the site of a small shipyard. The tired men dried their drenched hunting shirts in the shelter of the church. Woodford cantered down King Street to the harbor. In the gloom of the autumn daybreak, he made out British vessels riding in the bay, but all seemed quiet. He trotted a few miles to the home of Wilson-Miles Cary, the patriot slaveowner who had ridiculed Squire after recovering Aaron and Johnny following the storm. Like most of Virginia's elite, the two were well acquainted.

They shared a hot breakfast that would have been cooked and served by Cary's enslaved staff.

Squire's men had spent the wet night quietly sawing away at the hulks blocking the harbor entrance. Soon after Woodford rode off to breakfast, five vessels picked their way through the channel, anchoring just off the town's wharves. They caught the inhabitants completely by surprise; despite the previous day's events, no patriot sentry was on duty to warn of the incursion. "The people were so astonished at their unexpected and sudden arrival that they stood staring at them," John Page wrote Jefferson, and they "omitted to give the colonel the least notice of their approach." They also did not know he was at breakfast with Cary, oblivious to the danger. Squire sent a message to shore warning "that he would that day land and burn the town," according to a *Gazette* report.

The distant roar of cannon brought the colonel and Cary to their feet, their breakfast forgotten. Woodford rode off, only to find that "the people of the town had abandoned their houses," Page reported to Jefferson, while "the militia had left the breastwork which had been thrown up across the wharf and street." Another patriot rout seemed imminent. "Col. Woodford showed a great deal of coolness of courage, presence of mind, and judgement in the engagement at Hampton," Page wrote. The officer immediately turned his horse and galloped the three blocks to the church to gather his troops and deploy his secret weapon. The Culpeper County men grabbed their rifles and rushed out of the sanctuary and down King Street.

One man would have carried their flag sporting a coiled rattlesnake with LIBERTY OR DEATH above and DON'T TREAD ON ME below. Henry's stirring words were stamped on medallions worn on their chests or sewn across the front of their hunting shirts, which were secured with belts that held tomahawks and scalping knives. "Lord Dunmore is well acquainted with the skill of our riflemen, and the Shawnees have borne testimony of the coolness of their aim," noted a *Gazette*. Pendleton told Richard Henry Lee that the governor "is much afraid of the riflemen and has all his vessels caulked up on the sides, above men's height."

Squire had no experience with these western warriors and had not protected the sides of his five small vessels. As his crew hurled deadly iron projectiles, Woodford had the riflemen fan out among the crescent of buildings lining the harbor, "directing them to fire from the window, which they did with great spirit," one newspaper account said. From these sniper's nests they could aim at the British exposed on deck and then safely reload. "The fire was now general and constant on both sides," Page wrote. "Cannon balls, grapeshot, and musket balls whistled over the heads of our men, whilst our muskets and rifles poured showers of balls into their vessels." The British officers and crew found it hard to counter the rebel attack. "The sailors were not able to stand to their guns and serve them properly," Page noted. The firefight continued for more than an hour before Squire ordered a retreat.

The desperate British sailors sliced through their anchor cables for a quick getaway, but one of the smaller boats lost control and drifted to shore. The commander, a Lieutenant Wright, was shot in the knee and jumped overboard with Joseph Harris, the pilot who had already twice escaped the clutches of Hampton patriots. He helped Wright to land, where a Black man and a white man scrambled to rescue the pair. Taking careful aim, a rifleman shot the Black man from four hundred yards, but the others escaped into the surrounding woods. Wright was later "found dead on the shore," according to Richard Henry Lee, but Harris managed to return unscathed to Dunmore's service. The patriots, meanwhile, captured five white men, including an indentured servant who had fled Mount Vernon, an unidentified woman, and two enslaved men still aboard the tender. The whites were "treated with great humanity" while the Black men were "doubly confined" to "stand trial for life."

Lee informed Washington that Dunmore's "banditti" had been handily repulsed. "If the devil inspired them to come onshore" again, he added, "I make no doubt, but we shall have a good account of them." A patriot report boasted that they "had not a man wounded." Even Dunmore admitted "the loss of the rebels must have been very inconsiderable if they suffered at all," though one merchant later claimed that one patriot was killed and another badly wounded. The cannonade made a good deal of thunder and smoke, but damage to the town was surprisingly light. One local reported "a few windows broke, and a door panel."

Elated patriots crowded the King's Arms, Bunch of Grapes, and Lower Brick taverns. "The troops in this town are in high spirits," one observer noted, no doubt including the spirit of rum. "Lord Dunmore may now see he has not cowards to deal with." A triumphant report published in Williamsburg asserted that "officers and soldiers of the regular, minute, and militia acted with a spirit becoming freemen and Americans." The victory proved, the article boasted, that "Americans will die or be free." A chastened Squire steered his battered fleet back to Gosport. Moaning men and silent corpses littered the bloody decks. Accounts say that from two to twenty-one British were killed.

Since the June battle of Bunker Hill, the patriots had been locked in a largely bloodless stalemate with the British. The victory at Hampton provided a small but welcome morale boost. More importantly, it extended the war beyond New England. Pendleton reported to the Continental Congress that the success "will in some measure redeem the bleeding honor of Virginia" after the "degrading and mortifying accounts from Norfolk." He later apologized to the Philadelphia delegates for "the disgraceful patience and suffering of some of our people."

The British rout also served to reassure an anxious Congress that Virginia's patriots were prepared to fight for liberty as well as talk about it. "Lord Dunmore has commenced hostilities in Virginia," Jefferson wrote from Philadelphia on hearing of the battle. "It has raised our country into [a] perfect frenzy."

As bullets and cannonballs tore through Hampton's harbor, King George III processed through the House of Commons at Westminster in an ermine-trimmed robe and the glittering imperial crown. He mounted the throne to read the speech prepared by Lord North to open the new session of Parliament. The colonists, the king declared, "now openly avow their revolt, hostility, and rebellion." While anxious to prevent "the effusion of blood of my subjects," he was convinced the rebels intended to establish "an independent empire." He called on the legislators to support a full-scale war to restore the colonists' obedience. The monarch returned to his palace while the legislators discussed his request.

Near the end of that day's House debate, former South Carolina governor William Henry Lyttleton noted that "the southern colonies were weak, on account of the number of Negroes in them." He argued that "if a few regiments were sent there, the Negroes would rise, and imbrue their hands in the blood of their masters." This proposal appalled former West Florida governor George Johnstone. He called the idea "too black and horrid to be adopted." The motion was easily defeated. Parliament was eager to suppress the insurrection, but not enough to encourage those enslaved to join the cause. Many legislators either owned enslaved people in the West Indies or had a financial stake in the sugar plantations there. To support a slave rebellion in North America was to risk spreading rebellion to the Caribbean.

The House of Lords ultimately backed the king's appeal by a vote of more than two to one, and the House of Commons by nearly three to one, with Whigs deeply divided. Britain was now committed to snuffing out what had become the most menacing rebellion since Bonnie Prince Charlie's 1745 challenge to the Crown.

News of the Hampton defeat reached Gosport along with word of the patriot plans to burst their loyalist bubble. On November 1, Andrew Sprowle confided to a friend in Glasgow that two thousand armed rebels were on their way to Norfolk and Portsmouth "to burn these towns." Residents were "struck with such a panic, all removing into the country and their effects." Many merchants stored their goods in the shipyard warehouses and aboard merchant ships for "fear of the provincial forces." He added that "while the soldiers remain at Gosport, I am safe."

Many working-class and professional residents, however, could hardly afford to abandon their jobs, shops, animals, and homes. For Black and Scottish residents alike, the British fleet offered some measure of safety, but there was still cause to worry. Black inhabitants were familiar with the harsh punishments inflicted on their people, and rumors of a planned campaign of genocide terrified Scottish merchants. Sprowle noted darkly that the patriots were "all against the Scotsmen," even threatening "to extirpate them." That same day, a *Gazette* informed its readers that "the bulk of the inhabitants of Norfolk is composed of natives of North Britain doing all the mischief imaginable to the common cause of America." The writer argued that those who did not join the patriots "should be sent out of the country." A brother of Richard Henry Lee later compared the colony's community of Scottish merchants to "a wild onion" that "poison[s] the ground so that no wholesome plant can thrive" and is "extremely difficult to eradicate."

Norfolk merchant George Rae wrote to his brother in London, "These people at Williamsburg . . . now look upon us as enemies," while James Brown worried that the patriots shared "a great aversion to Scotsmen." If a merchant asked for repayment of a debt, he said, it was not uncommon "for the man that asks to be knocked down or the like." Given this antipathy, he calculated "a great probability" that patriots would destroy the town. James Parker had long before suspected the rebels' true motives. "Generally speaking, the more a man is in debt, the stronger he is possessed with the spirit of patriotism," he wrote in 1774. The merchant was convinced that talk of liberty was a way for wealthy white Virginians to avoid repaying their creditors, who were overwhelmingly Scottish.

Hunter remained upbeat when she wrote from Gosport on November 5 to a Miss Logan in Glasgow, who was caring for one of her daughters. "We are daily increasing in strength here and have got the Fourteenth Regiment almost completed." The grenadiers "are all mustered twice a day just before our windows with a band of music." She reported that the navy had captured nineteen rebel merchant vessels and that "five large ships of war [were] expected daily." Naval crews were being trained to fire cannon safely and efficiently, producing noise "both awful and agreeable." The "only distress I have is that [Gosport] may be the place of action," she confided. "If the rebels continue their present cowardice," Hunter added, "they will never venture this way." If they did find the courage "to strike a stroke," however, she predicted "it will be soon, before new troops come."

The chilling threat of a bloody assault by thousands of shirtmen wielding tomahawks did not keep her from carefully weighing her marriage prospects. She confided to Logan that she had recently turned down two proposals. "But this is not the time to marry here, as everybody is in the greatest confusion." She was, in fact, planning to wed her wealthy benefactor, Sprowle, and waved off Glasgow gossip that she was socializing too freely with unmarried officers. "Tell Susie she is a savage slut for not trusting me with a captain," she wrote, apparently referring to Leslie. She ended the letter abruptly. "I can write no more, all the redcoats are assembled with their music."

As the sound of the martial tunes drifted over the harbor, Norfolk's remaining leaders gathered at city hall to discuss the crisis. Parker claimed that Mayor Loyall was "almost the only rebel left in town, poor man." Their choice was stark: they could open the city to the shirtmen or ask for British help. The council selected the devil they knew over the one they did not, drawing up a petition formally asking Dunmore "to land himself and his forces for their protection."

Scottish merchant Charles Neilson explained to a Glasgow colleague that the borough's request was "owing to a body of provincials commanded by Patrick Henry threatening to come down (it is said they are now on their march) and destroy this town and Portsmouth." Burning the port, he explained, would force the British to abandon the area. Neilson was fearful. "Happy are you in being at a distance; our prospect is now truly alarming." His wife, he added, "wishes to be on the other side of the Atlantic." He regretted not sending "Mrs. Neilson and the poor little girls home in the summer. We must now all share our fate."

The governor accepted the urgent request, making himself responsible for the security of the city and its vulnerable residents. There were still no reinforcements from Boston, and white loyalists remained reluctant to take up arms. One patriot source in September estimated the earl had "about one hundred Negroes, and from twenty to thirty Tory volunteers" to go into battle alongside two hundred or so redcoats and marines. Black men continued to show up that fall, even without a public promise of freedom, and the governor was already quietly training them for war. Yet there were not enough to counter well over a thousand patriots under arms. He needed a larger army to occupy and defend Norfolk, and he needed it fast.

On Tuesday, November 7, Jefferson was desperate for news and fearful for the safety of his wife and children as the conflict in Virginia turned violent. "The suspense under which I am is too terrible to be endured," he wrote from Philadelphia to a friend who lived outside Williamsburg. "If anything has happened, for God's sake let me know it." Dunmore, meanwhile, retreated to the stern cabin of the *William* to draft what was arguably the most revolutionary decree yet made in British North America. "I have ever entertained hopes that an accommodation might have taken place between Great Britain and this colony," it began. Now the king's representative confronted "a body of armed men, unlawfully assembled, firing on his Majesty's tenders" and forming an army now marching "to attack his Majesty's troops, and destroy the well-disposed subjects of this colony." To restore "peace and good order," he was forced to take a "most disagreeable" but "absolutely necessary" step.

The document declared martial law throughout Virginia. Martial law was used by British monarchs in times of chaos and insurrection. Derived from England's Court of Marshal and Constable, it was not technically a law but a declaration of an emergency. The draft also "required every person capable of bearing arms to resort to his Majesty's standard." King Charles II had done this in 1642 when threatened with un uprising by Parliament, as had Bonnie Prince Charlie, acting on behalf of his father, whom he considered the rightful king, in his struggle against George II in 1745. The previous June, General Gage had issued the order in Massachusetts.

Declaring martial law and issuing a call to arms were sure to anger Virginia's patriots. But what made Dunmore's proclamation even more incendiary was its third aspect. "All indentured servants, Negroes, or others" who were bound to rebels would be freed if they were "able and willing to bear arms." They were to join the British "as soon as may be, for the more speedily reducing this colony to a proper sense of their duty to his Majesty's crown and dignity." The proclamation was an unprecedented and direct call for hundreds of thousands of enslaved Africans and tens of thousands of white indentured servants to rise up against their patriot owners and masters.

Spanish, Dutch, French, and Danish officials in Brazil, Florida, and the Caribbean had on occasion armed those they enslaved, but Britain had long resisted taking this step. One of those rare occasions was in 1676, when Virginia governor William Berkeley promised to liberate those in bondage who deserted a rebellion led by a recent English immigrant, Nathaniel Bacon. Bacon responded by granting "liberty to all servants and Negroes," and many Black men briefly joined his cause before their leader abruptly died and Berkeley reasserted control. In the aftermath, the shaken gentry approved strict laws preventing the enslaved from owning or using weapons and punishing fraternization between the races.

Dunmore signed his name in large letters at the bottom of the document, and then wrote beneath, "God Save the King." He gave the original to a messenger, who rowed it to the *Eilbeck*, recently rechristened the *Dunmore*. The printer in charge of Holt's confiscated press set the type and rolled copies off the machine for widespread distribution. Yet the governor hesitated to make the controversial decree public without the explicit approval of King George III. "I postponed as long as possible, in hopes of having instructions from your Lordship for my conduct, in this as well as in many other matters," he explained later to the colonial secretary. More than four months had passed with no word from London. With a hostile army on the march, time was running out.

Chapter Sixteen

A Conspicuous Light

As Dunmore scratched out his proclamation on November 7, Colonel Woodford launched the first Virginia offensive against Britain. The assault began at the birthplace of the American colonies, amid the ruins of the largely abandoned old capital of Jamestown. The first contingent of troops, consisting of some 250 men, boarded ferries for the half-mile crossing of the James River. Once on the opposite shore, they set up camp to await additional troops before proceeding on the long march to Norfolk.

Loyalist spies quickly relayed word to Montagu on the *Kingfisher* anchored off Gosport. He immediately set sail with four tenders to disrupt further troop crossings. When the convoy came into view of Jamestown, twenty Culpeper County riflemen were waiting. Page wrote Jefferson that in the ensuing skirmish, a six-pound shot from the warship smashed through a stone house, while "the other lodged in the bank over the heads of our men." The precision sniper fire forced a British withdrawal. The victorious shirtmen dug the iron ball out of the riverbank and sent it as a gift to Patrick Henry, who remained in the capital. "It is incredible how much they dread a rifle," Page said of the redcoats. "Small arms in the hands of a few men will keep numbers from landing." The attack nevertheless forced subsequent patriot troops to make a time-consuming journey upstream from Jamestown to avoid enemy fire.

The thunder of cannon could be heard in the capital, sparking fears that the British intended to attack. Patriot residents were already reeling from news that their leading citizen, the fifty-four-year-old

Peyton Randolph, was dead of a stroke suffered at a Philadelphia dinner party on October 22. "At nine o'clock he died without a groan," wrote Richard Henry Lee to Washington. As president of the Continental Congress, he had kept the peace between those who favored patient negotiation with Parliament and those who demanded a more aggressive stance. The representatives of the thirteen colonies remained deeply divided as the stalemate around Boston continued. New England delegates such as John Adams urged a faster military buildup, while middle-colony representatives such as John Dickinson of Pennsylvania backed public petitions and private bargaining to break the deadlock. Southern delegations were typically of two minds.

In Virginia, the rift was epitomized by the conflict between Committee of Safety president Edmund Pendleton, a cautious attorney, and Patrick Henry, the ambitious armed forces commander. The committee had passed over Henry to choose the more experienced and conservative Woodford, Pendleton's protégé, to lead the Norfolk expedition. The famous orator's regiment was confined to Williamsburg, and he was told to ensure Woodford's troops were "furnished with tents and kettles." Unlike Washington, Henry failed to grasp the critical importance of an adequate supply chain. The campaign quickly stalled "for want of arms, tents, etc.," wrote Page, as soldiers complained bitterly about inadequate rations.

Henry, meanwhile, sulked, refusing to take part in a council of war. "Without your presence," the men would look with "suspicion of our judgement and prudence," the Committee of Safety warned him on November 4. The commander's absence from a meeting "of such importance to the country," they added, "appears extraordinary." Not until November 10 did the first five hundred shirtmen depart their camp on the south side of the James. "Our troops are marching to Norfolk," the relieved committee reported the next day to the Continental Congress. The news that King George III had declared the colonies to be in open rebellion in August was printed in that same day's *Gazette*.

Those living around Norfolk's harbor feared the worst. Having been tarred and feathered, Anthony Warwick had no doubt the patriot army would seek vengeance. "It is generally believed they come with a professed intention of destroying by fire both towns," the merchant wrote that day to an associate in Scotland, since they "think them places of refuge for those inimical to what they call the liberties of America." He didn't dispute the point, estimating that there were "not twenty inhabitants now in both towns" who had not "publicly declared themselves friends to government and willing to take up arms in its defense." He predicted "a bloody work here," adding that Dunmore planned to "lay waste the whole country" to defend the king's cause. "A very few days will determine the fate of Norfolk and this place," he concluded somberly. "It is the expectation of every person that they will be destroyed."

Pendleton was aware of such sentiments; the patriots intercepted this and other loyalist letters. On November 11 he published an official notice denying reports that the troops were "empowered and directed to destroy the houses and properties." He declared "in the most solemn manner" that these were "false and malicious" claims. The patriot regiments, he insisted, were forbidden from damaging or destroying "the property of any persons whatsoever." This was not an army of vengeance, but of liberation, "destined to guard and protect the inhabitants of the counties of Norfolk and Princess Anne and the parts adjacent."

Senior Virginia patriots privately harbored quite different views. "The people at Norfolk are under dreadful apprehensions of having their town burnt," Page wrote on the same day to Jefferson. "They know they deserve it, but we seem to be at a loss what to do with them. Many of them deserve to be ruined and hanged," he insisted. "But at all events, rather than the town should be garrisoned by our enemies and a trade opened for all the scoundrels in the country, we must be prepared to destroy it."

Nearly two years before, during a heated debate in the House of Commons in the aftermath of the Boston Tea Party, one angry legislator suggested "the town of Boston ought to be knocked about the ears and destroyed." He quoted the Latin phrase "delenda est Carthago." This referred to the North African city of Carthage, a formidable rival to Rome in the early centuries BCE. After centuries of conflict, the Eternal City triumphed, and a humbled Carthage paid annual tribute. The continued existence of the African city nevertheless rankled the Roman senator Cato the Elder. He is said to have concluded every speech with the phrase "Carthage must be destroyed."

In 146 BCE, he got his wish. With the Senate's blessing, Roman general Scipio Africanus attacked and leveled the city without warning or provocation. Its inhabitants were killed or sold into slavery. One later telling holds that the victors sowed its ground with salt and placed a curse on the devastated site. Some historians consider Cato's call the first recorded incitement to genocide. When the British member of Parliament echoed the Roman senator in March 1774, he was not taken seriously; there is no evidence that legislators in London considered such an extreme act, which would have been certain to stoke further American outrage. That was borne out by the fact that after the year-long British occupation, Boston was "in a better state than we expected," Abigail Adams reported to her husband. Even the fine furniture in John Hancock's mansion, where Gage had lived during the siege, was untouched.

Thomas Jefferson, by contrast, viewed the Latin phrase as more than a rhetorical device. For him, the ancient fight between Rome and Carthage was a struggle pitting a republic led by noble and honest farmers against a gaudy and corrupt metropolis run by avaricious traders. In his later years, the Virginian associated Carthage with the British capital, speculating that some "Scipio Americanus" would leave the "ancient and splendid city of London" in ruins. In 1775, Norfolk loomed in the planter's mind as a colonial Carthage. Its dark and narrow alleys, squalid tenements, and grand mansions of wealthy merchants were at odds with his evolving vision of a republic of the soil.

A dozen years later, Jefferson would argue for a country that was "chiefly agricultural, and this will be as long as there shall be vacant lands in any part of America." He warned against urban expansion. "When they get piled upon one another in large cities, as in Europe, they will become corrupt as in Europe." The very existence of fast-growing Norfolk, with its belching factories and crowded taverns where Blacks and whites mingled, might tug Virginia down the wrong path.

One week before Dunmore penned his proclamation, Jefferson expressed this deep-seated loathing of the town to Page in large capital letters, a rarity in his correspondence: "DELENDA EST NORFOLK." Like Carthage, the port had to be destroyed, its thousands of residents dispersed, its buildings razed, and the colony cleansed of the deadly contagion of urban corruption. The anonymous author of the October 19 article urging Norfolk's destruction for "the general good" clearly shared Jefferson's view. So did Washington's nephew-in-law, Alexander Spotswood. In mid-November, he wrote to Pendleton that he would "rather burn the towns of Norfolk, [Gosport,] and Portsmouth, than hurt a hair of his Lordship's head." For Virginia's landed class, their largest city was more of a threat than Dunmore himself.

By early November, Major John Connolly had recovered from his long illness and prepared for the arduous journey from Gosport through enemy territory and indigenous lands to the Great Lakes. He hoped to reach distant Detroit by Christmas. Connolly went to great lengths to conceal his written instructions in the stuffed leather cushion at the rear of his enslaved servant's saddle. "In the night of the thirteenth of November 1775, I took my leave of Lord Dunmore," he wrote later. The governor sent with him a Scot named Allen Cameron, who had served as a South Carolina Indian agent, and Maryland physician John Smyth, who knew the route. The fourth member of the party was a literate African, possibly owned by Dunmore, who was described as "a man of great fidelity and adroitness." Though he would play a key role in the expedition, his name went unrecorded.

They sailed with their horses on a schooner up the Chesapeake, landing on its western Maryland shore and taking the road that led to the Appalachian Mountains. Late in the afternoon of November 18, they slid off their saddles in front of an inn in Frederick, which Smyth called "a fine large town, built of brick and stone." They were within a day or so of the relative safety of the forested and sparsely settled mountains. While their enslaved servant fed and stabled their steeds, the three white men relaxed in a tavern crowded with patriot militia. Smyth recalled that his party ordered "something different from the others," perhaps beer instead of cider. The suspicious rebels noticed this anomaly and told the strangers to meet with the local committee the next morning to explain their presence.

The patriots "got intoxicated overnight," giving the loyalists an opportunity to slip away at dawn as the men were sleeping it off. They rode through the next settlement, Hagerstown, and by day's end were "on the very border of the frontier, and almost out of danger," according to Connolly. In the waning light, they encountered "a hatter who knew Colonel Connolly at Pittsburgh," recalled Smyth. He greeted the major by name before heading in the opposite direction. The anxious Maryland physician proposed they change their route, but Connolly dismissed his concern. They halted at a small German-owned inn and bedded down for the night; the region was home to many German-speaking patriots. At two the next morning, Smyth said, three dozen German riflemen rushed "suddenly into our room, with their rifles cocked and presented close to our heads while in bed, [and] obliged us to surrender."

The riflemen forced the men out of the inn and onto their horses for the journey back to Hagerstown in the dark. "As we rode along," wrote Smyth, "some of them in the rear now and then fired off a rifle directed very near us, as I could hear the ball whistle past within a few feet of us every time they fired." They were confined during the next day and night in separate houses, and "suffered that kind of disturbance and abuse which might be expected from undisciplined soldiers, and a clamorous rabble, at such a crisis." Their baggage was carefully searched. "They examined everything so strictly as to take our saddles to pieces, and take out the stuffing, and even rip open the soles of our boots in vain." The patriots, however, had not bothered to confine the enslaved servant or search his possessions. He crept to the stable in the middle of the night, sliced open the undisturbed cushion containing the incriminating documents, and burned everything but Connolly's military commission. He informed the major, Connolly later recounted, "by means of a Negro girl," who delivered "a note informing me of what he had done."

Connolly had talked his way out of scrapes before, but he was unaware that the patriots had already learned of his plot. They intended "to arrest and secure Lord Dunmore's wicked agent," Richard

Henry Lee wrote Washington on November 13, after interception of Dunmore's August letter to Koquethagechton, the Delaware chief, asking for help in forming an alliance with the British. A copy had reached local minutemen just days before. The captives were taken back to Frederick, and a messenger was sent to bring Samuel Chase, the Maryland delegate to Congress who weeks before had urged Dunmore's seizure. At Frederick, a patriot officer revealed to Connolly that his plan had been discovered, and that "George Washington knew the time of my coming to, and the very day of my leaving Boston," the loyalist recounted ruefully. Only then was it clear to Connolly that his servant Cowley had betrayed his secrets after jumping ship in Newport. The men were confined to an upstairs room. Chase arrived and had the men stripped, searched, and questioned separately; all maintained they were simply private travelers on their way to Pittsburgh.

The wealthy Annapolis lawyer, who viewed the British "as one of the most abandoned and wicked people under the sun," was not fooled. He ordered a more thorough search, which produced a "soiled and besmeared" document in the baggage that had gone unnoticed. It was a damning draft outlining Connolly's plot to General Gage. "All attempts at denial were now idle," the major wrote. He feared the patriots would use the plot as an excuse to attack British garrisons on the frontier and was desperate to get word to them. "In this our good Negro again assisted us; she procured paper, and an inkhorn, which she contrived to leave between the bed and the sacking-bottom, unnoticed by the guard."

By the dim light of a candle, Connolly scribbled letters to British officers in the west. "I am now a prisoner, and the whole scheme at an end," he told one, urging him to gather troops to travel down the Mississippi. From there, they should sail around Florida to join Lord Dunmore at Norfolk. "Lose no time, for fear the rebels should be upon you from Pittsburgh." A second letter repeated that order and asked the officer to look after Connolly's wife. "God bless you, adieu, I write in bed, with two sentinels at the door, with hourly apprehensions of death." With dawn fast approaching, Smyth laboriously unscrewed the door lock. Just before first light, he opened the door, crept down the stairs, past the snoozing guard, and escaped out the door. "We scarce had time to screw the lock on again, and lie down, before the guard entered our room," Connolly said. The guard did not notice one man was missing, and "cried all safe, and retired."

When the missing man's absence was finally discovered later that day, Connolly and his companion were peppered with the "opprobrious epithets" to be expected from such "vulgar and exasperated men." Smyth was already fleeing west on foot through "a deep encrusted snow and most dreadful roads," his legs bleeding from the sharp ice. It was all for nothing; just shy of his goal of Pittsburgh, the loyalist physician was captured by a patriot posse.

Members of Congress celebrated their good luck in intercepting Dunmore's dangerous allies. They had just finalized the peace agreement with the Shawnees and other Ohio tribes. "This treaty with the Indians is the more likely to last, as Connolly, with his little corps of officers, are now in close custody in Maryland," Richard Henry Lee informed Washington on December 6. A week later, Washington wrote an officer that he was "exceeding happy" to learn "that that villain Connolly is seized," adding, "I hope if there is anything to convict him, that he will meet with the punishment due to his demerit and treachery." Connolly's capture crushed Dunmore's hopes for an alliance with the Ohio peoples and a second front against the rebels, but weeks passed before the news reached the earl's ship.

Washington's former business partner would languish for years in a grim Philadelphia cell with "both the iron and wooden door locked and chained close upon us, so as not to admit a breath of fresh air," recalled his fellow inmate Smyth. The unusually long and harsh incarceration underscored patriot fears of a British-Indian alliance. When the general paroled Connolly in late 1781, the determined colonel promptly fled to British lines. He later made his way to Detroit, where he was "preparing to invade this country" with British and Indian troops when the war ended in 1783.

"It is impossible to describe to you the unhappy situation I am in at this juncture," wrote the anxious Norfolk merchant John Laurence to a Liverpool colleague on November 12, the day before Connolly's party departed Gosport. "This place in a very few days is likely to become the seat of war in this colony." He estimated that "there is now not ten people in this place or Portsmouth but what have removed their effects into the country, where I think they cannot at any rate be safe." Laurence had stored "much rum, sugar, and wine on board the sloop *Betsey*." He intended to find room for all his effects—"except the slaves"—since "in all probability this town will be burnt down in a very few days."

Dunmore and his officers disagreed over how and even whether to defend the port. The governor urged construction of fortifications, a step Leslie and other army officers appear to have seen as useless. "They have quarreled again amongst themselves as usual," wrote one Portsmouth merchant. "Our poor town," he concluded, "is devoted to destruction." Word that six hundred North Carolina patriot troops under Colonel Robert Howe were marching north to rendezvous with Woodford's men only added to the general distress. "God only knows what I have suffered since my first embarking, not knowing how to act in innumerable instances that occur every day," Dunmore wrote Dartmouth in despair. He seesawed between abandoning the city and assembling an army to combat the rebels. Sailing away meant deserting thousands who had placed their faith in him, yet he feared "inevitable ruin should the rebels march a body against us that we were not able to withstand."

On November 14 came news that jolted the governor out of his despondency. "I was informed that a hundred and twenty or thirty North Carolina rebels had marched into this colony, to a place called the Great Bridge," he wrote the colonial secretary. This was the flourishing village named for the forty-foot-long plank crossing over the headwaters of the southern branch of the Elizabeth River, a dozen miles south of Norfolk, just before the stream was lost in the Great Dismal Swamp. Great Bridge stood at a strategic juncture in the road network linking the port with the rest of Virginia and North Carolina, a system one traveler described as "mere tracks large enough for wagons, occasionally bridged, across ditches, streams, or mudholes, by small tree trunks placed close together." The paths from North Carolina and Williamsburg skirted the swamp, intersecting on the outskirts of the village. Anyone without a boat who wanted to reach Norfolk had to cross at that point.

As the autumn light waned that day, Dunmore ordered his troops to assemble. Among them were African men under arms. "The king of the blacks, alias pirate, alias Dunmore, and his banditti, consisting of regular soldiers, sailors, Negroes, and Scotchmen, in number about 350, marched to Great Bridge," reported a Williamsburg newspaper. The real figure was much smaller, but the force included at least 109 members of the Fourteenth Regiment led by Captain Leslie, 22 white volunteers from Norfolk, and an unknown number of Black loyalists. They set off in tenders after dark and made their way up the southern branch of the Elizabeth River.

Just before dawn on November 15, the multiracial fighting force disembarked a few miles downstream from Great Bridge and prepared for a rebel attack. But when they arrived at the village, Leslie laconically reported, the Carolinian patriots had "thought proper to retire and disperse upon our approach." Dunmore and his officers took the opportunity to examine the area. Recognizing the site's strategic importance, the earl immediately ordered construction of a wooden fort on the shore opposite that of the village. This would protect the road that wound northeast to Kemp's Landing, where a short span crossed the eastern branch of the Elizabeth, and then turned west to Norfolk. Surrounded by swamp, the ground proved too wet to build durable earth fortifications that might withstand artillery, so work began on a modest wood structure.

The governor also discovered that the bridge planks were designed to be taken up in case of flooding. By removing that decking and securing the eastern side of the shore, the British could effectively block the militia advance. It was, Dunmore told Dartmouth, "by nature a very strong pass, and the only one by which they can enter Princess Anne County by land, and a great part of Norfolk County."

A messenger soon arrived with word that "between three and four hundred of our rebels assembled at a place called Kemp's Landing," Dunmore wrote the colonial secretary. "I was then determined to disperse them if possible." The landing lay fifteen miles to the northeast, and they set off that afternoon past thick woods and marsh that made for perfect ambush cover. The governor sent an advance party ahead of the main body of troops and gave strict orders for his men not to fire unless fired upon, and "even then to march close up to the enemies with fixed bayonets before they should discharge their muskets." The British army was known and feared across Europe for its fierce bayonet charges that terrified their foes and gave them little time to reload. Few if any of the Virginia militiamen had witnessed such an assault.

The rebels, alerted to the approaching troops, were waiting a mile or so outside of Kemp's Landing. As the column's advance guard came into view, two shots rang out from the thick woods along the road. Had the impatient Americans held their fire, the ambush might have trapped and overwhelmed the Crown's outnumbered soldiers. The governor acted decisively. "I immediately ordered the main body, who were within two or three hundred paces, to advance, and then detached a party with the volunteers to outflank them," he later wrote. The advance guard and the brawny grenadiers in their high black hats sprinted into the woods as white puffs of smoke floated through the cool autumn air. "The rebels fled on all quarters," reported Dunmore, "and we pursued them above a mile."

Pendleton later specified that Dunmore's loyalists, not the grenadiers, were sent after the fleeing patriots. Two of them, one armed only with a sword, dashed into the forest. They soon were hot on the heels of the patriot leader Colonel Joseph Hutchings, the Norfolk delegate to the Virginia Convention who had fled the British on their October foray to Kemp's Landing and had failed to halt the raid on Holt's press. The middle-aged officer, separated from his comrades, desperately tried to outrun his pursuers in the fading light. When they were just a few paces behind, he turned and pointed his pistol at a sword-carrying enemy.

The shock of seeing the familiar face may have shaken his aim, since the gun flashed and the bullet missed its target. The loyalist took advantage of the moment to rush forward and slashed him in the face. He and his companion then took the injured commander into custody and escorted him to Kemp's Landing. The colonel and his assailant were acquainted: under Virginia law, Hutchings owned the unnamed man who had just captured him.

The colonel was the prize prisoner among eight taken that day. Five patriots lay dead and two drowned while trying to escape through the cold waters of a nearby creek. Others lay injured. The British and loyalists were nearly unscathed. "We had only one grenadier wounded in the knee," Leslie reported later. Dunmore forbade his men from pursuing the other militia in the dimming light, lest his victory become a massacre. "His Excellency's humanity appeared in a conspicuous light," wrote Norfolk merchant Neil Jamieson, "as he could easily have surrounded and cut off most of these people, but he was satisfied with taking some prisoners."

Helen Maxwell, who had witnessed the previous skirmish at the landing, recalled being on hand to watch as "Lord Dunmore entered the town in triumph at the head of his soldiers." A patriot report says that the governor went personally "to Dr. Reid's shop, and, after taking the medicines and dressings necessary for his wounded men, broke all the others to pieces." He then proceeded to the home of George Logan, a Scottish businessman who owned a local store and lived in an "extremely elegant and commodious mansion house, with extensive gardens." He and his wife, Isabel, had suffered from "abuse and insults" in recent weeks. A patriot had fired at Isabel while she was riding in her carriage; the ball had missed her but injured a servant. The frightened couple were delighted to host the governor, and Isabel gave him and his officers "very strenuous aid and every possible assistance."

The earl immediately drew up an oath of allegiance renouncing those "endeavoring to overturn our happy constitution" through "actual rebellion against our gracious sovereign." Signers pledged to do "the utmost of my power and ability" to "support, maintain, and defend his crown against all traitorous attempts and conspiracies." The pledge resembled the one the British government had demanded from Dunmore, his father, and other Jacobites after their defeat at Culloden. Maxwell recalled that "those who could not conveniently run away went at once and took the oath of allegiance." Some of the patriot militia, she added, "turned back to town to submit themselves to the conqueror." Since wars began, she added, there had never been "a victory more complete or won with so little loss of blood."

If Dunmore had harbored doubts about the fighting abilities of Black men, they would have been dispelled by Hutchings' dramatic capture by a soldier whose name is lost to history. As an autumnal chill crept up from the nearby river, the governor decided to declare martial law, raise the king's standard, and make his emancipation proclamation public. Lacking the king's personal flag, he instead used the banner of the Fourteenth Regiment, a squared-off version of the Union Jack, with its red cross of England's St. George, blue cross of Scotland's St. Andrew, and red cross of Ireland's St. Patrick, with the Latin numeral XIV wrapped in roses sewn in the center. The irony could not have been lost on the earl; it was the same standard carried by the regiment when fighting the Jacobites at Culloden.

The ceremony may have taken place at the riverbank or on the stone steps of the Logans' brick mansion.* A soldier unfurled the flag while the earl or an officer read the proclamation to a multiracial crowd that would have included the Black men who had just emerged from combat. They would have been joined by local enslaved Africans who worked as unpaid field hands, house servants, stevedores, laundresses, boatmen, and carriage and cart drivers. White farmers, artisans, and merchants who had come to sign the oath also would have been present.

Dunmore then ordered the printed broadsides of the decree distributed throughout the Chesapeake by Royal Navy ships, tenders, and loyalist vessels. For the first time in the empire's history, the call for mass emancipation rang out. The document did not free all those enslaved; only Black men of fighting age owned by patriots qualified, though this did not prevent women, children, and the elderly from loyalist as well as patriot owners from seeking British protection. Few if any were turned away. "Lord Dunmore has taken into his service the *very scum* of the country to assist him in his diabolical schemes against the good people of this government," carped a *Gazette* report. A patriot committee reported that "a number of about two hundred slaves immediately joined him and were furnished with arms." Dunmore now had to turn these eager recruits into a crack fighting force, even as the patriots closed in on Norfolk.

* The precise location of the Logan home, in today's Virginia Beach, remains a matter of dispute.

Chapter Seventeen

Black Rascals

Civilians present that fateful day at Kemp's Landing pinned "a badge of red cloth on their breast" to signal their support for the Crown, and the item proved so popular that Helen Maxwell said that "the price of the article rose in the stores." She and her sister, however, refused to take the oath, and instead hurried out of town to stay at the nearby home of a patriot. They had their trunks brought to the dwelling, which was empty when they arrived.

"We had hardly got there," she recalled, "when an ugly looking Negro man, dressed up in a full suit of British regimentals, and armed with a gun, came upon us, and asked with a saucy tone, 'Have you got any dirty shirts here?'" This was the derogatory term for shirtmen. "I want your dirty shirts!" he demanded. When she insisted there were none, he refused to believe her. "But you have," he insisted, "and I will find them." He went upstairs to search, which Maxwell took as a ruse to rob the house. He came down empty-handed, warning them he would be back. The Black redcoat would have been part of a patrol Dunmore sent to round up patriot militia still in the vicinity. The sisters quickly decided to go back to Kemp's Landing "before that horrid wretch" returned.

When they arrived, the village exuded a festive air, with "the houses all lighted up, and Mrs. Logan's, particularly, appeared most illuminated." Leaving her sister at a nearby inn, Maxwell marched to the Logan house, stalked up the stone steps, and knocked boldly on the door, which Isabel Logan opened. The two women knew each other, and she received Maxwell "with great kindness." She then introduced her to the earl, who was "sitting at his ease, and apparently highly pleased with his day's work," Maxwell recalled. "So, I told him my tale."

Dunmore responded with amused sympathy. "Why Madam, this is a provoking piece of insolence, indeed, but there is no keeping these Black rascals within bounds," he told her. "It was but the other day that one of them undertook to impersonate Captain Squire, and actually extorted a sum of money from a lady in his name." He waved off her protests. "We must expect such things while this horrid rebellion lasts," he explained. She later thought this a poor excuse, since "he had excited the Negroes himself." The governor then asked about her husband, and she claimed not to know his whereabouts. "Well, madam, when you do, you must be sure and tell him for me that this is no time for a man like him to be out of the way. His Majesty wants his service." He promised finally, "I will give him any place he will name if he will come to join us. But join us he must."

After chatting a while longer, she rose to go. "His Lordship followed me to the door, and, offering me his arm, insisted on seeing me safe to my lodgings." She declined, with the excuse that "there was some risk" to her person—and perhaps to her reputation—were she seen strolling at night with the governor. "Oh, don't trouble yourself, my Lord," she told him. "It is but a step, and besides, I am afraid there is danger by the way, as some of our men may be lurking about and watching for a chance to shoot you." The truth was, she added later, "I was only afraid that they might miss their mark and shoot me." He persisted. "Never fear—my sentries are all about and I can't be caught napping." She took his arm, she said, "and he escorted me very politely to Billy White's door, where he bade me good night, but not 'til he had charged me again to be sure and tell Mr. Maxwell that he was very anxious to see him."

When she entered the inn, loyalist guests "had a rousing fire below and were very merry." She went upstairs to her room, across the hall from her sleeping sister. As she prepared for bed, "a servant girl"—almost certainly an enslaved woman—"came in to say that there was someone at the bottom of the garden wanting to see me." She followed to find her patriot husband standing in the shadows and warned him that Dunmore wanted him to enlist, then convinced him to spend the night with her before going back into hiding.

They were awakened in the middle of the night to moonlight glinting off two tall grenadiers apparently acting on a tip, perhaps from the Black servant. "What do you want?" demanded the husband. "What do you mean by breaking in here in this dead hour of the night?" One of the soldiers ordered him to hush "or you are a dead man." Maxwell's husband told them to leave, "for your officers are below and I will call them up." The grenadier "made a pass at him with his bayonet, which went through his shirt and even grazed his breast." Both soldiers then fled, with the husband in pursuit. Maxwell rushed to her sister's room and was alarmed to find it empty. She threw on a dressing gown and "followed the chase." Her sister and several other anxious guests, awakened by the commotion, stood anxiously at the bottom of the stairs. Her husband was pointing out the open window that the soldiers had used for a quick escape. "I know them and will have them punished for this outrage in the morning," he told the others. Everyone shuffled back to bed.

When Maxwell awoke the next morning, her husband was gone. She spotted him again a few days later wearing "a bit of red cloth on the breast of his coat." Outraged, she told him, "I would rather had seen you dead than to have seen you with this red badge." Her husband interrupted her. "Don't you see how Dunmore is carrying all before him?" he replied. "If I can save my property by this step, ought I not in common prudence wear it, for your sake and the children? But I tell you again, you may be perfectly sure that I shall never join the enemy."

More than one hundred patriots who fought against the British and loyalists at Kemp's Landing took the oath in the wake of the battle, according to the governor, as did some five hundred other Princess Anne County residents. They vowed to reject "a factious set of men styling themselves committees, conventions, and congresses" intent on exposing "us all to the horrors of civil war." Those who signed became members of the "Association of Loyal Virginians" and promised to "oppose their marching into this county . . . to the last drop of our blood." Like Maxwell's husband, many of these white converts were simply hedging their bets. For those enslaved, however, there was no turning back.

Dunmore marched out of Kemp's Landing late on the morning of November 16 at the head of his multiracial troops with fifteen patriot officers as prisoners, including the wounded Colonel Hutchings. They traveled on the road paralleling the Elizabeth's eastern branch until they came to the intersection with Church Street and turned left to cross Norfolk's isthmus into downtown. By two in the afternoon, a celebratory crowd had gathered in Market Square, where the tall brick courthouse looked over the river and Portsmouth beyond.

Scottish eyewitness John Brown said that "an entertainment was provided by the inhabitants for His Excellency and those under his command, and the standard erected before the courthouse, and the whole county striving who can get first to the book" to sign the loyalty oath. Brown was optimistic that "through the vigilance of Lord Dunmore," trade would be restored. "The earl was," he added, "so much admired in this part of the country, that he might have 500 volunteers to march with him to every part of Virginia."

An army required cash, so Dunmore's next stop that afternoon was to the palatial Portsmouth home of Neil Jamieson, also known as "complete master of trade in the bay." A sea captain who had come to Norfolk in the 1750s, he had worked for a large Glasgow firm before establishing his own business. He had bought wheat from Washington, sold enslaved Africans to tobacco planters, and purchased shares in Norfolk's distillery and tannery businesses. He also owned twenty-six houses and numerous vessels. His sixty-foot-wide brick home was part of a compound with two warehouses and its own wharf.

Unlike Sprowle and Parker, Jamieson had kept a low profile amid the growing conflict. Like other residents of the port, though, he lived in constant terror. "It is a disagreeable situation to be in, to be lying all night in fear, with loaded arms at your bedside, for fear of being alarmed or set upon," he confided to a Glasgow friend. "I don't know a man who had any property left here but myself." Jamieson had bought, at a high price, three small vessels on which to stow his rum and sugar stocks, and packed his personal effects so that they could be carried from his home to a vessel within half an hour.

"Lord Dunmore has applied to me to negotiate money matters," he wrote a colleague in Scotland on November 17. "I am not fond of this business, but if he urges it, and gives the necessary security, I suppose I must comply." He was reluctant to choose a side but felt obliged to help a fellow Scot. He also trusted Dunmore. "His Lordship is a humane good man and will use as much lenity as in prudence may be necessary." He agreed to loan the staggering sum of 5,000 pounds, and also to import clothing, sailcloth, potatoes, and other needed supplies from Glasgow. They agreed to keep the deal secret to protect Jamieson's publicly neutral stance.

In the days that followed, Dunmore's gamble seemed to have paid off. At least five hundred white men in Norfolk took the pledge. With those in neighboring counties, the governor on paper had more than three thousand loyalists at his back. "The whole counties of Norfolk and Princess Anne to a man has come into the standard which is now erected at Norfolk," wrote one local merchant. "I think the government will have such a party here that the shirtmen dare not face." He even urged his brother in Glasgow to send a vessel from Scotland packed with cloth, canvas, linens, nails, and stockings. "You'll never have such a [chance] to make money in dry goods in this country."

A second trader was also upbeat. "The late engagement at Kemp's, I believe, has been sufficient for numbers who have been constrained to throw off the yoke and boldly to stand forth and confess themselves friends of government." A third merchant echoed their optimism. "Things seem to take a favorable turn in favor of government in this neighborhood, but up the country continued as violent as ever," he wrote, adding that "we are in great hopes this proclamation may be of service." A fourth observed a "great many" from neighboring counties and North Carolina who were "daily coming into the governor for protection, which has entirely changed the face of affairs here." He was suddenly confident that "with the assistance of the king's ships and forces here, [they could] withstand the whole united force of the rest of the colony." A team of Scottish and Black men had completed the small stockade at Great Bridge, dubbed Fort Murray after the governor's clan, and pulled up the span's planks to block a rebel advance. "Lord Dunmore has gained the hearts of the people so much that they come flocking," wrote John Ewing, a Portsmouth loyalist, "like bees to the hive."

However, a Portsmouth baker named John Johnson provided one of the most astute analyses of the fast-moving events in a letter to his brother. He doubted that the last-minute attempt to recruit Black soldiers would alter the balance of power in favor of the loyalists. "This, I am afraid, will bring many of these poor wretches to a violent death." He added that if Woodford's army overwhelmed the city, "I am afraid it will be as bad if not worse than the rebellion in Scotland," referring to the bloody aftermath of Bonnie Prince Charlie's failed revolt.

Johnson dismissed the Committee of Safety's solemn promise to safeguard lives and property, predicting the patriots still "intend burning the town, either because they think many are well-disposed to government, or that it will be made a garrisoned place, and a station for troops and ships." Were the rebels to seize the town and force the loyalists on board vessels, he predicted the shirtmen would "gall the ships by taking station behind houses, and with their rifles firing at men who appear on the ships' decks." This scenario would force the warships to respond, which "may cause the destruction of this place."

For another Portsmouth businessman from Scotland, Andrew Miller, disaster was inevitable. "We expect that both Portsmouth and Norfolk will be blowed to pieces," he wrote on November 17. "For our governor John Earl of Dunmore has unsheathed his sword against the shirt army." He was certain he would be called up to fight, but he did relish one thought. Scots taking up arms were sure to enrage the patriots. This, he wrote gleefully, would "stink in their noses."

When the mass slave insurrection long feared by whites came to Virginia in the fall of 1775, it was not in the form of nighttime murders, mealtime poisoning, or other grisly forms of retribution long anticipated by their anxious owners. Instead, those in bondage walked, paddled, sailed, and rode away. Long before Dunmore made his proclamation, they arrived at Gosport or at the refugee camps that sprang up in and around Norfolk. Yet while there is voluminous correspondence from the far smaller community of Scottish merchants, not a single first-person account of the enslaved people who made the dangerous dash to Dunmore is known to survive. It is not even clear how many arrived behind British lines before and after the proclamation; estimates vary from eight hundred to several thousand.

Remnants of individual stories can be found in the back pages of the *Gazettes*, where owners placed ads for their lost human property along with those for horses and real estate. In September, an unnamed man on a Potomac River plantation stole a boat and was presumed to be heading to Norfolk, where, his owner said, "he may expect to be harbored and protected." Soon after, Daniel from Princess Anne County took two boys—possibly his sons—and was thought to be "lurking about Norfolk."

On November 7, as Dunmore penned his proclamation, Charles slipped away from his owner Robert Brent who lived not far from Mount Vernon, taking several of Brent's shirts, two mares, and "a pair of new saddle bags." He escaped with a white servant and the help of a white man named Kelly who provided them with an oyster boat to take them to Norfolk. Brent described Charles as "a very shrewd sensible fellow" who could read and write, and insisted he had "always been remarkably indulged, indeed, too much so." His departure was not due to "a dread of whipping," Brent concluded, "but from a determined resolution to get liberty, as he conceived, by flying to Lord Dunmore." Washington's cousin Lund understood this desire. "Liberty," the Mount Vernon caretaker wrote to George Washington, "is sweet."

By the middle of autumn, Royal Naval vessels patrolling Virginia waters provided many enslaved people with door-to-door transportation. "Lord Dunmore sails up and down the river and where he finds a defenseless place, he lands, plunders the plantation, and carries off the Negroes," one Norfolk resident reported on October 28. A patriot complained of the earl's "piratical expeditions up and down our rivers in quest of hen-roosts, sheepfolds, cow-pens, and Negro-quarters, which he never omitted an opportunity of pillaging." Many of these expeditions would have been guided by the very people who had abandoned their forced labor camps and knew where provisions were kept. These missions used British ships and Virginia's waterways as a nautical Underground Railroad, with those already freed returning to offer escape to their friends and relatives still in bondage. During a November 28 raid on a plantation near Jamestown, for example, "some of Dunmore's bandits, about twelve, mostly Negroes, came ashore [and] carried off two Negro women."

Those who left represented only a small fraction of those who stayed, but they made up the largest single flight to freedom of enslaved people in colonial North America. Their absence would have been keenly felt. Tobacco went uncured, seed beds lay untended, and horses and cattle grew thirsty. Laundry languished in bins, and fewer pitchers of fresh water were set daily on an owner's dressing table. The boycott of British goods meant that Virginians required more, not less, enslaved labor. Flax had to be processed and woven to make clothes, herbs gathered to imitate tea, and iron tools mended that couldn't be replaced. The November 15 proclamation threatened to accelerate the alarming labor drain, wreaking havoc not just on the social order but on an economy deeply dependent on unpaid workers.

Within two days of the decree's publication, patriots rushed to stem escapes using a mixture of threats and promises. "Be not, ye Negroes, tempted by this proclamation to ruin yourselves," declared one in the November 17 *Gazette*. "If they were told what a risk they run of being hanged if taken, and of having their wives and children cut off by our riflemen from the back country," then they would stay put, wrote another anonymous author in that issue. The riflemen, "who never wish to see a Negro," were sure to pour out their vengeance upon them. Those in bondage should instead patiently await "a better condition in the next world."

Pendleton had chosen this moment to take a mountain vacation, so Committee of Safety member John Page—one of Virginia's largest slaveowners—penned a counter-proclamation. It was published in the November 24 *Gazette*, next to the earl's document, along with a preface from the editor noting "the baseness of Lord Dunmore's heart, his malice and treachery." As Lee had done in scratching Shakespearean lines into a column at the Capitol, Page drew on *Macbeth*, the tragedy of a power-hungry Scottish lord. "Not in the legions of horrid hell, can come a devil more damn'd in evils, to top Dunmore."

Page's unsigned counter-proclamation was addressed directly to those enslaved and designed to be read out loud by their owners. Even the author admitted the goal of freedom was "very flattering and desirable to them." But he warned that those foolish enough to trust the British—the very people responsible for the "horrid traffic" in Africans—would suffer terrible consequences. Dunmore would "either give up the offending Negroes to the rigors of the laws they have broken or sell [them to] the West Indies," where they would "perish, either by the inclemency of the weather, or the cruelty of their barbarous masters." The governor was said to offer freedom not "out of any tenderness to them, but solely upon his own account." Their owners, in contrast, "wish, in general, to make it as easy and comfortable as possible."

If this was a kind of carrot, then came the stick. Anyone who escaped should expect harsh reprisals against their families, who would be "at the mercy of an enraged and injured people." Desertion would "provoke the fury of the Americans against their defenseless fathers and mothers, their wives, their women, and children." He urged those in bondage to consider what they "must expect to suffer if they fell into the hands of the Americans" during their escape, a reference to the legal code that punished insurrectionists with execution.

On the day of publication, Page lamented to Jefferson that "numbers of Negroes and cowardly scoundrels flock to [Dunmore's] standard." Two days later, a half dozen enslaved African men—Aaron, Harry, Lewis, Matthew, and two who were not named—stole a two-masted sailboat and set off down the James River for Norfolk under cover of a gale. A patriot patrol intercepted the craft, capturing two of the men, while the others managed to reach the port. Even as they made their escape, treasurer Robert Carter Nicholas noted, British ships were cruising up and down the rivers "using every art to seduce the Negroes." A multiracial band was reported to be terrorizing the countryside around the capital, in one case stealing "household furniture, four Negroes, a watch," and even "the bed on which several sick infants were reposing." The whites among them had "their faces blacked like Negroes, whose dear companions they are."

On November 25, a terrified patriot committee on the Eastern Shore sent John Hancock in Congress an urgent letter pleading for help. The peninsula shared by Virginia, Maryland, and Delaware was home to many enslaved people as well as poor whites who felt little love for the patriots. The committee feared an internal uprising combined with a seaborne invasion by Dunmore. Africans "would crowd to his standard, and his army become formidable in numbers," exposing residents to "the fury of his soldiers and slaves." The patriots had had little luck raising militia among "the fishermen and lower class of people," and they feared that white indentured servants would ally with enslaved people.

In one Maryland coastal county just to the north, a patriot raid on a Black arsenal netted "about eighty guns, some bayonets, swords, etc." The committee blamed "malicious and imprudent speeches of some among the lower classes of whites" aimed at convincing those in bondage "that their freedom depended on the success of the king's troops." The patriots also monitored those "who promote and encourage this disposition in our slaves." One man was tarred and feathered and exiled for "his intimacy and connections with the Negroes."

The threat of an uprising by "the lower classes of whites" and those enslaved extended to the Appalachians. On November 29, two white men in an iron foundry in far western Virginia made common cause with "a country-born Negro" named Will, who wore an iron collar, "being a notorious runaway." They fled across two hundred miles of dangerous territory to reach Norfolk.

Word of the proclamation prompted North Carolina militias to mobilize, while Maryland's patriots banned all mail from Virginia in a fruitless attempt to impose a news blackout. This was no longer a crisis—or opportunity—confined to Virginia. Even before word of the proclamation spread, enslaved people were on the move. The day after the proclamation was published, twenty-one-year-old and six-foot-tall Titus Cornelius escaped from his notoriously cruel Quaker owner in New Jersey, home to more than eight thousand people in bondage. Once he learned of Dunmore's pledge he headed south, evading patrols for hundreds of miles to reach Gosport. He would go on to become what one historian called "one of the war's most feared loyalists, white or black," known throughout the colonies as Colonel Tye. He led a loyalist brigade that harassed Washington's forces until patriots fatally wounded him in battle in 1780.

"Letters mention that slaves flock to him in abundance," Pendleton wrote of Dunmore in a November 27 letter to delegates in Congress after returning from his vacation, "but I hope it is magnified." Newspapers even solicited the views of enslaved Africans, or at least claimed to do so. A December 9 *Gazette* article highlighted the governor's hypocrisy in offering liberty only to those he did not own. An enslaved Yorktown barber named Caesar was reported to say that he "did not know anyone foolish enough" to accept Dunmore's offer. If the governor intended to emancipate Africans, the man is quoted as saying, "he ought first to set his own free."*

Subsequent ads in the three Williamsburg publications show an uptick in boats and horses stolen along with a larger number of runaways than usual, prompting increased patrols. "Rivers will henceforth be strictly watched, and every possible precaution taken," a patriot officer ordered on December 2. Many of those who fled were intercepted by these patrols, and Virginia's county jails were soon bursting at the seams. "The Negroes we have from divers quarters found going over to the governor and secured, are become too numerous," complained one Hampton patriot, who noted fourteen people were crammed into the small space.

Those fleeing slavery now differed not just in sheer numbers but in age and gender from those who had fled in the past. Before 1775, the typical runaway was a young man, often carrying a musical instrument, who was more likely seeking precious time with a distant wife or girlfriend than complete liberation. Dunmore's November proclamation may have declared freedom only for those "able and willing to bear arms," but that autumn, whole families and single women made the dash to freedom along with fighting-age men. In late November,

* Classical names such as Caesar were commonly bestowed by owners on those enslaved, either in mockery or to showcase the white man's superior education—or both.

two enslaved women joined seven men in an attempt to reach Norfolk by boat, though they were captured near Hampton and jailed.

In countless shacks, barns, attics, basements, and cabins throughout Virginia and beyond, enslaved Africans held whispered debates and endured heartbreaking leave-takings. Choosing the possibility of emancipation over continued captivity was very possibly a life-or-death decision. The rapidly changing situation made it difficult to determine which side had the upper hand. The pro-patriot newspapers warned that Dunmore could not be trusted, and promised vengeance against those who joined the loyalists. Anyone who left might endanger those who stayed behind. Yet the communications network of the enslaved confirmed that those who succeeded in the dangerous dash would be safe and, possibly, free.

Even if Dunmore lived up to his pledge, the risks in running were enormous. Many no doubt believed the patriot propaganda, feared retribution against their loved ones, or simply did not want to risk torture or execution if caught. Others would have waited for a more propitious moment, such as the arrival of a large British force or an attack on Williamsburg by Dunmore that would force a patriot retreat. Yet even if they chose to remain, each of Virginia's 200,000-plus enslaved people, as well as the roughly 300,000 who lived in the other dozen colonies, could suddenly imagine a clear path to liberation.

Chapter Eighteen

To Quicken All in Revolution

Ten days after Dunmore made his proclamation, Colonel Woodford crossed the Nansemond River with the first of his troops, including "forty gentlemen volunteers." They landed November 25 on a wharf at Suffolk, a small trading town midway between Jamestown and Norfolk. The settlement marked the porous boundary between the patriot-friendly territory to the west and the loyalist-leaning Norfolk and Princess Anne Counties to the east.

A feisty pastor named John Agnew had long preached here against the patriot cause. The Glasgow-born minister, whom Jefferson called "an irascible old gentleman," warned that the colony's gentry sought war with Britain for their own ends and at the expense of small farmers and laborers. This view was not uncommon. "The American opposition to Great Britain is not calculated or designed for the defense of American liberty or property," asserted one Maryland farmer, "but for the purpose of enslaving the poor people."

In March 1775, Agnew had mounted the pulpit to preach that "the great men" intended to "ruin the poor people, and that after a while they would forsake them and lay the whole blame on their shoulders, and by this means make them slaves." Before the service was over, armed patriots had then burst into the church, taking the parson into custody as the mortified worshipers looked helplessly on. He was later confined in Williamsburg's notorious jail, but other less vocal loyalists still resided in the area.

Woodford now ordered his men to confiscate the townspeople's weapons and detain eight loyalist suspects. Among them was Betsy Hunter, a relation of Andrew Sprowle, who was in Suffolk to attend a wedding. The colonel, who called her "a Scotch lass," deemed the entire wedding party suspicious and held them in custody. There were rumors that Dunmore intended to attack Woodford's strung-out forces, which lacked sufficient bullets and powder to put up a fight. Logistical complications continued to hamper their stop-and-start three-week march. Horses escaped, food was meager, and discipline was difficult to maintain. The dry and sunny fall weather soon gave way to the cold and damp of the approaching winter.

After making camp and posting sentries, Woodford sent an advance party of some two hundred men to Great Bridge under the command of thirty-six-year-old Lieutenant Colonel Charles Scott, a future governor of Kentucky. Their purpose was to reconnoiter British and loyalist lines ahead. The rough twenty-two-mile track skirted the northern boundary of the Great Dismal Swamp. Washington, Tucker, Parker, and other entrepreneurs had tried without success to transform this quagmire of peat, roots, and fallen trees into fertile farmland. Many of the unfree workers given this onerous task had chosen instead to flee deeper into the swamps, already sprinkled with small communities of those who had escaped bondage.

Connolly's unlucky companion John Smyth, now confined in a Philadelphia jail, left a vivid description of this wilderness when he followed the same track on his way to Norfolk in the early fall of 1775. He had evaded a patriot patrol on the road with the help of a local Black man. "I gave the Negro two dollars to carry me immediately into a private place in the Great Dismal Swamp," he wrote. They entered the thirty-mile-wide wilderness filled with "astonishing numbers of bears, wolves, panthers, wildcats, opossums, raccoons, snakes, some deer, and every kind of wild beasts." Cypress grew "in almost impenetrable closeness" that made for a "dark and dreary shade altogether impervious to the rays of the sun." A strange silence hung in the air, "for the woods are so close as to prevent the vibration of the air for any distance through them; even the report of firearms is smothered." At the center of the swamp lay mysterious

Lake Drummond, an oval body of water fed by no visible stream that geologists believe was formed by an ancient meteorite strike.

Scott and his shirtmen made their way cautiously down the road cut through the edge of the dense marsh. The lieutenant colonel found the locals "a cowardly set," and relayed word back to Woodford that "the inhabitants are all Tories and have taken the oath to defend the governor." That oath, Woodford believed, was "worse than the proclamation" in drawing recruits, suggesting that it had an even more electrifying effect on white inhabitants than the edict had on those enslaved.

Night had fallen when the tired men reached a small church at a fork in the road. To the right was the path leading south to North Carolina. Ahead was the village of Great Bridge. They moved quietly past the darkened brick and clapboard homes and shops lining the sole street; many of the residents had fled. Scott dispatched scouts to cross the two short spans over marshy creeks that led to a treeless causeway dotted with warehouses. This was where farmers and merchants stored their corn, pork, pine, cedar shingles, and turpentine, which were then sent by barge or ship downstream to Norfolk.

Beyond was the plankless bridge over the southern branch of the Elizabeth River. The newly built Fort Murray rose on the opposite shore, next to the road that continued on to Kemp's Landing. Marsh and river surrounded three sides of the wooden redoubt, manned that night by two dozen British regulars, a similar number of white volunteers, "and about fifty Negroes, whom," Dunmore said, "I now arm and discipline as fast as they come in." Peering through the darkness, Scott's scouts made out "some soldiers and many Negroes" and noticed "several officers there nearly drunk."

Just after midnight, the patriots encountered a small party on horseback, including "Lord Dunmore's secretary, a young gentleman from Maryland, and a Negro." The secretary was John Hunter, Sprowle's stepson and brother of the incarcerated Betsy. "After firing three or four shot[s], the Marylander surrendered," Scott reported. Hunter and "the Negro escaped, aided by the night." The captive said they had been sent by Dunmore to check on the redoubt's progress. He also revealed that the earl was arming Black volunteers. "Several of the principal Scottish Tories in Norfolk, I'm told, command Black companies," Woodford added in a report to Pendleton, "and speak with great confidence of beating us with the odds of five to one." He also had heard, however, that "none of them it is expected will fight."

The brief November 25 shootout ruined Scott's chance of surprising the small garrison, but he still saw a golden opportunity. "I can't help thinking that no time should be lost in attacking them while unprepared to receive us," he scribbled to Woodford. "If the attack is delayed a day or two, his Lordship (if he intends to defend the bridge) will have it in his power to place his cannon and render our passage over with all our troops rather difficult." A rider relayed the message to Suffolk. Woodford, however, feared the advance party lacked the necessary men, shot, and powder, and ordered Scott to stand down. The North Carolina militia was said to be within a day's march. By that time, the Virginian colonel would have his forces in place at Great Bridge. The combined troops would then outnumber the governor's men.

Both sides prepared for a showdown as a damp wind swirled the fallen leaves and a cold rain began to soak the unprotected shirtmen. Hearing of the patriot forces' arrival, Captain Leslie ordered Fort Murray reinforced with "twenty-five British regulars, some volunteers, and many Negroes," along with two four-pound cannons, swivel guns, and other smaller mounted weapons brought from the ships. "The rebels could not easily get possession of that post," Leslie wrote General Howe, the British commander in Boston, on November 28, "unless they brought artillery against it, which, by all accounts, they have not any at present."

That day, a unit of patriot riflemen arrived while Scott's men were digging breastworks between the village and the causeway. Twenty of these western men shouldered their highly accurate guns and sauntered past, wearing moccasins, hunting shirts, and coonskin caps, and crossed the four-hundred-yard-long causeway. When they were seventy yards from the bridge, they raised their weapons and opened fire. Unlike at Hampton, however, the enemy was safe behind a palisade. The British responded with a hail of cannon balls. One soared across the marsh and slammed into a corporal, ripping his body apart and killing him instantly. A second man was badly injured.

After a couple of hours of desultory fire, the patriots withdrew. The battle of Great Bridge had begun.

"We took possession of this town the 23rd [of November] and are now busy entrenching ourselves in the best manner we can," Leslie wrote General Howe from his new headquarters in Norfolk. "A large body of the rebels, consisting of eight or nine hundred men, are within ten or twelve miles of us," he added. "They marched from Williamsburg about a fortnight ago, with an intention to pillage and burn this town, which, however, we shall do everything that is possible to prevent."

The governor, army officers, and naval commanders had finally agreed to prepare for a lengthy land siege of what one patriot called a town "well calculated for defense." As the British had done in Boston, they built earthen fortifications across the narrow neck that led into town. Norfolk's land bridge, however, stood between shallow creeks rather than deep bays. And while the Massachusetts capital lay wholly on a large peninsula, the Virginia port's suburbs and industrial areas were exposed on the mainland. The British in New England also had spent months perfecting their defensive line, while Dunmore had only days. Black and white volunteers immediately began to labor on the earthen walls amid worsening weather. A Williamsburg paper, no doubt exaggerating conditions to discourage enslaved Africans from joining the effort, reported that many had fled after "digging entrenchments in wet ground" and suffering from "hungry bellies, naked backs, and no fuel."

Leslie intended to install ship's cannons along the earthworks to repel a patriot assault from land. To ensure a clear field of fire, crews set to work on November 30 demolishing thirty-two buildings, including the homes of tavern keeper James Atkinson, carpenter Sam Denny, silversmith Rich Pickadrick, cooper William Smith, and merchant William Chisholm. They also pulled down the regal residence of Samuel Boush Jr., a wealthy Norfolk burgess who by then had left town for his country home near Great Bridge.

The British defenses of Boston were manned by more than 6,000 redcoats. Dunmore had fewer than 150 British soldiers. Local white loyalists who had signed the oath were unlikely to fill the gap. In a December 6 letter to Dartmouth, the earl estimated that only one in ten was "in any degree capable of bearing arms, and the greatest part of these hardly ever made use of the gun." Hundreds of enslaved men provided a large new pool of motivated recruits, but they required extensive training as well. Virginia law forbade those in bondage from owning a firearm, and most Scottish merchants had no experience with warfare either. All had to learn to handle a weapon, march, understand and follow commands, and fight as a cohesive force even as a large army was approaching. It was a task even Bonnie Prince Charlie would have found daunting.

The governor nevertheless exuded optimism. "I hope a short time (if they are willing) will make them as good if not better than those who are come down to oppose them," he wrote Dartmouth. "I am now endeavoring to raise two regiments. One of white people, called the Queen's Own Loyal Virginia Regiment, the other of Negroes, called Lord Dunmore's Ethiopian Regiment." The former had five hundred recruits of local white men divided into ten companies, while the latter consisted of some two to three hundred Black volunteers.

The name of the Black unit sent a powerful message, since the governor attached his own name, and "Ethiopian" was a rare term of respect accorded to Africans by Europeans. The name referred to the East African Christian kingdom and stems from an Amharic term that ancient Greeks translated to mean "burnt faces" or "born under the sun's path." Homer praised the Ethiopian king in the *Iliad*, a fact that would have been known to the well-read governor. Europeans, noted sociologist W. E. B. Dubois, came to "refer to the ancient Ethiopians in exalted terms, and consider them the oldest, wisest, and most just of men."

Dunmore assigned "white officers and non-commissioned officers" to oversee the Black soldiers, who likely were organized in a similar fashion to the white troops. At least four Black men were eventually promoted to the ranks of corporal and sergeant. The enlisted men ranged from teenagers to middle-aged men, and included a broad mix of field hands, house servants, sailors, and artisans, both free and enslaved. Among them was Peter Anderson, one of Talbot Thompson's sailmakers. There was also Will, the "notorious runaway" who had fled from the western part of the state wearing an iron collar, and Aaron, Harry, Lewis, and Matthew, who had escaped to Norfolk by boat.

Twenty-four-year-old Major Thomas Taylor Byrd, an officer in the Fourteenth Regiment, commanded both new regiments. He carried the name of one of Virginia's oldest and most conflicted wealthy families. While Thomas remained true to the king, his brother Francis had just resigned from the British Navy to serve under Washington. Their father, William Byrd III—an infamous gambler said to have driven their mother to suicide—had been a staunch loyalist and had cut Francis out of his will. But when Dunmore proclaimed emancipation, the volatile patriarch threw in with the rebels and spurned Thomas instead. The stresses would prove too much; within a year the men's father would be dead by his own hand. One of the Ethiopian Regiment's early members was one William Byrd, almost certainly enslaved by the elder white man.

With limited numbers of muskets, some soldiers had to make do with swords, lances, pikes, and other weapons for hand-to-hand combat. At least some Ethiopian Regiment soldiers were issued surplus Fourteenth Regiment coats, though most of them would have made do with coarse white linen or whatever clothes they could obtain. A December 2 *Gazette* article reported that Black soldiers, like the shirtmen, sported a motto, either stamped on metal or sewn into their uniforms. If true, the slogan was a direct rebuke to Patrick Henry's followers. Rather than "Liberty or Death," it read "Liberty for Slaves." In the conflict about to unfold, both sides claimed to fight for freedom.

Dunmore's decree and loyalty oath produced the men he desperately needed to oppose the advancing patriots, but at a cost. "The inhabitants of this colony are deeply alarmed at this infernal scheme," one white traveler in western Virginia reported soon after it was made public. "It seems to quicken all in revolution." The governor's move promised to draw undecided white colonists to the American cause. "The proclamation from Lord Dunmore has had a most extensive good consequence," one Virginia planter wrote Richard Henry Lee. "Men of all ranks resent the pointing a dagger to their throats, through the hands of their slaves."

Lee agreed with that assessment. "Lord Dunmore's unparalleled conduct in Virginia has, a few Scots excepted, united every man in that large colony," he wrote his British friend and historian Catharine Macauley on November 29. "If administration had searched through the world for a person the best fitted to ruin their cause, and procure union and success for these colonies, they could not have found a more complete agent."

The impact of the earl's decree rippled far beyond the colony's borders. South Carolina patriot Edward Rutledge declared it would "more effectively work an external separation between Great Britain and the colonies than any other expedient which could possibly be thought of." Members of Congress were said to be anxious, as "great numbers of people, white and black, had repaired to the King's standard," according to a letter published in a Philadelphia newspaper on December 6. Many of Virginia's eastern elite were tempted to join "this Jacobite Scotch fortunist," even though "all the Virginia and North Carolina troops are in full march against him," the correspondent wrote. "Hell itself could not have vomited anything more black than his design of emancipating our slaves," the writer concluded, adding, "we know not how far the contagion may spread. The flame runs like wildfire through the slaves." The author noted ominously that "the subject of their nocturnal revels, instead of music and dancing, is now turned upon their liberty."

The decree also upended old rules of racial behavior. Another Philadelphia paper reported that when a white woman reprimanded a Black man for failing to give way on a narrow sidewalk, as custom demanded, he bridled. "Stay, you damned white bitch, 'til Lord Dunmore and his Black regiment come, and then we will see who is to take the wall." Even if the story was a patriot fabrication, it conveys the unease and even terror felt by whites in the proclamation's wake.

Hancock received a copy of Dunmore's decree on December 2 and immediately informed Washington. "Lord Dunmore has erected his standard at Norfolk, proclaimed martial law, invited the Negroes to join him, and offered them freedom," he wrote. Norfolk and Princess Anne Counties "have been obliged to submit to him," the Continental Congress president added. He hoped that measures were being taken "as will speedily and effectually repel his violence and secure the peace and safety of that colony."

The bland language disguises deep dismay. The bold stance taken in Philadelphia by Virginia delegates such as Henry and then Jefferson masked the political and military vulnerability within their home colony. Dunmore's proclamation made it clear that the province had become a key battleground in the conflict. The loss of Virginia would sever contact between North and South, inspire loyalists to take up arms, and give Britain a chance to negotiate separate agreements with individual colonies. The large and wealthy province also was essential to provide the men, provisions, and finances essential to take on Great Britain. Without Virginia's firm support, the patriot cause might collapse into small regional rebellions, uprisings more easily extinguished by London.

Within two days of the decree's arrival in Congress, delegates called for Pennsylvania, given its proximity, to send three companies to its southern neighbor to fight "the enemies of America." In the meantime, they urged Virginians to "resist to the utmost the arbitrary government intended to be established by Governor Lord Dunmore," and criticized his proclamation for "tearing up the foundations of civil authority and government."

They also urged the Virginia Convention to form its own independent representative government to "most effectually secure peace and good order in the colony." This last recommendation reflected fears that Virginia was descending into a chaotic civil war, with patriot planters caught between Dunmore and unruly white farmers demanding a larger share of power. The Philadelphia delegates also forbade individual provinces from seeking accommodation with the enemy, a warning clearly aimed at conservative leaders like Pendleton, who had long championed negotiation over war.

Inaction, incompetence, and infighting among Virginia's patriots had given Dunmore precious time to build up his forces. "All this would have been prevented if our troops could have crossed the James in the proper time," Richard Henry Lee lamented to Washington on December 6. "It seems this unlucky triumph over Hutchings, with his less than half-armed militia, so dispirited the miserable wretches in that neighborhood, that many have taken an oath of Lord Dunmore's," Lee added.

The Virginia delegate had spent the fall pressing his colleagues in the Continental Congress to create a navy to take on the royal governor, citing "our water-intersected country," where "a small number of men provided with naval force can harass us extremely." Given the expense, Maryland's Samuel Chase dismissed the suggestion as "the maddest idea in the world," but Congress finally approved the purchase of a small fleet of merchant vessels. The day after Lee wrote Washington, a promising young Scottish-born lieutenant named John Paul Jones stood on the deck of the *Alfred* anchored off Philadelphia and "hoisted the flag of America with my own hands, the first time it was ever displayed," Jones later recalled. "The object of the first expedition was against Lord Dunmore in Virginia." A month would pass before formal orders were issued, but the inaugural mission of what would become the United States Navy was to attack the earl's multiracial force of British troops and loyalists.

The governor's decree only reached distant Massachusetts in mid-December. From Philadelphia, Samuel Adams wrote a friend in his home state with the distressing news, adding that Norfolk was "a town inhabited by Scotch Tories, and such weak and timid people as they prevail upon to join them." One Massachusetts militia officer told John Adams, "We are somewhat alarmed with Dunmore['s] ferocity . . . but hope that he will be soon crushed." When Washington learned of the proclamation, he responded to Hancock in the calm manner typical of his official correspondence. "I make no doubt but that the Congress will take every necessary measure to dispossess Lord Dunmore of his hold in Virginia," he wrote evenly on December 14. "The sooner steps are taken for that purpose, the more probability there will be of their being effectual."

Three days later, Dunmore's letters intended for General Howe and Admiral Graves in Boston fell into Washington's hands after a patriot privateer captured the British sloop carrying the dispatches, as well as "Indian corn, potatoes, and oats" for hungry Boston troops. Those revealed that the governor had enough food to ship a cargo north. "We keep them in continual hot water," Dunmore had written Howe of Virginia's rebels, and "the Negroes are flocking in from all quarters." He begged for field pieces, troops, and "one of the line of battle ships," adding, "We have thrown up an entrenchment on the land side of Norfolk which I hope they will never be able to force."

A dismayed Washington sent the correspondence to Philadelphia via express messenger rather than trust it to "a common express." He again called upon Congress "to dispossess his Lordship of the strong hold he has got in Virginia," but this time strayed from his usual dry language to make the point more forcefully. "I do not mean to dictate," he told Hancock, "but I am sure they will pardon me for giving them freely my opinion, which is, that the fate of America a good deal depends on his being obliged to evacuate Norfolk this winter."

No patriot knew Dunmore better than the head of the Continental Army. Washington realized the governor was a potent threat to the rebellion, not the drunken degenerate of the newspapers. He confessed his worries to Lee. "If, my dear sir, that man is not crushed before spring, he will become the most formidable enemy America has—his strength will increase as a snowball by rolling; and faster, if some expedient cannot be hit upon to convince the slaves and servants of the impotency of his designs." He also grasped that forcing Dunmore and his troops onto ships was not enough. With the earl bent on "the total destruction of the colony," the general warned, "nothing less than depriving him of life or liberty will secure peace to Virginia."

This was no momentary outburst. Washington repeated the snowball analogy in a letter to one of his officers. Defeating the earl, he explained, was "indispensably necessary" primarily because of "the Negroes; for if he gets formidable, numbers of them will be tempted to join who will be afraid to do it without." He added, "If the Virginians are wise, that arch traitor to the rights of humanity, Lord Dunmore, should be instantly crushed, if it takes the force of the whole colony to do it. Otherwise, like a snowball in rolling, his army will get size."

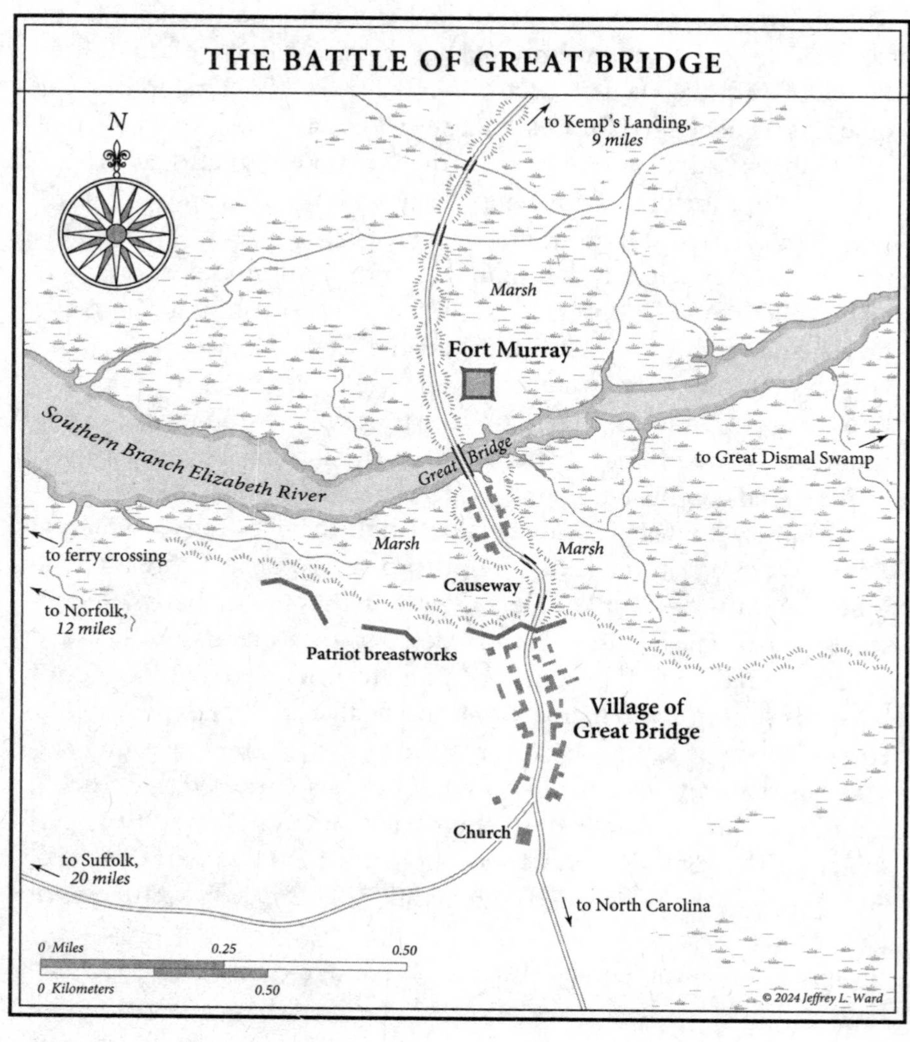
THE BATTLE OF GREAT BRIDGE
N
to Kemp's Landing, 9 miles
Marsh
Fort Murray
Southern Branch Elizabeth River
Great Bridge
to Great Dismal Swamp
to ferry crossing
Marsh
Marsh
Causeway
to Norfolk, 12 miles
Patriot breastworks
Village of Great Bridge
Church
to Suffolk, 20 miles
to North Carolina
0 Miles
0.25
0.50
0 Kilometers
0.50
© 2024 Jeffrey L. Ward

Chapter Nineteen

The Infernal Regions

During the first week that the two sides faced off at Great Bridge, neither gained the advantage. "Their riflemen keep up an almost constant fire, but hitherto without much success," wrote Captain Charles Fordyce, who led Britain's Fourteenth Regiment contingent at Fort Murray, on December 1. His own barrages had little effect against the stout breastworks the patriots had thrown up between the wooden span over the southern branch of the Elizabeth River and the village. After the initial skirmish the previous week, patriots counted only one man injured, though Colonel Woodford claimed that many Black spies—or suspected spies—were "killed or wounded by our people."

"What a pity it is that this colony should have been so much neglected," Fordyce wrote to a fellow officer, adding that "a couple of thousand men would settle everything." Now he watched with concern as the enemy trenches swelled with nearly a thousand soldiers. "Would to God we had a few more men," he wrote. "And I think we should give a very good account of these rascals; but we are at present a very handful." He feared the riflemen would infiltrate the warehouses on the causeway and use them as cover to pick off the few soldiers he had. That night he sent a party of Ethiopian Regiment soldiers to destroy five of the potential sniper's nests. The men slid along the sides of the bridge and crossed to the causeway to set the offending structures alight. Patriot sentinels briefly opened fire until the dancing flames backlit their positions, forcing them to withdraw.

Woodford arrived from Suffolk the next day to find the warehouses a smoldering heap. The enemy, he wrote, "keep up a constant fire," and "their numbers in the fort are said to be 250, chiefly Blacks," though the actual number was far smaller. The shirtmen disdainfully nicknamed Fort Murray "the hog pen." Their colonel did not share their contempt. "Their situation is very advantageous," he wrote, and there was "no way to attack them but by exposing most of the troops to their fire upon a large open marsh."

He begged Williamsburg to send more gunpowder and men, as well as cannon to smash through the vulnerable wooden stockade. "We are situated here in mud and mire, exposed to every hardship that can be conceived," he complained to Patrick Henry on December 3. He also noted "the want of provisions, of which our stock is but small," adding that the men were "suffering for shoes, and if ever soldiers deserved a second blanket in any service, they do in this." The regiment's orderly book cites "the filth in and about their camp and houses," warning that it would breed "infectious diseases amongst us." The shirtmen were restless, and at least one was tried for theft, while others wandered away from camp at will. Woodford needed a quick victory, as this marshy and remote site was no place to conduct a long winter siege.

The first skirmishes centered on a small earthwork on the far shore of a ferry crossing a half dozen miles downstream, halfway to Gosport. British regulars and some three dozen Black soldiers guarded the site to prevent shirtmen from crossing and encircling Fort Murray. When Lieutenant Colonel Charles Scott, who had led the first patriot troops to Great Bridge, learned of the enemy camp on December 3, he gathered a unit to reconnoiter. "A party of the king's troops and several Negroes" immediately crossed the river and attacked, "upon which some of our people gave ground," he reported. The sight of Black men wielding guns apparently unnerved many patriots, who fled. When the shirtmen soon returned with reinforcements, they gunned down at least seven of the enemy, including the British officer who had led the initial assault. Survivors retreated to the safety of their breastwork adjacent to the ferry house.

This minor clash at a forgotten ford marked the first recorded fight in British North America pitting a unit of organized Black soldiers against white Americans. Not only were members of the new Ethiopian corps willing to fight, but they also took the offensive.

At midnight on December 5, a party of one hundred patriots climbed quietly into small boats and paddled across the river to attack the same outpost. They outnumbered the British and loyalist defenders on the opposite shore by more than three to one. A watchful Black sentry sounded the alarm by shooting at the approaching shirtmen. "Our people, being too eager, began the fire without orders, and kept it up very hot for near fifteen minutes," Scott wrote later that day. "We killed one, burnt another in the house, and took two prisoners (all blacks), with four exceeding fine muskets." The remainder—twenty-six Black men and nine white—"escaped under cover of the night." Unsure if the enemy would regroup and launch a counterattack, the patriots crossed back to their camp, ending what proved a botched assault.

They took with them the prisoners, including "Negro Ned," an enslaved man from Kemp's Landing. He told them that he had come from Norfolk that day "with twenty-odd Blacks and three whites." Ned added that "all the Blacks . . . at the Great Bridge [were] supplied with muskets, ammunition, etc., and ordered to use them." The second captive was George from Suffolk, who estimated there were four hundred Black soldiers in Norfolk and ninety at Great Bridge. The captives could not or would not say how many redcoats and white loyalists were with them.

Fordyce rushed more men from Fort Murray to the smoking ruin of the ferry redoubt to secure the position. "We still keep up a pretty heavy fire between light and light," an exhausted Scott wrote later in the day to another patriot officer, adding that two of his men were dead. "Last night was the first of my pulling of my clothes for twelve nights successively. We are surrounded with enemies. Believe me, my good friends, I never was so fatigued with duty in my whole life." He had to break off the letter. "A gun fired," he wrote, with startling immediacy. "I must stop."

On the night of December 6, the patriots made another sneak attack on the redoubt downriver from Fort Murray, this time with a much larger force of 150 men, twice that of the enemy. They killed "one white man and three Negroes" and took three Ethiopian

Regiment members captive, "two of which are wounded (one mortally)," according to Woodford. The patriots confiscated six muskets and three bayonets, additional evidence that the Black soldiers used firearms. Despite their overwhelming numbers, the shirtmen abruptly abandoned the fort when four men approached with a cart carrying supplies to Fort Murray and began firing on them. "All escaped unhurt," Woodford noted. "One man only was grazed by a ball in the thumb." By then, some twenty soldiers from the Ethiopian Regiment were dead, a far higher toll than among the British or patriots.

Dunmore sent an additional ninety soldiers to Fort Murray, while men from Patrick Henry's First Regiment in Williamsburg marched into the patriot camp. Woodford's troops gave them the cold shoulder, reflecting the tension between the two commanders. "Our reception at the Great Bridge was to the last degree cool, and absolutely disagreeable," complained one officer in a letter to Henry. "We arrived there fatigued, dry and hungry, we were neither welcomed, invited to eat or drink, or shown a place to rest our weary bones." Pendleton sent with them five hundred pounds of powder and fifteen hundred pounds of lead, along with his "hope you will send some of them to the infernal regions."

The Committee of Safety president was facing his own battle for survival. Like the House of Burgesses, each Virginia Convention was made up of county representatives elected by white males who owned enough property to qualify to vote. In November, despite the conflict, they flocked to their county seats to cast their ballots for the Fourth Virginia Convention. Pendleton and several other conservative incumbents nearly lost to more radical candidates, and these results sent shivers through the gentry. One feared the "lower classes of whites" might attempt to seize the reins of the rebellion.

When delegates convened on December 4 at the College of William and Mary—the Capitol had been converted to winter barracks—one of their first acts was to agree to form an independent government with "full and free representation of the people" to secure "peace and good order." This government, of course, would be created by the colony's wealthy planters and lawyers. The plan had the full backing of the Continental Congress, which saw it as a way to stabilize a Virginia that seemed to its elite planters to be tottering between the twin dangers of royalist control and anarchy.

Nearly six weeks had passed since the first soldiers had embarked on the campaign to attack Dunmore. Poor logistical planning by Henry and Pendleton left the army with inadequate food, bedding, medicines, weapons, and ammunition, a problem exacerbated by cold and rain. Members took turns blaming Pendleton's protégé, Woodford, for the slow progress. "Our army has been for some time arrested in its march to Norfolk by a redoubt or stockade or hog pen, as they call it here by way of derision," proclaimed Thomas Ludwell Lee. The fort, he added, was "filled with a parcel of wild boars, which we appear not overfond to meddle with." Pendleton's right-hand man, John Page, joined the chorus. In a letter to Richard Henry Lee, he scorned Woodford for fearing "a body of Negroes headed by Scotchmen and a few regulars." This delay, he warned, would allow Dunmore to make Norfolk "impregnable by land."

By early December, the governor had moved his headquarters to the roomier *Dunmore*, evidently settling in for a long winter stay in the harbor. He would just have received word of Connolly's arrest in Maryland and was aware that no British, French, or indigenous army would be sweeping east in the spring. Worse news arrived on Friday, December 8, as a chill rain splattered the large windows of his flagship's stern cabin. North Carolina shirtmen were approaching Great Bridge with cannon in tow. Fort Murray, he conceded, "was not in a condition to stand anything heavier than musket shot." If the patriots seized the bridge and redoubt, there was nothing to stop them from marching on Norfolk. The frantic earl called an immediate war council.

His senior officers, including Squire from the *Otter*, Montagu from the *Kingfisher*, and Leslie of the Fourteenth Regiment, gathered in the governor's cabin around a long table littered with letters, reports, and maps. Dunmore relayed the bad tidings, adding that if they did not act quickly, the patriots would splinter the fort's palisades into kindling and swarm across the river to decimate its defenders. The road to Norfolk would be theirs, and "the well-disposed people of this part of the country" would be subject "to the resentment of the rebels," as he later told the colonial secretary. The governor proposed an immediate surprise attack to overwhelm the rebels before their artillery and reinforcements arrived.

He and the officers worked up a battle plan reflecting standard military technique of the day. Leslie would gather more than one hundred redcoats—the bulk of the regulars—along with white volunteers and two companies from the Ethiopian Regiment in Norfolk. The men would leave that same night to travel up the southern branch of the Elizabeth River to Fort Murray. The Ethiopian troops, meanwhile, would "make a detour, and fall in behind the rebels a little before break of day." At dawn, the Black soldiers would "fall upon the rear of the rebels." This diversion, presumably at the disputed ferry crossing to the south, halfway to Norfolk, would draw the patriots out of their Great Bridge trenches to aid their embattled comrades downstream. Other Black soldiers would rush out of Fort Murray to replace the bridge planks, and Leslie with his redcoats would then "sally out of the fort and attack their breastwork."

It was a complicated operation, and there was little time for the officers to coordinate details and prepare their men, many of whom had yet to fire a gun in war. Two widely separated forces had to move like clockwork in the dark. A frontal assault against breastworks manned with riflemen was dangerous business even with a diversion and required enormous courage and stamina. Much depended on the psychological effect of redcoats with bayonets marching inexorably toward untested soldiers. "We hinted to him, as far as delicacy in our situation would permit, the absurdity and extravagant folly of so unnecessary an attempt," another officer later claimed. "It was in vain." Yet the governor faced a stark choice. Either he abandoned the strategic pass, allowing the patriots to swarm to Norfolk's doorstep, or he gambled on a quick and decisive victory. "I thought it advisable," he later wrote, "to risk something to save the fort."

Leslie, not Dunmore, would command the attack. Just three weeks before, the earl had led troops to Great Bridge and then to victory at Kemp's Landing, and he had participated in a number of military actions to seize patriot arms. A year previously, he had marched into enemy territory at the head of a large army. And rather than flee when militia threatened Williamsburg in April, he had fortified the Palace and distributed weapons to his servants, personally taking charge of the compound's defense. He had never shied from a fight. On that wet December evening, however, the middle-aged earl may have been ill or exhausted. One source claims he had not slept for three nights, and a patriot report a few weeks later had him suffering from headaches and heart trouble. Whether tired, sick, or resigned, the governor was absent from the most pivotal moment of his career, and a decisive moment in the unfolding American Revolution.

The late autumn downpour had mercifully ceased by the time the British and loyalist troops began their journey in the dark from Norfolk to Great Bridge. The joint British and loyalist forces moved up the eastern riverbank, opposite patriot positions. The two units of the Ethiopian Regiment positioned themselves for the diversionary attack. Leslie's regimental soldiers moved on to Fort Murray, entering the fort's gate without alerting rebel sentries.

Three hours before dawn on December 9, the small redoubt was packed with several hundred redcoats, along with members of both the Ethiopian and Queen's Own Loyal Regiments. Sleep would have been difficult in the tense atmosphere amid whispers that the shirt-men scalped wounded enemies. Leslie, meanwhile, waited impatiently for word from the diversionary force. As the sky began to lighten, there was still no message or crack of distant gunfire.

The captain faced a difficult decision. A frontal assault without a diversion was extremely risky. The patriot breastworks were made up of a seven-foot-high palisade that stretched in a solid line south to north, crossing the road into the village. Another trench at an angle to the north was designed to inflict deadly crossfire. With many of the buildings on the causeway demolished, the enemy would have a clear shot at an advancing column. Yet given the impending arrival of rebel artillery, Leslie no doubt realized this might be the last dawn when defeating the patriots was feasible.

As a steely gray sky began to replace the darkness, the captain ordered Fordyce to attack. The first men out of the gate were Black soldiers carrying the long bridge planks. They worked to set them in place without alerting the enemy as drums sounded reveille on the far side of the causeway. Fordyce then had two small cannon rolled quickly over the bridge to provide cover for the infantry. The rumble of wheels finally caught the attention of the sleepy patriot sentries. Among them was William Flora, a free Black man from Portsmouth who had joined the Princess Anne County militia; he would have been one of a handful of Black shirtmen. The other men fired a few rounds before sprinting back to the safety of the breastworks. Flora, however, got off an impressive eight musket shots before turning to run. He coolly paused to pull up the planks of the short spans that linked the causeway to the path leading up to the patriot entrenchment.

"We were alarmed this morning by the firing of some guns just after reveille beating," one of Woodford's officers wrote in a letter in the December 15 *Gazette*. "Boys, stand to your arms!" called out another officer upon hearing the crack of muskets. "Col. Woodford and myself immediately got equipped and ran out." The British caught the patriots by surprise; of the hundreds of shirtmen bivouacked at or near Great Bridge, only a few dozen manned the main breastwork that dawn.

As the British cannon boomed, Fordyce led sixty grenadiers from the Fourteenth Regiment out of Fort Murray and across the bridge, marching six abreast. The planks rattled below their freshly polished black boots, though they would have left behind their tall bearskin hats in preparation for combat. Each man, chosen for height and stamina, wore white breeches and a bright-red coat with wings of red cloth at the shoulders; a burnished bayonet extended from each of their muskets. A second unit of a similar size followed close behind; among them were marines and sailors, as well as Leslie's twenty-year-old nephew. Members of the Queen's Own Loyal and Lord Dunmore's Ethiopian Regiments massed between the fort and the bridge to serve as the next wave.

The stunned patriots watched as a single column of men, roughly sixty feet long, moved with precision down the exposed causeway. As they passed the burned-out warehouses, their boots thumped in time to the beat played by the regimental drummer. Grapeshot flung by the cannon soared over their heads, forcing patriots to duck. "We marched up to their works with the intrepidity of lions," wrote one *Otter* midshipman. Stunned patriots emerged from their makeshift tents and lean-tos, grabbing boots and guns and sprinting for the nearest trench. "They were astonished at men marching up with such courage, or rather madness, to certain death," a redcoat recalled. Few of the men in hunting shirts had ever seen a British infantry unit, much less one in battle formation.

A patriot officer called out to his men to hold their fire until the British were within fifty yards. The hail of bullets and buckshot soon began. "As is the practice with raw troops, the bravest rushed to the works, where, regardless of order, they kept up a heavy fire on the front of the British column," recalled twenty-year-old Lieutenant John Marshall of the Culpeper riflemen, later chief justice of the United States Supreme Court.

Had they stood unprotected against the formidable onslaught, the rebels might have turned on their heels and fled as they did twice at Kemp's Landing. This time, however, they were safe behind their high mound of muddy earth studded with wooden spikes, free to pick off figures in the British column in complete safety. They also were better organized, led, and equipped than the local militias and had experienced riflemen in their ranks. As they fired and reloaded, patriots in a set of trenches to the north began to rake the causeway with deadly crossfire. "In less than ten minutes we were exposed to the enemy's fire, upwards of seventy of our little detachment were killed and wounded," recalled one British officer. "Perhaps a hotter fire never happened, or a greater carnage, for the number of troops," said Woodford.

When the advancing grenadiers faltered, Fordyce was a mere fifteen feet from the patriot redoubt. He waved his hat over his head to rally his hesitating men. "The day is our own," he shouted. A bullet then slammed into his knee, shattering the bone, but he wrapped it in a handkerchief and continued to urge his soldiers on. He had almost reached the base of the patriot entrenchment when he crumpled to the damp ground in a hail of bullets; by one count, his body was riddled with eighteen pieces of lead.

With Fordyce down, a bugler sounded the call to fall back. "Our men were so enraged, that all the entreaties, and scarcely the threats of their officers, could prevail on them to retreat, which at last they did," recalled the *Otter* midshipman. Rebel bullets whizzed over the treeless embankment in the growing light. Over planks that had become slippery with blood, the now-panicked men rushed from the relentless hail as Leslie ordered the cannon hauled back into the fort. It was just after dawn, and a mere half hour had passed, but the Battle of Great Bridge was over.

A sudden stillness descended, only broken by the piercing cries of the wounded. Bodies lay along the causeway and its muddy water-lapped rim. "I then saw the horrors of war in perfection, worse than can be imagined," one shocked rebel officer later wrote. "Ten and twelve bullets through many; limbs broke in two or three places; brains turned out. Good God, what a sight!" Woodford sent a messenger under a white flag to call for a truce so the victorious patriots could gather the British dead and injured. Leslie agreed, walking bravely out of the fort to bow in Woodford's direction.

A rebel party hauled a dozen corpses and seventeen injured from the field. Among the dead was Leslie's young nephew. "For God's sake, do not murder us!" some of the wounded were said to have called out, fearing they would be scalped and killed. While they were not harmed, many nevertheless died; the surgeon's supplies were in Williamsburg, still waiting to be transported to the front. All told, seventeen British soldiers died and forty-three were injured, a disastrous casualty rate of nearly 50 percent.

Though the bridge planks remained in place and the enemy was battered and demoralized, Woodford made no attempt to seize the sudden patriot advantage. The cautious colonel had word that Highlander troops had landed in Norfolk, though these later turned out to be civilian settlers from Scotland.

The next morning, no cooking smoke rose from the enemy fort across the river, so Woodford sent a party of riflemen led by Major Thomas Marshall—John Marshall's father—to investigate. The shirtmen crept cautiously along a causeway littered with debris from the previous day's retreat. A patriot scribe carefully counted thirty discarded muskets and bayonets, two dozen cartouche boxes, a dozen coats, and a scatter of waistcoats, garters, shoes, snuff boxes, knives, watches, breeches, stockings, gloves, and shirts. Amid the detritus was a pair of silver shoe buckles and a lone black handkerchief.

Rifles at the ready, they trod the bloodstained bridge planks, the smears now dried into a glossy reddish-brown. Fearing an ambush, they warily circled the fort but encountered only freshly dug shallow graves. When the men finally pushed open the wooden gate, they discovered two members of the Ethiopian Regiment, including a soldier named Caesar, owned by a Norfolk merchant, and Peter Anderson, a free Black man who had worked as a sailmaker for Talbot Thompson in Norfolk.

Anderson's forearm had been ripped open, while Caesar had six wounds in his thigh, with one bullet lodged deep beneath the skin. They may have been too badly injured to be moved, or Anderson may have volunteered to remain with his comrade. A December 30 *Gazette* letter asserts that Leslie was "unable to rally the Negroes, who could not stand the severe fire from hundreds of marksmen," and therefore "retreated into the fort." Though British accounts don't mention Ethiopian Regiment involvement in the frontal attack, the two soldiers' wounds are evidence that they took an active part. Woodford reported that his officers unanimously agreed the two gravely wounded men should be executed, but the colonel chose instead to send them to Williamsburg for judgement.

A search of the otherwise abandoned compound yielded a variety of equipment, which was later meticulously inventoried by the patriots, including twenty-nine spades, seven guns, two shovels, and one bayonet, along with two barrels of bread and two of rum, some beef, four or five iron pots, a box and a half of candles, and a few axes. Metal spikes filled the touchholes of a half dozen cannon, rendering them useless. The riflemen grabbed what spoils they could carry and returned to their palisade. A work detail soon buried the bullet-ridden body of the fallen Fordyce in the churchyard, while captive British soldiers were treated as prisoners of war. Loyalists, however, were not. Woodford ordered one Scottish volunteer "coupled to one of his Black brother soldiers with a pair of handcuffs." This, he told Pendleton on December 12, "shall be the fate of all those cattle, until I'm further instructed."

As his men enjoyed the liberated barrels of rum, the Virginia commander retired to his Great Bridge headquarters to relay the good news to Pendleton, his mentor and the Committee of Safety president. "This was a second Bunker's Hill affair, in miniature," he wrote. The gentry officer could not resist a dig at his New England allies. "With this difference: we kept our post."

In 1765, Sir Joshua Reynolds painted John Murray, Fourth Earl of Dunmore, in tartan and kilt, Scottish Highland clothes then illegal under British law. The sole exception was for military veterans like the earl, who fought for Britain in the Seven Years' War.

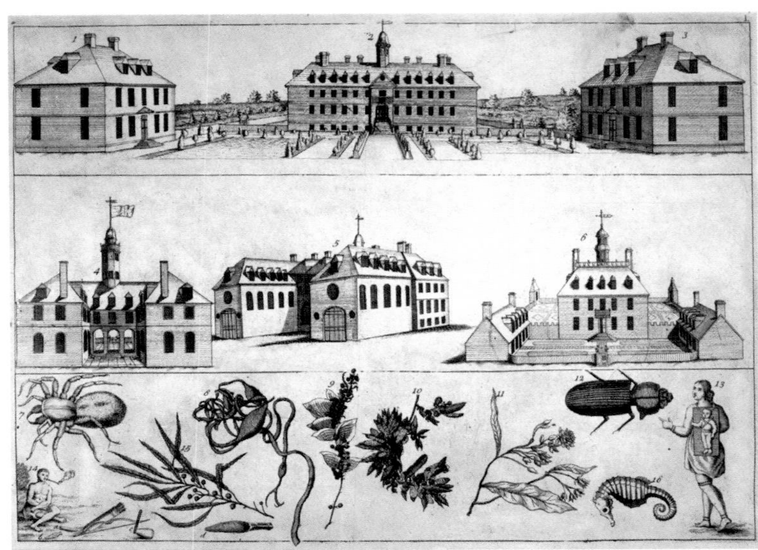

This copper plate dating to the 1730s provides the only known images of Williamsburg's public buildings in colonial times, including the College of William and Mary, the Capitol, and the Palace, with local flora, fauna, and indigenous people illustrated in the lower register.

A china plate with Dunmore's coat of arms found in the Palace during twentieth-century excavations.

George Washington chose to be portrayed in his old army clothes in this portrait made in 1772, more than a decade after he served in the Seven Years' War and soon after he befriended Dunmore.

Martha Dandridge Custis, shown in 1757, the year of her first husband's death. Two years later she married Washington.

There are no known images of colonial Norfolk, but artist Benjamin Latrobe painted this scene of its busy harbor in 1796.

Martha Tucker Newton and her son Thomas Newton III in 1770, later mayor of Norfolk. Her husband, Thomas Newton Jr., served in the House of Burgesses and the Virginia Conventions. Martha was the daughter of Robert Tucker, who owned Jane Thompson, wife of Talbot Thompson.

Scottish merchant Charles Steuart, who purchased the enslaved African James Somerset in Norfolk in 1749, and then attempted to sell him to Jamaica. A London court set Somerset free in 1772.

Thomas Jefferson (top), Patrick Henry (center), and Richard Henry Lee (bottom) quietly launched Virginia's patriot movement in Williamsburg's Raleigh Tavern in 1773; each would go on to play a critical role in the American Revolution.

"A Cure for the Refractory" is the motto on the post supporting a barrel of tar and bag of feathers on Williamsburg's Duke of Gloucester Street. A menacing crowd of men and women patriots "encourage" Scottish merchants to sign a pledge to boycott British goods.

Edmund Pendleton effectively led Virginia's patriot movement in the critical year between August 1775 and July 1776. His cautious and conservative stance irritated more radical colleagues.

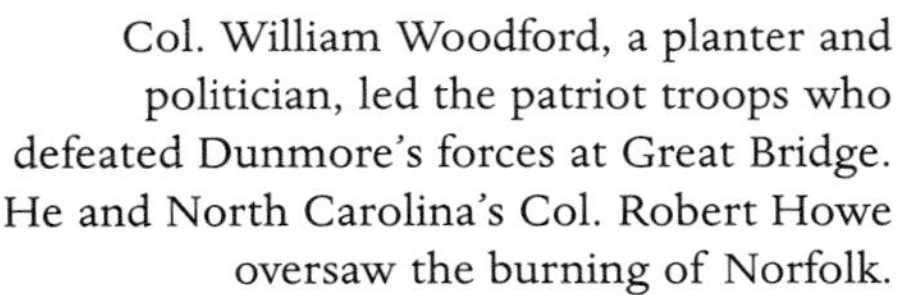

Col. William Woodford, a planter and politician, led the patriot troops who defeated Dunmore's forces at Great Bridge. He and North Carolina's Col. Robert Howe oversaw the burning of Norfolk.

Benjamin Latrobe's portrayal of a white overseer smoking as two enslaved women clear land to grow tobacco outside Fredericksburg.

Latrobe's "Preparations for the Enjoyment of a Fine Sunday Evening" portrays Black residents of Norfolk grooming and shaving. Tight surveillance in Virginia's forced labor camps contrasted with the port's less restrictive conditions.

Dunmore and his father sided with Bonnie Prince Charlie (right) against King George II in 1745–1746.

Phillis Wheatley, an enslaved Massachusetts poet, became the most celebrated Black American in late colonial America.

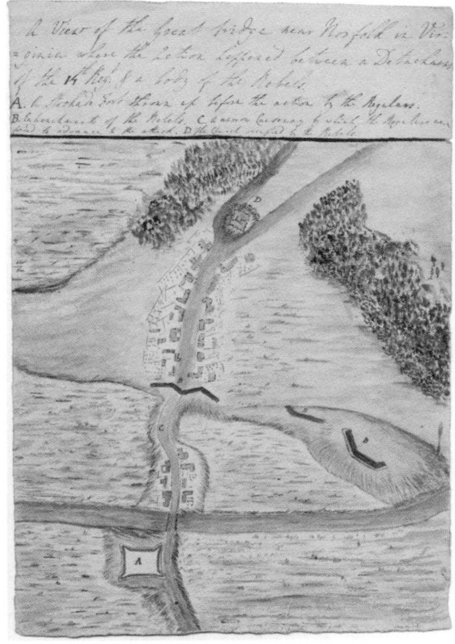

Bridge and causeway over the southern branch of the Elizabeth River, separating Fort Murray (bottom) from patriot breastworks (middle).

By His Excellency the Right Honorable JOHN Earl of DUNMORE, His MAJESTY's Lieutenant and Governor General of the Colony and Dominion of VIRGINIA, and Vice Admiral of the ſame.

A PROCLAMATION.

AS I have ever entertained Hopes, that an Accommodation might have taken Place between GREAT-BRITAIN and this Colony, without being compelled by my Duty to this moſt diſagreeable but now abſolutely neceſſary Step, rendered ſo by a Body of armed Men unlawfully aſſembled, firing on His MAJESTY's Tenders, and the formation of an Army, and that Army now on their March to attack His MAJESTY's Troops and deſtroy the well diſpoſed Subjects of this Colony. To defeat ſuch treaſonable Purpoſes, and that all ſuch Traitors, and their Abettors, may be brought to Juſtice, and that the Peace, and good Order of this Colony may be again reſtored, which the ordinary Courſe of the Civil Law is unable to effect; I have thought fit to iſſue this my Proclamation, hereby declaring, that until the aforeſaid good Purpoſes can be obtained, I do in Virtue of the Power and Authority to ME given, by His MAJESTY, determine to execute Martial Law, and cauſe the ſame to be executed throughout this Colony: and to the end that Peace and good Order may the ſooner be reſtored, I do require every Perſon capable of bearing Arms, to reſort to His MAJESTY's STANDARD, or be looked upon as Traitors to His MAJESTY's Crown and Government, and thereby become liable to the Penalty the Law inflicts upon ſuch Offences; ſuch as forfeiture of Life, confiſcation of Lands, &c. &c. And I do hereby further declare all indented Servants, Negroes, or others, (appertaining to Rebels,) free that are able and willing to bear Arms, they joining His MAJESTY's Troops as ſoon as may be, for the more ſpeedily reducing this Colony to a proper Senſe of their Duty, to His MAJESTY's Crown and Dignity. I do further order, and require, all His MAJESTY's Leige Subjects, to retain their Quitrents, or any other Taxes due or that may become due, in their own Cuſtody, till ſuch Time as Peace may be again reſtored to this at preſent moſt unhappy Country, or demanded of them for their former ſalutary Purpoſes, by Officers properly authoriſed to receive the ſame.

GIVEN under my Hand on board the Ship WILLIAM, off NORFOLK, the 7th Day of NOVEMBER, in the SIXTEENTH Year of His MAJESTY's Reign.

DUNMORE.

(GOD ſave the KING.)

Dunmore's proclamation, published November 15, 1775, promised to free and arm those enslaved by patriots, and willing to fight for the Crown. The document helped lay the foundations for Lincoln's later and more famous edict.

Combatants at the Battle of Great Bridge, which culminated on December 9, 1775, included soldiers from Britain's Fourteenth Regiment (top), Lord Dunmore's Ethiopian Regiment (center), and patriot riflemen from the western county of Culpeper (bottom).

After its 1776 destruction, Norfolk was slow to rebuild. Thomas Jefferson's daughter noted in 1789 that the city had not recovered from the war. Seven years later, Benjamin Latrobe painted ruins that still littered its northwestern suburbs.

British General Sir Henry Clinton visited Virginia in February 1776, but chose to focus his forces on a disastrous campaign against Charleston.

Captain Andrew Snape Hamond commanded the Royal Navy's Chesapeake fleet in 1776.

In spring 1776, patriot general Charles Lee failed to dislodge Dunmore and his loyalist allies, while urging wholesale depopulation of the Norfolk region.

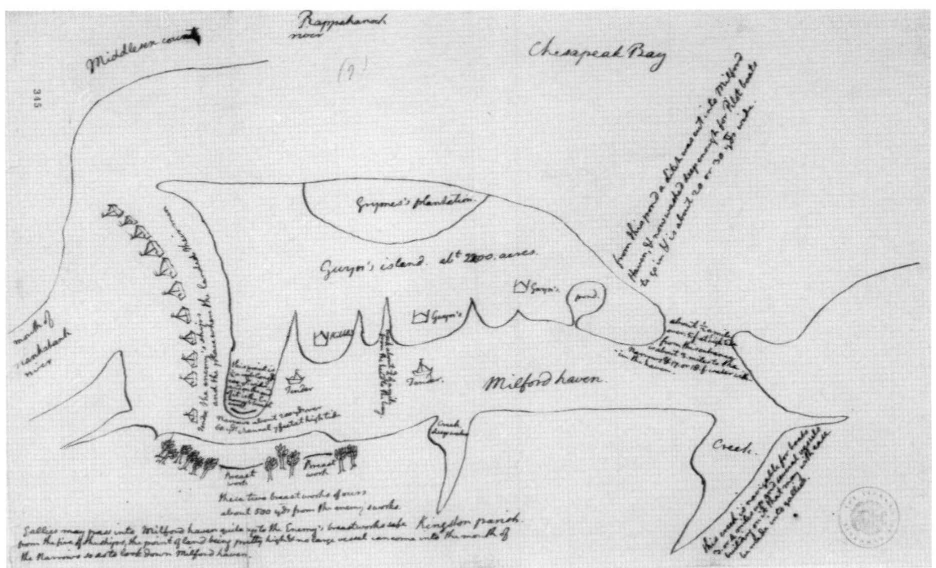

In June 1776, while drafting the Declaration of Independence, Thomas Jefferson obtained this map of Gwynn's Island detailing patriot as well as British and loyalist forces.

French artist Jean-Baptiste-Antoine DeVerger portrayed patriot soldiers at the Battle of Yorktown, including a Black soldier in the First Rhode Island Regiment.

The grandson of Dunmore and King George III sits on the lap of his mother, Lady Augusta Murray.

An enormous stone pineapple adorns the top of Dunmore's garden house outside Edinburgh. The Caribbean fruit was a symbol of hospitality in colonial Virginia.

This miniature shows Dunmore just prior to his 1809 death at about age 79.

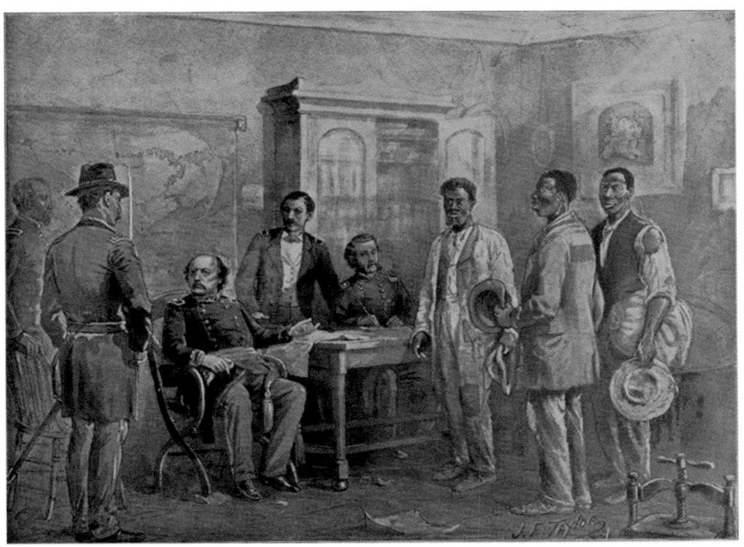

In May 1861, three enslaved men escaped Confederate lines in Norfolk and asked the commander of Fort Monroe, Union General Benjamin Butler, for refuge. He declared them "contrabands of war." Their flight set off a chain of events that would lead to emancipation.

Furious Confederates later burned nearby Hampton to prevent the town's use as a sanctuary for those fleeing bondage.

This cannonball was found in the ground below Norfolk's Borough Church, now St. Paul's, in the nineteenth century and cemented back into the indentation it made in the wall above. The British warship *Liverpool* is said to have fired the shot on New Year's Day 1776. Despite clear evidence to the contrary, Dunmore remains the popular culprit for the town's destruction.

Chapter Twenty

Dunmore's Dunkirk

Just before midnight on Saturday, December 9, eighteen hours after the Battle of Great Bridge, the ubiquitous Helen Maxwell and several of her friends had just returned from a visit with her mother when they spotted the shattered remnants of Dunmore's retreating troops on the road outside Norfolk. The men had abandoned Fort Murray in the middle of the previous night. Many were strewn on carts and wagons that had bumped for hours on the long road leading to Kemp's Landing and then to the port. "We saw them coming with the poor creatures in them, crying 'Water! Water!'" she recalled. "I and the young women, moved with pity, went out and carried them pitchers of water." The parched men, she added, "drank with a rabid thirst which it seemed impossible to satisfy."

The grim parade turned down Church Street; any dead would have been left in the sanctuary's darkened churchyard for later burial. The living continued across the isthmus and past the town's eerily empty new fortifications, abandoned to supply troops for the Great Bridge assault. Word of the defeat was already sweeping the city as the exhausted troops trudged into the port. Despite the slow exodus that had been underway since late September, at least a thousand residents remained in town. Now an army of rural white men eager to destroy a hated "nest of Tories" was presumably on its way, with no force to stop it.

Maxwell met a British sailing master amid the tumult. "He told us it was time for us to be moving, and we set about sending all our valuable articles of furniture" to a friend's home on the marshy peninsula between Norfolk and Portsmouth. Her family rushed "to get out of the way of the balls"—the British cannonballs expected to rain down from the ships when the rebels arrived. The family found passage across the river while leaving "a Negro woman, old Sarah, behind to take care of the house and lot and look after a sow and pigs which she was raising for herself with great care."

As an enslaved person, Sarah had little choice but to remain. The Maxwells were among the well-to-do with friends or family in the countryside who would take them in, or the means to pay an innkeeper for food and lodging. For those like Sarah, fearful of losing what little she had, the options were far fewer and the consequences far greater. A patriot takeover spelled disaster for Norfolk's Black community. Those who had escaped could at best expect to be returned to their owners; or they might instead face torture and execution. Even free Black families like the Thompsons could expect harsh treatment from rampaging shirtmen unlikely to respect their hard-earned manumission papers. Everything Jane and Talbot Thompson had worked for decades to create—a prosperous business, extensive real estate holdings, and a safe haven for the friends and relatives they had purchased—was now at risk. Their most precious asset, their hard-won liberty, might at any moment be taken.

Some determined patriots decided to stay, sure that their devotion to the cause would protect them and their property from harm. Others believed Pendleton's public assurances of a peaceful takeover. Whites sympathetic to the rebel cause, meanwhile, feared that those enslaved might turn on their owners at any moment. "I was told to report the least suspicious activity on the part of the blacks," recalled one, who at the time was a six-year-old white girl in a household that included five enslaved people. "I remember my grandmother carrying a silver-mounted dirk in her bosom."

Many remaining residents prepared to flee. They packed trunks with clothes, gathered precious china, silver flatware, and copper pots, and swiftly determined which chairs, clocks, and tables to leave behind. Merchants ransacked their desks to fill saddlebags with important papers and cash, while their employees wrestled crates heavy with valuable merchandise onto carts. Enslaved men leading packhorses competed for space in the narrow streets with heavily laden wagons.

There were only two ways out of town, up Church Street and into the countryside or across the harbor by boat. Both choices held risks: the land route was vulnerable to patriot militia, while vessels could be cramped, leaky, and dangerous as winter closed in.

One Norfolk patriot later claimed that he was "present when his Lordship received news of the defeat," and insisted that the governor "raved like the madman he is" and threatened to hang the messenger. No other source mentions such a tantrum, but Dunmore acted swiftly to address the crisis. Without sufficient troops to man the town's rudimentary entrenchments, he ordered both British and loyalist soldiers to board the Royal Navy ships, while directing their crews to make room for their families and other civilians aboard the *Otter*, *Kingfisher*, *William*, and *Dunmore*. The town's merchant captains summoned their own vessels, mostly brigantines. Jamieson hurried aboard the *Fincastle*, while Jonathan Eilbeck herded his family and servants onto the *Peace & Plenty* and Sprowle and his relatives fled to the *Hammond*. Prior to the upheaval, the aging shipyard owner had found time to wed; his new wife was Katherine Hunter, his nephew's widow with seven children back in Scotland.

"Most of the other vessels are small craft and occupied by trades people and Negroes," a Maryland patriot later reported. Rowboats, barges, tenders, schooners, and anything that could float collected beneath the guns of the warships like waterfowl seeking their mother's protection. Refugees rushed to obtain a dry place to stow themselves and their belongings. How long they would have to endure life on the water was uncertain.

The earl painted a bleak and heartrending picture of the hurried evacuation. "All who were friends to government took refuge on board of the ships, with their whole families, and their most valuable effects," he wrote Lord Dartmouth. "Some in the men of war, some in their own vessels, others have chartered such as were here, so that our fleet is at present numerous though not very powerful." It was, he assured the colonial secretary, "a most melancholy sight to see the numbers of gentlemen of very large property with their ladies and whole families obliged to betake themselves on board of ships, at the season of the year, hardly with the common necessaries of life." He added that "great numbers of poor people" were "without even these." They "must have perished had I not been able to supply them with some flour, which I purchased for his Majesty's service some time ago." The town's displaced inhabitants, he observed, were plunged "into despair, and they at present give themselves up as lost."

Samuel Boush Jr., grandson of Norfolk's first mayor, was determined to rescue his hometown and his investments from ruin. The wealthy patriot was among a handful of landlords who owned much of the port's real estate, which brought in as much as 10,000 pounds a year, or some $1 million today, in rent. Five years before, he had sold the Thompsons their Cumberland Street home. By the time the British occupied the town, Boush had retreated to his country house of Westwood near Great Bridge, and the British had subsequently demolished his town residence to secure the fortifications around Norfolk.

In the wake of the Saturday battle, Boush put out feelers to Dunmore to avoid "the effusion of more blood and the total destruction that is threatened." He arranged for the earl's representatives to meet him at Westwood the following day. "I am told his Lordship is not averse that a deputation be sent to the provincial troops," he wrote Mayor Loyall and two other members of the town's leadership on Sunday, December 10. "For God's sake, gentlemen, if you can possibly come, do." When no one arrived, an anxious Boush went to Woodford at Great Bridge to present a petition assuring the commander that Norfolk's residents "have at all times wished for liberty," yet "now lie under a dread of having our small substance destroyed." The document, which the real estate magnate likely wrote himself, begged the rebel army to protect rather than ravage the town "so that we remain in safety as true Sons of Liberty."

That day, the first contingent of North Carolina patriot militia arrived with six cannon. Dunmore's intelligence had been correct, but his assumption these weapons could batter Fort Murray proved wrong. They lacked carriages, rammers, and other vital accessories. A disgusted Woodford pronounced the equipment "almost useless."

Without artillery, the patriots would be hard-pressed to threaten the heavily armed Royal Navy ships riding in Norfolk's harbor.

On Monday morning, December 11, town leaders rode to Great Bridge to plead with Woodford. The party included Mayor Loyall and Dr. Archibald Campbell, a wealthy Scottish physician who lived on Cumberland Street near the Thompsons. Though of different ethnicities and political opinions, the men were united in their desire to rescue the borough from annihilation. Escorted to the colonel's headquarters, each man was questioned separately by Woodford. They all described a city in crisis. A feeling of "great dejection" had swept through town with news of the military defeat, said one. The quarter mile or so of fortifications were low and poorly made and had collapsed under the heavy autumn rains. Food was running short, and the British regulars had evacuated to the naval ships.

One member of the delegation claimed to have heard Captain Leslie, deeply grieving the loss of his nephew, swear that he would sacrifice no more of his men. Leslie's men were also said to resent Dunmore's recruitment of Black soldiers. Members of the British regiment "do not like to fight with the Negroes," one told Woodford. The British army in that era tended to exclude foreigners and people of color from their ranks, in contrast to the Royal Navy, which employed a wide diversity of seamen, including many free Black men. This institutional difference no doubt accounts for the more progressive racial views of naval officers such as Squire.

As a Scot sympathetic to the loyalists, Campbell was taking a risk entering the camp; one patriot planter later said he was "as artful as vicious." He may have recalled that the doctor had armed twenty of his enslaved men in 1768 to protect his home from a white mob opposing his effort to inoculate friends and family from smallpox. Woodford, however, called him "one of the most considerable men" in Norfolk, and listened respectfully when the physician explained that "it had been currently reported that the town was to be plundered and burnt." He and his colleagues sought "to avoid such calamities" by "praying [for] the protection of [the Virginia] Convention on behalf of its inhabitants." When Loyall was interrogated, the patriot mayor revealed that Dunmore "would be very glad to save the town" and was "very agreeable" to talks. If Norfolk's leaders "were now satisfied" that the patriots "would not burn the town," he hinted the earl might be willing to withdraw. The colonel then allowed the delegation to return to the borough.

Almost certainly as a result of this meeting, Woodford issued a statement that day to white residents of Norfolk and Princess Anne Counties, the region that lay on the other side of the bridge. "The late action at this place, it is hoped, will convince you that we are able to give you that protection which we were sent down to afford you," he wrote. "It is not my design to injure any of your persons or properties." He added that an advance guard would occupy Kemp's Landing, the halfway point on the route to Norfolk.

As dusk fell that Monday afternoon, Woodford heard the strange sound of drumming mixed with fiddling. The second group of North Carolinians had arrived, 340 shirtmen whom Woodford judged "tolerably good men but badly armed." At their head was Colonel Robert Howe of the Continental Army. Like Washington, Howe was a forty-three-year-old slave-owning planter who had served in the French and Indian War, married a wealthy heiress, and gone into debt trying to maintain a lavish lifestyle. Also like the Virginia general, he was tall and athletic, called "a man of the world, the sword, and the senate."

In contrast with Washington, however, he was suspected of siphoning government funds to stay afloat; a North Carolina royal governor complained of his "misapplication of the public money." His frequent affairs also prompted his wife to leave him, and one woman noted in her diary that he had a reputation as a "women-eater that devours everything that comes his way." He had little use for those who did not fall for his charms. When one loyalist lady chided him at a social gathering, he only half-jokingly threatened to have her tarred and feathered. Josiah Quincy Jr. of Massachusetts dismissed him as a "libertine," while a Scottish merchant contended that Howe "has the worst character you ever heard through the whole province," adding, perhaps without irony, that he was "very like a gentleman." The colonel also was no fan of democracy. A few years before, he had backed an army of redcoats which put down a rebellion by North Carolina's poor white farmers furious at a tax hike.

As a newly minted colonel in the expanding Continental Army, Howe outranked Woodford. He reported to Washington rather than to North Carolina patriots but, given the five hundred miles separating Cambridge from Norfolk, he had considerable latitude in his actions. He immediately assumed command of the combined forces. A North Carolinian, not a Virginian, was now in charge of defeating Dunmore.

When news of the Great Bridge victory reached Williamsburg, there was little time to celebrate. Enlistments were lagging, ammunition was in short supply, and the British blockade had proven highly effective. The price of sugar quintupled, while a gallon of rum purchased at the start of the year for two shillings now cost more than twelve. Salt, critical for preserving meat and fish and pickling vegetables for winter, had soared from a shilling to fifteen shillings a bushel. "For salt is all the farmer's cry; if we've no salt we sure must die," went one 1770s couplet. A Virginia county issued an order forbidding hoarding of the vital mineral "to prevent riots and tumults." The crisis prompted a worried Continental Congress to exempt the colony from the general ban on salt imports.

Of even greater concern was the governor's emancipation proclamation. On December 12, the Fourth Virginia Convention promised "the severest punishments" to those in bondage who joined the loyalists. The next day, delegates issued their first public manifesto explaining their decision to take up arms against the king. It was a simple matter of self-defense that required "repelling force by force." The royal governor was "the source of innumerable evils," who had "broken the bonds of society, and trampled justice under his feet." The patriot leaders accused him of plotting to "draw upon us a merciless and savage enemy," a reference to the Connolly plot to engage indigenous allies; a similar phrase would reappear six months later in the Declaration of Independence.

The capstone of their grievances was the earl's offer of "freedom to the servants of those he is pleased to term rebels, arming them against their masters" and exposing the colonists to "the dangers of a general insurrection." That last term also would show up in the July 1776 document. Dunmore also was charged with "the pilfering and plundering of the property of the people, and the actual seduction and seizure of their slaves." If a governor, they wrote, could "give freedom to our servants and slaves, and arm them for our destructions, let us bid adieu to everything valuable in life . . . and hug the chains prepared for us." Neither taxes nor the "Intolerable Acts" were mentioned.

The delegates ordered the white residents in Norfolk and Princess Anne Counties to denounce Dunmore as a "horrid supporter of tyranny" through his act of "declaring our servants and slaves free and inviting and arming them to assassinate their masters, our innocent wives and helpless children." White men over sixteen were required to take an oath pledging to "defend and support this colony against all invasions and insurrections whatsoever that shall or may be made against the rights and liberties of America." Those who refused were to be disarmed, confined to within five miles of their home, and required to pay triple taxes.

The following day, the Virginia Convention directed Woodford to forgive those who had joined Dunmore "through necessity," an amnesty that applied only to white residents. Just how this distinction would be made was unclear. "It is enacted," the patriot leaders declared, "that all Negro or other slaves, conspiring to rebel or make insurrection, shall suffer death." If, however, they turned themselves in to a patriot commander within ten days of publication of the notice, and agreed to return to lifetime servitude, they wrote, "we hereby promise to pardon them."

That same morning, December 14, more than twelve hundred men mostly clad in fringed hunting shirts and leather leggings tramped across the bridge planks still spotted with dried blood and passed the deserted Fort Murray. The track leading to Norfolk, already rutted from the British retreat, was a thick mire. Howe and Woodford sent a messenger ahead with a stark message for the town's mayor, aldermen, and residents. "We are marching to Norfolk with no intention to injure the inhabitants of the town either in their persons or property," the note read, "unless they should attempt to resist our entrance, or omit to inform us of the intention of any other persons to oppose us." The commanders added, "The magistrates of the town must give a positive answer that we may take our measures accordingly."

The terrified borough leaders immediately consulted with Dunmore, and then sent a reply agreeing to the patriot demands. A waning moon lit the way for the troops as they filed into town after dark. The hastily built fortifications were abandoned and their cannon spiked. The bulk of the men camped outside town, while others were detailed to secure the downtown. There was no resistance. "We have taken possession of Norfolk in a manner more peaceable than we expected," Howe wrote Pendleton that evening. Those floating in the harbor would have watched uneasily as the lamps and torches of shirtmen spread through the streets of the otherwise darkened town.

At ten o'clock that night, Woodford was writing his report to the Committee of Safety president after the "fatigues of the day" when gunfire rang out. "We have just exchanged shots in the streets, three of our people wounded," he scratched. "People say they received fire from the houses." Sleepy shirtmen were roused to fend off an attack. "The whole line at present [is] under arms," the commander reported to Pendleton. In fact, the wounds apparently came from friendly fire when patriot troops disobeyed orders and shot a dozen rounds at the silhouettes of the British ships, striking some of their comrades by accident. Woodford, however, felt only scorn for the occupied city. "The Convention may be assured, the town of Norfolk deserves no favor," he wrote, adding later, "I have the worst opinion of the people here and have no doubt, but everything related to us is laid before his Lordship."

As the sky lightened, the awe-inspiring sight of the vast armada slowly emerged. "All the principal Tories, with their families and effects, have removed on board the ships of war and other vessels in the harbor, of which there is a very large fleet," reported Woodford. "What they intend I know not." What they were capable of doing was not in question. The black snouts of cannon poked out of the square gunports on each of the four warships. Smaller cannon and swivel guns bristled on four schooners, four sloops, and several pilot boats. Though a minor squadron by Boston standards, the vessels nonetheless made up the most powerful naval force seen in Virginia up to that time. The flotilla was the first hostile fleet in the Chesapeake since 1652, when Oliver Cromwell sent warships during the

English Civil War to subjugate Virginia's gentry, staunch backers of the Stuart king over the forces of Parliament.

After sunrise, a boat shoved off from the *Otter* with a white flag fluttering in the frigid breeze. A British midshipman stepped out onto the wharf, and shirtmen escorted him to Howe and Woodford's headquarters. The sailor presented a letter addressed to the "officer commanding at Norfolk." In the note, the *Otter*'s Captain Squire protested the shots fired at the ships the night before, adding that he did "not mean to fire on the town of Norfolk unless first fired at." Howe and Woodford sent back a reply acknowledging the shots were "fired by mistake."

As at Great Bridge, the two enemies were cheek by jowl, separated only by a short stretch of water. The two rebel commanders struggled to discipline their troops. Aside from the stray shots, "many of the stores and cellars in the town were broke open and plundered by the soldiers" in the early days of the occupation, according to one patriot. One ransacked home was that of Thomas Newton Jr., a member of the town's Committee of Safety and delegate to the Virginia Convention who had married Martha Tucker, daughter of Jane Thompson's former owner. In this tense situation, a single rifleman who defied orders could provoke the British to bombard the town.

Howe and Woodford, who seem not to have visited the port before, spent the rest of the day examining the area. Howe concluded that the port provided any seaborne enemy with the capacity to "convey their men to any part of this colony to which they may choose to detach them." Those who controlled the port had access to a hinterland rich with grain and pork that could easily feed a vast army. The officers told Pendleton that they could secure the town if they had extensive military stores, multiple cannon, and "a large body of troops." The alternative was that it could be "totally destroyed to prevent its furnishing the enemy with good barracks." They made clear they preferred the second option.

Laying waste to the largest city in the largest colony—even a city despised by most patriots—was a weighty matter, and Pendleton was reluctant to lay this momentous decision before the Virginia Convention. In June, British forces had burned the small port of Charlestown, which faced Boston from the opposite bank of the

Charles River, to flush out snipers during the Battle of Bunker Hill, and in October they had bombarded Falmouth in Maine to avenge an attack on a naval ship. These attacks prompted widespread patriot outrage. Those incidents would pale beside the destruction of Norfolk, which would undermine the patriot claim of moral superiority over British barbarity. Pendleton kept the officer's recommendations secret, sharing them only with select committee members.

Maryland's *Gazette* reported on December 14 that Dunmore's proclamation had drawn "about 2000 men, including his black regiment, which is thought to be a considerable part." The newspaper was among the dozen or so throughout the colonies relaying word that they wore the LIBERTY FOR SLAVES inscription on their breast, while assuring readers that white surveillance of the area's rivers would stanch the flow of enslaved people fleeting to British lines. The article also noted that Norfolk's jail had been "set on fire," presumably by those imprisoned by patriots before the British occupation.

Six days later, Dunmore received welcome reinforcements and provisions when the 28-gun *Liverpool* manned by 160 sailors dropped anchor off Norfolk. The vessel carried 3,000 sets of arms for Virginia's and North Carolina's royal governors, as well as the first correspondence from London that Dunmore had seen since May. Among the pile was a letter from Dartmouth with the king's permission for Dunmore to return to Britain if he found his situation dire. He set it aside.

"This late acquisition of strength has much elated Lord Dunmore and his party," reported the next day's Williamsburg *Gazette*. "And Norfolk, Hampton, and all the river settlements are threatened with fire and sword." Woodford, meanwhile, worried the *Liverpool*'s arrival would put fresh wind in loyalists' sails. The colonel found that most of Norfolk's remaining residents at best "are to be considered neutrals," he wrote Pendleton, adding, "I have seen none of them who take arms, or appear inclined to do so." Yet he suspected they "only wait a change of the times, to again change their masters."

In the meantime, he was having trouble with his own officers, many of whom demanded leaves of absence as Christmas approached.

When Woodford refused, several threatened to resign. "The men I fear will follow this bad example and where it will end is hard for me to say," wrote the troubled colonel. The frosty relations between Henry's First Regiment and Woodford's Second Regiment had only grown icier. "A difference at this critical moment between our troops," one Convention delegate cautioned Henry, "would be attended with the most fatal consequences."

On the first day of winter, December 21, a damp, cold breeze blew across the harbor, sending civilians below deck—if their vessel had a protected space. Howe noted that the warships "ride with springs upon their cables" and "seem prepared for hostilities." Springs were typically installed on an anchor line to prevent the cable from snapping from the backlash of a cannonade. The detail suggested that the British were ready to bombard the town. According to patriot spies, some naval commanders favored an attack, while Dunmore opposed the idea. "The number of ships that surround this town obliges us to keep a great many guards, as it's impossible to say what may happen," Woodford told Pendleton. The mounting tension between the enemy forces left remaining residents "much alarmed," and many packed their belongings and left town.

Howe continued to press his case with Pendleton for Norfolk's destruction, arguing that the port was a dangerous trap in which defenders would become "prey to disgrace and famine." He concluded, "Upon the whole, I think Norfolk cannot be maintained with any troops you can place there against an attack by sea and land." Occupation "could answer no purpose but merely keeping it in subjection." Therefore, while the town was "extremely desirable to your adversaries who have shipping, it must ever remain, in the kind of war we are waging, a place disadvantageous and dangerous to you."

By the next day, the damp breeze had blown into a fierce northeaster, covering town and flotilla with a blanket of wet snow. Woodford complained that the weather "is very severe and the duty is very hard in our present situation." The bitter cold spelled greater misery for the thousands of people packed on the exposed vessels. The swells may have made it too dangerous to light cooking fires, forcing passengers to subsist on cold food and sending many scurrying to clutch the icy rails.

The last snow showers dissipated on Christmas Eve and a wan winter sun appeared. By then, the patriot army consisted of at least fifteen hundred men. Many had deserted after Great Bridge, but their numbers were at least triple those that the governor could field. "Lord Dunmore, with a rashness which has marked his whole conduct, has exposed the Fourteenth Regiment to disgrace and ruin," one Virginia delegate wrote to Richard Henry Lee in Philadelphia. Dunmore's "regiment of sables"—the Ethiopian Regiment—"is now dispersed," he claimed, "and the poor deluded wretches are daily brought into our camp in great numbers." Their fate, he added ominously, "is not yet determined."

In fact, many if not all members of the regiment who had escaped Great Bridge were safely aboard the ships, at least some accompanied by family members. During protracted negotiations with the rebels to exchange prisoners, Dunmore attempted to exchange shirtmen for Black soldiers, a sign of the value he placed on their service. The patriots refused to take this offer seriously. A Williamsburg official scoffed that instead of considering the Black soldiers as prisoners of war who might be traded, "he supposed we must sell them."

Chapter Twenty-One

Palpitation at the Heart

At two o'clock on the afternoon of Christmas Day, the roar of cannon thundered across Norfolk harbor, bringing patriot troops rushing out of their barracks and alarming shirtmen as far away as Hampton. The noise turned out to be "only a Christmas frolic between Lord Dunmore and the captains of the navy, upon visiting each other on board their ships." The festiveness masked the dire effects of the patriot policy of denying food and water to the flotilla. One Virginia delegate explained to Richard Henry Lee that the embargo forced Dunmore's troops to raid the surrounding coastline to find "provisions and fuel, which we have reason to believe is exceedingly scarce." This, in turn, inflamed white anger at the governor, who was already being mocked as "the piratical peer." Such forays were not, however, sufficient to keep misery at bay.

In the wake of the blizzard, hunger and sickness took their toll on those trapped in the harbor. "The women and children aboard the fleet are in great distress," Woodford reported to Pendleton. "We are told several are dead and many ill; they suffer for water, wood, and fresh provisions." The patriots, he added, had ensured "destruction of all the bake houses and other places where they receive any supplies from." The flour mill at Tucker's Point, however, was still under British control, as were the warehouses at Gosport, while the belly of the *Liverpool* and its companion vessel were filled with cheese, peas, dried beef, and other essentials. Yet these stockpiles were quickly being depleted. Poor sanitation, low morale, and the danger of snipers onshore added to the twin perils of hypothermia and starvation.

On Christmas Eve, the *Liverpool*'s captain, Henry Bellew, had sent Robert Howe a letter under a flag of truce warning of "the effects of numbers of men set loose to satisfy their hunger after fresh provisions." Starving men were violent men, and he preferred to avoid "the effusion of blood of the innocent and helpless." Howe replied with unusual sympathy, but said his hands were tied. "You may be assured it will not be my inclination to prevent your obtaining supplies," he wrote. Those were, however, his orders. Perhaps moved by the pitiful plight of thousands of shipbound civilians, the North Carolina colonel attempted to persuade Pendleton to ease the ban, citing Bellew's "moderate conduct" and the "sentiments of humanity" guiding his request.

The delegates in Williamsburg would not be swayed by the accelerating humanitarian crisis. "This Convention are fully sensible of the hardships which many innocent persons aboard his Majesty's ships may be exposed to for want of regular supplies of fresh provision," resolved the delegates. But "the duty we owe our country" they added, made any softening of their stance impossible. Captain Bellew, the members added, "must excuse the inhabitants of Virginia if they totally declined contributing towards their own destruction." Woodford had suggested that women and children be permitted to disembark from the flotilla, but only "with no intention to return." Men would be imprisoned, while Black refugees would have been dealt with far more harshly.

At year's end, the two sides eyed each other warily. "We have had a few popping shots now and then at our people and a broadside from the *Otter*," Howe reported to Pendleton on December 30. The shots, however, proved "all bloodless." The impasse laid the governor low, if a sardonic report in that day's Williamsburg *Gazette* was accurate. "Lord Dunmore, we hear, is sadly tormented with a violent headache and palpitation at the heart." Even the normally unflappable Bellew grew testy at the sight of shirtmen strolling along Norfolk's wharves, brandishing their muskets and rifles at the fleet. "I desire you will cause your sentinels in the town of Norfolk to avoid being seen," he wrote Howe. If they did not, he warned, the borough's women and children might suffer, "and it would not be imprudent if both were to leave the town."

The borough inhabitants, Howe responded curtly, "have nothing to do in this matter," and he requested time for them to "remove with their effects." The exchange is evidence that a significant civilian population remained. The colonel then reassured the captain that, despite their bluster, "our sentinels have received orders not to fire upon your people or any others unless approaching the shore in a hostile manner."

Black patriots had fought and died at the Battle of Bunker Hill in June 1775, but when George Washington assumed command of the Continental Army the following month, he refused to consider reenlistment of Black men when their service ended at the close of the year. In October, Continental Army officers unanimously voted to remove all enslaved Africans from their ranks and to refuse all Black volunteers in the future. The Continental Congress agreed. On November 12, 1775, three days before Dunmore made his proclamation, Washington ordered that "neither Negroes, boys unable to bear arms, nor old men" could enlist in the army.

In the middle of December, he received a patriotic verse written in praise of him by Phillis Wheatley, the enslaved Black Massachusetts poet. He was impressed enough by her talent to send a note of congratulations and an invitation for her to pay a visit. Meanwhile, the general watched anxiously as white soldiers packed up to go home "by hundreds and by thousands." When news of the governor's emancipation decree arrived, along with evidence that it was drawing large numbers of the enslaved to British lines, Washington suddenly reversed course. "It has been represented to me," he wrote Hancock on New Year's Eve, "that the free Negroes who have served in this army are very much dissatisfied at being discarded." Those "discarded" men, he feared, might decide to serve the enemy instead. "I have presumed to depart from the resolution respecting them and have given license for their being enlisted," he explained. Always careful to follow civilian direction, he added, "If this is disapproved of by Congress, I will put a stop to it."

Nearly half of the Philadelphia delegates were slaveowners, but many recognized that sagging enlistments and Dunmore's bold recruiting efforts forced their hand. They agreed "that the free Negroes who had served faithfully in the army at Cambridge may be reenlisted therein, but no other." For the remainder of the war, Black soldiers would form an important contingent in the American army; not until the Korean War would it again be so integrated.

In Norfolk, the frigid dawn of New Year's Eve arrived with a hard frost coating the borough's cedar-shingled roofs and the flotilla rigging. One merchant on board a vessel wrote that the rebels "began to insult us, by firing at us, and particularly attempting to shoot our worthy governor in his ship." That afternoon, a patriot squad hidden in a warehouse at the western end of the town docks attacked a British tender shuttling between vessels. "Fired two six pounders at them to cover our boat," Squire noted tersely in his log. The warehouses were ideal posts "from whence they used to annoy our boats as they passed," complained Dunmore. This minor incident in the waning hours of 1775 proved a final straw. The snipers could at any moment pick off anyone on deck, and the rebel commanders seemed unable or unwilling to restrain them.

As British and patriots traded shots in Norfolk's harbor, Williamsburg's elite and Virginia Convention delegates huddled in their woolen coats in the high-backed pews of Bruton Parish Church, a block from the empty Palace. Washington's friend and minister, the patriot pastor David Griffith, preached a Sunday sermon laced with references to the lash, wicked masters, and oppression. The devout Anglican clergyman, a favorite with the gentry, compared the rule of King George III to that of the ancient tyrannical pharaoh who enslaved the Hebrews. The dispute with Britain, he added, centered on the king's capacity to be in absolute control of "their lives and property," a situation he described as "truly slavish."

Griffith was not making a call for independence, a notion that few Virginians contemplated even then. He backed the restoration of colonial justice, not the creation of a new social order, and certainly not the emancipation of those who lived daily under the threat of a real lash. "I am very fully convinced of the necessity of subordination in society," he explained. "I am, by no means, an advocate for anarchy."

The colony had been roiled by class rebellion a century before, in 1676, when enslaved Africans and poor whites had briefly allied during Bacon's Rebellion and "so threatened the better sort of people that they durst not stir out of their houses." On the eve of 1776, Dunmore's success in rallying Black and white loyalists, coupled with several reports of cooperation among white laborers and unfree workers, raised the specter of another descent into what the gentry viewed as chaos. The pastor acknowledged that the conflict with Britain threatened "the preservation of order and justice." Yet Virginia Convention delegates were well aware that a militia made up solely of "the better sort" had proven insufficient to maintain the proper "subordination in society." To defeat Dunmore and his allies, the province's upper crust needed to fire up the volatile men in hunting shirts who carried rifles and tomahawks, but without ceding their own position at the top of the social pyramid.

From the high pulpit overlooking the upturned faces of colonial Virginia's patriot leaders, Griffith also noted that "the spirit of freedom" could be "attended with disagreeable consequences" if pursued by "imprudent conduct in rulers." He was thinking of misguided kings, but his words would take on a different and more sinister meaning the following day.

Part Three

January 1776 to October 1803

NORFOLK
N
PRINCESS ANNE ROAD
to Kemp's Landing,
7 miles
Windmills
Magazine
GUNPOWDER
STREET
Paradise Creek
PRINCESS
AMELIA
YORK
BOTETOURT
DUNMORE
YARMOUTH
BUTE
QUEEN
CHARLOTTE
CATHERINE
CUMBERLAND
CHURCH
DUKE
BOUSH
GRANBY
FREEMASON STREET
Town Bridge
Masonic Hall
FALKLAND
MARINER
HOLT
St. Paul's
Back Creek
Elizabeth River
Town Point
CHURCH
Courthouse
Prison
MAIN
Market Place
BERMUDA
MAIN
Newton's Creek
INDUSTRIAL AREA
Tannery, Shoe Factory,
Worker Housing
Wharves, Warehouses, and Piers
Public
Wharf
0 Miles
0.25
0 Kilometers
0.25
© 2024 Jeffrey L. Ward

Chapter Twenty-Two

Keep Up the Jig

The first morning of 1776 dawned mercifully clear and unseasonably warm in Norfolk, a welcome change from the drizzle of November and bitter cold of December. The sun glowed in the east as a light breeze sprang up from the north-northwest, drying the damp clothes hanging on lines strung across ship decks and between patriot barracks. It was a fine day for the New Year's Day tradition of visiting neighbors and friends, giving gifts, and sharing terrapin stew, apple toddy, eggnog, and the heated spiced punch called wassail. In colonial Virginia, the first day of the year surpassed Christmas as a day of celebration.

On this New Year's, the thousand or more residents who remained in town had no time to revel. The previous day, Dunmore had sent ashore notices of an impending attack so that "women, children, and innocent persons might have time to remove out of danger," according to the governor's shipboard *Gazette*. Much as they had done at Great Bridge, the British intended to destroy several warehouses along the town's western wharves used by patriot riflemen as sniper's posts. The warning sent a new stream of refugees on foot, on horseback, and in carts crammed with beds, dressers, tables, and clothes lumbering up Church Street and out of town. Others found whatever could float to join the makeshift fleet sheltered under British guns. Still others stayed, including stubborn patriots, the elderly, the infirm, and women in labor. Some, like "old Sarah," were determined to protect their valuable property at any cost or had been ordered to protect that of their white owners.

Civilians on board the four warships were also on the move, vacating gun decks as the cannon crews prepared their weapons. The men stacked cannonballs and filled buckets with water to wet the swabs used to put out any embers left after a shot, while others rolled barrels of black powder from the magazines deep in each hold. Early that afternoon, Helen Maxwell and her family gathered in the warm sunshine on the waterfront outside of their friend's home on the swampy peninsula between Norfolk and Portsmouth. Their outing had the air of a picnic. "We saw the ships all drawn up in a line before the town, from the upper wharf to Town Point, and heard the drums beating on board of them," she said. The clamor signaled the landing parties to assemble. Select redcoats and members of both the Queen's Own and Ethiopian Regiments readied to board boats to shuttle them to shore.

The weather conditions for the limited operation were ideal. The gentle offshore wind, blowing away from rather than toward the town, assured a controlled burn of the buildings south of Main Street. At three o'clock, Bellew stood on the deck of the *Liverpool* as patriot troops were "parading in the streets," using "every mark of insult." One account has the shirtmen perching their coonskin caps on top of their firearms, taunting the British to make good on their threat. The captain obliged. He ordered three cannonballs lobbed at "the rebels' guardhouse to disperse them."

The gun crews snapped into action, loading a gunpowder charge and iron ball into each barrel and stuffing a wad of cloth on top to keep them in place. Then, using all their strength, the entire crew pushed the heavy mass—a twenty-four-pounder could weigh two tons—forward so the barrel poked well outside the ship's hull and used iron wedges and rope tackle to adjust the angle of the barrel to point at the offending guardhouse. At the shout of "Fire!" a crew member applied a spark or ember to the touchhole, igniting a priming-powder charge, which then set off the main charge, propelling the ball outward as the carriage violently rebounded. Depending on the angle and height from which it was fired, a twenty-four-pound cannonball might soar for a mile. A well-trained crew could reload and fire within two minutes.

Three iron balls flew from a dense cloud of powder smoke with a deafening roar. "When at length the first heavy gun of the fleet broke the horrible suspense," recalled a woman who had been a six-year-old girl at the time, "we all simultaneously started up with a sort of mournful cry or wail." The *Liverpool* shuddered with the recoil of the guns, a terrifying moment for those civilians—most, if not all—who had never experienced a naval cannonade. The patriot sentinels on the wharves leapt out of the path of flying metal. As the shots echoed across the harbor, the captain's "example was immediately followed by all of us," wrote Dunmore. Within fifteen minutes, his flagship, along with Montagu's *Kingfisher* and Squire's *Otter*, joined in the thunder. The fleet had a combined arsenal of nearly one hundred pieces of heavy artillery. White smoke filled the harbor, shrouding the ships in a choking haze.

"Under cover of the cannon, I sent some boats onshore to burn some detached warehouses on the lower part of the wharfs," the governor later reported. An hour after the first roar of cannon, the heavily laden tenders pushed off from the *Dunmore* and reached the docks unopposed. One patriot later reported that the landing parties were "principally Negroes . . . with torches." By 4:30 p.m., Bellew noted, "many of the storehouses were on fire upon the wharves." There were few if any initial casualties. According to the governor, the landing parties' success inflamed "the ardor of the men" watching from the ships' decks, which "could be not repressed." They boarded "a great number of boats" to assist their fellows in the burn, "by which means the fire soon became general on the wharves." One unidentified sailor aboard the *Otter* conveyed the sense of spontaneous excitement in an intercepted letter printed later by a patriot newspaper. "What a glorious fight ensued!" he exulted. "We firing as if heaven and earth were coming together, and every moment the horrid noise of the buildings tumbling in the town."

The British and loyalists targeted some warehouses to punish their rebel owners as well as deny cover to snipers. One patriot later claimed to hear Montagu order a party to destroy a building belonging to John Hutchings, brother of Joseph, the captive patriot commander. Shirtmen initially drove the king's forces back, but on a second try they succeeded in firing the storage facility. Howe told Pendleton that "under the fire of their ships, they landed in many places, and set fire to the houses on the wharves," though he claimed the enemy "were every time repulsed" as his men acted "with steadiness and spirit." Woodford also claimed later that the enemy attacks "never failed being repulsed by our people." Other than the skirmish at Hutchings's warehouse, however, there is no evidence that the patriots resisted the British and loyalist onslaught. The rebel commanders may have believed the British goal was to capture the city, rather than burn a handful of warehouses and then retreat.

The din from the guns, the crashing balls, the pop of muskets, and the billowing smoke convinced some remaining civilians to flee the mayhem. Maxwell observed a British tender intercept passengers in one fleeing boat that included "Old Sarah and her sow and pigs." Directed by the enslaved woman, the tender's crew towed the boat toward the shore where Maxwell's family was staying. Their hosts, however, assumed the British were making a hostile landing, and the husband, sons, and wife grabbed muskets and rushed to the beach. Helen didn't wait to see the outcome of the impending clash. "I instantly caught up my daughter Helen in my arms, and taking little Max by the hand, I set off to make my escape." She hurried to find refuge at the home of her host's sister a few miles away, "where I thought I should be more safe."

At five o'clock the winter sun slid below the horizon, and an eerie orange twilight suffused the harbor as the ships continued the bombardment and the warehouses blazed. Smoke from the burning buildings drifted over the flotilla, mingling with the puffs of gunpowder, as even the breeze died away. "The roar of the cannon was more and more dreadful in my ears," Maxwell recalled, as she and her two small children "trudged through wood and marsh" to put distance between herself and the awful noise. They quickly became lost as night fell. "A Negro man named Jack" owned by a friend's family came to their rescue. He took her daughter in his arms and led them toward their destination.

In the growing darkness, a buggy passed by with her brother and their mother. They recognized Maxwell only by her voice. "Oh Nelly, is that you?" her mother cried out. At that moment, a woman rode up "in the greatest alarm, saying that she had just heard that the British were going to set fire that night to all the houses along the river, and she was flying to her brothers for safety." Moments later, Maxwell's father appeared. He explained to the frightened group that their hosts and the British barge men had "succeeded in making peace." Sarah and her sow and piglets presumably had been landed safely at the dock without bloodshed. Reassured, the family returned to their lodging by the point. They "put down beds on the floor" and tried to sleep amid the thunder of heavy guns and the crackle of musket fire.

There was no rest for the thousands of civilians clustered tightly together on the vessels in the harbor. Howe reported that the cannonade "continued till near ten at night, without intermission; it then abated a little, and continued till two this morning." Squire said the firing halted at eleven o'clock. The ear-piecing booms of each shot, the quaking warships, the cries of the gun crews, the acrid vapors pouring from the gun barrels, and the fumes from the burning warehouses continued for between seven and eleven hours, transforming the harbor into a nightmarish maelstrom. "The horror of the night exceeds description and gives fresh occasion to lament the consequences of civil war," one "Norfolk gentleman" wrote in a letter later published in a Williamsburg *Gazette*. "The thunder of artillery, the crash of falling houses, the roar of devouring flames, added to the piteous moans and piercing shrieks of the few remaining wretched, ruined inhabitants, form the outlines of a picture too distressing to behold without a tear. I pray God I may never see the like again."

The barrage diminished as the landing parties returned to the ships, their mission accomplished only after dark. By then, the flaming warehouses were collapsing into vast fiery heaps. Remarkably, despite the hours of cannon, musket, and rifle fire, few casualties are recorded on either side. "The only damage we received, was one man losing his arm; a man from the *Otter* was wounded in the groin, and a carpenter killed belonging to the *Dunmore*," reported a midshipman on the *Liverpool*. On the patriot side, Howe noted, "We have not one man killed, and but a few wounded," though some later died of their injuries. Woodford later wrote that a "gentleman volunteer" named Smith had been injured by an iron missile, though "the surgeons have hope" of his recovery.

The North Carolina commander painted a far more dramatic picture of the British attack. "I cannot enter into the melancholy consideration of the women and children running through a crowd of shot to get out of the town," Howe wrote the following day, "some of them with children at their breasts; a few of them I hear have been killed." The heinous act, he insisted, required retribution. "Does it not call for vengeance both from God and man?" There is only one confirmed account, however, of a civilian casualty of the bombardment. Mary Wesley, a young mother with three young children and a disabled husband, later testified she was suckling her youngest at home when a cannonball—its velocity nearly spent—smashed into her leg, breaking at least one bone.

Meanwhile, a young white girl was taking shelter with her family in a downstairs room of a home in the northern suburbs when she heard the cry "The town is on fire!" She rushed with an enslaved woman from the relative safety of the first floor to peer out a second-story window. "I saw smoke and flames rising up from several points along the riverbank," she recalled many decades later. Her companion prayed loudly for God's mercy moments before "a ball crashed through the building carrying her head with it and her lifeless body sunk down at my feet pouring upon me a stream of blood." The child fainted and was carried to the safety of the cellar, which the family soon abandoned as the fire spread. They found "the town lit up with the ghastly glare of the burning buildings," while civilians headed "towards the open country loaded with a few of their most valuable articles which they were seeking to save from the general doom." However, the fact that this anonymous account, which was "received from the lips of a venerable old woman," did not appear in print until more than eighty years after the event puts its veracity in doubt.

The shelling did surprisingly little damage to the town. The balls were neither heated nor packed with powder to explode and were therefore unlikely to start a conflagration or destroy a building. With most residents gone, there were also few cooking fires and lit candles to spread fire. The barrage seems to have been concentrated in the southwestern part of the town's peninsula, where the landing parties needed cover, though some cannonballs soared over the downtown and into the northern suburbs. James Parker later found that the brick wall surrounding his compound in the Norfolk suburbs was "greatly battered with the cannon shot." A twenty-four-pounder, said to have come from the *Liverpool*, smashed into the southeastern corner of the borough church just beyond the isthmus. The ball lodged about three feet below the eaves, though it did not otherwise damage the sturdy brick sanctuary. The scatter of shots that landed beyond the wharves seems to have been the result of poor aim by cannon crews rather than of intentional efforts to damage the commercial and residential areas north of Main Street.

Those on the flotilla felt deep relief when the noise ceased, the smoke drifted away, and they saw their town largely intact. Relief turned to horror, however, when pinpricks of orange light multiplied along the streets beyond the isthmus. "The rebels," wrote Squire, who stood on the quarterdeck of the *Otter*, "set fire to many parts of the back of the town," that is, the northern suburbs. As flames began to lick at buildings far from the warehouse district, the Thompsons, Parkers, and numerous other families watched the fires spread. The sky turned a luminous ruby color, catching the attention of a patriot soldier stationed in Hampton, more than a dozen miles to the northwest. The clouds, he wrote his wife, "appeared as red and bright as they do in an evening at sun setting." As the first day of 1776 drew to a close, the thriving port that until recently had been home to more than six thousand people was a roaring inferno.

Among the patriot troops in Norfolk on that first day of January was the young John Marshall, who would become the nation's fourth and most influential chief justice. He and his comrades watched "with great composure" as "the flames spread from house to house without making any attempt to extinguish them." He also suggested the men may in fact have "contribute[d] to extend them," given that they held "a strong prejudice" against the port. One shirtman put it more colorfully. "The people in Norfolk were a foul nest of damned Tories," a resident heard a rebel soldier say, "and ought to have all their houses burnt and themselves burnt with them!"

Other eyewitness accounts of the first days of January 1776 provide extensive proof that Norfolk's destruction was an intentional act perpetrated by the patriots with the encouragement of their leaders.

These vivid reports, made under oath and transcribed in third person by a clerk as part of a 1777 patriot investigation, provide a close-up glimpse into an orgy of destruction that lasted two full days and nights. Late on the afternoon of January 1, local resident James Nicholson stood near Main Street as British and loyalist troops torched the waterside storehouses. He then watched "rejoicing" patriot troops "coming up from the warehouses loaded with plunder, which he saw them divide among them." After parceling out the goods, the men "went from house to house plundering and firing them, determined as they said to 'keep up the jig.'" This cry—echoed in the modern expression "to give up the jig"—equated pillaging and burning with the lively African-derived dance popular among Virginians. It became the patriot refrain in the days to come.

When Nicholson spotted a house ablaze on Church Street, several blocks north and east of the burning wharves, he rushed to put out the flames. Shirtmen threatened to arrest and imprison him if he didn't desist. Then he "observed several parties of the soldiers, particularly the riflemen, set fire to the houses in different parts of the town." Patriot officers urged them on. Lieutenant Colonel Edward Stevens of the Culpeper riflemen was overheard encouraging his men to take what they could from homes they were setting on fire.

Another Norfolk resident, Matthew McCrae, also witnessed the British set fire "to several warehouses on different wharves." Soon after, he saw "a number of the provincial troops going from house to house with torches in their hands, firing the different dwellings." When he accosted the soldiers, "they told him they had general orders for destroying all the houses, and they would be damned if they would not keep up the jig." He declared himself "positively certain" that the fire could not have spread from house to house "had they not been wantonly destroyed by the provincial troops."

A local patriot sailor named John Rogers made a particularly dogged if doomed effort that night to prevent his fellow troops from laying waste to the port. A sergeant in a company led by Captain George Nicholas, son of the colony's treasurer, had set fire to the house of Charles Thomas, a former Norfolk mayor and staunch patriot. Rogers repeatedly extinguished the flames, only to have the sergeant return to reignite the building. A North Carolina officer standing nearby refused to intervene. Rogers then hurried to Main Street, where he tried to dissuade another officer and a group of patriot soldiers from burning the house of watchmaker Samuel Bacon. They ignored his pleas. "It was better to destroy the town than be at the expense of arranging provisions to support the troops," the officer explained, neatly summing up the view espoused by Howe and Woodford.

A distraught Rogers watched a gang of shirtmen prepare to burn the pharmacy owned by Dr. Alexander Gordon, a Scottish physician censured by Virginia patriots for breaking the boycott when he imported remedies from Britain. The sailor saw through its windows "a large quantity of medicine in the shop which he was desirous of saving." He strode up with an air of authority and informed the men that he had personal orders from Howe to rescue the valuable pharmaceuticals. They agreed to spare the building, and Rogers rushed off to find the patriot commander before the men called his bluff. The commander refused to help, insisting that it was too dangerous to send a horse-drawn wagon through the flaming streets to recover the medicines. Gordon's valuable pharmaceuticals were lost.

Rogers nevertheless continued his tireless quest to limit—or at least record—the devastation. At eleven o'clock that night he was on the wharves making a careful inventory as patriot troops broke into an undamaged warehouse. They made off with "a small cask of rum and a cask of about forty gallons of wine, two boxes of soap, five or six boxes of candles, a number of speaking trumpets, and other articles," he said. The men took most of this loot to Captain Richard Meade, who led a battalion of the Second Virginia Regiment and was quartered on Main Street in the former printshop of printer John Hunter Holt. Meade would go on to serve as Washington's aide-de-camp.

Some soldiers hawked their looted goods openly in the streets even as the buildings burned. One patriot officer told Norfolk shoemaker James Leitch that if the enemy did not burn the town, "the state would do it for them." He did, however, help Leitch procure two wagons to transport his belongings out of the conflagration. As he made his way through the streets, Leitch noted "several houses in the town, particularly belonging to Mr. Boush in Cumberland Street, set on fire by the soldiers, who encouraged each other to 'keep up the jig.'" Then they torched the home of Archibald Campbell, the

Scottish physician, who also lived on that street, as did Jane and Talbot Thompson. Standing just a few hundred yards away on a vessel deck, the couple would have watched in impotent horror as their clapboard house and outbuildings, the fruits of decades of toil, vanished in the raging flames.

When a warehouse owned by Sprowle caught fire, the flames leapt to the adjacent residence of an elderly Mr. Phripp. Norfolk resident Paul Wallington rushed in and carried the frail man to safety, then went back inside to recover "two looking glasses," along with other valuables. Meanwhile, "a man with a hunting shirt" absconded with one of the costly mirrors as Phripp cowered outside the burning home. An outraged Wallington confronted several shirtmen busy looting the house of another local patriot. "One of them threatened to knock him down with a tomahawk and observed that as all the houses were to be burnt, he might as well have part of what is in it, then let it be destroyed." The outraged citizen sought out a patriot lieutenant, who agreed to order the soldiers to vacate the houses, "though not before they had carried off some of the liquor and other things." It was a Pyrrhic victory; the building was later destroyed. Wallington then walked down Main Street to Market Square as shirtmen torched the market house, the town's economic heart.

Even women in labor could expect little sympathy from the patriots. Parnell Archdeacon Ingram was "very far gone with child and had the midwife with her, and several other women," reported William Ingram, the brother of her absent Scottish merchant husband. He was stunned when shirtmen burst into the home. "They declared they would burn it unless" she showed proof of her patriot credentials. Despite her condition, Archdeacon managed to produce a note from Colonel Howe assuring the men of her loyalty to the cause. The intruders, Ingram added, left to set fire to a nearby house owned by an orphan named John Gilchrist—but not before they told Archdeacon that "they had orders to burn every house in the town."

Shortly before midnight, as flames rose from neighboring roofs, she gave birth to a healthy daughter named Nancy. Mother and child managed to escape Norfolk before their home was reduced to ash. When Nancy married in 1797, her guardian noted in the registry that she was born on "a remarkable day for this town."

Chapter Twenty-Three

A Feeling Bosom

At dawn on Tuesday, January 2, a midshipman on the *Liverpool* made out "a dismal sight of ruins, and the town still in flames." He predicted, accurately, that the fires would rage for another three to four days. By seven o'clock, a quarter hour before the sun crept above the flat horizon, the crack of gunshots broke the morning stillness. "As soon as the shirtmen could see, they peppered us with their rifle barrels," he wrote. "As they have every advantage over us, they do not fail to make use of it, which renders our firing useless, as we cannot see one of them." After taking a shot, "they tumble down flat on their bellies, load again, and then rise up and fire."

The racket jolted awake any civilians on the flotilla snatching a few hours of rest after enduring the sight of their town's fiery demise. "The rebels began to fire upon us with musketry," reported the *Liverpool*'s Captain Bellew, "which we returned with great guns until they dispersed." The *Otter* joined in with its full complement of cannon, swivel guns, and muskets. Soon, white clouds of exploding gunpowder mixed with the black plumes of smoke again surging into the windless sky. Gangs of patriot soldiers and officers took little notice. In those early hours, inured to the sound of cannon, they roamed the streets, lighting new fires and gathering loot from abandoned shops and homes.

A local early riser named John Smith stepped outside his Norfolk home and saw a line of attached houses called Red Row on fire. He asked a group of nearby soldiers who was responsible and "was assured it was a matter of little consequence who did it, as there were orders from the commanding officer to burn all the houses on that side of the church." He apparently was referring to tenement housing for enslaved or free Black laborers who worked in the nearby Scottish factories east of Church Street. Smith later encountered a sergeant who bragged that "he burnt Red Row, and it ought to have been burnt long before."

Local resident Richard Jarvis watched helplessly that morning as two Carolina militia officers prepared to set a still-intact residence ablaze. Jarvis begged them to spare the house "as it belonged to an orphan child." At first the officers agreed, but they soon returned. "'We must keep up the jig,'" they told him, "and set fire to it, and it was burnt to the ground." Jarvis was convinced the blaze in that part of town would have died down "had it not been frequently renewed by the soldiers, who during the whole time were carrying household furniture and goods about the streets and offered the same for sale, at very trifling prices."

Arthur Smith, a patriot captain, reported that the fires raged on through Wednesday, "though he believes none of the enemy were onshore in the town all that time." Howe noted that the warships "kept up a pretty smart fire" that wounded several men. For the most part, however, the British and loyalists could only watch helplessly from a distance as shirtmen laid waste to their own city. According to Smith, "many of the officers in the service of the state" urged Howe and Woodford to halt the arson and looting. They feared "if some means were not used," then "the whole town would be consumed." Both commanders ignored their protests. The captain testified that it was not until Wednesday that "orders were issued that no more houses should be fired on pain of death, and that the fire ceased soon after." No such written command has been found, and Howe made no mention of such a decree in his January 3 letter to Pendleton, in which he estimated that "seven-eighths of the town" had been "reduced to ashes."

Not even privies were spared. Resident William Goodchild watched a shirtman set fire to his neighbor's "necessary house." He encountered an officer who told him, "Yes, damn them, we will burn them all." One of the few female eyewitnesses on record, Sarah Smith, "observed a soldier taking down the pales which enclosed the garden" of the Calvert property as others looted the wine and set fire to the house. She boldly berated the man for his behavior, but was told "she need not complain, for she might think herself worse off that she was not burnt with the house." Shirtmen also stooped to blackmail. An officer later confided to Smith that his men had taken "two dollars from a certain Mr. Baker," in exchange for agreeing "to delay burning his house, until he could remove his wife and children out of it."

William Ivey, a patriot merchant captain, became furious on January 3 when he saw that "several houses were then on fire belonging to persons whom he thought friendly to the American cause." These included George Abyvon, the former mayor. Ivey later said under oath that he sought out a senior patriot officer named Francis Eppes and "remonstrated with him on the impropriety of burning the houses of such persons." Eppes brusquely dismissed his complaint by saying that "all the houses were to be destroyed." As they spoke, Howe appeared. When Eppes repeated Ivey's criticism, the North Carolinian "threatened the deponent with confinement in the guard house, for giving his opinion."

Even as the city burned around him, Howe pressed his case with Pendleton for total demolition. "Norfolk is a post which would require at least five times our number of men to maintain it," he insisted, and those "would be in danger and might certainly be shut in and starved out." Patriot forces would be unable to halt loyalists in Norfolk and Princess Anne Counties from provisioning the British ships, "notwithstanding all our efforts to prevent it." He concluded that the town was "almost useless if maintained," and recommended falling back to Great Bridge.

By three o'clock the next afternoon, Thursday, January 4, Woodford estimated that "nine-tenths of the town is destroyed, but the fire is out." The once-bustling downtown was now dominated by a forest of charred black chimneys and heaps of smoking rubble as refugees fled the desolate scene. "The distress of these miserable people in the suburbs and along the road is scarcely to be described," Woodford added. "We have afforded them all the assistance in our power, for which purpose all the wagons have been detained, but how they will be removed further is not in our power to say."

Two days later, Howe gave an update to Pendleton. "The town of Norfolk, sir, is in a very ruinous condition, seven-eighths of it being reduced to ashes." The North Carolinian insisted that his "feeling bosom" was filled with compassion for "the unfortunate inhabitants of this town." He did not, however, admit blame or express remorse for his role in the ruination. "Though my heart bleeds for the sufferings of individuals whose distress I truly deplore," he wrote to the Committee of Safety president, Norfolk's loss was nevertheless "greatly beneficial to the public."

Before he knew Norfolk was in flames, Jefferson's close friend John Page had second thoughts about obliterating the port. "I think it would be better not to destroy the town, for it is possible that matters may be accommodated in a short time," he wrote Woodford on January 2. "In that case, we shall have done ourselves a great injury to no purpose and shall be laughed at by our enemies." Instead of demolition, he proposed bottling up the British there, as was done in Boston. "Let them take the houses, and let us confine them there, and cut off all communication between them and the rest of the country. It may be wise to draw their attention to so worthless a part of our country; it may mean saving some more valuable place." He also worried that setting fire to one town set a disturbing precedent. "If our enemies oblige us to burn Norfolk," Page added, "may they not oblige us to burn Portsmouth, Hampton, and York?"

What Page apparently did not know was that Pendleton, who served with him on the Committee of Safety, had already sent Howe a secret directive at the start of January, before news of the conflagration reached the capital. The patriot commanders were told to destroy Norfolk's key industrial plants. These instructions have since been lost, but the colonel referred to them soon after. "In consequence of your order," Howe wrote Pendleton January 6, "a party was sent out to the distillery under the command of Major Eppes, who was directed to destroy the pumps, fill up the wells, and do everything else which could promote the end proposed by you."

The Scottish-owned Thistle Distillery, one of two such plants near Norfolk, converted sugar and molasses imported from the West Indies into rum. The January 4 assault, Woodford reported, "drew a heavy cannonade and fire of musketry," since the *Dunmore* "lay abreast of that place." Eppes, however, "had the good fortune to lose never a man," even when the British and loyalists attempted to land boats. His troops, he said, "killed several of them" before proceeding to their task, which included, Howe added, destroying "a great quantity of molasses."

The second industrial target was Sprowle's sprawling shipyard, which stood a quarter mile upstream on the river's southern branch. Gosport had served as Dunmore's main land base and remained a critical depot for supplies and water. When the fleet moved downstream to anchor off Norfolk in November, the compound was left vulnerable to attack. On January 4, just after sunset, the British skirmished with a patriot contingent that landed at the site. "They were fired upon very smartly both from cannon and musketry, but providentially lost not a man," Howe wrote of the shirtmen. "They burned the pumps, houses, and everything at that place, and attempted to destroy a windmill from which the ships receive their chief supply," he added. "But the fire going out and a number of [enemy] boats approaching . . . , they retreated." The *London Chronicle* reported that patriots "broke open all the warehouses and plundered them, and that night set fire to all the buildings on the place and burnt them to the ground." According to the January 8 *Gazette*, Gosport is "burnt by our people, on which account old Sprowle has lost considerable property."

For the aging Scot, who had taken refuge on one of the British warships, the bright glow of his slave-powered fiefdom visible from the harbor must have been a bitter sight. His new wife, who had just wed a man purported to be the richest in the colony, no doubt stood pale at his side as his accumulated wealth dissolved in smoke. "The destruction of that place is a very heavy loss to Mr. Andrew Sprowle," noted one eyewitness. "Besides all the dwelling houses there was in his store many heavy and bulky goods of considerable value."

Pendleton's third goal was to raze the milling and baking operation at Tucker's Mill Point to cut off Dunmore's bread supply. Jane

Thompson's former owner, Robert Tucker, had built the complex run by enslaved labor on a knob of land along the Elizabeth River just below and opposite Norfolk, and his son had recently expanded and modernized a plant that was the largest in the South. Many of its unfree workers were relations or friends of the Thompsons, and many if not most had fled to the flotilla in December.

Squire reported on January 6 that "the rebels attempted to set fire to the mills at the point," and his ship "fired several six pounders and dispersed them." While Woodford admitted the expedition "was not so successful," he added that it "must be the business of another night." At ten o'clock on the evening of January 8, the same night the patriots attacked Gosport, Squire "perceived the mills to be on fire" and had his gunners shoot "several six-pounders," which again "dispersed the rebels." It was too late; the flames spread through buildings filled with highly combustible material. When the sails of the windmills caught fire, they flared briefly like twin burning Greek crosses above the harbor.

By the end of the first week of 1776, the fire that first engulfed Norfolk's downtown had expanded into a blazing arc encircling the flotilla. A *Gazette* reported with satisfaction on January 12 that "all the mills at Tucker's Point, with the Scotch distillery, and Mr. Sprowle's houses at Gosport, are totally demolished, as is likewise the chief part of Norfolk, a few houses only remaining above the church which are occupied."

This was just the start of the patriot campaign to punish the twenty thousand or more inhabitants of Norfolk and Princess Anne Counties for their failure to back the rebel cause. On January 4, Eppes met with a Scottish-born captain named William Chisholm, who had lost his Norfolk home and now squatted near the recently ruined distillery. Eppes relayed orders from Woodford "that it was his intention to burn all the houses between Kemp's Landing and the Cape which were within a mile of the water." The cape was Cape Henry, the promontory ten miles northeast of Kemp's Landing where the Chesapeake met the Atlantic. Hundreds of small farms and plantations lined the area's many creeks and inlets. A frightened Chisholm again fled with his family, and this time "encamped in the woods." Others followed suit. The directive spawned a second wave of desperate refugees as winter wore on.

Virginia Convention delegates worried that Norfolk and Princess Anne Counties remained thick with people loyal to Dunmore and the king. While reluctant to force thousands from their homes, the delegates "recommended" that residents "as may be exposed to the attacks of the enemy . . . remove themselves and their effects, and that the poorer sort be assisted in their removal by the public." Among the handful of remaining Norfolk residents, meanwhile, a rumor passed that the few surviving structures would be torched. Sarah Smith lived in one of those untouched homes. She sought out Howe and bluntly "asked him if he intended to burn the house in which she lived." After hesitating for a moment, the patrician colonel gave a chilling reply. "Yes," he told her, "I believe we shall burn up the two counties."

Later, in Britain, the famous parliamentarian and patriot sympathizer Edmund Burke would finger Lord Dunmore as the "principal actor in burning and destroying the best town in his government." He mourned the fate of Norfolk, the linchpin of the province's commerce that had been "growing and flourishing before these unhappy troubles." Burke estimated the total loss at a staggering 300,000 pounds, or about $30 million in today's currency.

The claim that the royal governor was to blame for this disaster was made even before the final cannonade subsided. In a joint letter written to Pendleton at ten o'clock at night on January 1, Howe and Woodford insisted a brisk southerly breeze fanned the warehouse inferno started by the British that afternoon, like bellows on fireplace coals. Howe wrote that these fires "spread with amazing rapidity," though his men "strove to prevent them."

There are, however, no eyewitness accounts of patriots dousing a single blaze, and several experienced sailors on both sides agreed that the day's gentle breeze blew in the opposite direction. "At the time the fire began in the town, the wind was at north northwest and very moderate, blowing off from the town," said local mariner John Rogers when questioned later under oath. Such an offshore breeze would have contained the fires set by the governor's troops. These sources, highly attuned to the weather, also confirm that even this light wind died out completely after dusk. Without a steady southern wind, particularly given the wet conditions, witnesses insisted the conflagration could not have spread on its own.

The patriot press was first to describe the disaster, drawing heavily on the correspondence of Howe and Woodford and accepting their fabrications as truth. A *Gazette* editor further embellished the story to create a suitably lurid and melodramatic tale of British cruelty. The account published January 6 stretched a sporadic ships' barrage of seven to eleven hours into a sustained bombardment lasting more than a full day. "It is affirmed that one hundred cannon played on the town almost incessantly for 25 hours," stated the article. "Notwithstanding this heavy firing and the town in flames around them, our men had the resolution to maintain their posts, and the coolness to aim as usual."

In this telling, the British were "repulsed with considerable loss in every attempt." Six of the enemy were said to have been killed, "and great numbers were supposed to be carried off in their boats" while "we did not lose a man." A brief mention of fleeing citizens became "poor women and children running about through the fire, and exposed to the guns from the ships, and some of them with children at their breasts." The article also repeated Woodford's unsubstantiated contention that "some poor women were killed in endeavoring to move out of town." The identity of the culprits was obvious. "Let our countrymen view and contemplate the scene!" the article proclaimed.

Members of the Fourth Virginia Convention meeting in Williamsburg were quick to condemn the governor for waging "an open and avowed war with the good people of this colony," conducted with "unrelenting fury." King George III and Dunmore were guilty of "burning and destroying open and defenseless towns, contrary to the practices of war among civilized nations," as well as "exciting insurrections among our slaves, investing the savages, and arming them against us." The rebel committee of Sussex County lambasted "the tyrannical, cruel, and destructive executioner of ministerial violence, Lord Dunmore, and his banditti of Blacks and Scotch Tories and Jacobites." From her plantation west of Richmond, patriot Judith Bell named the governor "as the cause of all the disturbances and all the bloodshed in Virginia," including Norfolk's destruction, and accused him of taking "pleasure in killing his fellow men."

Dunmore tried to provide a more accurate account in the January 18 edition of his shipboard newspaper. The article noted that residents had been warned to leave town before the barrage began and assured readers that the New Year's Day's "wind was moderate and from the shore," making it certain "the destruction would end with that part of the town next [to] the water, which the king's ships meant only should be fired." Blame for the rest of the devastation lay solely with the patriots. "The rebels cruelly and unnecessarily completed the destruction of the whole town by setting fire to the houses in the streets back, which were before safe from the flames." They also spread additional havoc by burning the Scottish-owned distillery, "a work of great value and public utility with a large stock of rum and molasses."

Though undoubtedly more factual, this dry and defensive commentary had limited circulation and little impact on public opinion. Patriot presses continued to paint a grim picture of a port "reduced to ashes, and become desolate, through the wicked and cruel machinations of Lord North and the junto, aided by their faithful servants, my Lord Dunmore, with his motley army." One British army officer lamented that the rebels had taken "the inhumanity of the action off their shoulders" to place it "upon our own." Dunmore may have had superior firepower, but Williamsburg's editors, once again, had outgunned the governor in print. For generations to come, the royal governor would be reviled as the new country's most notorious arsonist.

Chapter Twenty-Four

Flaming Arguments

Talk of independence from Great Britain was still taboo among most patriots at the start of 1776. Those in the Continental Congress who strongly favored separation from Britain, such as Jefferson and John Adams, feared alienating more moderate and conservative colleagues by pressing the point. Virginia's Pendleton was not alone in believing a peace accord might still be reached; Pennsylvania's John Dickinson and others continued to urge negotiation, while Maryland's delegation insisted they "never did, nor do, entertain any desires of independency."

In December 1775, Massachusetts representative Elbridge Gerry replaced the conservative Thomas Cushing, nudging that delegation in the direction of autonomy. Some Southerners, however, suspected independence was a ploy by such radical New Englanders to replace Britain as the new masters of the continent. One Virginia planter dismissed the notion of self-rule as "a delusive bait which men inconsiderately snatch at, without knowing the hook to which it is affixed."

News of King George III's October speech to Parliament declaring independence as the rebels' true goal reached Philadelphia at the end of the first week of 1776. On January 8, Dickinson drafted a response "to assure his Majesty that he is misinformed." That same day, "an express came with letters from Baltimore informing that Lord Dunmore has destroyed the town of Norfolk in Virginia," according to a diary entry by New Jersey delegate Richard Smith. The shocking news seemed proof that Britain would show no mercy in stamping out the rebellion. A major American port lay in ruins under the relentless guns of British warships. Philadelphia, New York, or Charleston might be next. Dickinson's resolution never made it to the floor.

The January 9 edition of Philadelphia's *Pennsylvania Evening Post* carried the text of the king's speech as well as an advertisement for a new pamphlet by an anonymous writer. The forty-seven-page tract, *Common Sense*, went on sale the next day, and it remains the most popular American title ever published. Setting aside arcane philosophical arguments and political jargon, the writer—later revealed to be an obscure English immigrant named Thomas Paine—made a passionate and persuasive argument for both separation from Britain and a more egalitarian system of government. "Until an independence is declared," the author insisted, "the continent will feel itself like a man who continues putting off some unpleasant business from day to day, yet knows it must be done, hates to set about it, wishes it over, and is continually haunted with the thoughts of its necessity."

When John Hancock confirmed the loss of the Virginia port a week later, he wrote Washington, "Lord Dunmore has endeavored to exercise the same barbarity against the defenseless town of Norfolk as was exercised against Falmouth" two months previously in Maine. The congressional president criticized an act that was "contrary to the rules of war . . . by all civilized nations." He added that "it would seem as if the rancorous ministry, despairing of their measures to conquer and enslave, had determined to glut their revenge with destruction and devastation."

The next day, Virginia delegate Benjamin Harrison cursed "our devil of a governor," adding, "I hope providence in its good time will bring him to account for all his misdoings." The king's belligerent stance coupled with the earl's alleged atrocities made compromise unthinkable. "We have nothing to expect but fire and sword," he added.

The loss of Norfolk, purportedly at the hands of the British, prompted Congress to issue final orders for the colonies' first fleet, anchored off Philadelphia, to sail to Chesapeake Bay to relieve "the peculiar distresses" in Virginia. The commander was to carry on the topmast of his flagship "a Jack with the Union flag and striped red and white in the field." This was the first flag of the nascent United States, which Lieutenant John Paul Jones had hoisted in December.

Fifty-seven-year-old Esek Hopkins, a Rhode Island captain, was given the grand title of "commander in chief of the fleet of the United Colonies."

The five small merchant ships converted to armed vessels were no match for even a single British ship of war, much less a fleet of four with a hundred cannon. A Maryland patriot leader in Annapolis warned Hancock that given "the strength of Lord Dunmore," it was "imprudent to hazard" an encounter with the British. What the patriot fleet lacked in size and firepower, however, the naval committee hoped to make up for in speed and secrecy. "You will discern, gentlemen, that the greatest dispatch will be necessary," Hopkins's orders read, "the success of the stroke being more sure as it [may] be most sudden and unexpected."

The commander was ordered to halt at the mouth of the Chesapeake and watch for a white flag waved by a sentinel at Cape Henry in Princess Anne County. He would "furnish the commander in chief with the most accurate information of the then strength and situation of Lord Dunmore's fleet and land forces." The next step was up to Hopkins. "If by such intelligence you find that they are not greatly superior to your own, you are immediately to enter the said bay, search out and attack, take, or destroy all the naval force of our enemies that you may find there." He was directed to take on two hundred "expert riflemen . . . before they come in sight of the enemy." Fast vessels bristling with the barrels of skilled snipers might not be able to sink a frigate, but they could harry it and even force a surrender. The commander was granted permission to "follow such courses as your best judgement shall suggest to you as most useful to the American cause."

The Continental Congress recognized that land troops were needed to supplement the fleet. Three Pennsylvania companies ordered to Virginia the previous month had been reassigned to the faltering American campaign in Canada. Maryland was tasked with supplying minutemen companies in their place, and Pennsylvania was asked to distribute half a ton of precious gunpowder. These combined land and sea forces were the patriots' best hope to neutralize the governor and his loyalist allies before the expected British invasion of the southern colonies. But outfitting the ships and organizing the troops would take at least a month.

Meanwhile, word of Norfolk's fiery end spread north and south, serving as a warning for any American port. New Yorkers read about the town's destruction on January 25. The following day, Charleston's *South Carolina and American General Gazette* reported that Dunmore had left "three parts of the town . . . in ashes." At Continental Army headquarters in Cambridge, Hancock's letter and a copy of Paine's pamphlet landed on Washington's cluttered desk at almost the same moment. "The destruction of Norfolk and threatened devastation of other places will have no other effect than to unite the whole country," the general predicted on January 31. Britain "seems to be lost to every sense of virtue, and those feelings which distinguish a civilized people from the most barbarous savages." The earl's old friend concluded that "a few more of such flaming arguments" coupled with the "unanswerable reasoning contained in *Common Sense* will not leave numbers at a loss to decide upon the propriety of a separation."

This sudden shift in public opinion alarmed loyalists and the British. Dunmore's February 3 *Gazette* argued that an American victory was an impossibility, given "a defenseless coast without a navy, a country without manufactures, a treasury without money, [and] an army without clothing, arms, ammunition, or discipline." But January's alchemy of Paine's pamphlet, the king's speech, and Norfolk's "flaming argument" had abruptly altered the political landscape. "The propriety of a separation" no longer seemed so far-fetched. For many, the unthinkable was now necessity.

On Christmas Day 1775, members of "Jack Dunmore's hopeful gang, consisting of soldiers, sailors, and Negroes," had marched into Williamsburg under "a strong guard" of patriots. Another bleak procession took place ten days later. Some had been captured at sea by patriot privateers, while others were apprehended at Great Bridge and in and around Norfolk. Many of the British and other white prisoners were confined in the spacious Public Hospital, one of North

America's first mental institutions, which had opened under Dunmore's tenure. Patriot captives taken by the British were confined to ships in Norfolk's harbor. They doubtless endured harsh conditions, though officers like the wounded Hutchings were allowed to receive food and clothing from patriots onshore.

Africans taken into rebel custody were sent to the capital's notorious public jail, which stood in a small ravine within sight of the Capitol. From the outside, it looked like any brick story-and-a-half Virginia building, save for the high wall enclosing an exercise yard. Its eight cells had once held the pirate crew of the famous renegade Blackbeard, but its more typical prewar inmates were a half dozen or so local men and women of both colors waiting to be tried, branded, whipped, or executed for a host of crimes. The unlikely superintendent was a genial English-born composer and musician named Peter Pelham, who also served as the organist at Bruton Parish Church and tutored young women in music. The jail job provided the additional income and comfortable lodgings Pelham needed to support a wife and fourteen children. As an added benefit, he could bring a prisoner to Sunday service to pump the sanctuary's organ while he played hymns for the congregation.

Pelham struggled to cope with the sudden influx of Black people accused of rebellion, prompting the Virginia Convention to appoint a panel "to inquire into the several cases of the prisoners confined in the public jail." On January 17, the committee chair reported that there were nearly fifty people jammed into the small facility. Two enslaved women, Rachel and Amy, were imprisoned for theft, while Neptune, owned by the prominent lawyer and congressional delegate George Wythe, had run away from his absent owner.

The rest were suspected insurrectionists. Forty-one Black men had been captured in battle or while trying to join the British. Among them were twenty-nine enslaved Africans taken at Great Bridge. "Some of them have been active, and some of them borne arms, under Lord Dunmore," the chair noted. Five others had been taken in the vicinity, while seven men had been seized in Hampton before they could reach British lines. Many were shackled by their feet or hands. A loyalist sergeant named Henry Crouch also was incarcerated;

his two names and rank suggest that he was a white man who served as an officer in the Ethiopian Regiment.

The committee did not directly address the obviously dire conditions in the jail. Only after many enslaved people expired in custody in subsequent months did angry slaveowners demand an inquiry to protect their human property. That May 1776 report found the jail "badly planned . . . for the purpose of admitting a free air." Given the lack of facilities and the "large and unusual number of prisoners," it said, Black inmates were confined to rooms that "abound[ed] with filth" and were filled with an "offensive smell . . . [that] would be injurious to the most robust health."

The unheated rooms, unsanitary cesspits, poor food, and severe overcrowding bred a host of illnesses, including the dreaded "gaol fever," now known as typhus. Lice and fleas typically spread bacteria that assaulted victims with high fevers, intense chills, delirium, and purple rashes, often leading to death. Dysentery, then called by the more graphic term "bloody flux," took hold when germs or parasites infected a person's intestines, leading to severe diarrhea, nausea, vomiting, stomach cramps, and weight loss. Bleeding gums, bruised skin, and severe joint pain accompanied scurvy, a vitamin C deficiency stemming from a lack of fresh fruit and vegetables.*

Rather than address the appalling conditions in the jail, members of the Virginia Convention argued instead over what to do with the growing number of Black prisoners. They determined that those found innocent of any involvement with Dunmore were to be returned to their owners, so long as their food and board tab was paid. If owners did not claim their property, the enslaved people were to be sold at public auction, with the money going to the colony's treasury. Rachel and Amy were to be transferred to their own county's jail, while Crouch was to remain in the prison.

Black insurrectionists confronted a far bleaker future. Death was the established punishment, though it was also costly; owners had to be compensated for the worth of their lost human property. One

* Archaeologists excavating the site in the 1930s uncovered two underground dungeons with iron leg restraints within each. A male skeleton lay next to a set of shackles and a large padlock.

alternative was to put them to work in distant lead mines. The deposits lay three hundred miles to the west, in the Appalachians, at an altitude of two thousand feet. Entrepreneur John Chiswell discovered the lode of ore close to the New River in 1761. With the help of Welsh experts, he transformed the remote and rugged site into the only major source of this vital metal in the American colonies. A group of Virginia investors led by wealthy planter William Byrd III eventually bought the concern. Since it was cheaper to import lead from Britain, the Chiswell mine remained a small operation; at the start of 1776, Byrd employed only four enslaved Africans—Big Joe, Little Isaac, Lewis, and Sligo—along with a handful of Welsh experts.

The end of trade with Britain made the mine a critical asset for patriots who needed a steady supply of domestically produced bullets. Soon after Byrd joined the patriot cause in the wake of Dunmore's declaration, Pendleton began negotiating with him to remedy "the want of lead for public use." The committee president agreed the colony would pay rent, "that the public may work the lead mines," and asked to lease Byrd's forced laborers, "if it would be convenient to you to part with either for a year." A former burgess named James Callaway, an old friend of Washington's who had built an iron foundry, was put in charge of the new patriot-funded facility.

The expanded operations required additional labor, and the sudden influx of Black prisoners in Williamsburg provided a welcome solution. Those found guilty of carrying arms for Dunmore would serve as "public Negroes" to produce the bullets needed to kill the British. This decision outraged some slaveowners. On January 8, eleven patriot planters from Norfolk and Princess Anne Counties argued that the delegates were too "lenient and merciful . . . respecting the slaves who bore arms against us." They urged that the convicts be transported "to some of the West India islands, or elsewhere."

The Virginia Convention gave in to their demands. Those Africans "who have been active under Lord Dunmore or have borne arms in his service" would be imprisoned until they could be "properly valued and sent to the foreign West India islands, or the Bay of Honduras, there to be sold" to the brutal forced-labor sugar camps dotting the Caribbean. The proceeds would be "repaid to their respective owners, provided they are not unfriendly to American liberty."

At least one patriot brig sailed for the West Indies with seven or eight Black prisoners the following month, with plans to trade the men for "a supply of powder and ammunition for the use of the state." The ship, crew, and manacled passengers were captured by the Royal Navy. Profits from selling both the vessel and the human cargo went instead to the treasury in London. British control of the sea made such voyages too risky, so the Convention reversed itself. Those insurrectionists who survived the rigors of Williamsburg's jail were forced to make the grueling march to the Chiswell lead mines.

Among the men imprisoned in the Williamsburg jail were Peter Anderson and Caesar, the wounded men captured at the Battle of Great Bridge. As a free Black man deemed to have been armed, Anderson was tried, found guilty of treason, and sentenced to die. He soon escaped the fetid prison and, after making a daring dash through enemy territory, later reunited with Dunmore's forces. Caesar, meanwhile, was brought before the Committee of Safety on February 7 for questioning; his enslaved status precluded a trial. Described later as a five-foot, seven-inch man "of a square athletic make," he claimed that his loyalist owner in Norfolk ordered him to Fort Murray. When he attempted to give himself up to shirtmen during a skirmish, one of them shot him. Pendleton and other committee members dismissed his claim of innocence, though they decided the teenager had not borne arms. After he was "valued," the captive was "taken and employed for the benefit of this colony in the lead mines." Patrick Henry assigned soldiers to escort him and other prisoners west.

After completing the arduous journey by foot, Caesar and his fellow convicts faced a torturous existence. Extracting and processing the ore was a dirty and dangerous business. "The metal is mixed, sometimes with earth, sometimes with rock, which requires the force of gunpowder to open it," Jefferson explained in his 1785 book *Notes on the State of Virginia*. Caesar would have been issued a heavy iron pickaxe to work in horizontal shafts and deep vertical pits. He also may have been tasked with transporting the heavy rock over a swift, broad stream. "The present furnace is a mile from the ore bank, and on the opposite side of the river," Jefferson noted. "The ore is first wagoned to the river a quarter of a mile, then laden on board of canoes and carried across the river, which is there about two hundred yards wide, and then again taken into wagons and carried to the furnaces."

Enslaved workers then smelted the rock, a process that required constant logging to fuel the furnaces. The final step was to pour the resulting molten lead into bullet molds. When cool, they were packaged and shipped out by wagon. Daily hazards included rockfalls inside the mines, drowning in the swift and frigid river, lead poisoning, and respiratory illnesses from toxic furnace fumes. Caesar and his fellow unfree workers also suffered from inadequate food, clothing, and shelter in the harsh environment. Jefferson wrote that workers were even required to "cultivate their own corn." One slaveowner, concerned that his valuable human property was being misused, bitterly complained of the mines' "unwholesome service."

Eventually, the unfree workers were joined by enslaved women who cooked, cleaned, and repaired worn and damaged clothing, which may have somewhat eased their extreme hardships, though not the dangers they faced. In his description of the mines, Jefferson estimated that between thirty and fifty men produced between twenty and sixty tons of lead each year, though he did not reveal that they were enslaved laborers.

In July 1776, as nineteen African convicts were trudging west to Chiswell from Williamsburg, Jefferson wrote Henry to request that fifteen to twenty tons of lead be sent immediately to Philadelphia. That same month, North Carolina patriots asked for five tons, "as the inhabitants of our frontier have scarcely any and are in the most distressed situation." By August, a *Gazette* reported that "15,000 weight of pure lead have been got from our mines in the backcountry, which, after being cast into bullets, we hope will be unerringly directed against our enemies." Two months later, ten tons had been shipped to Washington's army then encamped outside New York.

Chiswell became a grim state-sponsored Appalachian gulag essential to the patriot cause. Production soared to nearly 65,000 pounds in 1779, and the British tried unsuccessfully to attack the facility the following year. Jefferson called it "an object of vast importance" and added that it was "impossible they can be worked to too great an extent" given that they were "perhaps the sole means of supporting the American cause." The ore, he added, would also benefit Virginia by bringing in "no trifling sum of money."

As late as 1781, a Virginian told Washington that the lead mines were "of much consequence to the United States." By then, they were overseen by Charles Lynch, famous for punishing Black and white loyalists without benefit of a trial; his extrajudicial activities gave rise to the term "lynching." Even after the American victory at Yorktown in October of that year, Black men convicted of siding with the enemy were sentenced to years of hard labor. In 1785, after nearly a decade in the mines, Caesar managed to escape the mountain prison camp. He was last seen wearing the blue-and-white uniform of the disbanded Continental Army that had depended so heavily on the lead he and his fellow inmates had arduously produced.

Chapter Twenty-Five

Ill-Judged Measures

Norfolk's occupying force of roughly fifteen hundred shirtmen predictably grew hungry, sick, and cold after they had laid waste to the borough. Around them were the smoking heaps of debris from the very homes, tenements, mills, distilleries, and warehouses that might have kept them well fed, clothed, and housed during the harsh winter. Woodford acknowledged to his troops that he was "very sensible that many of the men suffer from want of shoes," but the large footwear factory lay in ruins. He added, a touch defensively, that it was not in his power to alter "this bad weather." Sanitary conditions were abysmal, and discipline frayed. A rash of gambling and horse stealing led to a series of courts martial, while a local woman named Miss Ophelia was robbed by soldiers. Sentinels had to be told repeatedly "never to set down upon their posts."

Many officers were eager to return home. At their insistence, Colonel Howe journeyed to Williamsburg "to lay the state of affairs relative to the army" before the Virginia Convention. On the afternoon of January 13, he arrived at the college building to be "examined concerning the present situation of Norfolk." Tall and urbane, the hero of Great Bridge was at ease, having long served in North Carolina's legislature. He reiterated his position that holding the town was impractical, a point with more urgency given the dearth of food and shelter for the troops. At the same time, Howe argued that abandoning it in a partially ruined state might still provide the enemy with a vital base from which to strike the rest of Virginia. The only solution, he insisted, was complete demolition.

While most of the downtown, with its strategic wharves and warehouses, was rubble, sections of the northern suburbs and some of the town's most prominent buildings remained intact. The borough church still stood, despite the cannonball that had struck its wall, as did the neighboring Glebe House and the Mason's Hall. Fine townhomes, modest residences of artisans and shopkeepers, and workers' tenements were scattered among the burned-out hulks of other structures. According to a later detailed accounting, more than 400 buildings—nearly a third of the town's 1,333 structures—survived the conflagration, including Mary Rose's tavern, the home of bricklayer John Shore, the ropewalk owned by Thomas Newton's father, and James Leitch's shoe shop—presumably long before looted by the shoeless soldiers.

On January 15, the Convention agreed to pull the army back to Great Bridge, once "the mills and entrenchments be destroyed." In a tense session, the delegates then debated a second resolution "for demolishing the remaining buildings in the town and suburbs." Some members expressed "reluctance for either the entire or partial destruction of this unhappy town," as one nineteenth-century historian put it. After a heated debate, they rejected the resolution, handing Howe and Pendleton an embarrassing defeat. But the committee president was undeterred. "I do not see the propriety of leaving such comfortable lodgings to our enemy," he wrote Woodford after the vote, criticizing "our slow-moving body." Pendleton then engineered a second vote. This time he had a majority. Howe was granted permission to demolish all those houses that "in his judgement may be useful to our enemies."

Page's apprehension that other settlements might suffer Norfolk's fate proved astute. The Virginia Convention's new target, almost certainly at Howe's urging, was Portsmouth, the suburb across the Elizabeth River that was home in prewar days to as many as a thousand people. After approving the resolution, the delegates granted Pendleton the power to determine "whether it will be for the general good of the community to have the town destroyed" while "taking the utmost care of the security of the inhabitants."

Like Howe, Pendleton seems to have felt no remorse about his role in ensuring Norfolk's annihilation. But he did his best to cover his tracks, insisting in his letter to Howe that he had initially opposed Norfolk's burning and evacuation. "While the town was entire, I could not think it right for you to abandon it," he wrote. "As it was too shocking to think of our making a conflagration of our own town." The governor, he added, had forced their hand. "But after Lord Dunmore had done that horrid work, fit only for him, I saw no reason for your stay."

It was a disingenuous claim, given that Pendleton personally gave an order for Howe to destroy Norfolk's industrial plants before hearing of the January 1 attack. Perhaps with an eye to history, the conservative attorney sought to distance himself from what became the largest single war crime of the American Revolution. The only comparable act was a patriot expedition that destroyed forty Iroquois villages in 1779 with Washington's approval.* Though there is no written evidence that Howe relayed the truth about Norfolk's destruction to Pendleton or other patriot leaders, the colonel undoubtedly would have debriefed the Committee of Safety president in private. Woodford would have done the same when he later returned to the capital, while thousands of officers and troops had seen and participated in the officially sanctioned destruction.

On January 20, the Fourth Virginia Convention disbanded until spring, leaving Pendleton and his committee to oversee the conflict. The next day at four in the afternoon, British and loyalist forces set off for Town Point wharf at the western end of downtown. It was their first landing since January 1. Under cover of cannon fire from the *Liverpool* and *Otter*, soldiers swarmed on the shore to obtain supplies. "We had three fine men killed with cannon shot," Woodford reported, "and one wounded, who, it is thought, will lose his arm." The patriots recovered the bodies of "one sailor and two Negroes" killed in the skirmish, a sign that the Ethiopian Regiment was active. But the patriots found themselves running dangerously low on powder. When the three dead shirtmen were laid to rest in the churchyard, the honor guard was instructed to fire only a single round rather than the traditional three. The patriot troops grew

* Washington had long before embraced the label Conotocaurius—"Town Destroyer"—bestowed on him by an Iroquois leader during the Seven Year's War.

increasingly restless amid foul weather, inadequate rations, illness, and impotence against the impregnable British warships.

On February 5, to the delight of his men, Howe finally ordered "that the whole of the troops at this place hold themselves in readiness to march at an hour's warning." At four o'clock the next morning, a sleepless loyalist on a ship's deck heard "a signal" from the town, perhaps an arcing flare or the single crack of a rifle. As the anonymous eyewitness watched, "every house from Mr. Farmer's plantation, tan-works, windmills, church, etc. were set on fire, and so quick you cannot tell which began first," according to the account published in the April 13 *London Chronicle*. Patriot mariner John Rogers, who had attempted to douse the January 1 blazes, stepped out of his house in the predawn darkness as soldiers dashed through the streets of the town's northern suburbs torching surviving structures. A dozen or so homes that stood "between the church and the boundaries of the town" were "burnt at the same time," while other shirtmen set two ropewalks and public workhouses on fire. Resident John Smith watched "a brick mill in the borough" catch fire and collapse.

Sleepy flotilla passengers, awakened by cries on deck, would have emerged from their crowded berths to watch in horror as what remained of their town was swallowed in a wall of flame. Though a Freemason and enthusiastic dancer, Howe did not spare the Mason's Hall, where the 1774 ball had taken place. And while he was an Anglican, he left the brick church a gutted shell. By the light of flames shooting from windows and sparks flying from collapsing timbers, the shirtmen marched down Church Street and turned east on the road to Kemp's Landing, the first stop on the retreat to Great Bridge.

"The town of Norfolk is now said to be entirely consumed," a Williamsburg newspaper reported with satisfaction on February 10. One tradition holds that only a single dairy and pigeon house survived intact. A Maryland newspaper article, reprinted in New York and other cities, was both an obituary and a warning. "Thus, in the course of five weeks, has a town which contained upwards of six thousand inhabitants, many of them in affluent circumstances, a place that carried on an extensive trade and commerce, affording bread to many thousands, been reduced to ashes and become desolate."

Never before or since has an American city experienced such complete destruction. Quebec City suffered from British bombardment in 1759, while Atlanta, Richmond, and Columbia, South Carolina, were set alight during the Civil War. Fire ravaged New York City in 1776 and Chicago in 1871, and a massive earthquake devastated San Francisco in 1906. Much of the urban fabric of each of these cities, however, remained intact, while Norfolk was utterly flattened. "Nothing is here but a ruinous town, nothing but brick walls and chimneys is to be seen," wrote one patriot soldier a few months after its destruction. "Nobody can conceive that did not see it, how much it is altered," added a British woman who viewed the devastation. "It shocks me exceedingly."

Two men on opposite sides of the conflict separately had to reach back to antiquity to describe the staggering extent of the catastrophe. They recalled not Carthage but a Syrian city ruled by Queen Zenobia. She rebelled against Rome, only to be utterly vanquished in 272 CE. "Desolation and ruin have overspread the face of the country," wrote a patriot "gentleman at Norfolk," adding that "the once populous town" now resembled "the ruins of Palmyra!"

James Parker, the Scottish merchant trapped on the flotilla, likewise ruminated on the devastated ancient metropolis. One bleak winter day after the patriots' departure, Parker had a boat take him to shore for an anguished walk amid what was left of his formerly grand compound. The brick mansion was burnt, the thick walls surrounding the property lay shattered, and even the carefully planted trees in the garden were scorched and dead. "I viewed the wreck of our Little Eden the other day," he wrote his wife, Margaret, mournfully. "Palmyra is not more complete in ruin."*

News of Norfolk's destruction traveled across the stormy winter North Atlantic, reaching Britain two months later. The House of Lords, where Dunmore was still a member, debated the scandalous

* Many of Palmyra's ancient structures remained standing, albeit in ruins, until their 2015 destruction by the Islamic State.

event on March 5. Even during the most brutal European wars of the sixteenth and seventeenth centuries, cities had been damaged during fighting but were never intentionally annihilated. The New Year's Day attack, by contrast, left behind "devastation hitherto unprecedented in the annals of mankind" that "would shock the most barbarous of nations," declared an appalled Charles Lennox, Third Duke of Richmond. While he may have exaggerated, not even the notorious 1631 sack and burning of Magdeburg during the Thirty Years' War had destroyed the entire German town.

Patriot accounts reached Parliament faster than the governor's version, and Whigs like Lennox, who opposed the government of Lord North, expressed outrage. The port "was reduced to ashes by the wanton act of one of our naval commanders," and the "wretched inhabitants" were left "to perish in the cold." Norfolk, after all, "was supposed to contain many friends of government," yet "even friends are fired upon in hopes of hurting the enemy." Lennox did not overtly blame Dunmore, not wanting to "condemn an absent man," but he denounced those who "command this wanton ruin, this unnecessary ravage, this useless desolation." Those who gave into a "barbaric rage" had placed "an indelible blot on the dignity and honor of the English nation" that "would render us despised and abhorred." The duke insisted that the government's policy was not only morally wrong but politically counterproductive. It would, he added, "turn the whole continent into the most implacable enemies." The Americans would be "forced into independency."

James Brydges, Third Duke of Chandos, was not so charitable. The Earl of Dunmore was directly responsible for what he derisively called "the notable success of firing the town of Norfolk." The governor, he acknowledged, was not acting on his own, but simply carrying out the government's orders "to burn the towns, to ravage the plantations, drive off the slaves, to kill those that resist." These, he added mockingly, "are the warlike achievements of the governor of Virginia."

The criticism stung and embarrassed supporters of the government. The thankless task of responding to these vitriolic attacks fell to John Montagu, Fourth Earl of Sandwich and First Lord of the Admiralty, whose youngest son was captain of the *Kingfisher*, which had taken part in the bombardment. Montagu does not seem to have received intelligence yet from his son, and he dismissed reports of damage as wildly exaggerated. "I do not believe it is yet burnt," he said. Then he immediately contradicted himself by insisting, "It was not the man of war's men that burnt Norfolk; it was the inhabitants themselves. The Norfolk people set fire to the town. That is, the fire from the man of war set fire to part of it, and the inhabitants burnt the rest."

This explanation would have elicited hoots of derision from the chamber's dubious Whigs, Parliament's minority faction. That a people would level the largest city in their own province was too ludicrous an idea to credit. John Page had worried that the patriots would be ridiculed by their enemies if they destroyed Norfolk. He did not anticipate that those foes would find the entire notion absurd.

Ten months later, in November 1776, the port town's influential citizens sent a plaintive call for assistance to Virginia's newly created General Assembly, which by then had replaced the Convention. "Numberless widows and orphans" had been driven "from their peaceful habitations into the woods without food or raiment, at a most inclement season, whereby many have perished," the former residents lamented. "Such scenes of distress have presented themselves to our view as would melt the heart of the most unrelenting savage." Though proclaiming their devotion to the patriot cause, they did not blame Dunmore. Instead, they insisted that the town had been "wantonly destroyed by the provincial troops" engaged in "licentious and disorderly conduct," despite the Committee of Safety's promise to protect life and property.

In subsequent months, the new patriot government was deluged with claims by Norfolk citizens demanding compensation for their losses. In 1777, the new legislative body created a panel to investigate. The four committee members arrived at the desolate site on September 8, 1777, and spent several weeks deposing eyewitnesses and employing experienced local carpenters and masons "to measure and value the buildings which had been destroyed." They painstakingly recreated the vanished borough on paper, complete with spreadsheets containing the worth of all the significant buildings, the names and occupations of their owners, the identities of the people who destroyed the buildings, and the dates the destruction took place.

The committee's conclusions were unambiguous. Out of the 1,333 buildings, the British and loyalists had ruined nineteen, mostly warehouses, during their January 1 raid. "Very few of the houses were destroyed by the enemy," the committee members unanimously concluded, "either from the cannonade or by the parties which landed on the wharves." Their efforts were, in fact, "so feeble, that we are induced to believe that the houses which they did set fire to might have been saved, had a disposition of that kind prevailed among the soldiers." Instead, these patriots "most wantonly set fire to the greater part of the houses within the town, where the enemy never attempted to approach, and where it would have been impossible for them to have penetrated." There was, the commissioners added, no doubt that "the burning of the greater part of the houses in almost any street" was due to the "unremitting endeavors" of the Virginian and North Carolinian troops "to burn all that came in their way."

During the first two weeks of the year, the patriots torched 863 of Norfolk's buildings, while the British and loyalists fired only three additional buildings after January 1, all during the raid at Town Point wharf. On February 6, at Howe and Woodford's orders, the shirtmen burned the town's 416 remaining buildings. The committee pegged the total loss at 176,426 pounds and 1 shilling and 10 pence, or nearly $18 million in today's dollars, a staggering sum in the eighteenth century. In total, the rebels destroyed 1,279 buildings, compared to Dunmore's 54. Ninety-six percent of the damage to the town was the intentional work of the provincial troops.

The data provided incontrovertible evidence that the patriots, with the consent of their leaders, had destroyed Norfolk and then blamed Dunmore. Washington, Jefferson, Pendleton, and other rebel leaders almost certainly knew the truth, but the event's propaganda value made it imperative to insist on British culpability. Virginia's General Assembly responded to the committee's blunt findings by hiding the twelve-page report from public view. This skewed the works of early historians of the Revolution. Sixty years passed before the report was released. By then, no amount of data could dislodge Dunmore's reputation as a war criminal.

More difficult to quantify than the loss of structures was the sudden and complete dispersal of thousands of laborers, sailors, artisans, merchants, and a host of professionals. Julia Wheatley, for example, was a prosperous midwife who specialized in curing "the most inveterate ringworms," as well as "many other disorders incident to both the sexes." She notified *Gazette* readers that she was moving her practice from Norfolk to Richmond. Archibald Campbell, the Scottish physician, fled to Bermuda, and in late 1776, the Assembly ordered deportation of all British merchants.* The port's loss dissolved tight-knit communities, terminated its multiracial tavern culture, and unmoored Virginia from the wider world. The unusual social and economic ecosystem in which Jane and Talbot Thompson thrived against all odds was swept away.

Many patriots predictably celebrated the downfall of this "nest of Tories," though a few were nagged by remorse. John Page's conscience still gnawed at him on July 15, 1776, when he wrote Jefferson in Philadelphia. "I would have agreed to be hanged" if that act would have saved Norfolk and destroyed the enemy fleet, he insisted. Five days later, though busy substituting for ill governor Patrick Henry, Page wrote again. Had they mounted cannon the previous October to threaten the ships "as I advised," he wrote, "Norfolk would not have been burnt."

Virginia colonel Adam Stephen, later put in charge of defending the harbor, complained to Jefferson on July 29. "Norfolk might have been easily saved," he wrote. "We feel the loss of it daily." The port, Stephen noted, would have provided vital naval stores as well as outfitting and repair facilities for Virginia's nascent war fleet. He told Pendleton that the town's ruins were "a standing monument of the weakness of our counsels and feeble efforts." Neither Jefferson nor Pendleton, the architects of the borough's destruction, replied.

* In late 1776, Virginia's General Assembly gave "all natives of Great Britain, who were partners with, factors, agents, storekeepers, assistant storekeepers, or clerks here, for any merchant or merchants of Great Britain" forty days to leave the state.

Only one of the nation's founders personally participated in the city-killing act of early 1776. It was not until after he was confirmed a quarter century later as Supreme Court chief justice that John Marshall—who emerged as Jefferson's great rival—reflected publicly on the town's intentional destruction by the patriots. "Thus, was destroyed the most populous and flourishing town in Virginia," he concluded. "Its destruction was one of those ill-judged measures, of which the consequences are felt long after the motives are forgotten."

Chapter Twenty-Six

Fatal Lethargy

Though most viewed King George III's declaration of rebellion as a clear call to war, Dunmore saw in it a last opportunity for peace. The king had pledged to "give authority to certain persons upon the spot to grant general or particular pardons and indemnities" and to "receive the submission of any province or colony which shall be disposed to return to its allegiance." It would be as if his subjects "had never revolted." For the governor, "this generous, this humane, this truly noble sentiment" was a sincere gesture of mercy. George II had hanged more than one hundred rebels for treason in the wake of the uprising led by Bonnie Prince Charlie. British troops confiscated estates, broke the power of rebel families, and decimated Highland culture. Under a less forgiving ruler, Virginia patriots might expect similar treatment.

To begin negotiations, Dunmore needed a go-between. The obvious candidate was sixty-two-year-old Richard Corbin, who had served a series of royal governors as receiver general, the officer responsible for financial transactions between Virginia and the Crown. Corbin had helped a young Washington obtain his first military commission and had made an immense fortune as a slave-owning businessman. "He is as rich as a Corbin" was a common local saying. His manor house on a tributary of the York was so large, one visitor joked that the planter rode in his coach drawn by four horses to meet his wife for tea in her distant reception room.

Dunmore had stored many of the colony's records in the Corbin home's cavernous cellars before fleeing to Norfolk, and he trusted the man he characterized as "a long faithful servant to the Crown, strongly attached to government by principle and the mother country by affection." King George III had made "our trusty and well-beloved Richard Corbin" acting governor in July 1775 in case Dunmore had been forced to abandon Virginia. By then, Corbin had retreated to his palatial mansion. "I cannot condemn the revolution, but I cannot support it," he once declared. With the exception of Patrick Henry, who felt only contempt for him, leading patriot gentry continued to hold him in high regard.

The governor had long considered Corbin a potential mediator. "You have it with all my heart and from my soul wishing that you could be the means of reconciling these very unfortunate differences between two countries," the governor had written him in the summer of 1775. On January 27, he wrote again, citing the king's offer as an opportunity for "an honorable, permanent, speedy, and happy reconciliation between this colony and its parent state." The earl warned of "all the horror of a most destructive civil war" that could only end in the patriots' ruin. He was convinced that "the bulk of the colony" would "return to their duty" rather than "totally throw off their allegiance to the best of sovereigns." He requested that Corbin discuss negotiations with "whomsoever you shall think proper" and assured him of his "willingness to undergo any fatigue or difficulty" to forge a peace deal.

Corbin was encouraged when he received the letter, smuggled to his manor across enemy lines. His niece, Martha Tucker Newton, had lost her home when Norfolk burned, and he was eager to put an end to the spiraling violence. But he also realized the timing of the earl's offer was anything but propitious. With Dunmore and his forces confined to ships, the patriots were more confident and less likely to consider talks. Only an overwhelming external threat, he would have realized, could bring the rebels to the negotiating table.

He put the letter away to wait for a better moment. No one in Virginia yet knew that hundreds of British troops under General Henry Clinton had left Boston by ship on January 20 for New York. Their early February arrival alarmed Washington, who sent seven hundred men by land under Major General Charles Lee from Cambridge to prevent the British from occupying the city.

Lee believed Clinton intended to bypass Virginia and land in North Carolina, where he would join five regiments sent from Britain. Benjamin Harrison, the Virginia delegate, heard from a spy that Clinton's real destination was the Chesapeake. "He gave out that he was to go to the southward, but you must prepare for him, for I think he will most assuredly stop with you," he wrote a friend in Williamsburg on February 13. "He certainly intends to Hampton Road to wait for his troops which are to rendezvous there." Harrison feared the prospect of Clinton's men joining forces with Dunmore. "Should he land them, God know what will become of you." Enlistments lagged, with Page fretting that "several counties have not raised a man." Harrison predicted that Virginia patriots would not awake from their "fatal lethargy" until "the shackles jingle on our feet."

Across the ocean, the first British invasion of the South was underway. A fleet of fifty vessels led by Admiral Peter Parker had departed Ireland with five regiments, two companies of artillery, and some ten thousand stands of arms. The 2500-man-strong force was led by Major General Charles Cornwallis. Two months behind schedule due to bad weather and logistical problems, the fleet steered through the stormy North Atlantic for Cape Fear, off the southeastern coast of North Carolina, to rendezvous with Clinton and his troops.

The king insisted that the general be permitted to determine the target, but Lord George Germain, the new colonial secretary, made clear his preference for Savannah, which lay close to loyalist East Florida. Others favored Charleston, the largest southern port. The Chesapeake ranked a distant third. Yet Harrison was right to raise the alarm; even then, Clinton's fleet was making its way through the Atlantic to Hampton Roads.

Howe and Woodford's shirtmen left a path of destruction on their retreat from Norfolk. Dr. James Taylor, a town alderman and physician, later declared that "houses four miles outside of said borough were also to be destroyed." A February 17 letter "from a gentleman on board the *Liverpool*" reported the rebels were "burning the houses and driving the cattle" as they marched back to Great Bridge.

Dunmore claimed the troops perpetrated "many excesses such as robbing, plundering, and ravishing young women before their parents." Another wrote, "The people are in great distress." Captain William Chisholm, the loyalist forced from his home in early January, remained in hiding with his family, where he nurtured a deep hatred of the rebels. "Thank God we are all healthy, and have plenty of provisions at present," he wrote to a merchant friend in Liverpool, adding that they were "in great hopes of soon having forces to drive those savages into their lurking holes."

Though a small patriot contingent remained at Kemp's Landing and occasional patrols roamed the shores, the rebels had for all intents and purposes abandoned southeastern Virginia. This eased the plight of those trapped in Norfolk harbor. This flotilla included the British warships and local merchant brigantines, schooners, snows, and sloops numbering a hundred or so. But these were only the larger vessels; the fleet also would have included pilot boats, tenders, and even open barges and rowboats, accommodations that would have left passengers dangerously exposed in the middle of winter.

Nothing like it had ever been seen in American waters. How many people crowded aboard this scrappy armada is difficult to estimate. One report mentions that "several hundred families" were afloat, or perhaps a thousand or more people. This figure would have referred only to local white families. Large numbers of free, enslaved, and recently emancipated Africans had sought refuge on the water, along with the hundreds of British sailors, marines, and soldiers aboard the warships. The population may have totaled three thousand people or more, crowded onto some two hundred vessels. With Norfolk's destruction, this would have made the flotilla the colony's largest settlement.

The ships, boats, and barges also were packed with an array of valuable merchandise, including rum, molasses, cloth, and tobacco, not to mention cash and precious household items that refugees had snatched before abandoning their homes. Patriots salivated at the immense treasure this represented. "We learn that the Tory property on float in a number of small vessels amounts to more than £150,000," Richard Henry Lee wrote Sam Adams on February 7, "and it is protected by three ships of war only."

One British officer christened this hodgepodge of vessels as Lord Dunmore's "floating town." Wealth and rank determined accommodations, with the richest merchants, such as Sprowle, commanding their own vessels or the best cabins on the warships. Poorer passengers made do in more crowded accommodations, where buckets served as communal toilets, fresh food was hard to come by, and infectious diseases were apt to spread more rapidly. Given frequent mentions of the death of Black soldiers, members of the Ethiopian Regiment, along with their families and friends, seem to have suffered more than whites.

No one, however, could escape the stench permeating each ship or the nauseating bucking each time a strong wind whipped up the harbor chop. The refugees endured "the inconveniences of living aboard miserable little vessels, with the remains of their prosperity, [rather] than trust themselves in the hands of the rebels," one Royal Navy captain noted. Other than a handful of the governor's letters and dry naval logs, almost no firsthand accounts are known, but the few clues suggest a shipboard society unique in the colonies, if not in the British Empire. "It was," historian James Corbett David concludes, "a place of remarkable intercultural engagement."

The residents hailed from African Guinea, Glasgow, the Scottish Highlands, London, rural Ireland, France, Spain, the German states, Portugal, the Netherlands, and various Caribbean islands, as well as Virginia, North Carolina, Maryland, and other colonies. The community boasted its own newspaper, Dunmore's *Gazette*, which printed occasional editions using Holt's confiscated press. The two-masted *Unicorn* had a blacksmith's shop. A civilian and military police force and court system appear to have maintained order and adjudicated disputes. Suffolk's outspoken John Agnew, who had been released from prison in Williamsburg, ministered to those within the Anglican church. A fiery Black Methodist preacher, "Daddy" Moses Wilkinson, was also on board. He had escaped from a plantation near Suffolk and joined the Ethiopian Regiment. Later members of his congregation described him as a man who combined Old Testament and African traditions in a new way. "He worked himself to such a pitch that I was fearful . . . something might happen to him," one impressed white worshiper later wrote.

There are also suggestions that multiracial entertainments took place on the flotilla. According to a Williamsburg newspaper, the governor hosted "a promiscuous ball" on his flagship, with "Black ladies" as guests. Such radical racial mixing—whether real or imagined—clearly shocked and even terrified Virginia's patriots. Of course, shipboard society would not have been integrated in any modern sense of the word; wealthy Scots, for example, continued to be served by their enslaved staff. Yet the cramped conditions made it impossible to maintain the strict class and color distinctions that prevailed on land. Those still in bondage rubbed shoulders with those recently freed, and both inevitably shared tables with white soldiers and civilians. Carpenters mingled with merchants, and dockworkers with pig farmers. Those with vital skills, such as the sailmaker Talbot Thompson, would have gained a measure of respect harder to obtain on land.

A Philadelphia silversmith named John Leacock provided a fictional glimpse of life aboard Dunmore's flagship, albeit through the lens of a prejudiced patriot playwright. His satire written in the spring of 1776 was never performed, but *The Fall of British Tyranny* was widely printed and demonstrates the impact of Dunmore's flotilla on the popular imagination far beyond Virginia's borders. The script devotes a full act to the antics of a "Lord Kidnapper," who lives "near Norfolk, in Virginia, on board a man of war." This was the earl in thin disguise. The act opens with the crew of his flagship bringing aboard a new batch of men fleeing bondage. The lecherous royal governor is offstage in his stern cabin, having sex with Jenny Bluegarter and Kate Common and is too preoccupied to keep a lookout for the impending arrival of Commander Hopkins's Continental fleet. He takes a brief break from lovemaking to welcome the new recruits. "The Kidnapper seems as fond of these Black regulars as he is of the brace of whores below," remarks a cynical boatswain. With a leer, he tells the earl that once he is done with their services—if they don't "get their brains knocked out"—he can sell them to the West Indies for a profit.

The white sailors, meanwhile, grumble that they will have to make room belowdecks "for these black regulars," who look like "a parcel of frozen half-starved dogs." The men go on to complain of "no fire, nothing to eat or drink, but suck our frosty fists like bears, unless we turn sheep-stealers again, and get our brains knock'd out" by brave shirtmen onshore. The ship's cook appears to announce that he is out of provisions and has "no fire, coal, or wood," and insists that even if he did, he would refuse to cook for "a parcel of scape gallows, convict Tory dogs, and runaway Negroes."

Meanwhile, Lord Kidnapper meets the twenty-two escaped Africans. "They have no right to make you slaves," he says of the enemy. "I wish all the Negroes would do the same, I'll make 'em free." On the spot he gives a man named Cudjo, one of the first Black characters in an American play, the rank of major. When Kidnapper asks if he is willing to shoot his owner, Cudjo responds in a parody of Black dialect. "Eas massa, you terra me, me shoot him down dead." The earl then explains to the men that their job is to "shoot all the damn rebels" and orders a sergeant to teach them how to load and fire a gun. Kidnapper quietly tells an officer to "set a guard over them every night, and take arms from them, for who knows but they may cut our throats."

Later, the governor assures Captain Squires and an obsequious chaplain—modeled on Suffolk's Anglican minister Agnew—that "the thoughts of emancipation will make them brave, and the encouragement given them by my proclamation will greatly intimidate the rebels—internal enemies are worse than open foes." The decree, he explains, is "a grand maneuver in politics, making dog eat dog." Then he lays out his strategy. "If we can stand our ground this winter and burn all their towns that are accessible to our ships, and Colonel Connolly succeeds in his plan" to rouse the western Indians, he says, then he will "drive the rebels like hogs in a pen."

By early 1776, Dunmore's efforts to engage Native Americans and the enslaved on behalf of Britain was common knowledge throughout the colonies. At least one Black mother in New Jersey celebrated by giving her newborn his name, according to a May 2 article in the *New York Journal*. The article's author, likely editor John Holt, a former Williamsburg mayor, wondered whether this "act of justice to Dunmore" was "a cruelty to the innocent Negro." He added a biting racist poem. "Hail! Doughty Ethiopian Chief! Though Ignominious

Negro-Thief! This Black shall prop thy sinking name and damn thee to perpetual fame."

A turning point in Dunmore's stalled effort to combat the rebellion came on February 9, three days after the shirtmen departed Norfolk. The 886-ton *Roebuck*, with two decks, forty-four cannon, and more than two hundred crew, arrived in Chesapeake Bay with guns blazing. Upon anchoring near Hampton, the crew spotted "some rebels that were upon the beach entrenched up to their chins" and blasted the outpost. Although the warship was unable to dislodge the men, it did pick up seven Black men seeking sanctuary; six joined the Ethiopian Regiment and one remained as a seamen with crew. Admiral Graves had dispatched the ship from Halifax when he learned that Hopkins's Continental fleet was on its way to attack Dunmore; after checking on the governor, the vessel was to proceed to Delaware Bay to blockade Philadelphia.

The next morning, the *Roebuck* captain climbed the ladder of the governor's flagship and stood before the beaming earl. A friend of Dunmore's, Andrew Snape Hamond was also the British naval officer most familiar with the colony's coastline and high society. His first sea voyage as a fourteen-year-old midshipman had taken him to Virginia, where he had met George Washington and "heard him relate all the dangers he had gone through both from the Indians and the French," he later recalled. In 1772, as a captain, Hamond had returned to Williamsburg, where, he wrote, "I had an opportunity of renewing my acquaintance with General Washington." He spent most of his time at the Palace, departing "with some difficulty on account of the hospitality and great affability of Lord Dunmore."

After a four-year absence, the captain was appalled by the grim wreckage of Norfolk and the dire situation of the fleet. "I found his Lordship and the loyal inhabitants," he wrote, "without provisions or water, with active enemy at their back." The ships' cables and sails needed repair, and only a month's supply of meat and two months' worth of flour remained on the naval ships. Conditions were almost certainly far worse on the civilian vessels. "No water was to be had but under the cover of the ship's guns," he added, "and the boats were continually fired upon" by patriot patrols, though the situation was easing with the recent departure of Howe and Woodford. "No time was to be lost," concluded Hamond, who was now the senior naval commander. "The whole fleet looked to me for protection."

Dunmore and Hamond weren't aware that ice had trapped the little Continental fleet in Delaware Bay for more than a month. As the governor and captain met in the stern cabin of the *Dunmore*, the patriot vessels had just freed themselves and sailed to the bay's mouth to gather provisions for the voyage south. When word of the *Roebuck*'s arrival in Norfolk reached the rebel flotilla, several men jumped ship rather than face what was clearly an overwhelming force. The commander Esek Hopkins then aborted the mission to attack Dunmore. He steered the squadron past the mouth of the Chesapeake and headed for the Caribbean to procure arms and gunpowder. The British, however, continued to expect an imminent assault.

A more pressing challenge was sickness. Hamond worried that "the ague and fever on board the *Otter* has shown itself to be an epidemic, and many died of it." The March 8 issue of the patriots' *Gazette* noted that the "jail distemper rages with great violence on board Lord Dunmore's fleet, particularly among the Negro forces." This outbreak of typhus was accompanied by a host of other illnesses, including dysentery and scurvy. The report estimated 150 had died. "As fast as they expire," it said, the bodies "are tumbled into the deep to regale the sharks." This gruesome detail was not patriot propaganda. The governor later wrote that "there was not a ship in the fleet that did not throw one, two, three, or more dead overboard every night." Corpses littered the shore. Hamond was alarmed to find the small *Otter*, which was "crammed so full of people," in a particularly sorry state. Only 20 of 160 crew were fit for duty.

With the high windows of Dunmore's flagship cabin framing Norfolk's ruins, the earl and captain agreed it was "absolutely necessary to fix upon some piece of ground that could be easily defended in order to get water ashore in safety and have a place to put the sick," recalled the captain. They chose Tucker's Mill Point, the four-acre point of land protruding into the river just a few hundred yards downstream. This was the site of a ruined distillery as well as the damaged flour complex. "The rebels had destroyed the mills but left the ovens standing and part of the dwelling house," wrote Hamond. If these could be restored to working order, the fleet would have fresh bread to feed the hungry multitudes. The area also offered level ground, fresh water sources, and was strategically surrounded on three sides by water. Every able-bodied person disembarked to dig a three-hundred-yard-long trench across the exposed south end. About ten feet wide and six feet deep, it would serve as a protective moat.

Less than a week after the *Roebuck* dropped anchor, a Scotsman from Norfolk reported the excavation was in no way "retarded by the rebels, and the work is near complete." When the trench was opened on either end, the brackish Elizabeth River water surged through to make Tucker's Mill Point an island. The men also constructed breastworks paralleling the moat to absorb cannon fire and cleared the field beyond to create a no-man's-land to counter any frontal assault. Up to five hundred soldiers patrolled the fortification, including redcoats, marines, white loyalists, and members of the Ethiopian Regiment. Hamond then ordered the *Roebuck*'s surgeon "to fit up a sort of hospital ashore and receive the sick men of the squadron." The physician would have ordered canvas tents set up in neat rows on one side to quarantine the sick.

On February 17, as the new encampment took shape, a lookout on the flotilla rejoiced. "A man of war, with several transports, are in view," he reported. "It is supposed General Clinton is at their head and will touch at this place." Another unnamed eyewitness, this one aboard the *Liverpool*, was relieved at the prospect of "all sorts of provisions in great plenty as soon as the forces arrive." Harrison's intelligence from New York proved correct. The British officer chosen by King George III to lead a southern invasion had indeed arrived in Virginia.

"We took advantage of a favorable breeze to pay a visit to the Earl of Dunmore in Virginia," Clinton wrote in his memoirs, as if describing a social engagement, which is precisely how he viewed it. "We found his Lordship on board a ship in Hampton Roads, driven from the shore and the whole country in arms against him." He saw Dunmore's plight as hopeless. "I must confess I could not see the use of his Lordship's remaining longer there." The earl, he added, "seemed to flatter himself that some opportunity might yet offer for his acting to advantage." That opportunity, of course, was precisely the appearance of a senior general tasked with leading an invasion.

Clinton's modest fleet included the *Mercury*, which had spent much of the previous year in Virginia, along with two troop transports and a supply vessel. To the roar of a celebratory cannonade and the shrill piping of whistles, the general climbed aboard the *Dunmore* on February 18. Dunmore was ecstatic; after more than six lonely months battling the Virginia rebellion with minimal assistance from the empire, significant help had finally arrived.

The governor believed Tucker's Mill Point was a natural springboard for the long-awaited British invasion of the South. Clinton's Boston troops combined with the fleet and army crossing the Atlantic could sweep up Virginia's vulnerable rivers, capture its capital, and set the disorganized patriots to flight. By spring, Dunmore was confident that he could be back in the Palace as the rebellion collapsed and the chastened gentry sought an accommodation. With Virginia sidelined, other southern rebels would lose heart. The middle colonies, already wary of violence, might sue for peace. The continental conflict would ebb into a regional uprising confined to troublesome New England.

The governor's vision was not shared by the king, his ministers, or generals like Clinton. Unlike Dunmore, they were not aware that Virginia's rebels were afflicted with that "fatal lethargy" decried by Benjamin Harrison. Nor did they grasp that the colony's economic muscle and large population made it critical to the patriot cause. At a time when maps of the region were few, they also failed to appreciate that the extensive network of waterways in the province made the land-bound patriots uniquely vulnerable.

In addition, the British civilian and military leaders were skeptical that Black soldiers would prove good fighters and were reluctant to accept them into the ranks. As a result, they concluded that armed Highlanders in eastern North Carolina offered a better chance to defeat the rebels than the loyalist forces gathered by the earl. And, for a winter campaign, the warmer waters of Cape Fear two hundred miles south of the chillier Chesapeake seemed a safer bet.

Even as Clinton gave the Virginia governor the bad news of his imminent departure, hundreds of these Scottish warriors assembled outside Wilmington, North Carolina, in anticipation of a British landing. Many had left Scotland after the 1746 Battle of Culloden. Now, like Dunmore, the former rebels were staunch supporters of the Crown. The combined British and loyalist forces were to crush the patriots there before moving on to take the South Carolina capital of Charleston. The famed Flora MacDonald is said to have given a rousing speech in Gaelic, "exciting all to a high military pitch." She had risked her life to hide Bonnie Prince Charlie in the wake of the failed uprising, and then emigrated with her husband. Now she urged the men to defend King George III with their lives.

Dunmore responded to Clinton's disclosure with "inexpressible mortification." He retreated to his stern-cabin desk to vent his outrage to Lord Dartmouth, unaware that the office of colonial secretary was held now by Lord Germain, an army veteran who had crushed the Highland clans in the wake of the Jacobite rebellion. "North Carolina," the governor protested, was "a most insignificant province, when this is the first colony on the continent, both for its riches and power." He had spent more than half a year struggling to create a loyalist army, only to be yet again ignored. The earl argued that, at the very least, the fleet might rendezvous in Norfolk, "because this is a safe harbor, both for access and riding in, where pilots are to be had." Dunmore groused at "being imprisoned on a ship between eight and nine months . . . left without a hope of relief, either to myself, or the many unhappy friends of government that are now afloat suffering with me." Virginia, he wrote bitterly, "is totally neglected."

A fierce gale swept through Norfolk's harbor the next afternoon, swirling ash from the ruined town and driving one of Clinton's transports into the *Mercury*. The damage took time to mend, forcing the two men to keep one another's company for another awkward week. John Page, meanwhile, informed Richard Henry Lee in Philadelphia of Clinton's arrival. "We are still ignorant who they are or what force they bring, and what is worse, sir, we have not a force sufficient to oppose them if they have not brought a single soldier." Page estimated that Dunmore was able to field six to seven hundred "sailors and marines, exclusive of the Tories and Negroes." The patriots, by contrast, "have not three hundred men at Hampton, not one hundred at York, nor three hundred in this city." The rest were deployed on rivers and bays to the north or had deserted their posts. Worse, "the country people and militia are not only without arms but are lulled into a stupid security by the tales which flatter them with peace."

Even as he scratched out the letter in his Williamsburg office, a messenger interrupted him. "I am called to the committee, where they are to consider a letter from Lord Dunmore," Page hurriedly scribbled. Then he set down his quill and dashed to an emergency meeting of the Committee of Safety. Richard Corbin, the aging counselor, had chosen this moment to leave his self-imposed exile and present Dunmore's letter to the patriot leaders. The canny envoy seems to have waited until rumors of an impending invasion permeated Williamsburg before revealing the earl's proposal to open peace talks.

Anxious committee members, fearful that thousands of British troops might land at any time, were willing to talk. Pendleton composed a letter assuring the governor he "would be made exceeding happy by a just and honorable reconciliation with Great Britain, without the farther effusion of blood." He added, however, that the committee was "not authorized or inclined to intermeddle in the mode of negotiations" with the mother country, a power held only by the Continental Congress. In a significant concession, he promised to submit the request to the House of Burgesses, which, though it remained dormant, was slated to meet in March if a quorum could be assembled. Until that time, Pendleton suggested that Dunmore "avoid making the breach still wider." This meant "suspending his hostilities against the inhabitants" until formal negotiations could begin.

Before it adjourned, the committee gave its blessing to Corbin to meet with Dunmore under a flag of truce. Picking up his pen where he had left off his letter to Lee, Page explained that the patriot leaders had imposed one stringent condition. "We gave him to understand that his Lordship should deliver us the slaves now with him immediately," he wrote. The price of discussing peace would be dissolution of the Ethiopian Regiment and the return of the hundreds of formerly enslaved Africans who had fled their owners to seek liberty with the British.

After dawn the next morning, "the old gentleman went off in great hopes of procuring a month's truce at least," wrote Page. He was accompanied by a carefully chosen delegation tasked with spying as well as negotiating. Among them was Captain Andrew Leitch, a Glasgow-born patriot officer who had hosted Washington at least once at his home in Alexandria and who must have known the governor. He was joined by another Alexandria merchant and friend of Washington, Irish-born John Fitzgerald, who had just received his captain's commission two weeks previously. Also with Corbin was the popular pastor David Griffith. A clerk named Edmund Wilcox and the minuteman Leven Powell joined the party. They arrived in Hampton in time to secure a vessel that afternoon to make the dozen-mile trip to the governor's flagship anchored off Tucker's Mill Point.

The voyage across Hampton Roads and up the Elizabeth River proved a nerve-racking ordeal. With Clinton in the harbor, security was tight. "We had some difficulty before we got to the ship," Powell wrote his wife later. They passed three troop transports along with several tenders and the *Mercury* and *Kingfisher*. "The commanders of these vessels treated us roughly, and we were brought to and boarded by everyone." The officers on the *Kitty* transport, however, proved "exceedingly kind and polite"—so kind, in fact, that Powell later sent them twenty bushels of oysters, thirty loaves of bread, a goose, and a turkey—"such things as I understood they were most in want of."

The Scottish merchant James Parker had joined the Queen's Own Loyal Regiment, and he was on the *Dunmore*'s deck when the "truce boat from Hampton" came alongside the flagship after dark. He watched the aging Corbin slowly climb the gangway with "some rebel officers." Parker had heard that they carried "a letter from the Committee of Safety offering to lay down their arms if all the acts of Parliament are repealed that have been made since 1763," terms highly unlikely to be accepted by the British side. Having arrived late, the men spent the night on board as guests of the governor.

The next morning an awed Powell found himself in august company. "I had the honor of breakfasting on the best Hyson tea"—a fine Chinese green—with the earl and several officers, including Clinton, recalled Powell. Dunmore must have delighted in serving these patriots the forbidden drink.

Corbin later noted that the three principal British negotiators—Lord Dunmore, General Clinton, and Captain Hamond—"all appear in good humor." The captain kicked off the talks by assuring the peace delegation that he would not allow "injury to individuals or their property." With plentiful supplies in the hold of the *Roebuck*, raiding local plantations—and, presumably, encouraging defections by those enslaved—was not on his agenda. He insisted his sole job was "to watch the water" in order to enforce an embargo on patriot shipping. Dunmore then suggested that "the gentlemen of the country"—wealthy Virginia planters—sign a document agreeing to begin talks. He also offered to go to England "as an ambassador of peace."

Both the earl and the general, however, insisted that they would only negotiate through the House of Burgesses, which the British considered the colony's sole legitimate body. "If we relied on the Congress, we had nothing to expect from Parliament," Clinton had warned. In the end, the two sides could not even agree on the outlines of a ceasefire. The Committee of Safety demand that Dunmore turn over all the enslaved people he had emancipated was almost certainly a major stumbling block; the governor's Black allies were vital to his efforts to fight the rebellion.

During the discussion, Clinton was tight-lipped about his invasion plans. Corbin reported to Pendleton that he had "under four hundred men," who were headed "out of the country." Powell also was unsure of their goal. "Whether General Clinton intended to strike a stroke here or to go further, I cannot tell," he wrote his wife, "but, from everything I could gather when I was on board, their destination is to one of the Carolinas." The rebel army captains were more enterprising. Perhaps while sharing beer or rum at a late-night mess table, they coaxed the truth out of several young officers. The British, they learned, were bound for Cape Fear, and then would sail south to attack Charleston. They may even have done some outright eavesdropping; one patriot officer overheard Dunmore beg Clinton for troops to drive the rebels from Kemp's Landing, where they maintained a small force. "I don't think it worth the while to meddle with them" was the general's dismissive response.

Though the talks failed, the intelligence gleaned by the patriots from the visit assured the Committee of Safety that Virginia was no longer in British crosshairs. That allowed Pendleton to take a harder line with the governor. He wrote that the earl's attempt to entice "the gentlemen of the country" to sign a document was doomed to fail, and his refusal to acknowledge the authority of Congress or the Convention precluded further discussion. In the end, he concluded, Corbin's "errand produced nothing." The patriot leaders were relieved to know that the British invasion of the South would pass Virginia by. For Dunmore, it was yet another blow. With Clinton preparing to sail and the patriots intent on war, he would have to depend on a homegrown fighting force.

Chapter Twenty-Seven

Boiling Water

Clinton bid farewell to Dunmore and sailed out of the Chesapeake bound for Cape Fear on February 27. He was several weeks behind a scheduled meeting with Scottish loyalists in coastal North Carolina. Rather than waiting, the impatient Highlanders marched against a patriot force outside Wilmington "with broadswords at their side, in tartan garments and feather bonnet, and keeping step to the shrill music of the bagpipe." They were gunned down at a crossing over Moore's Creek in a bloody repeat of Great Bridge. When Clinton received the dispiriting news, he began to doubt whether Britain could conquer, much less hold, the Carolinas.

Dunmore's position suddenly seemed more advantageous. "The provinces bordering on the Chesapeake," the general later wrote, "naturally attracted my attention." He envisioned "a secure asylum" from the Elizabeth River to the Albemarle Sound in northeastern North Carolina. Protected by the ocean on the east, the Chesapeake on the north, and the Great Dismal Swamp to the west, the British could create a large territory for those willing "to join the king's standard in a country abounding with provisions." From this bastion, troops could be "perfectly safe from affront and might be reinforced or withdrawn at pleasure (as we could have command of both waters)," and the "adjoining provinces might be kept in constant alarm by desultory excursions along their shores." Clinton even cited Tucker's Mill Point as a perfect headquarters, "that base having struck me very forcibly when I was there with Lord Dunmore as an excellent position for covering the king's frigates and other small vessels which might be employed in these waters."

Clinton's analysis precisely matched the strategy that Dunmore had long championed, though the governor lacked the necessary troops and vessels to secure the region. The combination of the general's men and ships and the flotilla under Admiral Peter Parker, then crossing from Ireland, could have posed a formidable threat to Virginia's fractious patriots. Hamond already anticipated his return. "Clinton, I think will certainly be here," he wrote on March 13, "by the last words he said to me in confidence." When the general learned in April that Charleston was heavily defended and hostile to the British, a return to Norfolk grew even more appealing.

Parker's fleet did not arrive off Cape Fear until early May. When Clinton floated the idea of targeting the Chesapeake, the imperious officer, son of a rear admiral, rejected it out of hand. Naval careers were made by daring captures of strategic cities, not by seizing a ruined port and a few hundred square miles of swampy farmland. Parker also spurned Germain's preference for capturing the smaller city of Savannah. He insisted on attacking the South Carolina capital, home to twelve thousand people and the largest port in the southern colonies.

Clinton's Virginia visit did have one unexpected and far-reaching consequence. The general's extended stay with Dunmore allowed him to see and even meet members of the Ethiopian Regiment. No British general had ever encountered Black loyalist Americans in uniform. When Clinton landed in North Carolina that spring, more than seventy men fleeing bondage immediately flocked to his camp. He organized a company called the Black Pioneers, many of whom would accompany him to New York later that year. He was too skittish to arm them, but they built fortifications, and the general prized their tenacity and toughness. "At the expiration of the present rebellion," he wrote April 20, they "shall be entitled (as far as depends upon me) to their freedom." The notion of liberating those enslaved, long anathema among British officials, had suddenly become de facto military policy.

The day after Clinton departed Virginia, Patrick Henry stood before the Committee of Safety in Williamsburg. Whip-thin and grim-faced, he read the paper handed to him. The letter from the Continental Congress named him colonel of the First Virginia Regiment under the Continental Army. The promotion was a diplomatic way to remove him from his position as commander of the colony's forces, a job for which he had proved unfit. Henry was not fooled. He brusquely refused the new post, resigned the old, and stalked out. When news of Henry's resignation spread, shirtmen dressed in mourning and gathered with their rifles outside his Williamsburg lodgings. They presented a letter, addressed to their "father and general," that denounced a "most glaring indignity."

Henry was immensely popular among the colony's shirtmen, mostly white Piedmont and mountain farmers and hunters of modest means. Many had left their fields, forests, and families when Henry warned that the British would seize their weapons and ammunition while inciting a slave insurrection. These were the men who wore his celebrated slogan LIBERTY OR DEATH on their hunting shirts or etched onto their powder horns. His fiery rhetoric drew far more to the cause than Pendleton's cool and cerebral arguments. That night, Henry's supporters held a raucous feast at Raleigh Tavern for their former leader. As the night went on and the soldiers grew drunk, they threatened to demand discharges rather than serve under another officer. A *Gazette* article soon denounced those who "strove to bury in obscurity his martial talents, fettered and confined with only an empty title, the mere echo of authority." This was a veiled reference to Pendleton, widely suspected of toppling their hero.

Had Henry used his famous rhetoric to fan the flames of dissent, he might have ordered his troops to arrest the Committee of Safety members and installed himself as the colony's premier political and military leader. Yet despite his populism, the lawyer remained a stalwart member of the gentry. He delayed his departure from the capital in order to calm the upset men, "visiting the several barracks, and [using] every argument in his power with the soldiery to lay aside their imprudent resolution and continue in the service." Pendleton, meanwhile, publicly denied that the Committee of Safety had any role in the demotion that had caused "much noise in the country."

The emergency subsided, but the incident exposed the simmering tension between the colony's wealthy planters and those who made up nine-tenths of white colonists. The Virginia Convention had refused to provide rent relief for tenants, while owners of large plantations and their overseers were exempted from military service to watch over the enslaved. "Many of your petitioners are poor men with families that are incapable of supporting themselves without our labor and assistance," argued more than one hundred men from the western county of Lunenburg. On no account should they be obliged to leave their farms, they protested, while overseers "are living in ease and affluence." Others complained of having to conduct slave patrol duty, since "a poor man was made to pay for keeping a rich man's slaves in order."

Williamsburg's patriot delegates held firm, even refusing to expand the colony's limited suffrage. As had been the case for forty years, only free white males over twenty-one who owned either one hundred acres of unimproved land, twenty-five acres with a house, or a lot or house in an incorporated town were eligible to vote. This all but assured that wealthy men would dominate the government after the April elections for the Fifth Virginia Convention. While many shirtmen resented the control imposed by the gentry, they feared more the enslaved people in their midst, the indigenous peoples to the west, and British troops with their armed Black comrades to the east.

"I think Virginia in danger and that you ought to take your precautions," Major General Charles Lee of the Continental Army warned in a December 1775 letter to Benjamin Franklin, who served on a military committee in the Continental Congress. "Virginia is our weak vulnerable part." While Lee professed to have "the highest opinion of Mr. Henry," he declared it foolish to place a man in charge "who has seen no service." He added, "I wish you would send some man who has the reputation of being a soldier."

With Henry now sidelined, that soldier would be the colorful and controversial Lee himself. "The history of his life is little less than the history of disputes, quarrels, and duels in every part of the world," summarized one acquaintance. The forty-five-year-old Englishman, who was no relation to the multitude of Virginia Lees, was also noted for his large nose, small hands, and sharp tongue. He suffered from gout, rheumatism, and what one biographer diagnoses as bipolar disorder and manic depression. As a young British officer, he fought in the French and Indian War, was adopted by the Mohawks, and married the daughter of a Seneca leader. They knew him as Ounewaterika, or "Boiling Water," for his hot temper; he once whipped a surgeon who he felt was not treating his wounds properly. Leaving his Seneca wife, he roamed Eastern Europe as a mercenary, socializing with kings and developing a hatred of monarchy. His encounters with Polish and Russian peasants engendered what he called "a greater horror of slavery than ever." That horror, however, did not extend to Africans in bondage. On the eve of the Revolution, the peripatetic soldier abandoned Britain and bought land in western Virginia, as well as a half dozen enslaved people.

When Lee visited Mount Vernon in late 1774, Washington was impressed by his military skill and enthralled with his exploits. Six months later, the adventurer was a close second when delegates in Philadelphia selected the Virginia planter as commander in chief. Lee was placed third in command, after Washington and the elderly Artemis Ward. The junior position rankled, and he surely lobbied Hancock for an independent command. With a British invasion in Virginia or the Carolinas looming, Hancock placed him in charge of the new Southern Department, which answered not to Washington but directly to Congress.

On March 7, 1776, Lee departed New York for Williamsburg, leaving behind unpaid bills from his tailor and wine supplier. He stopped in Philadelphia to receive his orders, which were to rid Virginia of Dunmore and fend off the impending invasion. Independence advocates like John Adams were busy using the royal governor's alleged crimes to bolster their stance. After contentious debate, delegates approved a March 23 resolution charging British officials with "spoiling and destroying the country, burning houses and defenseless towns, and exposing the helpless inhabitants to every misery from the inclemency of the winter, and not only urging savages to invade the country, but instigating Negroes to murder their masters." With the British in New

England bottled up in Boston, the legislation was aimed squarely at the real and alleged acts by Dunmore and his forces.

Six days later, Lee was riding in his Continental blues down Duke of Gloucester Street through an early spring downpour. He turned down Bowling Green, which led to the Palace and found the Committee of Safety ready to welcome their deliverer. The men enjoyed an elaborate meal in the same dining room where Dunmore and Washington had spent many evenings.

The suave Pendleton was foreordained to clash with the eccentric Lee, whom one contemporary called "a most troublesome and disagreeable guest." A New England pastor who dined with the general a few months previously in Cambridge summed him up as "a perfect original, a good scholar and soldier, and an odd genius; full of fire and passion." The bachelor also lacked manners and was "a great sloven, wretchedly profane." John Adams pegged him as "a queer creature," while Washington judged him "honest and well meaning," but with a temper "rather fickle and violent." Lee was, according to Benjamin Rush of Philadelphia, "obscene, profane, and at times impious." His constant companions were "a troop of dogs which he permitted to follow him everywhere and seemed to engross his whole heart." Abigail Adams tried her best to avoid Lee and his canines, though one evening she found it necessary to shake the paw of his Pomeranian at Lee's urging "for a better acquaintance." An unapologetic misanthrope, he made his feelings clear to her husband: "Once I can be convinced that men are as worthy objects as dogs, I shall transfer my benevolence."

At the Palace dining table, Lee immediately offended Pendleton and his colleagues by announcing that he would make the governor's abandoned home his headquarters as well as a dog kennel. He made no secret of his disdain for the colony's timid leadership. "I am sorry to grate your ears with a truth," he wrote Washington on April 5 from his new Palace desk, "but must at all events assure you that the Provincial Congress of New York"—notorious for its ambivalent views—"are angels of decision when compared with your countrymen—the Committee of Safety assembled at Williamsburg."

Lee was stunned to discover that the patriots had no forts or warships with which to oppose the British, only a few small cannon, and "a most horrid deficiency of arms." The troops were scattered in a useless 150-mile arc from Alexandria in the north to Great Bridge in the south. The shirtmen were "eternally petitioning to leave to visit their families," and their military knowledge was abysmal. "There is not a man here who knows the difference between a Chevaux de Frise"—a defensive device used to halt cavalry charges—"and a cabbage green," he wrote Hancock in disgust. He railed against Virginia's traditional aversion to public spending. "Their economy is of a piece with their wisdom and valor," he wrote acidly to Richard Henry Lee in Philadelphia. "To save money, we have no carriages for our guns; to save money, we have no blankets for our men, who are, from want of this essential, dying by dozens." When he heard of Pendleton's negotiations with Dunmore, he warned Washington that the Virginia patriots were susceptible to "what the milk-and-water people call reconciliation."

The general confided to Washington that he was at a loss "by which measure I should drive out the enemy and exclude 'em from the finest and most advantageous port in America." He was, he said, "like a dog in a dancing-school. I know not where to turn myself, where to fix myself." The challenges, he added, "would throw Julius Caesar into this inevitable dilemma." Without a navy, the patriots remained particularly vulnerable. Soon after his arrival, Royal Navy tenders cruising off Yorktown seized a French sloop packed with desperately needed small arms and gunpowder.

Pendleton, meanwhile, withdrew to his plantation, no doubt to escape the irritating general. He was notably absent on April 8, when Lee presented the committee with his blunt assessment that the colony's "multitude of slaves" and rivers made it the likely "immediate target" of the invasion force.

The patriot general was convinced the British would strike Virginia, either with Clinton's men or a second force. "I am apt to think that Williamsburg and Yorktown will be their object," he wrote Washington. Possessing these two towns "would give an air of dignity and decided superiority to their arms, which, in a slave country, is of the utmost importance." He was particularly concerned about the "important consequences" that the arrival of an army of redcoats would have in the "minds of the Negroes." He feared that the governor's call for emancipation exposed white Virginia's vulnerability. "Your dominion over the Black is founded on opinion," he lectured Richard Henry Lee. "If this opinion falls, your authority is lost."

This was precisely the "snowball" effect that worried Washington. Dunmore had primed Virginia's enslaved—and those of other colonies as well—to seek freedom. The arrival of a mass of British troops could light the fuse for an even larger mass exodus, with disastrous consequences for the patriot cause.

Lee viewed the thousands of white residents and refugees in the colony's southeast quadrant as an even greater strategic threat. After the shirtmen withdrew from much of Norfolk and Princess Anne Counties in February, local loyalists continued to provide provisions and intelligence to Dunmore, and the general feared they would back a British invasion force. Patriot leaders that winter had called for deporting residents, a policy that locals had strenuously opposed. Norfolk's Mayor Loyall presented a March 8 petition arguing that those displaced by such a move "would have homes to seek, and every necessary of life to procure without the means of obtaining either in consequence of the destruction of Norfolk." The petition insisted that "language is too weak to describe our distress" and urged consideration of the "principle of humanity." Unmoved by such pleas, Lee even blocked aid sent by Quakers alarmed by the "suffering of many of the late inhabitants of Norfolk, who are reduced to poverty and want by the destruction of that town."

The general insisted to Pendleton and his committee that "it will be difficult, if not impossible, to secure and preserve the province unless these inhabitants . . . are removed from the very spot where they can do such mischief." He proposed that "their wives and children should be carried into a place of security as hostages for the good behavior of the husbands and fathers." This would have to be done "at the point of the bayonet . . . unless their removal can be accomplished by some other means." Though he admitted the policy "must be attended with very considerable difficulties, and perhaps much distress to individuals," he saw no other option. "The preservation and [well-]being of the province, if not the whole continent, are at stake."

If the committee did not act, he declared, "I cannot be answerable for the execution of the important trust committed to my hands."

The plan required Virginia's patriot army to round up thousands of noncombatants, by force if necessary, and remove them from their homes, land, and animals during a lean winter. The troops would march women and children west of Great Bridge, where they would be kept as human shields against British and loyalist incursions.

The operation was unprecedented in its breadth and cost, as well as in its dire humanitarian implications. On April 10, the Committee of Safety dutifully consented, ordering "all inhabitants of Norfolk and Princess Anne counties at present residing between the enemy and our posts at Great Bridge and Kemp's Landing to the ocean, be immediately removed to some interior parts of the colony." Page insisted that the committee would "most cheerfully cooperate with General Lee," assuring him they had "entire confidence in his great military abilities."

The general remained convinced that Virginia's patriots were ill-prepared to oust Dunmore, much less oppose a massive invasion force. They needed outside help, and fast. On April 16, he wrote a delegate in Philadelphia that since Dunmore continued his "piratical war and can raise an insurrection of the Negroes, we must apply for some battalions to our middle colonies." The Continental Congress, he insisted, should send "three or four immediately."

As winter gales gave way to milder spring breezes, Hamond decided there was little to be accomplished hovering around Dunmore's floating town. The fortifications were adequate, the springs provided fresh water, and locals were now able to supply fresh food to the British and loyalists. The hospital at Tucker's Mill Point also was proving effective. "Since I got them ashore the disease has subsided," Hamond wrote on March 5, "and they are most of them in a fair way of recovery." The captain prepared the *Roebuck*, *Liverpool*, and *Otter* to sail to Delaware Bay to capture merchant vessels bound for Philadelphia and attack the elusive Continental fleet, and he even contemplated an attack on the rebel capital itself. Dunmore was adamant, however, that Hamond leave at least two ships for the flotilla's protection. The captain agreed, with the understanding that one would patrol the Virginia capes.

On March 21, the first day of spring, the *Roebuck* and *Liverpool* set off with the ebbing tide, bound for the open sea. Hamond did not yet know that four days previously, the British had withdrawn completely from Boston. Patriot crews had installed artillery on Dorchester Heights capable of obliterating the besieged town. The combined land and sea forces withdrew to Nova Scotia. The British intended to regroup and prepare for a new assault, which Washington suspected would be at New York, though others speculated that the Chesapeake might be their next target. This retreat made Tucker's Mill Point the sole significant British land base remaining in the thirteen colonies.

With Hamond's departure, the governor set about making the site a formidable military installation. The rebels "frequently come and take a few shot at us, and retire," the earl explained, though they never attempted to attack or even besiege the garrison. Workers rebuilt the damaged flour mill, guided by those enslaved men who had worked at the plant before the war, such as grinding experts Sam, George, Shallow, and Captain, and the bakers Robin, Bacchus, Cuffey, and London. White and Black carpenters and masons took part in the effort to repair the facility, which was soon churning out fresh bread for the thousands who lived at the point and on the ships anchored nearby.

The point soon resembled Gosport in the fall of 1775, though with far more Black people and with the strict segregation between the races even less evident. This bustling community included food production areas, a hospital, barracks, a military training ground, a bevy of workshops, and a cemetery filled with the fresh graves of the many who had succumbed to illness. Talbot Thompson would have been kept busy sewing canvas for tents and temporary roofs. Sprowle's former Gosport workers, enslaved and free, labored in rudimentary blacksmith shops and repair sheds to fix broken cables, muskets, and ship hardware. Women cooked meals, tended the sick, and fashioned uniforms and other clothing from local linen or flax. "I have bought a large quantity of Oznaburgs"—a cheap but sturdy fabric—"of which I am making summer clothing for our garrison," Dunmore reported at the end of March. The tailors almost certainly included many of the fifty female "Black banditti" who made their home on Tucker's Mill Point, according to a *Gazette*.

After a winter of disappointments, defeats, and disasters, Dunmore grew bullish. "We have in this little fort four ovens, and pretty good barracks for our Ethiopian Corps," he wrote to London. While he had trouble attracting whites to the Queen's Own Loyal Regiment, his effort to recruit Black soldiers was proceeding "very well."

Many—and perhaps most—of those who fled from bondage to reach the security of British lines were frustrated by stepped-up patriot patrols. In March, three Black men escaped from a forced labor camp, made their way to the shore, and boarded a vessel they presumed to be British. They "declared their resolution to spend the last drop of their blood in Dunmore's service," only to find the crew were patriots. Sent to the capital's squalid prison, two of the men "are under sentence of death and will be executed in a few days as an example to others," according to the April 13 *Gazette.* They were not the only examples. When eleven enslaved men on the Eastern Shore attempted to cross the bay, they were captured and also sentenced to death. At least some of these judgements were likely commuted to hard labor in the lead mines. This would have been done not out of mercy, but to avoid paying owners for destroying their property.

The enslaved nevertheless kept coming, slipping across the moat at night or arriving in small boats eager to join the fight for their freedom. Planter Edmund Ruffin complained that four of his human chattel were "in Lord Dunmore's service," while Landon Carter reported at month's end that "a slim Black fellow by name of Phil" had left his plantation wearing his new waistcoat and breeches, presumably "to increase the Black regiment forming in Norfolk harbor." On a single day in April, eighty-seven of those enslaved by John Willoughby Jr. of Norfolk joined the governor, including twenty-one women, twenty-three girls, twenty-seven boys, and sixteen men. The proclamation did not apply to those owned by loyalists, so it is possible Willoughby encouraged them to desert to Dunmore as a way to secure, rather than liberate, his human property. Nevertheless, fourteen of these men joined the Ethiopian Regiment and achieved freedom.

White officers taught Black enlisted men how to load and fire a gun, drill, and charge; Woodford reported in April that Thomas Byrd "is assuredly the major of the Blacks," even as his brother Francis

Otway Byrd served as an aide to General Charles Lee in Williamsburg. Patriot spies monitored with a mix of alarm and disdain this growing cadre of African soldiers. "We hear that Lord Dunmore's royal regiment of Black fusiliers is largely recruited," a *Gazette* reported in March, claiming that the men did double duty of menial tasks in the day, soldiering at night to the sound of a balafon—a West African xylophone made with gourds—rather than "the drowsy fife and drums." With grudging admiration, Pendleton reported on March 19 that the earl had four hundred Black troops under Major Byrd, "who have forgot the use of the hoe and ax and are the first troops in America."

The settlement, along with the floating town, posed more than a military menace to the patriots. It was also an existential threat. The Tucker's Mill Point community lay outside the jurisdiction of Virginia's strict laws that required Black subservience and punished the slightest infraction at the whipping post. The very existence of the little base demonstrated that an alternative society was possible, one in which those of European and African descent could cooperate, at least when faced with a common enemy.

As cherry, redbud, and then dogwood blossoms replaced bare branches, the earl once again contemplated his long-planned assault on Williamsburg. The colony's patriots, by their own admission, remained disorganized and divided. "Our army is a handful of raw, undisciplined troops, indifferently armed, wretchedly clothed, and without tents or blankets," bemoaned John Page to Richard Henry Lee on April 12. "Our people in some places [are] disconcerted about Henry's resignation," he wrote, while others opposed displacing Norfolk and Princess Anne residents. "God knows what will be the consequence if a vigorous push will be made by a fleet and six or seven regiments." He later told Jefferson that he feared the colony's disheartened patriots might be "tempted with the prospect of peace, security, and a trade equal to their wishes." He shuddered to think they might blame their leaders, "and be willing to sacrifice them to a reconciliation."

Even as the governor drilled the troops and pondered a spring campaign, he noted on March 30 that "a fever crept in amongst them which carried off a great many very fine fellows," referring to members of the Ethiopian Regiment, and using an unusually intimate phrase that suggests respect and even affection. "The medical people here thought, and I believe with reason, that it proceeded from their being much crowded aboard the ships and want of clothing." He was confident that with the coming of spring and construction of the base, the worst of the crisis had passed.

Then, in late March or early April, a resident in Dunmore's community woke with a runny nose. What this unfortunate person might have dismissed as a common cold grew steadily worse. The victim's head began to pound, and a wave of nausea and vomiting quickly rendered them weak and bedridden. Within two weeks, red lesions and a rash spotted the face of the sufferer, who simultaneously endured a painful backache and extreme fatigue. When the ugly red sores burst, the oozing pus infected other parts of their body—and other people with whom they came into contact.

At some early stage in this gruesome experience, the victim would have recognized smallpox. The microscopic brick-shaped variola virus thrived in crowded conditions, passing from person to person through infected bedding, bodily fluids, and face-to-face contact. The lesions on the more fortunate victims eventually hardened as they dried, often leaving deep scars, such as those apparent in more honest portraits of George Washington. Those less fortunate were left blind or lame, or both. For roughly half of those infected, the terrifying ordeal ended not in disfigurement but in death.

Smallpox established an invisible second front in the Revolutionary War. The epidemic began when the tenacious microorganism, which may have hitched a ride on a crowded British troop transport, appeared in the Massachusetts capital almost at the same time as the Battle of Bunker Hill. Six months later, Washington reported that "smallpox is in every part of Boston." The prospect mortified the general, who had endured the sickness while visiting Barbados as a teenager. "If we escape the smallpox in this camp and the country round about, it will be miraculous—every precaution that can be, is taken to guard against this evil." Only by imposing strict quarantine measures in Cambridge did he prevent its spread through his largely unvaccinated troops. The contagion by then had infected patriot troops marching into Quebec, ravaging the invasion force at the start of 1776. "This distemper is the king of terrors to America this year," John Adams wrote soon after. "The smallpox is ten times more terrible than Britons, Canadians, and Indians together," he lamented to his wife Abigail. "The smallpox! The smallpox! What shall we do with it?"

The virus next traveled south with General Lee's bodyguards; he left some of those with symptoms in Pennsylvania, and others in Fredericksburg, just a long day's ride from Williamsburg. Patriot leaders allocated funding "to prevent spreading of smallpox" beyond the town limits, and Pendleton's committee warned Lee "to take proper care" that the deadly illness did not spread to the capital. Its arrival, members feared, would "occasion a greater alarm . . . than would the appearance of ten thousand men from Russia." Fredericksburg was only a two-day sail from Norfolk's harbor, where unsanitary conditions created a perfect breeding ground for the invisible killer.

Chapter Twenty-Eight

Tomahawk Them All

As March gave way to April, leading patriots sensed that the largest, richest, and most populous colony was slipping from their grasp. "I am willing to allow the colony great merit for having produced a Washington," Abigail Adams wrote her husband on March 31, "but they have been shamefully duped by a Dunmore." The next day, the man she so admired expressed a similar concern. In a letter to lawyer Joseph Reed, Washington bemoaned the fact that "my countrymen"—Virginians—"from their form of government and steady attachment to royalty, will come reluctantly into the idea of independence."

In Philadelphia, there was alarm when a rumor spread that a British fleet had entered the Chesapeake. On April 15, Richard Henry Lee relayed reports that "Sir Peter Parker is arrived in Virginia with troops" to launch the long-feared southern invasion. The news proved false, but the apprehensions reflected growing fears that Dunmore might succeed in defeating or coopting the colony's patriots.

Jefferson had retreated to his mountaintop home on his return from Philadelphia in January to care for his sick wife and then to bury his mother, and he played little role in the unfolding drama in Virginia in the late winter and spring of 1776. It was the English-born General Charles Lee who spun into action. He reorganized Virginia's ill-prepared army and pushed to build a navy from scratch. Congress quickly agreed to his urgent request for "5000 blankets and many shoes" as well as three tons of gunpowder. He also lobbied hesitant planters to support separation from Britain.

April was election season for the small minority of the population qualified to vote for delegates to the Fifth Virginia Convention. While the question of independence was not on the ballot, candidates were split over whether to support the notion. Pendleton continued to argue forcefully for compromise. He "talked, or rather stammered, nonsense that would have disgraced the lips of an old midwife drunk with Bohea tea and gin," griped an exasperated Lee. Richard Bland, of the Committee of Safety, lambasted *Common Sense* author Thomas Paine as "a blockhead and ignoramus," while even Patrick Henry opposed declaring independence before the Americans could forge an alliance with France or Spain. As late as April 13, a *Gazette* published a letter from Pennsylvania dismissing independence as "the idol of those who wish to subvert all order among us and rise on the ruins of their country." Nine out of ten Pennsylvanians, he assured readers, "abhor the doctrine."

From Philadelphia, Richard Henry Lee kept up a steady stream of letters to his friends in Williamsburg, playing on their pride to make the case for a break with the mother country. "Virginia has hitherto taken the lead in great affairs, and many now look to her with anxious expectation" to rouse the colonies from a "fatal lethargy," he wrote Patrick Henry on April 20, borrowing Benjamin Harrison's telling phrase. If the Old Dominion acted, "it would set an example which North Carolina, Maryland, Pennsylvania, and New York will most assuredly, in my opinion, follow."

He also urged the orator to exert all his powers toward "the adoption of a wise and free government," which, he added, was "an indispensable necessity" to avoid anarchy. Lee enclosed John Adams's plan for a system which, he assured another fellow Virginian, would "be nearly the form we have been used to." Despite his revolutionary rhetoric, Henry privately agreed that any new government could not alter the gentry's firm grip on power, since "there is among most of our opulent families a strong bias to aristocracy."

Jefferson was far bolder. He pressed for more drastic changes, but his old friend Page warned him on April 26 that the new structure "should be formed as nearly resembling the old one as circumstances . . . permit" to "prevent disorders." Such arguments appealed to the colony's wealthy. Shorn of a royal governor and a distant king and ministers, Virginia's patriot government would be free to expand west, seize control of the slave trade, exile rapacious Scottish merchants, and do business with whomever they chose. This would usher in a wave of unlimited prosperity, with large planters as major beneficiaries of the coming boom.

When the votes across the colony were tallied, several well-known conservatives failed to win a majority in their counties. Pendleton himself was again nearly turned out of office. Some members of the gentry panicked. "Our freeholders, all mad, [are] determined to have a new House all together," wrote an anxious Major Josiah Parker, a Virginia Convention member and later a congressman. One in three incumbents would not return to Williamsburg, the biggest turnover in three decades.

Among the new faces was the twenty-five-year-old sickly James Madison, educated at the College of New Jersey, later known as Princeton, and a firm advocate of independence. Voters in James City County, which included half of Williamsburg, approved a measure calling for their Convention delegates to exert their "utmost ability in the next Convention towards dissolving the connection between America and Great Britain, totally, finally, and irrevocably."

The election results, however, did not mark the start of a popular uprising against Virginia's old guard. Most of those who would not return to Williamsburg had either retired or joined the patriot military. Nearly all the new delegates, including Madison, were tobacco planters who oversaw forced labor camps. They were united in their desire to keep the colony's small farmers in check, tamp down the slave insurrection, and obtain legal title to lands to the west. These men, not the famous firebrands of New England, would transform the rebellion into a truly continental revolution while deftly maintaining their own firm grip on power.

Only after the election results were in did Lee reconnoiter Tucker's Mill Point for himself. "I was the other day at Portsmouth with the general to view the enemy entrenchments, and visit my old neighbors," Woodford wrote his wife on April 30, sardonically referring to the Royal Navy's officers. "They saluted us with one gun from Captain Squire and a few swivels and small arms from a tender, which proved as impotent as usual." Squire's *Otter* lay just to the east of the point, close to Portsmouth. On the west side was the *Dunmore*. The *Liverpool*, recently returned, was anchored near the *William* and a sloop called the *Fincastle*—named for the earl's viscount son—along with twenty tenders outfitted with smaller guns. The British and loyalists had also constructed "a prodigious raft" that, when armed with cannon, could serve as a floating battery.

This firepower protected the loyalist civilians, the bulk of whom remained aboard the makeshift fleet now secured a safe distance downstream. Armed tenders constantly patrolled the shore, firing their cannon at any who dared to come too close. "One man . . . received a grapeshot in his body which I had cut out," wrote Major Parker. The king's supporters were careful not to stray beyond the range of their guns. "I found it impracticable to do anything there as the enemy would not venture out," groused Parker. The British and loyalists, he added, were as "busily engaged as possible in fortifying themselves. Indeed, they are now as secure as it is possible to be." He consulted an engineer, who agreed that the rebels could never take the base without a strong naval force.

During his brief visit, General Lee stayed at the family home of the ever-present Helen Maxwell. When he appeared at the door, she recalled, he was in green coveralls "with leather on the inward seam and a row of buttons on the out. He told her they were 'such as were worn in his Majesty the King of Prussia's service.'" Maxwell added that "he brought with him four ugly little dogs, which he petted and pestered everybody with in a nauseous style. One of them he called Lady Caroline, and another Lady Catherine; one named Busy, he said, he had been obliged to leave behind at Williamsburg to 'lie in.'" Lee was given the family's best bedroom. To the horror of Maxwell's mother, he slept with all the dogs in one bed.

The general was stunned to discover that newspaper reports of famine and deprivation aboard the flotilla were wishful thinking. Locals "amply and regularly supplied provisions and refreshment of every kind" despite strict patriot prohibitions on any such trade, he noted indignantly. Hamond reported a few days later that despite a shortage of fresh pork, "we have plenty of flour, and more can always be had." A patriot military court convened at Kemp's Landing on April 30 found several locals guilty of supplying the enemy with fish and livestock. Dunmore had even forbidden members of the fleet from trading with those onshore without authorization, in an apparent effort to prevent scarce hard currency from flowing into rebel pockets. The governor's pursers regularly purchased wheat, corn, pigs, sheep, and cattle from farmers on the James River, within a few miles of Williamsburg.

Lacking the artillery, troops, or ships necessary to combat Dunmore, an infuriated Lee decided to "intimidate the whole knot of these miscreants." His men arrested an aging loyalist named Joshua Hopkins as he was returning to Portsmouth from a visit with his son on the flotilla. During a long interrogation, the captive confessed to the crime of selling goods to the fleet. "We determined, after having seized his furniture, to set his house on fire in his presence," Lee reported. The general acknowledged that such an act "was not quite consistent with the regular mode of proceeding," but, he insisted, "there are occasions when the necessity will excuse deviations."

This was only a first step in a campaign of terror waged by Lee in the face of Dunmore's superior forces. Portsmouth's tidy streets were still lined with the mansions of Scottish merchants, and the shops and wharves remained largely intact. The general was outraged that locals went about their daily business within a quarter mile of the enemy encampment, blithely ignoring the evacuation order promulgated by the Committee of Safety. "I found the inhabitants of Portsmouth had universally taken the oaths to Lord Dunmore," he wrote to Pendleton on May 4, after returning to Williamsburg. The furious general said he had ejected "the people without exception, for even the women and children had learned the art and practiced with address the office of spies." Hundreds of inhabitants, including many who had fled Norfolk a few months previously, were turned out onto the muddy spring roads to seek shelter and sustenance.

"It perhaps be politic to destroy it totally," Lee mused of the town. Instead, he made do with torching the homes of "the most notorious traitors . . . in hopes of intimidating the neighborhood." Major Parker was put in charge of this effort, "taking care that all the houses, plank, vessels, etc. of the Sheddens, Goodriches, Jamiesons, and Sprowles were totally demolished." With the exception of the Goodrich house, these were the family homes of Virginia's wealthiest Scottish merchants

All, aside from Shedden, who was confined to a Suffolk jail, watched from the flotilla or the land base as their residences collapsed amid billowing black smoke. Goodrich's wife and child, who had remained in Portsmouth, escaped from their burning home and reached the safety of the fleet. The flames leapt to the property of an unlucky patriot neighbor, destroying his house, his outbuildings, a large warehouse, and the wharf. By month's end, Woodford reported that "all the inhabitants of that beautiful village and its neighborhood [were] removed, the gardens and wells destroyed."

Before having the homes torched, Lee had his men strip their interiors of "a considerable quantity of very valuable articles," as well as stockpiles of "molasses, salt, and other things much wanted for the public." Furniture, clocks, tableware, and other household goods removed from the mansions were sold to fill patriot coffers. The trove only whetted Lee's appetite. "How sure a prey these ships at Norfolk, with their immense treasure of goods, arms, ammunition would be," he wrote, estimating their worth at an astonishing 1.5 million pounds, or $150 million today. This was ten times the estimate that Richard Henry Lee had made in February. Yet without a patriot armada to engage the Royal Navy, stealth was his only option.

After midnight on Sunday, April 28, a small boat pushed off from the south shore of the Elizabeth River, the sound of its oars muffled by padding. A spring cloud cover may have dimmed the waxing moon, nearly full, as the patriot crew approached the shadowy hulk of the *Dunmore*. They positioned the boat under the protection of the slanting stern. A sudden noise from the governor's stateroom directly above their heads startled the jumpy shirtmen. Dunmore may have sensed trouble or may have simply been passing a restless night. Quiet soon returned, broken only by waves lapping gently against the ship's hull.

Two musket shots fired from shore at four o'clock that morning was to be the patriots' signal to board the ship, while another team would simultaneously surge through Portsmouth with lit torches to fire the town. The dual raids would distract the British and loyalists at Tucker's Mill Point, providing an opening for patriots to attack the compound and attempt to burn down the all-important flour mill. But no signal came. As the six o'clock dawn approached, the men reluctantly rowed away. Before they landed, however, they "shot a Negro going to shore in a canoe with a bottle of rum." The patriots then drank "to his health as he was expiring." After this gruesome toast, they returned to the home of Portsmouth resident Mary Veale, where they lodged.

They were unaware that one of the governor's many spies had been eavesdropping on them before they had left Veale's home the night before. The spy had heard one member of the party tasked with boarding the ship ask "what should be done with the Tories he found on board the vessel." The answer was unequivocal. "Damn them!" replied an officer, probably Major Parker. "Tomahawk them all and throw them overboard and give yourselves no further trouble about them." The mole had been unable to get word to the fleet, but when the patriots returned the next morning, the agent listened again as they reported on their failed mission.

Just why the attack was called off is not clear, and Lee did not mention the aborted effort to the Committee of Safety. He also had secretly ordered vessels assembled that could be set on fire and launched at the warships. "The shirtmen are and have been busy sometimes past constructing boats" designed to "destroy the fleet lying off Norfolk," a loyalist informer warned Dunmore on May 11.

By then, the little fire fleet was nearly complete. Once the boats were loaded with "a proper proportion of combustibles for burning the vessels"—cloth and wood soaked in turpentine—the patriots would await a favorable wind to set them alight "in the dead of night." A rebel team would then cut the British anchor cables, running the ships aground so they could not dodge the flaming vessels bearing down. These "infernal demons" would then "put to death all that attempt to put their foot ashore." The primary target, the agent reported, was the governor's flagship. "Such, my Lord, is the bloody plan intended to be perpetrated by those sons of murder and devastation."

The patriot general visited Portsmouth and Kemp's Landing for only a day or two before returning to Williamsburg on May 2 with little to show but a few wagons loaded with Scottish loot. "Lee is returned without doing anything," an unhappy planter informed Washington. Pendleton, by contrast, had nothing but praise for Lee's decision to expel Portsmouth residents and burn their homes and businesses, regardless of their political affiliation. "We much approve of the whole of your conduct to those people," he wrote on May 5.

The committee was pleased, however, that he had "confined the conflagration at present to the houses of the most notorious offenders." Members were nevertheless sympathetic to Lee's call "for the destruction of the whole," and the president promised that the next Convention would consider ordering the complete demolition of Portsmouth as it had of Norfolk. "What the public safety seems to require should be immediately done, even though some injury may arise to innocent individuals." Such suffering, he added, was "one of the inevitable consequences of this kind of war."

On Monday, May 6, forty-five members of Virginia's House of Burgesses filed into the chamber on the east side of the Capitol, but lacking a quorum, they "let that body die," wrote Pendleton. At the bottom of the last page of minutes, a clerk scrawled "Finis," a single-word epitaph for the western hemisphere's oldest legislature, established in 1619, the same year the first enslaved Africans arrived in the colony. The members filed out. Then a hundred or so bewigged gentlemen—including most of those who had just exited—paraded in. When the gavel came down convening the Fifth Virginia Convention, the colony's gentry had for all intents and purposes created a government outside British jurisdiction.

That week, word reached Williamsburg that the fleet sent from Ireland had arrived off Cape Fear. Thousands of British ground forces were poised to land in North Carolina, and Lee prepared to move south to counter the threat. First, he held a council of war with a half dozen senior colony officers to come up with "some plan for the safety and security of Virginia" during his absence. This included removal of all suspected white loyalists and "slaves of military age" from Norfolk and Princess Anne Counties, a move which the Committee of Safety had agreed to in April but hesitated to undertake. A delegation from the counties pointed to the "distresses and ruin" that would follow. Under pressure from Lee, the new Virginia Convention overrode these humanitarian objections. Delegates agreed that the thousands of residents "ought to be immediately removed with their families and effects to some interior parts of the colony."

Washington, now headquartered in New York in anticipation of a British attack, expressed his delight. "Your Convention are acting very wisely in removing the disaffected and stores from the counties of Princess Anne and Norfolk," he wrote a relative. Thomas Batchelor, who was in charge of taking care of the poor and handicapped in the local Norfolk parish, had a different reaction. He noted that the parish cared for three blind people and one "totally deprived of the use of her limbs." He queried the Virginia Convention as to what steps he should take "to prevent these unhappy people from perishing." A thousand pounds, or about $100,000, was set aside to pay for wagons to transport as far as Suffolk those without financial resources, a figure woefully inadequate to the scale of the mass relocation.

The departing Lee relegated to Woodford the unenviable task of overseeing one of the largest forced population displacements of nonindigenous people in American history. "I was to be left behind to execute the most disagreeable pieces of service that could have happened, the removing of all the inhabitants of these two Tory counties," Woodford complained to his wife after Lee had departed for Williamsburg. "The lowest estimate is 12,000 souls." He later upped that figure to "not less than 20,000." "Their distress will be great indeed," the colonel predicted, "and I expect to be witness to many more affecting scenes than even Norfolk afforded." It was an odd statement for a man directly responsible for that city's destruction, but he concluded piously, "The service of my country must be the first consideration, and where duty calls, pleasures and conveniences must give way."

Lee rushed south to North Carolina, and then to Charleston when he learned that the British invasion force intended to land there. He had failed to dislodge or even seriously challenge the governor, but he had jolted Virginia's patriots out of their "fatal lethargy." The question of whether the colony should separate from Britain was now on the Virginia Convention's agenda.

First, however, the delegates considered urgent petitions for payment by the many slaveowners recently deprived of their human chattel amid the mass escapes. Under Virginia law, the colony was bound to refund the value of an insurrectionist. Arthur Boush wanted "a reasonable allowance" for "Harry, a Negro man belonging to him [who had] fled to Lord Dunmore," had subsequently been captured, but had died in the Williamsburg jail. William Smith claimed compensation "for a Negro man slave who was shot for refusing to surrender himself to the troops when required." Delegates also had to consider the fate of "Chaney, a Negro woman" who was owned by a Tory and had been apprehended by patriot militia.

Not until May 14 did the Convention take up three resolutions backing independence. Sensing the voters' change in mood, Henry now supported separation before a European alliance had been achieved and wrote up a resolution. Knowing his unpopularity among conservatives, he had moderate Thomas Nelson present the document. Rising from his padded bench, paper in hand, the Yorktown businessman asserted that the British were "using every art to draw the savage Indians upon our frontiers and even encouraging insurrection among our slaves, many of whom are actually in arms against us." Therefore, he read, "a full declaration of independency appears to us to be the only honorable means under heaven of obtaining that happiness, and of restoring us again to a tranquil and prosperous situation."

When Nelson sat, Henry rose, and the chamber grew quiet. As usual, he began in a mild voice that built gradually to an evangelical fervor. Henry said that America would be led to the promised land of liberty as Moses had been led through the Sinai by a pillar of fire. Only one delegate publicly objected to the resolutions supporting independence for Virginia and all the colonies. Robert Carter Nicholas, the man who had introduced the 1774 resolution calling for a day of fasting and prayer, argued that the patriots lacked the strength to take on the British Empire, but Henry's rhetoric carried the day.

After the members adjourned to the capital's taverns to drink and gamble, Pendleton worked into the night on a final resolution based largely on Henry's words.

The first order of business on May 15 was to command patriot troops "to seize and secure any slaves which may be sent by Lord Dunmore or any of the Navy with flags of truce." The delegates then voted for independence; Nicholas abstained to make it unanimous. One hundred and twelve members agreed that the royal governor was "carrying out a piratical and savage war" against them, tempting their "slaves by every artifice to resort to him and training and employing them against their masters." Given this intolerable situation, they declared, "we have no alternative left but an abject submission to the will of those over-bearing tyrants, or a total separation from the crown and government of Great Britain." They directed Congress "to declare the United Colonies free and independent states absolved from all allegiance or dependence upon the crown or parliament of Great Britain."

The next day, the delegates set up a committee to fashion a new plan of government that would "secure substantial and equal liberty to the people." Then they joined a crowd of Williamsburg residents outside to hear the resolutions read aloud. Shirtmen paraded, toasts were made, and cannon fired "as the Union flag of the American states wave[d] upon the Capitol." This was the same banner John Paul Jones had first hoisted in late 1775, which combined the British flag with the red and white stripes of—ironically—the East India Company. That night, there were fireworks "and other demonstrations of joy . . . , everyone seeming pleased that the dominion of Great Britain was now at an end," reported the May 17 *Gazette*.

When news reached Philadelphia, an ecstatic Richard Henry Lee called the Virginia resolution "sensible and spirited," while John Adams declared it momentous. Another patriot was sure the decision would "have a wonderful good effect on the misguided councils" of wavering colonies, which included Maryland, Delaware, Pennsylvania, and New York. In previous weeks, patriot leaders in Rhode Island and North Carolina had backed independence, but the unanimous vote by the most important colony proved a tipping point on the road to revolution.

Virginia's resolution, however, contained a glaring caveat. The colony's ruling gentry demanded that "the power of forming government for and the regulation of internal concerns of each colony be left to the respective colonial legislatures." They were wary of trading a British king for a Philadelphia Congress that might interfere with their possession of human property or oppose their claims to indigenous lands.

This assertion of what became known as states' rights disturbed Richard Henry Lee. "Would not a uniform plan of government prepared for America by Congress and approved by the colonies be a surer foundation of unceasing harmony to the whole?" he asked John Adams. The pragmatic Massachusetts politician tried to allay his friend's sense of foreboding. Governing, he wrote, was a "matter of which the colonies are the best judges." It was also a matter that would divide the nations' founders when they created a new constitution a dozen years later. Two generations after that, the issue would thrust the nation into a bloody civil war. It haunts the country into the present day.

Chapter Twenty-Nine

A State of Society

Captain Hamond was relieved to be back at sea chasing patriot smugglers rather than chained to a cumbersome civilian flotilla. He spent April cruising Delaware Bay, even attempting unsuccessfully to attack Philadelphia, yet he remained anxious about Dunmore's ability to hold Tucker's Mill Point. "I am equally desirous to keep the little footing we have in Virginia secure," he wrote on April 8. But he lacked the ships he needed to blockade two major bays and protect the Virginia governor.

The British withdrawal from Boston on March 17 opened up a fresh opportunity for reinforcements. Vice Admiral Molyneux Shuldham and his fleet retreated to Nova Scotia, yet Hamond's urgent request for additional vessels to patrol the Delaware and Chesapeake was rebuffed. "It is utterly impossible for me to furnish you at this time with a greater number of ships," Shuldham curtly responded on April 11. The captain's plea for troops and artillery to bolster Dunmore's small corps was rejected as well. Worse, the *Roebuck* was ordered to join the invasion fleet expected to attack Charleston. The smaller and less powerful *Fowey*, then in Halifax, would be sent as a replacement.

When the *Fowey*, under George Montagu, sailed into Delaware Bay on April 30, a worried Hamond ordered him to Virginia to "give the surest protection to the lines of Tucker's Mills, and to the friends of government who have taken shelter on board vessels in the Elizabeth River." He told Montagu to "keep a strict watch over the motions of the enemy, and by a constant guard to prevent any designs they may put in execution against you." He explained the urgency in a May 4 letter to Clinton, who was still anchored off Cape Fear, waiting for Admiral Parker's full fleet to arrive from Ireland. "I cannot delay a moment to send her"—the *Fowey*—"to Lord Dunmore, as I find [General] Lee is getting into his neighborhood." He reiterated his certainty that occupying Virginia's southeast remained the best strategy for defeating the rebels in the south. As a sweetener, he proposed that it would serve as an ideal base to launch an attack on Philadelphia. Hamond confided to Clinton that "I would give the world to have an hour's conversation" with him and Parker.

By early May, Dunmore had learned of a patriot plan to install cannon on Craney Island, at the mouth of the Elizabeth, to trap the flotilla. The earl dispatched an urgent message to Hamond just as the captain was weighing anchor for Charleston. At first glance, the captain thought "his Lordship's apprehensions might be premature." He nevertheless altered course for Norfolk, stopping only to pluck "a dozen bullocks and some other stock" from an Eastern Shore island. The *Roebuck* sailed up the Elizabeth on May 19. It was a fine Sunday morning, and "a couple of lads belonging to the *Otter*" slipped away and had been "regaling themselves ashore with strawberries," when they were taken into custody by patriot sentries. After being questioned, according to a *Gazette* report, they were allowed to continue their berry-picking.

When Hamond climbed aboard the *Dunmore* that afternoon, he learned that the situation was far more dire than he had anticipated. A Craney Island battery and fireships were only two of a three-pronged threat. "Smallpox made its appearance among the Black troops," he later wrote. Those known to be ill were quarantined at Tucker's Mill Point, but nearly all the troops were in danger of infection. "In order to save them, the surgeons recommended that the whole be inoculated," Hamond recalled. "This was likely to be a great reduction of our force."

Inoculation typically brought on a mild illness, so those given the procedure would be unable to fight for a week or more, leaving the compound vulnerable to attack. The two men grimly agreed on an immediate evacuation of their well-fortified and strategic base downstream from Norfolk's ruins. "We thought it most advisable to move the fleet immediately" rather than wait "until the enemy had planted cannon at certain places on the riverside," Hamond wrote. "It would scarce have been possible to have got the vessels down the river, and they must have fallen into the hands of the rebels."

If Squire was present at this crucial meeting, he may have suggested the good anchorage and friendly locals on Gwynn's Island, both of which he had encountered during a March expedition up the Chesapeake Bay. The arrowhead-shaped piece of land, a little more than three miles in length, lay fifty miles to the north and was home to "many friends of government." Foremost among these was John Randolph Grymes, an England-educated loyalist with a thousand-acre plantation worked by thirty-five enslaved Africans.

The surrounding waters "formed an excellent harbor," while the land offered "plenty of fresh water" and "could easily be defended from the enemy," wrote Hamond. It was, he concluded, "the best rendezvous of any in Virginia for the fleet." It also lay within easy striking distance of the mainland, and close to tobacco-growing regions with large populations of enslaved Africans. Dunmore and Hamond could augment their forces while the existing troops recovered from their inoculations. Given that Gwynn's Island was roughly the same distance from Williamsburg as Norfolk, the governor and captain would have viewed the move more as pragmatic repositioning than as retreat.

To disguise their true intentions, the captain and earl leaked word that the flotilla was bound for North Carolina. As surgeons hurried to inoculate as many Black soldiers as possible, naval officers examined the more than one hundred ships to judge their seaworthiness and to inventory water and provisions. Those vessels unable to make the voyage—as many as forty—were sunk or burned to keep them from falling into patriot hands. Passengers on smaller boats were relocated to larger ones. The lack of able-bodied seamen made the task even more difficult; some ships lacked adequate crews to get underway.

Despite these enormous logistical challenges, the withdrawal began only three days after Hamond's arrival, helped by "fine, pleasant weather." At daybreak on May 22, the troops and civilians abandoned Tucker's Mill Point. As a band of patriots fired their muskets and rifles from a distance, though without inflicting casualties, the last loyalist and British soldiers torched the barracks and temporary dwellings that had been so painstakingly constructed just six weeks before. "The troops evacuated the entrenchments and embarked aboard the transports," Hamond wrote.

The *Otter*, which had carried Dunmore to Norfolk in July 1775, was the last to leave the harbor. Squire's vessel weighed anchor, and the ruined port and roadstead that had been Dunmore's base for more than ten months fell behind. When patriots swarmed into the abandoned base, one officer found three hundred "fresh graves . . . some of them large enough to contain the carcasses of a corporal's command," or about a dozen soldiers each.

A patriot perched in Hampton's church steeple reported on May 23 that "their whole fleet is in motion." He estimated sixty or seventy "sail of different kinds, hovering about the mouth of the James River." Others counted eighty-eight vessels. This forest of masts made up the largest collection of ships ever seen in Chesapeake Bay. Their destination, however, was a mystery to the patriots.

The bright, cool, dry weather held, but not until May 25 was the entire squadron fully assembled. Pendleton reported to Jefferson the day before that the fleet "had taken on board the shattered remains of the Ethiopian Regiment and abandoned their entrenchments, which our troops are destroying." He added that the patriots "expected an attack" at Hampton and were rushing troops to that exposed town. The Committee of Safety president would have feared that the British and loyalist campaign to capture Williamsburg was finally underway. Under cover of darkness, however, the flotilla hurried north up the bay. On the morning of May 26, patriot lookouts spotted the fleet sailing toward Maryland, and Pendleton sent warnings to Annapolis, where Governor Robert Eden still held his post in an uneasy truce with patriots.

The flotilla halted near the mouth of the Piankatank River, a dozen miles shy of the Potomac River mouth that marked the boundary with Maryland. Just before dawn on May 27, the vessels dropped anchor off Gwynn's Island. The short trip in the sparkling May weather was a grueling journey for those recovering from the smallpox inoculation, and a final voyage for the many who had succumbed to the virus itself or other sicknesses. Black soldiers were particularly hard-hit. Hamond despaired that "our whole force . . . did not amount to more than two hundred effective men, so great had been the mortality among the Negroes." A patriot report estimated that 75 Black men died on the trip from Norfolk, while a *Gazette* article put the figure at 175. Corpses floated in the wake of the northbound vessels.

The island's harbor proved good, but the land was more exposed than expected. Its western tip lay within musket shot of the mainland. Hamond ordered the *Fowey* and two small armed tenders anchored close to this vulnerable spot to protect the men as they dug into the sandy soil to construct fortifications. Local patriots quickly gathered to take pot shots at the intruders, "but without doing us the least mischief," the British captain reported. Grapeshot and cannon fire put the rebels "in the utmost consternation, some running one way and some another," reported one disgusted patriot officer. A downpour finally dispersed the frightened militia.

That evening, a canoe paddled quietly to the side of the *Roebuck* while twenty-seven-year-old seaman William Barry was on watch. He had been plucked at least a month before from a captured merchant vessel in Delaware Bay to serve on the warship. "Three Negro men" climbed aboard, he later recalled. Barry was shocked to see them "kindly received and entertained by a second lieutenant and other officers." They even shook hands with the new arrivals, as if greeting equals.

Hamond was called, and the captain asked the three men "if there would come more of their people on board," adding that "if they did, they would be well used." The visitors assured him that many were eager to join the British. The captain then questioned them on the location of any large numbers of shirtmen. "They told him there were none nigher than six miles" and revealed that there were plentiful unguarded cattle in the area. Hamond then asked if the men could provide fowl and sheep, as they were badly off for some on board." The visitors said they could, and the captain promised to pay them a fair price.

Then Barry reported a remarkable comment made by Hamond. "Besides," he quoted the captain as saying, they "should be free when this disturbance was over, which he expected to be very soon, and then each of them should have a plantation on rebel land." If the sailor's recollection was accurate and Hamond was sincere, then the captain—and, by extension, Dunmore—considered land distribution to be the natural next step after emancipation. Three years later, General Clinton would offer "freedom and a farm" to enslaved Americans. The notion of breaking up forced labor camps to provide acreage for freed Black laborers would not, however, resurface until the close of the Civil War nearly eight decades later.

The men returned later that night with fowls, and one brought "his wife and two children, and another Negro man." Word quickly passed through the network of enslaved Africans in the area, and a steady stream of those seeking release from bondage began to flock to the island. For the British, the ability of these men to forage, fish, and spy proved invaluable. They were not alone in seeking freedom; William Barry was himself desperate to escape his impressment. "A man had better curse his mother and father, and be killed at once, than live such a life," he later told a rebel committee.

Slipping quietly below deck after the Africans had boarded for the second time, he wiggled through an open gunport and dropped into their moored canoe. Cutting the rope, Barry paddled for shore, and after dawn found a rebel encampment. He promptly reported to a patriot officer that the British and loyalists consisted of one hundred men of the Fourteenth Regiment, one hundred and fifty white volunteers, fifty seamen, and three hundred Black soldiers. He counted eighty-two ships lying offshore.

He also revealed Hamond's plan to seize grazing livestock. The patriot officer quickly dispatched "forty men and horses, and drove the stock ten miles in the country, and saved them from being carried off." The frustrated British later "burned some houses along the shore" when they discovered there were no animals to be found. Some of the men, Barry claimed, in an account published on June 20 in the *Pennsylvania Evening Post*, "had not tasted any fresh meat for seven weeks."

Surveying the island on the next day, Hamond fretted that it would be difficult to defend "if the enemy should make any serious attack upon us." That afternoon, the governor's flagship arrived. Dunmore at first was delighted. "A finer harbor never was seen," he later wrote

Lord Germain. A tenth of the size of Manhattan, its twenty-two hundred acres had livestock and "a great abundance of fish on all sides." The governor would have been greeted warmly by Grymes, the island's major landowner.

But the earl swiftly saw, as had the captain, that the site "lies too near the main." They ordered construction of a small redoubt with five cannon at the exposed northwestern point and dubbed it Fort Hamond. Similar fortifications were raised on the east side facing the bay, to fend off patriot naval attacks, while two smaller ones were thrown up in the protected center portion of the island.

The May 31 issue of the *Gazette* noted anxiously that the governor had landed "his black and white troops, to the number of about 500, and is entrenching" on an island that was "possessed of a considerable quantity of [live]stock and is well watered." The article assured readers that the "pirates and renegades" were in a "sickly, starving, and dirty situation."

There were enough healthy civilians and soldiers among them, however, to enjoy what one *Gazette* derided as "a promiscuous ball." Whether accurate or not, the report was sure to shock most white Virginians, who maintained strict social segregation. The dance "was opened, we hear, by a certain spruce little gentleman"—a reference to the diminutive Dunmore—"with one of the black ladies." Musical instruments were common aboard British and merchant ships of the day, and the party may have taken place on a flagship deck festooned with lamps. For a few brief hours on that warm spring night, the dancers would have left behind the hardships and horrors of the past six months.

As the members of Dunmore's flotilla secured their new base on May 27, the Virginia Convention began its work week by considering a petition from Bennett Tomkins: "Four of his best Negroes endeavored to make their escape to Lord Dunmore but are apprehended and delivered to justice." The two men and two women probably were couples who ran away together. The men were sentenced to work in the lead mines "on account of the public." The women,

Rachel and Amy, were accused of theft and jailed. One died in prison before trial—which one was not considered important enough to record—and Tomkins asked for "compensation for his loss as should be thought just and reasonable."

Soon after, delegate Archibald Cary rose to read "a declaration of rights" to the assembled delegates. Inspired by the 1689 English Bill of Rights and writings of philosophers such as John Locke, it ensured that individual liberties would be respected no matter what sort of government was adopted. The first section made a radical statement that alarmed many Convention members. "That all men are born equally free and independent," Cary read out, "and have certain natural rights, of which are . . . the enjoyment of life and liberty with the means of acquiring and possessing property and pursuing and obtaining happiness and safety."

This declaration went on to insist "that no part of a man's property can be taken from him or applied to public use without his own consent or that of his legal representative." As "one of the great bulwarks of liberty," freedom of the press was to be ensured, along with a "well-regulated militia" in peacetime, in lieu of a standing army. When it came to religion, no one should be forced to adopt a creed, since "the duty which we owe our creator" is based on "reason and conviction." Many of these assertions would be echoed in the Declaration of Independence, still six weeks away, the 1789 French Declaration of the Rights of Man, and the 1791 United States Bill of Rights.

Cary was the brother of Hampton's Wilson-Miles Cary, who had taunted Captain Squire after the 1775 hurricane, and he was an unlikely advocate of liberty. A wealthy conservative judge who loathed Baptists, he held ten whites in indentured servitude and owned some thirty enslaved Africans. He was known to whip his human property in public, and he repeatedly beat a man owned by Jefferson for not opening the gate to Monticello quickly enough. The words he uttered, in fact, were penned by George Mason. The obvious contradiction between ideals and reality was too much for the reliably stubborn Robert Carter Nicholas, who was said to have been "irate" about the claim that all people were born equally free.

Debate on the controversial measure was postponed until June 11. On that day, Nicholas immediately took the floor of the old House of

Burgesses chamber. He argued that Mason's claim was inconsistent "with the state of slavery then existing in Virginia," one delegate recalled decades later. Nicholas warned that it would "have the effect of abolishing that institution." This charge electrified the Convention. "All were struck with the force of [his] objection," the delegate noted. It was one thing for England to emancipate its own people in bondage, but inconceivable for Virginia's gentry to suggest that those born enslaved were, in fact, free.

Mason's supporters waved aside these concerns. They argued that slaves, "not being constituent members of our society, could never pretend to any benefit from such a maxim." That night, while others caroused in Williamsburg's taverns, Pendleton crafted compromise wording. "All men are by nature equally free and independent and have certain inherent rights," read his revision, but only "when they enter into a state of society." This clause addressed Nicholas's concerns. The inherent humanity of Africans was not yet a matter of much debate; the notion that those with darker skin were a separate species only took firm root among some white Americans after the Revolution. In the 1770s, they typically considered those from Africa and of African heritage to be a lower caste outside European society. Only whites, who made the rules, could alter that status.

The next day, June 12, the Convention approved Pendleton's revision. The members then ordered an army captain to collect the "large quantities of iron and a considerable number of nails . . . from the ruins of Norfolk." The delegates noted that "those articles are much wanted for public use." Patriots that month also auctioned off Dunmore's personal effects and lands. The earl's books, snapped up at bargain prices by Virginia's gentry, testify to his broad intellectual curiosity. Most ended up in James Madison's personal library. Jefferson obtained several ancient histories, including a study of the Mongol Empire and "General Collection of Treaties, Declarations of War, Manifestos, and other Public Papers, Relating to Peace and War, books on Common Law." Also sold to the highest bidder were eleven of Dunmore's enslaved workers.

On June 28, the Virginia Convention chose Patrick Henry as Virginia's first elected governor, in a nod to his numerous followers, though the position had been stripped of much of the powers exercised by his predecessors. The next day, members adopted the new state's constitution, which ensured the gentry's continued power. The following week, Richard Henry Lee wrote Samuel Adams that "our devil Dunmore" remained at Gwynn's Island, "but we expect shortly to make him move his quarters." He included an image of the new seal of Virginia, with an Amazon warrior with one breast bared standing above a king with a toppled crown, and the Latin motto SIC SEMPER TYRANNIS, translated as "thus always to tyrants."

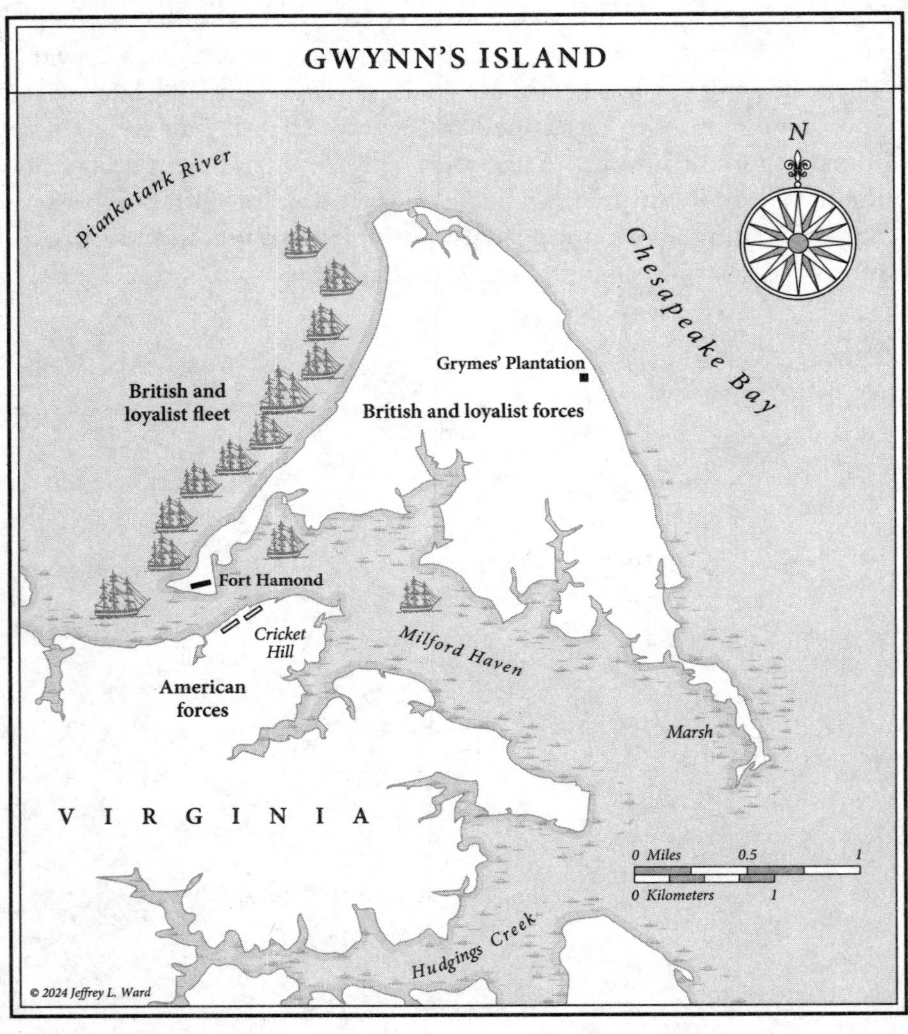
GWYNN'S ISLAND
N
Piankatank River
Chesapeake Bay
Grymes' Plantation
British and loyalist fleet
British and loyalist forces
Fort Hamond
Cricket Hill
Milford Haven
American forces
Marsh
VIRGINIA
0 Miles 0.5 1
0 Kilometers 1
Hudgings Creek
© 2024 Jeffrey L. Ward

Chapter Thirty

Misery, Distress, and Cruelty

Gwynn's Island, long an obscure rural backwater, was now King George III's sole land base in the wayward American colonies, and the nerve center for loyalist activity in the Chesapeake. Carpenters and masons immediately built ovens, windmills, and houses, according to John Emmes, a Delaware pilot. They also set up tents and constructed huts for the many suffering from illness, or recovering from vaccination.

The hottest part of the year, with its dreaded "fevers and agues," was only beginning. What we now know as the mosquito-borne illness malaria, which brings on fevers, chills, and nausea, becomes rampant with high temperatures. One prisoner of war grimly noted that "dozens died daily from smallpox and rotten fevers." A Williamsburg newspaper wrote of "a fever which has raged with great fury amongst them for some time past. From the funeral processions that have been seen there, [it] very probably has proved fatal to some persons of distinction." Foremost among those persons of distinction was Andrew Sprowle, the former Lord of Gosport, merchant, slave trader, slaveowner, and industrialist. Taken ill while on the way to Gwynn's Island, he died on May 29 aboard the *Roebuck*.

Dunmore would have led a solemn escort as the body of his friend was ferried to the island and buried in the center of what was quickly becoming a large cemetery of Black and white victims. His grave, a patriot later reported, was "neatly done up with turf." On the day of his death, he revised his will to make his soon-to-be widow, Katherine Hunter Sprowle, an heir. Soon after the funeral, she quarreled with Dunmore—possibly over her efforts to claim her late husband's enslaved property—and returned to Scotland, but she did not go quietly. In subsequent years she showered Jefferson, Franklin, and other American politicians with fruitless petitions to extract some remnant of Sprowle's fortune, though she succeeded in obtaining a pension from the British government.

Hamond ordered the *Otter* to patrol the capes and sent the *Fowey* to extricate Maryland governor Robert Eden from Annapolis and bring him to the safety of Gwynn's Island. The Continental Congress and Virginia's Committee of Safety had long urged Maryland's patriots to arrest the governor, but they had refused on the grounds that Eden had not threatened the American cause. Patriots had since intercepted his incriminating letters, and his position had grown precarious. The captain also armed his tenders with small cannon, muskets, pikes, swords, grapeshot, and powder to "harass" the rebels by "constantly moving about and making descents upon different parts of the coast." Dunmore chartered new vessels to strengthen the fleet, and the expeditions captured enemy vessels and secured livestock.

Despite the move to the more remote island, the earl maintained an intelligence network every bit as robust as the one in Norfolk. Richard Henry Lee complained to Washington on June 13 that a spy "was taking letters out of the post office in Virginia and carrying them to Dunmore," and warned that this "nefarious practice" was "of the greatest consequence."

The governor and Hamond also launched a disinformation campaign. They revealed to a visitor they correctly suspected of being an informant that commissioners from Britain were on their way to "treat with the Congress." They also assured him that "a very powerful fleet is expected with the troops from England." Neither claim was true, but the rumor was sure to unnerve the patriots, who made no immediate move to challenge the British and loyalist threat. This hesitation was not due to ignorance, given the frequent details passed on by deserters and spies and published in the capital's newspapers.

On May 31, a Black pilot steered a captured Spanish ship, the *Santa Maria*, to a safe anchorage off Gwynn's Island. On board was an immense treasure of fourteen thousand Spanish "hard dollars" and a man named Miguel Antonio Eduardo. He had been bound for Philadelphia on a secret mission for the Spanish Royal Agency for Negroes. The silver from the slave-trading organization was apparently destined for the patriots in exchange for Africans held in bondage. Eduardo managed to throw his orders overboard before being seized, but even after an unsuccessful search for hidden papers, the British remained suspicious. While a prisoner, the Spaniard counted "more than a hundred vessels" that included "barks, schooners, sloops, and numbers of large boats" riding off the island. In his diary, Eduardo estimated their troop strength at 250 redcoats and 300 Black men "who had fled the Americans to their freedom." These anemic numbers would represent only those healthy enough to report for duty.

The same day, a brig arrived filled with food supplies from the Caribbean. Provisions were now plentiful enough that Hamond dispatched a boat with bread and flour to the hungry garrison in St. Augustine. He hoped in return to receive beef, an essential part of the diet of British soldiers and sailors. "The other articles we are tolerably well off in," he wrote the Florida fort's governor on June 9. He also requested more cannon from St. Augustine and hinted that he could use more British regulars. There was sufficient gunpowder for the captain to order a twenty-one-gun salute from the *Fowey*, *Roebuck*, "and as many from the tenders as they can fire with convenience" to celebrate the king's birthday on June 4.

Despite illness and limited provisions, both Black and white loyalists from around Chesapeake Bay flocked to Gwynn's Island to fight under the royal governor. Emmes noted that "many Negroes came in and joined him." Those included eight of Landon Carter's enslaved men, who stole one of his boats, along with his son's gun, powder, and bullets. On one day alone, the *Fowey* brought one hundred volunteers and "several small vessels laden with cattle" from neighboring farms and islands. Gwynn's Island also drew delegations of loyalists from Delaware and Maryland's Eastern Shore eager to gain the support of the Royal Navy. Hamond was encouraged when they said their numbers topped three thousand. He was told that in one county nine in ten were "in favor of government and . . . ready to take up arms."

Virginia's patriots again were slow to react to an enemy camp alarmingly close to Williamsburg. Hamond noted on June 24 that they had not "been in the least interrupted by the rebels," though the Spaniard Eduardo said that the patriots occasionally fired at the men building earthworks. When Eduardo toured the island that day, he came away "wondering at the little or no resistance so small a number of men could be expected to present, and all so diseased."

The smallpox crisis soon was under control within the Ethiopian Regiment; Hamond reported that the "Negro troops got through the disorder with great success." But a wave of fever—likely typhus as well as malaria—continued to sweep the camp. In a June 26 letter to London, Dunmore reported that the illness "has proved a very malignant one and has carried off an incredible number of our people, especially the Blacks." Despite recruiting "six or eight fresh men every day"—mostly escaped Black men—there were soon only 150 "effective men" available for duty.

By then, smallpox was ravaging white loyalists, who may have resisted inoculation, arrived later, or been given a lower priority. As Washington had done at Cambridge, the governor "separated the sick from the well by the breadth of the island, and mean, if possible, to keep them from each other." Brush huts partially protected the ill from the harsh Tidewater summer sun, but the ranks thinned as the cemetery expanded. The June 14 *Gazette* reported, "Lord Dunmore's whole army is now reduced to forty regular soldiers, and two hundred of the black fusiliers."

Despite these appalling statistics, loyalists continued to arrive. On the evening of June 25 alone, five tenders brought between fifty and sixty white volunteers, "and would have brought many more had they room for them." Dunmore immediately enlisted the newcomers in the Queen's Own Loyal Regiment; the presence of armed Black men clearly did not dissuade many local white men from joining the king's cause. The June 28 *Gazette* guessed at two to three hundred new arrivals "from the number of tents which have been erected." The flow of men to Gwynn's Island prompted one Delaware patriot to send a warning to Hancock. "The most alarming circumstance," he wrote, was "the danger of Lord Dunmore's recruiting with success among the disaffected, who repair to him without reserve, and supply him with the produce of the country." Along with seeing to the training of these raw recruits, Dunmore even requisitioned the island's horses "to form a little troop" of cavalry to defend the island in case of attack.

A long drought combined with sickness proved more of a challenge than the patriots. Each man required at least half a gallon of fresh water for every hot summer day, but the normally plentiful wells began to dry up. Hamond was forced to detail ships to find other sources off the island. Filling and moving massive casks required tedious, backbreaking, and time-consuming labor, and patriot patrols made these forays dangerous. Beef remained in chronically short supply. A ship arrived with bread that had turned moldy in its hot and humid hold. By the end of June, even staples like oatmeal were running low. The June 25 capture of a brig "laden with rum from Barbados" along with "a few barrels of limes" no doubt lifted spirits, but the situation was growing dire.

Most of the thousands of civilians on the makeshift fleet remained on board their ships during the stifling days of summer, aside from the dead, like Sprowle, who were ferried ashore to be buried. Dunmore and Hamond were obliged to feed these noncombatant loyalists as well as their land-based soldiery. Reports from these vessels are sparse, but the Black and white civilians would have suffered the heat and humidity on a meager diet with limited water. If they lost just 10 percent of their body water, they would have endured muscle aches, vomiting, loss of appetite, a swelling tongue, and delirium that could end in death.

The soldiers on land may have received better rations, but the outbreak of typhus or malaria fatally crippled Dunmore's capacity to go on the offensive, despite the constant influx of new recruits. "Had it not been for this horrid disorder," the earl wrote ruefully to London, "I am satisfied I should have had two thousand Blacks, with whom I should have had no doubts of penetrating into the heart of this colony."

On May 26, the same day Dunmore and his forces landed at Gwynn's Island, the Virginia Convention's call for independence was read to the delegates in Philadelphia. Connecticut, New Hampshire, and Delaware quickly revised their instructions to their delegations to favor separation, though New York, Pennsylvania, South Carolina, Maryland, and New Jersey still hesitated.

On June 7, Richard Henry Lee rose from his seat, his right hand wrapped as usual in a black silk handkerchief that obscured fingers mangled in a gun accident, and spoke in a voice that one contemporary called "deep and melodious." He introduced a three-part resolution proposing that the colonies confederate, enter into foreign relations, and declare independence from Britain. No cheers erupted as the enormity of the moment sunk in. "All was silence," recalled John Adams. "No one would speak."

The voluble Massachusetts lawyer filled the void, but despite his pleas for members to approve the measures, it was clear advocates for separation needed more time to lobby. A vote was postponed for three weeks, but the Continental Congress soon appointed a five-member committee to draft a declaration explaining the reasons for separation.

Jefferson was largely responsible for the draft, which he wrote in his limited spare time between committee meetings. He drew heavily on Mason's declaration of rights, which was published June 12 in a Philadelphia newspaper, particularly in asserting that "all men are created equal and independent," and assembled a list of twenty-one accusations against the king, many of which reflected the complaints the Virginia Convention had made about Dunmore. "He has plundered our seas, ravaged our coasts, burnt our towns, and destroyed the lives of our people." Along with waging "cruel war against human nature itself" through the slave trade, "he is now exciting those very people to rise in arms among us" with the goal of murdering "the people." The king also had "endeavored to bring on the inhabitants of our frontiers the merciless Indian savages, whose known rule of warfare is an undistinguished destruction of all ages, sexes, and conditions of existence."

The British had fired Charlestown across from Boston, bombarded Falmouth in Maine, and sought indigenous allies in the north, but

Jefferson's denunciations clearly referred to the more recent and dramatic events in Virginia—Dunmore's alleged burning of Norfolk, the Royal Navy's raids along its coast, Connolly's plot to create a western front with the help of French and indigenous soldiers, and, of course, the earl's emancipation proclamation.

Along with his work on the draft and his other congressional duties, Jefferson kept a sharp eye on developments at Gwynn's Island. His papers include a careful sketch of the island, its bays and inlets, the enemy fortifications, and the patriot earthworks on the mainland, with detailed notes on the situation scribbled in the margins. On the brink of declaring independence, Virginia's delegation still feared Dunmore's presence and knew he was attracting recruits at an alarming rate.

The patriot leadership in Williamsburg put General Andrew Lewis in charge of ousting Dunmore. He had served under the governor in the Ohio frontier conflict, winning the Battle of Point Pleasant. One of the colony's few well-tested military officers, he may have held a personal grudge against the earl, who rebuked him for disobeying orders when he entered Shawnee territory during the 1774 peace negotiations. The governor had also refused his request to let his men plunder the villages of the conquered Shawnee. The loss of his brother at Point Pleasant also may still have rankled.

Lewis ordered his men to build fortifications on the mainland shore close to the island, but he himself preferred to remain in the more comfortable surroundings of Williamsburg. Deserters from the patriot camp warned Hamond that Lewis's men "worked day and night to finish a battery they were erecting opposite to our forts" and "meant to attack us as soon as their cannon were mounted." Yet aside from some patriot musket shots and answering cannon shot from the British, there was little violence throughout June.

At the end of the month, Maryland governor Eden arrived on the *Fowey* with a dozen sheep, three lambs, and seven sheep-goat hybrids given off as parting gifts when he left Annapolis, though his baggage had been impounded by the patriots. The small island was now home to two royal governors, both former friends of Washington.

Hamond, a man uncomfortable on land, grew restless seizing cattle to feed the thousands of loyalist soldiers and refugees. Bellew, cruising the Delaware on the *Liverpool*, wrote him that three "very sensible" white loyalists had asked for British support for a march on the Pennsylvania capital, claiming they could raise six or seven thousand men in a week. The Royal Navy captain was bullish, calling it "the very best opening that has appeared in our favor," given news that "the people of Philadelphia are full of disgust" with Congress.

That intelligence proved wishful thinking. On July 2, delegations from twelve colonies approved Lee's resolution declaring "that these United Colonies are, and of right ought to be, free and independent States." It was, however, a precarious unanimity; New York abstained, and one in five members voted against the measure. Nevertheless, two days later, Congress approved Jefferson's Declaration of Independence after striking his passages about the slave trade and his criticism of Scots. They also altered his charge that the king had urged those enslaved to murder their owners to the more euphemistic claim that he had "excited domestic insurrections."

Meanwhile on Gwynn's Island, Hamond, ever seeking action, decided to depart for the Delaware in the hope of capturing smugglers and threatening the rebel center of Philadelphia. Soon after, according to Eduardo, a messenger crossed the narrow strait from the mainland with "some written document" demanding "a general retirement from the island." This ultimatum prompted the captain and earl to send the ship's crews "to work on the fortifications that night." Still there was no sign of an imminent attack.

As of that day—July 5, 1776—there were two Virginia governors. Patrick Henry was sworn in as the first elected executive, despite opposition from conservatives. He immediately fell gravely ill. When planter Landon Carter heard—falsely—that Henry had died, he called the event a "glorious" intervention "by the hand of providence."

The *Fowey* returned from an expedition on July 7 with about one hundred loyalists—"a parcel of fine fellows"—and cattle. Eduardo counted 350 new arrivals. Hamond was now confident enough to order the earl's flagship—a converted merchant ship with few cannon and an inexperienced crew—to swap positions with the *Otter*, which lay close to the narrow point between mainland and island. Squire needed to clean from that ship's bottom the barnacles and algae that had built up in the warm southern waters.

At noon on July 8, amid the pealing of bells, crowds gathered in the yard of the Pennsylvania State House to hear a militia colonel make the first public reading of the Declaration of Independence. That afternoon, Hamond's marines boarded the *Roebuck*. The vessel was to leave on the next morning's tide. At dusk, Lewis and three other patriot officers arrived on the mainland shore to oversee the positioning of two pieces of eighteen-pound artillery trundled and barged from Williamsburg. Woodford joined the party.

Ten companies of shirtmen lay concealed behind the raw entrenchments, along with smaller cannon and an experimental wooden mortar designed by the eccentric French artillery captain Dohicky Arundel, who had joined the Continental Army. The officers had no plans for an immediate assault, but then they saw that the *Dunmore* "had exposed herself very prettily," Page wrote to General Lee. Anchored less than five hundred yards from the mainland, it now lay within easy range of the guns. The officers "determined not to lose this good opportunity of beginning their cannonade, in which they might severely and principally chastise the noble earl." Eduardo picked up on the deep animosity the patriots felt for Dunmore. "It is against this official that the Americans show their greatest rancor."

At eight o'clock on the morning of July 9, Lewis placed a burning match to the touchhole of one of the carefully aimed eighteen-pounders. With the ensuing boom, the rebels "opened several batteries on the fleet, and kept up a constant fire on the *Dunmore*," Hamond wrote in his log. One ball smashed into the ship's boatswain, slicing him in half, while another sailor lost an arm, according to a patriot report ten days later. Then a nine-pounder punctured the ship's hull, flew through the earl's stern cabin, and smashed into a wooden beam, "from the splinters of which Lord Dunmore got wounded in the legs, and had all his valuable china smashed about his ears."

According to a loyalist later captured by the patriots, "his Lordship was exceedingly alarmed, and roared out, 'Good God, that ever I should come to this!'" Landon Carter heard that the governor was injured in the groin and the planter could not contain his mirth. "I don't doubt this shot cooled his latitudinous virility for that night at least."

The British and loyalists were as surprised by the attack as the patriots had been at Great Bridge. "Their amazement and confusion was beyond description," wrote a jubilant Lewis to Richard Henry Lee. The panicked crew of the flagship managed a few shots at the enemy before using the ebbing tide to glide to safety, as did three tenders and a sloop. Even the exposed *Otter*, careened on the shore, was towed out of range by rowboats sent by Hamond. Lewis's guns were, however, effective in taking out the smaller British cannon and in "knocking down several tents which put their camp into great confusion." Eduardo said that "the royalists did not consider anything except a rapid retreat." The troops fled to the eastern side of the island, leaving the approach from the mainland undefended. The flagship boatswain and sailor were the only British or loyalist casualties. The sole patriot victim was Arundel; his experimental cannon exploded, instantly killing him.

In his eagerness to "chastise the noble earl," Lewis had failed to assemble vessels to ferry his men across the narrow strait to take advantage of his success. "Unhappily, we had not a boat on the shore," Page wrote. "These could not be procured till the next day."

This gave the king's forces precious time to consider their options. When the army officers, naval captains, and Governor Eden gathered to debate their next step, it was likely in the flagship's stern cabin, still littered with china sherds and with the governor's leg wrapped in bandages. They agreed Gwynn's Island "was no longer tenable," while Hamond declared that the flotilla must be dispersed. "I had come to the resolution to get rid of every vessel except the [troop] transports," he wrote later. A military officer tasked with blockading the two bays, the captain had grown "heartily tired of the predatory war, carried on by our little force merely for subsistence." He suggested the civilians be sent to St. Augustine. Eden and the others seconded the idea.

Dunmore alone objected. As governor, he was responsible for the health and well-being of the thousands of civilians he had protected for nearly a year. By removing them from their home colony, he would be admitting defeat. Without a large cadre of loyalists, moreover, there would be little hope of reestablishing British rule in the province. He may also have worried about the fate of the Black residents of the floating town, who might be re-enslaved or even sold to the West Indies by unscrupulous British officers. The governor, however, was overruled.

The exodus that followed was as chaotic as the departure from Norfolk six weeks earlier had been orderly. Its horror haunted Hamond. "The disgrace of [the] Gwynn's Island evacuation hangs so much about me," he confided to Dunmore ten days later. He found it "impossible to describe the distress and confusion that this floating town was thrown into, upon this sudden order of quitting the island." He almost certainly referred to the fate of the many sick and dying among the makeshift huts in the sweltering heat of the quarantined area. Bringing contagious patients aboard crowded ships would not only take precious time but would also imperil those uninfected. Captured white loyalists might expect to be nursed back to health by the patriots, but Black Americans could expect little mercy. If they survived, they would suffer imprisonment, hard labor in the lead mines, or death.

As Dunmore struggled on the evening of July 9 to direct the hurried evacuation, Washington listened with satisfaction to a public reading of the Declaration of Independence at New York's City Hall Park. The call for separation prompted a mob of patriot soldiers and civilians to swarm down Broadway and topple the two-ton equestrian statue of King George III on Bowling Green. Decapitated, the body of the figure was sent to Connecticut to be melted down into bullets to fire at the enemy. But even then, British ships under Admiral Richard Howe were gathering outside New York harbor to prepare for a massive August assault on the city by troops led by his younger brother, William.

As dawn lit up the western shores of the Chesapeake on July 10, two hundred shirtmen prepared to shuttle across the narrow strait in canoes gathered the night before. Three tenders, including a small sloop, the *Lady Charlotte*, were anchored to stymie the crossing. The crews began to fire small guns, but the patriots responded with two brass six-pounders. When the *Lady Charlotte* tried to escape and went aground, the rebels boarded the stranded vessel, taking prisoners and wounding the commander in the thigh and arm, while the crews of the other two tenders abandoned their crafts. Shirtmen then landed on Gwynn's Island. "This took so much time in our small vessels that the enemy had an opportunity of retreating to their ship," one patriot officer said, "in so precipitate a manner, that they left behind one of their cannon, several of their sick, and a great part of their effects."

The patriots were appalled by what they found. "The deplorable situation of the miserable wretches left behind is beyond description," wrote one. "Such a scene of misery, distress, and cruelty my eyes never beheld," said another. He was "struck with horror" by the "number of bodies in putrefaction" forming a gruesome line that he claimed stretched nearly two miles "without a shovelful of earth upon them." Even worse were those not yet dead. He saw "others gasping for life and some crawled to the water's edge, who could only make known their distress by beckoning to us." Another patriot saw Black people strewn across the island, "dying of the putrid fever," and added that "a child was found sucking at the breast of its dead mother." Some of the victims made desperate signs for water, while others sought to crawl away "from the intolerable stench of the dead bodies lying by their sides."

These dramatic accounts, published in the *Gazettes*, were purposely exaggerated to discourage further escapes by enslaved people to Dunmore's fleet. One patriot eyewitness, for example, wrote that many dead bodies "had been torn to pieces by wild beasts," but it is highly doubtful there were "wild beasts" on a small island that had been home to hundreds of hungry men. Colonel Adam Stephen provided what may be a more accurate picture. He insisted in private correspondence that there were only a dozen "unburied Negro corpses," presumably those who died during the frantic evacuation when burial was impractical. Yet the overall estimates of 500 Black victims and perhaps 150 whites may be roughly accurate. One rebel soldier counted 130 graves—"or rather holes loosely covered"—many of which apparently held more than one corpse.

What patriots glossed over was the fire in the quarantine area that killed Black and white loyalists. One shirtman noted that many "were burnt alive in brush huts, which in their confusion had got on fire." That ghastly conflagration was set on purpose by patriots seeking to cleanse the island of smallpox. "We must have run a great risk of taking the infection of the terrible disorders," said one. Another rebel fighter described the "firing of the enemy camp," while Eduardo noted that "at midday, the Americans went there and set fire to everything that remained." Any loyalists still alive almost certainly perished in the flames.

Chapter Thirty-One

Lands, Whores, and Dice

At eight o'clock on the morning of July 11, 1776, the Spanish captive Eduardo counted ninety-six ships setting sail from the anchorage off Gwynn's Island. One patriot watched as "the fleet went off in a sad plight and must be at a great loss where to go," adding that they "could not return to Norfolk, as the harbor there is well fortified." The flotilla moved north, passing the broad mouth of the Potomac River that separated Virginia from Maryland. It was now clear there was no safe place to land. Yet the thousands of crew members and passengers were in desperate need of water and provisions. They could not even flee the bay without first replenishing their supplies.

That night, "a strong wind struck us from the north and high seas," the Spaniard reported. "It lasted all night." The fierce gale snapped the mast of the already damaged *Dunmore*, shredded sails and rigging, and grounded dozens of smaller vessels. When twenty of these could not be rescued, Hamond was forced to set them on fire to prevent them from falling into enemy hands. Maryland's patriot forces, meanwhile, monitored the fleet's progress, ordering a battalion to the river's north shore to prevent a landing.

Before sunset on July 12, the ships anchored off the little slip of land called St. George Island, just off the mainland. The troops gathered cattle, sheep, and pigs but found only three shallow wells. They would have to sail up the Potomac, deep into enemy territory, for the vital water. Delays in transferring empty casks to two transports left the captain livid. His three warships were trapped "in a

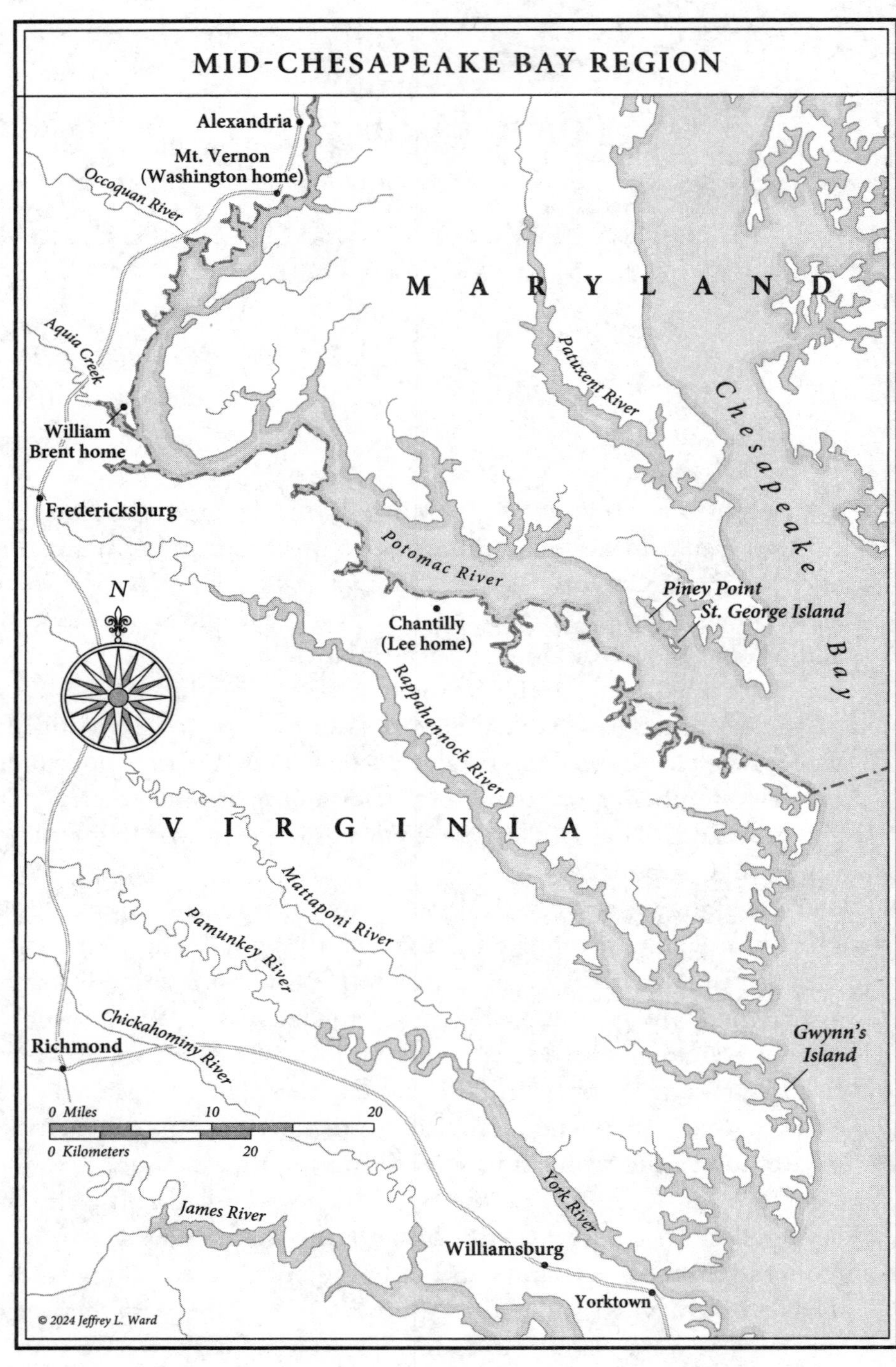
MID-CHESAPEAKE BAY REGION
Alexandria
Mt. Vernon
(Washington home)
Occoquan River
MARYLAND
Aquia Creek
William
Brent home
Fredericksburg
Patuxent River
Chesapeake Bay
Potomac River
N
Piney Point
St. George Island
Chantilly
(Lee home)
Rappahannock River
VIRGINIA
Mattaponi River
Pamunkey River
Chickahominy River
Richmond
Gwynn's
Island
0 Miles
10
20
0 Kilometers
20
York River
James River
Williamsburg
Yorktown
© 2024 Jeffrey L. Ward

state of perfect inactivity," he complained to Dunmore, "when it is necessary to strain every nerve to its utmost in prosecuting the war."

The divergent goals of the Royal Navy captain and Virginia's royal governor strained their long collaboration. Hamond hinted that Dunmore should remain with the flotilla at St. George, but the governor insisted on joining the expedition up the river. On July 19, Joseph Harris, the intrepid Hampton pilot who had served the British for a year and had rescued Squire during the 1775 hurricane, succumbed, likely to disease. The same day, the *Roebuck*, the *Dunmore*, two transports, and tenders set off with an innovative rowing galley constructed on Gwynn's Island that was impervious to the dreaded riflemen. The craft carried a crew of fourteen, with a six-pound cannon mounted on its bow and swivel guns to the stern, and drew only sixteen inches of water. Its sheltered sides made what patriots called a covered gondola into a kind of armored landing craft, presaging the ironclads that would steam through the Chesapeake in the Civil War. When patriots first saw the strange vessel, they were puzzled that there was "not a man to be seen" as it sliced through the water.

The convoy sailed into the Potomac River on a course that would take it past Richard Henry Lee's home of Chantilly. The Virginia delegate had left Philadelphia for Williamsburg a few weeks before, and he rushed home when he heard Dunmore was on the move. He was relieved to find the action confined to the northern shore in Maryland. Lee wrote sardonically to Jefferson on July 21 that "our African hero" was "now disturbing us in Potomac," then thanked Jefferson for sending a copy of his draft of the Declaration. By sunset that day, however, his nonchalance had turned to apprehension. Four British ships and three tenders suddenly appeared, and Lee rushed to join a militia unit patrolling the shore. The vessels, however, continued upstream; the expedition's goal was to find fresh water, not pillage. The next day, July 22, he wrote that Maryland patriots and the British were "continually blasting away at each other."

By that afternoon, the small fleet was within ten miles of Mount Vernon amid an increasingly desperate search. "Ought the precept, 'if thine enemy thirst, give him a drink,' to be observed toward such a fiend, and in such a war?" George Wythe asked Jefferson. "Our countrymen will probably decide in the negative."

After encountering fire from patriots on the Virginia shore, the ships retreated a few miles downstream, anchoring near the entrance to Aquia Creek. By the next morning, a rebel force had gathered by the "elegant brick house" of William Brent that stood on its banks. A disgusted John Parke Custis, Martha Washington's sole surviving child, wrote his stepfather that the men "all got drunk, and kept challenging the men of war to come ashore, and upbraiding them with cowardice." Hamond patiently waited. At noon, he sent several boats filled with more than one hundred soldiers toward Brent's home while the ships' gunners prepared grapeshot and nine-pound shot to cover their arrival. "The militia were asleep after their drunken frolic," Custis wrote, "and did not discover the enemy until they landed, and their vessels began to fire." The patriot officer in charge "desired his men to shift for themselves and ran off without firing a gun." An appalled Pendleton wrote Jefferson that he would "willingly conceal the shame of some of our militia on that occasion."

The landing party then went about the time-consuming business of filling the casks with Aquia's fresh water. Dunmore came ashore, entered Brent's house, and found newspapers trumpeting a resounding patriot victory in Charleston over Clinton's troops and Parker's ships. If true, the report was a devastating loss for the British and loyalist cause. He then ordered the building, along with outbuildings and haystacks, burnt. That afternoon, a boat arrived with "three of George Washington's servants," who then boarded the *Roebuck*. Whether they were white indentured servants or enslaved Africans is unclear. One of them may have been a middle-aged man named Harry Washington, who worked in the general's stables, would go on to serve in the British Royal Artillery and, much later, foment a rebellion in the West African colony of Sierra Leone.

Eventually, another less-inebriated militia contingent was spotted by lookouts on the *Roebuck*. The crew hoisted a white flag to warn the men ashore. In the hurried retreat, Hamond acknowledged a half dozen were wounded, but one patriot claimed that "three white men and four Negroes were found dead on the shore, two of the whites sewed up in hammocks and shot through the breast." These last were wearing "fine Holland shirts," and among them was a "gold-laced hat . . . with a bullet hole through both sides of the crown." They may have been killed during a previous skirmish and laid to rest on land as the expedition loaded the precious water.

The same day, July 23, Maryland patriots in small craft attacked the battered flotilla waiting seventy miles downstream at the mouth of the Potomac at St. George Island, forcing an evacuation "with the loss of some dead, various wounded, and others [taken] prisoners." The British and merchant ships returned to the island after two days, and "the royalists avenged themselves on the Americans by setting fire to all the houses, fields, and woods on the island," according to the Spaniard captive Eduardo. Eight ships deemed unseaworthy also went up in flames. Five days later, on the morning of July 28, a new and terrifying threat emerged. A new frigate with twenty guns manned by Maryland patriots suddenly bore down on the helpless flotilla. At that moment Hamond's *Roebuck* sailed out of the Potomac, driving the rebel craft away. The incident made clear, however, that the British had lost their unchallenged naval superiority.

Yet unfree workers continued to make their dash to freedom. Hamond reported "two Negroes came on board" the morning of July 30. There is even an intriguing mention in the July 26 *Gazette* that an African-born man named Abraham was sent "with many others from Barbados"—the British sugar island in the Caribbean—"by his master to fight for Lord Dunmore." New recruits, however, were no longer enough to turn the tide in this increasingly hostile land.

Distributing the casks took three anxious days, followed by several more of contrary winds. Not until August 2 could Hamond order the ships to depart. "Dunmore's fleet is gone off from the mouth of [the] Potomac, very sickly and in great distress," the Maryland patriot committee reported. The rebels remained unsure of the ships' destination, and one Maryland rebel warned that the fleet still posed a grave danger. Hamond, however, was intent on leaving the Chesapeake. His role supporting "Lord Dunmore and his floating town" was "now nearly at an end," and he would "be much more at liberty to act offensively against the enemy," he wrote. The events of the previous three months, he added, were "too painful for me to relate."

Aside from the hundreds of dead and dying left on Gwynn's Island, he had lost thirty of the *Roebuck*'s crew. At that moment, seventy-six were too ill to man the rigging. The earl's "troops have been so few in number, such a motley set, and so full of disease, that it has been totally impossible to do or attempt anything of consequence." Their men had been reduced to "burning and destroying houses on the banks of the rivers, and taking the cattle off the farms, which decides nothing." He was certain, however, that a strict blockade would weaken the patriots, who "have scarcely a second shirt, and their coats are already in rags."

Two days later, the flotilla anchored just west of Cape Henry, near the entrance to the Atlantic and only ten miles from Kemp's Landing. Nine months before, the governor had beaten a larger patriot force, proclaimed emancipation for those enslaved, and won the support of thousands. Now he led a crippled and demoralized band closely monitored by rebel forces. "Being fifty-two sails, a most beautiful sight," wrote a patriot soldier stationed near the cape. The local commander rushed two hundred men to the site, fearing an invasion.

Meanwhile, a British tender arrived with mail that confirmed the disastrous failure of the massive southern invasion. Admiral Peter Parker and General Henry Clinton wrote Dunmore that they could provide no assistance to the beleaguered governor. "I must say this is truly discouraging," given "the forlorn state in which they have left us," Dunmore wrote Lord Germain on August 4. He had spent fourteen months "constantly penned up in a ship hardly with the common necessities of life," but what "makes it now a thousand times worse, is that I am left without even the hope of being able to render his Majesty the smallest service." He found himself "in the utmost difficulty to determine what to do."

Hamond implored the earl to accept the "total impracticability of rendering his Majesty any service." The next day, Dunmore bid farewell to Captain Squire and the *Otter*, which accompanied more than thirty vessels with hundreds of Black and white civilian loyalists to their destination of St. Augustine. An unknown number of these remained enslaved by pro-British planters. Soon after, the *Fowey* unfurled her sails to escort seven ships, one of which carried the Maryland governor, on the first leg of the journey to England.

On August 6, seeking additional water and food, three British tenders made a beeline for the shore. A squadron of sixty rebels rushed to the beach, the very place where English settlers paused in 1607 on their way to settle Jamestown. The two sides exchanged shots before the landing force withdrew. "We took one prisoner who came ashore with two Negroes," the patriot soldier noted, "but the Negroes made their escape." The prisoner informed his captors that "they suffer very much on board for want of water and fresh provisions and they die very fast on board, having not hands enough to man the vessels."

The brief skirmish, the last confrontation between Virginia's patriots and their royal governor, apparently convinced Dunmore that retreat to New York harbor was the only option. On August 7, the *Roebuck* and *Dunmore*, along with five transports and two ships "laden with rum, sugars, and dry goods," weighed anchor, and the sands of Cape Henry receded in the summer haze. The surviving members of the Ethiopian Regiment, totaling more than two hundred men, were on board with their families. Passengers included preacher "Daddy" Moses Wilkinson, blinded by smallpox, Jane and Talbot Thompson from Norfolk, Harry Washington from Mount Vernon, and Ralph, who had escaped lifetime servitude under Patrick Henry. The August 9 *Gazette* reported that the fleet had on board "near 400 regulars, Negroes, and Tories," who were "tolerably healthy and had lately gotten a supply of provisions."

American patriots celebrated the earl's departure. A Massachusetts man was delighted to hear of the end to "Lord Dunmore's piratical depredations," while a Williamsburg newspaper bid good riddance to a man they asserted had "perpetrated crimes that would even have disgraced the noted pirate Blackbeard." That notorious renegade was reviled by white Virginians as much for treating his Black crew members as equal partners as for his relentless marauding.

"I thought all London was afloat," recalled one astonished Maryland private in the Continental Army. Not even a veteran sailor like Hamond had seen anything like it. The roadstead off New York's Staten Island on August 14 was a dense forest of some 350 ships spread over three miles. Two hundred warships and innumerable transports and supply vessels lay at anchor. Aboard were 32,000 redcoats preparing to land on Long Island as a first step to conquering New York City. The British boasted twice the manpower of Washington's army.

Patriot sentries passed word to Washington's Manhattan headquarters that the earl had arrived, and the general informed Hancock in Philadelphia, without comment, of his former friend's unexpected appearance. Jefferson in turn relayed his news to Page in Virginia on August 20, adding that Dunmore "had the blacks shipped off to the West Indies." In fact, the members of the Ethiopian Regiment were readying for battle against Washington's forces on Long Island.

That afternoon the governor attended a "great formal dinner" hosted by Admiral Richard Howe on his flagship, the sixty-four-gun *Eagle*. Richard's brother William, head of ground troops, attended, as did Parker—some of his defeated fleet had arrived that same day from Charleston—and Lord Campbell, the royal governor of South Carolina; the Scottish earl had been injured in the battle at Charleston and would eventually die of his wounds.

Seated at a table crowded with some of Britain's most senior officers, Dunmore made a pitch for reinforcements to be sent to Virginia. He had Hamond's backing; the captain wrote that with a thousand men and a dozen warships, the British could bring the Chesapeake patriots to heel and even threaten Philadelphia. The Howe brothers "approve very much of our conduct, yet they seem very unwilling to part with any of their force at present," the disappointed earl informed Germain in a September 4 letter. Any Virginia campaign would have to wait until New York was firmly in British hands.

Dunmore and some members of the Ethiopian Regiment soon found themselves in the thick of the Battle of Long Island, which began on August 26. The September 14 issue of the *Gazette* reported that the earl accompanied Highlanders and Hessians "the whole day," while his Black soldiers took part in various skirmishes. The patriots claimed to have captured "Major Cudjo, commander of Lord Dunmore's Black regiment," though whether he was real or imagined is unclear.

The British and loyalists quickly overwhelmed the patriots, pushing them to the Brooklyn shore, but Washington used the rain and fog in the night of August 29 to 30 to ferry most of his nine thousand men across the East River to Manhattan. A September 15 British assault captured New York City, and the patriots abandoned Manhattan Island in October, eventually retreating to White Plans, then across the Hudson River into New Jersey and then Pennsylvania to regroup.

In the aftermath of the victory, Dunmore hoped to gain a military commission to carry on the fight, and he leased a house on Broadway, only a few blocks from the Black encampment near today's Astor Place where members of the Ethiopian Regiment and their families settled. The corps eventually was absorbed into Clinton's Black Pioneers and included both sexes. Though they were not issued weapons, they received the same pay as whites, and a few achieved the rank of corporal and sergeant. Among them were several people the governor had owned and then freed. These included a middle-aged blind woman named Sarah, who had probably lost her sight from smallpox; Roger Scott, "formerly slave to Lord Dunmore" and an "ordinary fellow" of fifty who said he "got his freedom" from the earl; and a thirty-two-year-old "stout wench" named Cathern Scott.

While General Howe refused the earl's request for a commission, Dunmore would have influenced the commander's decision to protect rather than return those enslaved who had fled patriot owners. Even in New York, Dunmore remained closely associated with Africans. When he met Lord Stirling, a British officer who had joined the patriot cause and was now a captive, the earl said he was sorry that Stirling kept company with the rebels. The prisoner tartly replied, "My Lord, I have kept whiter company than your Lordship has of late."

On November 11, the governor boarded the familiar *Fowey*, which had housed him and his family when he fled Williamsburg for Yorktown in June 1775. His departure alarmed delegates in Congress. "Lord Dunmore is to take the command of a fleet bound for the southward," Hancock warned Maryland patriots. He added that, as "it is by no means certain against which of the southern states the expedition is designed, it is highly necessary you should be on your guard." In fact, the earl arrived in Britain on December 21 after a six-year absence.

Though reunited with his family after eighteen long and difficult months, Dunmore found mostly cold shoulders in London when he resumed his seat in the House of Lords. He had lost North America's prize colony and freed many enslaved people, a deeply unpopular move among the British elite, which profited from human trafficking and enslaved Caribbean labor. He was presented to the French king during an August 1777 Paris visit, but a full year passed before the earl gained an audience with his own sovereign, a sign of the monarch's displeasure.

When they finally met, in December 1777, Dunmore offered to raise four thousand Highlanders and sought a commission as a colonel. The king dismissed both ideas, writing to Lord North that they had enough Scotsmen in uniform, and that the earl had "quitted the army several years ago, and only as a captain." In the space of two years, the governor had raised two armies, won a frontier war, fought a grinding second conflict, and knew Virginia like no other British official. This practical experience did not trump strict military protocol.

The following month, a Scottish court stunned Europe and America by declaring slavery illegal in that kingdom. Two weeks later, Parliament finally addressed Dunmore's emancipation proclamation and British efforts to win indigenous support against the rebels. Patriots had long predicted that legislators would revoke the governor's decree, and on February 6, 1778, patriot sympathizer Edmund Burke launched the long-awaited attack in the House of Commons.

In a marathon three-hour speech behind closed doors, he charged, "Our national honor has been deeply wounded, and our character as a people debased" by what he called "shameful, savage, and servile alliances" with Black and indigenous peoples that had served only "to unite and arm all the colonies against us." He claimed that the primary aim of "all of the Negroes" who considered revolt was murder, rape, "and horrid enormities of every kind." Dunmore's proclamation, he asserted, "was the grand cause" that prompted Virginia and its sister southern colonies to declare for independence. Burke, who would later emerge as an opponent of the slave trade, urged Parliament to make "the most marked and public disapprobation" of a policy "disgraceful to a great and civilized nation."

Lord North and his government held firm, refusing to repudiate the governor's actions and those of other British officials seeking indigenous backing. After "a warm debate of seven hours," Burke's measure failed by nearly two to one. The king and his ministers no doubt supported Dunmore's policy out of pragmatic rather than ethical reasons, but the vote put Parliament on record as supporting mass emancipation, at least during time of war.

The same day Burke stood to denounce Dunmore's policy, American and French negotiators signed a treaty of alliance. It was the ultimate marriage of convenience. The French had long been the primary enemy of American colonists. They had dominated the regions to the north and west of British territory, were overwhelmingly Catholic, and were led by one of Europe's most autocratic rulers. But American patriots were eager to win the assistance of French troops and fleets, while the French saw a chance to weaken their ancient foe. This alliance, combined with renewed patriot efforts to recruit Black soldiers, forced Britain's conservative military leaders to reconsider the latent power of enslaved Americans.

On June 7, 1779, the British commandant of New York City decreed that "all Negroes that fly from the enemy's country are free—no person whatever can claim a right to them." Three weeks later, General Clinton issued a more guarded proclamation from his headquarters in Phillipsburg, just north of New York. He promised "every Negro who shall desert the rebel standard full security" to choose "any occupation they shall think proper." He also warned any Black American captured while on military duty for the rebels would be sold into slavery. There was no explicit promise of full emancipation, nor did Clinton make a provision for Black men to take up arms, but it turned Dunmore's isolated decree into official British policy.

Even then, three years later and three hundred miles north of Virginia, patriots still recalled the royal governor with fear and loathing. A Connecticut newspaper that summer advertised the sale of a twenty-four-year-old pregnant black woman who "bids fair to make more recruits for Lord Dunmore."

Despite the infusion of French money, ships, and men into the patriot cause, the foes remained locked in a stalemate outside New York. British military leaders by 1779 came to the belated conclusion that Virginia was "the province which of all others gives sinews to the rebellion from its extensive traffic," as one British admiral put it. By then, Georgia's capital Savannah was firmly back in British hands. Charleston would fall to them in May 1780. "If offensive war is intended, Virginia appears to be the only province in which it can be carried on," General Cornwallis wrote one year later. He marched a large army of redcoats through North Carolina that spring with orders to establish a base at a deep-water port in southern Virginia.

Thousands of enslaved people abandoned their forced labor camps to follow in the protective wake of the British army. Cornwallis treated this cadre not as an asset but as a nuisance that could, at best, provide some convenient labor. He complained that summer that he was "in great want of Negroes to work, as the heat is too great to admit of the soldiers doing it." A man with deep racial prejudices, he refused to give the Black refugees significant responsibilities, much less weapons. "Every soldier had his Negro who carried his provisions and bundles," noted one German mercenary.

On June 25, 1781, ten years after Dunmore first arrived in Williamsburg, the British army marched triumphantly down Duke of Gloucester Street. The Virginia capital had recently moved to the less vulnerable site of Richmond, and the settlement was now little more than a sleepy village. Among those in bondage who deserted to the conquerors were the people owned by Peyton Randolph's widow Betty. "The good old lady was left without a human being to assist her in any respect," one white patriot wrote on July 11.

Cornwallis did not linger. "Having no harbor, and requiring an army to occupy the position, [it] would not have suited us," he explained. He set out to find a suitable base, crossing the James River to survey Portsmouth, which he rejected as too unhealthy and exposed to French warships. He abandoned large numbers of sick and dying Black refugees there and settled on Yorktown. Dunmore had concluded in July 1775 that the tobacco port with its high bluffs was difficult to defend and too deep in hostile territory. Washington, who had spent time with the governor at his Portobello plantation just upriver, also was well aware of Yorktown's vulnerabilities.

When a French admiral agreed to blockade the Chesapeake, cutting off any escape for Cornwallis, Washington and French general Comte de Rochambeau marched their combined armies of seven thousand men, including hundreds of Black patriots, four hundred miles south to encircle the enemy. When they reached Philadelphia in early September, many Continental troops refused to continue unless they were paid in hard currency, and Rochambeau provided the needed gold coins. A British fleet under Admiral Thomas Graves, meanwhile, arrived at the Chesapeake capes to relieve Cornwallis, only to find a larger French flotilla waiting. In the subsequent sea battle, Graves was forced to withdraw. Nine days later, Washington and Rochambeau arrived in Williamsburg. The trap was set.

Bombarded and besieged for three weeks, the British general and his eight thousand soldiers surrendered on October 19, 1781, but not before expelling large numbers of sick and hungry Black men devastated by smallpox and typhus from their protection. "We had used them to good advantage and set them free," a German officer wrote in dismay, "and now, with fear and trembling, they had to face the reward of their cruel masters." A Williamsburg patriot who attended the surrender ceremony wrote that "an immense number of Negroes have died in the most miserable manner in York." Sarah Osborn, a patriot laundress, noted "a number of dead Negroes" around their encampment whom "the British had driven out of the town and left to starve, or were first starved and then thrown out."

Many who survived desperately sought refuge with French officers. "We gained a veritable harvest of domestics," chortled one Frenchman. Six days after the surrender, Washington forbade "such Negroes or mulattoes be retained in their service" and ordered the Black loyalists locked up before being returned to their American owners. Meanwhile, one of his officers worked his way through the enemy camp, seizing any Black person without papers proving they had been legally purchased by a British or Hessian soldier. The officer suggested to Washington that some of those recovered be sent to labor in the lead mines.

Though the war sputtered on for another two years, the American Revolution came to an effective military conclusion at the very spot where Dunmore had begun his campaign against the rebels, and where enslaved people had first found refuge with the British. They were the first of tens of thousands of people who escaped bondage during the half dozen years of conflict. For most of those who remained alive, the patriot victory at Yorktown meant a return to a lifetime of servitude.

Even as Washington's men rounded up the Black loyalists, the governor was on a ship bound for America, fully anticipating a Cornwallis victory that would put him back in the Palace, where he could resume his interrupted tenure as governor. Lord Germain explained to General Clinton in an October 4, 1781, letter that the earl was "unwilling to remain inactive in England whilst military operations are carrying on within the province of which he is governor," adding archly, "and where he imagines he still retains influence and connections sufficient to enable him to be useful."

On December 21, after an absence of nearly five years, Dunmore landed on a Charleston wharf to news of the bitter British defeat at Yorktown, 350 miles to the north. The next evening, "some malicious person" torched the Williamsburg Palace, according to a Charleston paper. "We have no water or buckets to put it out," wrote a rueful Rochambeau to Washington, who had spent so much time in the mansion. The building was in use as a hospital for one hundred ill and wounded soldiers from the Yorktown campaign. The French general added that all the sick were evacuated, although another account has a single soldier perishing in the blaze that raged for three hours.

When dawn arrived, the seven-decade-old residence that had been home to seven appointed and two elected governors lay in a smoking heap, like the British government's hopes of squelching the rebellion. "Oh God, it is all over!" Lord North was said to have cried on learning in late November of the Yorktown defeat. Dunmore, however, was not yet ready to concede defeat.

Chapter Thirty-Two

A Glaring Piece of Injustice

On his arrival in Charleston, the earl was given "a grand reception" and elegant accommodations by Charleston loyalists grateful for his efforts in London to obtain compensation for those who had lost property during the conflict. One claimant was Peter Anderson, the Black sailmaker wounded at Great Bridge, sentenced to death by the patriots, and who later escaped and made his way back to Dunmore's camp. Anderson later requested a modest payment from the British government for his losses, including four featherbeds and twenty hogs. The governor provided a certificate attesting that "he was a free man and joined me in the first breaking out of the rebellion," and that he "had some small property in Virginia."

Dunmore also encountered rebel ridicule on his return to America. Wrote one patriot poet:

> That a silly old fellow much noted of yore / and known by the name of John, earl of Dunmore / has again ventured over to visit your shore.

Putting words into the earl's mouth, he went on:

> Though a brute and a dunce, like the rest of the clan, / I can govern as well as most Englishman can; / And if I'm a drunkard, I still am a man

The poet also had him address enslaved Americans:

> Give me lands, whores and dice, and you still may be free; / Let who will be master, we sha'nt disagree; / If king or if Congress—no matter to me;

Dunmore's conviction that the war could only be won with the help of Black troops had not wavered during his long absence, and he wasted little time on his arrival. Within two weeks, he backed a campaign even more ambitious—or quixotic—than his 1775 effort with Major Connolly to invade Virginia with the support of indigenous peoples of the Ohio Valley. He partnered with a North Carolina loyalist named John Cruden, who oversaw British confiscation of patriot estates and their enslaved workers. Cruden prepared a January 5, 1782, memo for the governor that called for arming ten thousand unfree workers to conquer Virginia.

In a February 2 letter to General Clinton in New York, the earl argued this plan was "the most efficacious, expeditious, cheapest, and certain means of reducing this country to a proper sense of their duty." Africans were "not only fitter for service in the warm climate than white men, but they are also better guides, may be got on much easier terms, and are perfectly attached to our sovereign." And, he added, "from my own knowledge of them, I am sure they are as soon disciplined as any set of raw men that I know of."

While Cruden's draft called for armed Black men to be led by white officers, Dunmore proposed "to fill up the vacancies of the non-commissioned officers now and then with black people, as their services should entitle them to it." A handful of his Ethiopian Regiment members had already achieved non-commissioned rank, but this new plan would make such promotions accepted military policy. To encourage enlistments, the British would offer "a promise of freedom to all that should serve during the continuance of the war." That promise, he insisted, would "be held inviolate." But the new Black soldiers would earn more than freedom. Each man would be paid a guinea and a crown—roughly $300 today—presumably a one-time payment. Dunmore, eager to enlist the support of his superiors, copied the letter to Lord Germain in London.

The January 5 memo apparently was leaked within days to Nathaniel Greene, the patriot general stationed outside Charleston. This would explain his January 24 letter to Washington suggesting that he "raise some black regiments," since "to fill up the regiments with whites is impracticable." In another letter, he assured the South Carolina patriot governor that "they would make good soldiers, I have not the least doubt." In exchange, the enslaved men "should have their freedom, and be clothed and treated, in all respects, as other soldiers; without which they will be unfit for the duties expected from them." Greene's language is notably similar to that of the Cruden memo. Dunmore quickly learned of the plan and warned London.

South Carolina rebels, however, were appalled by the general's recommendation; they had rejected a similar plan put forward in 1779 by John Laurens, an officer under Washington who was from a wealthy South Carolina planter family. A patriot judge was "not a little startled at the proposition" made by Greene and expressed distaste at the idea of "servile hands" defending republican freedom. The legislators not only rejected the idea but decided instead to give an enslaved African from loyalist plantations to each white soldier. The South Carolina physician David Ramsay was a rare patriot who disagreed with this policy. The "great obstacles in the way of Black liberty," he concluded, were "white pride and avarice."

Meanwhile, Dunmore's persistent lobbying apparently helped convince Lt. General Alexander Leslie, Britain's commander in South Carolina, to form a cavalry unit called the Black Dragoons made up of former and current enslaved men. In a February 25 skirmish with patriots under Francis Marion, they drove the enemy away, and even made off with the Swamp Fox's tent and liquor. Leslie, impressed by their bravery and no doubt encouraged by Dunmore, wrote to Clinton suggesting that the unit be expanded, and their members promised freedom.

But the Virginia governor was well aware that the leader of the British military in America had always refused to arm Black men, so he set off for New York to make the case personally. On the day he departed, March 30, he warned Germain that "by neglecting to make a proper use of those people, who are so much attached to us," they would be committing a grave error. Patriot owners, he added, "are now carrying them up the country as fast as they can find them," and he suggested evacuating Black refugees to the safety of Louisiana.

Peace talks between American and British negotiators in Paris had just begun when Dunmore arrived in New York on April 11. For more than five years, the port city had been home to many former members of the Ethiopian Regiment, which had been absorbed into the Black Pioneers in September 1776. During the conflict, thousands of others had fled from lifetime servitude to find safety inside British lines, including many of Jane and Talbot Thompson's relatives. Most lived in cramped and crowded barracks; one housed thirty-seven people in just three and a half rooms. Others made do in a ramshackle encampment called Canvas City built on the ruins left by a massive fire that swept the city after the British occupation in 1776, which may well have been the result of patriot arson.

Clinton welcomed the Virginia governor to his headquarters at 1 Broadway, across from the empty plinth on Bowling Green that had once held the equestrian statue of King George III. He was intrigued enough by Dunmore's plan to approve an operation to build forts near Norfolk and Hampton to blockade the James River. Yet the general cautioned that "the arming of Negroes requires a little consideration." What neither man knew was that in the wake of the debacle at Yorktown, King George III had called for an end to fighting on February 14 and Lord North had resigned his position as prime minister on March 20.

Sir Guy Carleton, the longtime governor of Canada, arrived in May to relieve Clinton of his command and oversee the British evacuation of New York. Dunmore was pointedly not invited to his inaugural dinner. The earl's bellicose views were out of favor, and Carleton, who had fought against the Jacobites at the Battle of Culloden, may have had little affinity for the Scottish noble. The governor prepared to go home, but he almost certainly lobbied the commanders on behalf of Black loyalists trapped in New York and other British-controlled ports. He knew better than any other British official that if they fell back into the hands of the victorious rebels, they faced imprisonment, torture, death, or re-enslavement.

On May 16, 1782, Dunmore boarded a ship for Britain, never to return to North America. After a speedy voyage, he arrived in London in time to attend a June 19 reception for the king and took part in a private debriefing session with the sovereign, Clinton, and Cornwallis. Details of the meeting are not known, but in August Dunmore was pressing "to raise several corps of Blacks upon the promise of freedom" to attack the new nation. He also backed a proposal to arm indigenous people along the Mississippi River who would seize American lands in the Ohio. The goal, he explained, was "to drive the thirteen united provinces into the sea."

That summer, the Royal Navy began to evacuate Savannah and Charleston loyalists—both Black and white—to nearby British havens. East Florida's governor reported over three thousand Black refugees had arrived in St. Augustine, "and more are daily coming." Some were free, while others remained in bondage to loyalist planters. This exodus alarmed patriot leaders, many of whom assumed the British would sell them in the West Indies at an immense profit.*

In September, James Madison proposed in Congress that the British pay for "slaves and other property which had been carried off or destroyed in the course of the war by the enemy." The American delegation in Paris, made up of Benjamin Franklin, John Adams, and John Jay, was, however, unenthusiastic about forced servitude, though Jay himself had lost an enslaved man named Massey to the British. Then, on November 30, the day the final treaty was being drafted at the Hotel d'York, South Carolina's Henry Laurens appeared.

The wealthy planter was the father of John Laurens who had pushed unsuccessfully to liberate Black men to fight the British, and he had spent fifteen months in the Tower of London. Released from that grim prison, he rushed to the French capital, still grieving the loss of his son in one of the Revolution's last engagements. "Mr. Laurens said there ought to be a stipulation that the British troops should carry off no Negroes or other American property," Adams noted. "We all agreed. Mr. Oswald consented." Richard Oswald, the British negotiator, owned a slave business in Sierra Leone, and Laurens had once served as his South Carolina purchasing agent.

* While a loyalist inspector in the Caribbean, Cruden conducted an investigation that found some Black refugees "had been fraudulently taken away," though such incidents appear to have been isolated.

The last-minute addition suddenly called into question the fate of tens of thousands of Black Americans, since it obligated Britain to withdraw from the United States "without causing any destruction, or carrying away any Negroes, or other property of the American inhabitants." Adams reported that the document was "signed, sealed, and delivered, and we all went . . . to dine with Dr. Franklin."

News of the treaty article would not arrive in America until early 1783. By then, Royal Navy commanders had evacuated as many as eight thousand Black southern loyalists to destinations as diverse as Louisiana and Germany. Those who had fled with Dunmore to New York, however, remained in limbo, enduring another bitter winter in Manhattan as rumors swirled that "all the slaves, in number two thousand, were to be delivered up to their masters," recalled Boston King, a Black loyalist from South Carolina, "which filled us all with inexpressible anguish and terror." By spring, Southern patriots were "seizing upon their slaves in the streets of New York," he added. "We lost our appetite for food, and sleep departed from our eyes."

Washington remained at his Newburgh headquarters upstream on the Hudson River. With fighting over, his new mission was to ensure that General Carleton withdrew his men and ships from New York, the last British outpost in the colonies, in a timely fashion. But he faced other challenges as well. In mid-March 1783, he squelched a mutiny of officers demanding payment from Congress.

With spring's arrival the following week came a letter with a bold proposal from the Marquis de Lafayette, who had served the general during the war and had become like a son to the childless Virginian. "Let us unite in purchasing a small estate," the French officer suggested, "where we may try the experiment to free the Negroes and use them only as tenants" and then spread the model across the South and the West Indies. On April 5, Washington replied that the scheme to "encourage the emancipation of the black people of this country from that state of bondage in which they are held, is a striking evidence of the benevolence of your heart." He added, "I shall be happy to join you in so laudable a work," but he deferred discussing details until, as he wrote, "I have the pleasure of seeing you." This was, at best, a polite brush-off; he never took the marquis up on his innovative idea.

Ten days later, on April 15, Congress ordered Washington to arrange for "the delivery of all Negroes and other property of the inhabitants of the United States in the possession of the British forces." Virginia governor Benjamin Harrison even asked the head of the Continental Army to assume the role of slave catcher. "I observe by a clause in the articles we are to have our Negroes again," Harrison wrote on March 31. "I have thirty missing, many of which I understand are dead, but there are still some that are very valuable." He added: "If it is not too much to ask, I shall ever be under the greatest obligation if you will fall on some method to secure them." He assured his fellow planter that he would cover the cost of their sea passage back to Virginia and added, "My well-being depends on their being recovered."

Washington himself was negotiating with a New York–based merchant named Daniel Parker to recover the three enslaved individuals from Mount Vernon lost to Dunmore, as well as the seventeen who had taken refuge on a passing Royal Navy warship in 1781. "Some of my own slaves, and those of Mr. Lund Washington who lives at my house, may probably be in New York," he wrote Parker on April 28. "If by chance you should come at the knowledge of any of them, I would be much obliged by our securing them so I may obtain them again." He assured him that while his efforts might be "troublesome to yourself," they were fully legal, and he helpfully included a list of human chattel.

That same day, a delegation of Norfolk slaveowners presented their case in person to Carleton's staff in Manhattan. Their petition complained that "passports have been granted several Negroes to embark on board transports," and they were "apprehensive of a total loss." Nearly 750 enslaved men and women from Norfolk County alone were unaccounted for, the highest figure for any Virginia county. A member of the group told Virginia legislators on May 3 that Carleton's aide had insisted "no slaves were to be given up, who claimed the benefit of their former proclamations for liberating such slaves." The British general, in other words, had no intention of returning those enslaved people already liberated under Dunmore's and Clinton's proclamations. Hundreds were already on their way to Nova Scotia, far from the grasp of their owners. The Norfolk businessman was irate. He called it a "glaring piece of injustice, and open violation" of the draft treaty. The injury, he added, "will be inconceivable."

The thirty-six-gun British frigate was new and sleek and bore the ironic name *Perseverance*. On the morning of May 6, 1783, Washington stood stiffly in his buff-and-blue dress uniform on a Hudson River dock north of New York City as sailors rowed Sir Guy Carleton, the new British commander in chief of American forces, to shore. The Continental Army general sized up his able adversary as the fifty-eight-year-old officer drew closer. Like the American, he hid his thinning hair under a wig, but his round face and double chin were a striking contrast to the lean, tall Virginian who was seven years his junior.

An Irish-born soldier who had long governed Canada, Carleton had successfully ousted the rebels from the northern province during the Revolution. Washington had requested to meet with him in order to pin down details of the British withdrawal. When Carleton stepped onto the dock, the two men exchanged formal greetings and climbed into a carriage as their aides followed on foot behind. The party halted at a nearby one-story brick-and-stone house with a steeply pitched roof braced by two massive chimneys. For an hour, the company of officers and politicians from both sides chatted politely, a scene unimaginable just months before. "When all seated, Washington opened the business," recalled New York chief justice William Smith, who was in the audience. Smith had clashed with Dunmore a decade before when the earl was provincial governor.

Speaking "with great slowness" in a "low tone of voice," the Virginian said the first order of business was "the preservation of property from being carried off, and especially the Negroes." Washington pointed out to Carleton that the draft treaty article required King George III to turn over "any Negroes or other property of the American inhabitants." The British general then made a stunning announcement. Black loyalists even then were on their way to Nova Scotia.

"Already embarked!" Washington exclaimed. It was a rare public outburst by a man famous for his self-control, but it was pure theater from a man who, like Dunmore, adored stage plays. Two weeks before, he had informed Carleton that he wanted to discuss "the carrying away by the British of American property including Negroes." His spies and Virginia friends surely had informed him of the transports filled with Black refugees. The British, Washington continued more evenly, had violated a solemn preliminary treaty made between two nations. Carleton calmly replied that the agreement could not be "inconsistent with prior engagements binding the national honor, which must be kept with all colors"—Black or white. He cited the 1775 proclamation made by the Virginia general's erstwhile friend, as well as Clinton's 1779 decree, as evidence of "prior engagements." He then added his worry that "delivering up the Negroes to their former masters" might expose some to "execution" and "others to severe punishments." The British had promised and granted freedom, and they could not undo it. Their honor was at stake. There were, therefore, no "slaves" to return.

The British commander offered a way for the visibly irritated Virginian to save face. He assured Washington that he had kept a careful record of all Black emigrants in a ledger that provided the name, age, physical description, former owner, and escape date of each one; it came to be called *The Book of Negroes*. He added that a joint military commission could be set up to settle future disputes. "If the sending off of the Negroes should hereafter be declared an infraction of the treaty, compensation must be made by the crown of Great Britain to the owners," Carleton explained. Washington was not fooled. He peppered the general with questions: How would they put a price on each person, given that "the value of the slave consist[s] in his industry and sobriety" rather than age and occupation? What if they had changed their name, or did not accurately identify their master? Carleton was unmoved. The Black loyalists, he said, had no reason to lie, and their worth could be established by their age and description. Besides, he added, if the British did not provide them with a home, they were sure to escape on their own, leaving the patriots with no chance for compensation.

The men went on to discuss the precise timing for the British evacuation of New York, but here, too, they could not reach a satisfactory agreement. The strained meeting was deadlocked. "Washington pulled out his watch," Smith wrote, "and observing that it was near dinner time offered wine and bitters." The negotiators drifted outside to enjoy drinks under a large tent on the lawn, followed by an elaborate meal prepared by Samuel Fraunces. A famous chef and owner of New York City's renowned Fraunces Tavern, he was also one of Washington's spies. The sun was low by the time Carleton and his aides returned to their ship. After their departure, Washington bemoaned to aides the "diffuse and desultory" conference.

He stayed up late penning a letter of protest to the British general. "The carrying away of any Negroes or other property belonging to the American inhabitants" was "under your control," he noted. "I was surprised to hear you mention that an embarkation had already taken place, in which a large number of Negroes had been carried away." Washington reiterated that Carleton's view was against the letter and spirit of the preliminary treaty, and he requested his justification in writing. Then he dropped an ominous threat. He was prepared to "take any measures which may be deemed expedient to prevent the future carrying away of any Negroes or other property of the American inhabitants." The commander in chief implied that he was willing to attack British-controlled New York to recover those he considered patriot property.

Carleton was eager to avoid another such encounter, so the next day he pleaded illness and skipped a second elaborate meal planned by Washington. The patriot general, meanwhile, wrote to Virginia governor Harrison. "I have discovered enough . . . in the course of the conversation which was held to convince me that the slaves which have absented from their masters will never be restored to them," he said, expressing more resignation than anger. "Vast numbers of them are already gone to Nova Scotia." The British commander's response to the general's letter confirmed this view. "The Negroes in question, as I have already said, I found free when I arrived in New York," Carleton explained a week later. He had no right "to prevent their going to any part of the world they thought proper." In a swipe at patriot prejudice, he declared that "breach of public faith towards people of any complexion" reflected poorly on the Americans.

Carleton's intransigence outraged slaveowners. From Richmond, Edmund Pendleton wondered whether the general had met with Washington solely "for amusement whilst the Negroes were car-r[ied] away." Virginia's House of Delegates proposed "prisoners of war should be detained, until an answer be given as to the delivery of slaves." In Philadelphia, Continental Congress president Elias Boudinot warned Benjamin Franklin in Paris, that "sending away the Negroes . . . has irritated the citizens of America to an alarming degree." James Madison rose to call the British move "a shameful evasion."

Lawmakers even debated whether to halt the disbanding of the Continental Army to signal that they would consider marching on New York to regain their human property. Hamilton stepped in to calm the furor, warning members that the "renewal of hostilities might be a consequence of such declaration." Only amid much grumbling among slaveowners was the resolution dropped.

King George III, however, gave Carleton's decision, "in the fullest and most ample manner, his royal approbation," while a minister wrote the general from London that his decision to protect the Black loyalists was "certainly an act of justice due to them from us." A later British memo reasserted the government's right "to withdraw Negroes," and accused Washington of acting in the matter "with all the grossness and ferocity of a captain of Banditti." It was the very term patriots had used to describe Dunmore.

At ten o'clock on a Wednesday morning in the summer of 1783, soon after Carleton and Washington met, Jane Thompson stood in line at the imposing three-story Fraunces Tavern on Pearl Street in lower Manhattan, holding the hand of her five-year-old grandchild and whatever papers she had rescued from her long-gone home on Cumberland Street. She was now a widow. Her husband, Talbot, the Norfolk sailmaker who had made history by gaining freedom for himself and his wife, had died a year before in their adopted home of New York.

A panel of British officers questioned Thompson while a clerk made notes in *The Book of Negroes*. As Washington had feared, she fudged the details to increase her chances of achieving permanent freedom. She spelled her name "Thomson," gave her age as seventy, claimed to have been born free, and said she'd left Norfolk—where she "lived with Col. Tucker"—in 1777. Almost none of this was accurate. She was, in fact, born into bondage, was a decade or so younger, and had left by the start of 1776. Slavecatchers would be less inclined to seize an old woman born free, and Colonel Tucker was long dead. The clerk described her as "worn out." Then they called the next in line.

Brigadier General Samuel Birch later met with the officers and clerk to look over the day's paperwork. He signed a slip of paper declaring that "Jane Thomson, a Negro, has hereby His Excellency Sir Guy Carleton's permission to go to Nova Scotia, or wherever else she may think proper." This was one among more than three thousand certificates of freedom Birch signed that summer, including one for a man enslaved by Jefferson and three for people who had been owned by Washington. Dozens appear to have served in Dunmore's Ethiopian Regiment in Virginia. The chance to obtain the certificates "dispelled all our fears, and filled us with joy and gratitude," recalled Boston King.

On July 31, 1783, Thompson stood anxiously on the deck of *L'Abondance* as British inspectors examined her certificate before allowing her to depart New York harbor aboard the captured French vessel. She was surrounded by friends, relatives, and neighbors clutching their precious slips of paper. Among them were two of her daughters with their husbands and children, the blind Methodist preacher "Daddy" Moses Wilkinson, and Harry Washington, who had fled Mount Vernon. Most of the 410 Black loyalist passengers on the cargo vessel had been Virginia residents, and many had fled Norfolk and Princess Anne Counties, including a thirty-year-old baker named Norfolk Virginia. They were among the three to four thousand Black refugees evacuated from New York that year, who in turn were part of the ten-thousand-strong diaspora of Black loyalists. Most fled the young nation to escape a lifetime bondage.

Two weeks later, *L'Abondance* dropped anchor in a fir-fringed harbor in southeastern Nova Scotia, and Thompson and others disembarked at a crowded refugee camp called Port Roseway, soon renamed Shelburne after Dunmore's old friend who served as the new prime minister. "I was now become a new creature," wrote an elated Boston King, his freedom finally secure. Yet the promised supplies and land grants never fully materialized, and Black loyalists confronted animosity from both local whites and white loyalist immigrants.

Mobs brutally attacked Black residents in the summer of 1784, and Thompson and fifteen hundred others moved across the harbor to a town they dubbed Birchtown for the British general who had signed their freedom certificates. For a time, it was the largest free Black community in the Western Hemisphere. They learned from local indigenous Micmac people how to construct rough huts dug into the ground and eventually built a church, a school, and small clapboard homes. The rocky soil, dense swamp, and harsh weather made life difficult, however, and famine and illness stalked residents. "Some killed and ate their dogs and cats, and poverty and distress prevailed on every side," King recalled.

Complaints about their plight eventually spawned an effort to settle freed African Americans in Sierra Leone on the West African coast. Their goal was not just to find a better life for themselves, but "to put a stop to the abominable slave trade," wrote King. On January 15, 1792, one month after ratification of the U.S. Bill of Rights, nearly twelve hundred Black loyalists—including King, Harry Washington, and most members of Thompson's family—set sail for the new colony.

King went on to become a celebrated teacher and preacher in Freetown, while Harry Washington prospered as a respected farmer. Many of the settlers, however, chafed at the tight control the British exerted over the colony's governance. A few months after his former owner died at Mount Vernon in December 1799, Washington joined a rebellion that was quickly put down. He was banished to a remote coastal settlement, and his final fate is unknown. The aging Jane

Thompson, meanwhile, was either too frail or unwilling to endure another displacement and remained in Birchtown. Her death in poverty on the bleak Canadian coast also went unrecorded.

Five years passed before Lady Dunmore and her sister could secure a new job for the perpetually indebted earl. In 1787, as the Constitutional Convention met in Philadelphia, he again left his family behind, this time to serve as governor of the Bahamas. Like Nova Scotia, the subtropical archipelago off Florida served as a refuge for American loyalists. Many were Southerners who had fled East Florida when it was returned to Spain under the Treaty of Paris, bringing their enslaved laborers to work tobacco, tomato, and pineapple plantations in the brutal heat and humidity. Some free American Black loyalists transported to the islands by the British soon found themselves forced back into bondage and even sold to Caribbean plantations.

"The Negroes who came here from America with the British general's free passes are treated with unheard of cruelty by men who call themselves loyalists," one white visitor wrote. "Those unhappy people after being drawn from their masters by promises of freedom, and the king's protection, are every day stolen away from these islands, shipped, and disposed of, to the French at Hispaniola."

Dunmore immediately pardoned those who had fled their owners. A week later—the twelfth anniversary of his proclamation's signing—he set up a "Negro Court" to adjudicate the matter. White Bahamians were outraged. One planter said the governor's behavior was "such as what . . . one might naturally be expected from the lordly despot of a petty clan." The earl did have support from the local press; the two Scottish printers seized in the 1775 raid on Holt's newspaper in Norfolk followed the governor to his new post in Nassau.

Dunmore acknowledged that "this enquiry has given umbrage to some persons here who have detained several of these unhappy people under various pretenses in a state of slavery." The new governor also protected Black residents in a slum near his mansion from white assault and granted lands to freed Black men and women; they named their settlement Dunmore Town, further angering whites.

Yet the court proved largely toothless; only one out of thirty claimants gained freedom. And even as he defended Black residents, the earl purchased plantations and enslaved Africans to work the land. Dunmore had freed hundreds, yet as with other planters—including Washington, Jefferson, and Madison—he remained willing to close his eyes to the suffering of those who made him wealthy.

White Americans, meanwhile, grew alarmed at the governor's sudden reappearance so close to their shores and suspected that he intended to arm Creek and Choctaw warriors to attack the nation's vulnerable western frontier. "Our Virginia papers say that he is trying to raise the Indians to cut our throats," a wealthy matron wrote in 1789 to Jefferson while he was minister to France. Another contact warned the diplomat that the earl was "spiriting up the savages bordering on the frontiers to commit hostilities against the people of the United States." There was even a rumor that Dunmore would send one of his sons to organize a province near the Mississippi made up of Native, white, and Black inhabitants. The governor was more likely interested in profiting from his dealings with the indigenous peoples on the mainland; he cultivated commercial ties with them to divert trade from the United States to the Bahamas.

After nearly a decade on the sweltering island, the earl was recalled to London amid claims by Bahamian planters that he had misused his office for personal gain. The more pressing reason for Dunmore's abrupt dismissal was that his daughter, Augusta Murray, had secretly married the king's son and borne a child from the union. Had the marriage been accepted, Dunmore's grandson, rather than Queen Victoria, might have sat on the throne. Since the couple had wed without the monarch's permission, however, Parliament declared the bond illegal, and Augusta was temporarily banished. The two lovers continued to meet surreptitiously on the continent, producing a second child, but the husband ultimately abandoned her amid rumors of her infidelity. Augusta Murray was left alone to raise their son and daughter.

An indignant Dunmore confronted the monarch in October 1803 at London's St. James Palace. Granted a private audience, he accused the British sovereign and his son of mistreating his daughter and grandchildren. "Bastards, bastards!" cried the furious king. "Such bastards as yours are," the earl stated evenly, implying that George III's own children were then also illegitimate. The king turned "red as a Turkey cock," Dunmore's son later related, and asked what he meant. "I say, sir, that my daughter was legally married to your son and that her children are just such bastards as Your Majesty's are." Speechless with rage, the offended ruler stalked out of the room.

"God damn him," the earl thundered to his mortified wife and children when he returned home. "It was as much as I could do to refrain from attempting to knock him down when he called them bastards." This verbal assault on the leader of the British Empire, a man he had so long defended, abruptly ended the earl's career, and turned the entire family into social outcasts.

The Murray family retreated to a small and inexpensive English seaside resort, far removed from Britain's aristocratic social circles. Dunmore, however, continued to cultivate friends among prominent thinkers, including Jeremy Bentham, the philosopher who asserted that right and wrong are best judged by whether an act improves or detracts from human happiness. "Lord Dunmore used to call on me," he recalled. They "used to stimulate one another" by making "trifling chemical experiments together." Bentham, who argued publicly that emancipating those enslaved benefitted the greater good, also hashed out social issues with the earl. "For a Church-of-England man," he observed, "Dunmore was free of prejudices, and we had many common sympathies."

He characterized the Scottish noble "as a sort of liberal," but even Bentham—a notorious critic of religion—was shocked by Dunmore's radical ideas. "He told me his notion was, there had been several revelations—Jesus' one, Mahomet's another, at which I was very much scandalized."

Dunmore's willingness to flout convention extended to his estate outside Edinburgh, where he built a sophisticated hothouse, fueled by a neighboring coal seam, to cultivate pineapples, a prized luxury in that day. Any profits he might have made were eaten up by construction of an intricate forty-six-foot-high stone carving of the exotic delicacy on top of his neoclassical garden house, which stood on a rise above the broad Firth of Forth. The fruit, Washington's favorite, was also a widely used symbol of hospitality in colonial Virginia; its wooden and brass facsimiles adorned the gentry's doors and rooftops. Dunmore left behind no explanation for this eccentric structure, widely considered the oddest building in Scotland. If he relished irony, this peculiar folly, visible for miles, may have been his public response to exile from both the Old Dominion and the British elite.

Epilogue

Thomas Jefferson exempted Paris from his categorical dislike of cities. While serving as the American ambassador on the eve of the 1789 French Revolution, he delighted in the capital's bookshops, architecture, and intellectual stimulation. He avoided an opportunity to visit Lady Dunmore and one of her daughters when they were in town, later expressing "something of regret" for not seeing a woman he noted was "respected by all Virginians."

In 1785, he published his only book, *Notes on the State of Virginia*, with a Parisian press. "Norfolk will probably be the emporium for all the trade of the Chesapeake Bay and its waters," he predicted, adding that it was "the most populous town we ever had." He made no mention of its previous destruction. The volume also postulated that those of African descent were "inferior to the whites in the endowments both of body and mind."

When the revolution in France broke out in the summer of 1789, Jefferson returned to a young country that had ratified a constitution and elected Washington as president. On board his ship were his two daughters, his enslaved chef James Hemings, and James's light-skinned sixteen-year-old enslaved sister, Sally Hemings. She was likely the half-sister of Jefferson's late wife and may already have been pregnant with his child. After a fast Atlantic crossing, the ship anchored in Norfolk's harbor in late November. Ten-year-old Maria Jefferson is said to have burst into tears at the sight of the still-scarred town, exclaiming in French, "But this is very different from Paris!" His elder daughter, Martha, noted more soberly that "Norfolk had not recovered from the effects of the war" fourteen years before.

The party picked its way among shacks pieced together with scrap wood leaning against burned-out buildings. Lonely chimneys still dotted the devastated landscape. British architect Benjamin Latrobe, who arrived seven years later, described the shattered landscape of Norfolk with its "innumerable retinue of narrow and filthy lanes and alleys" and "ruins of the old houses" that were "almost as numerous as the inhabited houses." A contemporary French visitor was shocked by "the many charred ruins that still remain." He counted only five hundred new buildings, a fraction of the number that stood before the destruction. When Jefferson arrived, the sole hotel was full, but a guest gave his rooms to the famous diplomat and his daughters. There, he learned from a newspaper that the president had appointed him secretary of state.

Before they had settled into their lodgings, disaster struck. Their ship caught fire in the harbor with their luggage still aboard, including some of the eighty-six crates stuffed with European furniture, fabric, and books. Smoke billowed from its hold, and only the combined efforts of the port's sailors and the thickness of the heavy trunks saved Jefferson's possessions from the flames.

The family and enslaved staff did not linger, soon boarding a boat to Richmond. Latrobe made a similar journey, and related that the shores of the Elizabeth River were lined with "wagon loads of the bones of men, women, and children, stripped of the flesh by vultures and hawks" that "covered the sand for a most considerable length." Local white residents explained that these were the skeletons of the enslaved people whom Dunmore had abandoned in 1776. Any such gruesome boneyard, however, would have marked the resting place of those who joined the governor's fight rather than endure slavery under the patriots, choosing liberty even at the price of death.

By the following March, Jefferson was in the temporary capital of Philadelphia to take up his new post in Washington's Cabinet. He emerged as the leading opponent of Treasury secretary Alexander Hamilton, who supported the growth of towns, a national bank, and a powerful central government to protect the fledgling nation from predatory European powers. The Virginia planter, who at that time owned some ten thousand acres and more than one hundred people, held that urban areas subverted democratic values by placing wealth in the hands of the few. "For general occupations of manufacture, let our workshops remain in Europe" to preserve an agrarian society and prevent "the mobs of great cities," which he likened to "sores" on the body politic.

In 1800, the year Jefferson defeated John Adams to win the presidency, yellow fever ravaged Baltimore and Norfolk. Rather than press for public health improvements, the new chief executive instead expressed his belief that such deadly epidemics would "discourage the growth of great cities in our nation," which he called "pestilential" to morals and to the "health and liberties of man." New York, he asserted, was "a cloacina of all the depravities of human nature." Such depravities, according to the president, included sex between those of European and African descent.

For Jefferson, cities were not just vectors of greed and disease, but sites of unfettered miscegenation. He articulated the white supremacist notion that "the two races, equally free, cannot live in the same government." The enslaved, if manumitted, had to be "removed beyond the reach of mixture." That mixing, of course, was already taking place in his own household. His liaison with Sally Hemings that began in Paris produced children who later would blend successfully into white society; one went on to serve as a colonel in the Union Army during the Civil War.

Jefferson's vision of an affluent, democratic, educated, and white agrarian Virginia proved a dismal and even tragic failure. Boston, New York, Philadelphia, Baltimore, and Charleston powered their states' progress as the industrial revolution gained steam in the early nineteenth century. Virginia's economy, by contrast, stagnated. Norfolk never fully regained its commercial muscle, exhausted soil forced farmers west, and foreign immigrants bypassed a land of enslaved rather than free labor. Ever-frugal legislators refused to fund a public school system. "Virginia is fast becoming the Barbary of the union and in danger of falling into the ranks of our own Negroes," Jefferson himself despaired in 1820, six years before his death.

The state's enslaved people became its most lucrative export, as planters sold them to the fast-expanding cotton fields of the Deep South. Tens of thousands were marched south in chains. Jefferson, who, like Dunmore, was perpetually in debt, recognized the potential financial gains. "I consider the labor of a breeding woman as no object," he wrote in 1819, since "a child raised every two years is of more profit than the crop of the best laboring man."

The new states of Tennessee, Kentucky, Alabama, and Mississippi adopted and vastly expanded Virginia's colonial model of forced labor camps, low taxes, and tight control over the Black population. As in the House of Burgesses, a small planter caste dominated their legislatures and kept the power of white farmers in check. Cotton barons replaced the tobacco gentry, but they closely imitated the homes, manners, and traditions of their Old Dominion predecessors. They would also prove willing to wage war to defend their way of life, including the use of enslaved people, in the name of liberty.

On February 25, 1809, as Thomas Jefferson was in his last two weeks in the White House, the president wrote a French Catholic abolitionist that his doubts about the intellectual capacity of Black people were based on "personal observation on the limited sphere of my own state, where the opportunities for the development of their genius were not favorable." He looked forward to a day of "their reestablishment on an equal footing with other colors of the human family."

On that winter Saturday, nearly four thousand miles to the east, Lord Dunmore died "of decay" at age seventy-six ; a small portrait made just before his death shows a balding man with knobby knees sloughed in a chair and wrapped in a tartan shawl. "My loved father has endeared to me every grey headed old man I see," lamented Augusta Murray.

Despite his blueblood lineage, the profligate Dunmore left his family in financial straits. Even before his passing, the earl's children turned to his old enemies for support. When Virginia Murray was born in 1774, the family claimed, the House of Burgesses promised her land now worth 100,000 pounds. In 1803, John Murray, her brother, made the trek to Monticello to plead his case with Jefferson, who was then president. In 1816, two years before her death, Lady Dunmore asked the American ambassador to Britain, John Quincy Adams, to pay her a visit in London. He described her as an "old lady, who must be at least seventy-five, and who is so deaf that she can hear only by an ear-trumpet." Adams wrote that "the countess talked much of the politeness which was shown to her by the Virginians," and explained that her daughter was nearly destitute. Virginia Murray later penned a plea to Jefferson noting, "I am totally unprovided for," and adding, "You are too just to visit what . . . may seem the sins of the father upon his luckless daughter." Jefferson and Adams politely deflected the petitions, which predictably came to nothing.

The late royal governor's descendants eventually gave up their claim but continued to be drawn to Virginia. Dunmore's grandson Charles Augustus Murray visited Virginia in the 1830s, boarding a steamer named *Patrick Henry* for the trip to "that now desolate spot" of Jamestown. He found Williamsburg "little better than a deserted village." Murray strolled around the Palace ruins before riding to Hampton, where he watched workers putting the final touches on nearby Fort Monroe. A young Robert E. Lee, who had married Martha Washington's granddaughter, had overseen construction of the nation's largest fortification, a moated stone structure designed to protect Hampton Roads from enemy invasion and barrack enough troops to put down a slave insurrection.

From there, Murray caught a ferry to Norfolk, which he said had "little to interest the stranger, but the bay affords a noble harbor." His visit to the state left him repelled by the "inhuman unholy nature" of slavery, in which owners kept "all glimpses of knowledge or liberty" from those they held in bondage.

Two decades later, when the Civil War broke out, Dunmore's great grandson Charles Murray crossed Union lines to visit Richmond and then traveled on to Charleston. One contemporary called the Seventh Earl of Dunmore "a man of a very venturesome disposition"; he would later spy for the British in the Himalayas. Captured by a Federal ship when he attempted to leave Charleston aboard a blockade runner, he was imprisoned and searched. The earl had secreted a Confederate flag around his body, which he explained was a gift from a rebel captain. Only the intervention of a British minister won the jailed peer his freedom.

By the time Abraham Lincoln took the oath of office as president on March 4, 1861, seven states had seceded to form the Confederate States of America. Later that month, Alexander Stephens, the vice president of the newly declared country, told a cheering audience in Savannah, "We are passing through one of the great revolutions in the annals of the world." The cornerstone of the new government, he said, "rests upon the great truth that the Negro is not equal to the white man; that slavery, subordination to the superior race, is his natural and moral condition."

Many white Southerners viewed their struggle as a reprise of the Revolutionary War, with the Confederates as the new patriots. A tyrannical Lincoln, eager to deprive them of their enslaved property, was the new King George III. "We are fighting for independence," declared President Jefferson Davis. Any opponents, he added, would "smell Southern powder and feel Southern steel."

Once again, Virginia's support was eagerly sought by both sides of an accelerating conflict. Confederate forces fired on Charleston harbor's Fort Sumter, controlled by Federal forces, on April 12, sparking full-fledged war. Five days later, Virginia's secession convention voted to join the rebels. One week after that, Federal troops burned the Gosport shipyard—rebuilt and enlarged following the 1776 conflagration—along with eleven Navy ships to prevent them from falling into Confederate hands. By May, enslaved men had been conscripted to build a gun battery along a Norfolk shore in anticipation of a Union naval assault. Above them fluttered a flag given to the corps by citizens of Hampton, a blue field embossed in gold with Patrick Henry's famous words, GIVE ME LIBERTY OR GIVE ME DEATH.

On May 23, a majority of Virginia's adult white male voters approved a state referendum to secede. That same day, three of the unfree workers conscripted in Norfolk—Frank Baker, Shepard Mallory, and James Townsend—learned that they were slated for transfer to North Carolina to labor on rebel earthworks. After nightfall, they stole a boat and paddled across the broad expanse of Hampton Roads. Federal sentries apprehended the men when they landed on the far shore and the next morning escorted them across the drawbridge that led to Fort Monroe, which remained under the control of Union forces. The new commander of the moated fortress was

Major General Benjamin Butler, a short and balding Massachusetts lawyer and abolitionist familiar with laws pertaining to slavery and emancipation, and decrees such as those promulgated by Dunmore and Clinton.

As Butler questioned the refugees, an aide interrupted to inform him that Major John Baytop Cary of the men's Virginia militia unit was waiting outside under a flag of truce. Cary, a native of Hampton, was a descendant of wealthy slaveowners Archibald Cary, who had read out George Mason's declaration of rights in the Williamsburg Capitol in 1776, and Wilson-Miles Cary, who had sparked the 1775 battle at Hampton by demanding the return of his enslaved men. The rotund Butler mounted a horse and clattered across the plank bridge. The tall, slim Confederate officer, neatly dressed in a gray uniform, greeted the fort commandant and demanded the return of Baker, Mallory, and Townsend. Butler refused. "I shall hold these Negroes as contraband of war," he later reported saying, "since they are engaged in the construction of your battery and are claimed as your property." A furious Cary trotted away empty-handed. The Black men would now labor for the Union.

"Out of this incident," two of Lincoln's secretaries later wrote, "seems to have grown one of the most sudden and important revolutions in popular thought which took place during the whole war." Within days, nearly fifty enslaved Africans had appeared at Fort Monroe seeking protection. Within two weeks, five hundred were granted refuge. A New York City newspaper published an image of crowds eagerly seeking refuge inside Fort Monroe, with the caption, "Stampede Among the Negroes of Virginia." When he learned of Butler's action, Lincoln was reluctant to overturn the decision, though one Cabinet member reminded the general that his job was "war, not emancipation."

Whites on both sides accused the Massachusetts officer of piracy, the same charge leveled at Dunmore by patriots. Nevertheless, Union commanders across the South quietly began to accept "contrabands" into their camps. Confederates were outraged. That summer, in a distant echo of Norfolk's destruction, a rebel general had his own troops burn Hampton rather than allow it to serve as a sanctuary for Black refugees. Just as Norfolk was the only city completed devastated during the American Revolution, Hampton was the only town leveled in the Civil War.

As the conflict intensified in the summer and fall of 1861, Virginia's last royal governor and his decree loomed large in the minds of people in both the North and the South. "The meanness, vandalism, and cowardice of the Yankees exceeds anything experienced by Virginia in the days of Lord Dunmore," thundered the *Richmond Enquirer* in August. Even a staunchly pro-Union Maryland paper warned against a reprise of his proclamation. That "scheme of very questionable wisdom" had produced "violent irritation without affording adequate benefits."

The unfavorable public view of Dunmore, who nearly a century later was still reviled by many white Americans, may explain why Lincoln avoided mention of the earl or his proclamation, with which he was doubtless familiar. In 1862, Massachusetts senator and fervent abolitionist Charles Sumner said the royal governor's decree was the first in a series of legal precedents that gave the president the political cover he needed to emancipate those enslaved in enemy territory. "Slavery should be struck to save precious blood," Sumner argued, noting that "in our Revolution, this appeal was made by three different British commanders—Lord Dunmore, Sir Henry Clinton, and Lord Cornwallis." He quoted Dunmore's 1775 decree, as well as his 1782 call to arm Black men in South Carolina to defeat the rebels. Sumner, who made the same arguments privately with the president, insisted these examples vindicated a move to free those enslaved by rebels.

Like Dunmore, Lincoln moved cautiously on the inflammatory matter of legal emancipation. Both men were pragmatic politicians who realized that African American troops might turn the tide in their favor. Yet they also knew that granting freedom to enslaved people could boomerang by enraging whites and strengthening the rebels. At a July 22, 1862, Cabinet meeting, secretary of state William Seward urged Lincoln to wait for a battlefield victory so that the proclamation did not seem "the last resource of an exhausted government . . . stretching out its hand to Ethiopia." The president drafted a proclamation that was, like Dunmore's, cast not as a moral statement but as "a fit and necessary war measure."

The next month, he penned a public letter designed to assure white Americans that emancipation was a step of last resort to win the conflict. "If I could save the Union without freeing any slave, I would do it," he wrote. "What I do about slavery and the colored race, I do because I believe it helps to save the Union."

When Union troops repulsed Confederate forces outside the Maryland town of Sharpsburg near Antietam Creek on September 17, 1862, Lincoln seized the moment, much as Dunmore had done after his victory at Kemp's Landing. "I made a solemn vow before God, that if General Lee was driven back from Pennsylvania," the president told his Cabinet soon after, "I would crown the result by the declaration of freedom to the slaves."

His decree was, like Dunmore's, highly conditional. The governor had promised to free only those enslaved by patriots, and then only those capable of fighting. Lincoln's document freed only those enslaved in rebel states, and then only in areas not occupied by Federal troops, to avoid a constitutional challenge by the courts. The president did not require unfree workers to fight in exchange for freedom, as the earl had done, but he did provide a path for Black men to serve the Union under arms. "Such persons of suitable condition will be received into the armed service of the United States to garrison forts, positions, stations, and other places, and to man vessels of all sorts in said service."

The "snowball" so feared by George Washington in 1775 had finally rolled to the door of the White House. Lincoln, born two weeks after Dunmore died, issued his proclamation on January 1, 1863, precisely four score and seven years after the burning of Norfolk. Nearly two hundred thousand Black men subsequently flocked to the Union standard, providing desperately needed troops to defeat the Confederates. As they had in the Revolution, these soldiers not only fought but piloted ships, dug trenches, foraged for supplies, cooked meals, and performed countless essential logistical tasks. Their presence also gave the conflict a moral compass beyond simply preserving a nation. Like Dunmore's Ethiopian Regiment, they faced greater risks than their white counterparts. Capture by the Confederates meant execution or re-enslavement. This time, however, victory over the rebels removed the threat of exile or continued bondage.

Six days after the Confederate surrender on April 9, 1865, Lincoln was dead. As he shot the president at Washington's Ford's Theatre, John Wilkes Booth called out the Virginia state motto: "Sic semper tyrannis"—thus always to tyrants. Full emancipation came nine months later, in December 1865, ninety years after Black loyalists clashed with patriot shirtmen at Great Bridge.

The ratification of the Thirteenth Amendment ended chattel slavery. This did not, of course, end prejudice, segregation, or the denial of basic rights, much less economic inequity. It did, however, bring the stirring words of slaveowners George Mason and Thomas Jefferson in the Virginia Bill of Rights and the Declaration of Independence a step closer to reality. The founders had made a promise, Lincoln said in his first inaugural address, "that in due time the weights should be lifted from the shoulders of all men, and that all should have an equal chance." White patriots and Black loyalists fought and died on opposite sides in the American Revolution with the word "liberty" on their breasts. Slavery's demise narrowed the glaring gap between those whose ancestors had fought for and those who fought against independence.

Nearly a century ago, a scholar researching the life of Virginia's last royal governor noted in bewilderment that "few historians have tried to find the truth about Dunmore's blackened name." The reason for that enduring disrepute is not difficult to discern. Patriot propaganda created a convenient caricature that allowed later Americans to avoid the complicated and sometimes ugly reality of the Revolutionary War.

As historians first began to tell the tale of the nation's birth, the earl emerged as a dependable villain, like Benedict Arnold, if more obscure. "A needy Scottish peer of the House of Murray, passionate, narrow, and unscrupulous in his rapacity" was the damning judgement of George Bancroft, the famous nineteenth-century Harvard historian. Words like "inept and ineffectual," "stubborn," and "weak and unstable" were used to describe the governor's personality. According to one academic, "he was rude and coarse, jealous for his office, hot tempered, untruthful, and excelled in the art of making excuses."

That view has changed little in the past two and a half centuries. Though sympathetic to the Black loyalist cause, a twenty-first-century writer more colorfully dismissed Dunmore as a "pink-cheeked timeserver" with "a political tin ear" and "a fatally imperfect grasp of military tactics" who "blustered his way through a sorry, unwinnable predicament." Another chastised Dunmore for adopting "the fatal course of bluster, sneers, sarcasm, and blunt antagonism." Even the earl's undisputed love of learning and culture has been dismissed with contempt, as if it were a thin disguise over his native Scottish barbarism. "His fine library and collection of musical instruments," asserted one historian, "gave him the trappings of sophistication." A recent biographer summed him up as an arrogant imperialist who ignored conventions solely to expand the empire while enhancing his personal privilege.

The earl also continues to carry much of the blame for the loss of Virginia's largest city, the greatest single war crime of the conflict, despite the glaring fact that the patriots themselves admitted responsibility and exonerated him in 1777. His "bombardment of Norfolk was a crowning piece of stupidity," wrote H. J. Eckenrode in 1916, long after the hidden report by Virginia's legislature had been made public. Six decades later, during the Bicentennial, the *New York Times* recalled that Dunmore "laid waste to much of Norfolk, Va.," while Philadelphia's Museum of the American Revolution opened in 2017 with a plaque citing January 1, 1776, as the day "British forces burn Norfolk, Virginia."

Historians also continue to dismiss the royal governor's attempts to enlist Black and indigenous allies as cynical, ineffective, or even farcical. Harvard's Bancroft argued that "the cry of Dunmore did not rouse among Africans a passion for freedom." Another scholar in the nineteenth-century claimed that even those who did heed his call to join the Ethiopian Regiment proved feckless. "The Negroes behaved very shabbily," he wrote, "and saved themselves by flight." In 1908, at the height of the Jim Crow era, Virginia historian William H. Stewart concluded that "Dunmore's efforts to incite the slaves to the midnight murder of innocents and also to set Indian warriors on the warpath for indiscriminate scalping resulted in making his name a synonym for horror and loathing everywhere." The governor's proclamation, he contended, "made the ploughmen halt in the fresh furrows to shoulder their muskets for battle."

It's a revealing comment, with its suggestion that Virginia patriots broke with Britain more from a desire to keep the enslaved in bondage than to obtain liberty for themselves. Even a twenty-first century scholar insisted that the plight of those enslaved "never really touched [the governor], even during the years of the war when they would become his allies." Another brushed aside the proclamation's significance because it was "not founded upon any moral or religious objection to slavery"—a charge that some Southern whites also leveled at Lincoln's 1863 edict. The royal governor, concludes historian Gordon Wood: "wasn't an abolitionist—he was desperate." Yet what was in the mind and heart of Dunmore and Lincoln mattered little to those released from lifetime servitude. Those freed by the earl might take issue with historians who reckon Dunmore's decree as a colossal mistake benefitting only the patriot cause.

The hard truth is that the royal governor and his Ethiopian Regiment are an awkward reminder that the Revolution was fought, in part, to maintain slavery rather than extend liberty to all. This realization has begun to creep into recent popular histories, such as *The 1619 Project* sponsored by the *New York Times*, which places slavery, controversially, at the heart of America's origins. One academic has asserted that the earl's emancipation policy, inspired by those African Americans who risked their lives for liberation, had "the most farthest-reaching consequences of any in the American Revolution."

What is beyond dispute is that tens of thousands of African Americans joined the rush to freedom during the conflict. In so doing, they laid the foundation for a more just and equitable society. Given what we now know, it is no stretch to accept the provocative conclusion of the scholar who suggested in 2014 that Dunmore "could well be considered a Founding Father of the Republic." The governor and Washington, those close friends turned bitter adversaries, each played a key role in making the nation.

After her husband's death, the elderly and nearly blind Lady Dunmore lived for another decade in virtual seclusion and genteel poverty with their daughter, Lady Augusta, and her two illegitimate children by the son of King George III. One of their rare visitors noted that Augusta was a proud Scot as well as an "intellectual and intelligent" woman, one who no doubt had spent long hours as a child among her father's vast collection of books in Williamsburg's Palace. Those volumes had long since been dispersed to the Virginia gentry, but she transformed the ground floor of her seaside home into a library.

In the summer of 1811, when she had just turned fifty, Augusta Murray converted the space into a stage for a performance of Shakespeare's "Scottish play." Her ten-year-old daughter took the role of Lady Macbeth, the wicked wife of the ambitious Scottish lord whom Virginia patriots associated with Dunmore. Though she "ranted a little" in her delivery, the visitor recalled, "she looked the part well."

Among those who would have assisted Lady Augusta with the production of *Macbeth* was "Black George" Murray, "the Negro of my dear parents." He undoubtedly was an enslaved worker in the Palace who had crossed the ocean a half century previously with the earl or countess, and receipts show he was paid for a variety of services. Britain would not outlaw slavery throughout its empire for another two decades, but Scotland and England had by then banned the practice within their borders.

As with nearly all the millions of Virginians born into bondage over the course of a quarter millennium, almost nothing is known of the appearance, likes and dislikes, and personality and opinions of Lady Augusta's servant. But unlike the vast majority who remained behind in the wake of the Revolutionary War—including the hundreds of people owned by Patrick Henry, Thomas Jefferson, and George Washington—"Black George" Murray spent his last years in a land that forbade slavery. He lived, and died at some unrecorded date, as a free man.

Timeline

October 1770 – Lord Dunmore arrives in New York harbor to serve as the colony's royal governor

September 1771 – Dunmore arrives in Williamsburg to serve as Virginia's royal governor

September 1771 – James Somerset flees his owner in London

June 22, 1772 – Lord Mansfield orders James Somerset freed

May 10, 1773 – Parliament grants British East India Company a monopoly on tea sales in American colonies

December 16, 1773 – Boston Tea Party

February 26, 1774 – Lady Dunmore and children arrive at Yorktown

March 31, 1774 – Britain orders closure of Boston harbor

May 26, 1774 – Lord Dunmore dissolves Virginia's House of Burgesses

August 5, 1774 – Virginia Convention names delegates to Continental Congress

October 19, 1774 – Ohio Valley indigenous leaders sign treaty to end Lord Dunmore's War

October 20, 1774 – Continental Congress adopts resolution to halt British imports

January 19, 1775 – Virginia Murray, daughter of Lord and Lady Dunmore, christened in Williamsburg

January 20, 1775 – House of Commons rejects reconciliation with American colonies

March 23, 1775 – Patrick Henry proclaims "liberty or death" at Virginia Convention in Richmond

April 19, 1775 – Battles of Lexington and Concord in Massachusetts

April 21, 1775 – British forces seize gunpowder stores in Williamsburg's Magazine

April 22, 1775 – Lord Dunmore threatens to arm those enslaved if physically threatened by patriots

April 29, 1775 – Virginia patriot militia gather to march on Williamsburg

May 3, 1775 – Troops under Patrick Henry threaten capital

June 1, 1775 – House of Burgesses convenes in Williamsburg

June 3, 1775 – Booby trap at Williamsburg Magazine injures three

June 8, 1775 – Lord Dunmore flees to HMS *Fowey* off Yorktown

June 15, 1775 – George Washington selected as commander in chief of Continental Army

June 17, 1775 – Battle of Bunker Hill

June 18, 1775 – Lady Dunmore and children depart for Britain

July 15, 1775 – Lord Dunmore arrives in Norfolk harbor

July 17, 1775 – Gosport shipyard becomes base for Lord Dunmore and Royal Navy ships

July 31, 1775 – British troops arrive in Gosport from St. Augustine

August 5, 1775 – Patrick Henry selected to command Virginia's army

August 9, 1775 – Virginia Convention creates Committee of Safety to serve as executives in patriot government

August 23, 1775 – King George III declares the American colonies to be in rebellion

September 2, 1775 – Major hurricane devastates Norfolk

September 30, 1775 – British forces seize press owned by John Hunter Holt

October 18, 1775 – British forces seize guns and ammunition at Kemp's Landing; patriots flee

October 26, 1775 – Royal Navy ships attack Hampton but withdraw in defeat

October 26, 1775 – King George III asks Parliament to wage war on American rebels

November 7, 1775 – Lord Dunmore writes proclamation declaring martial law and emancipating those enslaved by patriots

November 7, 1775 – Virginia's patriot army begins march from Williamsburg to Norfolk

November 14, 1775 – With British and white and Black loyalist troops, Dunmore defeat patriots at Kemp's Landing

November 15, 1775 – Dunmore makes proclamation public

December 9, 1775 – Patriot forces defeat British and loyalists troops at the Battle of Great Bridge

December 14, 1775 – Patriot forces occupy Norfolk; loyalists flee to "Lord Dunmore's floating town"

January 1, 1776 – British attack Norfolk, patriots burn and loot

January 9, 1776 – News of King George III's call to war reaches Philadelphia

January 10, 1776 – *Common Sense* goes on sale

February 6, 1776 – Patriot troops march out of Norfolk, and burn all remaining buildings

February 10, 1776 – Dunmore and Captain Hamond establish land base at Tucker's Mill Point downstream from Norfolk

February 17, 1776 – British General Henry Clinton arrives in Norfolk harbor

February 21, 1776 – Dunmore and Clinton discuss ceasefire with Virginia patriot delegation in Norfolk harbor

March 29, 1776 – Patriot General Charles Lee arrives in Williamsburg

Late March/early April 1776 – Smallpox appears on "Lord Dunmore's floating town" and Tucker's Mill Point.

May 15, 1776 – Virginia Convention unanimously approves colony's declaration of independence

May 22, 1776 – Dunmore and Hamond evacuate Tucker's Mill Point

May 27, 1776 – Lord Dunmore's floating town anchors off Gwynn's Island

June 7, 1776 – Richard Henry Lee introduces resolution of independence in Continental Congress

June 12–13, 1776 – Thomas Jefferson composes draft of Declaration of Independence

June 29, 1776 – Patrick Henry elected patriot governor of Virginia

July 4, 1776 – Continental Congress adopts Declaration of Independence

July 9, 1776 – Virginia patriots attack Gwynn's Island

July 9, 1776 – Patriot troops tear down statue of King George III in New York City

July 11, 1776 – Dunmore's fleet departs Gwynn's Island

July 22, 1776 – Skirmish between patriot and British/loyalist forces south of Mount Vernon

August 4, 1776 – At entrance to Chesapeake Bay, Lord Dunmore's floating town departs Virginia for New York, Britain, St. Augustine

August 7, 1776 – Dunmore and Hamond sail with Black loyalists to New York

August 26, 1776 – Dunmore and Ethiopian Regiment fight at Battle of Long Island

November 11, 1776 – Dunmore returns to Britain

June 30, 1779 – Clinton signs Philipsburg Proclamation

October 19, 1781 – British surrender to Americans and French at Yorktown

December 21, 1781 – Dunmore arrives in Charleston from Britain

March 20, 1781 – Lord North resigns as prime minister

March 30, 1782 – Dunmore leaves for New York to lobby for Black troops

May 16, 1782 – Dunmore departs New York for Britain

May 6, 1783 – Washington meets Carleton

July 31, 1783 – *L'Abondance* departs New York with Black loyalists for Nova Scotia

November 1787 – Dunmore arrives to govern Bahamas

October 1803 – Dunmore confronts King George III

February 25, 1809 – Dunmore dies in Ramsgate, England

May 23, 1861 – Three enslaved Virginians escape to Fort Monroe

September 22, 1862 – Lincoln issues Emancipation Proclamation

December 6, 1865 – Thirteenth Amendment ratified

Acknowledgments

Nearly everyone quoted in this book is long dead, so in-person interviews were out of the question. I therefore relied heavily on librarians, historians, historical interpreters, museum curators, and well-informed local history enthusiasts to help me piece together the puzzle of Virginia's early revolutionary drama.

Among the many librarians who assisted me were Patrick Kerwin and Muthara Mobashar at the Library of Congress, Endrina Tay at the Jefferson Library, Marianne Martin at the Rockefeller Library, Virginia Dunn at the Library of Virginia, and the staff at many other institutions, including Old Dominion University's Perry Library, William and Mary's Swem Library Special Collections Research Center, the Sargeant Room at Norfolk Public Library, Clements Library, the National Library of Scotland, Scotland's Blair Castle archives, the National Archives at Kew, the Caird Library at Greenwich, the Massachusetts Historical Society, and the Maine Historical Society.

The Colonial Williamsburg Foundation gave me access to their many sites as well as to their knowledgeable historical interpreters; Corinne Dame, aka Lady Dunmore, in particular went out of her way to share her formidable files. Peggy McPhillips, former Norfolk historian, was generous with her time, as was Richard Fisher at the Great Bridge Battlefield and Waterways Foundation. Patrick Hannum provided an informed tour and detailed explanation of that battle, Christopher Pieczynski walked me through the much-altered landscape at Kemp's Landing, and Michael Cecere devoted a cold Sunday morning to showing me the key landmarks in the Battle of Hampton. Julia Sienkewicz assisted in my understanding of Benjamin Latrobe's postwar visit to Norfolk.

Frank W. Garmon Jr. provided critical help in transcribing daunting eighteenth-century handwriting, while Juhwan Cho, Andrew Hoffman, Jenna Martin, and Victoria McFarlane assisted my efforts in archives. I am particularly indebted to Ellie Woolard, who took part in assembling the endless endnotes. Also, thanks to Bernard Morin for his valuable insights.

Among those historians who kindly offered valuable suggestions were James Corbett David, Cassandra Pybus, Robert Parkinson, Andrew O'Shaughnessy, Brett Tartar, Cassandra Newby-Alexander, and Gordon Wood. Douglas Egerton generously provided me with a preview of his forthcoming book on the upheavals along the Revolution-era frontier, while Lincoln scholar Jon White patiently educated me on the politics behind the 1863 Emancipation Proclamation. Special thanks are due Gerald Horne and Woody Holton, who graciously looked over the manuscript and provided sage feedback. All errors in fact and interpretation are, of course, solely my responsibility.

Several friends and family members hosted me during research and writing stints, including Fred Schwab, Betsy Brown, and Ann Lawler, while Paul Farago, Nathan Boniske, and Brahman Bloukos kept me in functioning order. My agent, Ethan Bassoff of William Morris, was an enthusiastic early supporter of this project, which gave me a coveted opportunity to work with George Gibson, the Grove Atlantic editor who brought many decades of wisdom to bear. As always, special gratitude is due Mahan Kalpa Khalsa, who patiently endured my frequent sojourns into the late eighteenth century.

Bibliography

The literature of the American Revolution is vast. What follows are selected books, articles, and dissertations focused primarily on Virginia in the first half of the 1770s.

Books

Atkinson, Rick. *The British Are Coming: The War for America, Lexington to Princeton, 1775–1777*. New York: Henry Holt, 2019.

Bannister, Jerry. *The Loyal Atlantic: Remaking the British Atlantic in the Revolutionary Era*. Ontario, Canada: University of Toronto Press, 2012.

Bennett, Charles E., and Donald R. Lennon. *A Quest for Glory: Major General Robert Howe and the American Revolution*. Chapel Hill: University of North Carolina Press, 1991.

Black, Jeremy. *Culloden and the '45*. Charleston, SC: History Press, 2021.

Bogger, Tommy. *Free Blacks in Norfolk, Virginia, 1790–1860: The Darker Side of Freedom*. Charlottesville: University of Virginia Press, 1997.

Bradley, Patricia. *Slavery, Propaganda, and the American Revolution*. Jackson: University Press of Mississippi, 1999.

Brands, H. W. *Our First Civil War: Patriots and Loyalists in the American Revolution*. New York: Anchor, 2022.

Breen, T. H. *American Insurgents, American Patriots*. New York: Hill and Wang, 2011.

Brown, Christopher Leslie, and Philip D. Morgan, eds. *Arming Slaves: From Classical Times to the Modern Age*. New Haven, CT: Yale University Press, 2006.

Brown, Kathleen M. *Good Wives, Nasty Wenches, and Anxious Patriarchs: Gender, Race, and Power in Colonial Virginia*. Chapel Hill: University of North Carolina Press, 1996.

Carr, Lois Green, Phillip D. Morgan, and Jean B. Russo, eds. *Colonial Chesapeake Society*. Chapel Hill: University of North Carolina Press, 1988.

Cawthon, Elizabeth A. *The James Somerset Case*. New York: Infobase Publishing, 2018.

Cecere, Michael. *March to Independence: The Revolutionary War in the Southern Colonies, 1775–1776*. Yardley, PA: Westholme Publishing, 2021.

———. *A Universal Appearance of War: The Revolutionary War in Virginia, 1775–1781*. Berwyn Heights, MD: Heritage Books, 2019.

Chernow, Ron. *Washington: A Life.* New York: Penguin, 2010.

Cogliano, Francis D. *A Revolutionary Friendship: Washington, Jefferson, and the American Republic,* Cambridge, MA: Harvard University Press, 2024.

Cowie, Jefferson. *Freedom's Dominion: A Saga of White Resistance to Federal Power.* New York: Basic Books, 2022.

Crow, Jeffrey J., and Larry E. Tise, eds. *The Southern Experience in the American Revolution.* Chapel Hill: University of North Carolina Press, 1978.

David, James Corbett. *Dunmore's New World.* Charlottesville: University of Virginia Press, 2015.

Drury, Bob, and Tom Clavin. *Blood and Treasure: Daniel Boone and the Fight for America's First Frontier.* New York: MacMillan, 2021.

Egerton, Douglas R. *Death or Liberty: African Americans and Revolutionary America.* New York: Oxford University Press, 2009.

Eller, Ernest McNeill, ed. *Chesapeake Bay in the American Revolution.* Centerville, MD: Tidewater Publishers, 1981.

Ellis, Joseph J. *American Sphinx: The Character of Thomas Jefferson.* New York: Knopf, 1996.

———. *Revolutionary Summer: The Birth of American Independence.* New York: Vintage Books, 2014.

Fenn, Elizabeth A. *Pox Americana: The Great Smallpox Epidemic of 1775–82.* New York: Hill and Wang, 2001.

Flanders, Alan B. *Bluejackets on the Elizabeth: A Maritime History of Portsmouth and Norfolk, Virginia from the Colonial Period to the Present.* Portsmouth, VA: Portsmouth Naval Shipyard Museum, 1998.

Frey, Sylvia. *Water from the Rock: Black Resistance in a Revolutionary Age.* Princeton, NJ: Princeton University Press, 1991.

Friedenberg, Daniel M. *Life, Liberty, and the Pursuit of Land.* Buffalo, NY: Prometheus Books, 1992.

Gilbert, Alan. *Black Patriots and Loyalists: Fighting for Emancipation in the War for Independence.* Chicago: University of Chicago Press, 2012.

Gilroy, Paul. *The Black Atlantic: Modernity and Double-Consciousness.* Cambridge, MA: Harvard University Press, 1995.

Gordon-Reed, Annette. *The Hemingses of Monticello: An American Family.* New York: W. W. Norton, 2009.

Hast, Adele. *Loyalism in Revolutionary Virginia: The Norfolk Area and the Eastern Shore.* Ann Arbor: University of Michigan Research Press, 1982.

Hayes, Kevin J. *The Mind of a Patriot: Patrick Henry and the World of Ideas.* Charlottesville: University of Virginia Press, 2008.

Higginbotham, A. Leon, Jr. *In the Matter of Color: Race and the American Legal Process: The Colonial Period.* New York: Oxford University Press, 1978.

Hoffman, Ronald, et al, eds. *The Economy of Early America: The Revolutionary Period.* Charlottesville: University of Virginia Press, 1988.

Holton, Woody. *Forced Founders: Indians, Settlers, Slaves, and the Making of the American Revolution in Virginia.* Chapel Hill: University of North Carolina Press, 1999.

———. *Liberty Is Sweet: The Hidden History of the American Revolution.* New York: Simon & Schuster, 2022.

Hook, Andrew. *Scotland and America: A Study of Cultural Relations, 1750–1835.* Sheffield, UK: Humming Earth, 2008.

Horne, Gerald. *The Counter-Revolution of 1776: Slave Resistance and the Origins of the United States of America.* New York: New York University Press, 2014.

Hume, Ivor Noël. *1775: Another Part of the Field.* New York: Knopf, 1966.

Isaac, Rhys. *Landon Carter's Uneasy Kingdom: Revolution and Rebellion on a Virginia Plantation.* New York: Oxford University Press, 2004.

———. *The Transformation of Virginia, 1740–1790.* Chapel Hill: University of North Carolina Press, 1982.

James, Edward Wilson, ed. *The Lower Norfolk County Virginia Antiquary.* 5 vols. Chesapeake, VA: Friedenwald Company, 1897.

Jasanoff, Maya. *Liberty's Exiles: American Loyalists in the Revolutionary World.* New York: Knopf, 2011.

Karras, Alan L. *Sojourners in the Sun: Scottish Migrants in Jamaica and the Chesapeake, 1740–1800.* Ithaca, NY: Cornell University Press, 1992.

Kranish, Michael. *Flight from Monticello: Thomas Jefferson at War.* New York: Oxford University Press, 2010.

Kulikoff, Phillip David. *Tobacco and Slaves: The Development of Southern Cultures in the Chesapeake, 1680–1800.* Chapel Hill: University of North Carolina Press, 1986.

Lepore, Jill. *These Truths: A History of the United States.* New York: W. W. Norton, 2018.

Lindsay, Lisa A., and John Wood Sweet, eds. *Biography and the Black Atlantic.* Philadelphia: University of Pennsylvania Press, 2013.

Linklater, Andro. *Measuring America: How the United States Was Shaped by the Greatest Land Sale in History.* New York: Plume, 2003.

Maier, Pauline. *American Scripture: Making the Declaration of Independence.* New York: Vintage Books, 1998.

Malcolm, Joyce Lee. *Peter's War: A New England Slave Boy and the American Revolution.* New Haven, CT: Yale University Press, 2009.

Mays, David John. *Edmund Pendleton, 1721–1803: A Biography.* Vol. 1. Cambridge, MA: Harvard University Press, 1952.

McDonnell, Michael A. *The Politics of War: Race, Class, and Conflict in Revolutionary Virginia.* Chapel Hill: University of North Carolina Press, 2007.

Mintz, Steven, ed. *African American Voices: A Documentary Reader, 1619–1877.* Hoboken, NJ: Wiley-Blackwell, 2009.

Morgan, Edmund S. *American Slavery, American Freedom: The Ordeal of Colonial Virginia.* New York: History Book Club, 2005.

Morgan, Philip D. *Slave Counterpoint: Black Culture in the Eighteenth-Century Chesapeake and Lowcountry.* Chapel Hill: University of North Carolina Press, 1998.

Morris, Brent J. *Dismal Freedom: A History of the Maroons of the Great Dismal Swamp.* Chapel Hill: University of North Carolina Press, 2022.

Morrow, George T., II. *A Cock and Bull for Kitty: Lord Dunmore and the Affair That Ruined the British Cause in Virginia.* Williamsburg, VA: Telford Publications, 2011.

Moss, Bobby G., and Michael C. Scoggins. *African-American Loyalists in the Southern Campaign of the American Revolution.* Blacksburg, SC: Scotia-Hibernia Press, 2005.

Mullin, Gerald W. *Flight and Rebellion: Slave Resistance in Eighteenth-Century Virginia.* New York: Oxford University Press, 1972.

Musselwhite, Paul. *Urban Dreams, Rural Commonwealth: The Rise of Plantation Society in the Chesapeake.* Chicago: University of Chicago Press, 2019.

Nash, Gary B. *Race and Revolution.* Lanham, MD: Rowman & Littlefield, 1990.

———. *The Unknown American Revolution: The Unruly Birth of Democracy and the Struggle to Create America.* New York: Penguin, 2006.

Norton, Mary Beth. *1774: The Long Year of Revolution.* New York: Knopf, 2020.

O'Shaughnessy, Andrew Jackson. *The Men Who Lost America: British Leadership, the American Revolution, and the Fate of the Empire.* New Haven, CT: Yale University Press, 2014.

Papas, Phillip. *Renegade Revolutionary: The Life of General Charles Lee.* New York: New York University Press, 2014.

Parkinson, Robert G. *The Common Cause: Creating Race and Nation in the American Revolution.* Chapel Hill: University of North Carolina Press, 2016.

———. *Thirteen Clocks: How Race United the Colonies and Made the Declaration of Independence.* Chapel Hill: University of North Carolina Press, 2021.

———. *Heart of American Darkness: Bewilderment and Horror on the Early Frontier.* New York: W. W. Norton, 2024.

Parramore, Thomas C. *Norfolk: The First Four Centuries.* Charlottesville: University of Virginia Press, 2000.

Penningroth, Dylan C. *Before the Movement: The Hidden History of Black Civil Rights.* New York: Liveright Publishing Corp, 2023.

Phillips, Kevin. *1775: A Good Year for Revolution.* New York: Penguin, 2013.

Pybus, Cassandra. *Epic Journeys of Freedom: Runaway Slaves of the American Revolution and Their Global Quest for Liberty.* Boston: Beacon Press, 2007.

Quarles, Benjamin. *The Negro in the American Revolution.* Chapel Hill: University of North Carolina Press, 1961.

Ragsdale, Bruce. *A Planters' Republic: The Search for Economic Independence in Revolutionary Virginia.* Madison, WI.: Madison House, 1996.

———. *Washington at the Plough: The Founding Farmer and the Question of Slavery.* Cambridge MA: Harvard University Press, 2021.

Randolph, Roy. *Captain Charles Fordyce, 14th Foot.* Self-published, Roy Randolph, 2019.

Richard, Carl J. *Greeks and Romans Bearing Gifts: How the Ancients Inspired the Founding Fathers.* Lanham, MD, Rowman and Littlefield, 2008.

Roberts, Andrew. *The Last King of America: The Misunderstood Reign of George III.* New York: Penguin, 2023.

Royster, Charles. *The Fabulous History of the Dismal Swamp Company.* New York: Vintage Books, 2000.

Rutyna, Richard A, and Peter C. Stewart, eds. *Virginia in the American Revolution: A Collection of Essays.* 2 vols. Norfolk, VA: Old Dominion University, 1977.

Ryan, William R. *The World of Thomas Jeremiah: Charles Town on the Eve of the American Revolution.* New York: Oxford University Press, 2010.

Saunt, Claudio. *West of the Revolution: An Uncommon History of 1776.* New York: W. W. Norton, 2015.

Schama, Simon. *Rough Crossings: Britain, Slaves, and the American Revolution.* New York: HarperCollins, 2006.

Selby, John E. *Dunmore.* Williamsburg: Virginia Independence Bicentennial Commission, 1977.

———. *The Revolution in Virginia, 1775–1783.* Williamsburg, VA: Colonial Williamsburg Foundation, 1988.

Sharples, Jason T. *The World That Fear Made: Slave Revolts and Conspiracy Scares in Early America.* Philadelphia: University of Pennsylvania Press, 2020.

Smith, Julia Abel. *Forbidden Wife: The Life and Trials of Lady Augusta Murray.* Charleston, SC: History Press, 2020.

Sobel, Mechal. *The World They Made Together: Black and White Values in Eighteenth-Century Virginia.* Princeton, NJ: Princeton University Press, 1987.

Taylor, Alan. *The Internal Enemy: Slavery and War in Virginia, 1772–1832.* New York: W. W. Norton, 2014.

Thompson, Mary V. *"The Only Unavoidable Subject of Regret": George Washington, Slavery, and the Enslaved Community at Mount Vernon.* Charlottesville: University of Virginia Press, 2019.

Tinner, Florence. *Gateway to the New World: A History of Princess Anne County, Virginia, 1607–1824.* Greenville, SC: Southern Historical Press, 2020.

Walker, James W. St. G. *The Black Loyalists: The Search for a Promised Land in Nova Scotia and Sierra Leone, 1783–1870.* Ontario, Canada: University of Toronto Press, 2017.

Whichard, Rogers Dey. *History of Lower Tidewater, Virginia.* 3 vols. New York: Lewis Historical Publishing, 1959.

Whitehead, Ruth Holmes. *Black Loyalists: Southern Settlers of Nova Scotia's First Free Black Communities.* Halifax, NS: Nimbus Publishing, 2013.

Wiencek, Henry. *An Imperfect God: George Washington, His Slaves, and the Creation of America.* New York: Farrar, Straus and Giroux, 2004.

Williams, Glenn F. *Dunmore's War: The Last Conflict of America's Colonial Era.* Yardley, PA: Westholme Publishing, 2017.

Williams, Tony. *The Hurricane of Independence.* Naperville, IL: Sourcebooks, 2008.

Williamson, Gene. *Guns on the Chesapeake: The Winning of America's Independence.* Jacksonville, FL: Heritage, 2007.

Willis, Sam. *The Struggle for Sea Power: A Naval History of the American Revolution.* New York: W. W. Norton, 2016.

Wingo, Elizabeth B. *The Battle of Great Bridge.* Chesapeake: Norfolk County Historical Society of Chesapeake, Virginia, 1964.

Wood, Gordon S. *The Radicalism of the American Revolution.* New York: Vintage Books, 1993.

Wrike, Peter Jennings. *The Governors' Island: Gwynn's Island, Virginia, During the Revolution.* Richmond, VA: Brandylane Publishers, 1993.

Articles

Dewey, Frank L. "Thomas Jefferson and a Williamsburg Scandal: The Case of Blair v. Blair." *Virginia Magazine of History and Biography* 89, no. 1 (Jan. 1981): 44–63.

———. "Thomas Jefferson's Law Practice: The Norfolk Anti-Inoculation Riots." *Virginia Magazine of History and Biography* 91, no. 1 (Jan. 1983): 39–53.

Evans, Emory G. "Private Indebtedness and the Revolution in Virginia, 1776–1796." *William and Mary Quarterly* 28, no. 3 (Jul. 1971): 349–374, http://www.jstor.org/stable/1918823.

Frey, Sylvia. "Between Slavery and Freedom: Virginia Blacks and the American Revolution." *Journal of Southern History* 49, no. 3 (Aug. 1983): 375–398.

Gara, Donald J. "Loyal Subjects of the Crown: The Queen's Own Loyal Virginia Regiment and Dunmore's Ethiopian Regiment, 1775–76." *Journal of the Society for Army Historical Research* 83, no. 333 (Spring 2005): 30–42, https://www.jstor.org/stable/44231142.

Jackson, L. P. "Virginia Negro Soldiers and Seamen in the American Revolution." *Journal of Negro History* 27, no. 3 (Jul. 1942), 247–287, https://doi.org/10.2307/2715325.

Kaplan, Sidney. "The 'Domestic Insurrections' of the Declaration of Independence." *Journal of Negro History* 61, no. 3 (Jul. 1976): 243–255, https://www.jstor.org/stable/2717252/.

McDonnell, Michael A. "Class War? Class Struggles during the American Revolution in Virginia." *William and Mary Quarterly*, 3rd ser., 63, no. 2 (Apr. 2006): 305–344, https://www.jstor.org/stable/3877355.

———. "Popular Mobilization and Political Culture in Revolutionary Virginia: The Failure of the Minutemen and the Revolution from Below." *Journal of American History* 85, no. 3 (Dec. 1998): 946–981.

Nicholls, Michael L. "Aspects of the African American Experience in Eighteenth-Century Williamsburg and Norfolk." *Colonial Williamsburg Foundation Library Research Report Series – 330.* Colonial Williamsburg Foundation Library. Williamsburg, VA, 1991.

Pybus, Cassandra. "Jefferson's Faulty Math: The Question of Slave Defections in the American Revolution." *William and Mary Quarterly*, 3rd ser., 62, no. 2 (Apr. 2005): 243–264.

Rasmussen, Barbara. "Anarchy and Enterprise on the Imperial Frontier: Washington, Dunmore, Logan, and Land in the Eighteenth-Century Ohio Valley." *Ohio Valley History* 6, no. 4 (Winter 2006): 1–26.

Sellick, Gary. "'Undistinguished Destruction': The Effects of Smallpox on British Emancipation Policy in the Revolutionary War." *Journal of American Studies* 51, no. 3 (Aug. 2017): 865–885.

Sienkewicz, Julia A. "Shattered Landscapes: Revolutionary Ruins in the Virginian Watercolors of Benjamin Henry Latrobe." *Art Inquiries* 17, no. 2 (2017): 155–171.

Soltow, J. H. "Scottish Traders in Virginia, 1750–1775." *Economic History Review* 12, no. 1 (Aug. 1959): 83–98, https://doi.org/10.1111/j.1468-0289.1959.tb01835.x.

Tate, Thad W. "The Coming of the Revolution in Virginia: Britain's Challenge to Virginia's Ruling Class, 1763–1776." *William and Mary Quarterly* 19, no. 3 (Jul. 1962): 323–343, https://doi.org/10.2307/1920086.

Quarles, Benjamin. "Dunmore as Liberator." *William and Mary Quarterly* 15, no. 4 (Oct. 1958): 494–507.

Walker, James W. St. G. "Black American Loyalists: The Slaves' War for Independence." *Historical Reflections / Réflexions Historiques* 2, no. 1 (Summer 1975): 51–67.

Dissertations and Theses

Bialko, Nicole Rigney. "The Shawnee and the Long Knives: Loyalty and Land in Lord Dunmore's War." Master's thesis, Liberty University, 2022.

Bogger, Tommy L. "The Slave and Free Black Community in Norfolk, 1775–1865." PhD diss., Old Dominion University, 1976.

Caley, Percy Burdelle. "Dunmore: Colonial Governor of New York and Virginia, 1770–1782. PhD diss., University of Pittsburgh, 1939.

Carey, Charles W., Jr. "Lord Dunmore's Ethiopian Regiment." Master's thesis, Virginia Polytechnic Institute and State University, 1995.

Costa, Thomas M. "Economic Development and Political Authority: Norfolk, Virginia, Merchant-Magistrates, 1736–1800." PhD diss., College of William and Mary, 1991.

Davis, Camille Marie. "Why the Fuse Blew: The Reasons for Colonial America's Transformation from Proto-Nationalists to Revolutionary Patriots: 1772–1775." Master's thesis, University of North Texas, 2015.

Duncan, Todd Grant. "Princess Anne County: A Study in Material Wealth." Master's thesis, Old Dominion University, 1980.

Ferrari, Mary. "Artisans of the South: A Comparative Study of Norfolk, Charleston and Alexandria, 1763–1800." PhD diss., College of William and Mary, 1992.

Henley, William Albert. "Independence and the Beginnings of a New Government: A Study of the Virginia Conventions, 1774–1776." Master's thesis, Ohio State University, 1971.

Long, Charles Thomas. "Green Water Revolution: The War for American Independence on the Waters of the Southern Chesapeake Theater." PhD diss., George Washington University, 2005.

McBride, John David. "The Virginia War Effort, 1775–1783: Manpower Policies and Practices." PhD diss., University of Virginia, 1977.

Mitchell, Peter M. "Loyalist Property and Revolution in Virginia." PhD diss., University of Colorado, 1965.

Moomaw, W. Hugh. "The Naval Career of Captain Hamond, 1775–1779." PhD diss., University of Virginia, 1955.

Palladino, Brian David. "'From a Determined Resolution to Get Liberty': Slaves and the British in Revolutionary Norfolk County, Virginia, 1775–1781." Master's thesis, College of William and Mary, 2000.

Ridgewood, Robert Glenn Parkinson. "Enemies of the People: The Revolutionary War and Race in the New American Nation." PhD diss., University of Virginia, 2005.

Rife, James Phillip. "'So Calamitous a Situation': The Causes and Course of Dunmore's War, 1744–1774." Master's thesis, Virginia Polytechnic Institute and State University, 1999.

Shepard, E. Lee. "The Administration of Justice in Revolutionary Virginia: The Norfolk Courts, 1770–1790." Master's thesis, University of Virginia, 1974.

Smyth, Edward A. "Mob Violence in Pre-Revolutionary Norfolk, Virginia." Master's thesis, Old Dominion University, 1975.

Stewart, Byron James. "The Revolutionary Generation: Weighing the Ultimate Fates of Black Patriots and Loyalists, 1776–1836." Master's thesis, Howard University, 2013.

Walker, Francis Moorman. "Lord Dunmore in Virginia." Master's thesis, University of Virginia, 1933.

Williams, Glenn Franklin. "LORD DUNMORE'S WAR: No Other Motive Than the True Interest of This Country." PhD diss., University of Maryland, 2016.

Wrick, Elizabeth Ann. "Dunmore—Virginia's Last Governor." Master's thesis, West Virginia University, 1937.

Illustration Credits

Insert 1.1: National Galleries of Scotland. Insert 2.1: A. D. White Architectural Photographs, Cornell University Library; Insert 2.2: The Colonial Williamsburg Foundation. Archaeological Collections. Insert 3.1: Museums at Washington and Lee University; Insert 3.2: Museums at Washington and Lee University. Insert 4.1: Maryland Center for History and Culture; Insert 4.2: The Colonial Williamsburg Foundation. Gift of M. Knoedler and Company, Inc; Insert 4.3: The Colonial Williamsburg Foundation. Gift of Miss Sylvia Steuart. Insert 5.1: Gift of Mrs. Henry S. McNeil in memory of Mr. Henry S. McNeil. The Diplomatic Reception Rooms, U.S. Department of State, Washington, D.C.; Insert 5.2: Colonial Williamsburg Foundation; Insert 5.3: National Portrait Gallery. Insert 6.1: Library of Congress; Insert 6.2: Library of Virginia; Insert 6.3: Private Collection. Insert 7.1: Maryland Center for History and Culture; Insert 7.2: Maryland Center for History and Culture. Insert 8.1: Accepted in lieu of Inheritance Tax by H M Government from the Trustees of the Wemyss Heirlooms Trust and allocated to the Scottish National Portrait Gallery, 2016; Insert 8.2: Library of Congress; Insert 8.3: William L. Clements Library, University of Michigan Library Digital Collections. Insert 9.1: Library of Congress. Insert 10.1: Don Troiani; Insert 10.2: Don Troiani; Insert 10.3: Don Troiani. Insert 11.1: Maryland Center for History and Culture. Insert 12.1: American Museum & Gardens; Insert 12.2: Private Collection; Insert 12.3: Library of Congress. Insert 13.1: Library of Congress; Insert 13.2: Anne S.K. Brown Military Collection, Brown University Library. Insert 14.1: DACOR-Bacon House; Insert 14.2: Image by author; Insert 14.3: The Colonial Williamsburg Foundation. Museum Purchase. Insert 15.1: The Miriam and Ira D. Wallach Division of Art, Prints and Photographs: Picture Collection, The New York Public Library; Insert 15.2: The Miriam and Ira D. Wallach Division of Art, Prints and Photographs: Picture Collection, The New York Public Library. Insert 16.1: Image by author

Notes

Prelude

xiv "that arch traitor": George Washington, "From George Washington to Lieutenant Colonel Joseph Reed," December 15, 1775, *Founders Online*, National Archives, https://founders.archives.gov/documents/Washington/03-02-02-0508.

xiv "had searched through": Richard Henry Lee to Catherine Macaulay, in *The Letters of Richard Henry Lee*, ed. James Curtis Ballagh, (New York: Macmillan, 1911), 162.

xiv "be placed securely": William James Van Schreeven and Robert L. Scribner, eds., *Revolutionary Virginia, the Road to Independence* (Charlottesville: University Press of Virginia, 1973–1983), 5:61. (hereafter cited as *RV*).

xiv "there was never a viler": "Judith Bell to Alexander Spears," February 16, 1776, #TD 131/18, bundle 8, Mitchell Library, Glasgow City Archives.

xiv "the first full-fledged": Benjamin Quarles, "Lord Dunmore as Liberator," *William and Mary Quarterly* 15, no. 4 (Oct. 1958): 494, https://doi.org/10.2307/2936904.

xvi "most formidable enemy": George Washington, "From George Washington to Richard Henry Lee," December 26, 1775, *Founders Online*, National Archives, https://founders.archives.gov/documents/Washington/03-02-02-0568.

xvii "The American war is over": Benjamin Rush, *Address to the People of the United States in the Documentary History of the Ratification of the Constitution*, digital edition, ed. John P. Kaminski et al. (Charlottesville: University of Virginia Press, 2009), 13:45–49.

xviii "right of the people to": US Constitution, amend. 2.

Part One

Chapter One: A Kind of Friction

3 "Clear, with very little wind": George Washington, "Diary entry: 26 February 1774," February 26, 1774, *Founders Online*, National Archives, https://founders.archives.gov/documents/Washington/01-03-02-0004-0004-0026.

3 "bold, gravely cliff": Adam Gordon, "Journal of Lord Adam Gordon," in *Narratives of Colonial America 1704–1765*, ed. Howard H. Peckham (Chicago: Lakeside Press Donnelly, 1971), 254.

3 "I take the liberty" George Washington, "Letters of George Washington to Lord Dunmore," ed. John Stewart Byron and E. G. Swem, *William and Mary Quarterly* 20, no. 2 (1940): 166, https://doi.org/10.2307/1922674.

4 "FURTH FORTUNE": Ed Crews, "Town Coach: Elegant, Eye-Catching Eighteenth-Century Vehicle Travels Colonial Williamsburg Streets," *Colonial Williamsburg Journal*, Autumn 2006, https://research.colonialwilliamsburg.org/Foundation/journal/Autumn06/coach.cfm.

4 "short, strong built, well-shaped": William Johnson, *The Papers of Sir William Johnson*, ed. Milton W. Hamilton (Albany: University of the State of New York, 1931), 7:945.

4 "muscular and healthy": Edmund Randolph, *History of Virginia*, ed. Arthur H. Shaffer (Charlottesville: University of Virginia Press, 1970), 197.

5 "By ramming the rod too violently": Clementina Rind, *Virginia Gazette*, March 3, 1774. Rockefeller Library Collections, accessed January 8, 2024, https://research.colonialwilliamsburg.org/DigitalLibrary/va-gazettes/. (All *Virginia Gazette* articles published in Williamsburg were accessed through the John D. Rockefeller Jr. Library's digital archives.)

5 "arms, face, and eyes": ibid.

5 "gave great pain": ibid.

5 "a very elegant": Jared Sparks, *The Life of Gouverneur Morris: With Selections from His Correspondence and Miscellaneous Papers* (London: Forgotten Books, 2018), 1:21.

5 "the two greatest": Augustine Prevost and Nicholas B. Wainwright, "Turmoil at Pittsburgh: Diary of Augustine Prevost, 1774," *Pennsylvania Magazine of History and Biography* 85, no. 2 (Apr. 1961): 124, http://www.jstor.org/stable/20089384.

6 "so very low and flat": François Jean de Beauvoir, *Travels in North America in the Years 1780, 1781, and 1782, By the Marquis de Chastellux*, vol. 2, trans. George Grieve and J. Kent (Dublin, 1787), 53–54, https://link.gale.com/apps/doc/U0103693800/MOME?u=ashv45734&sid=summon&xid=2c5d1ff0&pg=272.

6 "wholly built upon smoke": "America and West Indies: November 1627," in *Calendar of State Papers Colonial, America and West Indies*, ed. Noel Sainsbury, vol. 1, 1574–1660 (London: Her Majesty's Stationery Office, 1860), 86, British History Online, accessed December 19, 2023, http://www.british-history.ac.uk/cal-state-papers/colonial/america-west-indies/vol1/p86a.

6 "We have no merchants": Raymond B. Pinchbeck, *The Virginia Negro Artisan and Tradesman*, Phelps-Stokes Fellowship Studies, no. 7 (Richmond, VA: William Byrd Press, 1926), 25, https://hdl.handle.net/2027/uc1.$b69371.

7 "The shrieks of the": Olaudah Equiano, *The Interesting Narrative of the Life of Olaudah Equiano, or Gustavus Vassa, the African, Written by Himself*, vol. 1, electronic ed. (Chapel Hill: University of North Carolina, 2001), 79, https://docsouth.unc.edu/neh/equiano1/equiano1.html.

7 "be a man of humanity": John Michael Vlach, "Afro-American Domestic Artifacts in Eighteenth-Century Virginia," *Material Culture* 19, no. 1 (Spring 1987): 6, http://www.jstor.org/stable/29763792.

7 "I wish you could": George Washington, "From George Washington to William Pearce," June 7, 1795, *Founders Online*, National Archives, https://founders.archives.gov/documents/Washington/05-18-02-0153.

7 "thirty-nine lashes": William Waller Hening, ed., *The Statutes at Large; Being a Collection of All the Laws of Virginia from the First Session of the Legislature, in the Year 1619*, vol. 4, (Richmond, VA: R. W. & G. Bartow, 1823), 122.

8 "all corruption": Ruth Holmes Whitehead, *Black Loyalists: Southern Settlers of Nova Scotia's First Free Black Communities* (Halifax, Nova Scotia: Nimbus, 2013), 71.

8 "which locked her mouth": Equiano, *The Interesting Narrative of the Life of Olaudah Equiano*, 91–92.

8 "They live in huts": Whitehead, *Black Loyalists*, 140.

8 "Freedom is to them": David Hackett Fischer, *Fairness and Freedom: A History of Two Open Societies: New Zealand and the United States* (New York: Oxford University Press, 2012), 44.

9 "There are an incredible number": "Letters Exchanged by Lord Dunmore and Lord Dartmouth, Including Answers to the Heads of Enquiry," Correspondence; Report, The National Archives, Kew, CO 5/1352 1774/03/18-1774/04/06, Accessed January 9, 2024, http://www.colonialamerica.amdigital.co.uk.proxy171.nclive.org/Documents/Details/CO_5_1352_001.

10 "whatever he has for sale": ibid.

12 "an enemy to the liberties": Association of the Sons of Liberty of New-York, pamphlet (New York, 1773), Library of Congress, accessed December 12, 2023, https://www.loc.gov/item/2020767487/.

12 "What think you, captain": Committee of Tarring and Feathering, "To the Delaware Pilots and To Capt. Ayres," 1773, Library of Congress, Broadsides, leaflets, and pamphlets from America and Europe, https://www.loc.gov/item/2020767545/.

12 "unlimited extension of taxes": Alexander Purdie and John Dixon, *Virginia Gazette*, March 3, 1774.

13 "The Bostonians did wrong": Edmund Pendleton, "Edmund Pendleton to Joseph Chew, June 20, 1774," in *The Letters and Papers of Edmund Pendleton*, vol. 1, ed. David John Mays (Charlottesville: University Press of Virginia, 1967), 93.

13 "Americans will never": George Washington, "From George Washington to George William Fairfax," June 10–15, 1774, *Founders Online*, National Archives, https://founders.archives.gov/documents/Washington/02-10-02-0067.

13 "our northern brethren": Purdie and Dixon, *Virginia Gazette*, February 10, 1774.

13 "A great number": Rind, *Virginia Gazette*, March 3, 1774, 3.

14 "free from the plague": James Blair, "The Third of Five Student Speeches written by Francis Nicolson and James Blair," May 1, 1699, *Encyclopedia Virginia*, accessed December 18, 2023, https://encyclopediavirginia.org/entries/the-third-of-five-student-speeches-written-by-francis-nicolson-and-james-blair-may-1-1699.

15 "A magnificent structure": Hugh Jones, *The Present State of Virginia*, pdf, Library of Congress, 31, https://www.loc.gov/item/rc01002788/.

15 "On those occasions": Jane Carson, *We Were There: Descriptions of Williamsburg* (Charlottesville: University of Virginia Press, 1965), 15.

15 "dance or die": Philip Vickers Fithian, *Philip Vickers Fithian, Journal and Letters*, pdf, Library of Congress, 235, www.loc.gov/item/01030673/.

15 "There was not an ill dancer": William Q. Maxwell, "Governor's Palace Report, Block 20 Building 3A," Colonial Williamsburg Foundation Library, November 1954, https://research.colonialwilliamsburg.org/DigitalLibrary/view/index.cfm?doc=ResearchReports%5CRR1463.xml&highlight=.

15 "resembles a good": Peter Martin, *The Pleasure Gardens of Virginia: From Jamestown to Jefferson* (Charlottesville: University of Virginia Press, 2001), 81.

16 "very disagreeable": John Ferdinand Smyth, *A Tour in the United States of America* (New York: New York Times and Arno Press, 1968), 19.

16 "the great polis.": George Washington, *George Washington's Barbados Diary, 1751–52*, ed. Alicia K. Anderson, Lynn P. Price, and William M. Ferraro (Charlottesville: University of Virginia Press, 2018), 109–110.

16 "they return to their plantations": Andrew Burnaby and Francis Fauquier, *Burnaby's Travels Through North America* (New York: A. Wessels Company, 1904), 35.

16 "Our city has long expected": Emmanuel Jones Jr., "To George Washington from Emmanuel Jones, Jr., 18 February 1774," February 18, 1774, *Founders Online*, National Archives, https://founders.archives.gov/documents/Washington/02-09-02-0363.

16 "great preparations": John Byrd, "John Byrd to William Byrd," quoted in *Virginia Magazine of History and Biography* 38 (1930), 356.

16 "an illumination": "Williamsburg—The Old Colonial Capital," *William and Mary College Quarterly Historical Magazine* 16, no. 1 (1907): 39, https://doi.org/10.2307/1916115.

16 "arranged upon the walls": William Wirt and George Tucker, "William Wirt's Life of Patrick Henry," *William and Mary College Quarterly Historical Magazine* 22, no. 4 (1914): 257, https://doi.org/10.2307/1914815.

17 "boys of ten": Ebenezer Hazard and Fred Shelley, "The Journal of Ebenezer Hazard in Virginia, 1777," *Virginia Magazine of History and Biography* 62, no. 4 (1954): 410, http://www.jstor.org/stable/4246052.

17 "beds, bedding, looking glasses,": "Memorial to the Loyalist Claims Commission," February 24, 1784, DC, 815–823, 12/54/118–20.

17 "a number of valuable pictures": A. Lawrence Kocher, "Architectural Report: Palace of the Governors of Virginia Block 20 Building 3," accessed December 19, 2023, https://research.colonialwilliamsburg.org/DigitalLibrary/view/index.cfm?doc=ResearchReports%5CRR0133.xml&highlight=.

18 "well pleased with everything": John Blair, "To Thomas Jefferson from John Blair, 2 March 1774," March 2, 1774, *Founders Online*, National Archives, https://founders.archives.gov/documents/Jefferson/01-01-02-0080.

18 "While cannon roar": Purdie and Dixon, *Virginia Gazette*, March 3, 1774.

18 "May his example liberty inspire": Purdie and Dixon, *Virginia Gazette*, March 3, 1774, 2.

19 "effectual steps . . .": *Public Advertiser*, January 28, 1774.

Chapter Two: A Gentleman of Benevolence

21 "Damn Virginia!": William Smith, *Historical Memoirs of William Smith* (London: Colburn & Tegg, 1956), 1:106.

21 "Virginia, where the": John Murray, "Dunmore to Gower," March 9, 1771, box 3, Dunmore Family Papers, Special Collections Research Center, Swem Library, College of William and Mary.

21 "tiresome": John Murray, "Dunmore to Hillsborough," July 2, 1771, private DC, 69, or C.O. 5/154/20.

21 "a more distinguishing": "Johnson to Dunmore," March 16, 1771, in *The Papers of Sir William Johnson*, ed. Milton W. Hamilton (Albany: University of the State of New York, 1931), 8:28–30.

22 "health and good society": James Corbett David, "Dunmore's New World: Political Culture in the British Empire" (PhD diss., College of William and Mary, 2010), 81.

22 "to fit yourself with all": George III, "Instructions to Lord Dunmore," *Collections of the Massachusetts Historical Society* (Boston: Massachusetts Historical Society, 1871), 10:630.

22 "perfectly sober": John Murray, "Dunmore to William Johnson," August 24, 1771, in *The Papers of Sir William Johnson*, 8:234.

22 "a gamester": William Aitchison to Charles Steuart, October 17, 1770; and James Parker to Charles Steuart, April 19, 1771, Charles Steuart Papers, National Library of Scotland, Edinburgh, Scotland.

22 "a very active": William Leete Stone, *History of New York City: From the Discovery to the Present Day* (New York: Virtue & Yorston, 1872), 230.

22 "easy and affable": William Johnson, *The Papers of Sir William Johnson*, 7:945.

23 "convivial disposition": David, "Dunmore's New World," 81.

23 "He may be described": J. M. Toner, "George Washington as an Inventor and Promoter of the Useful Arts," in *Early Sketches of George Washington*, ed. W. S. Baker, (Agawam, MA: Silver Street Media, 2020), 13.

24 "cutting a flash": Helen Duff, "To the Lord Viscount Macduff, at Duff House," April 25, 1762, in *Lord Fife and His Factor: Being the Correspondence of James, Second Lord Fife, 1729–1809*, ed. Alistair Norwich Tayler and Henrietta Tayler (Portsmouth, NH: Heinemann, 1925), 9.

24 "such hazardous": George Washington, "From George Washington to John Posey," June 24, 1767, *Founders Online*, National Archives, https://founders.archives.gov/documents/Washington/02-08-02-0001.

24 "God knows I have": George Washington, "From George Washington to Carlyle & Adam," February 15, 1767, *Founders Online*, National Archives, https://founders.archives.gov/documents/Washington/02-07-02-0331.

25 "among the poorer folk,": Thomas Bisset, "Thos. Bisset, Dunkeld, to Duke of Atholl," NRAS 234, box 49/5/198, National Archives, Blair Castle.

25 "Though none but": "Duke of Atholl to John Mackenzie of Delvine," June 11, 1766, Delvine MSS, Lauriston Castle Collection, MS 1405, f. 96, National Library of Scotland, Edinburgh, Scotland.

25 "teased every minister": Horace Walpole, *The Letters of Horace Walpole: Fourth Earl of Orford*, ed. Helen Wrigley Toynbee and Paget Jackson Toynbee (Oxford: Clarendon Press, 1904), 409, n. 4.

25 "kissed his Majesty's": *South Carolina and American General Gazette*, February 14, 1770.

25 "may turn out": John Murray, "E. of Dunmore, London, to Duke of Atholl," NRAS 234, box 54/1/140, National Archives, Blair Castle.

25 "The welfare of": David, "Dunmore's New World," 38.

25 "create suspicions of a decay": George Washington, "From George Washington to George Mason," April 5, 1769, *Founders Online*, National Archives, https://founders.archives.gov/documents/Washington/02-08-02-0132.

25 "a settlement in": Landmark Trust, *The Pineapple History Album* (Dunmore Park, Scotland: Landmark Trust), 57.

26 "I can never look": George Washington, "From George Washington to William Crawford," September 17, 1767, *Founders Online*, National Archives, https://founders.archives.gov/documents/Washington/02-08-02-0020.

26 "Not even a second": Rind, *Virginia Gazette*, January 14, 1773.

26 "land stealers.": A. K. Christian, "Mirabeau Buonaparte Lamar," *Southwestern Historical Quarterly* 24, no. 1 (1920): 43, http://www.jstor.org/stable/30234792.

26 "punctually obeyed": George Washington, "From George Washington to Lord Dunmore," April 15, 1773, *Founders Online*, National Archives, https://founders.archives.gov/documents/Washington/02-09-02-0163.

27 "the atmosphere seemed in a glow": George Milligen-Johnston, James Glen, *Colonial South Carolina: Two Contemporary Descriptions*, ed. Chapman J. Milling and Robert L. Meriwether (London, Forgotten Books, 2018), 109.

27 "I do sincerely": John Murray, "To George Washington from Lord Dunmore," July 3, 1773, *Founders Online*, National Archives, https://founders.archives.gov/documents/Washington/02-09-02-0193.

27 "much addicted to": Charles Augustus Hanna, *The Scotch-Irish* (New York: G. P. Putnam's Sons, 1902), 82.

27 "Upon my arrival": John Murray, "Dunmore to Dartmouth," March 18, 1774, in *Documents of the American Revolution, 1770–1783: Transcripts, 1774*, ed. K. G. Davies (Newbridge, County Kildare, Ireland: Irish University Press, 1972), 65.

28 "a very sensible": George Washington, "Remark & Occurs. in Novr. [1770]," November 22, 1770, *Founders Online*, National Archives, https://founders.archives.gov/documents/Washington/01-02-02-0005-0031.

28 "a gentleman of benevolence": John Connolly, "To George Washington from John Connolly," August 29, 1773, *Founders Online*, National Archives, https://founders.archives.gov/documents/Washington/02-09-02-0238.

28 "exceedingly sorry": George Washington, "From George Washington to Lord Dunmore," September 12, 1773, *Founders Online*, National Archives, https://founders.archives.gov/documents/Washington/02-09-02-0246.

28 "likely to give": David, "Dunmore's New World," 120.

28 "I do not mean": John Murray, "To George Washington from Lord Dunmore," September 24, 1773, *Founders Online*, National Archives, https://founders.archives.gov/documents/Washington/02-09-02-0253.

29 "Its situation beautiful": Rind, *Virginia Gazette*, November 30, 1769.

29 "With the flour": George Washington, "From George Washington to Thomas Newton, Jr.," December 14, 1773, *Founders Online*, National Archives, https://founders.archives.gov/documents/Washington/02-09-02-0305.

29 "Should this prove": John Armstrong, "To George Washington from John Armstrong," December 23, 1773, *Founders Online*, National Archives, https://founders.archives.gov/documents/Washington/02-09-02-0314.

29 "may be advantageous": Joseph Redington, ed., *Calendar of Home Office Papers of the Reign of George III: 1770–1772* (London: Longman & Company and Trűbner & Company, 1881), 473.

29 "strong coarse stockings": James Minzies, "James Minzies to John Norton," June 12, 1773, Folder 85, John Norton and Sons Papers (1750 [1763–1798] 1902) MS 1936.3, Special Collections, John D. Rockefeller Jr. Library, Colonial Williamsburg Foundation.

29 "his Lordship was determined": William Wirt Henry, *Patrick Henry; Life, Correspondence and Speeches* (New York: Charles Scribner's Sons, 1891), 206.

Chapter Three: A Notion Now Too Prevalent

30 "He is as popular": James Parker to Charles Steuart, February 11, 1775, Charles Steuart Collection, Scotland National Library, Edinburgh, Scotland.

30 "North Britons": Daniel Szechi, "Constructing a Jacobite: The Social and Intellectual Origins of George Lockhart of Carnwath," *Historical Journal* 40, no 4 (Dec. 1997): 944, n. 104, doi:10.1017/S0018246X97007541.

31 "from the usurpation": William Marquis of Tullibardine, "Circular Letter to The Laird of Asshentilly and Other Gentlemen in Atholl," *Jacobite Correspondence of the Atholl Family, during the Rebellion* (Edinburgh: Abbotsford Club, 1840), pdf, accessed January 10, 2024, https://www.yourphotocard.com/Ascanius/documents/Jacobite%20correspondence%20of%20the%20Atholl%20family.pdf.

32 "the progress of the human": *Gazette Littéraire de l'Europe*, April 4, 1764, 98.

32 "lawyers, university men,": Benjamin Franklin, *The Autobiography of Benjamin Franklin: 1706–1757* (Auckland, New Zealand: Floating Press, 2009), 25. https://www.ebooks.com/en-us/book/413176/the-autobiography-of-benjamin-franklin/benjamin-franklin/.

32 "talked very well,": James Boswell, *Boswell, Laird of Auchinleck, 1778–1782*, ed. Joseph W. Reed and Frederick A. Pottle (New York: McGraw Hill, 1977), 118–119, 236.

33 "No one is born": Adam Ferguson, *Institutes of Moral Philosophy* (Edinburgh: A. Kincaid & J. Bell, 1769), 222.

33 "supposed property": ibid.

33 "There is not": Adam Smith, *The Theory of Moral Sentiments* (Cambridge: Cambridge University Press, 2002), 242,

33 "nations of heroes": Daniel B. Klein, "Adam Smith's Rebuke of the Slave Trade, 1759," *Independent Review* 25, no. 1 (2020): 93, https://www.jstor.org/stable/48583696.

33 "in continual fear": Adam Smith, *Lectures on Jurisprudence*, ed. R. L. Meek, D. D. Raphael, and P. Stein (Oxford: Clarendon Press, 1978), 183.

33 "the more intolerable": ibid., 185.

33 "Love of dominion": ibid., 187.

33 "I am apt to suspect": David Hume, "Of National Characters," in *David Hume on Morals, Politics, and Society*, ed. Angela Conventry and Andrew Valls (New Haven, CT: Yale University Press, 2018), 170, n. 32, https://doi.org/10.2307/j.ctv6gqxqj.26.

33 "As freedom is": Richard K. MacMaster, "Arthur Lee's Address on Slavery: An Aspect of Virginia's Struggle to End the Slave Trade, 1765–1774," *Virginia Magazine of History and Biography* 80, no. 2 (Apr. 1972): 154.

35 "Near 200 Blacks": Purdie and Dixon, *Virginia Gazette*, September 3, 1772.

35 "was determined": Rind, *Virginia Gazette*, November 12, 1772.

35 "Slaves are devils": Howard Bodenhorn, "'To Set Devils Free': Manumission in Nineteenth-Century Virginia," (Seminar paper, Clemson University and NBER, September 2009), 2, https://websites.umich.edu/~baileymj/Bodenhorn.pdf.

35 "slave holding might": ibid.

35 "put into the heads": Nini Rodgers, *Ireland, Slavery, and Antislavery: 1612–1865* (London: Palgrave Macmillan, 2007), 78.

36 "where they imagine": Purdie and Dixon, *Virginia Gazette*, September 30, 1773.

36 "to get on board some": *Purdie and Dixon*, Virginia Gazette, June 30, 1774.

36 "a large scar": Alexander Purdie, *Virginia Gazette*, January 19, 1774.

36 "the mischief": Rind, *Virginia Gazette*, February 27, 1772.

37 "of great inhumanity": H. R. McIlwaine and J. P. Kennedy, eds., *Journals of the House of Burgesses, 1619–1776* (Richmond: Virginia State Library, 1905–1915), 12:256–257.

37 "to be kind": "Corbin Genealogy (Continued)," *Virginia Magazine of History and Biography* 30, no. 1 (1922): 80.

37 "as the number": MacMaster, "Arthur Lee's 'Address on Slavery,'" 148.

37 "the introduction": Alan Gilbert, *Black Patriots and Loyalists: Fighting for Emancipation in the War for Independence* (Chicago: University of Chicago Press, 2012), 53.

37 "the evil consequences": *Fourteenth Report of the Royal Commission on Historical Manuscripts* (Burlington, Ontario: TannerRitchie, 2013), 113.

37 "to infuse that spirit": McIlwaine and Kennedy, *Journals of the House of Burgesses of Virginia, 1619–1776*, 6:317.

38 "Academicus": Purdie and Dixon, *Virginia Gazette*, August 5, 1773.

39 "at the request": Thomas Jefferson, "Plan for an Addition to the College of William and Mary," n.d., HM 9387, Huntington Library, San Marino, CA.

39 "capable of being made": Thomas Jefferson, *Notes on the State of Virginia* (Paris, 1784–1785), 280.

40 "forwardness and zeal": Thomas Jefferson, *Autobiography of Thomas Jefferson, 1743–1790: Together with a Summary of the Chief Events in Jefferson's Life* (New York: G. P. Putnam's Sons, 1914), 9.

40 "various rumors": Kennedy, *Journals of the House of Burgesses of Virginia, 1619–1776*, 13:28.

40 "unity of action.": Thomas Jefferson, "Thomas Jefferson's Notes on Early Career (the so-called 'Autobiography')," July 29, 1821, *Founders Online*, National Archives, https://founders.archives.gov/documents/Jefferson/03-17-02-0324-0002.

40 "a little ill humor,": Percy Scott Flippin, *The Royal Government in Virginia, 1624–1775* (New York: Columbia University Press, 1919) 84:144.

Chapter Four: A Mysterious War Dance

41 "Possession is eleven points": Robert Christy, ed., *Proverbs, Maxims, and Phrases of All Ages: Classified Subjectively and Arranged Alphabetically* (New York: G. P. Putnam's Sons, 1887), 1:144.

42 "many hundreds": William Crawford, "Crawford to Washington," May 8, 1774, *Founders Online*, National Archives, https://founders.archives.gov/documents/Washington/02-10-02-0042.

42 "an entire depopulation": *Journal of the House of Delegates of the Commonwealth of Virginia* (Richmond, VA: Samuel Shepherd, 1835), document no. 30, 1.

43 "a general asylum": Brent J. Morris, *Dismal Freedom: A History of the Maroons of the Great Dismal Swamp*, (Chapel Hill: University of North Carolina Press, 2022), 45.

45 "that disasters of the sort": Johann David Schöpf, *Travels in the Confederation [1783–1784]*, trans. Alfred James Morrison (Philadelphia: William J. Campbell, 1911), 227.

45 "as fine a one": "Letters Exchanged by Lord Dunmore and Lord Dartmouth" (Correspondence; Report, National Archives, Kew, CO 5/1352 1774/03/18-1774/04/06), accessed January 9, 2024, http://www.colonialamerica.amdigital.co.uk.proxy171.nclive.org/Documents/Details/CO_5_1352_001.

45 "perhaps the most": *RV* 3:217

45 "the finest and most": Charles Lee, "To George Washington from Major General Charles Lee," April 5, 1776, *Founders Online*, National Archives, https://founders.archives.gov/documents/Washington/03-04-02-0031.

45 "The country is thinly": John Clayton, "A Letter from Mr. John Clayton Rector of Crofton at Wakefield in Yorkshire, to the Royal Society, May 12, 1688," in Peter Force, ed., *Tracts and Other Papers Relating Principally to the Origin, Settlement, and Progress of the Colonies in North America, III* (Washington, DC, 1844), 12:21.

46 "Norfolk has more": William Byrd, *The Westover Manuscripts: Containing the History of the Dividing Line Betwixt Virginia and North Carolina: A Journey to the Land of Eden: and A Progress to the Mines* (Petersburg, VA: E. and J. C. Ruffin, 1841), 10.

46 "remain in a happy": ibid.

46 "The sewage ditches": Médéric Louis Elie Moreau de Saint-Méry, *American Journey*, trans. Kenneth Lewis Roberts and Anna Mosser Roberts (New York: Doubleday, 1947), 42.

46 "receptacles of the filth": Benjamin Henry Latrobe, *The Virginia Journals of Benjamin Henry Latrobe, 1795–1798*, ed. Edward Carter II and Angeline Polites (New Haven, CT: Yale University Press, 1977), 75.

46 "putrid bilious fevers": ibid., 53.

46 "people could not": Byrd, *The Westover Manuscripts*, 10.

47 "spirit of trade": "Observations in Several Voyages and Travels in America in the Year 1736," *William and Mary College Quarterly Historical Magazine* 15, no. 4 (Apr. 1907): 222–223.

47 "All the merchants": John Rogers Williams, "Journal of Philip Fithian, Kept at Nomini Hall, Virginia, 1773–1774," *American Historical Review* 5, no. 2 (1899): 294, https://doi.org/10.2307/1834612.

47 "Norfolk is the port": *Narratives of Colonial America 1704–1765* (Chicago: R. R. Donnelley, 1971), 254.

48 "Negro shoes": Purdie and Dixon, *Virginia Gazette*, October 4, 1770.

48 "put out the muzzle": James Parker to Charles Steuart, May 1769, Charles Steuart Papers, National Library of Scotland, Edinburgh, Scotland.

49 "Perhaps he may": Purdie and Dixon, *Virginia Gazette*, June 11, 1772.

49 "a great concourse": Norfolk County Deedbook 10, 1718–1719, f. 11, Microfilm, Virginia State Library, Richmond, VA.

49 "When they saw": ibid.

49 "by imprisonment": William Gooch, G. McLaren Brydon ed., "The Virginia Clergy," *Virginia Magazine of History and Biography* 32 (1924): 323.

49 "insult and abuses": Brent Tarter, "The Order Book and Related Papers of the Common Hall of the Borough of Norfolk, Virginia, 1736–1798" (1979): 55–56.

49 "unlawful and tumultuous": ibid., 59.

49 "a good market": Prevost and Wainwright, "Turmoil at Pittsburgh," 121.

50 "keeping a disorderly": Michael L. Nicholls, "Aspects of the African American Experience in Eighteenth-Century Williamsburg and Norfolk," 1990, 35.

50 "dispose or apprehend": Tarter, "Order Book and Related Papers," 62–63.

51 "own liking": "Petition of Talbot Thompson," *Executive Journals of the Council of Colonial Virginia*, ed. Benjamin J. Hillman (Richmond: Virginia State Library, 1966), 6:200.

52 "meritorious service": William Waller Hening, *The Statutes at Large; Being a Collection of all the Laws of Virginia . . .* (Richmond and Philadelphia, 1819), 4:132.

52 "pride of a manumitted": William Gooch, "Governor Gooch to Mr. Popple (1736)," Slavery, Law & Power in the British Empire and Early America, website, accessed January 8, 2024, https://slaverylawpower.org/governor-gooch-popple/.

52 "according to his": "Petition of Talbot Thompson," *Executive Journals of the Council of Virginia*, 6:200.

53 "an honest, industrious": "American Loyalist Claims Commission," n.d., A. O. 13/25/479, National Archives, Kew, Richmond, Greater London, United Kingdom.

53 "in a way that no": Cassandra Pybus, "Recovered Lives as a Window into the Enslaved Family," in *Biography and the Black Atlantic*, ed. Lisa A. Lindsay and John Wood Sweet (Philadelphia: University of Pennsylvania Press, 2014), 123, http://www.jstor.org/stable/j.ctt4cgh6w.9.

54 "live in peace": H. Roy Kaplan, *American Indians at the Margins: Racist Stereotypes and Their Impacts on Native Peoples* (Jefferson, NC: McFarland, 2022), 109.

54 "their heads powdered": Edward Wilson James, *The Lower Norfolk County Virginia Antiquary* (Chesapeake, VA: Friedenwald Company, 1897), 5:33–35n.

55 "in the character": Maximilian Schele de Vere, *The Romance of American History: Early Annals* (New York: G. P. Putnam & Sons, 1872), 31.

55 "By and by," James, *The Lower Norfolk County Virginia Antiquary*, 5:33–35n.

55 "But the poor captain": ibid.

55 "to some Negro tune,": Nicholas Cresswell, *The Journal of Nicholas Cresswell, 1774–1777* (New York: Dial Press, 1924), 52–53.

55 "encircled their king": Schele de Vere, *The Romance of American History*, 31.

Chapter Five: Twenty-Two Days for Nothing

57 "You would swear": William Wirt Henry, *Patrick Henry; Life, Correspondence and Speeches*, 1:127.

57 "of their ancient": Kennedy, ed., *Journals of the House of Burgesses of Virginia 1619-1776*, 5:xii.

58 "prudence and moderation": Purdie and Dixon, *Virginia Gazette*, May 12, 1774.

58 "We were under": Thomas Jefferson, *The Writings of Thomas Jefferson*, "Letterpress Edition," ed. Paul Leicester Ford (New York, 1892–1899), 1:9–11.

58 "fasting, humiliation": ibid.

58 "destruction of our": "Resolution of the House of Burgesses Designating a Day of Fasting and Prayer," May 24, 1774, *Founders Online*, National Archives, https://founders.archives.gov/documents/Jefferson/01-01-02-0082.

58 "much retard the settlement": Lynda Lee Butler and Margit Livingston, *Virginia Tidal and Coastal Law* (Charlottesville, VA: Michie, 1988), 377.

58 "dined and spent": Jared Sparks, *The Life of George Washington* (London: Colburn, 1839), 2:189.

59 "the best horsemen": Francis D. Cogliano, *A Revolutionary Friendship* (Cambridge, MA: Harvard University Press, 2024), 20.

59 "Mr. Speaker": Thomas Jefferson, "Resolution of the House of Burgesses Designating a Day of Fasting and Prayer," May 24, 1774, *Founders Online*, National Archives, https://founders.archives.gov/documents/Jefferson/01-01-02-0082&sa=D&source=docs&ust=1704819561277826&usg=AOvVaw1SRH-R6MkWGCPKlcgBUIF4.

59 "I have in": Letter 206, June 17, 1774, in Charles Steuart Papers, National Library of Scotland, Edinburgh, Scotland.

59 "This dissolution": George Washington, "From George Washington to George William Fairfax," June 10–15, 1774, *Founders Online*, National Archives, https://founders.archives.gov/documents/Washington/02-10-02-0067.

60 "inflame the whole": Peter Force, ed., *American Archives*, Fourth Series, (Washington, DC: M. St. Claire Clark and Peter Force, 1837), 1:352.

60 "The governor dissolved": Cogliano, *A Revolutionary Friendship,* 84.

60 "Jollity, the offspring": George Humphrey Yetter, *Williamsburg Before and After: The Rebirth of Virginia's Colonial Capital* (Williamsburg VA: Colonial Williamsburg Foundation, 1998), 91.

60 "formed and pressed": "Association of Members of the Late House of Burgesses, 27 May 1774," *Founders Online*, National Archives, https://founders.archives.gov/documents/Jefferson/01-01-02-0083.

60 "meet in a general": ibid.

61 "a disorder in his breast": C. W. Coleman, "The County Committees of 1774–75 in Virginia," *William and Mary College Quarterly Historical Magazine* 5, no. 2 (July 1896), 96.

62 "the effect of the day": Jefferson, "Thomas Jefferson's Notes on Early Career."

62 "cement among": Edmund Randolph, "Edmund Randolph's Essay on the Revolutionary History of Virginia, 1774–1782: The History of the Revolution," *Virginia Magazine of History and Biography* 43, no. 3 (Jul. 1935), 215.

62 "the postponing of a dinner": "The Plea for Moderation by the King's Attorney General," July 1774, in *RV* 1:214.

62 "murdered and scalped.": *Maryland Gazette*, June 30, 1774, Maryland Gazette Collection MSA SC 2731, January 9, 1772–September 10, 1779, M 1282, Archives of Maryland Online, accessed January 9, 2024, https://msa.maryland.gov/megafile/msa/speccol/sc4800/sc4872/001282/html/m1282-0636.html.

62 "since the first settlement": George Washington, "From George Washington to George William Fairfax," June 10–15, 1774, *Founders*

Online, National Archives, https://founders.archives.gov/documents/Washington/02-10-02-0067.

62 "send terror into": John Connolly, "To George Washington from John Connolly," June 7, 1774, *Founders Online*, National Archives, https://founders.archives.gov/documents/Washington/02-10-02-0063.

62 "this useless people may now": William Preston, "Circular Letter of Colonel William Preston," July 20, 1774, in *Documentary History of Dunmore's War*, eds. Rueben Gold Thwaites and Louise Phelps Kellog, (Madison, WI: Wisconsin Historical Society, 1904), 91–93.

62 "crisis could be": John W. Shy, "Dunmore, the Upper Ohio Valley and the American Revolution," in *Ohio in the American Revolution: A Conference to Commemorate the 200th Anniversary of the Ft. Gower Resolves* (Columbus: Ohio Historical Society, 1976), 15.

63 "may have a dangerous": Force, *American Archives*, 462.

63 "I am determined": "John Connolly to Arthur St. Claire," July 19, 1774, in *The St. Clair Papers: The Life and Public Services of Arthur St. Clair, Soldier of the Revolutionary War; President of the Continental Congress; and Governor of the North-Western Territory; with His Correspondence and Other Papers*, ed. William Smith (Cincinnati, OH: R. Clarke, 1882), 327.

63 "the growing discontents": "Petition to Lord Dunmore," June 16, 1774, Virginia Official Correspondence, 1768–1776, in Bancroft Transcripts, Library of Congress, Washington, DC.

63 "The Indians is": Arthur Campbell. "Major Arthur Campbell to Colonel William Preston," October 12, 1774, in *Documentary History of Dunmore's War*, 246–247.

63 "as many prisoners": Force ed., *American Archives*, 1:473.

63 "Lord Dunmore is": Thomas Wharton, "Letters of Thomas Wharton: 63–1783," *Pennsylvania Magazine of History and Biography* 33 (1909): 445.

63 "conscious of the injustice": Thomas Jefferson, "Memorandum Books, 1775," *Founders Online*, National Archives, https://founders.archives.gov/documents/Jefferson/02-01-02-0009.

64 "very warm in a debate": Prevost and Wainwright, "Turmoil at Pittsburgh," 121.

65 "the masterly manner": ibid., 123.

65 "hatred, ill-temper,": Frank L. Dewey, "Thomas Jefferson and a Williamsburg Scandal: The Case of Blair v. Blair," *Virginia Magazine of History and Biography* 89, no. 1 (1981): 49, http://www.jstor.org/stable/4248451.

65 "impotence and hidden": ibid., 50.

66 "fever and agues,": "Dunmore to Gower," March 9, 1771, box 3, Papers 1749–1797, Dunmore Family Papers, Special Collections Research Center, Swem Library, College of William and Mary.

66 "We never before": George Washington, "From George Washington to Thomas Johnson," August 5, 1774, *Founders Online*, National Archives, https://founders.archives.gov/documents/Washington/01-03-02-0004-0004-0026.

66 "inviolable and unshaken": "Resolutions and Association of the Virginia Convention of 1774, [1–6 August 1774]" *Founders Online*, National Archives, https://founders.archives.gov/documents/Jefferson/01-01-02-0091.

67 "I will raise": John Adams, "[August 1774]," August 31, 1774, *Founders Online*, National Archives, https://founders.archives.gov/documents/Adams/01-02-02-0004-0005.

67 "reduce us from": George Washington, "Fairfax County Resolves," July 18, 1774, *Founders Online*, National Archives, https://founders.archives.gov/documents/Washington/02-10-02-0080.

67 "The African trade": Force, *American Archives*, 1:541.

67 "neither ourselves import,": "Continental Association," October 20, 1774, *Founders Online*, National Archives, https://founders.archives.gov/documents/Jefferson/01-01-02-0094.

67 "we view it": "The Association of the Virginia Convention," August 1–6, 1774, The Avalon Project, accessed January 9, 2024, https://avalon.law.yale.edu/18th_century/assoc_of_va_conv_1774.asp.

67 "inimical to this": Daniel Reaves Goodloe, *The Birth of the Republic: Compiled from the National and Colonial Histories and Historical Collections, from the American Archives and from Memoirs, and from the Journals and Proceedings of the British Parliament* (Chicago: Belford, Clarke, 1889), 285.

68 "A Summary View": Thomas Jefferson, "Draft of Instructions to the Virginia Delegates in the Continental Congress," July 1774, *Founders Online*, National Archives, https://founders.archives.gov/documents/Jefferson/01-01-02-0090.

68 "the laziest man in reading": Jefferson, *Autobiography of Thomas Jefferson*, 15.

68 "The abolition": ibid.

69 "most indecent": Frank Moore, ed., *American Eloquence: A Collection of Speeches and Addresses; By the Most Eminent Orators of America* (New York: D. Appleton and Company, 1871), 2:251.

Chapter Six: Lord Feathers and the Big Knife

71 "which made my Lordship": Prevost and Wainwright, "Turmoil at Pittsburgh," 131.

72 "kind of loose frock,": Joseph Doddridge, *Notes on the Settlement and Indian Wars of the Western Parts of Virginia and Pennsylvania from 1762 to 1783*, ed. Alfred Williams (Albany, NY, 1876), 140.

72 "peculiar": John Adams, "John Adams to Abigail Adams," June 11, 1775, *Founders Online*, National Archives, https://founders.archives.gov/documents/Adams/04-01-02-0146.

72 "His Lordship . . .": Prevost and Wainwright, "Turmoil at Pittsburgh," 143.

72 "very much like those": ibid., 132.

73 "to put an end": *RV*, 2:15.

73 "little or no": Prevost and Wainwright, "Turmoil at Pittsburgh," 143.

73 "Great Dunmore,": Philip Alexander Bruce and William Glover Stanard, "Orderly Book and Journal of James Newell: During the Point Pleasant Campaign, 1774," *Virginia Magazine of History and Biography* 11 (1903): 248.

74 "Be Strong!": John Stuart, "Narrative by Captain John Stuart of General Andrew Lewis' Expedition against the Indians in the Year 1774 and the Battle of Point Pleasant, Virginia," *Magazine of American History* 1 (November 1877): 678.

74 "Never did the": William Fleming, "Fleming to Bowyer," October 13, 1774, in *Documentary History of Dunmore's War*, 256.

74 "The Big Knife": John Stuart, "Narrative by Captain John Stuart of General Andrew Lewis' Expedition against the Indians," 747.

74 "I have heard": Alexander Scott Withers, *Chronicles of Border Warfare or, a History of the Settlement by the Whites of North-Western Virginia and of the Indian Wars and Massacres in that State* (Clarksburg, VA: Joseph Israel, 1831), 185–186.

74 "they could not": Andrew Lewis, "Colonel Andrew Lewis to Dr. Samuel Campbell," n.d., in *The Virginia Historical Register and Literary Advisor*, ed. William Maxwell (Richmond, VA: McFarlane and Fergusson, 1848), 1:32.

75 "any violence upon": John Dixon and William Hunter, *Virginia Gazette*, January 28, 1775.

75 "exert every power": Purdie and Dixon, *Virginia Gazette*, December 22, 1774.

75 "military league.": Force, *American Archives*, 1:1672.

76 "We look upon": George Washington, "From George Washington to William Milnor," January 23, 1775, *Founders Online*, National Archives, https://founders.archives.gov/documents/Washington/02-10-02-0174.

76 "those cruel": "Fincastle Resolutions" in Purdie, *Virginia Gazette*, February 10, 1775.

76 "The original purchase": "Botetourt Resolutions," in Dixon and Hunter, *Virginia Gazette*, March 11, 1775.

76 "never more take": Purdie and Dixon, *Virginia Gazette*, December 1, 1774.

77 "cheerfully undergoing": Virgil Anson Lewis, *History of the Battle of Point Pleasant Fought Between White Men and Indians at the Mouth of the Great Kanawha River (now Point Pleasant, West Virginia) Monday, October 10th, 1774: The Chief Event of Lord Dunmore's War* (Chicago, Tribune Printing Company, 1909), 92.

77 "tall, manly, well-shaped": Cresswell, *Journal of Nicholas Cresswell*, 49.

77 "They are in white": ibid., 50.

77 "strictly to refrain": Dixon and Hunter, *Virginia Gazette*, January 28, 1775.

77 "restrain the Americans": John Murray, "Dunmore to Dartmouth, December 24, 1774," in *Documentary History of Dunmore's War*, 371.

77 "Everything here": Cresswell, *Journal of Nicholas Cresswell*, 43–44.

78 "carried me through": William Smith to Jeremiah Morgan, April 3, 1766, Fauquier Papers, 3:1351–1352.

78 "universally condemned": Rind, *Virginia Gazette*, August 25, 1774.

79 "Lord Feathers": James Parker to James Steuart, December 6, 1774, Charles Steuart Papers, National Library of Scotland, Edinburgh, Scotland.

79 "lives were": James R. Fichter, "The Mystery of 'the Alternative of Williams-Burg,'" *Journal of the American Revolution*, April 22, 2019, https://allthingsliberty.com/2019/04/the-mystery-of-the-alternative-of-williams-burg/.

79 "entirely disregarded": David, "Dunmore's New World," 167.

80 "very dim-sighted": Dixon and Hunter, *Virginia Gazette*, March 18, 1775.

81 "of gunpowder or any": Force, *American Archives*, 1:881.

81 "take the most": ibid.

82 "dinner alone.": George Washington, "Diary Entry: 19 January 1775," January 19, 1775, *Founders Online*, National Archives, https://founders.archives.gov/documents/Washington/01-03-02-0005-0001-0019.

83 "warming machine": Graham Hood, *The Williamsburg Collection of Antique Furnishings* (Williamsburg, VA: Colonial Williamsburg Foundation, 1978), 9.

83 "near 100 dishes": Graham Hood, *The Governor's Palace in Williamsburg: A Cultural Study* (Williamsburg, VA: Colonial Williamsburg Foundation, 1992), 169.

83 "until his Majesty's": Dixon and Hunter, *Virginia Gazette*, January 19, 1775.

84 "There is no time": William Cobbett, *Parliamentary History of England from the Earliest Period to the Year 1803*, vol. 18, 1774–1777 (London: T. C. Hansard, 1814), 149.

Chapter Seven: My Right Well-Beloved Cousin

85 "The cherry buds": George Washington, "Memm. [March 1775]," *Founders Online*, National Archives, https://founders.archives.gov/documents/Washington/01-03-02-0005-0007.

85 "collection of villages": John Peyton Little, *History of Richmond* (Richmond, VA: Dietz Printing Company, 1933), 55.

85 "most ardent wish": W. F. Dunaway Jr., "The Virginia Conventions of the Revolution," *Virginia Law Register* 10, no. 7 (Nov. 1904): 574.

85 "animated debate": *RV*, 2:366 and 69, n. 8.

86 "immediately into a posture": ibid.

86 "a distraught": Robert Douthat Meade, *Patrick Henry: Patriot in the Making: Practical Revolutionary* (Philadelphia: Lippincott, 1969), 473.

86 "Every word he": Charles Wells Moulton, *The Library of Literary Criticism of English and American Authors* (Buffalo, NY: Moulton Publishing, 1902), 351.

86 "It is natural": William Wirt Henry, *Patrick Henry; Life, Correspondence and Speeches*, 262.

86 "totally disarmed": ibid., 265.

86 "There is no": ibid., 266.

87 "Is life so": William Wirt Henry, *Sketches of the Life and Character of Patrick Henry* (Ithaca, NY: Andrus, Gauntlett, 1850), 94.

87 "an imaginary": *RV*, 2:369.

87 "I know not": Henry, *Sketches of the Life and Character of Patrick Henry*, 94.

87 "he plunged": *RV*, 2:369.

87 "repel the invaders": ibid., 2:366 and 69, n. 8.

87 "prepare a plan": George Washington, "Diary entry: 23 March 1775," March 23, 1775, *Founders Online*, National Archives, https://founders.archives.gov/documents/Washington/01-03-02-0005-0005-0023.

87 "for his truly": *RV*, 2:376.

88 "no right to": Thomas Jefferson, "Draft of Instructions to the Virginia Delegates in the Continental Congress," July 1774, *Founders Online*, National Archives, https://founders.archives.gov/documents/Jefferson/01-01-02-0090.

88 "has rather the air": 37. Cogliano, *A Revolutionary Friendship*, 37.

89 "disgrace even": Isaac William Stuart, *Life of Jonathan Trumbull, Sen., Governor of Connecticut* (Boston: Crocker and Brewster, 1859), 175.

89 "depraved, malignant": David M. Roth, *Connecticut's War Governor: Jonathan Trumbull* (Essex, CT: Globe Pequot, 2017), 68.

89 "the first of the": George Washington, "From George Washington to Jonathan Trumbull, Jr.," October 1, 1785, *Founders Online*, National Archives, https://founders.archives.gov/documents/Washington/04-03-02-0257.

89 "right trusted": James Phillip Rife, "'So Calamitous a Situation': The Causes and Course of Dunmore's War, 1744–1774," (master's thesis, Virginia Polytechnic Institute and State University, 1999), 80.

90 "unwarrantable proceedings": John Pinkney, *Virginia Gazette*, March 30, 1775.

90 "Had the above": Purdie, *Virginia Gazette*, March 31, 1775 (supplement).

91 "Would anyone believe": Patrick Henry, "Patrick Henry to Robert Pleasants," January 18, 1773, in *The Founders' Constitution*, vol. 1, ch. 15, doc. 7, accessed January 11, 2024, http://press-pubs.uchicago.edu/founders/documents/v1ch15s7.html.

91 "We have no": "Felix's Petition for Freedom," January 6, 1773, wwnorton.com, accessed April 18, 2024, https://wwnorton.com/college/history/america7_brief/content/multimedia/ch06/research_01a.htm.

91 "We have in common": Jared Ross Hardesty, *Unfreedom: Slavery and Dependence in Eighteenth-Century Boston* (New York: New York University Press, 2018), 170.

91 "Would you desire": Ceasar Sarter, *Essex Journal*, August 17, 1774.

91 "will make us as tame": "George Washington to Bryan Fairfax," August 24, 1774, *Founders Online*, National Archives, https://founders.archives.gov/GEWN-02-10-02-0097.

92 "the constant example": Charles S. Hyneman and Donald S. Lutz, *American Political Writing During the Founding Era 1760-1805* (Indianapolis, IN: Liberty Press, 1983), 934.

92 "they would fight": Abigail Adams, "Abigail Adams to John Adams," September 22, 1774, *Founders Online*, National Archives, https://founders.archives.gov/documents/Adams/04-01-02-0107.

92 "confessed that their": *New-York Journal*, March 2, 1775.

92 "We are to set": Frank Moore, *The Diary of the Revolution* (Hartford, CT: J. B. Burr, 1876), 124.

92 "some disturbance": Robert G. Parkinson, *The Common Cause: Creating Race and Nation in the American Revolution* (Chapel Hill: University of North Carolina Press, 2016), 81.

92 "unhappy wretches": James Madison, "From James Madison to William Bradford," November 26, 1774, *Founders Online*, National Archives, https://founders.archives.gov/documents/Madison/01-01-02-0037.

92 "If America and": ibid.

93 "Your fear with": William Bradford, "To James Madison from William Bradford," January 4, 1775, *Founders Online*, National Archives, https://founders.archives.gov/documents/Madison/01-01-02-0038.

93 "emancipating your": Arthur Lee, December 6, 1774, Lee Family Papers, 1638–1867, Virginia Historical Society, Richmond, Virginia.

93 "humbling the high": Edmund Burke, "The Speech of Edmund Burke, Esq; on Moving His Resolutions for Conciliation with the Colonies," March 22, 1775, Eighteenth Century Collections Online, accessed January 11, 2024, https://quod.lib.umich.edu/e/ecco/004895777.0001.000/1:3?rgn=div1;view=fulltext.

93 "The people with": George Livermore, *An Historical Research Respecting the Opinions of the Founders of the Republic on Negroes as Slaves, as Citizens, and as Soldiers Read Before the Massachusetts Historical Society*, Boston: New-England Loyal Publication Society, 1863), 169.

93 "I am informed": William Lee, *Letters of William Lee: Sheriff and Alderman of London; Commercial Agent of the Continental Congress in France; and Minister to the Courts of Vienna and Berlin, 1766–1783* (London: Historical Printing Club, 1891), 1:143.

94 "We patrol and go": Woody Holton, *Forced Founders: Indians, Debtors, Slaves, and the Making of the American Revolution in Virginia* (Chapel Hill: University of North Carolina Press, 1999), 141.

94 "a parcel of": Michael A. McDonnell, *The Politics of War: Race, Class, and Conflict in Revolutionary Virginia* (Chapel Hill: University of North Carolina Press, 2007), 49.

94 "about fifteen": Pinkney, *Virginia Gazette*, March 30, 1775.

Chapter Eight: The Smoldering Spirit of Revolt

95 "for the avowed": Thomas Gage, "Thomas Gage to Lieut. Colonel Smith," April 18, 1775, Digital History, accessed January 10, 2024, https://www

.digitalhistory.uh.edu/active_learning/explorations/revolution/account2_lexington.cfm.

96 "a large number": McIlwaine and Kennedy, eds., *Journals of the House of Burgesses of Virginia: 1619–1776*, 13:223–4.

96 "made me think": William Clark, ed., *Naval Documents of the American Revolution* (Annapolis, MD: US Department of the Navy, 1964), 1:259. (hereafter cited as *NDAR*)

97 "a great commotion": William Pasteur, "Deposition of Dr. William Pasteur In regard to the Removal of Powder from the Williamsburg Magazine," *Virginia Magazine of History and Biography* 13, no 1 (Jul. 1905): 49.

97 "many of them": ibid.

97 "continued threats": *NDAR*, 1:259.

97 "humbly": "Municipal Hall to Governor Dunmore, An Humble Address," April 21, 1775, in *RV*, 3:54–55.

98 "some disturbance": Edmund Pendleton, "To George Washington from Edmund Pendleton," April 21, 1775, *Founders Online*, National Archives, https://founders.archives.gov/documents/Washington/02-10-02-0265.

98 "milder in terms": *NDAR*, 1:259.

98 "saw no further": Pasteur, "Deposition of Dr. William Pasteur," 49.

98 "had a strong": Pendleton, "To George Washington from Edmund Pendleton," April 21, 1775.

99 "suspicion of": Norfolk County Minute Book, March 17, 1774–November 11, 1775, Court Proceedings, Clerk's Office, Chesapeake, VA.

99 "practice physic": Mary A. Stephenson, "Apothecary Historical Report, Block 30-2 Building 13G," Colonial Williamsburg Foundation Library, November 1949, https://research.colonialwilliamsburg.org/DigitalLibrary/view/index.cfm?doc=ResearchReports%5CRR0008.xml&highlight=.

99 "exceedingly exasperated": Pasteur, "Deposition of Dr. William Pasteur," 49.

100 "swore by the living": ibid.

100 "fix up the royal": John Randolph, "Deposition of John Randolph in Regard to the Removal of the Powder," *Virginia Magazine of History and Biography* 15, no 2 (Oct. 1907): 149.

100 "had lost the confidence": "Testimony of Benjamin Waller," in McIlwaine and Kennedy, eds., *Journals of the House of Burgesses of Virginia, 1619–1776*, 5:232.

101 "You will see": McDonnell, *The Politics of War*, 66.

101 "an insult to every": Pinkney, *Virginia Gazette*, April 28, 1775 (supplement).

101 "has justly forfeited": Purdie, *Virginia Gazette*, June 2, 1775.

101 "the monstrous": *South Carolina Gazette*, June 6, 1775.

101 "entertained ideas": John Drayton, *Memoirs of the American Revolution* (Charleston, SC: A. E. Miller, 1821), 1:231.

101 "The Negroes have": John Adams, "1775. Sept. 24. Sunday." *Founders Online*, National Archives, https://founders.archives.gov/documents/Adams/01-02-02-0005-0003.

102 "embrace this opportunity": *NDAR*, 1:215.

102 "public insult": Spotsylvania Independent Company, "To George Washington from Spotsylvania Independent Company," April 26, 1775, *Founders Online*, National Archives, https://founders.archives.gov/documents/Washington/02-10-02-0271.

103 "if a large body": William Pasteur, deposition, quoted in "Committee on the Late Disturbances, report," June 14, 1774, in *Journals of the House of Burgesses of Virginia, 1773–1776*, McIlwaine and Kennedy, eds, 231.

103 "being heavy": Thomas Jefferson, "Enclosure: Thomas Jefferson's Biography of Peyton Randolph (ca. 1723–75), [ca. 26 July 1816]," *Founders Online*, National Archives, https://founders.archives.gov/documents/Jefferson/03-10-02-0158-0002.

103 "that upwards of": *Pennsylvania Evening Post*, May 9, 1775.

104 "a candid relation": *RV*, 3:63.

104 "His Excellency": Philip Alexander Bruce and William Glover Stanard, "Virginia Legislative Papers," *Virginia Magazine of History and Biography* 13 (1905): 50.

104 "without provocation": ibid.

104 "I have spoken": Purdie, *Virginia Gazette*, April 29, 1775.

105 "well armed and": Purdie, *Virginia Gazette*, May 12, 1775.

105 "a council of": "Proceedings of a Council in Fredericksburg," April 29, 1775, in Pinkney, *Virginia Gazette*, May 11, 1775.

105 "peaceable measures": *RV*, 3:70–71.

105 "I am extremely": Alexander Spotswood, "To George Washington from Alexander Spotswood," April 30, 1775, *Founders Online*, National Archives, https://founders.archives.gov/documents/Washington/02-10-02-0276.

106 "incredible": George Washington, "From George Washington to Lord Dunmore," April 3, 1775, *Founders Online*, National Archives, https://founders.archives.gov/documents/Washington/02-10-02-0247.

106 "I despair of it": George Washington, "From George Washington to John Dickinson," April 13, 1775, *Founders Online*, National Archives, https://founders.archives.gov/documents/Washington/02-10-02-0261.

106 "a pusillanimity little comporting": James Madison, "From James Madison to William Bradford," May 9, 1775, *Founders Online*, National Archives, https://founders.archives.gov/documents/Madison/01-01-02-0044.

107 "If this is the case": John Murray, "To George Washington from Lord Dunmore," April 18, 1775, *Founders Online*, National Archives, https://founders.archives.gov/documents/Washington/02-10-02-0262.

Chapter Nine: Virginia's Rubicon

108 "He has fortified": Parker to Steuart, May 6, 1775, Charles Steuart Collection.

108 "The inhabitants of most": *NDAR*, 1:258.

108 "make an effectual": *NDAR*, 10:175.
109 "one of the large ships": *NDAR*, 1:257.
109 "be effected without force" ibid, 1:259.
110 "Commotions and insurrections": *RV*, 3:77.
110 "Mr. Page,": ibid., 3:86.
110 "You may in vain": Patrick Henry, *Patrick Henry in His Speeches and Writings and in the Words of His Contemporaries*, ed. James M. Elson (Lynchburg VA: Warwick House, 2007), 83.
111 "believed at the": Randolph, *History of Virginia*, 219.
111 "there being some": William E. White, "The Independent Companies of Virginia, 1774–1775," *Virginia Magazine of History and Biography* 86, no. 2 (Apr. 1978): 158.
111 "spread before their eyes": William Wirt Henry, *Patrick Henry; Life, Correspondence and Speeches*, 138.
112 "all men of property": Purdie, *Virginia Gazette*, May 5, 1775.
112 "the many innocent": John Burk, Skelton Jones, and Louis Hue Girardin, *History of Virginia: From Its First Settlement to the Present Day, 4 vols.*, (Petersburg, VA: Dickson & Pescud, 1816), 4:3.
112 "at daybreak": *NDAR*, 1:280.
112 "defending myself": ibid, 1:259.
112 "armed his servants": Burk, Jones, and Girardin, *History of Virginia*, 3:403.
112 "parties of Negroes": ibid, 409.
113 "now settled.": ibid., 403.
113 "did actually bully": William Cabell Rives, *History of the Life and Times of James Madison* (Boston: Little, Brown, 1859), 1:94.
113 "a spirit of cruelty": Dixon and Hunter, *Virginia Gazette*, May 6, 1775.
113 "a great number": ibid.
113 "abhorrence of": Force, *American Archives*, 2:525.
113 "not to aid": *NDAR*, 1:290.
113 "gained him great honor": James Madison, "From James Madison to William Bradford," May 9, 1775, *Founders Online*, National Archives, https://founders.archives.gov/documents/Madison/01-01-02-0044.
114 "Even in the place": *NDAR*, 1:341.
114 "appears so very alarming": Thomas Gage, "General Thomas Gage to William Legge, Lord Dartmouth," May 15, 1775, *NDAR*, accessed January 8, 2024, https://www.ndar-history.org/?q=node/699.
114 "Gage's ignorance about": Nick Bunker, *An Empire on the Edge: How Britain Came to Fight America* (New York: Vintage Books, 2015), 290.
114 "might be of some": *NDAR*, 1:338.
114 "We hear by private": ibid.
114 "offered to join": Pinkney, *Virginia Gazette*, May 4, 1775.
114 "to go about": John Randolph, "Deposition of John Randolph in Regard to the Removal of the Powder," 150.

114 "The rebels are called": NDAR, 3:622.

115 "any club, staff": *Acts of Assembly, Passed in the Colony of Virginia: From 1662, to 1715* (London: John Baskett, printer to the King's most excellent majesty, 1727), 1:136.

115 "the most speedy": Robert Bissett, *The History of the Reign of George III: To the Termination* (Albany, NY: B. D. Packard, 1816), 529.

115 "conciliatory resolution": William MacDonald, ed., "No. 48. Report on Lord North's Conciliatory Resolution," *Documentary Source Book of American History, 1606–1913* (New York: Macmillan, 1916), 184–188.

115 "I would make": Rhys Isaac, *The Transformation of Virginia, 1740–1790* (Chapel Hill: University of North Carolina Press, 1982), 259.

116 "It is no longer": Kennedy, ed., *Journals of the House of Burgesses of Virginia, 1619–1776*, 5:xxiii.

116 "great joy of": Purdie, *Virginia Gazette,* May 12, 1775 (supplement).

116 "Such a scene": Dixon and Hunter, *Virginia Gazette*, June 3, 1775.

116 "a pompous military": *NDAR*, 1:259.

116 "other respectable": Pinkney, *Virginia Gazette*, June 1, 1775.

117 "I have called": Dixon and Hunter, *Virginia Gazette*, June 3, 1775.

117 "convivial banquets": Theodorick Bland, *The Bland Papers* (Carlisle, MA: Applewood Books, 2009), 43.

117 "his most catholic": Pinkney, *Virginia Gazette*, May 25, 1775.

118 "was frostbitten": Kennedy, ed., *Journals of the House of Burgesses of Virginia, 1619–1776*, 5:184.

118 "unlawful concourse": Isaac, *Transformation of Virginia*, 196.

118 "was very much lacerated": Burk, Jones, and Girardin, *History of Virginia*, 4:25.

118 "The cry among": *NDAR*, 1:259.

119 "the barrels very": Lyon Gardiner Tyler, *Tyler's Quarterly Historical and Genealogical Magazine* (1941), 22:136.

119 "totally destroyed": McIlwaine and Kennedy, eds., *Journals of the House of Burgesses of Virginia, 1619–1776*, 13:224.

119 "blow up the": Pinkney, *Virginia Gazette*, June 8, 1775.

119 "thanks for his kind": McIlwaine and Kennedy, eds., *Journals of the House of Burgesses of Virginia, 1619–1776*, 13:199.

Chapter Ten: Black as an Ethiop

121 "now fully persuaded": McIlwaine and Kennedy, eds., *Journals of the House of Burgesses of Virginia, 1619–1776, 13*:206.

121 "His Excellency": ibid, 13:207.

121 "impracticable": ibid, 13:207.

121 "no doubt some": Parker to Steuart, June 27, 1775, MS 5029, f. 89. 5, Charles Steuart Collection, Scotland National Library, Edinburgh, Scotland.

122 "some foolish": Burdelle Caley, "Dunmore: Colonial Governor of New York and Virginia," (PhD diss., University of Pittsburgh, 1939), 506.

122 "it was from": John Adams, "Notes of Debates, Continued Oct. 6. (from the Diary of John Adams)," October 6, 1775, *Founders Online*, National Archives, https://founders.archives.gov/documents/Adams/01-02-02-0005-0004-0003.

122 "Daniel, a Negro": McIlwaine and Kennedy, eds., *Journals of the House of Burgesses of Virginia, 1619–1776*, 13:224.

123 "At eleven a.m.": *NDAR*, 1:650.

123 "the pivot": Washington Irving, *Life of George Washington* (New York: G. P. Putnam and Company, 1855–1859), 5:563.

123 "Small as it is": John Murray, "Lord Dunmore to General Thomas Gage," June 17, 1775, Thomas Gage Papers, Clements Library, University of Michigan, Ann Arbor.

123 "I will return": McIlwaine and Kennedy, eds., *Journals of the House of Burgesses of Virginia, 1619–1776*, 13:215.

124 "The British Parliament": Thomas Jefferson, "Virginia Resolutions on Lord North's Conciliatory Proposal," June 10, 1775, *Founders Online*, National Archives, https://founders.archives.gov/documents/Jefferson/01-01-02-0106.

124 "base deserters": ibid.

124 "We examined it": ibid.

125 "a reconciliation": McIlwaine and Kennedy, eds., *Journals of the House of Burgesses of Virginia, 1619–1776*, 13:236.

125 "for the preventing": *NDAR*, 1:710.

125 "a band of assassins": Parker to Steuart, June 12, 1775, Charles Steuart Collection.

125 "an improper place": *RV*, 3:21.

125 "some irregularities": McIlwaine and Kennedy, eds., *Journals of the House of Burgesses of Virginia, 1619–1776*, 13:258.

125 "a well-grounded": ibid.

125 "subjugate America": ibid, 13:256.

125 "It is imagined": James Madison, "From James Madison to William Bradford," June 19, 1775, *Founders Online*, National Archives, https://founders.archives.gov/documents/Madison/01-01-02-0047.

126 "No harum scarum": John Avlon, *Washington's Farewell: The Founding Father's Warning to Future Generations* (New York: Simon & Schuster, 2017), 116.

126 "immediate presence at home": McIlwaine and Kennedy, eds., *Journals of the House of Burgesses of Virginia, 1619–1776*, 13:279.

127 "A considerable body": *NDAR*, 1:259.

127 "We never imagined": Pinkney, *Virginia Gazette*, June 29, 1775.

127 "When the hurly-burly's": James Grahame, *The History of the United States of North America: From the Plantation of the British Colonies Till Their Assumption of National Independence* (Boston: C. C. Little & J. Brown, 1845), 4:50.

128 "He tried every stratagem": *NDAR*, 2:183.

128 "difficult to be": ibid, 1:259.

128 "to assist the citizens": *NDAR*, 1:873.

128 "any attempts that he": Richard Arthur Roberts, ed., *Calendar of Home Office Papers of the Reign of George III: 1773–1775* (London: Longman & Company and Trűbner & Company, 1899), 412.

128 "wantonly cutting": *NDAR*, 1:873.

129 "We had but just" ibid, 1:259.

129 "within three or four minutes": Roberts, *Calendar of Home Office Papers of the Reign of George III*, 412.

129 "no injury was": Benjamin Harrison, "To George Washington from Benjamin Harrison," July 21–24, 1775, *Founders Online*, National Archives, https://founders.archives.gov/documents/Washington/03-01-02-0088.

129 "A servant, who": *NDAR*, 1:873.

129 "If the head of": James Parker to Charles Steuart, April 14, 1775, Charles Steuart Papers, National Library of Scotland, Edinburgh, Scotland.

130 "full of men": *NDAR*, 1:872

130 "The men are": ibid, 1:873.

130 "The great scarcity": George Washington, "From George Washington to John Hancock," July 14, 1775, *Founders Online*, National Archives, https://founders.archives.gov/documents/Washington/03-01-02-0065.

130 "What he now procured": *NDAR*, 1:337.

130 "a few pales": ibid., 1:886.

130 "Negro slaves": Pinkney, *Virginia Gazette*, July 13, 1775.

131 "harbor the slaves": *NDAR*, 1:1130.

131 "We have not": Purdie, *Virginia Gazette*, July 14, 1775.

131 "not to be contradicted": Ivor Noël Hume, *1775; Another Part of the Field* (New York: Knopf, 1966), 267.

131 "Lord Dunmore is": Jonathan H. Poston, "Ralph Wormeley V of Rosegill: A Deposed Virginia Aristocrat," (master's thesis, College of William and Mary, 1979), 47.

Part Two

Chapter Eleven: Lieutenant Governor of Gosport

138 "Williamsburg did well": *NDAR*, 1:294.

138 "broad stairs of": Ernest M. Eller, *Chesapeake Bay in the American Revolution* (Centreville, MD: Tidewater Publishers, 1981), 69.

139 "scandalous": Nellie Norkus, *Francis Fauquier, Lieutenant-governor of Virginia, 1758–1768: A Study in Colonial Problems* (Pittsburgh, PA: University of Pittsburgh, 1977), 223.

139 "cuts as droll": John Mason and Frances Norton, eds., *Merchants of London and Virginia*, 2nd ed. (Devon, UK: Newton Abbot, 1968), 76.

139 "in the winter": Kevin Phillips, *1775: A Good Year for Revolution* (New York: Penguin, 2013), 408.

140 "No one does anything": *RV*, 3:303–304.

140 "If we permit": Michael L. Nicholls, *Aspects of the African American Experience in Eighteenth-Century Williamsburg and Norfolk*, Colonial Williamsburg Foundation Library Research Report Series – 330 (Williamsburg, VA: Colonial Williamsburg Foundation Library, 1991), 103.

140 "an old, shattered": Henry King Carroll, *The Francis Asbury Centenary Volume: The Makers and Making of American Methodism, the Customs, Morals, and Social Conditions of the Pioneer Days, Drawn from the Best Historical Sources* (Nashville, TN: Methodist Book Concern, 1916), 60.

141 "lieutenant governor": *RV*, 3:303–304.

141 "lands in the": *The Proceedings of the Convention of Delegates for the Counties and Corporations in the Colony of Virginia, Held at Richmond Town, in the County of Henrico, on the 20th of March 1775* (Richmond, VA: Ritchie, Trueheart & Du-Val, 1816), 4.

141 "set fire to the": *RV*, 3:323.

141 "a sufficient armed": *Proceedings of the Convention of Delegates for the Counties and Corporations in the Colony of Virginia*, 5.

142 "consisted entirely": Kate Mason Rowland, *The Life of George Mason, 1725–1792* (New York: G. P. Putnam's Sons, 1892), 1:195.

142 "Gone": Michael A. McDonnell, "Popular Mobilization and Political Culture in Revolutionary Virginia: The Failure of the Minutemen and the Revolution from Below," *Journal of American History* 85, no. 3 (Dec. 1998): 956.

142 "shilly shally . . .": Lund Washington, "To George Washington from Lund Washington," February 29, 1776, *Founders Online*, National Archives, https://founders.archives.gov/documents/Washington/03-03-02-0286.

142 "many insults": William Byrd, *The Correspondence of the Three William Byrds of Westover, Virginia, 1684–1776* (Charlottesville: Virginia Historical Society, 1977), 2:812.

142 "the ravages of": Force, *American Archives*, 1:542.

142 "truly alarmed": *RV*, 3:322.

142 "totally devoid of": William Henry Stewart, *History of Norfolk County, Virginia, and Representative Citizens* (Chesapeake, VA: Biographical Publishing Company, 1902), 352.

142 "the time may come": ibid., 353.

142 "a fear to offend": Michael Cecere, "Williamsburg Becomes an Armed Camp, 1775," *Journal of the American Revolution*, June 16, 2020, https://allthingsliberty.com/2020/06/williamsburg-becomes-and-armedcamp-1775/.

143 "The independent companies": Parker to Steuart, August 4, 1775, Charles Steuart Papers, National Library of Scotland, Edinburgh, Scotland.

143 "very laudable": *RV,* 3:362.

143 "wild irregular sallies": McDonnell, "Popular Mobilization and Political Culture in Revolutionary Virginia," 962.

144 "Hampton town": Joseph R. Frese, "The Royal Customs Service in the Chesapeake, 1770: The Reports of John Williams, Inspector General," *Virginia Magazine of History and Biography* 81, no. 3 (Jul. 1973): 314.

144 "intelligence concerning": *NDAR*, 1:938.

144 "always appeared": ibid.

145 "His happy talent": John Adams, "From John Adams to Timothy Pickering," August 6, 1822, *Founders Online*, National Archives, https://founders.archives.gov/documents/Adams/99-02-02-7674.

145 "ambitious designs of separating": "A Declaration by the Representatives of the United Colonies of North-America, Now Met in Congress at Philadelphia, Setting Forth the Causes and Necessity of Their Taking Up Arms," The Avalon Project, accessed January 12, 2024, https://avalon.law.yale.edu/18th_century/arms.asp.

145 "brother the Big Knife": *RV*, 3:214.

145 "a committee of": John Connolly, "A Narrative of the Transactions, Imprisonment, and Sufferings of John Connolly, an American Loyalist and Lieut. Col. in His Majesty's Service," *Pennsylvania Magazine of History and Biography* 12, no. 3 (Oct. 1888): 315.

145 "in the most open": Percy B. Caley, "The Life Adventures of Lieutenant-Colonel John Connolly: The Story of a Tory," *Western Pennsylvania Historical Magazine* (1928): 106.

145 "secretly frustrated": F. R. Diffenderffer, "Col. John Connolly," *Journal of the Lancaster County Historical Society* 7, no. 6 (1902–3): 117.

145 "a large belt of": Connolly, "A Narrative of the Transactions, Imprisonment, and Sufferings of John Connolly," 316.

146 "I have finished": Philip Alexander Bruce and William Glover Stanard, "Virginia Legislative Papers," *Virginia Magazine of History and Biography* 13 (1905): 79.

146 "a ministerial tool": Caley, "Life Adventures of Lieutenant-Colonel John Connolly," 109.

146 "inflammatory and": Connolly, "A Narrative of the Transactions, Imprisonment, and Sufferings of John Connolly," 323.

146 "immediately obtained": ibid.

146 "Proposals for raising": Daniel Wunderlich Nead, *The Pennsylvania-German in the Settlement of Maryland* (Lancaster, PA: Press of the New Era Printing Company, 1913), 264.

147 "such serviceable": Caley, "Life Adventures of Lieutenant-Colonel John Connolly," 148.

147 "This would not only": John Connolly, "Narrative of John Connolly, Loyalist," *Pennsylvania Magazine of History and Biography* 12, no 4 (1889): 407.

147 "such troops as": Caley, "Life Adventures of Lieutenant-Colonel John Connolly," 149.

148 "Our foolish men": Force, *American Archives*, 3:72.

148 "many of the more western": Dixon and Hunter, *Virginia Gazette*, August 26, 1775.

148 "to induce them": Purdie, *Virginia Gazette*, September 8, 1775.

148 "to see the Indians": *RV*, 4:291.

Chapter Twelve: The First Law of Nature

149 "He was not handsome": James, *The Lower Norfolk County Virginia Antiquary*, 2:137.

149 "under no apprehensions": *NDAR*, 1:947.

149 "protect the property": *RV*, 3:431, 443.

149 "a number of slaves" *RV*, 3:385, 453.

150 "this town and": *NDAR*, 1:1048.

150 "ill-treated": *Norfolk Intelligencer*, July 5, 1775; August 16, 1775.

150 "Last week several": *NDAR*, 1:1162.

150 "The governor of": McDonnell, *The Politics of War*, 86.

150 "a new government": *NDAR*, 1:1046.

151 "furnish themselves": *RV*, 3:407.

151 "sincere repentance": ibid., 3:414.

151 "beat and bruised": ibid., 3:286

151 "The populace were": *RV*, 3:420.

152 "a severe fever": Adele Hast, *Loyalism in Revolutionary Virginia: The Norfolk Area and the Eastern Shore* (Ann Arbor, MI: UMI Research Press, 1982), 65.

152 "Suppose yourselves": *RV*, 3:433.

152 "Such accusations": *NDAR*, 1:1130.

152 "give great offense": *RV*, 3:452.

153 "a letter of thanks": ibid., 3:474.

153 "wench of forty": Graham Russell Hodges, *Slavery and Freedom Among Early American Workers* (New York: Routledge, 2016), 66.

153 "commands an ignorant": *RV*, 3:385.

154 "stumps and roots": Pinkney, *Virginia Gazette*, August 24, 1775.

154 "of daring and": Thomas Jefferson, *The Writings of Thomas Jefferson: Correspondence, cont* (Washington, DC: Taylor & Maury, 1854), 442.

154 "It is likely he" Purdie, *Virginia Gazette*, August 4, 1775.

154 "their mortal enemy": *NDAR*, 1:1064.

154 "It is our desire,": *RV*, 3:385.

154 "for the defense and": ibid., 395.

154 "We are of as many": McDonnell, *The Politics of War*, 99.

154 "I never was in such": George Mason, "To George Washington from George Mason," October 14, 1775, *Founders Online*, National Archives, https://founders.archives.gov/documents/Washington/03-02-02-0156.

155 "very unfit to be": Moses Coit Tyler, *Patrick Henry* (Boston: Houghton, Mifflin, 1899), 185.

155 "He was chosen": Henry Mayer, *A Son of Thunder: Patrick Henry and the American Republic* (New York: Grove, 2007), 270.

155 "My countrymen made": George Washington, "From George Washington to Lieutenant Colonel Joseph Reed," February 26–March 9, 1776, *Founders Online*, National Archives, https://founders.archives.gov/documents/Washington/03-03-02-0274.

155 "he was met and": Moses Coit Tyler, *Patrick Henry* (Boston: Houghton, Mifflin, 1896), 156.

156 "an old man, almost": Force, *American Archives*, 3:379–380.

156 "the first order": David John Mays, *Edmund Pendleton, 1721–1803: A Biography* (Cambridge, MA: Harvard University Press, 1952), 2:126.

156 "cool, smooth and": ibid., 130.

156 "the worst form": ibid., 131.

156 "not an inclination": *Letters of Delegates to Congress, 1774–1789: August 1774–August 1775* (Washington, DC: Library of Congress, 1976), 403.

156 "rash measures without": McDonnell, *The Politics of War*, 68.

156 "very injurious to": ibid., 70.

157 "intends soon to put": Purdie, *Virginia Gazette*, August 11, 1775.

157 "Lord Dunmore was meditating": *NDAR*, 1:1147.

157 "whether the king may": *Proceedings of the Convention of Delegates for the Counties and Corporations in the Colony of Virginia*, 17.

157 "his repeated and horrible": ibid., 28.

157 "I can hardly think": George Washington, "From George Washington to Lund Washington," August 20, 1775, *Founders Online*, National Archives, https://founders.archives.gov/documents/Washington/03-01-02-0234.

158 "You may depend": Lund Washington, "To George Washington from Lund Washington," October 5, 1775, *Founders Online*, National Archives, https://founders.archives.gov/documents/Washington/03-03-02-0274.ibid.

158 "Englishmen, and more": *Publications of the Navy Records Society* (London: Navy Records Society, 1926), 60:250.

158 "the very cement": John Laffin, *Jack Tar: The Story of the British Sailor* (London: Cassell, 1969), 88.

159 "a fashionable suit": *RV*, 3:485.

159 "unjustly censured": *NDAR*, 1:1130.

159 "I confess I feel": ibid., 1:1148.

159 "alarm and intimidate": ibid., 1:1198.

Chapter Thirteen: Terror of Oyster Boats and Canoes

161 "Many vessels": *Norfolk Intelligencer*, September 6, 1775

162 "only one vessel": Parker to Steuart, September 25, 1775, Charles Steuart Collection.

162 "one of the severest": *Norfolk Intelligencer*, September 6, 1775.

162 "strong gales": *NDAR*, 1:1296.

162 "We had to turn": William F. Stark, *The Last Time Around Cape Horn: The Historic 1949 Voyage of the Windjammer Pamir* (New York: Basic Books, 2009), 176.

162 "violent hard squalls": *NDAR*, 1:1296.

162 "all as snug": ibid.

163 "She being in great": ibid.

163 "Lord Dunmore, it seems": Pinkney, *Virginia Gazette*, September 7, 1775.

163 "had very near": ibid.

164 "small mulatto": *RV*, 3:122.

164 "like scrolls of parchment": Rick Schwartz, *Hurricanes and the Middle Atlantic States* (Dehradun, Uttarakhand, India: Blue Diamond Books, 2007), 44.

164 "much heavy rain": ibid., 45.

164 "every soul on board": Tony Williams, *Hurricane of Independence: The Untold Story of the Deadly Storm at the Deciding Moment of the American Revolution* (Naperville, IL: Sourcebooks, 2009), 35.

164 "securing the rigging": Dixon and Hunter, *Virginia Gazette*, September 9, 1775.

164 "harboring gentlemen's": Purdie, *Virginia Gazette*, September 8, 1775.

165 "During the gale": *NDAR*, 2:4.

165 "irrecoverably gone": ibid., 2:42.

165 "made great destruction": *Norfolk Intelligencer*, September 6, 1775.

165 "Houses were blown": Francis Asbury, *Journal of Rev. Francis Asbury: Bishop of the Methodist Episcopal Church* (New York: Lane & Scott, 1852), 1:162.

165 "Everything at home": Carmeline V. Zimmer, ed., *Selected Letters from the Parker Family Papers; The Correspondence of Margaret Parker* (Norfolk, VA: ODU Publications, 1977), 59.

166 "one of the most active": "Wilson-Miles Cary," Library of Virginia, accessed April 25, 2024, https://www.lva.virginia.gov/public/dvb/bio.asp?b=Cary_Wilson-Miles.

166 "two of my neighbors": *NDAR*, 2:17.

167 "And there may": ibid., 2:56.

167 "At four began to": ibid., 2:42.

167 "anchored abreast": ibid., 2:54.

167 "a very artful": ibid., 2: 85.

167 "disagreeable": ibid., 2:72.

168 "the service of their": *Norfolk Intelligencer*, September 6, 1775.

168 "the crimes daily": *Norfolk Intelligencer*, September 20, 1775.
168 "a saucy coward": Pinkney, *Virginia Gazette*, September 14, 1775.
168 "the terror of Norfolk": *NDAR*, 2:173.
168 "the people of Hampton": ibid., 2:74.
169 "the several slaves": ibid., 2:111.
169 "a pillaging or": ibid., 2:123.
169 "Joseph Harris": ibid., 2:125.
169 "the impudence of": ibid., 2:167.
169 "a servant of": ibid., 2:111.
170 "we shall cease": *Norfolk Intelligencer*, August 30, 1775.
170 "many falsities": *NDAR*, 2:56.
170 "an old woman or two": ibid., 2:154.
170 "too free with people": Parker to Steuart, October 2, 1775, Charles Steuart Collection.
171 "desist in his personal": *RV*, 4:156.
171 "inflaming the minds": ibid., 4:345.
171 "five hundred spectators": ibid.
172 "all the types and every": *NDAR*, 2:257.
172 "After getting to": ibid., 2:342.
172 "It was prostitute": *RV*, 4:337.
172 "were beating to arms": ibid., 4:345.
172 "spirited gentlemen": *NDAR*, 2:343.
172 "but these were all": ibid., 2:267.
172 "landed in the most": ibid., 2:258.
173 "We have ever preserved": ibid.
173 "poisoning the minds": ibid., 2:259.
173 "to truth," ibid., 2:260.
173 "the public press": ibid., 2:316.
173 "fine new ship": Purdie, *Virginia Gazette*, August 25, 1775.
174 "so diabolical a scheme": *NDAR*, 2:343.
174 "some ink and paper": Parker to Steuart, October 9, 1775, Charles Steuart Collection.

Chapter Fourteen: Burn the Scoundrels

175 "We need not be tender": Clarence E. Carter, ed., *The Correspondence of General Thomas Gage with the Secretaries of State, 1763–1775* (New Haven, CT, 1931–1933), 1:403–404.
175 "cultivate the friendships": "Lernoult to Gage," May 14, 1775, American Series 128, April 23–May 14, 1775, Clements Library, University of Michigan, Ann Arbor.

176 "When my proposition": John Connolly, "A Narrative of the Transactions, Imprisonment, and Sufferings of John Connolly," 410.

176 "take arms against his": William Edward Hartpole Lecky, *A History of England in the Eighteenth Century* (London: Longmans, Green, 1923), 4:221.

176 "outrageous actions and rebellious": William Cowley, "To George Washington from William Cowley," September 30–October 12, 1775, *Founders Online*, National Archives, https://founders.archives.gov/documents/Washington/03-02-02-0063.

176 "a short fit of sickness": Connolly, "A Narrative of the Transactions, Imprisonment, and Sufferings of John Connolly," 410.

176 "Your good friend Lord": *NDAR*, 2:557.

177 "A small detachment entered": *New York Gazette and Weekly Mercury*, November 25, 1775.

177 "You will no doubt": Richard Henry Lee, "To George Washington from Richard Henry Lee," October 22–23, 1775, *Founders Online*, National Archives, https://founders.archives.gov/documents/Washington/03-02-02-0192.

178 "in the hearing of women": *NDAR*, 2:275.

178 "The situation of Norfolk": Purdie, *Virginia Gazette*, October 27, 1775.

178 "dared to offer violence": Pinkney, *Virginia Gazette*, October 19, 1775.

179 "the guardian deities": ibid.

180 "very threatening condition": John Adams, "John Adams diary 23, notes on Continental Congress, 22 [i.e., 23] September–25 October 1775," *Adams Family Papers*, Massachusetts Historical Society, accessed January 13, 2024, https://www.masshist.org/digitaladams/archive/doc?id=D23.

180 "the principal families": George Mason, "To George Washington from George Mason," October 14, 1775, *Founders Online*, National Archives, https://founders.archives.gov/documents/Washington/03-02-02-0156.

180 "Lord Dunmore has been": ibid., 23.

180 "Virginia is pierced": ibid.

181 "I look on the plan": ibid., 21.

181 "I wish he had": John Adams, "John Adams diary 23, notes on Continental Congress, 22 [i.e., 23] September–25 October 1775," 21.

181 "seizing the king's": ibid.

181 "they can't be more irritated": ibid., 22.

181 "He is fond of his": ibid., 21.

181 "it was from a reverence": ibid., 24.

181 "take such measures": ibid.

181 "Franklin is not dangerous": ibid., 22.

182 "An informer is such": *NDAR*, 2:266.

182 "No man can give": Parker to Steuart, October 8, 1775, Charles Steuart Collection.

183 “A villain has given”: *NDAR*, 2:465.

183 “sincere repentance.”: *NDAR* 3:618.

184 “a great quantity of artillery”: *NDAR*, 2:844.

184 Many people rode out”: Parker to Steuart, October 9, 1775, Charles Steuart Collection.

184 “Our men all went out”: D. R. Anderson, ed., “Letters of Colonel William Woodford, Colonel Robert Howe and Major-General Charles Lee,” *Richmond College Historical Papers* 1, no. 1 (June 1915): 1:98.

184 “A fine ditch”: Catesby Willis Stewart, *The Life of Brigadier General William Woodford of the American Revolution* (Richmond, VA: Whittet and Shepperson, 1973), 1:398.

184 “The captain then gave”: Parker to Steuart, October 9, 1775, Charles Steuart Collection.

185 “full of Dutch courage.”: Hume, *1775: Another Part of the Field*, 391.

185 “Is it thus you”: Anderson, ed., “Letters of Colonel William Woodford, 98.

185 “good many small arms”: *NDAR*, 2:1148.

185 “broke open a blacksmith’s shop”: *NDAR*, 2:545.

185 “Poor Robinson went”: Parker to Steuart, October 9, 1775, Charles Steuart Collection.

185 “delivered themselves up to”: *RV*, 4:35.

185 “turned king’s evidence,”: Parker to Steuart, October 9, 1775, Charles Steuart Collection.

186 “twenty pieces of cannon”: *NDAR*, 2:148.

186 “some powder”: ibid., 2:546.

186 “without the smallest opposition,”: ibid., 2:844.

186 “was done in the face of day”: “Extract of a Letter from Alexandria (Virginia),” in Force, *American Archives*, 3:1193, https://digital.lib.niu.edu/islandora/object/niu-amarch%3A102889.

186 “The people of this province”: *RV*, 4:344.

187 “As our situation”: *NDAR*, 2:844.

187 “half an army”: Gilbert, *Black Patriots and Loyalists*, 28.

187 “full of intelligence”: John Dalrymple, “Project for strengthening General Howe’s Operations in the North by a Diversion in the south, without taking off the Troops,” George Germain Papers, vol. 4, Clements Library, University of Michigan, Ann Arbor.

187 “the most agreeable situation”: *RV*, 4:379.

187 “Indeed, Gosport is the”: ibid., 304.

188 “The old gentleman”: ibid.

188 “formidable, outspoken, and educated”: John G. M. Sharp, “Andrew Sprowle, 1710–1776: ‘Lord of Gosport,’” USGenWeb Archives Project, accessed January 13, 2024, http://www.usgwarchives.net/va/portsmouth/shipyard/sharptoc/asprowle.html.

188 "a very bad woman": William Alexander, "To Benjamin Franklin from William Alexander," November 6, 1783, *Founders Online*, National Archives, https://founders.archives.gov/documents/Franklin/01-41-02-0126.

188 "very great folks": *RV*, 4:304.

188 "The officers of both army": ibid.

188 "well paid": ibid., 364.

188 "the only people we now": *RV*, 4:345–6.

Chapter Fifteen: A Most Disagreeable Step

191 "He has acquitted": "To Mrs Roberston of Lude from Janefield, August 3, 1775," courtesy of Corinne Dame at the Colonial Williamsburg Foundation.

191 "a great number of frigates": *NDAR*, 2:393.

191 "lined with crimson": ibid., 2:407.

191 "to put a stop to all": ibid., 2:465.

192 "olive branch": "The 'Olive Branch' Petition to King George III of England from the Second Continental Congress," 1775, New York Public Library Digital Collections. Accessed April 19, 2024. https://digitalcollections.nypl.org/items/af2242e0-7f2b-0132-7d52-58d385a7b928.

192 "open and avowed rebellion.": George III, "His Majesty's most gracious speech to both houses of Parliament, on Friday, October 27, 1775," broadside portfolio 108, no. 38, Library of Congress, accessed January 13, 2024, https://lccn.loc.gov/2020768864.

192 "A very considerable number": Donald L. Robinson, *Slavery in the Structure of American Politics, 1765–1820* (San Diego, CA: Harcourt Brace Jovanovich, 1970), 99.

192 "Every means of distressing America": George III, *The Correspondence of King George the Third from 1760 to December 1783: Printed from the Original Papers in the Royal Archives at Windsor Castle* (New York: Macmillan, 1928), 3:269.

192 "withdrawing himself unnecessarily": Force, *American Archives*, 3:1190.

193 "to march to the neighborhood": *RV*, 4:270.

193 "seemed as much afraid": Michael Cecere, "Williamsburg Becomes an Armed Camp, 1775," *Journal of the American Revolution*, June 10, 2020, https://allthingsliberty.com/2020/06/williamsburg-becomes-and-armed-camp-1775/.

193 "I hope the riflemen": Abigail Adams, "Abigail Adams to John Adams," March 31, 1776, *Founders Online*, National Archives, https://founders.archives.gov/documents/Adams/04-01-02-0241.

193 "More particularly, you": *RV*, 4:271.

193 "Two or three vessels of tolerable": Richard Henry Lee, "To George Washington from Richard Henry Lee," November 13, 1775, *Founders Online*, National Archives, https://founders.archives.gov/documents/Washington/03-02-02-0336.

194 "There are none of": *NDAR*, 2:1144.

194 "our affairs may, perhaps": Force, *American Archives*, 3:1067.

194 "Make no doubt,": *RV*, 4:279.

194 "took away a valuable Negro": *NDAR*, 2:630.

195 "So soon as the rebels": *NDAR*, 2:1309.

195 "The people were so": John Page, "To Thomas Jefferson from John Page," November 11, 1775, *Founders Online*, National Archives, https://founders.archives.gov/documents/Jefferson/01-01-02-0134.

196 "that he would that day": *NDAR*, 2:630.

196 "the people of the town": John Page, "To Thomas Jefferson from John Page," November 11, 1775, *Founders Online*, National Archives, https://founders.archives.gov/documents/Jefferson/01-01-02-0134.

196 "Lord Dunmore is well acquainted": Force, *American Archives*, 3:1191.

196 "is much afraid of the riflemen": *NDAR*, 2:465.

196 "directing them to fire from": ibid., 2:991.

197 "The fire was now general": John Page, "To Thomas Jefferson from John Page," November 11, 1775, *Founders Online*, National Archives, https://founders.archives.gov/documents/Jefferson/01-01-02-0134.

197 "found dead on the shore": *NDAR*, 2:1013.

197 "treated with great": Purdie, *Virginia Gazette*, November 3, 1775.

197 "banditti": Richard Henry Lee, "To George Washington from Richard Henry Lee," November 13, 1775, *Founders Online*, National Archives, https://founders.archives.gov/documents/Washington/03-02-02-0336.

197 "had not a man": *NDAR*, 11:631.

197 "the loss of the rebels": ibid., 2:1310.

197 "a few windows broke": Pinkney, *Virginia Gazette*, October 26, 1775.

198 "The troops in this town": ibid.

198 "Lord Dunmore may now": ibid.

198 "officers and soldiers": *NDAR*, 2:843.

198 "will in some measure": Robert Leroy Hilldrup, *The Life and Times of Edmund Pendleton* (Chapel Hill: University of North Carolina Press, 1939), 138.

198 "the disgraceful patience": Edmund Pendleton, *The Letters and Papers of Edmund Pendleton*, ed. David John Mays (Charlottesville: University Press of Virginia, 1967), 128.

198 "Lord Dunmore has commenced": Thomas Jefferson, "Thomas Jefferson to John Randolph," in Force, *American Archives*, 3:1706, https://digital.lib.niu.edu/islandora/object/niu-amarch%3A97579.

198 "now openly avow": Cobbett, *Parliamentary History of England*, 18:695.

199 "the southern colonies": ibid., 18:733.

199 "too black and horrid": ibid., 18:747.

199 "to burn these towns": Purdie, *Virginia Gazette*, December 29, 1775.

200 "all against the Scotsmen": *RV*, 4:313.

200 "the bulk of the inhabitants": Force, *American Archives*, 3:1073.

200 "a wild onion": Robert W. Coakley, "Virginia Commerce during the American Revolution" (PhD diss., University of Virginia, 1949), 52.

200 "These people at": *RV*, 4:337.

200 "a great aversion": "Virginia Legislative Papers," *Richmond College Historical Papers* 1, no. 1 (1915): 134.

200 "Generally speaking": Parker to Steuart, May 17, 1774, Charles Steuart Papers.

200 "We are daily": *RV*, 4:323.

201 "But this is not": ibid., 4:304.

201 "almost the only": Parker to Steuart, October 9, 1775, Charles Steuart Papers.

201 "to land himself": Paul Musselwhite, "'This Infant Borough': The Corporate Political Identity of Eighteenth-Century Norfolk," *Early American Studies* 15, no. 4 (2017): 827.

201 "owing to a body": *RV*, 4:329.

201 "Happy are you": ibid.

201 "about one hundred": Hume, *1775; Another Part of the Field*, 323.

202 "The suspense under which": Thomas Jefferson, "From Thomas Jefferson to Francis Eppes," November 7, 1775, https://founders.archives.gov/documents/Jefferson/01-01-02-0131.

202 "I have ever": *NDAR*, 2:920.

202 "required every person": ibid.

202 "All indentured servants": Gilbert, *Black Patriots and Loyalists*, 10.

203 "liberty to all": Justin Iverson, *Rebels in Arms: Black Resistance and the Fight for Freedom in the Anglo-Atlantic* (Athens: University of Georgia Press, 2022), 18.

203 "God Save the King": "Lord Dunmore's Proclamation," *Encyclopedia Virginia*, accessed January 30, 2024, https://encyclopediavirginia.org/8974hpr-dfab138fa60b3d9/.

203 "I postponed": *NDAR*, 2:1310.

Chapter Sixteen: A Conspicuous Light

204 "the other lodged in": John Page, "To Thomas Jefferson from John Page," November 11, 1775, *Founders Online*, National Archives, https://founders.archives.gov/documents/Jefferson/01-01-02-0134.

204 "At nine o'clock": Richard Henry Lee, "To George Washington from Richard Henry Lee," October 22-23, 1775, *Founders Online*, National Archives, https://founders.archives.gov/documents/Washington/03-02-02-0192.

205 "furnished with tents": Pendleton, *The Letters and Papers of Edmund Pendleton*, 126.

205 "for want of arms": *NDAR*, 2:1061.

205 "Without your presence": *RV*, 4:321.

205 "Our troops are marching": *NDAR*, 2:994.

205 "It is generally believed": James Henry Eckenrode, *Revolution in Virginia* (Boston: Houghton Mifflin, 1916), 65.

206 "empowered and directed": Force, *American Archives*, 3:1659.

206 "The people at Norfolk": John Page, "To Thomas Jefferson from John Page," November 11, 1775, *Founders Online*, National Archives, https://founders.archives.gov/documents/Jefferson/01-01-02-0134.

206 "the town of Boston": Force, *American Archives*, 1:46.

207 "in a better state": Abigail Adams, "Abigail Adams to John Adams," March 31, 1776, *Founders Online*, National Archives, https://founders.archives.gov/documents/Adams/04-01-02-0241.

207 "Scipio Americanus": Thomas Jefferson, "Thomas Jefferson to Francis C. Gray," March 4, 1815, *Founders Online*, National Archives, https://founders.archives.gov/documents/Jefferson/03-08-02-0245.

207 "chiefly agricultural": Thomas Jefferson, "To James Madison from Thomas Jefferson," December 20, 1787, *Founders Online*, National Archives, https://founders.archives.gov/documents/Madison/01-10-02-0210.

208 "DELENDA EST NORFOLK.": Thomas Jefferson, "From Thomas Jefferson to John Page," October 31, 1775, *Founders Online*, National Archives, https://founders.archives.gov/documents/Jefferson/01-01-02-0130.

208 "the general good": Pinkney, *Virginia Gazette*, October 19, 1775 (supplement).

208 "rather burn the towns": *RV*, 4:412.

208 "In the night of the": Connolly, "A Narrative of the Transactions, Imprisonment, and Sufferings of John Connolly," 411.

208 "a man of great fidelity": ibid., 416.

208 "a fine large town": Smyth, *A Tour in the United States of America*, 2:256.

208 "something different from": ibid., 2:249–250.

209 "got intoxicated overnight": ibid.

209 "on the very border": Connolly, "A Narrative of the Transactions, Imprisonment, and Sufferings of John Connolly," 413.

209 "suddenly into our room": Smyth, *A Tour in the United States of America*, 2:252.

209 "As we rode along": ibid., 2:253.

209 "to arrest and secure": Richard Henry Lee, "To George Washington from Richard Henry Lee," November 13, 1775, *Founders Online*, National Archives, https://founders.archives.gov/documents/Washington/03-02-02-0336.

210 "George Washington knew": Connolly, "A Narrative of the Transactions, Imprisonment, and Sufferings of John Connolly," 414.

210 "as one of the most": James Haw, *Stormy Patriot: The Life of Samuel Chase* (Baltimore: Maryland Historical Society, 1980), 50.

210 "soiled and besmeared": Connolly, "A Narrative of the Transactions, Imprisonment, and Sufferings of John Connolly," 415.

210 "I am now a prisoner": Force, *American Archives*, 4:617.

210 "God bless you,": ibid., 4:618.

210 "We scarce had time": Connolly, "A Narrative of the Transactions, Imprisonment, and Sufferings of John Connolly," 417.

211 "opprobrious epithets": ibid.

211 "a deep encrusted": John Smyth, "Narrative or Journal of Capt. John Ferdinand Dalziel Smyth, of the Queen's Rangers," *Pennsylvania Magazine of History and Biography* 39 (1915): 158.

211 "This treaty with the": Richard Henry Lee, "To George Washington from Richard Henry Lee," December 6, 1775, *Founders Online*, National Archives, https://founders.archives.gov/documents/Washington/03-02-02-0452.

211 "exceedingly happy": George Washington, "From George Washington to Lieutenant Colonel Joseph Reed," December 15, 1775, *Founders Online*, National Archives, https://founders.archives.gov/documents/Washington/03-02-02-0508.

211 "both the iron and": Smyth, *A Tour in the United States of America*, 291.

211 "preparing to invade": Benjamin Harrison, "To George Washington from Benjamin Harrison, Sr.," March 23, 1782, *Founders Online*, National Archives, https://founders.archives.gov/documents/Washington/99-01-02-08035.

211 "It is impossible": *RV*, 4:390.

211 "This place in a very": ibid., 4:391.

212 "They have quarreled": *RV*, 4:354.

212 "God only knows what I": *NDAR*, 2:1309.

212 "I was informed that": Force, *American Archives*, 3:1713.

212 "mere tracks large enough": Saint-Méry, *American Journey*, 69.

213 "The king of the blacks": Rind, *Virginia Gazette*, November 16, 1775.

213 "thought proper to": *NDAR*, 2:1148.

213 "by nature a very": ibid, 13:1311.

213 "between three and four": ibid, 3:1310.

213 "even then to march": ibid, 2:1309.

214 "I immediately ordered": ibid, 13:1310.

215 "We had only one": Force, *American Archives*, 3:1717.

215 "His Excellency's humanity": ibid., 4:844.

215 "Lord Dunmore entered": James, *The Lower Norfolk County Virginia Antiquary*, 2:133.

215 "to Dr. Reid's shop": Force, *American Archives*, 4:202.

215 "extremely elegant and": Helen Calvert Maxwell Read, *Memoirs of Helen Calvert Maxwell Read* (Chesapeake, VA: Norfolk County Historical Society, 1970), 54.

215 "endeavoring to overturn": Force, *American Archives*, 3:1671.

215 "those who could not": James, *The Lower Norfolk County Virginia Antiquary*, 2:133.

216 "Lord Dunmore has taken": Purdie, *Virginia Gazette*, November 17, 1775.

216 "a number of about": Force, *American Archives*, 3:1670.

Chapter Seventeen: Black Rascals

217 "a badge of red cloth": Read, *Memoirs of Helen Calvert Maxwell Read*, 54.
217 "We had hardly got there": ibid., 54–55.
218 "Well, madam, when you": ibid., 56.
218 "His Lordship followed": ibid.
218 "had a rousing fire": ibid.
219 "What do you want?": ibid., 57.
219 "a bit of red cloth on the breast": ibid.
219 "If I can save my": ibid., 57–58.
219 "a factious set of men": *NDAR*, 2:1309–1311.
220 "an entertainment was": *RV*, 4:446.
220 "complete master": Thomas Costa, "Economic Development and Political Authority: Norfolk, Virginia Merchant-Magistrates, 1736–1800," (PhD diss., College of William and Mary, 1991), 82.
220 "It is a disagreeable": *RV*, 4:423.
221 "Lord Dunmore has applied": ibid., 4:424.
221 "The whole counties": ibid., 4:439.
221 "You'll never have": ibid.
221 "The late engagement": ibid., 4:447.
221 "Things seem to take": ibid., 4:448.
221 "great many": ibid., 4:457.
222 "Lord Dunmore has gained": ibid., 4:436.
222 "This, I am afraid": ibid., 4:415.
222 "intend burning the town": ibid., 4:426.
222 "gall the ships": ibid.
223 "We expect that both": ibid., 4:428.
223 "he may expect to": Dixon and Hunter, *Virginia Gazette*, September 2, 1775.
223 "lurking about Norfolk": Dixon and Hunter, *Virginia Gazette*, August 26, 1775.
223 "a pair of new": Purdie, *Virginia Gazette*, November 17, 1775.
223 "from a determined resolution": Dixon and Hunter, *Virginia Gazette*, November 18, 1775.
223 "Liberty": Lund Washington, "To George Washington from Lund Washington," December 3, 1775, *Founders Online*, National Archives, https://founders.archives.gov/documents/Washington/03-02-02-0434.
223 "Lord Dunmore sails": Benjamin Quarles, *The Negro in the American Revolution* (Williamsburg, VA: Institute of Early American History and Culture, 1961), 22.
223 "piratical expeditions": Force, *American Archives*, 3:1104.
224 "some of Dunmore's bandits": Dixon and Hunter, *Virginia Gazette*, December 2, 1775.

224 "Be not, ye negroes,": Purdie, *Virginia Gazette*, November 17, 1775.
224 "the baseness of Lord Dunmore's": *Virginia Gazette*, November 17, 1775.
225 "very flattering and": ibid.
225 "out of any tenderness": Force, *American Archives*, 3:1387.
225 "at the mercy of an": ibid.
225 "numbers of Negroes": Quarles, *The Negro in the American Revolution*, 26.
225 "using every art": *RV*, 4:470.
225 "household furniture": Hume, *1775; Another Part of the Field*, 400.
226 "would crowd to": Force, *American Archives*, 3:1670.
226 "about eighty guns": Ira Berlin and Ronald Hoffman, eds., *Slavery and Freedom in the Age of the American Revolution* (Charlottesville: University of Virginia Press, 1983), 291.
226 "malicious and imprudent": Parkinson, *The Common Cause*, 88.
226 "a country-born": Pinkney, *Virginia Gazette*, November 23, 1775.
227 "one of the war's most": Hodges, *Slavery and Freedom Among Early American Workers*, 66.
227 "Letters mention that": Force, *American Archives*, 4:202.
227 "did not know anyone": Pinkney, *Virginia Gazette*, December 9, 1775.
227 "Rivers will henceforth": Dixon and Hunter, *Virginia Gazette*, December 2, 1775.
227 "The Negroes we": *RV*, 5:46.
227 "able and willing": "Lord Dunmore's Proclamation," Digital History, accessed January 16, 2024, https://www.digitalhistory.uh.edu/active_learning/explorations/revolution/dunsmore.cfm.

Chapter Eighteen: To Quicken All in Revolution

229 "forty gentlemen": Catesby Willis Stewart, *The Life of Brigadier General William Woodford of the American Revolution*, 438.
229 "an irascible old gentleman": "Seeds Of Revolution Began At Glebe Church," Glebe Episcopal Church, accessed April 26, 2024, https://www.glebechurch.org/history.
229 "The American opposition": Force, *American Archives*, 5:1224.
229 "the great men": McDonnell, *The Politics of War*, 31.
230 "a Scotch lass": *RV*, 4:478.
230 "I gave the Negro": Smyth, *A Tour in the United States of America*, 2:234.
230 "astonishing numbers": ibid., 2:236.
230 "in almost impenetrable": ibid., 2:235.
231 "a cowardly set,": *RV*, 4:477.
231 "worse than the proclamation": ibid.
231 "and about fifty": *NDAR*, 13:1311.

231 "some soldiers": *RV*, 4:476.

231 "Lord Dunmore's secretary": ibid.

232 "I can't help thinking": ibid.

232 "twenty-five British": Force, *American Archives*, 4:349.

232 "The rebels could": Force, *American Archives*, 4:349.

233 "We took possession": *NDAR*, 2:1148.

233 "well calculated for": Richmond College, *Richmond College Historical Papers* (Richmond, VA: Richmond College, 1915–1917), 138.

233 "digging entrenchments": *Pennsylvania Gazette*, December 13, 1775.

233 "hungry bellies": Pinkney, *Virginia Gazette*, December 13, 1775.

234 "in any degree capable": *NDAR*, 13:1311.

234 "I hope a short time": ibid.

234 "burnt faces": Stefan Goodwin, *Africa in Europe: Antiquity into the Age of Global Expansion* (Lanham, MD: Lexington Books, 2009), 16.

234 "born under the sun's": W. E. B. Du Bois, *The Negro* (New York: H. Holt, 1915), 37.

234 "refer to the ancient": W. E. B. Du Bois, *Black Folk Then and Now,* The Oxford W. E. B. Du Bois, ed. Henry Louis Gates Jr. (New York: Oxford University Press, 2007), 12.

234 "white officers": Force, *American Archives*, 3:1714.

235 "notorious runaway": Pinkney, *Virginia Gazette*, November 23, 1775.

235 "Liberty for Slaves.": *Pennsylvania Gazette*, December 13, 1775.

235 "The inhabitants of": Holton, *Forced Founders*, 158.

236 "The proclamation from": *NDAR*, 3:277.

236 "Lord Dunmore's unparalleled": Richard Henry Lee to Catherine Macaulay, November 29, 1775, leefamilyarchive.org, accessed January 16, 2024, https://leefamilyarchive.org/history-papers-letters-transcripts-gw-delegates-div0248/.

236 "more effectively work": Gilbert, *Black Patriots and Loyalists*, 15.

236 "great numbers of": *NDAR*, 13:1307.

236 "Hell itself could not": Margaret Wheeler Willard, ed., *Letters on the American Revolution, 1774–1776* (Port Washington, NY: Kennikat Press, 1968), 233.

236 "Stay, you damned": *Pennsylvania Evening Post*, December 14, 1775.

236 "Lord Dunmore has erected": John Hancock, "To George Washington from John Hancock," December 2, 1775, *Founders Online*, National Archives, https://founders.archives.gov/documents/Washington/03-02-02-0426.

237 "the enemies of": *Journals of the American Congress: From 1774–1788: In Four Volumes* (Washington, DC: Way and Gideon, 1823), 1:197.

237 "All this would": Richard Henry Lee, "To George Washington from Richard Henry Lee," December 6, 1775, *Founders Online*, National Archives, https://founders.archives.gov/documents/Washington/03-02-02-0452.

238 "our water-intersected": Force, *American Archives*, 4:201.

238 "the maddest idea": John Adams "[Notes of Debates, Continued] Oct. 7. [from the Diary of John Adams]," *Founders Online*, National Archives, https://founders.archives.gov/documents/Adams/01-02-02-0005-0004-0004.

238 "hoisted the flag": Henry Edward Waite, ed., *Extracts Relating to the Origin of the American Navy* (Boston: New England Historic Genealogical Society, 1890), 29.

238 "a town inhabited": John Adams, Samuel Adams, and James Warren, *Warren-Adams Letters: Being Chiefly a Correspondence Among John Adams, Samuel Adams, and James Warren, 1743–1814* (Boston: Massachusetts Historical Society, 1917), 72:191.

238 "We are somewhat": Joseph Hawley, "To John Adams from Joseph Hawley," December 18, 1775, *Founders Online*, National Archives, https://founders.archives.gov/documents/Adams/06-03-02-0191.

238 "I make no doubt": George Washington, "From George Washington to John Hancock," December 14, 1775, *Founders Online*, National Archives, https://founders.archives.gov/documents/Washington/03-02-02-0503.

239 "Indian corn, potatoes,": George Washington, "From George Washington to John Hancock," December 18, 1775, *Founders Online*, National Archives, https://founders.archives.gov/documents/Washington/03-02-02-0528.

239 "We keep them in": *NDAR*, 13:1210.

000 "a common express": George Washington, "From George Washington to John Hancock," December 18, 1775, *Founders Online*, National Archives, https://founders.archives.gov/documents/Washington/03-02-02-0528.

239 "If, my dear sir": George Washington, "From George Washington to Richard Henry Lee," December 26, 1775, *Founders Online*, National Archives, https://founders.archives.gov/documents/Washington/03-02-02-0568.

239 "indispensable necessary": George Washington, "From George Washington to Lieutenant Colonel Joseph Reed," December 15, 1775, *Founders Online*, National Archives, https://founders.archives.gov/documents/Washington/03-02-02-0508.

Chapter Nineteen: The Infernal Regions

241 "Their riflemen keep": Force, *American Archives*, 4:350.

241 "What a pity it is": ibid.

241 "Would to God": ibid., 4:351.

242 "keep up a constant fire": Catesby Willis Stewart, *The Life of Brigadier General William Woodford of the American Revolution*, 445.

242 "the hog pen.": *NDAR*, 4:26.

242 "Their situation is": *RV*, 5:49.

242 "We are situated here": William Wirt Henry, *Patrick Henry; Life, Correspondence and Speeches*, 1:36.

242 "the want of provisions": William Wirt Henry, *Sketches of the Life and Character of Patrick Henry*, 169.

242 "the filth in and about": Brent Tarter, "The Orderly Book of the Second Virginia Regiment: September 27, 1775–April 15, 1776 (Continued)," *Virginia Magazine of History and Biography* 85, no. 3 (1977): 303, http://www.jstor.org/stable/4248140.

242 "A party of the king's": Force, *American Archives*, 4:171.

243 "Our people, being": *NDAR*, 2:1299.

243 "Negro Ned": "The Woodford, Howe, and Lee Letters," in *Richmond College Historical Papers*, ed. Dice Robins Anderson (Richmond, VA: Richmond College, 1915), 113.

243 "We still keep up": *NDAR*, 13:1274.

243 "one white man": The Woodford, Howe, and Lee Letters," 114.

244 "All escaped unhurt": ibid.

244 "Our reception at": *RV*, 5:122.

244 "hope you will send": ibid., 5:76.

244 "lower classes of": Parkinson, *The Common Cause*, 88.

244 "full and free representation": John Adams, "[Thursday October 26. 1775.] [from the Diary of John Adams]," *Founders Online*, National Archives, https://founders.archives.gov/documents/Adams/01-03-02-0016-0050.

245 "Our army has been": *NDAR*, 3:26.

245 "a body of Negroes": Mays, *Edmund Pendleton, 1721–1803: A Biography*, 2:69.

245 "was not in a condition": *NDAR*, 3:141.

245 "the well-disposed people": ibid.

246 "make a detour": ibid.

246 "We hinted to him": Terrance Leon Mahan, *Virginia Reaction to British Policy, 1763–1776* (Madison: University of Wisconsin Press, 1960), 2:364.

246 "I thought it advisable": *NDAR*, 3:141.

248 "We were alarmed this": Purdie, *Virginia Gazette*, December 15, 1775.

249 "We marched up to": Force, *American Archives*, 4:452.

249 "They were astonished": *NDAR*, 3:40.

249 "As is the practice": John Marshall, *The Life of George Washington, Commander in Chief of the American Forces, During the War which Established the Independence of His Country* (Philadelphia: James Crissy, 1832), 69.

249 "In less than ten": Dorothy Volo and James M. Volo, *Daily Life During the American Revolution*, (Westport, CT: Greenwood Publishing, 2003), 85.

249 "Perhaps a hotter fire": Force, *American Archives*, 4:228.

249 "The day is our": Norman Fuss, "Billy Flora at the Battle of Great Bridge," *Journal of the American Revolution*, October 14, 2014, https://allthingsliberty.com/2014/10/billy-flora-at-the-battle-of-great-bridge/.

249 "Our men were so": *NDAR*, 3:29.

250 "I then saw the horrors": Jean Edward Smith, *John Marshall: Definer of a Nation* (New York: Henry Holt, 1998), 49.

250 "For God's sake,": *NDAR*, 3:220.

251 "unable to rally": *NDAR*, 3:309.

251 "coupled to one of": *RV*, 5:117.

251 "shall be the fate": ibid.
252 "This was a second": *NDAR*, 3:40.

Chapter Twenty: Dunmore's Dunkirk

253 "We saw them coming": Read, *Memoirs of Helen Calvert Maxwell Read*, 60.
253 "He told us it was": ibid., 49.
254 "a Negro woman": ibid.
254 "I was told to report": *Sacramento Bee*, June 18, 1861.
255 "present when his Lordship": "The Woodford, Howe, and Lee Letters," 121.
255 "Most of the other": *NDAR*, 5:1022.
255 "All who were": ibid., 3:142.
256 "the effusion of more": *RV*, 5:96.
256 "I am told his Lordship": ibid.
256 "have at all times": ibid., 5:97.
256 "almost useless": Catesby Willis Stewart, *The Life of Brigadier General William Woodford of the American Revolution*, 510.
257 "great dejection": *RV*, 5:116.
257 "do not like to fight": ibid.
257 "as artful as vicious": *NDAR*, 3:227.
257 "one of the most considerable": *RV*, 5:165.
257 "it had been currently": Force, *American Archives*, 4:86.
257 "would be very glad": *RV*, 5:158.
257 "were now satisfied": ibid., 5:115.
258 "The late action": ibid., 5:109.
258 "tolerably good men": ibid., 5:117.
258 "a man of the world": ibid., 5:136.
258 "misapplication of the": Janet Schaw, *Journal of a Lady of Quality: Being the Narrative of a Journey from Scotland to the West Indies, North Carolina, and Portugal, in the Years 1774 to 1776*, ed., Evangeline Walker Andrews and Charles McLean Andrews (New Haven, CT: Yale University Press, 1921), 317.
258 "women-eater that": ibid., 176.
258 "libertine": Charles E. Bennett and Donald R. Lennon, *A Quest for Glory: Major General Robert Howe and the American Revolution* (Chapel Hill: University of North Carolina Press, 1991), 1.
258 "has the worst character": Stephen R. Taaffe, *Washington's Revolutionary War Generals* (Norman: University of Oklahoma Press, 2019), 184.
259 "For salt is all the": Randall M. Miller, ed., *The Greenwood Encyclopedia of Daily Life in America* (New York: Bloomsbury, 2008), 137.
259 "to prevent riots": McDonnell, *The Politics of War*, 151.
259 "the severest punishments": Jacob Neff Brenaman, *A History of Virginia Conventions: The Making of the Modern Law* (Richmond, VA: J. L. Hill, 1902), 62:30.

259 "repelling force by force": Force, *American Archives*, 4:82.

260 "horrid supporter of": "Virginia Legislative Papers," *Virginia Magazine of History and Biography* 18, no. 4 (Oct. 1910): 391.

260 "through necessity": Force, *American Archives*, 4:84.

260 "It is enacted": ibid., 4:85.

260 "We are marching to": *RV*, 5:140.

261 "We have taken possession": ibid., 5:141.

261 "fatigues of the day": "The Woodford, Howe, and Lee Letters," 127.

261 "I have the worst": Force, *American Archives*, 4:227.

261 "All the principal": ibid.

262 "officer commanding at": ibid., 4:279.

262 "fired by mistake": *NDAR*, 3:119.

262 "many of the stores": John Rogers, "Commissioners to Examine Claims in Norfolk, Depositions 1777," box 1081445, folder 1, deposition 3, Library of Virginia, Richmond, VA.

262 "convey their men": "The Woodford, Howe, and Lee Letters," 138.

262 "a large body of": *RV*, 5:160.

263 "about 2000 men": *Maryland Gazette*, December 14, 1775.

263 "This late acquisition": Purdie, *Virginia Gazette*, December 22, 1775.

263 "are to be considered" *RV*, 5:193.

264 "The men I fear will": "The Woodford, Howe, and Lee Letters," 135.

264 "A difference at this": William Wirt Henry, *Sketches of the Life and Character of Patrick Henry*, 191.

264 "ride with springs upon": *RV*, 5:217.

264 "The number of ships": ibid., 5:220.

264 "much alarmed": Stewart, *The Life of Brigadier General William Woodford*, 534.

264 "prey to disgrace and": *RV*, 5:217.

264 "is very severe": "The Woodford, Howe, and Lee Letters," 137.

265 "Lord Dunmore, with a": *NDAR*, 3:227.

265 "he supposed we must sell": The Woodford, Howe, and Lee Letters," 146.

Chapter Twenty-One: Palpitation at the Heart

266 "only a Christmas": *NDAR*, 3:297.

266 "provisions and fuel": ibid., 3:288.

266 "the piratical peer.": Harry M. War, *Between the Lines: Banditti of the American Revolution* (New York: Bloomsbury Academic, 2002), 62.

266 "The women and children": "The Woodford, Howe, and Lee Letters," 145.

267 "the effects of numbers": *NDAR*, 3:228.

267 "You may be assured": ibid., 3:229.

267 "moderate conduct": ibid., 3:244.

267 "This Convention": ibid., 3:295.

267 "with no intention to": "The Woodford, Howe, and Lee Letters," 145.

267 "We have had a few": *RV*, 5:286.

267 "Lord Dunmore, we hear": Catesby Willis Stewart, *The Life of Brigadier General William Woodford of the American Revolution*, 1:576.

267 "I desire you will": William Henry Stewart, *History of Norfolk County, Virginia*, 45.

268 "have nothing to do": "The Woodford, Howe, and Lee Letters," 146.

268 "neither Negroes, boys": George Washington, "General Orders, 12 November 1775," *Founders Online*, National Archives, https://founders.archives.gov/documents/Washington/03-02-02-0326.

268 "by hundreds and": Rufus Rockwell Wilson, ed. *Heath's Memoirs of the American War* (New York: A. Wessels Co., 1904), 43–44.

268 "It has been represented": George Washington, "From George Washington to John Hancock, December 31, 1775," *Founders Online*, National Archives, https://founders.archives.gov/documents/Washington/03-02-02-0579.

268 "that the free Negroes": George Washington, "General Orders, 30 December 1775," *Founders Online*, National Archives, https://founders.archives.gov/documents/Washington/03-02-02-0575.

269 "began to insult us": H. S. Parsons, "Contemporary English Accounts of the Destruction of Norfolk in 1776," *William and Mary College Quarterly Historical Magazine* 13, no. 4 (1933): 221, https://doi.org/10.2307/1919768.

269 "Fired two six pounders": *NDAR*, 3:325.

269 "from whence they used": ibid., 3:618.

269 "their lives and": David Griffith, *Passive Obedience Considered: In a Sermon Preached at Williamsburg, December 31st, 1775* (Farmington Hills, MI: Gale, Sabin Americana, 2012): 21.

270 "so threatened the better": William Berkeley, *The Papers of Sir William Berkeley, 1605–1677*, ed. Warren M. Billings (Richmond: Library of Virginia, 2007), 537.

270 "the preservation of": Griffith, *Passive Obedience Considered*, 22.

270 "the spirit of freedom": ibid., 12.

Part Three

Chapter Twenty-Two: Keep Up the Jig

273 "women, children, and": *NDAR*, 3:808.

274 "We saw the ships": Read, *Memoirs of Helen Calvert Maxwell Read*, 40.

274 "parading in the streets": Charles Brinson Cross, *A Navy for Virginia: A Colony's Fleet in the Revolution* (Richmond: Virginia Independence Bicentennial Commission, 1981), 12.

274 "the rebel's guardhouse": *NDAR*, 3:563.

274 "When at length": *Sacramento Bee*, June 18, 1861.

275 "example was immediately": *NDAR*, 3:618.

275 "Under cover of the": ibid.

275 "principally Negroes . . .": ibid, 3:662.

275 "many of the storehouses": ibid., 3:563.

275 "the ardor of the men": ibid, 3:618.

275 "What a glorious fight": *The Freeman's Journal*, March 14, 1776, Newspapers.com, accessed January 17, 2024, https://www.newspapers.com/image/61102437/?terms=Norfolk&match=1.

275 "under the fire of their": *NDAR*, 3:617.

276 "never failed being repulsed": ibid.

276 "Old Sarah and her": Read, *Memoirs of Helen Calvert Maxwell Read*, 40.

276 "trudged through wood": ibid., 52.

276 "Oh Nelly, is that": ibid.

277 "continued till near ten": *NDAR*, 3:579.

277 "The horror of the night": Pinkney, *Virginia Gazette*, January 20, 1776.

277 "The only damage we": *NDAR*, 3:621.

277 "We have not one": ibid., 3:580.

277 "gentleman volunteer": *RV*, 5:346–347.

277 "I cannot enter into": ibid., 3:580.

278 "The town is on fire!": *Sacramento Bee*, June 18, 1861.

278 "greatly battered with": Zimmer, *Selected Letters from the Parker Family Papers; The Correspondence of Margaret Parker*, 70.

279 "The rebels,": *NDAR*, 3:565.

279 "appeared as red": John E. Selby, *Dunmore* (Williamsburg: Virginia Independence Bicentennial Commission, 1977), 49.

279 "with great composure": Marshall, *The Life of George Washington*, 2:372.

279 "a strong prejudice": Marshall, *The Life of George Washington*, 2:372.

279 "The people in Norfolk": Robert Brett, Commissioners to Examine Claims in Norfolk, Depositions 1777, box 1081445, folder 1, deposition 14, Library of Virginia, Richmond, VA.

280 "rejoicing": James Nicholson, Commissioners to Examine Claims in Norfolk, Depositions 1777, box 1081445, folder 1, deposition 1, Library of Virginia, Richmond, VA.

280 "observed several parties": Nicholson, Commissioners to Examine Claims in Norfolk.

280 "to several warehouses": Matthew McCrae [McPhee], Commissioners to Examine Claims in Norfolk, Depositions 1777, box 1081445, folder 1, deposition 17, Library of Virginia, Richmond, VA.

281 "It was better to destroy": Rogers, Commissioners to Examine Claims in Norfolk.

281 "a large quantity of medicine": ibid.

281 "a small cask of rum": ibid.

281 "the state would do it": James Leitch, Commissioners to Examine Claims in Norfolk, Depositions 1777, box 1081445, folder 1, deposition 11, Library of Virginia, Richmond, VA.

282 "two looking glasses": Paul Wallington, Commissioners to Examine Claims in Norfolk, Depositions 1777, box 1081445, folder 1, deposition 18, Library of Virginia, Richmond, VA.

282 "very far gone with": William Ingram, Commissioners to Examine Claims in Norfolk, Depositions 1777, box 1081445, folder 1, deposition 16, Library of Virginia, Richmond, VA.

282 "a remarkable day": George Holbert Tucker, ed., "Abstracts from Norfolk City Marriage Bonds, 1797–1850" (Genealogical.com, 2009), 3.

Chapter Twenty-Three: A Feeling Bosom

283 "a dismal sight of ruins,": *NDAR*, 3:621.

283 "The rebels began to fire": ibid., 3:580.

283 "was assured it was a matter": John Smith, Commissioners to Examine Claims in Norfolk, Depositions 1777, box 1081445, folder 1, deposition 15, Library of Virginia, Richmond, VA.

284 "as it belonged to an orphan": Richard Jarvis, Commissioners to Examine Claims in Norfolk, Depositions 1777, box 1081445, folder 1, deposition 7, Library of Virginia, Richmond, VA.

284 "though he believes none": Captain Arthur Smith, Commissioners to Examine Claims in Norfolk, Depositions 1777, box 1081445, folder 1, deposition 9, Library of Virginia, Richmond, VA.

284 "necessary house.": William Goodchilde, Commissioners to Examine Claims in Norfolk, Depositions 1777, box 1081445, folder 1, deposition 12, Library of Virginia, Richmond, VA.

284 "observed a soldier taking": Sarah Smith, Commissioners to Examine Claims in Norfolk, Depositions 1777, box 1081445, folder 1, deposition 19, Library of Virginia, Richmond, VA.

285 "several houses were then": William Ivey, Commissioners to Examine Claims in Norfolk, Depositions 1777, box 1081445, folder 1, deposition 10, Library of Virginia, Richmond, VA.

285 "Norfolk is a post which": *RV*, 5:319.

285 "nine-tenths of the town": *NDAR*, 3:662.

285 "The distress of these miserable": *RV*, 5:346.

286 "The town of Norfolk": ibid., 5:355.

286 "feeling bosom": ibid., 5:356.

286 "I think it would be better": Mays, *Edmund Pendleton, 1721–1803: A Biography*, 2:83.

286 "In consequence of your": Catesby Willis Stewart, *The Life of Brigadier General William Woodford of the American Revolution*, 1:589.

287 "drew a heavy cannonade": *RV*, 5:346.

287 "a great quantity of": *RV*, 5:355.

287 "They were fired upon": ibid.

287 "broke open all the": *NDAR*, 4:38.

287 "burnt by our people": *Virginia Gazette*, January 8, 1776.

287 "The destruction of that": *NDAR*, 4:38.

288 "the rebels attempted": *RV*, 5:663.

288 "was not so successful,": ibid., 5:346.

288 "perceived the mills": *NDAR*, 3:686.

288 "all the mills at Tucker's": Purdie, *Virginia Gazette*, January 12, 1776.

288 "that it was his intention": William Chisholm, Commissioners to Examine Claims in Norfolk, Depositions 1777, box 1081445, folder 1, deposition 5, Library of Virginia, Richmond, VA.

289 "recommended": *RV*, 5:405.

289 "asked him if he": Sarah Smith, Commissioners to Examine Claims in Norfolk.

289 "principal actor in burning": Burke, *The Annual Register of World Events*, 32.

289 "spread with amazing": *RV*, 5:319.

289 "At the time the fire began": Rogers, Commissioners to Examine Claims in Norfolk.

290 "It is affirmed that one": Pinkney, *Virginia Gazette*, January 6, 1776.

290 "repulsed with considerable": ibid.

290 "an open and avowed war": *RV*, 5:435.

290 "unrelenting fury.": ibid, 5:436.

291 "the tyrannical, cruel, and": *RV*, 6:35.

291 "as the cause of all the disturbances": "Judith Bell to Alexander Spears," February 16, 1776, #TD 131/18, bundle 8, Mitchell Library, Glasgow City Archives.

291 "wind was moderate": Earle of Dunmore, January 18, 1776, *Virginia Gazette*, Library of Congress, Washington DC, sn87062000.

291 "reduced to ashes,": Purdie, *Virginia Gazette*, February 9, 1776.

291 "the inhumanity of the action": *RV*, 5:17.

Chapter Twenty-Four: Flaming Arguments

292 "never did, nor do": "Proceedings of the Conventions of the Province of Maryland, 1774–1776," Archives of Maryland Online, accessed April 26, 2024, https://msa.maryland.gov/megafile/msa/speccol/sc2900/sc2908/000001/000078/html/am78--120.html.

292 "a delusive bait": Carter Braxton, "Carter Braxton to Landon Carter," April 14, 1776, in *Letters of Members of the Continental Congress*, ed. Edmund

Cody Burnett (Washington, DC: Carnegie Institution of Washington, 1921), 420.

292 "to assure his majesty": "On a Petition to the King," January 9–24, 1776, in *Letters of Delegates to Congress*, vol. 3: January 1, 1776–May 15, 1776, ed., Paul H. Smith and Ronald M. Gephart (Washington, DC: Library of Congress, 1976), 3:63.

292 "an express came": *NDAR*, 3:681.

293 "Until an independence": Thomas Paine, *Common Sense* (New York: P. Eckler, 1918), 49.

293 "Lord Dunmore has endeavored": Force, *American Archives*, 4:687.

293 "contrary to the rules of": John Hancock, "To George Washington from John Hancock," January 6–21, 1776, *Founders Online*, National Archives, https://founders.archives.gov/documents/Washington/03-03-02-0026.

293 "our devil of a governor": Benjamin Harrison, "Benjamin Harrison to Robert Carter Nicholas," January 17, 1776, in *Journals of the Continental Congress, 1774–1789*, ed. Worthington C. Ford et al. (Washington, DC: Library of Congress, 1904–1937), 3:107.

293 "the peculiar distresses": *NDAR*, 3:640.

294 "commander in chief of": ibid., 3:637.

294 "the strength of Lord": Force, *American Archives*, 4:575.

294 "You will discern,": *NDAR*, 3:640.

294 "furnish the commander": ibid.

294 "If by such intelligence": ibid., 3:638.

295 "three parts of the town": *South Carolina and American General Gazette*, January 26, 1776.

295 "The destruction of Norfolk": George Washington, "From George Washington to Lieutenant Colonel Joseph Reed," January 31, 1776, *Founders Online*, National Archives, https://founders.archives.gov/documents/Washington/03-03-02-0163.

295 "a defenseless coast": Earle of Dunmore, February 3, 1776, *Virginia Gazette*, Library of Congress, Washington DC, s87062000.

295 "Jack Dunmore's hopeful": *NDAR*, 3:662.

296 "to inquire into": Force, *American Archives*, 4:127.

296 "Some of them have": ibid., 4:128.

297 "badly planned . . .": *Proceedings of the Convention of Delegates for the Counties and Corporations in the Colony of Virginia*, 36.

298 "the want of lead for": *RV*, 6:81.

298 "that the public may": ibid.

298 "public Negroes": Sean Gallagher, "The Prison of Public Works: Enslaved People and State Formation at Virginia's Chiswell Lead Mines, 1775–1786," *Journal of Southern History* 86, no. 4 (2020): 782.

298 "lenient and merciful": *RV*, 5:363.

298 "who have been active": *RV*, 5:423.

299 "a supply of powder": Randal L. Hall, *Mountains on the Market: Industry, the Environment, and the South* (Lexington: University Press of Kentucky, 2012), 23.

299 "of a square athletic": James Hayes, *Virginia Gazette and American Advertiser*, May 4, 1785.

299 "valued," *RV*, 6:69.

299 "The metal is mixed": Jefferson, *Notes on the State of Virginia*, 38.

299 "The present furnace is": ibid., 39.

300 "cultivate their own": ibid.

300 "unwholesome service": Gallagher, "The Prison of Public Works," 792.

300 "as the inhabitants": Force, *American Archives*, 1:613.

300 "15,000 weight of pure": ibid., 1:937.

300 "an object of vast": Thomas Jefferson, "Virginia Delegates in Congress to the Executive of Virginia (Patrick Henry)," July 15, 1776, *Founders Online*, National Archives, https://founders.archives.gov/documents/Jefferson/01-01-02-0182.

301 "of much consequence": David Ross, "To George Washington from David Ross," October 23, 1781, *Founders Online*, National Archives, https://founders.archives.gov/documents/Washington/99-01-02-07248.

Chapter Twenty-Five: Ill-Judged Measures

302 "very sensible that": Tarter, "The Orderly Book of the Second Virginia Regiment," 316.

302 "never to set down": ibid., 319.

302 "to lay the state of affairs": *RV*, 5:403.

302 "examined concerning": Force, *American Archives*, 4:124.

303 "the mills and entrenchments": *RV*, 5:405.

303 "for demolishing the": Burk, Jones, and Girardin, *History of Virginia*, 4:110.

303 "I do not see the": ibid.

303 "whether it will be": *RV*, 5:416.

304 "While the town was": Pendleton, *The Letters and Papers of Edmund Pendleton*, 7:148.

304 "Town Destroyer": "Quotes," Onondaga Nation website, accessed January 29, 2024, https://www.onondaganation.org/history/quotes/.

304 "We had three fine men": *NDAR*, 3:905.

305 "that the whole of the": Tarter, "The Orderly Book of the Second Virginia Regiment," 322.

305 "a signal": *NDAR*, 4:23.

305 "between the church": John Rogers, Commissioners to Examine Claims in Norfolk.

305 "a brick mill in": John Smith, Commissioners to Examine Claims in Norfolk.

305 "The town of Norfolk": Dixon and Hunter, *Virginia Gazette*, February 10, 1776.

305 "Thus in the course": Force, *American Archives*, 4:947.

306 "Nothing is here but": Peter Minor, "Peter Minor to Brother" June 19, 1776, Garrett Minor Papers, Library of Congress, Washington, DC.

306 "Nobody can conceive": Jenny Stuart, "Letters from Virginia, 1774–1781," ed. William Abbot, *Magazine of History with Notes and Queries* 3, no. 4 (1906): 215.

306 "Desolation and ruin": *NDAR*, 3:673.

306 "I viewed the wreck of": Zimmer, *Selected Letters from the Parker Family Papers; The Correspondence of Margaret Parker*, 70.

307 "devastation hitherto": T. C. Hansard, ed., *The Parliamentary Debates: Official Reports* (Richmond, UK: H.M. Stationery Office, 1813), 18:1196.

307 "condemn an absent": ibid., 18:1205.

308 "I do not believe it is": ibid., 18:1219.

308 "Numberless widows and": "Petitions and Letters, To the Convention, Governor, or House of Delegates praying for Relief, 1775–1783," *Richmond College Historical Papers* 2 (1915): 338.

308 "to measure and value": "Doc. No. 43," *Journal of the House of Delegates of the Commonwealth of Virginia* (Richmond, VA: Samuel Shepherd, 1835), 15.

309 "Very few of the houses": ibid., 16.

310 "the most inveterate": Pinkney, *Virginia Gazette*, January 20, 1776.

310 "all natives of": American Archives, Correspondence, Proceedings, etc. December 1776, p. 1287.

310 "I would have agreed": John Page, "To Thomas Jefferson from John Page," July 15, 1776, *Founders Online*, National Archives, https://founders.archives.gov/documents/Jefferson/01-01-02-0183.

310 "as I advised": John Page, "To Thomas Jefferson from John Page," July 20, 1776, *Founders Online*, National Archives, https://founders.archives.gov/documents/Jefferson/01-01-02-0189.

310 "Norfolk might have": Adam Stephen, "To Thomas Jefferson from Adam Stephen," July 29, 1776, *Founders Online*, National Archives, https://founders.archives.gov/documents/Jefferson/01-01-02-0199.

311 "Thus was destroyed": Marshall, *The Life of George Washington*, 69.

Chapter Twenty-Six: Fatal Lethargy

312 "give authority": *NDAR*, 2:778.

312 "this generous, this": Mays, *Edmund Pendleton, 1721–1803: A Biography*, 1:88.

312 "He is as rich as": Alfred Bagby, *King and Queen County, Virginia* (New York: Neale Publishing, 1908), 78.

313 "a long faithful": Robert Doares, "The Man Who Would Not Be Governor," *Colonial Williamsburg Journal* 22, no. 4 (Winter 2000–2001): 74–78.

313 "our trusty and well-beloved": ibid.

313 "I cannot condemn": ibid.

313 "You have it with": "Corbin Genealogy, (Continued)," *Virginia Magazine of History and Biography* 3, no. 1, (1922): 84.

313 "an honorable, permanent": *NDAR*, 3:1021.

314 "He gave out that he": *NDAR*, 3:1263.

314 "houses four miles": James Taylor, Commissioners to Examine Claims in Norfolk, Depositions 1777, box 1081445, folder 3, file Q, Library of Virginia, Richmond, VA.

315 "from a gentleman": Margaret Wheeler Willard, *Letters on the American Revolution, 1774–1776* (Boston: Houghton Mifflin, 1925), 261.

315 "many excesses such": Hume, *1775; Another Part of the Field*, 447.

315 "The people are in": *NDAR*, 4:23.

315 "Thank God we": ibid., 4:24.

315 "several hundred families": Andrew Snape Hamond, *The Autobiography of Captain Sir Andrew Snape Hamond, Bart., R.N., 1738–1828, Covering the Years 1738–1793* (Charlottesville: University of Virginia Press, 1953), 65.

315 "We learn that the Tory": Richard Henry Lee, "Richard Henry Lee to Samuel Adams," February 7, 1776, Lee Family Archives, accessed April 26, 2024, https://leefamilyarchive.org/history-papers-letters-transcripts-ballagh-b082/.

316 "floating town": *NDAR*, 6:66.

316 "the inconveniences of": *RV*, 6:xxvi.

316 "It was,": David, "Dunmore's New World," 171.

316 "He worked himself": Grant Gordon, *From Slavery to Freedom: The Life of David George, Pioneer Black Baptist Minister* (Nova Scotia, Canada: Lancelot Press, 1992), 101.

317 "a promiscuous ball": Purdie, *Virginia Gazette*, May 31, 1776.

317 "Lord Kidnapper": John Leacock, *The Fall of British Tyranny: Or, American Liberty Triumphant: The First Campaign. A Tragi-comedy of Five Acts, as Lately Planned at the Royal Theatrum Pandemonium, at St. James's. The Principal Place of Action in America. Publish'd According to Act of Parliament* (Philadelphia: J. Douglass M'Dougall, 1776), vii.

317 "The Kidnapper seems as": ibid., 44.

317 "for these black regulars": ibid.

318 "They have no right": ibid., 46.

318 "the thoughts of emancipation": ibid., 48.

318 "act of justice to": *New York Journal*, May 2, 1776.

319 "some rebels that were": *RV*, 6: 85.

319 "heard him relate": Hamond, *The Autobiography of Captain Sir Andrew Snape Hamond*, 50.

319 "I had an opportunity": ibid., 59.

319 "with some difficulty": George B. Oliver, *Liberalism and the United States Supreme Court, 1932–1955* (Ashland, VA: Randolph-Macon College, 1955), 28.

319 "I found his Lordship": Hamond, *The Autobiography of Captain Sir Andrew Snape Hamond*, 65.

320 "No water was to be": Sir Andrew Snape Hamond papers, 1766–1825, Library of Congress, Microfilm 13,932–3P, Hamond Account 1775–1777.

320 "the ague and fever": *NDAR*, 4:182.

320 "jail distemper": Purdie, *Virginia Gazette*, March 8, 1776.

320 "there was not a ship": Force, *American Archives*, 2:158.

320 "crammed full of": Sir Andrew Snape Hamond papers, 1766–1825, Library of Congress, Microfilm 13,932–3P, Hamond Account 1775–1777.

320 "absolutely necessary": ibid.

321 "The rebels had destroyed": ibid.

321 "retarded by the": *The Remembrancer, Or Impartial Repository of Public Events* (London: J. Almon, 1776), 2:359.

321 "to fit up a sort": ibid.

321 "A man of war": Willard, *Letters on the American Revolution*, 261.

321 "all sorts of provisions": *NDAR*, 3:1338.

321 "We took advantage": ibid., 4:102.

323 "exciting all to a": John Patterson MacLean, *Flora MacDonald in America: With a Brief Sketch of Her Life and Adventures* (Lumberton, NC: A. W. McLean, 1909), 47.

323 "inexpressible mortification": *NDAR*, 3:1349.

323 "being imprisoned": ibid., 3:1350.

323 "We are still ignorant": ibid., 4:14.

324 "I am called to": ibid.

324 "would be made": *RV*, 6:113.

324 "We gave him to": *NDAR*, 4:22.

325 "the old gentleman went": ibid.

325 "We had some difficulty": *The John P. Branch Historical Papers* (Ashland, VA: Randolph Macon College, 1901), 1:30.

325 "truce boat from": *NDAR*, 4:32.

325 "I had the honor": *John P. Branch Historical Papers*, 1:30.

326 "all appear in good": *NDAR*, 4:101.

326 "under four hundred": *RV*, 6:432.

326 "Whether General Clinton": *John P. Branch Historical Papers*, 1:31.

327 "I don't think it worth": *NDAR*, 4:101.

327 "the gentlemen of the": *RV*, 6:142.

Chapter Twenty-Seven: Boiling Water

328 "with broadswords at": John Petterson MacLean, *An Historical Account of the Settlements of Scotch Highlanders* (Cleveland, OH: Helman-Taylor, 1900), 127.

328 "The provinces bordering": W. Hugh Moomaw, "The Naval Career of Captain Hamond, 1775–1779" (PhD diss., University of Virginia, 1955), 86.

328 "that base having struck": William Willcox, ed., *The American Rebellion: Sir Henry Clinton's Narrative of His Campaigns, 1775–1782* (New Haven, CT: Yale University Press, 1971), 27.

329 "Clinton, I think will": "The Aspinwall Papers," in *Collections of the Massachusetts Historical Society* (Cambridge, MA: John Wilson and Son), 4:786.

329 "At the expiration": Whitehead, *Black Loyalists*, 77.

330 "father and general": William Wirt Henry, *Sketches of the Life and Character of Patrick Henry*, 180.

330 "strove to bury in": Purdie, *Virginia Gazette*, March 15, 1776.

330 "visiting the several": William Wirt Henry, *Sketches of the Life and Character of Patrick Henry*, 134.

330 "much noise in the": Mays, *Edmund Pendleton, 1721–1803: A Biography*, 92.

331 "Many of your petitioners": *RV*, 7:114.

331 "a poor man was": Force, *American Archives*, 6:390.

331 "I think Virginia": Charles Lee, "To Benjamin Franklin from Charles Lee," December 10, 1775, *Founders Online*, National Archives, https://founders.archives.gov/documents/Franklin/01-22-02-0174.

331 "the history of his": James Thatcher, *A Military Journal during the American Revolutionary War from 1775 to 1783 . . . To which is added an appendix, containing biographical sketches of several General Officers* (Boston: Richardson and Lord, 1823), 565.

332 "Boiling Water": Rupert Hughes, *George Washington: The Rebel and the Patriot, 1762–1777* (New York: W. Morrow, 1927), 237.

332 "a greater horror of": Charles Lee, *The Lee Papers* (New York: New-York Historical Society, 1872), 4:41.

332 "spoiling and destroying": John Adams, "[Saturday March 23. 1776.]" *Founders Online*, National Archives, https://founders.archives.gov/documents/Adams/01-03-02-0016-0083.

333 "a most troublesome": William Gordon, *The History of the Rise, Progress, and Establishment of the Independence of the United States of America* (New York: Samuel Campbell, 1801), 3:329.

333 "a perfect original": Jeremy Belknap, *Life of Jeremy Belknap, D. D.: The Historian of New Hampshire: with Selections from His Correspondence and Other Writings* (New York: Harper and Brothers, 1847), 94.

333 "a queer creature": John Adams, "From John Adams to James Warren," July 24, 1775, *Founders Online*, National Archives, https://founders.archives.gov/documents/Adams/06-03-02-0052.

333 "honest and well": George Washington, "From George Washington to John Augustine Washington," March 31, 1776, *Founders Online*, National Archives, https://founders.archives.gov/documents/Washington/03-03-02-0429.

333 "obscene, profane": Mays, *Edmund Pendleton, 1721–1803: A Biography*, 2:99.

333 "for a better acquaintance": Abigail Adams, "Abigail Adams to John Adams," December 10, 1775, *Founders Online*, National Archives, https://founders.archives.gov/documents/Adams/04-01-02-0221.

333 "Once I can be convinced": Charles Lee, "To John Adams from Charles Lee," October 5, 1775, *Founders Online*, National Archives, https://founders.archives.gov/documents/Adams/06-03-02-0094.

333 "I am sorry to": Charles Lee, "To George Washington from Major General Charles Lee," April 5, 1776, *Founders Online*, National Archives, https://founders.archives.gov/documents/Washington/03-04-02-0031.

334 "a most horrid": ibid.

334 "There is not a man": Force, *American Archives*, 5:1222.

334 "Their economy": *NDAR*, 4:672.

334 "what the milk-and-water": Charles Lee, "To George Washington from Major General Charles Lee," April 5, 1776.

334 "multitude of slaves": *RV*, 6:352.

334 "I am apt to think": Charles Lee, "To George Washington from Major General Charles Lee," April 5, 1776.

334 "important consequences": Charles Lee, *The Lee Papers*, 4:372.

335 "Your dominion": ibid., 4:379.

335 "would have homes": *RV*, 6:185.

335 "suffering of many": Dixon and Hunter, *Virginia Gazette*, April 23, 1776.

335 "It will be difficult": *RV*, 6: 352.

335 "I cannot be answerable": ibid.

336 "all inhabitants of": ibid., 370.

336 "most cheerfully cooperate": ibid., 373.

336 "piratical war and can": Philip Papas, *Renegade Revolutionary: The Life of Charles Lee* (New York: New York University Press, 2014), 157.

336 "Since I got them": Wm. P. Palmer, ed., *Calendar of Virginia State Papers and Other Manuscripts* (Richmond, VA: R. F. Walker, 1875), 8:108.

337 "frequently come and": "Lord Dunmore to Lord Germain, March 30, 1776," in Force, *American Archives*, 2:160.

337 "I have brought a": ibid.

337 "Black banditti": Dixon and Hunter, *Virginia Gazette*, August 31, 1776.

338 "We have in this": "Lord Dunmore to Lord Germain, March 30, 1776," in Force, *American Archives*, 2:160.

338 "declared their resolution": Gerald W. Mullin, *Flight and Rebellion: Slave Resistance in Eighteenth-Century Virginia* (Oxford: Oxford University Press, 1972), 133.

338 "are under sentence": Dixon and Hunter, *Virginia Gazette*, April 13, 1776.

338 "in Lord Dunmore's service": Purdie, *Virginia Gazette*, January 6, 1776.

338 "a slim Black fellow": Purdie, *Virginia Gazette*, April 5, 1776.

338 "is assuredly the major": *RV*, 6:282.

339 "We hear that Lord": Purdie, *Virginia Gazette*, March 15, 1776.

000 "who have forgot": Pendleton, *The Letters and Papers of Edmund Pendleton*, 160.

339 "Our army is a": William Wirt Henry, *Patrick Henry; Life, Correspondence and Speeches*, 356.

339 "tempted with the": John Page, "To Thomas Jefferson from John Page," April 26, 1776, *Founders Online*, National Archives, https://founders.archives.gov/documents/Jefferson/01-01-02-0151.

340 "a fever crept": Force, *American Archives*, 2:160.

340 "smallpox is in": George Washington, "From George Washington to Lieutenant Colonel Joseph Reed," December 15, 1775, *Founders Online*, National Archives, https://founders.archives.gov/documents/Washington/03-02-02-0508.

341 "This distemper is": John Adams, "From John Adams to James Warren," July 24, 1776, *Founders Online*, National Archives, https://founders.archives.gov/documents/Adams/06-04-02-0179.

341 "to prevent the": *RV*, 7:95.

341 "to take proper": *RV*, 6:351.

Chapter Twenty-Eight: Tomahawk Them All

342 "I am willing": Abigail Adams, "Abigail Adams to John Adams," March 31, 1776, *Founders Online*, National Archives, https://founders.archives.gov/documents/Adams/04-01-02-0241.

342 "my countrymen": George Washington, "From George Washington to Lieutenant Colonel Joseph Reed," April 1, 1776, *Founders Online*, National Archives, https://founders.archives.gov/documents/Washington/03-04-02-0009.

342 "Sir Peter Parker": Ballagh, *The Letters of Richard Henry Lee*: 1762–1778, 175.

342 "5000 blankets": Richard Henry Lee, "Richard Henry Lee to Charles Lee, 22 April 1776" Lee Family Archive, accessed April 26, 2024, https://leefamilyarchive.org/history-papers-letters-transcripts-gw-delegates-div0280/.

343 "talked, or rather": John Hazelton, *The Declaration of Independence: Its History* (New York: Dodd, Mead, and Company, 1906), 72.

343 "a blockhead and": ibid.

343 "the idol of": Dixon and Hunter, *Virginia Gazette*, April 13 1776.

343 "Virginia has hitherto": Ballagh, *The Letters of Richard Henry Lee: 1762–1778*, 176.

343 "the adoption of": ibid, 180.

343 "be nearly the form": ibid, 184.

343 "there is among": Patrick Henry, "To John Adams from Patrick Henry," May 20, 1776, *Founders Online*, National Archives, https://founders.archives.gov/documents/Adams/06-04-02-0087.

343 "should be formed": John Page, "To Thomas Jefferson from John Page," April 26, 1776, *Founders Online*, National Archives, https://founders.archives.gov/documents/Jefferson/01-01-02-0151.

344 "Our freeholders": Mays, *Edmund Pendleton, 1721–1803: A Biography*, 2:368.

344 "utmost ability in": Force, *American Archives*, 5:1047.

344 "I was the other": William Woodford and John W. Jordan, eds., "Unpublished Letters of General Woodford, of the Continental Army, 1776–1779," *Pennsylvania Magazine of History and Biography* 23, no. 4, (1899): 454.

345 "a prodigious raft": Lee, *The Lee Papers*, 5:5.

345 "One man . . .": ibid., 2:4.

345 "with leather on": James, *The Lower Norfolk County Virginia Antiquary*, 1:99.

345 "amply and regularly": Charles Lee, *The Life and Memoirs of the Late Major General Lee*, Edward Langworthy, ed., (New York: Richard Scott, 1813), 301.

346 "we have plenty": *NDAR*, 4:1408.

346 "intimidate the whole": Lee, *The Life and Memoirs of the Late Major General Lee*, 301.

346 "I found the inhabitants": Lee, *The Lee Papers*, 468.

346 "It perhaps be politic": *RV*, 6:529.

346 "taking care that": Lee, *The Lee Papers*, 5:5.

347 "all the inhabitants": Catesby Willis Stewart, *The Life of Brigadier General William Woodford of the American Revolution*, 1:651.

347 "a considerable": Mays, *Edmund Pendleton, 1721–1803: A Biography*, 101.

347 "How sure a prey": Lee, *The Life and Memoirs of the Late Major General Lee*, 292.

348 "shot a Negro": *NDAR*, 4:1396.

348 "what should be": Force, *American Archives*, 2:164.

348 "The shirtmen are": *NDAR*, 5:57.

348 "a proper proportion": ibid.

348 "infernal demons": ibid.

348 "Such, my Lord,": ibid.

349 "Lee is returned": Landon Carter, "To George Washington from Landon Carter," May 9, 1776, *Founders Online*, National Archives, https://founders.archives.gov/documents/Washington/03-04-02-0195.

349 "We much approve": *RV*, 6:535.

349 "let that body": Mays, *Edmund Pendleton, 1721–1803: A Biography*, 105.

349 "Finis": *RV*, 7:19.

349 "some plan for": ibid., 7:65.

350 "slaves of military age,": ibid., 7:66.

350 "distresses and": *RV*, 6:514.

350 "ought to be": *RV*, 7:96.

350 "Your Convention": George Washington, "From George Washington to John Augustine Washington," May 31–June 4, 1776, *Founders Online*,

National Archives, https://founders.archives.gov/documents/Washington/03-04-02-0333.

350 "totally deprived of": *RV*, 7:95.

350 "I was to be left": William Woodford et al., "Unpublished Letters of General Woodford, of the Continental Army, 1776–1779," *Pennsylvania Magazine of History and Biography* 23, no. 4 (1899): 453.

350 "not less than": *RV*, 1:164.

350 "Their distress will": Woodford et al., "Unpublished Letters of General Woodford, 453.

351 "a reasonable allowance": *RV*, 7:78.

351 "for a Negro man": ibid., 7:79.

351 "Chaney, a Negro": ibid., 7:93.

351 "using every art": ibid., 7:146.

352 "to seize and secure": ibid., 7:141.

352 "carrying out a": Thomas Jefferson, "Resolutions of the Virginia Convention Calling for Independence," May 15, 1776, *Founders Online*, National Archives, https://founders.archives.gov/documents/Jefferson/01-01-02-0152.

352 "secure substantial": *RV*, 7:158.

352 "and other demonstrations": Purdie, *Virginia Gazette*, May 17, 1776.

352 "sensible and spirited": Lee, *The Lee Papers*, 5:47.

352 "have a wonderful good": ibid.

353 "the power of": Virginia Convention, May 15, 1776, *Virginia. In convention. Present 112 Members*, pdf, https://www.loc.gov/item/2020774962/.

353 "Would not a uniform": Richard Lee, "To John Adams from Richard Lee," May 18, 1776, *Founders Online*, National Archives, https://founders.archives.gov/documents/Adams/06-04-02-0083.

353 "matter of which": John Adams, "From John Adams to Richard Lee," June 4, 1776, *Founders Online*, National Archives, https://founders.archives.gov/documents/Adams/06-04-02-0105.

Chapter Twenty-Nine: A State of Society

354 "I am equally desirous": *NDAR*, 4:729.

354 "It is utterly impossible": ibid., 4:765.

354 "give the surest": ibid., 4:1407.

355 "I cannot delay": ibid., 4:1408.

355 "I would give the": W. Hugh Moomaw, "The British Leave Colonial Virginia," *Virginia Magazine of History and Biography* 66, no. 2 (1958): 159, http://www.jstor.org/stable/4246423.

355 "his Lordship's apprehensions": Ernest M. Eller, *Chesapeake Bay in the American Revolution* (Centreville, MD: Tidewater Publishers, 1981), 92.

355 "a couple of lads": *NDAR*, 5:240.

355 "Smallpox made its": Gilbert, *Black Patriots and Loyalists*, 33.

355 "In order to save": ibid.

356 "We thought it most": ibid.

356 "many friends of": John E. Selby, *The Revolution in Virginia, 1775–1783*, (Williamsburg, VA: Colonial Williamsburg Foundation, 2007), 105.

356 "formed an excellent": ibid.

356 "fine, pleasant weather": Sir Andrew Snape Hamond papers, 1766–1825, Library of Congress, Microfilm 13,932–3P, Hamond Account 1775–1777.

357 "the troops evacuated": Sir Andrew Snape Hamond, "Narrative Account of Activity in the Revolutionary War, 1775–1777 and Heads of the Life of Sir Andrew Snape Hamond, Bart," Hamond Naval Papers, Alderman Library, University of Virginia, Charlottesville.

357 "fresh graves . . ." *RV*, 7:265.

357 "their whole fleet": *NDAR*, 5:222.

357 "had taken on board": Edmund Pendleton, "To Thomas Jefferson from Edmund Pendleton," May 24, 1776, *Founders Online*, National Archives, https://founders.archives.gov/documents/Jefferson/01-01-02-0157.

358 "our whole force": *NDAR*, 5:322

358 "but without doing": ibid.

358 "in the utmost": Thomas Posey, "Thomas Posey's Revolutionary War Journal," May 27, 1776, Thomas Posey Papers, Indiana Historical Society Library, Indianapolis.

358 "Three Negro men": Force, *American Archives*, 6:811.

358 "Besides,": ibid.

359 "his wife and": ibid.

359 "A man had better": *NDAR*, 5:485.

359 "forty men and horses": Force, *American Archives*, 6:811.

359 "had not tasted": *NDAR*, 5:485.

359 "if the enemy should": *NDAR*, 5:460.

359 "A finer harbor": Force, *American Archives*, 2:162.

360 "his black and white": Purdie, *Virginia Gazette*, May 31, 1776.

360 "a promiscuous ball": ibid.

360 "Four of his best": Force, *American Archives*, 6:1537.

360 "on account of the": ibid., 6:1539.

361 "compensation for his": ibid., 6:1537.

361 "a declaration of": George Mason, "The Virginia Declaration of Rights," National Archives, accessed January 19, 2024, https://www.archives.gov/founding-docs/virginia-declaration-of-rights.

361 "that no part of a": ibid.

362 "with the state of": *RV*, 7:454.

362 "All were struck": ibid.

362 "not being constituent": William Wirt Henry, *Patrick Henry; Life, Correspondence and Speeches*, 1:425.

362 "All men are by nature": William H. Samuel, ed., *The Debates and Proceedings of the Constitutional Convention of the State of Virginia* (Richmond, VA: Printed at the Office of the New Nation, 1868), 1:241.

362 "large quantities of iron": McIlwaine and Kennedy, *Journals of the House of Burgesses, 1619-1776*, 13:17.

363 "our devil Dunmore": Ballagh, *The Letters of Richard Henry Lee: 1762–1778*, 208.

Chapter Thirty: Misery, Distress, and Cruelty

365 "dozens died daily": ibid., 5:1344.

365 "a fever which has": ibid., 5: 431.

365 "neatly done up": ibid., 5:1150.

366 "harass": ibid., 5:840.

366 "was taking letters": Richard Henry Lee, "To George Washington from Richard Henry Lee," June 13, 1776, *Founders Online*, National Archives, https: / / founders.archives.gov / documents / Washington / 03-04-02-0403.

366 "treat with the": ibid., 5:341.

367 "hard dollars": Moomaw, *The Naval Career of Captain Hamond*, 202.

367 "more than a hundred": *NDAR*, 5:1341.

367 "who had fled the Americans: ibid., 5:1344.

367 "The other articles": ibid., 5:542.

367 "and as many from the" ibid., 5:365.

367 "many Negroes came": ibid., 5:668.

367 "several small vessels": ibid., 5:1078.

367 "in favor of government": ibid., 5:719.

368 "been in the least": ibid., 5:719.

368 "wondering at the": ibid., 5:1345.

368 "Negro troops got through": ibid., 5:840.

368 "has proved a very": ibid., 5:756.

368 "separated the sick": *NDAR*, 5:756.

368 "Lord Dunmore's whole army": ibid, 5:535.

368 "and would have brought": ibid. 5:757.

368 "from the number": ibid, 5:756.

368 "The most alarming": Force, *American Archives*, 1:9.

369 "to form a little": *NDAR*, 5:758.

369 "laden with rum from Barbados": ibid, 5:743.

369 "Had it not been for this horrid": ibid, 5:756.

370 "deep and melodious": Harlow Giles Unger, *First Founding Father: Richard Henry Lee and the Call to Independence* (New York: New York, 2017), 37.

370 "All was silence": John Adams, "The Works of John Adams, vol. 3 (Autobiography, Diary, Notes of a Debate in the Senate, Essays)" Online Library of Liberty, accessed April 26, 2024, 44, https://oll.libertyfund.org/titles/adams-the-works-of-john-adams-vol-3-autobiography-diary-notes-of-a-debate-in-the-senate-essays.

370 "all men are created": *The Papers of Thomas Jefferson*, ed. Julian P. Boyd, vol. 1, *1760–1776* (Princeton, NJ: Princeton University Press, 1950), 1:243–247.

371 "worked day and": *NDAR*, 5:840.

372 "very sensible": ibid., 5:719.

372 "that these United": "Lee's Resolution (1776)," *Encyclopedia Virginia*, accessed January 20, 2024, https://encyclopediavirginia.org/entries/lees-resolution-1776/.

372 "excited domestic": "Declaration of Independence: A Transcription," *America's Founding Documents*, National Archives, accessed January 20, 2024, https://www.archives.gov/founding-docs/declaration-transcript.

372 "some written document": *NDAR*, 5:1345.

372 "glorious": Landon Carter, *The Diary of Colonel Landon Carter of Sabine Hall, 1752–1778*, 1057.

372 "a parcel of fine": Moomaw, The *Naval Career of Captain Hamond*, 233.

373 "had exposed herself": Harry M. Ward, *Major General Adam Stephen and the Cause of American Liberty* (Charlottesville: University of Virginia Press, 1989), 138.

373 "It is against": *NDAR*, 5:1346.

373 "opened several": *NDAR*, 5:996.

373 "from the splinters": ibid., 5:1150.

373 "his Lordship was exceedingly": ibid.

373 "I don't doubt": Rhys Isaac, *Landon Carter's Uneasy Kingdom: Revolution and Rebellion on a Virginia Plantation* (New York: Oxford University Press, 2004) 12.

373 "Their amazement and confusion": Lewis to Richard Henry Lee, July 16, 1776," *Southern Literary Messenger Journal* 26, (1858): 28.

374 "knocking down several": ibid., 5:1149.

374 "chastise the noble": Moomaw, *The Naval Career of Captain Hamond*, 235.

374 "Unhappily, we": Force, *American Archives*, 1:214.

374 "was no longer": *NDAR*, 5:1079.

374 "heartily tired of": Moomaw, *The Naval Career of Captain Hamond*, 248.

375 "The disgrace of": *NDAR*, 5:1149.

375 "This took so much": Richard L. Jarvis, *My Hudson Ancestors from Virginia* (British Columbia, Canada: Trafford, 2004), 113.

376 "The deplorable situation": *NDAR*, 5:1044.

376 "Such a scene of misery,": *NDAR*, 5:1150.

376 "dying of the putrid": Dixon and Hunter, *Virginia Gazette*, July 20, 1776.

376 "had been torn": Michael Cecere, "Battle of Gwynn's Island: Lord Dunmore's Last Stand in Virginia," Journal of the American Revolution,

accessed April 26, 2024, https://allthingsliberty.com/2016/05/battle-of-gwynns-island-lord-dunmores-last-stand-in-virginia/.

376 "unburied Negro corpses": Harry M. Ward, *Major General Adam Stephen and the Cause of American Liberty*, 138.

376 "or rather holes": *NDAR*, 5:1150.

376 "were burnt alive": *NDAR*, 5:1150.

376 "We must have run": Dixon and Hunter, *Virginia Gazette*, July 20, 1776.

376 "at midday, the Americans": *NDAR*, 5:1346.

Chapter Thirty-One: Lands, Whores, and Dice

377 "the fleet went": Stewart, *The Life of Brigadier General William Woodford*, 691.

377 "a strong wind": *NDAR*, 5:1346.

379 "state of perfect": Moomaw, "The British Leave Colonial Virginia," 153.

379 "not a man to": Force, *American Archives*, 1:382.

379 "our African hero": Richard Henry Lee, "To Thomas Jefferson from Richard Henry Lee," July 21, 1776, *Founders Online*, National Archives, https://founders.archives.gov/documents/Jefferson/01-01-02-0190.

379 "continuously blasting away": Richard Henry Lee, "Richard Henry Lee to Landon Carter," July 21, 1776, Lee Family Archives, accessed May 5, 2024, https://leefamilyarchive.org/history-papers-letters-transcripts-ballagh-b090/.

379 "Ought the precept": George Wythe, "To Thomas Jefferson from George Wythe," July 27, 1776, *Founders Online*, National Archives, https://founders.archives.gov/documents/Jefferson/01-01-02-0195.

380 "elegant brick house": Pinkney, *Virginia Gazette*, September 6, 1776.

380 "all got drunk": John Parke Custis, "To George Washington from John Parke Custis," August 8, 1776, *Founders Online*, National Archives, https://founders.archives.gov/documents/Washington/03-05-02-0465.

380 "willingly conceal": Edmund Pendleton, "To Thomas Jefferson from Edmund Pendleton," July 29, 1776, *Founders Online*, National Archives, https://founders.archives.gov/documents/Jefferson/01-01-02-0198.

380 "three of George": Sir Andrew Snape Hamond papers, 1766–1825, Library of Congress, Microfilm 13,932-3P, Hamond Account 1775–1777.

380 "three whitemen": *NDAR*, 5:1207.

381 "with the loss of": ibid., 5:1347.

381 "two Negroes": ibid., 5:477.

381 "with many others": Dixon and Hunter, *Virginia Gazette*, July 26, 1776.

381 "Dunmore's fleet is": *NDAR*, 6:65.

381 "Lord Dunmore and his": *NDAR*, 6:66.

381 "troops have been": ibid., 6:68.

382 "Being fifty-two": Gilbert, *Black Patriots and Loyalists*, 36.

382 "I must say this": *NDAR*, 6:51.

382 "total impracticability": ibid., 6:174.

383 "We took one prisoner": Gilbert, *Black Patriots and Loyalists*, 36.

000 "they suffer very": "Peter Minor to Garrett Minor," August 9, 1776, Minor and Watson Correspondence, Manuscript Division, Library of Congress.

383 "laden with rum, sugars": *NDAR*, 6:174.

383 "near 400 regulars": Purdie, *Virginia Gazette*, August 9, 1776.

383 "Lord Dunmore's piratical": "From Edward Bancroft," in *The Deane Papers* (New York: New-York Historical Society, 1886), 19:250.

383 "perpetrated crimes": *NDAR*, 6:132.

383 "I thought all London": Ron Chernow, *Washington: A Life* (New York: Penguin, 2010), 236.

384 "had the blacks": Thomas Jefferson, "From Thomas Jefferson to John Page", August 20, 1776, Founders Online, National Archives, https://founders.archives.gov/documents/Jefferson/01-01-02-0207.

384 "great formal dinner": *NDAR*, 6:184.

384 "approve very much": ibid., 6:678.

384 "the whole day": Dixon and Hunter, *Virginia Gazette*, September 14, 1776.

385 "formerly slave to": Graham Russell, Gao Hodges, and Edward Brown, eds., *The Book of Negroes: African Americans in Exile After the American Revolution* (New York: Fordham University Press, 2021), 170.

385 "stout wench": ibid., 173.

385 "My Lord, I": Parkinson, *The Common Cause*, 280.

385 "Lord Dunmore is": Force, *American Archives*, 3:697.

385 "quitted the army": George III, *The Correspondence of King George the Third*, (London: Macmillan and Company, 1927), 3:516.

386 "Our national honor,": Edmund Burke, *The Speeches of the Right Honourable Edmund Burke: In the House of Commons, and in Westminster-Hall* (London: Longman, Hurst, Rees, Orme, and Brown, 1816), 1:399.

386 "a warm debate": ibid: 1:394.

387 "all Negroes that fly from": Buskirk, "Crossing the Lines," 84.

387 "every Negro who shall": Massachusetts Historical Society, *Proceedings of the Massachusetts Historical Society* (Boston, John Wilson and Son, 1863), 219.

387 "bids fair to make": Gerald Horne, *The Counter-Revolution of 1776* (NY: New York University Press, 2016), 225.

387 "the province which of all": James Tormey, *The Virginia Navy in the Revolution: Hampton's Commodore James Barron and His Fleet* (Cheltenham, UK: History Press, 2016), 89.

388 "If offensive war": Henry Clinton, *Observations on Some Parts of the Answer of Earl Cornwallis to Sir Henry Clinton's Narrative* (London: J. Debrett, 1783), 107.

388 "in great want": Charles Cornwallis, *Correspondence of Charles, First Marquis Cornwallis* (London: J. Murray, 1859), 113.

388 "Every soldier had his": Don N. Hagist, "Mrs. Middleton Takes Prisoners," Journal of the American Revolution, accessed April 26, 2024, https://allthingsliberty.com/2013/06/mrs-middleton-takes-prisoners/.

388 "The good old lady": "The Southern Campaign, 1781, From Guilford Courthouse to the Siege of York, Narrated in the Letters from Judge St. George Tucker to His Wife," *Magazine of American History with Notes and Queries* 7, no. 2 (1881): 207.

388 "Having no harbor,": Cornwallis, *Correspondence of Charles, First Marquis Cornwallis*, 109.

389 "We had used them": Parkinson, *The Common Cause*, 519.

389 "an immense number": McDonnell, *The Politics of War*, 476.

389 "a number of dead": Whitehead, *Black Loyalists*, 807.

389 "We gained a veritable": Lloyd Dobyns, "Fighting . . . Maybe for Freedom, but Probably Not," *Colonial Williamsburg Journal*, Autumn 2007, accessed January 20, 2024, https://research.colonialwilliamsburg.org/Foundation/journal/Autumn07/slaves.cfm#.

389 "such Negroes or": George Washington, "General Orders, 25 October 1781," *Founders Online*, National Archives, https://founders.archives.gov/documents/Washington/99-01-02-07264.

390 "unwilling to remain": George Germain, "Lord Germain to General Henry Clinton," October 4, 1781, Henry Clinton Papers, Clements Library, University of Michigan, Ann Arbor.

390 "some malicious person": Minnie G. Cook, "The Susan Constant and the Mayflower," *William and Mary College Quarterly Historical Magazine* 17, no. 2 (1937): 235, https://doi.org/10.2307/1925278.

390 "We have no water": Jean-Baptiste Donatien de Vimeur, "To George Washington from Jean-Baptiste Donatien de Vimeur, comte de Rochambeau," December 24, 1781, *Founders Online*, National Archives, https://founders.archives.gov/documents/Washington/99-01-02-07583.

390 "Oh God, it is": Edward J. Larson, *American Inheritance: Liberty and Slavery in the Birth of a Nation, 1765–1795* (New York: W. W. Norton, 2023), 149.

Chapter Thirty-Two: A Glaring Piece of Injustice

391 "a grand reception": George E. Ellis, ed., *Memoir of Sir Benjamin Thompson, Count Rumford, with Notices of His Daughter* (Boston: American Academy of Arts and Sciences, 1871), 126.

391 "he was a free": Bobby G. Moss and Michael C. Scoggins, *African-American Loyalists in the Southern Campaign of the American Revolution* (Blacksburg, SC: Scotia-Hibernia Press, 2005), 4.

391 "That a silly old fellow": Philip Morin Freneau, *The Poems of Philip Freneau: Poet of the American Revolution* (Princeton, NJ: Princeton University Library, 1902), 2:114.

392 "the most efficacious": George Livermore, ed., *An Historical Research Respecting the Opinions of the Founders of the Republic: On Negroes as Slaves, as Citizens, and as Soldiers* (Boston: A. Williams and Company, 1863), 142.

392 "to fill up the vacancies": ibid., 146.

393 "raise some black": Nathanael Greene, "To George Washington from Nathanael Greene," January 24, 1782, *Founders Online*, National Archives, https://founders.archives.gov/documents/Washington/99-01-02-07729.

393 "they would make": Livermore, *An Historical Research Respecting the Opinions of the Founders*,191.

393 "not a little startled": ibid., 192.

393 "great obstacles in": Erskine Clarke, *Our Southern Zion: A History of Calvinism in the South Carolina Low Country, 1690–1990* (Tuscaloosa: University of Alabama Press, 2014), 103.

393 "by neglecting to": Livermore, *An Historical Research Respecting the Opinions of the Founders*, 190.

394 "the arming of": David, "Dunmore's New World," 242.

394 "to raise several corps": William Smith, *Historical Memoirs of William Smith* (New York: New York Times and Arno Press), 2:497.

395 "to drive the": David, "Dunmore's New World," 243.

395 "and more daily coming": Whitehead, *Black Loyalists*, 124.

395 "slaves and other": James Madison, "Motion on Slaves Taken by the British," September 10, 1782, *Founders Online*, National Archives, https://founders.archives.gov/documents/Madison/01-05-02-0049.

395 "Mr. Laurens said": John Adams, "From John Adams to Boston Patriot, July 30, 1811," *Founders Online*, National Archives, https://founders.archives.gov/documents/Adams/99-02-02-5665.

396 "without causing any": Jared Sparks, *The Diplomatic Correspondence of the American Revolution: Lafayette; Commissioners for Peace; Gerard; Luzerne*, (Boston: Nathan Hale and Gray and Bowen, 1830), 199.

396 "signed, sealed, and delivered": Adams, "From John Adams to Boston Patriot, July 30, 1811."

396 "all the slaves": Gilbert, *Black Patriots and Loyalists*, 189.

396 "Let us unite in": Gilbert du Motier, "To George Washington from Marie-Joseph-Paul-Yves-Roch-Gilbert du Motier, Marquis de Lafayette," February 5, 1783, *Founders Online*, National Archives, https://founders.archives.gov/documents/Washington/99-01-02-10575.

396 "encourage the emancipation": George Washington, "From George Washington to Marie-Joseph-Paul-Yves-Roch-Gilbert du Motier, Marquis de Lafayette," April 5, 1783, *Founders Online*, National Archives, https://founders.archives.gov/documents/Washington/99-01-02-10998.

397 "the delivery of all": Worthington Chauncey Ford, ed., *Journals of the Continental Congress, 1774–1789* (Washington, DC, 1904–37), 24:242–243.

397 "I observe by a": Benjamin Harrison, "To George Washington from Benjamin Harrison, Sr.," March 31, 1783, *Founders Online*, National Archives, https://founders.archives.gov/documents/Washington/99-01-02-10969.

397 "Some of my own": George Washington, "From George Washington to Daniel Parker," April 28, 1783, *Founders Online*, National Archives, https://founders.archives.gov/documents/Washington/99-01-02-11181.

397 "passports have been": Philip George Swan, "To Separate the Tares from the Corn: Debts and Slaves in Post-Revolutionary Virginia" (master's thesis, College of William and Mary, 1993), 20.

397 "no slaves were": Thomas Walke, "Thomas Walke to Virginia Delegates," May 3, 1783, *Founders Online*, National Archives, https://founders.archives.gov/documents/Madison/01-07-02-0003.

398 "glaring piece of": ibid.

398 "When all seated,": Smith, *Historical Memoirs of William Smith*, 2:586.

398 "with great slowness": ibid.

399 "Already embarked!": Chernow, *Washington: A Life*, 236.

399 "the carrying away": George Washington, "From George Washington to Guy Carleton," May 6, 1783, *Founders Online*, National Archives, https://founders.archives.gov/documents/Washington/99-01-02-11218.

399 "inconsistent with": Gilbert, *Black Patriots and Loyalists*, 178.

399 "If the sending off": "Account of a Conference between Washington and Sir Guy Carleton," May 6, 1783, *Founders Online*, National Archives, https://founders.archives.gov/documents/Washington/99-01-02-11217.

399 "the value of the": ibid.

400 "Washington pulled": Smith, *Historical Memoirs of William Smith*, 2:587.

400 "diffuse and desultory": George Washington, "From George Washington to Elias Boudinot," May 8, 1783, *Founders Online*, National Archives, https://founders.archives.gov/documents/Washington/99-01-02-11228.

400 "The carrying away": Washington, "From George Washington to Guy Carleton," May 6, 1783.

400 "I have discovered": George Washington, "From George Washington to Benjamin Harrison, Sr.," May 7, 1783, *Founders Online*, National Archives, https://founders.archives.gov/documents/Washington/99-01-02-11225.

400 "The Negroes in question": Guy Carleton, "To George Washington from Guy Carleton," May 12, 1783, *Founders Online*, National Archives, https://founders.archives.gov/documents/Washington/99-01-02-11252.

401 "for amusement": Edmund Pendleton, "To James Madison from Edmund Pendleton," June 2, 1783, *Founders Online*, National Archives, https://founders.archives.gov/documents/Madison/01-07-02-0063.

401 "prisoners of war": James Madison, "Notes on Debates," May 8, 1783, *Founders Online*, National Archives, https://founders.archives.gov/documents/Madison/01-07-02-0014.

401 "sending away the": Elias Boudinot, "To Benjamin Franklin from Elias Boudinot," June 18, 1783, *Founders Online*, National Archives, https://founders.archives.gov/documents/Franklin/01-40-02-0113.

401 "a shameful evasion": Ellen Gibson Wilson, *The Loyal Blacks* (New York: Capricorn Books, 1976), 55.

401 "renewal of hostilities": Sylvia R. Frey, *Water from the Rock: Black Resistance in a Revolutionary Age* (Princeton, NJ: Princeton University Press, 2020), 193.

401 "in the fullest and": K. G. Davies, ed., *Documents of the American Revolution, 1770–1783: Transcripts, 1774*, 202.

401 "certainly an act": ibid., 202.

401 "to withdraw": Gilbert, *Black Patriots and Loyalists*, 189.

401 "with all the grossness": ibid.

402 "lived with Col. Tucker": Hodges and Brown, *The Book of Negroes: African Americans in Exile After the American Revolution*, 117.

402 "worn out": ibid.

402 "Jane Thomson, a Negro": "Certificate of Freedom," Black Loyalists: Our History, Our People, accessed January 25, 2024, https://blackloyalist.com/cdc/documents/official/order_of_general_birch.htm.

402 "dispelled all our": Stephen Davidson, *Birchtown and the Black Loyalist Experience* (Halifax, Nova Scotia: Formac Publishing, 2019), 55.

403 "I was now become a new": Boston King, "Memoirs of Boston King," *Black Loyalists*, accessed April 26, 2024, https://blackloyalist.com/cdc/documents/diaries/king-memoirs.htm.

403 "Some killed and ate": ibid.

404 "The Negroes who": Jerry Bannister and Liam Riordan, *The Loyal Atlantic: Remaking the British Atlantic in the Revolutionary Era* (Toronto: University of Toronto Press, 2012), 200.

404 "Negro Court": Paul Daniel Shirley, "Migration, Freedom and Enslavement in the Revolutionary Atlantic: The Bahamas, 1783–c. 1800" (PhD thesis, University College London, 2011), 158.

404 "such as what . . .": Maya Jasanoff, *Liberty's Exiles* (New York: Knopf, 2011), 233.

404 "this enquiry has": ibid., 231.

405 "Our Virginia papers": Lucy Ludwell Paradise, "To Thomas Jefferson from Lucy Ludwell Paradise," May 5, 1789, *Founders Online*, National Archives, https://founders.archives.gov/documents/Jefferson/01-15-02-0098.

405 "spiriting up the": David Humphreys, "To Thomas Jefferson from David Humphreys," November 2, 1790, *Founders Online*, National Archives, https://founders.archives.gov/documents/Jefferson/01-17-02-0255.

405 "Bastards, bastards!": David, "Dunmore's New World," 332.

406 "red as a Turkey": ibid.

406 "God damn him": ibid.

406 "Lord Dunmore used": Jeremy Bentham, *The Works of Jeremy Bentham*, ed. John Bowring (Edinburgh: W. Tait, 1839), 124.

Epilogue

409 "something of regret": Thomas Jefferson, *The Papers of Thomas Jefferson: Retirement Series*, vol. 13, *22 April 1818 to 31 January 1819*, ed. J. Jefferson Looney (Princeton, NJ: Princeton University Press, 2018), 538.

409 "Norfolk will probably": Jefferson, *Notes on the State of Virginia*, 175.

409 "inferior to the whites": ibid., 239.

409 "But this is very": Catherine Kerrison, *Jefferson's Daughters: Three Sisters, White and Black, in a Young America* (New York: Random House, 2018), 117.

409 "Norfolk had not": Thomas Jefferson, "From Thomas Jefferson to John Trumbull," November 25, 1789, *Founders Online*, National Archives, https://founders.archives.gov/documents/Jefferson/01-15-02-0531.

410 "innumerable retinue of narrow": Benjamin Henry Latrobe, *Virginia Journals of Benjamin Henry Latrobe, 1795–1798*, ed. Edward C. Carter II (New Haven, CT: Yale University Press, 1977), 75.

410 "the many charred": Saint-Méry, *American Journey*, 48.

410 "wagon loads of": Jean H. Baker, *Building America: The life of Benjamin Henry Latrobe* (New York: Oxford University Press, 2020), 46–47.

411 "For general occupations": Jefferson, *Notes on the State of Virginia*, 275.

411 "the mobs of great cities,": ibid.

411 "discourage the growth": Thomas Jefferson, "From Thomas Jefferson to Benjamin Rush," September 23,1800, *Founders Online*, National Archives, https://founders.archives.gov/documents/Jefferson/01-32-02-0102.

411 "a cloacina of": Thomas Jefferson, "From Thomas Jefferson to William Short," September 8, 1823, *Founders Online*, National Archives, https://founders.archives.gov/documents/Jefferson/98-01-02-3750.

411 "the two races,": Thomas Jefferson, "Extract from Thomas Jefferson's Draft Autobiography," February 8, 1821, Thomas Jefferson Foundation, accessed January 20, 2024, https://tjrs.monticello.org/letter/1401.

411 "removed beyond the reach": Jefferson, *Notes on the State of Virginia*, 240.

411 "Virginia is fast": Ari Helo and Peter Onuf, "Jefferson, Morality, and the Problem of Slavery," *William and Mary Quarterly* 60, no. 3 (July 2003): 613.

412 "I consider the labor": Thomas Jefferson, "Extract from Thomas Jefferson to Joel Yancey," Jefferson's Monticello, accessed April 26, 2024, https://tjrs.monticello.org/letter/2117.

412 "personal observation": Thomas Jefferson to Henry Gregoire, February 25, 1825, https://www.loc.gov/resource/mtjl.043_0836_0836/?st=text

412 "decay": Jasanoff, *Liberty's Exiles*, 348.

412 "old lady, who": "Extract from John Quincy Adams' Diary, London, England, 31 January 1816," The Adams Papers, Microfilm reel #32.

413 "I am totally": Virginia Murray, "Lady Virginia Murray to Thomas Jefferson [before November 29, 1815]," *Founders Online*, National Archives, https://founders.archives.gov/documents/Jefferson/03-09-02-0140.

413 "that now desolate": Charles Augustus Murray, *Travels in North America During the Years, 1835 & 1836, Including a Summer Residence with the Pawnee Tribe of Indians in the Remote Prairies of the Missouri, and a Visit to Cuba and the Azore Islands* (London: Richard Bentley, 1839), 172, https://www.loc.gov/item/02000373/.

413 "little to interest": ibid.

413 "inhuman unholy": ibid.

413 "a man of a very": "Recollections of a Rebel Reefer" in Brian M. Thomsen, *Blue & Gray at Sea: Naval Memoirs of the Civil War* (New York: Macmillan, 2003), 95.

414 "We are passing": Alexander H. Stephens, "Cornerstone Speech," March 21, 1861, London's Global University, accessed January 20, 2024, https://www.ucl.ac.uk/USHistory/Building/docs/Cornerstone.htm.

414 "We are fighting": Jefferson Davis, *Jefferson Davis: The Essential Writings*, ed. William J. Cooper (New York: Modern Library, 2003), 196.

415 "I shall hold these": T. A. Bland, *Life of Benjamin F. Butler* (Boston: Lee & Shepard, 1879), 52.

415 "Out of this incident": Benjamin F. Butler, *Autobiography and Personal Reminiscences of Major General Benj. F. Butler: Butler's Book: A Review of His Legal, Political, and Military Career* (Boston: Thayer, 1892), 260.

415 "Stampede Among": "Stampede Among the Negroes in Virginia—Their Arrival at Fortress Monroe," Library of Congress Prints and Photographs Division, accessed February 29, 2024, https://www.loc.gov/pictures/item/99614015/.

415 "war, not emancipation": Louis P. Masur, *Lincoln's Hundred Days: The Emancipation Proclamation and the War for the Union* (Cambridge, MA: Belknap Press, 2012), 18.

416 "The meanness, vandalism": *Richmond Enquirer*, August 30, 1861.

416 "scheme of very": *Port Tobacco Times*, November 21, 1861.

416 "Slavery should be struck": Charles Sumner, *Charles Sumner: His Complete Works*, ed. George Frisbie Hoar (Boston: Lee & Shepard, 1909), 217.

416 "the last resource": Walter Stahr, *Seward: Lincoln's Indispensable Man* (New York: Simon & Schuster, 2012), 343.

416 "a fit and necessary": Abraham Lincoln, *The Emancipation Proclamation: January 1, 1863* (Washington, DC: National Archives and Records Administration, 1994), 8.

417 "If I could save": Abraham Lincoln, "Abraham Lincoln papers: Series 2. General Correspondence. 1858 to 1864: Abraham Lincoln to Horace Greeley, Friday, Augst 22, 1862 (Clipping from Aug. 23, 1862, *Daily National Intelligencer*, Washington, DC), manuscript/mixed material, https://www.loc.gov/item/mal4233400/.

417 "I made a solemn": Stephen Mansfield, *Lincoln's Battle with God: A President's Struggle with Faith and What It Meant for America* (Nashville, TN: Thomas Nelson, 2012), 165.

417 "Such persons of": Lincoln, *The Emancipation Proclamation*, 9.

418 "Sic semper tyrannis": Michael W. Kauffman, *American Brutus: John Wilkes Booth and the Lincoln Conspiracies* (New York: Random House, 2004), 274.

418 "that in due time": Abraham Lincoln, "Speech in Independence Hall, Philadelphia, Pennsylvania," February 22, 1861, University of Michigan Library, accessed January 29, 2024, https://quod.lib.umich.edu/l/lincoln/lincoln4/1:376?rgn=div1;view=fulltext.

418 "few historians have": Elizabeth Ann Wrick, "Dunmore—Virginia's Last Royal Governor," (master's thesis, West Virginia University, 1937), 6.

418 "A needy Scottish peer": George Bancroft, *History of the United States from the Discovery of the American Continent* (Boston: Little, Brown, 1856), 5:383.

418 "inept and ineffectual": Peter McQuilkin Mitchell, "Loyalist Property and the Revolution in Virginia" (PhD diss., University of Colorado, 1935), 81.

418 "stubborn": Frances Moorman Walker, "Lord Dunmore in Virginia" (master's thesis, University of Virginia, 1933), 18.

418 "weak and unstable": Claude Halstead Van Tyne, *The American Revolution: 1776–1783* (New York: Greenwood Press, 1969), 52.

418 "he was rude and coarse": Walker, "Lord Dunmore in Virginia," 2.

419 "pink-cheeked": Simon Schama, *Rough Crossings: Britain, The Slaves and the American Revolution* (New York: Harper Collins, 2006), 74.

419 "the fatal course": Bruce Tarter, "Some Thoughts Arising from Trying to Find out Who was Governor Dunmore's Mistress," (unpublished manuscript), 4.

419 "His fine library": Kevin Hayes, *The Mind of a Patriot: Patrick Henry and the World of Ideas* (Charlottesville: University of Virginia Press, 2008), 77.

419 "bombardment of Norfolk": Eckenrode, *Revolution in Virginia,* 88.

419 "laid waste to much": Israel Shenker, "North Carolina First to Give Approval," *New York Times*, April 13, 1976, 70.

419 "the cry of Dunmore": Bancroft, *History of the United States*, 6:225.

419 "The Negroes behaved": Carlo Botta, *History of the War of Independence* (Carlisle, MA: Applewood Books, 2009), 1:249.

419 "Dunmore's efforts": William H. Stewart, *The Spirit of the South: Orations, Essays, and Lectures* (New York: Neale Publishing, 1908), 12.

420 "never really touched": Whitehead, Black Loyalists, 66.

420 "not founded upon any": Byron James Stewart, "The Revolutionary Generation: Weighing the Ultimate Fates of Black Patriots and Loyalists, 1776–1836," (master's thesis, Howard University, 2010), 51.

420 "wasn't an abolitionist": Author interview with Gordon Wood, September 26, 2023.

420 "the most farthest-reaching": Murphy MacDuffey Wood, "The Impact of British Slave Emancipation in the American Revolution" (master's thesis, James Madison University, 2010), 10.

420 "could well be considered": Horne, *The Counter-Revolution of 1776*, 225.

421 "intellectual and intelligent": Elizabeth Grant, *Memoirs of a Highland Lady: The Autobiography of Elizabeth Grant of Rothiemurchus, Afterwards Mrs. Smith of Baltiboys*, 1797–1830 (London: John Murray, 1898), 147.

421 "ranted a little": ibid., 148.

421 "The Negro of my": Julia Abel Smith, *Forbidden Wife: The Life and Trials of Lady Augusta Murray* [translated by author from French] (Charleston, SC: History Press, 2020), 283.

Index

(*continued*)

(*continued*)

(*continued*)